Understanding Psychology for Medicine and Nursing

T0387986

The book presents a comprehensive updated approach to current psychological knowledge to facilitate a rapid review of the major subjects in psychology in medicine and to stimulate further detailed study.

The book is divided into five Parts. Part One provides an elaborate background of the various sub-disciplines of psychology, the various theories and schools of thoughts encompassing them. Part Two discusses the links between the physical and psychological state of being human. Part Three elucidates the basic psychological processes that shape human cognizance. Part Four talks about the different factors which influence the human psyche. Part Five discusses the various aspects of clinical psychology and their implications for the physical well-being of people.

Understanding Psychology for Medicine and Nursing distinguishes itself in providing a concise, clear understanding of most of the basic topics of psychology that are essential to all students of general psychology, but particularly to medical and nursing students, and to postgraduate trainees in psychiatry.

Mohamed Ahmed Abd El-Hay is Professor of Psychiatry in the Department of Neuropsychiatry in Tanta University, Egypt, with a particular interest in child and adolescent psychiatry. He teaches psychiatry and psychology to medical and nursing students. Dr. Abd El-Hay has published numerous scientific papers on psychiatry as well as books on psychiatry, psychology, and social psychology.

Understanding Psychology for Medicine and Nursing

Insights and Applications

Mohamed Ahmed Abd El-Hay

NEW YORK AND LONDON

First published 2020
by Routledge
52 Vanderbilt Avenue, New York, NY 10017

and by Routledge
2 Park Square, Milton Park, Abingdon, Oxon, OX14 4RN

Routledge is an imprint of the Taylor & Francis Group, an informa business

Library of Congress Cataloging-in-Publication Data
A catalog record for this title has been requested

ISBN: 978-0-367-42892-1 (hbk)
ISBN: 978-0-367-42893-8 (pbk)
ISBN: 978-1-003-00001-3 (ebk)

Typeset in Minion Pro
by Wearset Ltd, Boldon, Tyne and Wear

Printed and bound by CPI Group (UK) Ltd, Croydon, CR0 4YY

Contents

Illustrations

Photos

Figures

Tables

Preface

Psychology is a dynamic field of study that has grown in innumerable ways during its short lifetime. Each school of thought left an acknowledged mark on psychology, helping to shape it into the respected discipline that it now is.

This book tries to provide a concise, clear understanding of the most basic topics of psychology that are essential to all students of general psychology, but in particular, to medical and nursing students, and to postgraduate trainees in psychiatry. I have tried to do this in a simple understandable language, in a concise form, though in a comprehensive updated approach, that gives an outline of current psychological knowledge, facilitates the rapid review of psychological subjects, and stimulates further detailed study.

I hope this book will present psychology as an interesting rather than an incomprehensible subject, and that it will provoke more study of the introduced topics.

Mohamed Ahmed Abd El-Hay

Abbreviations

5-HIAA	5-hydroxyindoleacetic acid
5-HT	5-hydroxytryptamine
ACh	acetylcholine
AChE	acetylcholinesterase
Acrophase	phase position of the rhythm
ACTH	adrenocorticotrophic hormone
AD	Alzheimer's disease
ADHD	attention deficit hyperactivity disorder
ANS	autonomic nervous system
APA	American Psychological Association
ARAS	ascending reticular activating system
ASD	autism spectrum disorder
ATs	automatic thoughts
BNST	bed nucleus of the stria terminalis
cAMP	cyclic adenosine monophosphate
CBT	cognitive-behavioral therapy
CBZ	carbamazepine
CCK	cholecystokinin
CHC	Cattell–Horn–Carroll
CNS	central nervous system
CO	carbon monoxide
COMT	catechol-O-methyl-transferase
CRH	corticotropin-releasing hormone
CT	computerized tomography

CTF	central tegmental field
DAT	dopamine transporter
DNA	deoxyribonucleic acid
DSM	*Diagnostic and Statistical Manual*
ECT	electroconvulsive therapy
EEG	electroencephalography
EMG	electromyography
EOG	electrooculography
EPSP	excitatory postsynaptic potential
FASD	fetal alcohol spectrum disorders
FCT	fundamental cause theory
fMRI	functional magnetic resonance imaging
Ga	auditory processing
GABA	gamma-aminobutyric acid
GAD	glutamic acid decarboxylase
GAS	general adaptation syndrome
Gc	crystallized intelligence/comprehension knowledge
Gf	fluid intelligence/fluid reasoning
Gf-Gc	fluid-crystallized intelligence
Gh	tactile abilities
Gk	kinesthetic abilities
Gkn	general (domain-specific) knowledge
Glr	long-term storage and retrieval
Go	olfactory abilities
Gp	psychomotor abilities
GP	globus pallidus
GPCRs	G protein-coupled receptors
Gps	psychomotor speed
Gq	quantitative knowledge
Grw	reading and writing skills and knowledge
Gs	processing speed
Gsm	short-term memory
Gt	decision speed/reaction time
Gv	visual processing
ICD	International Classification of Diseases
IPSP	inhibitory postsynaptic potential
IPT	interpersonal therapy
IQ	intelligence quotient
KO	knockout
LDT	lateral dorsal thalamic nucleus
LHA	lateral hypothalamic area
LSD	lysergic acid diethylamide
LTD	long-term depression
LTM	long-term memory
LTP	long-term potentiation
mAChRs	muscarinic receptors
MAO	monoamine oxidase
MAO-A	monoamine oxidase-A

MAOIs	monoamine oxidase inhibitors
MAPK	mitogen-activated protein kinase
MDMA	methylenedioxymethamphetamine
MeA	medial amygdala
MMPI-2	Minnesota Multiphasic Personality Inventory-2
MPA	primary mental abilities
MPH	methylphenidate
MPOA	medial preoptic area
MRI	magnetic resonance imaging
MSLT	multiple sleep latency test
nAChRs	nicotinic receptors
NARI	noradrenergic reuptake inhibitor
NMDA	N-methyl-D-aspartate
NNT	number needed to treat
NO	nitric oxide
NOS	nitric oxide synthase
NREM	non-rapid eye movement
NSDUH	National Survey on Drug Use and Health
OCD	obsessive-compulsive disorder
PCP	phencyclidine
PD	Parkinson's disease
PDD	Bowlby's protest/despair/detachment model
PET	positron emission tomography
PHG	parahippocampal regions
PKU	phenylketonuria
PMA	primary mental abilities
PNS	peripheral nervous system
PPIs	positive psychology interventions
PPT	pedunculopontinethalamic nucleus
PSG	polysomnography
PTSD	post-traumatic stress disorder
PVN	paraventricular nucleus
REBT	rational emotive behavioral therapy
REM	rapid eye movement
RNA	ribonucleic acid
SCN	suprachiasmatic nucleus
SES	socio-economic state
SNr	substantia nigra pars reticulata
SNRIs	serotonin and norepinephrine reuptake inhibitors
SNS	somatic nervous system
SPECT	single-photon emission computed tomography
S-R	stimulus-response
SSRIs	selective serotonin reuptake inhibitors
STM	short-term memory
SWS	slow-wave sleep
TAT	thematic apperception test
tau	cycle length
TCA	tricyclic antidepressant

THC	tetrahydrocannabinol
TMN	tuberomamillary nucleus
TMS	transcranial magnetic stimulation
TOM	theory of mind
TV	television
VIP	vasoactive intestinal peptide
VLPO	ventrolateral preoptic nucleus
vmPFC	ventromedial prefrontal cortex
VTA	ventral tegmental area
WAIS	Wechsler Adult Intelligence Scale
WISC	Wechsler Intelligence Scale for Children
WPPSI	Wechsler Preschool and Primary Scale of Intelligence

PART ONE
Psychology
Science and
Application

one
Introduction

Learning Goals

- This chapter is intended to provide the reader with common definitions of psychology, and give a brief history of its birth as a science, and the scope of current psychology.

Introduction

Psychology is a popular major for students, an important perspective in clinical practice, a popular topic in the public media, and a part of our everyday life. During its relatively short history as a separate field of study, definitions of psychology have changed frequently, this change echoed the diverse, and sometimes conflicting, theoretical views regarding the nature of human beings and the most appropriate methods for investigating them. Generally speaking, psychology is defined as the scientific study of mental processes and behavior. The word "psychology" comes from the Greek words "psyche," meaning mind, soul, or spirit, and "logos," meaning knowledge or study. Literally speaking, psychology is the study of the mind. According to the British Psychological Society, psychology is the scientific study of people, the mind, and behavior. The focus of psychology is the human being, who is a complex subject. Psychologists study human issues that begin before birth and continue until death. A human being is at once a biological organism, a social organism, and an organism with a mind.

While contemporary psychology reflects a discipline with rich and varied history, the origins of psychology differ significantly from current conceptions of the field. By understanding the history of psychology, one can gain a better understanding of how topics in psychology were studied and what we have learned thus far.

The History of Psychology

More than 2,000 years ago, Socrates and his followers, Plato and Aristotle, wrote about topics such as pleasure, pain, knowledge, motivation, and rationality. They theorized about whether human traits are innate or the product of experience, a topic which continues to be a subject of debate in current psychology. They also considered the origins of mental illness, with both Socrates and Plato focusing on psychological forces as the root of such illnesses. Many of Aristotle's ideas remained influential until the beginnings of modern science in the seventeenth century (Kheriaty, 2007). However, philosophers could advance the understanding of human behavior only to a certain point. Their methods were limited to intuition, observation, and logic.

PHOTO 1.1.   Socrates, Aristotle, Plato.

Psychology as a separate field of study grew out of several other disciplines, both scientific (specifically physiology) and non-scientific (specifically philosophy). Prior to the 1870s, psychologists had trained mainly as physiologists, doctors, philosophers, or some combination of these, there were no laboratories devoted specifically to psychological research.

The emergence of psychology as a science was not clear until the French philosopher, René Descartes (1596–1650) proposed a doctrine called "interactive dualism": the idea that mind and body were separate entities that interact to form sensations, emotions, and other conscious experiences. This concept had a great impact on the development of both psychology as a science and science in general.

PHOTO 1.2. René Descartes.

Dualism allowed scientists to treat matter as inert and completely distinct from human beings, which meant that the world could be described objectively, without reference to the human observer. Descartes viewed the material world as comprised of objects which are assembled like a huge machine and operated by mechanical laws. He extended this view to living organisms, including, eventually, humans. Because the mind (unlike the physical world) is non-material, Descartes believed that it can be investigated only through introspection (observing one's own thoughts and feelings). Objectivity became the ideal of science, and was extended to the study of human behavior and social institutions in the mid-1800s by the French philosopher, Auguste Comte, who called it "positivism," which suggests that our way of thinking is divided into three major phases: theological, metaphysical, and the third is scientific, or rather, to be more precise, "positivist" (Comte, 1903).

The emergence of psychology as a distinct scientific discipline is generally dated to 1879, when the German physiologist Wilhelm Wundt opened the first psychological laboratory at the University of Leipzig in Germany. During the mid-1800s, Wundt used scientific research methods to investigate reaction times. His book, *Principles of Physiological Psychology*, published in 1874, outlined many of the major connections between the science of physiology and the study of human thought and behavior. Wundt defined psychology as the study of human consciousness and emphasized the use of experimental methods to study and measure consciousness. Wundt advanced the technique of introspection as the "scientific" tool that would enable researchers to reveal the structure of the mind. While Wundt's influence declined in the years to come, his early work in psychology helped set the stage for future experimental methods, and his impact on psychology is unquestionable.

By the early twentieth century, the validity and usefulness of introspection were seriously being questioned, particularly by John B. Watson, an American psychologist. Watson believed that the results of introspection could never be proved or disproved; introspection is subjective, and only the individual can observe his or her own mental processes. Ivan Pavlov's work on the conditioned reflex (induced under rigid laboratory controls, and therefore empirically observable and quantifiable) had given birth to an academic psychology in

PHOTO 1.3. Wilhelm Wundt.

the United States led by John Watson which came to be called "the science of behavior." Watson believed that only behavior is measurable and observable by more than one person. He proposed that psychologists should confine themselves to studying behavior. Watson's behaviorism largely replaced structuralism, advocating that people should be regarded as complex animals and studied using the same scientific methods as those used in chemistry and physics. Behaviorism totally rejected Freudian notions about unconscious influences. For Watson, psychology should match the natural sciences and adopt its own objective methods to be a scientific discipline. Watson (1919) defined psychology as the division of natural science which deals with human behavior "both learned and unlearned doings and sayings" as its subject matter.

PHOTO 1.4.   John B. Watson.

Perhaps the school of psychology that is most familiar to the general public is the psychodynamic approach to understanding behavior, which was championed by Sigmund Freud (1856–1939) and his followers.

Psychodynamic psychology focused on the role of unconscious thoughts, feelings, and memories. Freud developed his theories about behavior through extensive analysis of the patients whom he treated in his private clinical practice. Freud believed that many of the problems that his patients experienced, including anxiety, depression, and sexual dysfunction, were the result of the effects of painful childhood experiences that the person could no longer remember. So, while the behaviorists ignored the unconscious because they felt that its essential privacy and subjectivity rendered it inaccessible to scientific study, psychodynamic psychologists tended to regard behavior as a relatively superficial expression of unconscious drives.

In the late 1950s, many British and American psychologists were heavily influenced by computer science, in an attempt to understand more complex behaviors which they felt had either been neglected altogether or greatly oversimplified by learning theory (conditioning). These complex behaviors were what Wundt, Watson, and other early scientific psychologists had called "mind or mental processes." Instead, cognitive psychologists used the term "cognition or cognitive processes" to refer to the ways in which people come to know the world around them,

PHOTO 1.5.   Sigmund Freud.

how they attain, retain, and regain information, through the processes of perception, attention, memory, problem-solving, decision-making, language, and thinking in general. Cognitive psychologists see people as information processors, and human cognitive processes as similar to the operation of computer programs.

Contemporary psychology is interested in an enormous range of topics that look into human behavior and mental processes from the neural level to the cultural level. Contemporary psychology explores concepts such as perception, cognition, attention, emotion, phenomenology, motivation, brain functioning, personality, behavior, resilience, the unconscious mind, and interpersonal relationships. The resulting knowledge is then applied to various spheres of human activity, including the problems of individuals' daily lives and the treatment of mental illness. The multiple perspectives in modern psychology provide researchers and students a variety of ways to approach problems and to understand, explain, predict, and resolve human thought and behavior. Perhaps the field of psychology struggles to find a unifying paradigm because human beings are multifaceted and human experiences are so diverse and complex.

However, despite the dramatic growth and change that psychology displayed across its history, the story certainly does not end here. Psychology has continued to evolve and new ideas and perspectives are still being introduced. Today, the majority of psychologists do not identify themselves with a single school of thought. Instead, they often focus on a particular specialty area or perspective, often drawing on ideas from a range of theoretical backgrounds. This eclectic approach has contributed new ideas and theories that will continue to shape psychology for years to come. Studying psychology will reveal that there are many different ways to think about and deal with human experience, thought, and behavior.

Despite the differences in their interests, areas of study, and approaches, all psychologists have one thing in common: they rely on scientific methods. Research psychologists use scientific methods to create new knowledge about the causes of behavior, whereas practitioner psychologists, such as clinical, counseling, industrial, organizational, and school psychologists, use existing research to enhance the everyday life of others.

Summary

- Psychology is the scientific study of the mind and behavior of the human being.
- The development psychology as a separate field of study grew out of several scientific and non-scientific disciplines.
- Well-defined psychological schools and perspectives were developed during the relatively brief history of psychology.
- Contemporary psychology is interested in an enormous range of topics that look into human behavior and mental processes from the neural level to the cultural level.

Test Your Knowledge

- Define what is meant by psychology.
- How do the works of Wilhelm Wundt contribute to psychology?
- How does John B. Watson's view add to psychology?

Critical Thinking Question

- Evaluate the role of René Descartes in the development of psychology.

two

Major Areas of Applied Psychology

Learning Goals

■ This chapter is intended to provide the reader with an outline of the common areas of specialization in psychology, such as clinical psychology, counseling psychology, developmental psychology, educational and school psychology, personality psychology, social psychology, forensic psychology, organizational psychology, experimental psychology, and health psychology.

Introduction

The field of modern psychology has many scientific perspectives that share at least some common approaches and that work together and exchange knowledge to form a coherent discipline (Yang & Chiu, 2009). However, further specialization in psychology may stem from interest in a specific age group, a specific disorder, or specific situations. Because of the broad and diverse nature of the field of psychology, students may wonder which areas are most suitable for their interests and which types of careers might be available to them. Common areas of specialization in psychology include:

1. *Clinical psychology*: this studies the causes, diagnosis, treatment, and prevention of different types of behavioral and emotional disorders. Clinical psychologists attempt to use the principles of psychology to better understand, predict, and alleviate intellectual, emotional, and behavioral problems, mental disorders, drug addiction, and marital and family conflicts. It is important to distinguish clinical psychology from psychiatry. Psychiatrists are medical doctors who have received specialized training in psychiatry. Clinical psychologists go to graduate school and get a PhD, while psychiatrists go to medical school and get an MD.

2. *Counseling psychology*: while clinical psychologists are likely to deal with severe disorders (e.g., schizophrenia, bipolar disorder), counseling psychologists often deal with less severe behavioral and emotional problems. Counseling psychologists helps individuals of all ages to adjust, adapt, and cope with personal and interpersonal problems in such diverse areas as relationships, work, education, marriage, child rearing, and aging.

3. *Developmental psychology*: this is concerned with the study of the physical, cognitive, social, and psychological changes that occur at different ages and stages of the lifespan. Developmental psychologists might study a specific ability, such as language development, or study a particular period of life, such as infancy, adolescence, adulthood, or old age.

4. *Educational psychology*: this focuses on the study of all psychological aspects of the learning process, aiming at increasing the effectiveness of the learning experience. Educational psychologists help in the development of the instructional methods and materials used to train people in both educational and work settings. This usually includes the study of learning facilities, curricula, teaching techniques, and particular student problems.

5. *School psychology*: school psychologists are concerned essentially with psychological testing (e.g., assessment of learning disabilities), but they may also perform counseling, or guide students who have emotional or academic problems. They also develop programs to train teachers and parents to help students with emotional or learning problems.

6. *Personality psychology*: this is concerned with the study of individual differences in thoughts, emotions, and behavior, the sources and consequences of such differences, and the degree of consistency of characteristics within the individual across situations and over time.

7. *Social psychology*: this is interested in how people perceive and interpret their social world and how their beliefs, emotions, and behaviors are influenced by the real or imagined

PHOTO 2.1.
Development.

PHOTO 2.2. Studying.

presence of others. They are also concerned with the behavior of groups and with social relationships between and among people. Variable topics like conformity, obedience, persuasion, interpersonal attraction, helping behavior, prejudice, aggression, and social beliefs are studied by social psychologists.

8. *Forensic psychology*: this is concerned with the application of psychology to legal issues. Forensic psychologists may conduct psychological evaluations with defendants and present their findings as an expert witness in court. They may also provide evaluations for child custody arrangements, or be asked to predict dangerousness or competency to stand trial.

9. *Organizational psychology (work psychology)*: this is the branch of psychology concerned with selecting people who are most suitable for particular jobs or designing structures that facilitate cooperation and teamwork. It includes such topics as job analysis, personnel selection and training, worker productivity, job satisfaction, leadership, and group behavior within organizations.

10. *Neuropsychology*: this focuses on the relationship between the brain and behavior, emotion, and cognition. That is, how brain functioning affects those processes. In practice, a neuropsychologist uses different types of standardized tests to measure different brain functions, including emotions, memory, cognitive ability, personality, problem-solving, reasoning, and personality. Neuropsychologists can help in developing a treatment plan by explaining how the brain functions and how that functioning relates to behavior.

11. *Experimental psychology*: this is actually misleading, because many psychologists who are not defined as "experimental psychologists" do conduct experiments, but this name is often used for psychologists who study basic psychological processes (e.g., perception, cognition, learning, and other psychological processes).

12. *Health psychology*: this is interested in the role of psychological factors in the development, prevention, and treatment of illness. Health psychology includes topics such as stress and coping, the relationship between psychological factors and physical health, and ways of promoting health-enhancing behaviors.

Test Your Knowledge

- What is the difference between clinical and counseling psychology?
- What is the focus of developmental psychology?
- What is the difference between educational and school psychology?
- What is the focus of personality psychology?
- What is the interest of social psychology?
- What is the focus of forensic psychology?
- What is the focus of organizational psychology?
- What are the areas of interest of neuropsychologists?
- What is meant by experimental psychology?
- What is the focus of health psychology?

Critical Thinking Questions

- What is the role of psychologists in the field of human development?
- How can neuropsychology help in understanding human behavior and emotion?

three
Research in Psychology

Learning Goals

- This chapter is intended to provide the reader with a comprehensive overview of what is meant by psychological research and the scientific method. By the end of this chapter, one will have an idea of the different types of research designs and their distinguishing features, in addition to understanding the ethics of psychological research.

Introduction

Psychologists are not the only people who seek to understand human behavior and solve social problems. Philosophers, religious leaders, and politicians, among others, attempt to provide explanations for human behavior.

Psychologists depend on research as a tool for understanding human beings and their relationships with others. Like any science, psychology is based on verifiable or empirical evidence, that is the result of objective observation, measurement, and experimentation. As part of the overall process of producing empirical evidence, psychologists follow the basic steps of the scientific method. Following the basic guidelines of the scientific method does not guarantee that correct conclusions will always be reached, but it guards against bias and minimizes the chance of error and faulty conclusions. So, psychologists need to have a good understanding of the purposes, advantages, and disadvantages of different research methods. This will enable them to read research reports that are usually concisely written, and require a degree of knowledge of the topic and research methods. Research reports are much clearer and easier to understand once the basics of psychological research methods are known. There are four basic goals of psychological research: (1) to describe; (2) to explain; (3) to predict; and (4) to change behavior and mental processes. In other words, psychological research involves the following:

1. *Description* of what occurred: this is usually the first step in understanding a behavior. Psychologists attempt to describe or to name and classify particular behaviors by making careful scientific observations.
2. *Explanation* of certain behavior or mental process by elucidating possible reasons for its occurrence.
3. *Prediction* of the possibility of the occurrence of a future behavior or mental process through identifying conditions under which it is likely to occur.
4. *Change*: applying psychological knowledge to prevent unwanted outcomes or bring about desired goals, to help people improve their work environment, to stop addictive behaviors, to become less depressed, to improve their family relationships, and so on.

PHOTO 3.1.   A Laboratory Study.

The Scientific Method

The scientific method is the set of assumptions, rules, and procedures that scientists use to conduct research. All scientists (whether they are physicists, chemists, biologists, sociologists, or psychologists) share the basic processes of collecting data and drawing conclusions about those data. The methods used by scientists have developed over years and provide a common framework for developing, organizing, and sharing information. In its ideal form, the scientific method has six elements:

1. Identify the research problem.
2. Review the related literature.
3. Propose a hypothesis.
4. Design and conduct the research.
5. Analyze the data and report the results.
6. Draw conclusions and build a theory.

1. Identify the Research Problem

This entails identifying and specifying an area in which one is going to conduct the research. The research problem can be identified in many ways, including personal interest, scientific developments, social and clinical problems, etc.

2. Review the Related Literature

Conducting a search for other research findings related to the future research, in order to see how others have approached the same or similar issues. Also, reviews of the related literature can give some idea of the probable outcome of one's research.

3. Propose a Hypothesis

A hypothesis is a preliminary assumption or prediction that describes the relationship between two or more variables to be tested. A hypothesis is often stated as a specific prediction that can be empirically tested, such as "psychological stress increases the possibility of physical illness."

PHOTO 3.2.   Scientific Method.

The aim of the hypothesis is not to arrive at the perfect answer to the question but to provide a direction for the subsequent scientific investigation. Hypotheses should be carefully phrased in order to indicate the nature of the relationships being investigated (causal or otherwise relationships).

The *variables* contained in any given hypothesis are simply anything that can vary or change among individuals and can be observed and measured, such as age, gender, height, intelligence, years of education, or reading speed. The psychologist must provide an operational definition of each variable to be investigated. An *operational definition* describes the variable in specific terms and determines how it will be measured or manipulated. Operational definitions are important because many of the concepts that psychologists investigate, such as education, happiness, or stress, can be measured in more than one way, e.g., when verifying a hypothesis that premarital education enhances marital quality, a researcher would need to formulate an operational definition of premarital education and marital quality. This helps to determine items that researchers need to observe, and the measures that would reflect these factors. In looking at that hypothesis, Stanley et al. (2006) operationally defined premarital education as the couple's response to a question asking if they had attended a class, workshop, or counseling session designed to prepare them for marriage. Answering "no" was scored "0," and "yes" was scored "1." Marital quality was operationally defined as the person's 1–5 rating in response to several questions about their satisfaction with the marriage. Responding with 1 indicated that the person was not at all satisfied, and 5 indicated that the person was completely satisfied. A completely different operational definition could be found in another body of research.

4. Design and Conduct the Research

After reviewing the related literature and making hypotheses, the research is conducted. A variety of research designs is available to the researchers, who can choose the one that best suits their study (discussed later).

5. Analyze the Data

After collecting the information, the data will be tabulated and statistically assessed in order to see whether the findings prove or disprove the hypotheses. A statistically significant result is simply one that is not likely to have occurred by chance, but it does not mean that the finding is significant in the everyday sense of being important, e.g., in a study looking at factors that would help predict people who are at risk of attempting suicide (Mann et al., 1999), fewer years of education (12.7 years) were a statistically significant risk of suicide as compared to non-attempters (14 years). In practical terms, however, the difference was not substantial enough to be clinically meaningful in trying to identify people who represent a suicide risk. Evaluation of the effect size can give an idea of the magnitude or size of an effect. Effect size can be assessed using a variety of methods, such as (1) Cohen's d; or (2) the number needed to treat (NNT).

6. Draw Conclusions

Conclusions are drawn after a statistical analysis of the data. Accordingly, a decision is made about the rejection or acceptance of the hypothesis. As research findings accumulate from individual studies, eventually theories develop. A theory, or model, is a tentative explanation that tries to summarize and integrate diverse research findings and observations on a particular topic. A useful theory is one that promotes the understanding of behavior, allows testable predictions to be made, and stimulates new research. It is not unusual to find more than one theory that is useful in explaining a particular area of behavior or mental processes, such as the development of personality or the experience of emotion.

Types of Research Designs

Research methodology can be classified in many different ways, e.g., some researchers distinguish between quantitative and qualitative studies; others distinguish between experimental and non-experimental research; still others distinguish between research that is conducted in laboratories versus in the field, e.g., schools. However, there is overlap among different research categorizations, e.g., a non-experimental study can be either quantitative or qualitative, while an experimental study can include some qualitative components. The main types of research methods include:

- descriptive (observational) research
- correlational research
- true experiments
- quasi-experiments.

Descriptive Studies (Observational Studies)

Descriptive research involves strategies for observing behavior and describing in detail its characteristics objectively and systematically. Using descriptive methods, researchers can answer important questions, such as when certain behaviors take place, how often they occur, and whether they are related to other factors, such as a person's age, ethnic group, or educational level. Without descriptive data, it is difficult for research to progress effectively, e.g., it is difficult to imagine research about the causes of schizophrenia without a substantial body of knowledge which describes the major features of schizophrenia. However, descriptive research cannot give an etiological explanation of a phenomenon. Commonly used descriptive methods include:

1. *Naturalistic observation*: researchers observe and record behavior in its natural setting without attempting to influence or control it, e.g., in a school playground.

   The basic aim of naturalistic observation is to detect the behavior patterns that exist naturally, patterns that might not be apparent in a laboratory or if the subjects knew they were being watched. Psychologists should carefully define the behaviors that they will observe and measure before they begin their research. Naturalistic observation does not explain behavior, though descriptions can be revealing. In conducting observational research, scientists must guard against observer bias resulting from an observer's expectations.

   One advantage of naturalistic observation is that it allows researchers to study human behaviors that cannot ethically be manipulated in an experiment, e.g., suppose that a psychologist wants to study bullying behavior in children, it would not be ethical to deliberately create a situation in which one child is aggressively bullied by another child. However, it would be ethical to study bullying by observing aggressive behavior in children in a crowded school playground (Hawkins, Pepler, & Craig, 2001). Because the observations occur in the natural setting, the results of naturalistic observation studies can often be generalized more confidently to real-life situations than can the results of studies using artificially manipulated or staged situations.

PHOTO 3.3.   Naturalistic Observation.

2. *Case study*: this is an intensive, in-depth investigation of an individual, a family, or some other social unit. Case studies involve gathering a lot of information from numerous sources (e.g., friends, family, and co-workers) to construct a detailed profile of the person. Psychological, biographical, neurological, medical, and even school or work records may be examined. Other sources of information can include psychological testing and observations of the person's behavior.

   Clinical psychologists and psychiatrists routinely use case studies to develop a complete profile of a psychotherapy client. Case studies are also used in psychological research investigating rare or unusual conditions. In case-based research (case series), information from multiple case studies is systematically combined and analyzed. Case-based research can be particularly valuable in clinical psychology, where it can be used to evaluate and improve treatment strategies for people with specific psychological disorders.

3. *Surveys*: these are a direct way to learn about the behavior, attitudes, and opinions of people, by asking them a structured set of questions in a predetermined order about their experiences, beliefs, behaviors, or attitudes.

   One key advantage offered by survey research is that information can be gathered from a larger group of people than other research methods. Surveys usually involve carefully designed questionnaires, usually in a paper-and-pencil format, that are

PHOTO 3.4.   Surveys.

distributed to a selected group of people. Computer-based or internet-based surveys have become increasingly common. Surveys are still conducted over the telephone or personally, with the interviewer recording the person's responses. Surveys are administered to a segment of the population. Selecting a representative sample is the key to getting accurate survey results. A representative sample should parallel, or match, the larger group on relevant characteristics, such as age, sex, race, marital status, or educational level. Random selection is usually used to choose a representative sample. Random selection means that every member of the larger group has an equal chance of being selected for inclusion in the sample.

One potential problem with surveys and questionnaires is that people do not always answer honestly. Participants may misrepresent their personal characteristics or lie in their responses. These problems can be addressed in a well-designed survey. One strategy is to rephrase and ask the same basic question at different points in the survey or during the interview. The researchers can then compare the responses to make sure that the participant is responding honestly and consistently.

Correlational Studies (Associative Studies)

Two or more variables are measured more or less simultaneously in a sample of individuals, i.e., the extent to which measured variables are associated or correlated, at a single point in time, is examined.

A variable is anything that can be measured, and differs among individuals, such as age, gender, intelligence, years of education, reading speed, or behavior.

Correlational research is considered a type of observational research as nothing is manipulated by the researcher, i.e., correlational studies examine how variables are naturally related in the real world, without controlling either of them, e.g., correlation between people's height and weight, or correlations between scores on personality tests and number of friends.

Correlational studies are often carried out in areas of psychology such as social, personality, developmental, educational, and abnormal or clinical psychology. In these areas, such research designs have the advantage of enabling the researcher to measure a number of different variables at the same time. Any of these variables might possibly explain why something occurs. It is likely that anything that we are interested in explaining will have a number of different causes

PHOTO 3.5. Correlational Studies.

rather than a single cause. By measuring a number of different variables at the same time, it becomes possible to see which of the variables is most strongly related to what it is we are seeking to explain.

Correlational studies cannot be used to determine the causal relationship between the variables. In other words, we cannot make statements concerning cause and effect on the basis of this type of research, as we do not know the direction of the cause. Also, another unconsidered variable of which we are not aware may be causally involved, e.g., major depression was postulated to be associated with low levels of serotonin neurotransmitters, therefore, a causal relationship cannot be stated, as the depletion in serotonin may cause depression or depression may cause a depletion in neurotransmitter levels, or a third factor may be responsible for both lowering serotonin synthesis rates and triggering depression (Aan het Rot, Mathew, & Charney, 2009).

When working with continuous variables, the correlation coefficient to use is Pearson's r. The correlation coefficient (r) indicates the extent to which the pairs of numbers for these two variables lie on a straight line. A correlation can be expressed numerically as a coefficient, ranging from -1 to +1. Values above zero indicate a positive correlation, while values below zero indicate a negative correlation. A zero correlation occurs when there is no relationship between variables, e.g., the correlation between gender and intelligence. A positive correlation describes a situation where both variables either increase or decrease together, they move in the same direction, however, this is not a cause-and-effect relationship. In a negative correlation, the variables move in opposite directions. An increase in one variable predicts a decrease in the other variable and vice versa.

In designing a study, psychologists try to anticipate and control for *confounding variables* (also called extraneous variables or the third variable problem). These factors are not the focus of the experiment, but they might produce inaccurate experimental results by influencing changes in the dependent variable. Depending on the question being investigated, potential confounding variables in a psychology experiment may include unwanted variability in factors such as the participants' ages, gender, ethnic background, race, health, occupation, personal habits, education, and so on. Even though researchers try to minimize unwanted influences and variability, it is impossible to control every aspect of an experimental situation. This is why researchers use various experimental controls.

The advantages of correlational research are:

- Correlational research allows the researcher to investigate naturally occurring variables that may be unethical or impractical to test experimentally, e.g., it would be unethical to conduct an experiment on whether smoking causes lung cancer.
- Correlational research allows the researcher to assess the presence of a relationship between variables that can be displayed in a graphical form.

The disadvantages of correlational research are:

- A correlation does not imply causation. Even if there is a very strong association between two variables, we cannot assume that one causes the other, e.g., suppose we found a positive correlation between watching violence on TV and violent behavior in adolescence. The cause of both variables could be a third (extraneous) one, e.g., growing up in a violent home, where both watching TV and violent behavior are the outcome; being a violent adolescent may lead to more preference to watch violence on TV; or watching violence on TV may cause increased violence.

- Correlation does not allow us to go beyond the given data, e.g., suppose it was found that there was an association between time spent on homework (half an hour to 3 hours) and examination score (1–6). It would not be legitimate to infer from this that spending 6 hours on homework would be likely to generate a score of 12.

Experimental Studies

A true experiment is defined as a research study that imposes control over all other variables except the one under study. It is often easier to impose this sort of control in a laboratory setting, hence the erroneous notion that true experiments are only laboratory studies. Experimental studies are used to explore a cause-and-effect relationship between changes in one variable and the effect that is produced on another variable, e.g., the effect of a certain drug on alleviating a certain disorder.

Every experiment must have at least two groups: an experimental and a control group. All subjects should be randomly assigned to groups, and should be tested as simultaneously as possible, and the experiment should be conducted in a double-blind fashion. Conducting an experiment involves deliberately varying one factor, which is called the *independent variable*. The researcher then measures the changes, if any, that are produced in a second factor, called the *dependent variable*. The dependent variable is so named because changes in it depend on variations in the independent variable. Each experimental and control group will receive an independent variable. The dependent variable will be measured to determine if the independent variable has an effect.

A clinical trial is an example of experimental research that seeks to determine the clinical efficacy of a new treatment or drug. There are two groups: a treatment group (the group that receives the therapeutic agent) and a control group (the group that receives the placebo). Subjects are randomly assigned to groups, they are tested simultaneously, and the experiment should be conducted in a double-blind approach. In other words, neither the patient nor the person administering the drug should know whether the patient is receiving the drug or the placebo. The independent variable in the clinical trial is the therapeutic agent.

Experimental studies are not always feasible; the results may not generalize to other contexts; and it may not be ethical to manipulate certain variables. Experimental bias may occur when an experimenter influences participants and thinks that the effect is due to the variable being studied.

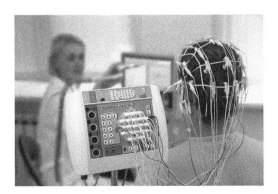

PHOTO 3.6. Studying Brain Activities by EEG.

Quasi-Experimental Studies

Quasi-experiments are very similar to true experiments but use naturally formed groups (young vs. old; men vs. women) or pre-existing groups that are not naturally formed. Quasi-experimentation is used in situations that are difficult or unethical to randomly assign to groups, e.g., if comparing young and old subjects on lung capacity, it is impossible to randomly assign subjects to either the young or old group (these are naturally formed groups). This limits the conclusions one can draw from such study. In that study, one may conclude that old age can result in less lung capacity, but other variables can actually account for this result, e.g., repeated exposure to pollutants as opposed to age may be responsible for the difference in lung capacity. It could also be a generational factor; the older group perhaps smoked more in their early years as compared to the younger group who have increased awareness of the hazards of cigarettes. Thus, we must be careful about making statements of causality with quasi-experimental designs, as many differences between the groups that we cannot control could account for differences in our dependent measures.

Another type of quasi-experimental research is comparing a group that gets a particular intervention with another group that is similar in characteristics but did not receive the intervention; no random assignment is used to form groups (Cook & Campbell, 1979), e.g., if a corporation wanted to test the effectiveness of a new program that will be implemented at a work site, as compared to another site as a control (no program). As the employees are not randomly assigned to work at each site, the study has pre-existing groups. After a few months of study, the researchers could then see if the new program site had less absenteeism and lower health costs than the old program site. The results are again restricted due to the quasi-experimental nature of the study. As the study has pre-existing groups, there may be other differences between those groups than just the presence or absence of a new program, e.g., the new program may be in a significantly newer, more attractive building, a bad manager may work at the old program site, or the employees on the old site are less efficient than those on the new program. Either way, if a difference is found between the two sites, it may or may not be due to the presence/absence of the new program. For this reason, researchers attempt to control for differences between non-randomly assigned groups in a number of ways. Two of the most common control methods include:

1. *Matching*: for example, when an enhanced and an old version of a third-grade reading curricula are being administered in different classrooms, and a researcher is interested in comparing the effects of the traditional reading curriculum with the effects of the enhanced version of the curriculum that includes extra homework assignments; the researchers try to match similar classrooms on other possible variables, e.g., matching classrooms on years of experience of the teacher.
2. *Statistical control*: the researcher can statistically control for variables that are related to the outcome. If the researcher knows that variables such as socio-economic status and prior reading ability are related to reading achievement, then the researcher can statistically control for these variables, in order to better assess the unique effects of the new curriculum.

Cross-Sectional Studies Versus Longitudinal Studies

Cross-sectional studies create comparisons at a single point of time, whereas longitudinal studies create comparisons over time. The research question will determine which approach is best. Both cross-sectional and longitudinal studies record information about their subjects without manipulating the study variables. Both may take either observational or correlational form.

Cross-Sectional Studies

The defining feature of a cross-sectional study is that it compares different population groups at a single point of time. A cross-sectional study involves assessment, at the same time, of people who are similar on some characteristics but different on a key factor of interest such as age, income levels, or geographic locations. Participants are usually separated into groups known as cohorts, e.g., researchers might create cohorts of participants who are in their twenties, thirties, and forties. The benefit of a cross-sectional study design is that it allows researchers to compare many different variables at the same time, e.g., comparison of age, gender, income, and educational level in relation to a personality trait.

The advantages of cross-sectional studies are:

- Cross-sectional studies are usually relatively inexpensive and allow researchers to collect a lot of information quite quickly (no long periods of follow-up). Participants are less likely to quit this type of studies for this reason.
- Researchers can collect data on different variables to see how these differences might correlate with the critical variable of interest.
- While cross-sectional studies cannot be used to determine causal relationships, they can provide a useful base to further research, e.g., cross-sectional study can be used to assess whether a particular behavior might be linked to a particular illness. Results of this study can serve as a clue to further experimental studies.

The disadvantages of cross-sectional studies are:

- Cross-sectional studies do not provide definite information about cause-and-effect relationships. It may be difficult to determine whether the outcome followed exposure in time or whether exposure resulted from the outcome. This is because such studies offer a snapshot of a single moment in time, they do not consider what happens before or after the snapshot is taken. However, cross-sectional studies can provide an understanding of correlations that may exist at a particular point in time.
- They are not suitable for studying rare diseases or diseases with a short duration.
- Cross-sectional studies usually require a large number of participants. It may be difficult to find participants who are precisely similar except in one specific variable.
- A group may have a unique experience that gives rise to cohort differences that can influence the results. Individuals born during the same period or in a given geographic region may share important experiences limited to times and location, e.g., individuals who were alive during World War II may share experiences that make them different from other age groups.

Longitudinal Studies

A longitudinal study is a type of correlational research that includes investigation of variables beyond a single moment of time. Data are collected at the beginning of the study, and are periodically gathered throughout the length of the study. Longitudinal research can extend over years or even decades, e.g., in a study about the effect of physical exercise during middle age on cognitive health at old age; data related to the physically fitness of the mid-forties to early fifties participants, how often they work out and how well they do on cognitive performance tests, are collected at the beginning of the study. Periodically over the course of the study, the researchers gather the same data from the participants to check activity levels and mental performance, and to test the study hypothesis that people who are more physically fit in their forties and fifties will be less likely to develop cognitive decay in their seventies and eighties.

There are three distinct kinds of longitudinal studies: panel, cohort, and retrospective. A panel usually involves a random representative sample of subjects who are followed at particular intervals over a long period, whereas a cohort study observes subjects in a similar group based on a specific variable, such as birth, geographic location or common experiences. A retrospective study involves looking at historical information such as medical records.

The advantages of longitudinal studies are:

- The key advantage to longitudinal studies is the ability to show changes affecting a variable over time. It is particularly useful when studying development and lifespan issues, e.g., looking at changes in development over time can help researchers to establish a sequence of events when looking at the aging process.
- Depending on the scope of the study, longitudinal observation can also help to discover connections between different events over a long period of time, events that might otherwise not be linked.
- Looking how identical twins reared together from childhood into adulthood differ from those reared apart on a variety of variables can help to explore how growing up in a different environment influences things such as personality and achievement. Since the participants share these same genetics, it is assumed that any differences would result from environmental factors. This can help also to identify which characteristics are more strongly influenced by either genetics or experience.
- Using longitudinal studies enables psychologists to measure the impact of various therapy practices over time, usually using a control group as a baseline.

The disadvantages of longitudinal studies are:

- Longitudinal studies require a long time and are often expensive.
- Because of the cost, these studies often include only a small group of subjects, which makes it difficult to apply the results to the general population.
- Participants may drop out of the study, leading to a shrinking of the sample size and the amount of data collected. The dropout of some participants from a study is known as selective attrition. In some cases, this can lead to an attrition bias and influence the results of the longitudinal study. If the final group no longer reflects the original representative sample, this attrition can also threaten the validity of the experiment, and it will be difficult to generalize the results to the rest of the population.
- Longitudinal data is collected at multiple pre-determined points, but those observation periods cannot take into account whatever has happened in between those points.
- Panel conditioning: during the study, respondents can often unknowingly change their qualitative responses to better fit what they consider to be the observer's intended goal. The process of the study itself has changed how the subject or respondent views the questions.
- It is difficult to account for all of the confounding factors that may affect the results. If one could guarantee to deal with all the confounding variables in this sort of research, it could be an ideal type of research method.

Ethics in Psychological Research

Many organizations, including universities, have ethics committees that supervise the research carried out by employees and other researchers who wish to do research in these organizations. The ethical standards provide enforceable rules for conduct as psychologists. Ethical behavior is not the responsibility of each individual psychologist alone but the responsibility of the entire psychological community. Monitoring the activities of fellow psychologists, seeking the advice of other psychologists when ethical difficulties come to light, and collectively advancing ethical behavior in their workplace, are all instances of the mutual concern that psychologists have about the conduct of the profession.

The American Psychological Association's ethical code amounts to a substantial ethical program for both psychological practitioners and researchers. This is important since unethical behavior reflects on the entire psychological community. Sanctions may be imposed on those violating ethical principles. This code is contained in the *Ethical Principles of Psychologists and Code of Conduct* (American Psychological Association, 2010). In general, psychologists must respect the dignity and welfare of participants. The psychologist must inform the participants of the purpose of the research, including significant information that might affect a person"s willingness to participate or quit the study. The psychologist must also explain that participants are free to decline to participate or to withdraw from the research at any time. Psychologists should not disclose personally identifiable information about research participants. Psychologists cannot deceptively expose research participants to dangerous or harmful conditions that might cause either physical or emotional harm. At most institutions, any psychological research using human or animal subjects is inspected by an institutional review board before approval is granted (Ghooi, 2014). The use of animals in psychological research is also governed by specific ethical guidelines. The APA ethical guidelines are based on five general principles:

1. *Beneficence and non-maleficence*: psychologists are obliged to do good and avoid harm to those they interact with professionally. Psychologists should do their best to be aware of how their own physical and mental health may impact their ability to provide professional services to others. They should be aware of and guard against those factors which may result in harm to others, including financial, social, and institutional considerations.
2. *Fidelity and responsibility*: psychologists are required to clarify their role and obligations in all aspects of their professional activities, to adhere to professional standards of conduct, and to take responsibility for their actions. Under this standard, psychologists are faithful, dependable, and conscientious. Psychologists should work to avoid possible conflicts of interest situations that could lead to harm.
3. *Integrity*: psychologists are expected to display honesty and truthfulness in all aspects of their professional work, e.g., by not stealing or cheating, and avoiding all forms of deception and dishonesty. Deception can range from relatively minor omissions, such as not telling people the full story of what you are doing, to a completely false story about your identity and the nature of the study. With full consideration of the ethical and practical problems in using deception, some researchers find instances where they feel it is justified. Following the publication of Stanley Milgram"s classic studies of obedience in which unaware volunteers were asked to apply allegedly painful electric shocks to another person, the use of deception in social psychological research increased in popularity along with criticism from those opposing it. Experimenters who employ deception are responsible for debriefing the participants by describing the

nature of the deception, why it was used, and allowing the participant to express their feeling about what happened.

4. *Justice*: this means that psychologists exercise careful judgment and take care to enable all people to experience just and fair treatment and psychological practices. Psychologists should be aware of the nature of their biases (potential and actual) and make sure that their biases, competence, and limitations do not lead to unjust practices. They should not engage in, or overlook, unjust practices and need to be aware of the ways in which injustice may manifest itself.

5. *Respect for people's rights and dignity*: psychologists respect the dignity and worth of all people, and the rights of all people to privacy, confidentiality, and self-determination. Consequently, psychologists need to be aware of the vulnerabilities of some individuals that make it difficult for them to make autonomous decisions, e.g., children. The principle also requires psychologists to be aware of and respect differences among cultures, individuals, and roles. Age, disability, ethnicity, gender, gender identity, language, national origin, race, religion, sexual orientation, and socio-economic status are among these differences. Psychologists should try to eliminate any of their own biases regarding such issues in their own professional interactions, while being vigilant for, and critical of, those who fail to meet this standard.

Clinical Notes

- Evaluation of research results necessitates a good understanding of the purposes, advantages, and disadvantages of different research.
- Consider the advantages and disadvantages of different research methodology; all methods can be appropriately used according to research circumstances.
- Adherence to ethical guidelines in research is the responsibility of each individual and the entire psychological community.

Summary

- The basic goals of psychological research are to describe, to explain, to predict, and to change behavior and mental processes.
- The scientific method is the set of assumptions, rules, and procedures that scientists use to conduct research.
- A hypothesis is a preliminary assumption or prediction that describes the relationship between two or more variables to be tested.
- A variable is anything that can vary or change among individuals and can be observed and measured, such as age, gender, height, and intelligence.
- An operational definition of a variable describes in specific terms how it will be defined, measured, or manipulated.
- An independent variable is the factor that is deliberately changed, while the dependent variable is the factor that shows changes as a consequence of changes in the independent variable.
- A statistically significant result denotes that it is not likely to have occurred by chance.
- The main types of research methods include descriptive research, correlational research, true experiments, and quasi-experiments.
- Descriptive research involves naturalistic observation, case studies, and surveys.

■ In correlational studies, two or more variables are measured more or less simultaneously in a sample of individuals. Correlational studies cannot be used to determine the causal relationship between the variables.

■ Confounding variables are factors that are not the focus of the experiment, but might produce inaccurate experimental results by influencing changes in the dependent variable.

■ A true experiment is defined as a research that imposes control over all other variables except the one under study.

■ Quasi-experiments use naturally formed groups or pre-existing groups that are not naturally formed.

■ Cross-sectional studies make comparisons at a single point in time, whereas longitudinal studies make comparisons over time.

■ A longitudinal study is a type of correlational research that involves looking at variables beyond a single moment of time.

■ The APA ethical guidelines are based on five general principles: beneficence and non-maleficence, fidelity and responsibility, integrity, justice, and respect for people's rights and dignity.

Test Your Knowledge

■ What are the basic goals of psychological research?
■ Define scientific method and describe its elements.
■ Enumerate different types of descriptive studies.
■ What is the value of observational study?
■ What is meant by surveys?
■ What are the advantages and disadvantages of correlational studies?
■ What are the differences between experimental and quasi-experimental studies?
■ What are the differences between cross-sectional versus longitudinal studies?
■ What are the advantages and disadvantages of cross-sectional studies?
■ What are the advantages and disadvantages of longitudinal research?
■ Describe the main ethical guidelines of psychological research.

Critical Thinking Questions

■ Propose a research problem and determine how could you test it.
■ Describe the most suitable methods of research to ascertain the effect of a certain drug on human behavior, elucidating the advantages and disadvantages.
■ How could you assess the monoamines hypothesis of major depression, according to your understanding of different research methods?
■ How could different research methodology be used to evaluate the etiology of schizophrenia?
■ How can researchers declare their ethical obedience when conducting a study?

four
Major Schools
of Psychology

Learning Goals

- This chapter is intended to provide the reader with a comprehensive overview of the different psychological schools, arranged approximately according their time of origin. These schools include structuralism, functionalism, the evolutionary school, the psychodynamic school, the behavioral school, the biological school, the cognitive school, the sociocultural school, Gestalt psychology, and the humanistic school. Characteristic features of each school will be briefly discussed, including its important ideas, and its contribution to shaping the field of psychology, its place in current psychology, criticism or limitations of that school, and its clinical application if still applicable.

Introduction

When psychology was first established as a science separate from biology and philosophy, there was a debate over how to describe and explain the human mind and behavior. Over decades, different psychological ideas were elaborated into a large number of psychological theories. The following is a brief outline of the major schools that have influenced our knowledge and understanding of psychology:

I. STRUCTURALISM

The emergence of psychology as a distinct scientific discipline can be traced to Wilhelm Wundt's research in his laboratory in Leipzig. Wilhelm Wundt and his student, Edward B. Titchener, began a field known as structuralism. Structuralism, as the name suggests, was centered on investigating the structure of the mind. Structuralism held that conscious experiences could be broken down into elemental structures or component parts. The goal of structuralism was to create a periodic table of the elements of human experiences, even the most complex ones, such as sensations and feelings, similar to the periodic table of elements that had been created in chemistry. Volunteers were trained to observe, analyze, and describe their own sensations, mental images, and emotional reactions through a method they called introspection. Introspection involves looking inwards, reflecting on, analyzing, and trying to make sense of internal experiences as they occur. Research participants

PHOTO 4.1.   Edward Titchener.

were presented with various forms of stimuli and asked to describe as clearly and objectively as possible what they experienced as they worked on mental tasks, such as viewing colors, reading a page in a book, or performing a math problem. Reports would then be examined to determine the basic elements of consciousness, e.g., if a participant was presented with a slice of cake, it would not be enough to simply identify the type of food; in addition to explaining the basic elements of the cake that a participant was able to sense, he or she might describe the taste, smell, texture, color, and shape of the cake in as much detail as possible. When a person views a simple stimulus, such as a book, he/she is asked to try to reconstruct their sensations and feelings immediately after viewing it. Persons might first report on the colors they saw, then the smells, and so on, in the attempt to create a total description of their conscious experience. In other studies, the structuralists used newly invented reaction time instruments to systematically assess not only what the participants were thinking but how long it took them to do so. Structuralism played a significant role in shaping the field of psychology during its formative years; its role can be summarized in the following:

- Wundt and his followers helped to establish psychology as an independent experimental science and their emphasis on scientific methods of inquiry remains a key aspect of the discipline today.
- Structuralists discovered that people took longer to report the type of the sound they had just heard than to simply report that they had heard the sound. These studies marked the first time researchers realized that there is a difference between the sensation of a stimulus and the perception of that stimulus. Also, the idea of using reaction times to study mental events has now become the mainstay of cognitive psychology.
- Structuralists were the first to realize the importance of unconscious processes, and that psychologists cannot expect research participants to be able to accurately report on all of their experiences.

The limitations of introspection are:

- Despite their honorable attempts at scientific study, introspection was an unreliable method of research. Different subjects often provided different introspective reports about the same stimulus. Even well-trained subjects in introspection varied in their responses to the same stimulus from trial to trial.
- Introspection could not be used to study children.
- Complex topics, such as learning, development, mental disorders, and personality, could not be investigated using introspection.
- The methods and goals of structuralism were simply too limited to accommodate the rapidly expanding interests of the field of psychology.

Clinical Notes

- Structuralism has no current clinical implications.

Summary

- The goal of structuralism was to break down conscious experiences, even the most complex ones such as sensations and feelings, into elemental structures, to create a table of the elements of human experiences, similar to the periodic table of elements that had been created in chemistry.

Test Your Knowledge

- What role did structuralism play in psychology?
- Give an account of introspection.
- What are the limitations of introspection?

Critical Thinking Question

- Is it possible to break down conscious human experiences into their basic elemental structures to create a table of the elements of human experiences?

II. FUNCTIONALISM

The American scientist William James (1842–1910) believed that the structuralists were misguided; the mind is fluid, not stable, consciousness is ongoing, and not static. Therefore, he presumed that attempts to study the structure of the mind would be fruitless at worst and frustrating at best. He emphasized the study of the function, as opposed to the structure, of the mind. Function in this sense can mean one of two things: (1) how the mind operates; that is, how the elements of the mind work together; and (2) how specific behaviors and mental processes promote adaptation to the environment. James believed that mental processes serve vital functions that enable us to adapt and survive in a changing world, a matter that reflected the influence of Charles Darwin's principle of natural selection (survival of the fittest) on James' thinking. The functionalists believed that Darwin's theory could be applied to

PHOTO 4.2.   William James.

psychological characteristics too. Just as some animals have developed strong muscles to allow them to run fast, the functionalists thought that the human brain had adapted to serve a particular function in human experience. Thus, while the structuralists asked what happens when we engage in mental activity, the functionalists were more concerned with how and why it happens. However, functionalism was criticized for providing a vague definition of the term "function."

Although functionalism no longer exists as a school of psychology, its basic principles have been absorbed into psychology and continue to influence it in many ways. Functionalism contributed greatly to the development of psychology. It extended both the subject matter of psychology as well as the range of methods used to acquire data, e.g., the functionalists' emphasis on adaptation led them to promote the study of learning since this is believed to improve adaptability and chances of survival. Their concern with why certain mental processes occur also meant that they did extensive work on motivation. Functionalists are also credited with bringing the study of animals, children, and abnormal behavior into psychology, as well as an emphasis on individual differences (Hergenhahn, 2009). In addition, while the structuralists established psychology as a pure science, the functionalists broadened its narrow interests by focusing on the practical application of psychology in real-life problems. Also, functionalists added to the existing collection of research methods using mental tests, questionnaires, and physiological measures (Schultz & Schultz, 2007). The work of the functionalists has developed into the field of evolutionary psychology.

Clinical Notes

- Functionalism has no current clinical implications.

Summary

- Functionalism focused on the study of the function of the mind, how the mind operates, and how specific behaviors and mental processes promote adaptation to the environment.

Test Your Knowledge

- What role did functionalism play in psychology?

Critical Thinking Question

- How would you evaluate the functionalism approach?

III. EVOLUTIONARY PSYCHOLOGY

The main assumption of evolutionary psychology is that the human mind adapts to the natural environment in which it evolves. Evolutionary psychology focuses on the extent to which a human being has a given characteristic that helps the individual organism to survive and reproduce at a higher rate than do other members of the species who do not have the characteristic over the long course of evolution, e.g., it has been argued that jealousy has survived over time in men because it is supposed that the experience of jealousy leads men to be more likely to protect their mates and guard against rivals, which increases their reproductive success, and thus they are fitter than men who do not feel jealous (Buss, 2000). Thus, evolutionary psychology accepts the functionalists' basic assumption that many human psychological systems, including memory, emotion, and personality serve key adaptive functions. The core principles on which evolutionary psychology is founded can be summarized into the following:

- Darwin believed that natural selection plays a role in the evolution of behavior, and that the human mind can be explained by the same physical laws as other body organs. Darwin sees the human mind as the product of evolution just like other body organs, and states that we can gain a better understanding of the mind by examining the evolutionary circumstances that shaped it (Workman & Reader, 2014).
- The brain has evolved specialized neural mechanisms for solving problems that have persisted over deep evolutionary time, that give modern people Stone Age minds.
- Most contents and processes of the brain are unconscious, and most mental problems that seem easy to solve are actually extremely difficult problems that are solved unconsciously by complicated neural mechanisms.

Though evolutionary psychology provides logical explanations for why we may have many psychological characteristics, it is extremely difficult to test many of evolutionary psychology predictions, e.g., we cannot know which psychological characteristics our ancestors possessed or did not possess, we can only guess about these (Gould & Lewontin, 1979).

Clinical Notes
- Evolutionary psychology has little current clinical implication.

Summary
- Natural selection plays a role in the evolution of behavior, and the human mind can be explained by the same physical laws as other body organs.

Test Your Knowledge
- How can evolutionary psychology explain human behavior?

Critical Thinking Question
- How would you evaluate the evolutionary approach in psychology?

IV. PSYCHOANALYTIC AND PSYCHODYNAMIC THEORIES

PHOTO 4.3.   Sigmund Freud with His Colleagues at the IPA Congress at The Hague, 1920.

In his psychoanalytic theory, Freud argued that human behavior is the result of the interactions among the three components of the mind: the id, the ego, and the superego. Conflicts among these three structures, and our attempts to find balance among them, determine how we behave and approach the world. The foundation for psychodynamic perspective lies in the work of Sigmund Freud, which was expanded and diverged by works of his followers, such as Carl Jung, Alfred Adler, Melanie Klein, John Bowlby, and Mary Ainsworth. Psychodynamic theories share the following ideas:

- Mind (psyche) consists of interacting (dynamic) structures.
- It emphasizes the role of the unconscious above all.
- It assumes that the patient's psychological problems are caused by a malfunction in the defense mechanisms meant to protect the conscious from the subconscious.

Some theories could be considered psychodynamic but not psychoanalytic, such as Transactional Analysis (TA) (Eric Berne), analytical psychology (Carl Jung), and so forth. The following are summaries of the major theories proposed by psychodynamic theorists, including Sigmund Freud, Carl Jung, Alfred Adler, Eric Berne, Erik Erikson, and Karen Horney.

Sigmund Freud's Psychoanalytic Theory

Psychoanalytic theory and practice originated in the late nineteenth century in the work of Sigmund Freud (1856–1939). This offers a distinctive way of thinking about the human mind and of responding to psychological distress. Freud developed his theories about behavior through extensive analysis of the patients whom he treated in his private clinical practice.

PHOTO 4.4.   Sigmund Freud.

Freud's psychoanalytic theory and his therapy are based on the concept that forces motivating our behavior are derived from unconscious mental processes. Freud introduced a number of new concepts and theories of mind that include:

a. the topographical theory of mind
b. the structural model of mind
c. the psychosexual stages of development
d. defense mechanisms (see p. 86).

The Topographical Theory of Mind

Freud (1949) supposed that psychic processes (mental functions) operate on three levels: unconscious, preconscious, and conscious (see Photo 4.5).

■ *The conscious mind*: this part of the mind holds information of which we are aware of at the current moment, i.e., what we are currently thinking and feeling. It is seen as the tip of the iceberg in the ocean. The conscious mind has the ability to direct our focus, and to imagine what is not real.

■ *The preconscious mind*: this contains thoughts and feelings that a person is not currently aware of, but which can easily be brought to consciousness. It exists just below the level of consciousness. The preconscious is like a mental waiting room, in which thoughts remain until they succeed in attracting the eye of the conscious, e.g., when considering events of last night meeting, that information was preconscious till one pulls it up into consciousness.

- *The unconscious mind*: Freud believed that we are only aware of a small part of our mind's activity, and most of this activity remains hidden in our unconscious. The unconscious comprises mental processes that are inaccessible to consciousness but influence judgments, feelings, or behavior. According to Freud, the unconscious mind is the primary source of human behavior. Freud used the analogy of an iceberg to describe the three levels of the mind: the most important part of the mind is the part you cannot see. The unconscious mind acts as a storehouse of primitive wishes and impulses. Freud emphasized the importance of the unconscious mind, and its role in governing behavior to a greater degree than people suspect, and stated that our feelings, motives, and decisions are powerfully influenced by our past experiences, which are stored in the unconscious. Freud believed that unconscious drives can become conscious only in disguised or distorted form, such as dreams, slips of the tongue, or neurotic symptoms. Indeed, the aim of cure in psychoanalysis is to revert unconscious processes into conscious ones. Unconscious processes originate from two main sources: (i) *repression* or blocking out of anxiety-filled experiences: Freud (1915) suggested that threatening or painful desires and thoughts that threatens self-esteem or feelings of comfort and pleasure, are pushed out of awareness into the unconscious, because awareness of them produces anxiety; and (ii) *inherited experiences* (phylogenetic endowment) that lie beyond an individual's personal experience. Feist and Feist (2010) explained this as the unconscious inherited images that have been passed down to us by our ancestors through many generations of repeated experience.

When patients become overly upset when a Freudian psychoanalyst suggests that there is a particular thought or wish in the patient's unconscious, psychoanalysts consider this as evidence that they are on the right track. In psychoanalytic theory, this is known as "resistance," referring to the idea that patients will resist suggestions that probe the anxiety-producing contents of the unconscious. However, the existence of the unconscious remains controversial, with some

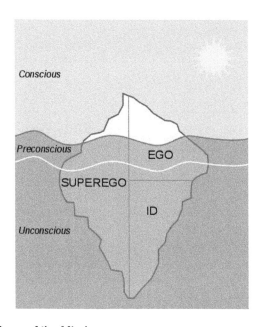

PHOTO 4.5. The Iceberg of the Mind.

researchers arguing that evidence for it is compelling and others challenging that unconscious processing can be accounted for without assuming the existence of a Freudian storehouse of repressed wishes and troubling urges and impulses (Eagle, 2011; Luborsky & Barrett, 2006).

Methods of Understanding the Unconscious Mind

Unconscious thoughts express themselves in a disguised form so as not to overly disturb the conscious mind. The unconscious resembles a boiler of threatening and anxiety-producing ideas, while the steam from this boiling pot can come into awareness and influence behaviors and disturb our emotions and cognitions, e.g., calling a partner by the name of a previous one, whom one liked better. According to Freudian theory, repressed information can flow out of the unconscious and express itself in dreams, slips, and free associations:

- *Dreams*: Freud suggested that sleep is a period of chaos during which the unconscious thoughts of the id attempt to find their way into consciousness. Freud proposed that the best place to look for clues to the unconscious is in dreams. Dreams, in Freud's view, represent gratification of unconscious instinctual impulses and wish fulfillment. Dreams are caused by conflict and are characterized by their power to bring up memories that the dreamer has forgotten, their strong use of symbolism, and their ability to reproduce repressed impressions of the dreamer's childhood. Freud suggested that dreams are not obvious and direct mirrors of unconscious ideas, but what is recalled from a dream is a disguised form of what we unconsciously wish for. That is, the manifest content of the dream (things that are present and the events that happen in a dream) are disguised versions of unconscious thoughts. The meanings of those dream elements are called the latent content of the dream. A dream must be analyzed and interpreted in order to understand the clues that it provides.

- *Slips*: Freud believed that all behavior (including slips of the tongue) is determined and there is no place for chance occurrence. According to Freud, a mistake is influenced by the unconscious, and has a hidden meaning. Freud said that such mistake is not accident, it is called a Freudian slip. He suggested that people reveal what is really on their mind by doing or saying something they do not intend, e.g., if a person unintentionally cut himself while peeling an orange after doing what he believed to be wrong, and this act made him feel guilty: the Freudian slip explanation assumes that the feelings of guilt in the unconscious direct the person to cut himself as a punishment. Similarly, when a person accidentally calls a boyfriend or girlfriend by the wrong name, it reveals something about unconscious thoughts and wishes. According to Freud, it does no good to ask a person whether this is true, as this information is in the unconscious, i.e., the person is not aware of it.

- *Free association*: Free association is a simple technique used by psychoanalysts, in which patients talk of whatever comes into their mind and the analyst draws conclusions based on what is said. This technique involves the therapist reading a list of words (e.g., mother, childhood, etc.) and observation of the patient's immediate response with the first word that comes to mind. It is hoped that fragments of repressed memories will emerge in the course of free association. Free association may not prove useful if the client shows resistance, or is reluctant to say what he or she is thinking. Freud reported that free associating patients occasionally experience an emotionally intense and vivid memory so that they almost relive the experience, this is called *abreaction*. This is like a flashback from a war or a rape experience. During abreaction, reliving or recalling a repressed experience results in the release of vivid, often cathartic, expression of repressed emotions or experience. If such a disturbing memory occurred in therapy or with a supportive friend and one felt better (relieved or cleansed), this is called *catharsis*. Successful therapy rests on the patient's transference of childhood sexual or aggressive feelings onto the therapist and away from symptom formation. Patients' resistance to change is seen as progress because it indicates that therapy has advanced beyond superficial conversation.

The Structural Model of Mind

Though the topographic model was helpful in understanding how people process and store information, it is not useful in explaining other important psychological phenomena, e.g., why some people develop psychological disorders and others do not. To extend his theory, Freud developed the structural model of the mind to account for normal and abnormal personality development. This model postulates that the mind could be divided into three interacting categories called the id, the ego, and the superego. Freud called it "the psychic apparatus." Freud did not mean that these are physical parts of our bodies or our brains, but a metaphorical mental framework. He coined these terms and proposed this division of the mind as abstract ideas meant to help us to understand how personality develops and works, and how mental illnesses can develop. In this model, the three different components interact with each other and create a constant two-way traffic between the conscious and unconscious parts of the mind. The essence of the structure described by Freud remains central to psychodynamic theory, although subsequent thinkers have significantly modified the way this model is seen to function.

Conflicts among these three structures, and efforts to find balance among desires of each of them determine how we behave and approach the world. The balance among these three structures in any given situation determines how one will resolve the conflict between two main behavioral tendencies: biological aggressive and pleasure-seeking drives vs. socialized internal control over those drives, e.g., the superego can make a person feel guilty if rules are not followed. When there is conflict between the goals of the id and superego, the ego must act as a judge and mediate this conflict. The ego can employ various defense mechanisms (Freud, 1894, 1896) to prevent it from becoming overwhelmed by anxiety. According to the structural model, personality reflects the interplay of these three psychic structures, which differ across individuals in relative power and influence. When the id predominates, instincts prevail, resulting in an impulsive personality style. When the superego is strongest, moral prohibitions dominate and a restrained over-controlled personality ensues. When the ego is dominant, a more balanced set of personality traits develop (Eagle, 2011; McWilliams, 2009).

The Id

The id is the first element of the structural model of mind (the "it" in Latin), that contains biological instincts (or drives) which Freud called Eros and Thanatos. Eros, or the life instinct, helps the individual to survive; it directs life-sustaining activities, such as respiration, eating, and sex (Freud, 1925). The energy created by the life instincts is known as libido. In contrast, Thanatos or the death instinct is viewed as a set of destructive forces present in all human beings (Freud, 1920). When this energy is directed outward onto others, it is expressed as aggression and violence. The destructive instinct aims to return a person to an inorganic state, but it is usually directed against other people resulting in aggression. Freud believed that Eros is stronger than Thanatos, thus enabling people to survive rather than to self-destruct. The two instincts can either operate against each other through hate or combine with each other through attraction.

The aim of the sexual instinct is pleasure, which can be gained through the erogenous zones, especially the mouth, anus, and genitals. The object of the sexual instinct is any person or thing that brings sexual pleasure. Both sadism (receiving sexual pleasure from inflicting pain on another) and masochism (receiving sexual pleasure from painful experiences) satisfy both sexual and aggressive drives.

Freud said that the id is totally unconscious, that is, we are unaware of its workings. The id is not rational; it imagines, dreams, and invents things to give us what we want. The id is driven by the pleasure principle, which struggles for immediate reduction of tension and gratification of all desires and needs. If these needs are not satisfied immediately, the result is a state of anxiety or tension, e.g., an increase in hunger or thirst should produce an immediate attempt to eat or drink.

The id is the only component of personality that is present at birth, so it is most clearly seen in the actions of babies and young children whose lives are dominated by their own needs, wishes, and feelings. The id is very important early in life, because it ensures that an infant's needs are met. If the infant is hungry or uncomfortable, he or she will cry until the demands of the id are met. The id plays an important role in the development of the bond between children and their parents through driving the baby to attach itself to caregivers and to satisfy its basic biological needs. However, the id's powerful drives do not disappear as we grow older, but (with variable success), they become increasingly hidden from view as we attempt to control them, by hiding their most unacceptable aspects in the unconscious part of mind. The way in which individuals handle biologically driven urges, desires, and emotions located in the id plays a vital role in shaping their inner world. If people are mainly ruled by the pleasure principle, they may find themselves taking things that they want out of other people's hands to satisfy their own needs. This sort of behavior would be both disruptive and socially unacceptable.

Because immediately satisfying personal needs is not always realistic or even possible, Freud assumed that the id tries to resolve the tension created by the pleasure principle through *primary process thinking*, which involves forming a mental image of the desired object in order to reduce the frustration of not having been gratified yet. This image can take the form of a dream, fantasy, hallucination, or delusion, e.g., a person who desires a piece of chocolate cake but does not have any at the moment, may deal with this by visualizing a delicious piece of cake. It is called primary because it comes first in human development. The experience of the mental image through the primary process is known as *wish fulfillment*. Primary process thinking is derived from the id and marked by illogical form, preverbal content, an emphasis on immediate wish fulfillment, and an equation of thought and action. In this type of thinking, the mechanisms of condensation, displacement, and symbolic representation are characteristic. Such a mode of thinking is characteristic of children, dreams, and in psychotic disorders.

The Ego

The second element of Freud's structural model is the ego (the "I" in Latin). In contrast to the instinctual id and the moral superego, the ego is the rational, pragmatic part of our personality. The ego is responsible for dealing with reality. It is less primitive than the id and it operates in both the conscious and the unconscious mind. It is what Freud considered to be the self, and its job is to balance the demands of the id and superego in the context of everyday reality. The ego is the seat of our capacity to learn, adapt, compromise, reflect, anticipate, and plan, and it works hard to integrate the different parts of our emotional and cognitive characters. It is also the source of our capacity to build successful relationships, as it manages the ongoing balance between our own wishes and needs and those of other people. The ego also drives us to seek approval and praise from significant others.

According to Freud, the ego develops from the id during infancy. The ego's goal is to satisfy the demands of the id in a safe and socially acceptable way. In contrast to the id, the ego is governed by what is known as the *reality principle*, that is, the ego must take the demands of reality and the outside world into account in addition to the id's basic needs and urges. The reality principle weighs up the costs and benefits of an action before deciding to act upon or abandon impulses. So, the ego attempts to help the id to get what it wants by judging the difference between real and imaginary. In many cases, the id's impulses can be satisfied through a process of *delayed gratification*; the ego will eventually allow the behavior, but only at the appropriate time and place. If a person is hungry, the id might begin to imagine food and even dream about food. The ego, however, will seek how to get some real food and helps a person satisfy id's primary process needs through reality using the secondary process. *Secondary process thinking* is based on logic, obeying the rules of causality, and is consistent with external reality. It separates internal fantasy from external reality, creating accurate internal representations, judging the results of one's actions, locating events in linear time, solving problems, and communicating clearly. The strength of the secondary process can vary depending upon a number of factors. If the id needs are very urgent, e.g., if you really need to get to a restroom as quickly as possible; these needs may override the ego and the secondary process and instead force you to act on such demands. The ability to restrain the basic demands of the id probably become stronger as one grows. According to Freud, a healthy adult personality is characterized by the ability to delay gratification until it is acceptable or realistic.

Ego defenses: in addition to being the logical, rational, reality-oriented part of the mind, the ego functions to manage anxiety through the use of ego defenses. Ego defenses are basically mental strategies that we use automatically and unconsciously when we feel threatened (Cramer, 2006). These defense mechanisms will be discussed later in detail on pp. 86–92.

The Superego

The last component of Freud's structural model of the mind to develop is the superego. The superego operates on the morality principle and motivates the person to behave in a socially responsible and acceptable manner. It is the aspect of personality that holds all of our internalized moral standards and ideals approved by parental and other authority figures as well as societal, and cultural traditions (*ego ideal*). Obeying these rules leads to feelings of pride, value, and accomplishment. It also includes prohibitions of things that are viewed as bad by parents and society (*the conscience*). These behaviors are often forbidden and lead to bad consequences, punishment, or feelings of guilt and remorse. The superego acts to perfect and civilize our behavior. It works to suppress all the unacceptable urges of the id and struggles to make the ego act upon idealistic standards rather than upon realistic principles. The superego develops during early childhood around age 5, when the child identifies with members of the family and the culture in which the child was raised. The superego is present in the conscious, the preconscious, and the unconscious.

The Interaction of the Id, the Ego, and the Superego

According to Freud, the key to a healthy personality is a balance between the id, the ego, and the superego. Freud believed that a healthy personality was one in which the id's demands are met but also the superego is satisfied in making the person feel proud and not overwhelmed by guilt. Competing forces may give rise to conflict between the id, the ego, and the superego. The struggle between the id and the superego is an example of intrapsychic conflict (conflict within the mind).

If the id is too strong, a person will be rude, arrogant, and selfish. An overly strong id makes one a psychopath, lacking a conscience, or selfishly meeting one's needs without concern for others. If the superego is too strong, a person is constantly worried, nervous, and so overwhelmed by guilt that it is difficult to find satisfaction and suffers from anxiety, and is always repressing the id's desires. Sometimes it is said that the ego is the mediator between the id and the superego, but this is not what Freud said. The ego does not help to find compromise, the ego helps the id to satisfy its desires by focusing on what is real. Freud used the term ego strength to refer to the ego's ability to function despite these competing forces. A person with good ego strength is able to effectively manage these pressures, while those with too much or too little ego strength can become too unyielding or too disrupting.

Only the ego feels anxiety, but the id, the superego, and the outside world can each be a source of anxiety. Neurotic anxiety stems from the ego's relation with the id; moral anxiety is similar to guilt and results from the ego's relation with the superego, while realistic anxiety is similar to fear, and is produced by the ego's relation with the real world.

The Psychosexual Stages of Development

The psychosexual stages of development are probably the most controversial aspect of psychodynamic theory. Freud believed that personality develops through a series of childhood stages in which the pleasure-seeking energies of the id become focused on certain erogenous areas. This psychosexual energy, or libido, was described as the driving force behind behavior. Freud outlined these stages as oral, anal, phallic, latency, and genital. Across these five stages, the child is presented with different conflicts between their biological drives (id) and their social and moral conscience (superego), and their biological pleasure-seeking urges focus on different areas of the body (what Freud called "erogenous zones"). The child's ability to resolve these internal conflicts determines their future ability to cope and function as an adult. If these psychosexual stages are successfully completed, the result is a healthy personality. Failure to resolve a stage can lead one to become stuck or fixated at that stage, with later influence on adult personality and behavior. A *fixation* means a persistent focus on an earlier psychosexual stage. Until this conflict is resolved, the individual will remain "stuck" in this stage, e.g., a person who is fixated at the oral stage may be over-dependent on others and may seek oral stimulation through smoking, drinking, or eating.

The Oral Stage (Birth–18 Months)

The mouth is the center of pleasure during the oral stage. Babies derive pleasure from sucking and mouthing various objects, including their own fingers. The child follows the pleasure principle during this stage.

The primary conflict at this stage is the weaning process, the child learns to become less dependent upon caretakers. Infants who receive either too little or too much gratification become fixated in the oral stage, and are likely to regress to these points of fixation under stress, even as adults, e.g., a child who was underfed or neglected will become orally dependent as an adult and is likely to manipulate others to fulfill his or her needs rather than becoming independent. On the other hand, the child who was overfed or overly gratified will resist growing up and try to return to the prior state of dependency by demanding satisfaction from others, and acting in a helpless or needy way.

The Anal Stage (18 Months–3 Years)

During the anal stage, Freud believed that the primary focus of the libido is to control the bladder and bowel movements. Thus, the major conflict at this stage is toilet training, the child has to learn to control his or her bodily needs. Developing this control leads to a sense of accomplishment and independence. The ego evolves during this stage as the child hesitates between id impulses (defecation at will) and parental demands (only on the toilet).

According to Freud, success at this stage is dependent upon the way in which parents approach toilet training. Parents who utilize praise and rewards for using the toilet at the appropriate time encourage positive outcomes and help children to feel capable and productive. Freud believed that positive experiences during this stage served as the basis for people to become competent, productive, and creative adults.

Freud believed that if toilet training was either too harsh or too tolerant, children would become fixated at the anal stage and become likely to regress to this stage under stress as adults. If parents take an approach that is too permissive, Freud suggested that an anal-expulsive personality could develop in which the individual has a lack of self-control, a tendency toward carelessness, untidiness, or an extravagant or destructive personality. If parents are too strict or begin toilet training too early, Freud believed that an anal-retentive personality develops in which the individual is strict, rigid, with a compulsive seeking of order and tidiness.

The Phallic Stage (3–6 Years)

During the phallic stage, the primary focus of the libido is on the genitals. At this age, children begin to discover the differences between males and females. According to Freud, boys begin to view their fathers as a competitor for the mother's affections. The *Oedipus complex* describes these feelings of wanting to possess the mother and the desire to replace the father. However, the child fears that he

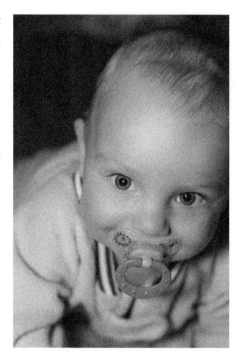

PHOTO 4.6.   The Oral Stage.

PHOTO 4.7.   The Anal Stage.

will be punished by the father for these feelings. Freud called this fear *castration anxiety*. Freud, however, believed that girls experience *penis envy*, and begin to hate their mother for not giving a penis to them. The girl then transfers her love to her father, and competes with her mother. The term *"Electra complex"* has been used to describe a girl's sense of competition with her mother for the affections of her father. The Oedipus complex is resolved when the parents allow their same-sex children to identify with them and learn how to properly mirror their behavior and learn how to properly act within society. Freud argued that boys will normally eventually abandon their love of the mother, and instead identify with the father, taking on the father's personality characteristics. For girls, however, Freud believed that penis envy was never fully resolved and that all women remain somewhat fixated at this stage. Psychologists such as Karen Horney disputed this assumption, calling it both inaccurate and demeaning to women. Instead, Horney proposed that men experience feelings of inferiority because they cannot give birth to children.

The Latent Period (6–Puberty)

This stage begins after age 5 or 6 years (end of phallic stage) till about 12 years. Freud believed a child entered the latent stage, when preoccupation with sexual concerns is very much reduced. Libidinal energy is weak and most behaviors focus on interaction with peers of the same sex. Boys and girls have little or no interest in members of the opposite sex. Sexual energy is directed into other areas, such as intellectual pursuits and social interactions. The child enters school at the beginning of this stage, meets new children, teachers, and hears about heroes of history. Children become more concerned with peer relationships, hobbies, and other interests. Children identify or imitate the morals of their relatives and follow their ideals. So, the child should be attached to an integrated person or persons during this stage to acquire from them the sound mature conduct. The development of the ego and the superego contributes to this period of calm. This stage is important in the development of social and communication skills and self-confidence.

PHOTO 4.8.   Children engaged in intellectual pursuits & social interactions.

The Genital Stage (Puberty to Death)

This stage begins at adolescence (with the onset of puberty) and lasts until death, sexual desires reappear in this stage. According to Freud, sexual impulses return during this time frame, and if development has proceeded normally to this point, the child is able to move into the development of mature romantic relationships. But if earlier problems have not been appropriately resolved, difficulties with establishing an intimate love relationship are likely.

Criticisms of Freudian Psychoanalytic Theory

Psychoanalysis served as a catalyst to many professionals in the field of psychology. Psychoanalysis enlightened health professionals about many aspects of the human mind and its inner working phenomena that had previously been incomprehensible. As a direct or indirect result of psychoanalysis, many approaches to psychological treatment were developed worldwide (Farrell, 1981). The criticisms of Freud's theory can be grouped into the following categories:

1. *Narrow focus*: Freud theories largely ignored "normal" healthy functioning and were highly focused on pathology. Freud's view of human sexuality as the main driver of human personality development received much criticism. In his singular emphasis on the structure of the human mind, Freud paid little or no attention to the impact of environment, sociology, or culture.

2. *Anti-feminist bias*: feminists criticized the assumptions and approaches of psychoanalytic theory that are patriarchal (male-dominated), and anti-feminist. The theory is focused mainly on male development with little mention of female psychosexual development.

3. *No scientific basis*: critics affirm that many of the principles upon which Freud's theory is based are inaccurate, and that it lacks empirical evidence and relies too heavily on therapeutic achievements. Psychoanalysis theory is not testable as it lacks operational definitions and there is no way to measure results, e.g., concepts such as the libido are impossible to measure, and therefore cannot be tested. Many psychoanalytic concepts are impossible to disprove because even contradictory information can be used to support Freud's theory.

4. *Flawed methodology*: the methods or techniques involved in psychoanalysis, such as Freud's ideas on the interpretation of dreams and the role of free association, have been criticized. Also, Freud's data are developed from a small number of upper-class patients or from self-analysis, and it could be a way of imposing his own ideas onto his patients or seeing only what he expected to see. Some opponents assert that Freud's clinical data are flawed, inaccurate, and selective at best.

5. *Highly subjective*: there are no clear objective shared lines of reasoning between theories and observations, e.g., the same phenomenon observed by two or more psychoanalysts may be interpreted in completely different ways that are contradictory to each other (Colby, 1960).

6. *Lack of predictions*: though psychoanalysts assume that certain childhood experiences, such as abuse or harassment, can produce certain outcomes or states of neurosis, one cannot predict that children who have had such experiences will become characterized by certain personality traits, or that a particular neurotic state indicates that those children have had this childhood experience.

Clinical Notes

■ Psychoanalytic theory was developed into a therapeutic technique that probes the patient's unconscious through techniques such as free association and dream analysis. It will be discussed in Chapter 22 on psychotherapy.

Summary

- Freud introduced a number of concepts and theories of mind that include the topographical theory of mind, the structural model of mind, the psychosexual stages of development, and defense mechanisms.
- The topographical theory of mind proposes that psychic processes operate on three levels: the unconscious, the preconscious, and the conscious.
- Unconscious processes originate mainly from repression and inherited experiences.
- Dreams, slips, and free associations are the main routes to explore the unconscious, according to Freud.
- The structural model of mind postulates that the mind can be divided into three interacting categories called the id, the ego, and the superego. Conflicts among these three structures, and efforts to find balance among desires each of them determine how we behave and approach the world.
- The id contains biological instincts, the ego is responsible for dealing with reality, while the superego operates on the morality principle.
- Primary process thinking involves forming a mental image of the desired object in order to reduce the frustration of not having received gratification yet.
- Secondary process thinking is based on logic, obeying the rules of causality, and is consistent with external reality.
- Freud believed that personality develops through a series of stages in which the pleasure-seeking energies of the id become focused on certain erogenous areas, these are called the psychosexual stages.
- Fixation means a persistent focus on an earlier psychosexual stage.
- The Oedipus complex describes feelings of wanting to possess the mother and the desire to replace the father.
- The Electra complex describes a girl's sense of competition with her mother for the affections of her father.

Test Your Knowledge

- What are the core features of psychodynamic theories?
- What is the topographical theory of mind?
- What is the difference between primary and secondary process thinking?
- What does Freud say about the unconscious?
- What is Freud's view of dreams?
- What is Freud's view of slips?
- What is Freud's view of free association?
- What is the structural model of mind?
- What are the psychosexual stages of development?
- Define the Oedipus complex.
- Define the Electra complex.
- What are the methods that Freud adopted to understand the unconscious?
- How do the id, the ego, and the superego interact?

Critical Thinking Questions

- As a Freudian psychoanalyst, how could you explain human behavior?
- As an opponent of Freudian psychoanalytic theory, how could you argue against it?

Alfred Adler

PHOTO 4.9.   Alfred Adler.

Alfed Adler (1870–1937) was an Austrian physician, who was one of the original members of Freud's inner circle. However, theoretical differences emerged between Adler and Freud. Adler attempted to understand human behavior in a way that is essentially different from that of Freud and Jung. Adler left Freud's circle and established a theory of personality that was nearly totally opposite to that of Freud, which became known as *individual psychology* (Ansbacher & Ansbacher, 1956). The 12 main principles of Adlerian theory are as follows.

1. *Striving for success and superiority*: Adler reduced all motivation behind human behavior to the striving for success and superiority. Future goals are often governed by goals which are set in childhood. Once the goal is set, we are determined by it in all our actions as if "caught in an iron shirt." Adler thought children develop feelings of inferiority because they are small and weak. If these feelings become overwhelming, a child develops an inferiority complex, which has to be overcome. The concept of moving from a sense of inferiority to a sense of mastery forms the cornerstone of Adler's personality theory. This means that people are continually directed by the need to overcome inferiority feelings and the desire for completion. The striving force can take one of two courses: the first course involves efforts to get *personal superiority*; when striving goes too far, a person develops a *superiority complex* in which this drive is wrongly self-directed and aimed at selfish goals, such as power and self-esteem. The second course involves *social interest* (see below). Psychologically healthy people strive for the success or perfection of all people, without losing their personal identity. In contrast, psychologically unhealthy individuals strive for personal superiority with little concern for others, and whenever they appear to be interested in other people, their basic motivation is personal benefit.

2. *Social interest*: Adler meant social interest not in terms of particular social behaviors, but in the broader sense of being useful to others. It manifests itself as caring for

family, helping others, kindness, and similar personal attributes directed for social advancement rather than for personal gain. In this, Adler distinguished between social interest and extraversion.

The natural inferiority of individuals necessitates their joining together to form a society. Without protection and nourishment from parents, a baby cannot survive, and our ancestors would have been eaten by animals that were stronger without protection from the family. Thus, social interest is crucial to individual and social health, and is a necessity for perpetuating the human species and achieving success.

Adler felt that social interest is a combination of being inborn and learned. It is based on an innate disposition (as shown in the way babies and small children often show sympathy for others without having been taught to do so, or the crying of babies in a nursery when one baby in the nursery begins to cry), though it has to be nurtured to persist.

Adler considered social interest as a measure of maturity, and as evidence that one has succeeded in the tasks of life. Contrarily, Adler considered lack of social interest a defining feature of mental illness; all failures (neurotics, psychotics, criminals, drunkards, problem children, suicides, perverts, and prostitutes) result from lacking in social interest, hence gaining social interest is considered a positive movement in therapy.

3. *Self-determination and uniqueness*: according to Adler, a person's fictional goal is influenced by hereditary and cultural factors, but its uniqueness originates from the creative power of the individual. People's creative power places them in control of their own lives, responsible for their final goal, determines their method of striving for that goal, and contributes to the development of social interest. People are not usually fully aware of their goal, but analysis of birth order, repeated coping patterns, and earliest memories, can lead the psychotherapist to infer the goal as a working hypothesis.

4. *Conscious behavior*: Adler believed that a person's conscious behavior, not their unconscious, was the mainstay of personality development. Because of this concept, Adler emphasized personal responsibility for how the individual chooses to interpret and adjust to life's events or situations.

5. *Subjective perceptions shape people's behavior and personality*: Adler assumed that people experience events within a highly personal framework (the apperceptive schema). This subjective meaning cannot be imposed from without but is defined from within. The result is personal beliefs about self, others, and the world. These beliefs become one's personal truth. Consequently, the manner in which people strive for superiority or success is not shaped by reality but by their subjective perceptions of reality, that is, by their fictions, or expectations of the future. *Fictions* are ideas that have no real existence, yet they influence people as if they really existed, e.g., men are superior to women; many people, both men and women, act as if this is a reality.

6. *Private logic and common sense*: private logic justifies socially inappropriate behavior, everyone can find a way to justify or excuse almost any activity. The person who lies, cheats, steals, or whatever, to advance his or her own personal benefit (without regard for the interests of others) is proof of the universality of private logic. Such reasoning helps the main goal of getting ahead instead of remaining behind, and disregards working in cooperation with others.

In contrast, common sense is the community's wisdom about ways people should behave among others, to encourage socially useful behavior. The child is exposed to this community wisdom in the words and actions of others, religious teachings, folk sayings, customs, etc.

7. *Unity of the individual*: Adler believed that a person (married, parent, in a job, with friends, and so on), is always the same, always follows the same goals, and uses to a greater extent the same approaches throughout his or her life. According to Adler (Ansbacher & Ansbacher, 1956), the whole person strives in a self-consistent fashion toward a single goal, and all thoughts, feelings, and behaviors can be understood only as parts of this goal. Adler supposed that each aspect of the personality points in the same direction, and that personality cannot be so separated. This personality unity or self-consistency was closely tied to the fictional final goal or guiding self-ideal, by which one organizes one's life in specific ways to achieve an ultimate, idealized solution to a basic life problem. Adler supposed that conscious and unconscious processes are unified and operate to achieve the single goal. Adler defined the unconscious as that part of the goal that is neither clearly formulated nor completely understood by the individual. With this definition, Adler avoided a dichotomy between the unconscious and the conscious, which he saw as two cooperating parts of the same unified system. In the same way, Adler assumed that there was no separate id, ego, or superego, no separate personal past, present, or future, nor separate actions unconnected to thoughts and/or feelings. It was this that led him to select the name for his approach as individual psychology.

8. *Style of life*: Adler used this concept to refer to the flavor or style of a person's life, which develops from the self-consistent personality structure. It includes a person's goal, self-concept, feelings for others, the unified and self-consistent pattern of beliefs, perceptions, attitudes, relationships, and actions, and attitude toward the world which make up the complete person. A person's style of life is fairly well established by age 4 or 5. Even though their final goal remains constant, healthy people see many ways of striving for success and continually seek to create new options for them.

   An ineffective lifestyle may have no consequences when life poses no challenge. However, ineffective lifestyles can lead to development of symptoms that protect self-esteem and help the individual to avoid dealing realistically with their problems. Neurotic symptoms develop when people maintain social interest but are blocked from life goals by these symptoms, whereas people with psychotic symptoms lose social interest and retreat into their own world.

9. *Birth order*: Adler believed that the birth of each child changed the family substantially. He thought that the birth order of children affects many aspects of their personality development:

   a. First-born children are usually high achievers, parent pleasers, conforming, and behave well. Children born seven or more years apart from siblings are more like first-born children.

   b. Second-born children are more outgoing, less anxious, and less constrained by rules than first-born children. They usually excel at what the first-born does not.

   c. Middle children have a feeling of being squeezed in and are troubled with perceived unfair treatment. These children learn to exceed in family politics and negotiation, and tend to develop areas of success that are not enjoyed by their siblings. However, they can become manipulative.

   d. The youngest child is the most likely to please or entertain the family. While they run the risk of being spoiled, they are the most likely to get what they want through their social skills and ability to please. They are often high achievers, because of the role models of their older siblings.

   e. Only children often take on the characteristics of their parents, as their parents are the only role model. While these children may mature early and be high achievers, they may be pampering, lack socialization skills, or be selfish.

10. *Family*: Adler saw the family as the basic socialization unit for the child. He believed that children's interpretation of the events in their life was determined by the interaction with family members before the age of 5. The family interactions teach children to perceive events and situations through certain subjective evaluations of themselves and the environment, called fictions. Basic mistakes could be made based on these fictions. Adlerians believe that some of those mistakes are as follows (Mozak, 1984):
    a. Over-generalizing, in which the individual believes that everything is the same or alike.
    b. False or impossible goals of security: this leads the individual to try to please everyone in seeking security and avoiding danger.
    c. Misperceptions of life and life's demands: this leads the individual to expect more accommodation than is reasonable and to interpret their failure to get accommodation as never getting any breaks.
    d. Minimization or denial of one's worth: this results in the individual believing that they cannot be successful in life.
    e. Faulty values: this results in a "me first" mentality with little or no regard for others.

11. *Psychological types*: Adler proposed four psychological types that could be distinguished based on the different levels of energy (the strength of their striving after personal power) they had. These types include:
    a. The socially useful type: one who has both social interest and energy, this is the healthy person.
    b. The ruling type: they are characterized by a tendency to be aggressive and dominant. Their energy is so great that they tend to push over anything or anybody who gets in their way. The most energetic of them are bullies and sadists. The less energetic ones hurt others by hurting themselves, and include alcoholics, drug addicts, and suicides.
    c. The leaning type: they are sensitive people who have developed a shell around themselves which protects them, but they rely on others to overcome life's difficulties. They have low energy levels and so become dependent. When overwhelmed, they develop neurotic symptoms: phobias, obsessions and compulsions, general anxiety, hysteria, amnesias, and so on, depending on the individual details of their lifestyle.
    d. The avoiding type: these have the lowest levels of energy and essentially survive by avoiding life, especially other people. When overwhelmed, they tend to become psychotic, retreating finally into their own personal worlds.

12. *Childhood*: like Freud, Adler saw personality or lifestyle as something established quite early in life. In fact, the prototype of lifestyle tends to be fixed by about 5 years old. New experiences tend to be interpreted in terms of the prototype rather than changing that prototype. Adler felt that there were three basic childhood situations that most contribute to a faulty lifestyle:
    a. Organ inferiorities, and early childhood diseases: these are what Adler called "overburdened." Children will remain focused on themselves if no one comes along to draw their attention to others. Most will go through life with a strong sense of inferiority. A few will overcompensate with a superiority complex. Only some will truly compensate with the encouragement of loved ones.
    b. Pampering: many children are taught that their wishes are everyone else's commands, and they can take without giving. Pampered children fail in two ways: first, children do not learn to do for themselves, and discover later that they are truly

     inferior; second, they do not learn any other way to deal with others except by giving commands.

  c. Neglect: a child who is neglected or abused learns inferiority, but in a far more direct manner than what the pampered child learns, because they are told and shown every day that they are of no value; they learn selfishness because they are taught not to trust anyone. They do not develop a capacity for love, as they have not known it. The neglected child includes not only orphans and the victims of abuse, but the children whose parents are never there, and the ones raised in a rigid, authoritarian manner.

Clinical Applications of Adlerian Theory

- Adlerian principles have been adopted in Adlerian individual psychotherapy, couple therapy, and family therapy.
- Adlerian therapy helps to raise patients' awareness of their lifestyle, how it is discordant with the demands of social reality, and how it may be reoriented. The therapist must awaken the patient's social interest, and the energy that goes with it. The goal of therapy is to replace exaggerated self-protection, self-enhancement, and self-indulgence with social interest.
- Current Adlerian therapy involves four stages: engagement, assessment, insight, and reorientation:
  a. Engagement: the therapist builds a trusting therapeutic with the person in therapy, that helps in working together to effectively address the problem. This relationship enables the therapist to provide the basic form of social interest, which the patient can then generalize to other relationships.
  b. Assessment: The therapist attempts to understand the person's history, beliefs, experiences, feelings and emotions, and motives, to reveal the overall lifestyle patterns of the individual.
  c. Insight: The therapist helps the individual to develop new ways of thinking about their mistaken assumptions, attitudes, behaviors, and feelings about themselves and the world.
  d. Reorientation: Clients are encouraged to apply their new insight to overcome their feelings of insecurity, develop deeper feelings of connectedness, and to redirect their striving for goals that have no social value into more socially beneficial directions. Adler avoided appearing too authoritarian and advised therapists never to allow the patient to force them into this role, because this allows the patients to play some of the same games they have played many times before.

Summary

Adler proposed the following concepts:

- Striving for success or superiority is the dynamic force behind people's behavior.
- Social interest: Adler stressed the importance of being useful to others. He considered social interest as a measure of maturity, and as evidence that one has succeeded in the tasks of life.
- Self-determination and uniqueness: a person's fictional goal is influenced by hereditary and cultural factors, but its uniqueness springs from the creative power of the individual.

- Adler believed that a person's conscious behavior, not their unconscious, is the mainstay of personality development.
- Adler assumed that people experience events within a highly personal framework.
- Private logic justifies socially inappropriate behavior, everyone can find a way to justify or excuse almost any activity.
- Common sense is the community's wisdom about ways people should behave among others, to encourage socially useful behavior.
- Unity of the individual: Adler believed that a person is always the same, follows the same goals, and uses to a greater extent the same approaches throughout his or her life.
- Style of life: the flavor or style of a person's life which develops from the self-consistent personality structure. This includes a person's goal, self-concept, feelings for others, the unified and self-consistent pattern of beliefs, perceptions, attitudes, relationships, and actions, and attitude toward the world.
- Birth order: Adler believed that the birth order of children affects many aspects of their personality development:
- The family interactions teach children how to perceive events and situations through certain subjective evaluations of themselves and the environment, called fictions.
- Adler proposed four psychological types that could be distinguished based on the different levels of energy.

Test Your Knowledge

Give an account of the following Adlerian concepts:

- striving for success
- social interest
- goal orientation
- self-determination and uniqueness
- subjective perceptions
- private logic and common sense
- unity of the individual
- style of life
- psychological types
- organ inferiorities
- pampering

Critical Thinking Question

How could you argue with and against Adlerian theory and therapy?

Carl Jung

Jung introduced a number of concepts that enriched psychodynamic theory and human thinking in general. These include levels and dynamics of psyche, psychological types, and theorizing about personality development.

Levels of the Psyche

Jung divided the human psyche into a conscious and an unconscious level, with the latter further subdivided into a personal unconscious and a collective unconscious.

The Conscious Level

Consciousness is the only part of the mind known directly by the individual. It appears early in life through the operation of four basic functions: thinking, feeling, sensing, and intuiting. In addition, there are two attitudes which determine the orientation of the conscious mind: extroversion and introversion. The development

PHOTO 4.10.   Carl Jung.

of consciousness also ushers in the beginning of individuation, the process by which a person becomes psychologically "individual," that is, a separate, indivisible unit or whole. From this process, the ego emerges, which provides a sense of identity and continuity, and is the central core of the personality.

Psychic images recognized by the ego are said to be conscious. Jung saw the ego as the center of consciousness, but the ego is just one small portion of the self. Jung believed that consciousness is selective, and the ego is the part of the self that selects the most relevant information from the environment and chooses a direction to take, based on it, while the rest of the information sinks into the unconscious. It may enter into the conscious mind later on in the form of dreams or visions. The origin of the ego lies in the self-archetype, which is formed over the course of early development as the brain attempts to add meaning and value to its various experiences.

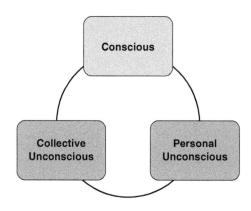

FIGURE 4.1.   Levels of the Psyche.

In a psychologically healthy person, the ego takes a secondary position to the unconscious self. Thus, consciousness plays a relatively minor role in analytical psychology, and an overemphasis on expanding one's conscious psyche can lead to psychological imbalance. Healthy individuals are in contact with their conscious world, but they also allow themselves to experience their unconscious self and thus to achieve *individuation*.

The Personal Unconscious Level

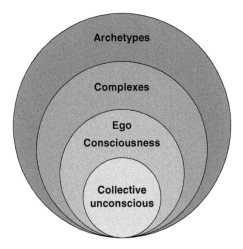

FIGURE 4.2. Personal Unconscious.

Perhaps Jung's greatest contribution was expanding the concept of the unconscious. Freud used the term unconscious to apply to the hidden thoughts and ideas of one person. In Freud's view, each person has his or her own unconscious, which is generally similar among people. However, Jung assumed that each one has a personal unconscious, and what is in one person's unconscious might not be in another person's unconscious. This conception is called by Jung "the personal unconscious."

The Freudian unconscious, in Jung's terms, is composed of the individual's particular and unique experiences which have been made unconscious through repression. For Jung, the personal unconscious is formed by our individual experiences and is therefore unique to each of us. Repressed material represents only one kind of unconscious content. The personal unconscious also includes forgotten events, and experiences originally perceived below the threshold of our consciousness. Some material in the personal unconscious can be recalled easily, some remembered with difficulty, and still others are beyond the reach of consciousness.

Associated groups of emotionally toned composites of suppressed memories, emotions, perceptions, and wishes may cluster together to form a complex, which is formed by experience and by an individual's reactions to that experience that cluster around a theme provided by some archetype. Unlike Freud, Jung believed complexes could be very diverse, rather than individuals simply having a core sexual complex, e.g., a person's experiences with an officer, father, or teacher may become grouped around an emotional core, so that any of those people, or even just naming any of them, sparks an emotional response that blocks the smooth flow of thought. Complexes are largely personal, but they are strongly influenced by the collective unconscious. In the previous example, a teacher complex comes not only from one's personal relationship with the teacher but also from the entire species' experiences with teachers. In addition, the teacher complex is partly formed by a person's conscious image of the teacher. Thus, complexes may be partly conscious and may stem from both the personal and the collective unconscious.

In a healthy individual, complexes are seldom a problem, and indeed are likely a key to balancing the one-sided views of the ego, so that development can occur. If the person is mentally unwell, however, and unable to regulate himself or herself (as seen in those experiencing dissociation between these states), complexes may become overt and more of an issue. In these cases, the ego is damaged, and is therefore not strong enough to make use of the complexes via sound reflection, granting them a full and uncontrollable life of their own. Complexes often prevent complete individuation from taking place, and one of the aims of therapy is to free the patient from their grip.

The Collective Unconscious

The collective unconscious refers to humans' innate tendency to react in a particular way whenever their experiences stimulate a biologically inherited response tendency, e.g., we do not have to learn to fear the dark or snakes through direct experience, because we are naturally predisposed to develop such fears through the inheritance of our ancestors' fears. Carl Jung suggested that all human beings share certain unconscious ideas which were created from similar evolutionary circumstances and common ancestors. The unconscious that we all share is called the collective unconscious. According to Jung, the collective unconscious is the storehouse of hidden memory traces that were inherited from our ancestral past. It is our minds' residue of human evolutionary development. Jung theorized that the components that make up the collective unconscious are universal types or propensities that we all share and that have a predominant mythological quality. The physical contents of the collective unconscious pass from one generation to the next as psychic potential. Distant ancestors' experiences with universal concepts such as God, mother, water, earth, and so forth have been transmitted through the generations, so that people everywhere and at any time have been influenced by their primitive ancestors' experiences. Therefore, the contents of the collective unconscious are more or less the same for people in all cultures.

The contents of the collective unconscious (called archetypes) influence a person's thoughts, emotions, and actions, and are responsible for many of people's myths and religious beliefs. The archetype also produces big dreams, which have meanings that extend beyond the individual dreamer and that are filled with significance for people of every time and place. Jung said that people have as many of these inherited tendencies as they have typical situations in life. At first, they are forms without content, representing merely the possibility of a certain type of perception and action. With more repetition, these forms begin to develop some content and to emerge as relatively autonomous archetypes.

Archetypes

An archetype is an unlearned tendency to experience things in a certain way. The archetype acts as an "organizing principle" on the things we see or do. At first, babies just want something to eat, without knowing what they want. They have an indefinite desire which can be satisfied by some things and not by others. Later, with experience, children begin to desire more specific things when they are hungry. Jung believed that symbols from different cultures are often very similar because they originated from archetypes shared by the whole human race. For Jung, our primitive past becomes the basis of the human psyche, directing and influencing present behavior. Though there are no fixed numbers of archetypes, Jung identified a large number of archetypes that overlap with each other, including birth, rebirth, death, power, magic, the hero, the child, the trickster, God, the demon, the wise old man, the earth mother, and the giant. Jung assumed that the archetypes color our world of experience and express themselves within our personalities. The archetypes may manifest in our dreams, influence those whom we are attracted to, and become part of our art, our folklore, and the symbols that we use in our cultures, e.g., the symbols for motherhood are the same from one culture to another. Jung gave special attention to the following archetypes:

1. *The persona*: this is derived from a Latin word for mask. It refers to the image a person presents to the world, to make a particular impression on others. At its best, it is just the "good impression" we all wish to present as we fill the roles required by the society. It can also be the "false impression" we use to manipulate people's opinions and behaviors. At its worst, it can be mistaken, even by ourselves, for our true nature. Persona conceals a person's true nature and Jung describes it as the "conformity" archetype. Although it begins as an archetype, by the time the person stops realizing it, it has become distant from the collective unconscious. Persons who identify too strongly with their personas can run into problems, e.g., the celebrity who becomes too involved with himself or herself as the "star," the person who cannot leave work at work, or the academic who treats others with superiority. Doing the aforementioned can impede someone's personal growth, as other aspects of the self cannot properly develop.

2. *The anima/animus*: this is the mirror image of the contra-sexual archetypes of the psyche, that is, the unconscious feminine side in males and the masculine tendencies in women, respectively. The psyche of a woman contains masculine aspects (the animus archetype) and the psyche of a man contains feminine aspects (the anima archetype). These are built from feminine and masculine archetypes the individual experiences, as well as experience with members of the opposite sex (beginning with parents), and seek to balance out one's otherwise possible one-sided experience of gender. These archetypes tend to be projected in a more idealized form, e.g., one looks for the reflection of one's anima or animus in a potential mate, accounting for the phenomenon of love at first sight.

3. *The shadow*: this represents qualities that a person does not wish to acknowledge, and attempts to hide from self and others. It may have positive or negative qualities, and may be the source of both creative and destructive energies. People who do not realize their shadow may come under its power and lead unhappy lives, constantly running into bad luck and discouragement for themselves. Jung believed that people who do not realize their shadow may project them onto others, meaning that we often cannot tolerate qualities in others that we have in ourselves and do not wish to admit this.

4. *The self*: this refers to our feelings of wholeness and unity, our sense of organization within our personality, and our identity, i.e., the sense of the totality of the personality. The self is the archetype of archetypes because it pulls together the other archetypes and combines them in the process of self-realization. The self represents the whole collection of all opposites, so that every aspect of your personality is expressed equally. You are then neither and both male and female, neither and both ego and shadow, neither and both good and bad, neither and both conscious and unconscious, neither and both an individual and the whole of creation. For Jung, the ultimate aim of every individual is to achieve a state of selfhood (similar to self-actualization), and in this respect Jung is moving in the direction of a more humanist orientation.

Dynamics of the Psyche

Jung thought of a number of principles that govern the operation of the psyche, these include:

1. *The principle of opposites*: every wish immediately suggests its opposite. In order to have a concept of good, you must have a concept of bad, just like you cannot have up without down or black without white. According to Jung, it is the opposition that creates the power (or libido) of the psyche. It is like the two poles of a battery, or the splitting of an atom. It is the contrast that gives energy, so that a strong contrast gives strong energy, and a weak contrast gives weak energy.

2. *The principle of equivalence*: the energy created from the opposition is given to both sides equally. So, when you hold a young bird in your hand, there is energy to help it, but there is an equal amount of energy to crush it. If you decide to help the bird, energy goes into various behaviors involved in helping it. The fate of the other energy depends on your attitude toward the fulfilled wish. If you acknowledge it, face it, keep it available to the conscious mind, then the energy goes toward a general improvement of your psyche, and hence you grow. But if you deny and suppress that evil wish, and pretend that you never had it, the energy will go toward the development of a complex.

3. *The principle of entropy*: this is the tendency for oppositions to come together, and for energy to decrease over a person's lifetime. Jung borrowed the idea from physics, where entropy refers to the tendency of all physical systems to "run down," that is, for all energy to become evenly distributed, e.g., if you have a heat source in one corner of the room, the whole room will eventually be heated. When we are young, the opposites will tend to be extreme, and so we tend to have lots of energy. As we get older, most of us come to be more comfortable with our different facets. We recognize that we are all mixtures of good and bad, and are less innocently idealistic than we expected before. We are less threatened by the opposite sex within us and become more androgynous. Even physically, in old age, men and women become more alike. This process of rising above our opposites, of seeing both sides of who we are, is called *transcendence.*

4. *Causality and teleology*: causality holds that present events have their origin in early childhood experiences, so that the past determines the present. Conversely, teleology holds that present events are motivated by goals and aspirations for the future that direct a person's destiny. Jung believed that both causality and teleology play a part. But he adds a middle alternative and called it "synchronicity." Jung believed that human behavior is shaped by both causal and teleological forces and that causal explanations must be balanced with teleological ones. In other words, humans are motivated both by their past experiences and by their expectations of the future.

5. *Progression and regression*: to achieve self-realization, people must adapt to both their outside environment and their inner world as well. Adaptation to the outside world involves the forward flow of psychic energy and is called progression, whereas adaptation to the inner world relies on a backward flow of psychic energy and is called regression. Progression pushes a person to react consistently to a given set of environmental conditions, whereas regression is a necessary backward step in the successful achievement of a goal. Both progression and regression are essential if people are to achieve individual growth or self-realization. Jung believed that the backward step is essential to a person's forward movement toward self-realization.

Psychological Types

Jung assumed that psychological types grow out of a union of two basic attitudes: introversion and extraversion, and four separate functions: thinking, feeling, sensing, and intuiting.

Attitudes

Jung defined an attitude as a predisposition to act or react in a characteristic manner. He insisted that each person has both an introverted and an extraverted attitude, although one may be conscious while the other is unconscious. The extraversion attitude orients a person toward the external world, while the introversion attitude refers to people's subjective world. Like other opposing forces in analytical psychology, introversion and extraversion serve in a complementary rather than an opposing relationship to one another. Introverts are people who prefer their internal world of thoughts, feelings, fantasies, dreams, and so on, while extroverts prefer the external world of things and people and activities. Extraverts are influenced more by the real world than by their subjective perception, whereas introverts rely on their individualized view of things. Introverts and extraverts often mistrust and misunderstand one another, but neither attitude is superior to the other. Most people have a blend of both, i.e., are ambiverts. Introversion/extraversion may be confused with ideas like shyness and sociability, partially because introverts tend to be shy and extroverts tend to be sociable, but Jung introduced them to refer more to whether the ego more often resorts to the internal world or toward the external world. In that sense, at times, the introvert is more fitting to a situation where the solution lies within, while the extrovert is more fitting to a situation where the solution resides in working with the external environment. However, most cultures usually value the extrovert much more.

Functions

Whether we are introverts or extroverts, people need to deal with their inner and outer world. People have their own comfortable and preferred ways of dealing with it. Jung suggested four basic ways or functions: two rational functions (thinking and feeling), and two irrational functions (sensing and intuition). The four functions usually appear in a hierarchy, with one function occupying a superior position, another occupying a secondary position, and the other two occupying tertiary or inferior positions. All persons have these functions in different proportions. Most people have only one superior function and characteristically approach a situation relying on that function. Some people develop two functions, and a few very mature individuals have cultivated three. Poorly developed functions are usually unconscious, so the person might deny their presence.

- *Thinking*: means logically evaluating information or ideas. It involves decision-making or judging, rather than simple intake of information. Extraverted people rely heavily on concrete thoughts, but they may also use abstract ideas if these ideas have been transmitted to them from outside, e.g., by parents or teachers. Introverted people react to external stimuli, but their interpretation of an event is colored more by the internal meaning they bring with them than by the objective facts themselves.
- *Feeling*: unlike the usual understanding of the word, Jung called feeling rational. Feeling is the evaluation of every conscious activity, even those valued as indifferent. The feeling function should be distinguished from emotion. Most of these evaluations have no emotional content, but they are capable of becoming emotions if their

intensity increases to the point of stimulating physiological changes within the person. Emotions, however, are not limited to feelings; any of the four functions can lead to emotion when their strength is increased. Extraverted feeling people use objective data to make evaluations. They are usually well liked because of their sociability, but in their search to conform to social standards, they may appear artificial, shallow, and unreliable. Introverted people base their value judgments primarily on subjective perceptions rather than objective facts. These people have an individualized conscience, ignore traditional opinions and beliefs, and have nearly complete indifference to the objective world (including people). This causes persons around them to feel uncomfortable and to cool their attitude toward them.

■ *Sensing*: this means getting information by means of the senses. A sensing person is good at looking and listening and generally getting to know the world. Jung called sensing the irrational function, meaning that it involved perception rather than judging of information. These perceptions are not dependent on logical thinking or feeling but exist as absolute, elementary facts within each person. Extraverted people perceive external stimuli objectively, in much the same way that these stimuli exist in reality. Their sensations are not greatly influenced by their subjective attitudes. Introverted people are largely influenced by their subjective sensations of sight, sound, taste, touch, and so forth. They give a subjective interpretation to objective phenomena yet are able to communicate meaning to others.

■ *Intuiting*: this is a kind of perception that works outside of the usual conscious processes. It is irrational or perceptual, like sensing, but comes from the complex integration of large amounts of information, often adding or subtracting elements from conscious sensation, rather than simple seeing or hearing. Extraverted people are oriented toward facts in the external world. Because strong sensory stimuli interfere with intuition, intuitive people suppress many of their sensations and are guided by hunches and guesses contrary to sensory data. Introverted people are guided by the unconscious perception of facts that are basically subjective and have little or no resemblance to external reality. Introverted intuitive people may appear peculiar to people of other types who have little comprehension of their motives. Jung believed that introverted intuitive people may not clearly understand their own motivations, yet they are deeply moved by them.

The Development of Personality

Jung believed that personality develops through a series of stages that are completed by individuation or self-realization. Jung divided development into four broad stages: (1) childhood: the period from birth until adolescence; (2) youth: the period from puberty until middle life, which is a time for extraverted development and for being grounded in the real world of schooling, occupation, courtship, marriage, and family; (3) middle life: from about 35 or 40 until old age. He considered this a time when people should be adopting an introverted, or subjective attitude; and (4) old age: which is a time for psychological rebirth, self-realization, and preparation for death.

In contrast to Freud, Jung emphasized the second half of life, the period after age 35 or 40, as the time when people may acquire the ability to attain self-realization. However, the opportunity for degeneration or rigid reactions is also present at that time. The psychological health of middle-aged people is related to their ability to achieve balance between the poles of the various opposing processes.

Analytical psychology is essentially a psychology of opposites, and self-realization is the process of integrating the opposite poles into a single homogenous individual. This process of "coming to selfhood" means that a person has all their psychological components functioning in unity, with no psychic process atrophying. People who have gone through this process have achieved realization of the self, minimized their persona, recognized their anima or animus, and acquired a workable balance between introversion and extraversion. In addition, those self-realized individuals have elevated all four of the functions to a superior position, an extremely difficult accomplishment. Self-realization is extremely rare and is achieved only by people who are able to assimilate their unconscious into their total personality. To come to terms with the unconscious is a difficult process that demands courage to face the evil nature of one's shadow and even greater courage to accept one's feminine or masculine side. This process is almost never achieved before middle life, when a person can remove the ego as the dominant concern of personality and replace it with the self. The self-realized person must allow the unconscious self to become the core of personality. To merely expand consciousness is to inflate the ego and to produce a one-sided person who lacks the soul spark of personality. The self-realized person is dominated neither by unconscious processes nor by the conscious ego but achieves a balance between all aspects of personality. Self-realized people are able to struggle with both their external and their internal worlds.

The goal of Jungian therapy is to help neurotic patients become healthy and to move healthy people in the direction of self-realization. Jung was eclectic in his choice of therapeutic techniques and treated older people differently than the young.

Evaluation of Jung's Ideas

Jung's work has contributed to mainstream psychology in at least one significant respect. He was the first to distinguish the two major attitudes or orientations of personality: extroversion and introversion. He also identified four basic functions (thinking, feeling, sensing, and intuiting) which in a cross-classification yield eight pure personality types. Psychologists like Hans Eysenck and Raymond Cattell have subsequently built upon these.

Though Jung's theory remains very popular, in many ways, it does not seem like a psychological theory, because it is influenced heavily by anthropology and spirituality, and by being unscientific. Many of the writings of Jung have more of a philosophical than a psychological flavor. As a scientific theory, it is criticized for its inability to generate research, or to withstand falsification.

Clinical Notes

Though it is of little use nowadays, Jung provided an in-depth analytical psychotherapy designed to bring together the conscious and unconscious parts of the mind to help a person feel balanced and whole. Jungian therapy focuses on the source of a problem rather than on the manifestations or symptoms. The analyst should explore the deep-rooted causes of relationship problems and blocked emotions to achieve "individuation" or wholeness. In Jungian therapy, various techniques, such as dream analysis, and creative experiences like art, movement, or music, are used to encourage self-expression. Jungian therapy can benefit persons with emotional problems, phobias, and relationship or trauma problems.

Summary

- Jung introduced a number of concepts that enriched psychodynamic theory and human thinking in general. These include the proposition of levels and dynamics of psyche, the proposition of psychological types, and theorizing about personality development.

- Jung divided the human psyche into conscious and unconscious levels, with the latter further subdivided into a personal unconscious and a collective unconscious.

- Personal unconscious is formed by our individual experiences and is therefore unique to each of us. Repressed material represents only one kind of unconscious content. The personal unconscious also includes forgotten events, and experiences originally perceived below the threshold of our consciousness. Some material in the personal unconscious can be recalled easily, some remembered with difficulty, and still others are beyond the reach of consciousness.

- The collective unconscious refers to humans' innate tendency to react in a particular way whenever their experiences stimulate a biologically inherited response tendency, e.g., we do not have to learn to fear the dark or snakes through direct experience, because we are naturally predisposed to develop such fears through the inheritance of our ancestors' fears.

- An archetype is an unlearned tendency to experience things in a certain way. The archetype acts as an "organizing principle" on the things we see or do.

- The persona is derived from a Latin word for mask. It refers to the image a person presents to the world, to make a particular impression on others.

- The anima/animus is the mirror image of the contra-sexual archetypes of the psyche, that is, the unconscious feminine side in males and the masculine tendencies in women, respectively.

- The shadow represents those qualities a person does not wish to acknowledge, and attempts to hide from self and others.

- Jung thought of a number of principles that govern the operation of the psyche, these include the principles of opposites, equivalence, entropy, causality and teleology, and progression and regression.

- Jung assumed that psychological types grow out of a union of two basic attitudes: introversion and extraversion, and four separate functions: thinking, feeling, sensing, and intuiting.

- Jung believed that personality develops through a series of stages that culminate in individuation, or self-realization.

Test Your Knowledge

From Jung's point of view, give an account on the following concepts:

- levels of the psyche
- the personal unconscious
- the collective unconscious
- archetypes
- the persona
- the anima/animus
- the shadow

- the dynamics of the psyche
- the principle of opposites
- the principle of equivalence
- the principle of entropy
- causality and teleology
- progression and regression
- psychological types

Critical Thinking Questions

- How would you evaluate Jung's contribution to psychology?
- How would you argue for and against Jungian therapy?

Eric Berne and Transactional Analysis

The belief that people have multiple natures can be found throughout history in religion, philosophy, and literature. Eric Berne (1910–1970) was a Canadian-born American psychologist/psychiatrist. Berne proposed a theory that entails a new structure of ego states, and discussed how these states are used in daily interactions (transactions). According to Berne, analysis of transactions could help the person to become better, and hence can be used as a way of therapy (Berne, 1961, 1964).

PHOTO 4.11. Eric Berne.

Ego States

Berne assumed that ego consists of three primary states that people consistently use (Parent-Adult-Child, PAC):

1. *The parent ego state (P)* is the collection of thoughts, feelings, and behaviors that are learned or introjected from parents or other caretakers during childhood. Parent ego state could be either nurturing (when soft, loving, and permissive) or controlling (in the case of a critical parent).
2. *The adult ego state (A)* is a reasonable, objective, and effective state dealing with present reality; the person behaves, feels, and thinks based on the facts, in a way that is going on the here-and-now and not on pre-judged thoughts or childlike emotions.

3. *The child ego state (C)* is the seat of emotions, thoughts, feelings, and memories that one retains from childhood. Responding in child ego state means using past internal experiences to determine current thinking, feeling, and behavior. The child ego state can be divided into the free and adapted states. The free child ego state is the source of spontaneous feeling and behavior, that lead to experiencing the world in a direct and natural way. It can be playful, genuine, expressive, and emotional. Persons who are in touch with their true selves (free child) have more intimate relationships. The adapted child ego state is the part that has learned to comply with the parental messages received while growing up. Though all people adapt in one way or another, a rebellious child ego state can develop to face restricting parental messages. It is still, however, a kind of adaptation to the parents' messages.

All ego states are manifested in each individual, and each ego state is mirrored in the individual's patterns of behavior, feelings, and thinking. However, each state is specific to each individual. Each ego state works normally in its appropriate situation. Psychopathology arises when certain ego state works in an inappropriate situation. Ego states may also become tainted (contaminated) by each other.

Transactions

Transactions are the method of communication or interaction with another person. In other words, it is the way by which an ego state addresses an ego state in others. Transactions can occur concurrently at both explicit and psychological levels, e.g., a lovely caring voice with sarcastic intent. Understanding of the real communication requires both apparent and non-verbal reading.

People frequently pressurize others or experience pressure from others to communicate in a way that matches their style, e.g., a boss who talks as a controlling parent to his employees will often create feelings of humiliation or other childlike responses. Employees who resist pressure may be fired or categorized as trouble-makers. Transactions can be experienced as positive or negative depending on the nature of the strokes within them. However, a negative transaction is preferred to no transaction at all, because of a fundamental craving or hunger for strokes. The nature of transactions is important to understanding communication.

Types of Transactions

1. *Reciprocal transactions (complementary transactions)*: these are simple forms of communication in which both partners share the same ego state as the other partner, e.g., adult-adult, or child-child. In this type of communication both partners exchange psychologically balanced strokes, and communication like this can continue indefinitely.
2. *Crossed transactions*: in crossed transactions, partners share different ego states, e.g., parent-child or adult-child interactions. It typically results in communication failures and produces problems in the workplace.
3. *Duplex transactions (ulterior transactions)*: in this class of transactions, two messages are sent in parallel, one is overt, and the other is covert and unspoken.

Strokes

A stroke is anything people do that provides another person with recognition and stimulation, e.g., a look, a nod, a smile, a spoken word, or a touch. Strokes can be positive or negative. A key idea is that people always search for recognition. Thus, if people do not get positive strokes, they seek recognition of a negative kind, since negative strokes are better than no strokes at all. Strokes may be internal (derived from fantasies, self-praise, and other forms of self-stimulation), or external (derived from others). Strokes can also be conditional or unconditional. Conditional strokes are based on some condition, e.g., something we do, or accomplish, and for a particular trait that we possess. Unconditional strokes are a very rich kind of strokes that come to you just for being you.

Games

A game is a repeated pattern of reciprocal transactions that has a predictable outcome. Games are learned patterns of behavior, and most people play a small number of their favorite games with other people in varying degrees of intensities. People who are used to a game are willing to play it, even as a different actor from what they originally were. Games are often characterized by a switch in roles of players toward the end. Each game has a reward (payoff) for those playing it. Breaking the game lies in depriving the actors of their payoff. Games vary in their length of time, varying from seconds or minutes to months or even years. Games play several functions, these include: structuring time, acquiring strokes, maintaining the substitute feeling and the system of thinking, confirming parental injunctions and furthering the life script, maintaining the person's life position, and making people predictable.

Life Scripts and Early Decisions

A life script is a personal unconscious life strategy that is based on an interpretation of the external and internal events, and decisions which people made in their early life. These decisions can be adaptive during childhood. However, they do not always make sense for adults who often repeat the patterns that provided those early decisions.

The early decisions are the most important part of the life script. People obtain direct and indirect messages from parents, and important people such as grandparents, siblings, and teachers, about how they should be to obtain strokes from them. Dealing with these messages is so important. People make decisions about themselves and their lives that allow them to adapt in the best possible way to the particular situation (Solomon, 2003).

Injunctions and Counter-Junctions (Drivers)

Injunctions are messages given to the child by the parent's child ego state, out of the circumstances of the parent's own anger, frustration, or unhappiness, regarding what not to do or not to be in order to get recognition. Counter-junctions or drivers are messages given to the child by the parent's parent ego state, out of the circumstances of the parent's own anger or unhappiness, regarding what they have to do or to be in order to get recognition. Both injunctions and counter-junctions can be given through direct expression or often inferred from modeling and rewarding certain behavior.

Life Positions

Based on the messages received and the decisions made, young children develop an attitude in life that reflects how they feel about their selves in relation to others (a life position). Life positions are also called "existential positions" because they influence how we view our own and others' existence. Life positions are personal basic beliefs about self and other people.. Life positions are categorized in different ways. Franklin Ernst supposed four basic life positions, which he called the OK Corral (Ernst, 1971). These are:

- I'm OK, You're OK.
- I'm OK, You're Not OK.
- I'm Not OK, You're OK.
- I'm Not OK, You're Not OK.

Clinical Notes

Transactional analysis can help personal understanding of self, and provides some tools to help change it. It focuses on the interactions (transactions) between the patient and the therapist occurring during the treatment session and between the patient and others in the social environment. Transactional analysis includes four components: (1) ego state analysis; (2) transactional analysis proper, i.e., the ascertaining of the dominant ego state (parent, child, or adult) used in the patient's transactions; (3) game analysis, identifying the games played in interactions and of the gratifications provided; and (4) script analysis, detecting the causes of the patient's emotional problems. Transactional analysis can be used in both individual and group psychotherapy.

Summary

- Berne assumed that ego consists of three primary states that people consistently use (Parent-Adult-Child, PAC).
- Transactions are the method of communication or interaction with another person. In other words, it is the way by which an ego state discourse relates to an ego state in others.
- There are three types of transactions: reciprocal or complementary transactions, crossed transactions, and duplex or ulterior transactions.
- A stroke is anything people do that provides another person with recognition and stimulation.
- A game is a repeated pattern of reciprocal transactions that has a predictable outcome.
- A life script is a personal unconscious life strategy that is based on an interpretation of the external and internal events, and decisions which people made in their early life.
- Based on the messages received and the decisions made, young children develop an attitude in life that reflects how they feel about their selves in relation to others, this is called the life position.

Test Your Knowledge

- What is meant by ego states, in Berne's view?
- Define a transaction.
- What is meant by life scripts and early decisions?

- What is meant by games in transaction theory?
- Define transactional analysis.
- Define injunction, and counter-injunction.
- What are life positions?

Critical Thinking Questions

- Explain the relationship between recognition hunger and strokes.
- How would you evaluate transaction theory and analysis?

Erik Erikson's Psychosocial Theory

Erik Erikson (1902–1994) proposed a psychosocial stage theory of development that encompassed human growth throughout the entire lifespan. Erikson emphasized that the ego makes positive contributions to development by mastering attitudes, ideas, and skills at each stage of development. This mastery helps children grow into successful contributing members of society. Erikson emphasized that the ego rather than the id functions as the center of personality and the unified sense of self. The ego develops within a given society and is influenced by child-rearing practices and other cultural customs.

PHOTO 4.12.   Erik Erikson.

While Erikson believed that each stage of psychosocial development is important, he placed a particular emphasis on the development of *ego identity*. Ego identity is the conscious sense of self that we develop through social interaction. The development of identity begins in childhood and becomes particularly important during adolescence, but it is a process that continues throughout life. Our personal identity gives each of us an integrated and cohesive sense of self that endures and continues to grow as we age, i.e., our ego identity is constantly changing due to new experiences and information we acquire in our daily interactions with others. Erikson perceived identity as developing in the context of social relationships and institutions that either promote or impede its development.

In addition to ego identity, Erikson also believed that a sense of competence motivates behaviors and actions. Each stage in Erikson's theory is concerned with becoming competent in an area of life. If the stage is handled well, the person will feel a sense of mastery, which is sometimes referred to as *ego strength* or *ego quality*. If the stage is managed poorly, the person will emerge with a sense of inadequacy.

Erikson used the term "epigenetic principle" to suggest that the development of certain ego abilities follows a predictable eight-stage sequence, given an average expectable environment. He thought that inherited factors determine the characteristic sequence of these developmental stages. Each stage builds on the preceding stages, and paves the way for subsequent stages. Each stage is characterized by a psychosocial crisis, which is based on physiological development, and demands put on the individual by parents and/or society.

During each of Erikson's eight stages, there is a psychological conflict that works as a turning point in development and must be successfully accomplished in order for a child to develop into a healthy, well-adjusted adult. Each stage involves a crisis of two opposing emotional forces, which Erikson termed "contrary dispositions." Erikson used the words "syntonic" for the first-listed "positive" disposition in each crisis (e.g., Trust) and "dystonic" for the second-listed "negative" disposition (e.g., Mistrust). According to Erikson, the individual is provided with a "sensitive period" to successfully resolve each crisis before a new crisis is presented. The results of the resolution, whether successful or not, are carried forward to the next crisis and provide the foundation for its resolution. Ideally, the crisis in each stage should be resolved, in order for development to proceed correctly. Successful completion of each developmental task results in a sense of competence and a healthy personality. Failure to master these tasks leads to feelings of inadequacy. However, the outcome of one stage is not permanent, but can be altered by later experiences. Everyone has a mixture of the traits attained at each stage, but personality development is considered successful if the individual has more of the good traits than the bad traits.

Stage 1 Trust vs. Mistrust

PHOTO 4.13.   Loving & caring parents.

- This occurs from birth to 12 months of age and is the most fundamental stage in life. Infants learn that adults can be trusted.
- Because an infant is completely dependent, the development of trust occurs when adults meet a child's basic needs for survival.
- Caregivers who are responsive and sensitive to their infant's needs help infants to develop a sense of trust; the infant develops attachment to the primary caregiver and begins developing communication skills.
- Caregivers who do not meet the needs of their babies, by being inconsistent, emotionally unavailable, or rejecting, contribute to feelings of mistrust in the children they care for.
- As no child is going to develop a sense of 100 percent trust or 100 percent mistrust, Erikson believed that successful development can be obtained by balance between the two opposing sides. When this happens, children acquire hope, which Erikson described as openness to experience tempered by some caution from possible danger. Failure to accomplish this stage contributes to depression, hopelessness, difficulties in engaging others, and suspiciousness.

Stage 2 Autonomy vs. Shame and Doubt

- This stage of development occurs during the toddler period (ages 1–3 years).
- A toddler's main task is to resolve the issue of autonomy vs. shame and doubt by working to establish independence. Toddlers begin to explore their world, learn that they can control their actions and act on their environment to get results, and begin to show clear preferences for certain elements of the environment, such as food, toys, and clothing. Toddlers begin developing socialization skills.

PHOTO 4.14.   A Child Seeking Autonomy.

- Like Freud, Erikson believed that toilet training is a vital part of this process. However, Erikson's reasoning was quite different than that of Freud's. Erikson believed that learning to control one's bodily functions leads to a feeling of control and a sense of independence. Other important events in this stage include gaining more control over food choices, toy preferences, and clothing selection.
- Children who successfully complete this stage feel secure and confident, while those who do not accomplish this stage may begin to doubt their abilities, have low self-esteem and feelings of shame, narcissistic vulnerability, delinquency, and obsessive behavior. Erikson believed that achieving a balance between autonomy and shame and doubt would lead to will, which is the belief that children can act with intention, within reason and limits.

Stage 3 Initiative vs. Guilt

- During the preschool years (3–6 years), children are capable of initiating activities and begin to assert their power and control over the world through social interactions and play.
- Initiative refers to a sense of ambition and responsibility; this occurs when parents allow a child to explore within limits, and support the child's choice. These children will develop self-confidence and feel a sense of purpose.
- During this stage, children develop a sense of purpose, master self-care skills, develop a sense of gender, identity, and family relationship.

PHOTO 4.15.   Children Asserting Power & control.

- Children who are successful at this stage feel capable and able to lead others. Failure to accomplish this stage may contribute to anxiety, phobias, inhibitions, impotence, or psychosomatic illness.

Stage 4 Industry vs. Inferiority

- This stage covers the elementary school years (6–12 years).
- Children begin to compare themselves with their peers to see how they measure up. They either develop a sense of pride and accomplishment in their schoolwork, sports, social activities, and family life, or they feel inferior and inadequate because they feel that they do not measure up. Children who are encouraged by parents, teachers, and peers develop a feeling of competence and belief in their skills.

PHOTO 4.16.   Sense of pride & accomplishment.

- Successfully finding a balance at this stage of psychosocial development leads to the strength known as competence or a belief in our own abilities to handle the tasks set before us.
- Children who do not accomplish this will doubt their abilities to be successful, and may develop feelings of inadequacy, inferiority, work inhibitions, or a compensatory search for money, power, and prestige.

Stage 5 Identity vs. Confusion

- During adolescence (ages 12–18), the main task is developing a sense of identity.
- Adolescents struggle with questions such as "Who am I?" and "What do I want to do with my life?" Along the way, most adolescents try on many different selves to see which ones fit; they explore various roles and ideas, set goals, and attempt to discover their "adult" selves.
- Preschool children describe themselves in terms of a

PHOTO 4.17.   Adolescents.

favorite activity. At 8 or 9, children give facts about themselves. At about age 11, children begin to describe themselves in terms of social relationships, personality traits, and other general stable psychological characteristics, suggesting changes in the ways they think of themselves and the beginning of the development of a unique personal identity.
- According to Erikson, events of late adolescence trigger an identity crisis, a struggle to create an integrated and unique self-image. In Western cultures during late adolescence, young people try out various behaviors to help resolve questions about sexuality,

self-worth, industriousness, and independence. By age 21, about half of the adolescents have resolved the identity crisis in a way consistent with their self-image and the historical era in which they are living.

- Personal identity may be affected by ethnic identity, which reflects one's racial, religious, or cultural group. A positive ethnic identity adds to self-esteem.
- Adolescents who receive proper encouragement and reinforcement through personal exploration will emerge from this stage with a strong sense of self and a feeling of independence and control. Those adolescents are able to retain their beliefs and values in the face of problems and other people's perspectives.
- Adolescents who failed to complete this stage may develop prolonged dependence, the revival of borderline and narcissistic traits, and display role diffusion at work.

Stage 6 Intimacy vs. Isolation

- This stage covers the period of early adulthood (twenties through early forties).
- During this stage, young adults can live independent from parental figures, make a personal commitment to others, such as a spouse, and adjust to companionship style. Erikson believed that a strong sense of personal identity was important for developing intimate relationships. Studies have demonstrated that those who do not develop a positive self-concept tend to have trouble developing and maintaining successful relationships and are more likely to suffer emotional isolation, loneliness, and depression.

PHOTO 4.18.   **Making a Family.**

- Those who are successful in this stage will form relationships that are committed and secure. This stage is marked by the ability to form lasting, meaningful relationships with other people.

Stage 7 Generativity vs. Stagnation

- When people reach their forties, they enter the time known as middle adulthood, which extends to the mid-sixties.
- Generativity involves finding life's work and contributing to the development of others through activities such as volunteering, mentoring, and raising children.
- During this stage people seek satisfaction through productivity in their career, family, and contributing positively to society, often through caring for others, or engaging in meaningful and productive work.
- Those who are successful during this phase will feel that they are contributing to the world by being active in their home and community. They feel proud of their accomplishments,

happy by watching their children grow into adults, and developing a sense of unity with their life partner.

- Those who fail to master this task may experience stagnation and feel as though they are not leaving a mark on the world in a meaningful way; they may have little connection with others and little interest in productivity and self-improvement.

PHOTO 4.19.   Satisfaction through Productivity.

Stage 8 Integrity vs. Despair

- This stage extends from the mid-sixties to the end of life (late adulthood).
- Erikson said that people in late adulthood reflect on their lives and deal with loss of friends and relatives, and prepare for retirement and death. People feel either a sense of satisfaction or a sense of failure.
- People who feel proud of their accomplishments feel a sense of integrity, and they can look back on their lives with few regrets and a general feeling of satisfaction. These individuals will attain wisdom, even when confronting death.

PHOTO 4.20.   Late Adulthood.

- People who are not successful at this stage may feel as if their life has been wasted and may experience regrets. They focus on what "would have," "should have," and "could have" been. They face the end of their lives with feelings of bitterness, depression, and despair.

One of the strengths of psychosocial theory is that it provides a broad unified framework to view development throughout the entire lifespan. It also allows us to emphasize the social nature of human beings and the important influence that social relationships have on development. Researchers have found evidence supporting Erikson's ideas about identity and have further identified different sub-stages of identity formation. Some research also suggests that people who form strong personal identities during adolescence are better capable of forming intimate relationships during early adulthood.

One major weakness of psychosocial theory is that the exact mechanisms and kinds of experiences necessary to successfully complete each stage are not well described or developed. The theory fails to detail exactly what types of experiences are necessary at each stage in order to successfully resolve the conflicts and move to the next stage.

James Marcia's Theory of Identity Status

Inspired by the work of Erikson, James Marcia (1966–) proposed six domains in which adolescents search for identity, and give rise to development of personal identity: vocational plans, values and preferences, religious beliefs, gender roles, ethnic identities, and political affiliations and beliefs. Marcia identified four identity statuses (Marcia, 1966):

- *Identity Achievement*: individuals have conducted a search for an appropriate identity and explored alternatives and finally become committed to a specific identity.
- *Identity Diffusion*: individuals did not search for an identity, and hence they did not make any commitments to a specific identity.
- *Identity Foreclosure*: individuals did not search for an identity, however, they committed to a specific identity without exploring alternatives.
- *Identity Moratorium*: individuals have conducted a search for an appropriate identity, but they did not have any firm commitments to a specific identity.

Clinical Notes

Despite the significant contributions of Erik Erikson's theory to a broad range of psychological disciplines, this theory has no recognizable contribution in clinical practice.

Summary

Erik Erikson developed an eight-stage psychosocial theory of development:

- Stage 1 Trust vs. Mistrust: infants learn that adults can be trusted. The infant develops attachment to primary caregiver and begins developing communication skills.
- Stage 2 Autonomy vs. Shame and Doubt: toddlers begin to explore their world, learn that they can control their actions and act on their environment to get results. They begin developing socialization skills.
- Stage 3 Initiative vs. Guilt: children are capable of initiating activities and begin to assert their power and control over the world through social interactions and play.
- Stage 4 Industry vs. Inferiority: children compare themselves with their peers and develop either a sense of pride and accomplishment, or they feel inferior and inadequate.
- Stage 5 Identity vs. Confusion: the main task of this stage is to develop a sense of identity.
- Stage 6 Intimacy vs. Isolation: young adults can live independent from parental figures, make a personal commitment to others, such as a spouse, and adjust to companionship style.
- Stage 7 Generativity vs. Stagnation: people seek satisfaction through productivity in career, family, and community interests.
- Stage 8 Integrity vs. Despair: people reflect on their lives and deal with loss of friends and relatives, and prepare for retirement and death. People feel either a sense of satisfaction or a sense of failure.
- James Marcia proposed six domains that give rise to development of personal identity, and identified four identity statuses.

Test Your Knowledge

Give an account of the following concepts of Erik Erikson's psychosocial theory

- Trust vs. Mistrust
- Autonomy vs. Shame and Doubt
- Initiative vs. Guilt
- Industry vs. Inferiority
- Identity vs. Confusion
- Intimacy vs. Isolation
- Generativity vs. Stagnation
- Integrity vs. Despair

Critical Thinking Questions

- How can you think about identity development considering Erikson's psychosocial theory and current psychological research?
- How would you evaluate Erik Erikson's psychosocial theory?

John Bowlby and Attachment Theory

John Bowlby (1907–1990) was a British psychoanalyst, notable for his interest in child development and his pioneering work on attachment theory. Attachment is a special emotional relationship that starts when a person is emotionally bonded with another person; it involves an exchange of comfort, care, and pleasure. The concept of infants' emotional attachment to caregivers has been known anecdotally for hundreds of years. Most early observers focused on the anxiety displayed by infants and toddlers when threatened with separation from a familiar caregiver. Freudian theory attempted a systematic consideration of infant attachment and attributed the infant's attempts to stay near the familiar person to motivation learned through feeding experiences.

PHOTO 4.21.   Attachment.

Bowlby believed that early relationships with caregivers play a major role in child development and continue to influence social relationships throughout life. Bowlby was influenced by ethological theory in general, especially by Lorenz's (1935) study of imprinting which showed that attachment was innate (in young ducklings) and therefore has a survival value. Bowlby believed

PHOTO 4.22.   Ethological Theory.

that babies are born with the tendency to display certain innate behaviors (called social releasers) which help ensure proximity and contact with the mother or attachment figure. When a child experiences heightened arousal, he or she sends signals to their caregiver. Crying, smiling, and locomotion are examples of these signaling behaviors. Instinctively, caregivers respond to their children's behavior, creating a reciprocal pattern of interaction. Bowlby postulated that the fear of strangers represents an important survival mechanism, in-built by nature.

The main points of Bowlby's theory are:

1. Bowlby hypothesized that both the mother and infant are biologically preprogrammed to develop an attachment relationship to stay in contact with each other, as this will help them to survive, however, their roles are different. The infant's role is to lead the relationship while the mother's part is to sensitively respond and cooperate. The infant produces innate "social releaser" behaviors, such as crying and smiling that stimulate caregiving from adults. This leads to adaptations in the infant either toward or away from cooperation, depending on how well the mother responds to the infant's cues. The attachment behaviors initially function like fixed action patterns and all share the same function.

2. Bowlby believed that there are four basic characteristics of attachment. These four attributes are very evident in the relationship between a child and his or her caregiver. They include:
   a. Safe haven: ideally, the child can rely on the caregiver for comfort at times whenever he or she feels threatened, this becomes evident in returning to the attachment figure for comfort and safety when the child faces fear or threat.
   b. Secure base: the attachment figure acts as a basis of security from which the child can explore the surrounding environment. Bowlby noted that security of attachment is strongly related to the degree of freedom of communication between caregiver and infant.
   c. Proximity maintenance: this refers to the desire of a child to explore the world but still tries to stay close to his or her caregiver, e.g., a teenager discusses peer problems with his mother.
   d. Separation distress: this means that the child becomes unhappy and sorrowful in the absence of the attachment figure, e.g., an infant cries loudly when his or her mother leaves for work.

3. Bowlby suggested that the determinant of attachment is not food but care and responsiveness. This was based on Harry Harlow's findings that infant monkeys spent more time with soft mother-like dummies that did not offer food than they did with dummies that provided food but were less pleasant to the touch.

4. A child has an innate need to attach to one main attachment figure (monotropy). Although Bowlby did not rule out that young children can form multiple attachment figures, Bowlby believed that a child would initially form only one attachment (usually the mother) which is more important than any other attachment, and that this attachment figure acts as a secure base for exploring the world. Bowlby believed that this attachment is qualitatively different from any subsequent attachments. This primary attachment relationship acts as a prototype for all future social relationships. So, disrupting it can have severe consequences. Bowlby's theory of monotropy led to the formulation of his maternal deprivation hypothesis: a warm, intimate, and continuous relationship with a mother figure is necessary for healthy psychological/emotional development. Mother-love in infancy/childhood is as important for mental health as

are vitamins and proteins for physical health. A child should receive continuous care of this single attachment figure for approximately the first two years of life.

5. Bowlby (1951) claimed that there is a critical period of mothering, and that it is almost useless if delayed until after age 2½ to 3 years and, for most children, if delayed till after 12 months, i.e., if the attachment period is broken or disrupted due to separation or loss of the mother as well as the failure to develop an attachment, during the critical two-year period, the child will suffer irreversible long-term consequences of this maternal deprivation. This risk continues until the age of 5. The underlying assumption of Bowlby's maternal deprivation hypothesis is that continual disruption of the attachment between infant and primary caregiver (i.e., the mother) could result in long-term cognitive, social, and emotional difficulties for that infant.

6. Bowlby and Robertson (1952) believed that short-term separation from an attachment figure leads to three progressive stages of distress (the PDD model):
   - Protest: the child cries, screams, and protests angrily when the parent leaves. They will try to cling on to the parent to stop them leaving.
   - Despair: the child's protest begins to stop and they appear to be calmer although still upset. The child refuses others' attempts at comfort and often seems withdrawn and uninterested in anything.
   - Detachment: if separation continues, the child will start to engage with other people again. They will reject the caregiver on their return and show strong signs of anger.

7. Bowlby (1988) suggested that the long-term consequences of failure to initiate, or a breakdown of, the maternal attachment possibly include an inability to form attachments in the future, delinquency (behavioral problems in adolescence), affectionless psychopathy (inability to feel remorse), and problems with cognitive development.

8. The child's attachment relationship with their primary caregiver acts as a prototype that guides their future relationships and responsiveness to others in general, via development of an internal working model (Bowlby, 1969). There are three main features of the internal working model: (a) a model of others as being trustworthy; (b) a model of the self as valuable; and (c) a model of the self as effective when interacting with others.

Criticism of Bowlby's View of Attachment

Schaffer and Emerson (1964) noted that, by 18 months, very few children (13 percent) were attached to only one person, some had five or more attachments. Rutter (1972) pointed out that several indicators of attachment (such as protest or distress when attached person leaves) have been shown for a variety of attachment figures, e.g., fathers, siblings, peers, and even inanimate objects. Rutter also criticized Bowlby for not distinguishing between deprivation (loss of or damage to an attachment), and privation (failure to develop an emotional bond) which Rutter suggested was more deleterious to the child. Rutter proposed that privation is likely to lead initially to clinging, dependent behavior, attention-seeking, and indiscriminate friendliness, then as the child matures, an inability to keep rules, form lasting relationships, or feel guilt. He also found evidence of affectionless anti-social behavior, and disorders of language, intellectual development, and physical growth among those children. Rutter argues that these problems are not due solely to the lack of attachment to a mother figure, as Bowlby claimed, but to factors such as the lack of intellectual stimulation and social experiences which attachments normally provide, i.e., the quality of the attachment bond is the most important factor, rather than just deprivation in the critical period. In addition, such problems can be overcome later in the child's development, with the right kind of care.

Mary Ainsworth's "Strange Situation" Assessment

During the 1970s, psychologist Mary Ainsworth further expanded upon Bowlby's work in her famous "Strange Situation" study. The study involved observing children between the ages of 12–18 months responding to a situation in which they were briefly left alone and then reunited with their mother. The child is observed playing for 20 minutes while caregivers and strangers enter and leave the room. Based on these observations, Ainsworth concluded that there are three major styles of attachment: (1) secure attachment; (2) ambivalent-insecure attachment; and (3) avoidant-insecure attachment (Ainsworth, 1964; Ainsworth, Bell, & Stayton, 1971; Ainsworth, Blehar, Waters, & Wall, 1978). Main and Solomon (1986) added a fourth attachment style known as disorganized-insecure attachment. Numerous studies have supported Ainsworth's conclusions and additional research has revealed that these early attachment styles can help predict behaviors later in life. The following summarizes characteristics of these attachment styles:

Secure Attachment

- Children who are securely attached to their caregivers (parents), feel happy whenever their caregivers are around, but are upset when their caregivers leave. When distressed or frightened, these children will seek comfort from the caregiver. Contact initiated by a caregiver is readily accepted by securely attached children and they greet the return of a parent with positive behavior. While these children can be comforted to some extent by other people in the absence of caregiver, they clearly prefer the caregiver to strangers.
- Parents of securely attached children tend to play more with their children. Additionally, these parents react more quickly to their children's needs and are generally more responsive to their children than parents of insecurely attached children. Studies have shown that securely attached children are more empathetic during later stages of childhood. These children are also described as less disruptive, less aggressive, and more mature than children with ambivalent or avoidant attachment styles.
- As adults, those who are securely attached tend to have trusting, long-term relationships. Other key characteristics of securely attached individuals include having high self-esteem, enjoying intimate relationships, seeking out social support, and an ability to share feelings with other people.

Ambivalent Attachment

- Observational research consistently links ambivalent-insecure attachment to low maternal availability. A child who is ambivalently attached becomes upset and sorrowful whenever he or she gets separated from his or her parent, but does not seem reassured or comforted by the return of the parent. In some cases, the child might passively reject the parent by refusing comfort, or may openly display direct aggression toward the parent. The child does not feel that he or she can rely on the caregiver whenever he or she is in need of something. As these children grow older, teachers often describe them as clingy and over-dependent (Cassidy & Berlin, 1994).
- Ambivalently attached children tend to be suspicious of strangers. As adults, those with an ambivalent attachment style often feel reluctant to become close to others and worry that their partner does not share their feelings. This leads to frequent breakups,

often because of cold and distant relationships. These individuals feel especially upset at the end of a relationship. Cassidy and Berlin described ambivalently attached adults who cling to young children as a source of security.

Avoidant Attachment

- A child who has an avoidant attachment tends to keep away from his or her parents. This avoidance often becomes especially pronounced after a period of absence, or it may result from neglect or abuse of children.
- These children do not reject parental attention, but neither do they seek their comfort or contact. Children with an avoidant attachment show no preference between a parent and a complete stranger.
- As adults, those with an avoidant attachment tend to have difficulty with intimacy and close relationships. Those individuals do not devote much emotion in relationships and experience little distress when a relationship ends. They often avoid intimacy by using excuses (such as long work hours). Other common characteristics include a failure to support partners during stressful times and an inability to share feelings, thoughts, and emotions with partners.

Disorganized Attachment

- Main and Solomon (1986) proposed that inconsistent behavior on the part of parents might be a contributing factor in this style of attachment. In later research, Main and Hesse (1990) argued that parents who act as figures of both fear and reassurance to a child contribute to a disorganized attachment style. Because the child feels both comforted and frightened by the parent, confusion results.
- Actions and responses of children with a disorganized-insecure attachment to caregivers are often a mix of behaviors, including avoidance or resistance. These children seem either confused or apprehensive in the presence of a caregiver.

Attachment Through Life

It is difficult to claim that infant attachment styles are identical to adult romantic attachment styles, as a long time elapses between infancy and adulthood, so intervening experiences play a large role in adult attachment styles. Consequently, those described as ambivalent or avoidant in infancy can become securely attached as adults, while those with a secure attachment in childhood can show insecure attachment styles in adulthood. However, research has shown that early attachment styles can help predict patterns of behavior in adulthood.

In one study, Hazan and Shaver (1987) found that the best predictor of adult attachment style was people's perceptions about the quality of their relationships with their parents, and their parent's relationship with each other; however, parental divorce seemed unrelated to attachment style. Hazan and Shaver found that securely attached adults tend to believe that romantic love is enduring and have happy and trusting love experiences. Ambivalently attached adults often report falling in love easily and frequently, though they have difficulty finding real love, while those with avoidant attachment styles tend not to believe in romantic love as shown in movies, do not believe that love lasts, do not fall in love easily, and report a fear of intimacy.

Clinical Notes

- Attachment theory provides a useful framework for understanding the importance of early relationships and working with children who have experienced developmental trauma and who have difficulties in experiencing a secure attachment. This has guided the development of a range of interventions to increased security of attachment for the infant and children.
- While working with adults in psychotherapy, attachment theory enhances the understanding of and responding to clients' need, and identification of the possible transference and the counter-transference reactions during therapy.

Summary

- Attachment is a special emotional relationship that starts when a person is emotionally bonded with another person, it involves an exchange of comfort, care, and pleasure.
- Bowlby hypothesized that both the mother and infant are biologically preprogrammed to develop an attachment relationship to stay in contact with each other, as this will help them to survive, however, their roles are different.
- Bowlby (1951) claimed that a child has an innate need to attach to one main attachment figure (monotropy).
- Bowlby believed that there are four basic characteristics of attachment: safe haven, secure base, proximity maintenance, and separation distress.
- Bowlby suggested that the determinant of attachment is not food but care and responsiveness.
- Bowlby claimed that there is a critical period of mothering, it is almost useless if delayed until after 2½ to 3 years.
- Bowlby and Robertson believe that short-term separation from an attachment figure leads to three progressive stages of distress: protest, despair, and detachment.
- Mary Ainsworth proposed three attachment styles: secure attachment, ambivalent attachment, and avoidant attachment. Main and Solomon added a fourth style of attachment: disorganized attachment.

Test Your Knowledge

- Give an account of Bowlby's view of attachment.
- Describe Bowlby's basic characteristics of attachment.
- Give an account of styles of attachment.
- Describe the theory of monotropy.
- Give an account of the maternal deprivation hypothesis.

Critical Thinking Questions

- How would you argue with and against Bowlby's view of attachment?
- Assess attachment across the lifespan.
- How useful is it to understand attachment theory while practicing psychotherapy?

Karen Horney

Karen Horney (1885–1952) was a German psychologist who made major contributions to psychology. Horney agreed with Freud that childhood experiences played a major role in development as an adult but thought that the greatest influence was social relationships not sexual ones. Her view of human beings and human behavior is more optimistic. Some of Horney's contributions include her theories on the psychology of women, her work on understanding and treating neuroses, and her ideas on the possibility of human growth and self-actualization, ideas that influenced humanist psychologists like Abraham Maslow and Carl Rogers. The keys elements of Karen Horney's theories include:

PHOTO 4.23.   Karen Horney.

1. *Theory of neurosis*: Horney assumed that all children need feelings of safety and security that can be attained only from loving parents. Horney introduced the term "basic evil" to refer to poor parenting, from neglect up to child abuse. This incorporates various inappropriate behaviors that parents may exhibit toward their children, including indifference toward the child, rejection of the child, hostility toward the child, obvious preferences for a sibling, unfair punishment, ridicule, humiliation, erratic behavior, broken promises, and isolation of the child from others. According to Horney, these inappropriate behaviors lead to the child's feelings of basic hostility toward parents. However, children seldom overtly express this hostility as rage, instead they repress their hostility toward their parents and have no awareness of it. Children who repress feelings of basic hostility develop a feeling of being isolated and helpless, of insecurity and a pervasive sense of apprehension, which Horney called basic anxiety (Horney, 1950). Thus, basic anxiety develops because of the conflict between dependency and hostility toward the mother, the father, or both. Horney argued that a child is tied to his or her parents because of dependence on the mother and father for food, shelter, and other basic needs, not sex (as Sigmund Freud argued). As the child realizes that he or she has no place to go, no matter how terribly the parents treat him or her, and that he or she is dependent on parents, anxiety generalizes, and everyone becomes a potential threat, and the world is seen as hostile and unreliable. Accordingly, Horney argued that bad parenting is the root of all our problems (Horney, 1950).

   Horney identified ten strategies and corresponding needs that neurotics develop to cope with their excessive anxiety and feelings of helplessness and loneliness. These include: (1) need for affection and approval; (2) need for over-reliance on a partner; (3) need for ambition and personal achievement; (4) need for power; (5) need to exploit others; (6) need for social recognition or prestige; (7) need for personal admiration; (8) need to restrict one's life within narrow borders; (9) need for self-sufficiency and independence; and (10) need for perfection and unassailability. Later on, Horney grouped these ten neurotic needs into three basic neurotic trends in personality: (1) moving toward people (the compliant type); (2) moving against people (the aggressive type); and

(3) moving away from people (the detached type). Normal people have the flexibility to use any or all of these approaches, but neurotics rely rigidly on only one, e.g., occasionally the need to hear reassurance that one is liked is healthy, but the need to hear this reassurance constantly is not healthy and would be the sign of a neurotic need. Thus, neurotic individuals are frequently trapped in a vicious circle in which their compulsive need to reduce basic anxiety leads to a variety of self-defeating behaviors; these behaviors then produce more basic anxiety, and the circle continues (Horney, 1937, 1942).

2. *Theory of self*: Horney believed that healthy people have an accurate conception of who they are, and they are free to realize that potential (self-realization) and achieve what they wish within reasonable boundaries. Thus, she believed that self-actualization is the healthy person's aim, as opposed to the neurotic's clinging to a set of key needs. Horney believed that people have two views of their self. The "real self" and the "ideal self." The real self is who and what they actually are. The real self contains potential for growth, happiness, will power, gifts, and so forth. As the real self has deficiencies that people do not like, people create what they "should" be in their ideal self. The ideal self is the type of person people feel that they should be and is used as a model to assist in developing their potential and achieving self-actualization. This ideal self is not a positive goal, nor is it realistic or possible. Horney recognized three aspects of the idealized self-image: (1) the neurotic search for glory: a comprehensive drive toward actualizing the ideal self; (2) neurotic claims: a belief that a person is entitled to special privileges; and (3) neurotic pride: a false pride that is not based on reality but on a distorted and idealized view of self. The neurotic person's self is split between an idealized self and a corresponding disliked self. Therefore, neurotic individuals dislike themselves because reality always falls short of their idealized view of self; they develop self-hatred, which can be expressed as: (1) relentless demands on self; (2) relentless self-accusation; (3) self-contempt; (4) self-frustration; (5) self-torture; and (6) self-destructive actions and impulses. On the other hand, neurotics may externalize their frustrations for their unfulfilled goals of perfectionism by projecting blame onto the world and the people around them. The neurotic, therefore, swings back and forth between pretending to be perfect and hating themselves. Horney called this inner battle to meet the unattainable goals of perfectionism, the "tyranny of the shoulds" and the neurotic's "striving for glory." She concluded that these two impossible selves prevent the neurotic from ever reaching their potential unless the cycle of neurosis is somehow broken, through treatment or otherwise (Horney, 1950).

3. *Personality theory*: Horney reformulated Freudian thought and presented a holistic, humanistic perspective that emphasized cultural and social influences, human growth, and the achievement of self-actualization. Horney believed that each person begins life with the potential for healthy development, but people need favorable conditions for growth. These conditions include a warm and loving environment, that should not be overly permissive. Children need to experience both genuine love and healthy discipline. Such conditions provide them with feelings of safety and satisfaction and permit them to grow in accordance with their real self. Horney insisted that modern culture is too competitive and that competition leads to hostility and feelings of isolation. These conditions lead to exaggerated needs for affection and cause people to overvalue love. Self-realization, according to Horney, should be a lifelong goal (Horney, 1950).

4. *Feminine psychology*: Karen Horney was the first woman to present a paper on feminine psychology at an international meeting. The 14 papers that she wrote between 1922 and 1937, and compiled to form a volume entitled *Feminine Psychology*, earned

Horney a distinguished position in psychology. Horney became a supporter for women in their ability to have both children and a career. She recognized issues such as women's dignity and equality within the workplace and the conflicts that stem from raising a family. Horney also recognized that social and cultural influences encouraged women to be dependent on men for love, prestige, wealth, care, and protection. She pointed out that the overemphasis on pleasing men and the overvaluation of men and love led women to gain value only through their husbands, children, and family. Thus culture and society can influence and even determine what a woman should do with her life goals.

5. *Womb envy*: Horney rejected Freud's suggestion that women were frustrated and unhappy because they were not males, and denied that women have penis envy. Horney developed the concept of "womb envy" in boys to counter Freud's concept of "penis envy" for girls. She asserted that women did not envy men's anatomy but envied the independence, success, and freedom that women often are denied. Also, Horney rejected Freud's notion of a woman having an inadequate superego, which comes from not being able to resolve the Oedipal conflict as a girl. Her view of the Oedipus complex differed markedly from Freud's in that she insisted that any sexual attraction or hostility the child feels for the parent would be the result of learning and not biology. Horney believed that psychological differences between men and women are not due to anatomy but to culture and social expectations.

Clinical Notes

Horney's assumption about the consciousness-unconscious relationship, the ego-others relationship, and the patient-therapist relationship had some implication on analytic psychotherapy. She developed a theory of neurosis, a theory of self, and contributed to feminine psychology.

Summary

- Basic evil refers to poor parenting, from neglect up to child abuse.
- Basic hostility refers to the child's repressed hostility toward their parents.
- Basic anxiety refers to a feeling of being isolated and helpless, insecurity, and a pervasive sense of apprehension, in children with basic hostility.
- Horney suggested that neurosis is more continuous with normal life than previous theorists. She defined neurosis in both intrapsychic and interpersonal terms.
- Horney identified ten strategies and corresponding needs that neurotics develop to cope with their excessive anxiety and feelings of helplessness and loneliness.
- Horney believed that self-actualization is the healthy person's aim, as opposed to the neurotic's clinging to a set of key needs. She believed that healthy people have an accurate conception of who they are, and they are free to realize that potential (self-realization) and achieve what they wish within reasonable boundaries.
- The real self is who and what people actually are. It contains the potential for growth, happiness, will power, gifts, and so forth.
- The ideal self is the type of person we feel that we should be.
- Horney believed that each person begins life with the potential for healthy development, but people need favorable conditions for growth. Horney reformulated Freudian thought and presented a holistic, humanistic perspective that emphasized cultural and social influences, human growth, and the achievement of self-actualization.

- Horney rejected Freud's suggestion that women were frustrated and unhappy because they were not males, and that women have penis envy, and she developed the concept of womb envy in boys. Horney believed that psychological differences between men and women are not due to anatomy but to culture and social expectations.

Test Your Knowledge

- Give an account of Horney's theory of neurosis.
- Describe Horney's theory of self.
- Give an account of Horney's contribution to feminine psychology.

Critical Thinking Questions

- How can you assess Horney's theory of neurosis?
- How can you assess Horney's objections to Freud's ideas about women?

Melanie Klein

Melanie Klein (1882–1960) is one of the founding figures in psychoanalysis. She extended and developed Sigmund Freud's understanding of the unconscious mind. Following World War I, Klein developed the technique of play therapy to uncover children's unconscious motivations, as a substitute for Freud's free association, of which very young children are incapable. She believed that children project their feelings in therapeutic play sessions. By analyzing children's play, Klein explored the unknown territory of the mind of the infant, finding an early Oedipus complex and the earliest roots of the superego. She showed that the way children played with toys revealed earlier infantile fantasies and anxieties.

PHOTO 4.24.   Melanie Klein.

Klein extended Freud's developmental stages down to the first 4–6 months after birth. Klein understanding of the child's fears, and defenses against them, enabled her to make original theoretical contributions to psychoanalysis, known as *object relations theory*. The term "object" in this theory refers to any person or part of a person that infants introject, or take into their psychic structure and project it later onto other people. Object relations refer to the emotional bonds that one person develops with another one, with emphasis on emotional relationships formed during the first two years of life, where such bonds are called "object relationships." So object relations theory is really something more like "interpersonal relations theory." Psychological disturbance in adults is supposed to result from problems in object relations during childhood. Object relations theory has been taken up and developed by Margaret Mahler, Ronald Fairbairn, Donald Winnicott, Harry Guntrip, Otto Rank, Sandor Ferenczi, and Scott Stuart.

Object relations theory assumed that personality can be understood as reflecting the mental images of significant figures (especially the mother) that we form early in life in response to interactions taking place within the family (Kernberg, 2004; Wachtel, 1997). These mental images (sometimes called introjects) serve as templates for later interpersonal relationships through our unconscious memories and patterns of relating. According to object relations theorists, children not only internalize the object itself, but also the entire relationship. The infant internalizes two sets of object relations (both positive and negative), which include representations of the self, the object, and the emotion that links between the two.

Transference occurs when people use representations of older relationships as a mean of understandings their new relationships. When an older relationship has been "transferred" onto a newer one, the older relationship will be the point of comparison against which the newer one is judged. The person doing the transference may read nonexistent characteristics or tendencies into the newer relationship, simply because of their presence in the older original relationship, e.g., reacting angrily toward an adult male therapist, by someone who had a difficult and distant relationship with his or her father.

Klein assumed that very young infants possess an active, unconscious fantasy life. Their most basic fantasies are images of the "good" breast and the "bad" breast. In attempts to reduce the conflict produced by good and bad images, infants organize their experience into positions or ways of dealing with both internal and external objects. These positions include the following.

The Paranoid-Schizoid Position

During this position, the infant develops the first object relationship with a part (e.g., the breast) rather than a whole person or object. The infant perceives the mother's breast as all good or all bad, according to the infant's experience of satisfaction or frustration. The infant's experience with the good breast and the bad breast leads to a struggle between two opposing feelings: a desire to harbor the breast which feeds it, and a desire to bite or destroy it when hungry. To tolerate these two feelings, the ego splits itself by retaining parts of its life and death instincts, while projecting other parts onto the breast. The object will become persecutory and overwhelm or destroy the ideal object and the self, which are then introjected, giving rise to paranoid anxiety. This anxiety is a central aspect of the paranoid-schizoid position. The capacity for whole object relations is not achieved until the depressive position, in which both good and bad parts can be tolerated at the same time.

According to Klein, children adopt various defense mechanisms to protect their egos against anxiety aroused by their own destructive fantasies. These include introjection, projection, splitting, and projective identification:

1. *Introjection*: Klein defined introjection as the fantasy of taking into one's own body the images that one has of an external object. Internal object is a term used to denote an inner mental and emotional image of an external figure, also known as an external object, together with the experience of that figure. The inner world is seen to be composed of internal objects. Infants usually introject good objects as a protection against anxiety, but they also introject bad objects in order to gain control of them.
2. *Projection*: The fantasy that one's own feelings and impulses reside within another person is called projection. Children project both good and bad images, especially onto their parents.
3. *Splitting*: Infants sort out experiences of themselves and of external objects into good or bad by splitting or mentally keeping apart, incompatible images, thus keeping

relatively safe aspects of self and the mother which promote life and growth, from internal or external forces that threaten life and safety. Also, splitting allows infants to like themselves while still recognizing some unlikable qualities.

4. *Projective identification*: this is an unconscious fantasy in which aspects of the self or an internal object are split off and attributed to an external object and finally introjected in an altered form.

The Depressive Position

The child arrives at the depressive position, when he or she adequately deals with the paranoid schizoid position, by bringing together conflicted feelings of love and hate, realizing the hated person and the loved person are the same one, leading to a sense of guilt, and a wish to repair. According to Klein, one would realize that the mother that one hated was also the mother that one loved. The depressive position emerges when one takes in the mother as a whole object. One would inhibit the need to attack, and contain the feeling in oneself. This led to taking in and tolerating more pain.

Modified Views of Object Relations: Margaret Mahler, Heinz Kohut

A number of other theorists have expanded and altered Klein's theory of object relations. Notable among them are Margaret Mahler, Heinz Kohut, John Bowlby, and Mary Ainsworth.

Margaret Mahler's View of Object Relationships

Margaret Mahler (1897–1986) focused on the development of ego within the context of object relationships. Mahler shifted the focus away from the Freudian emphasis on the gratification of instincts or biological needs as the basis for mental life, to an emphasis on how interpersonal relationships between the caregiver and child become internalized within the ego or self, resulting in an integrated sense of self. Mahler developed her theory of object relations from careful observations of infants as they bonded with their mothers during their first three years of life. *Separation-individuation* is the name she gave to the process by which internal maps of the self and of others are formed. These experiential maps, or internal representations, are built up through both positive and negative interactions with caregivers during the period from birth to 3 years of age. According to Mahler, it is the ability to integrate frustrating and pleasurable aspects of experience with another person that leads to a stable sense of self that can tolerate fluctuating emotional states within the self and with others. The inability to integrate these aspects of experience can lead to psychopathology (Mahler, Pine, & Bergman, 1975). In their progress toward achieving a sense of identity, Mahler proposed that children pass through a series of three developmental phases.

1. *Normal Autistic Phase*: this covers the first three or four weeks of life in which the infant is either sleeping or hardly conscious. The newborn acts to achieve a homeostatic equilibrium outside of the uterus. The infant is unable to differentiate, and this stage is objectless. At this stage, the mother needs to be available and meet the baby's needs with loving, tender, and caring interaction. Later, Mahler discarded this phase.
2. *Normal Symbiotic Phase*: (age 1–5 months), the infant perceives itself as one with its mother within the larger environment; the infant is now aware of its mother, but has

no sense of individuality of its own. Positive stimuli (cuddling, smiling, engaged attention) and relief of discomfort (feeding promptly when hungry, changing of soiled diapers, providing an appropriate sleep environment) all help the infant to develop a trust that their needs will be met, building a basis for security and confidence.

3. *Separation-Individuation Phase*: (from about 5 months until about 3 years), the infant begins to communicate with its environment and people. *Separation* refers to the child's emergence from a symbiotic state and development of differentiation in the infant's mind between the infant and the mother (caregiver), whereas *individuation* refers to the evolution of intrapsychic autonomy, concerned with the development and assertion of the infant's own unique characteristics. The separation-individuation phase is subdivided into four stages, which occur in the following order, but which often overlap in time:

   Stage one: differentiation: (5–9 months), the infant becomes increasingly aware of its surroundings and interested in them, using its mother as a point of reference or orientation. Infants smile in response to their own mother, indicating a specific bond with her. Psychologically healthy infants will expand their world beyond the mother, and will be curious about others and inspect them; unhealthy infants will fear and retreat from them.

   Stage two: practicing: (the period from about 7–10 months of age to about age 15–16 months), during this stage, children easily distinguish their body from their mothers, establish a specific bond with their mother, and begin to develop an autonomous ego. The infant begins to explore actively and becomes more independent of its mother. The infant still experiences itself as one with its mother. Some independent play time is enjoyed, but often the baby is only comfortable to play on their own when the mother is within the child's sight. Encouraging children to begin independent exploration while staying nearby will provide children with the ability to take pleasure in their growing world.

   Stage three: rapprochement: (16–24 months), children begin to realize the limits of their omnipotence and have a new awareness of their distinction from the caregiver; children get a first real sense that they are individuals, separate from their mothers. The increase in cognition and motor development leads the young child to run away from his or her mother, refusing her attention or wishes, and to be anxiously clinging to her. Mahler referred to this as "ambitendency," and explained this behavior by the child's simultaneous need for autonomy and need for support. Toilet training often begins at this stage, leading to further struggles with autonomy and control.

   Stage four: consolidation and object constancy: (24–36 months), children develop a constant inner representation of their mother, so that they can tolerate being physically separate from her. This makes it possible for children aged 2 years old to admit that they are unique from their mothers without anxiety, allowing the child to accept substitutes for the mother when she is absent. If object constancy is not developed, children will continue to depend on their mother's physical presence for their own security. In addition to object constancy, children consolidate their individuality, that is, they learn to function without their mother and to develop other object relationships (Mahler et al., 1975).

Ronald Fairbairn's View of Object Relationships

Ronald Fairbairn (1889–1964) proposed that development of the personality structure occurs in terms of object relationships rather than in terms of Freud's id, ego, and superego. Fairbairn suggested the existence of (1) an ego at birth, which splits during the paranoid-schizoid position in response to frustrations and excitement experienced in the relationship with the mother, into the central ego, which resembles Freud's concept of the ego; (2) the libidinal ego, which resembles the id; and (3) the antilibidinal ego, which resembles the superego.

Fairbairn viewed personality development as three stages of a gradual process during which individuals evolve from a state of complete infantile dependence on the caregiver, to a state of quasi-independence, and finally to a state of mature dependence.

Donald Winnicott's View of Object Relationships

Donald Winnicott (1896–1971) asserted that the interaction of mothers and infants over time is crucial in infant growth and development, and stressed the importance of the raising environment on the ability of children to develop a sense of independence. Adequate parental care includes psychological and physical protection of the child from discomfort. The developing child may develop either a true self (the part of the infant that feels creative, spontaneous, and real) with good enough care, or a false self (built on the basis of compliance) with inadequate care.

Clinical Notes

Though controversy about object relations theory exists, some clinicians have applied its theoretical concepts to classify character pathology into hierarchical levels of organizations, and its concepts were adapted in psychoanalytic practices. Therapy is directed at resolving bad or persecutory objects relationships internalized by the patients in order for them to develop mature relationships with people and not just use them for their personal satisfaction (Kernberg, 1978).

Summary

- Klein developed the technique of play therapy to uncover children's unconscious motivations, as a substitute for Freud's free association.
- Klein's understanding of the child's fears, and defenses against them, enabled her to make original theoretical contributions to psychoanalysis, known as object relations theory.
- Object relations refer to how experience with another comes to be represented in the mind. So object relations theory is really something like "interpersonal relations theory."
- Klein assumed that very young infants possess an active, unconscious fantasy life. Their most basic fantasies are images of the "good" breast and the "bad" breast. In attempts to reduce the conflict produced by good and bad images, infants organize their experience into positions, or ways of dealing with both internal and external objects. These positions include the paranoid-schizoid position and the depressive position.
- Mahler developed her theory of object relations (separation-individuation) from careful observations of infants as they bonded with their mothers during their first three years of life. The ability to integrate frustrating and pleasurable aspects of experience with another person leads to a stable sense of self that can tolerate fluctuating emotional states within the self and with others.

Test Your Knowledge

- Describe the defenses proposed by Mahler during establishing object relations.
- What is meant by the paranoid-schizoid position?
- What is meant by the depressive position?
- Describe Margaret Mahler's view of the separation-individuation process.

Critical Thinking Questions

- How can we evaluate object relations theory?
- How can object relations theory be used in assessment and therapy?

Defense Mechanisms

Defense mechanisms are classically defined as automatic psychological processes adopted by a person in response to emotional conflicts, unacceptable impulses, and internal or external dangers or stressors. The ego manipulates, denies, or distorts reality to keep conflicts out of consciousness, thus protecting the mind/self/ego against feelings of anxiety or guilt, providing a guard against a situation with which one cannot cope, and maintaining one's self-esteem. Individuals are usually unaware of these processes as they occur. Sigmund Freud (1894, 1896) coined a number of ego defenses which he referred to throughout his written works. His daughter, Anna Freud, developed these ideas and elaborated on them, adding five of her own (A. Freud, 1937, 1946). Many psychoanalysts have also added further types of ego defenses.

Although the concept of "defense mechanisms" was criticized and disputed for a number of years, empirical studies show renewed interest in these defenses. Cognitive psychologists confirmed the presence of unconscious psychological processes, a prerequisite for defenses. Also, developmental, personality, and social psychologists have found evidence for defense mechanisms (Cramer, 2000). Functional brain imaging studies revealed that affects generated in the limbic system and the hippocampus are shut off by the defense mechanisms (suppression and repression) in the prefrontal cortex (Baddeley, Eysenck, & Anderson, 2009).

Defense mechanisms are not to be confused with *conscious coping strategies*, which are strategies that are deliberately used to deal with stress. Although there is an overlap between coping and defense mechanisms, there are definite theoretical differences. Coping is a conscious process, intentional, determined by situation not a disposition, and is not hierarchically arranged.

It is noteworthy that other psychological theoretical perspectives have addressed the psychoanalytic defenses, giving them different labels. Social psychologists addressed the cognitive processes of projection under the name of attribution (or later, the false consensus effect); displacement formed the basis of early work on scapegoating; aspects of denial have been reorganized as positive illusions; and undoing has been relabeled "counterfactual thinking" (Paulhus, Fridhandler, & Hayes, 1997).

PHOTO 4.25.   Anna Freud.

Defense mechanisms may result in healthy or unhealthy consequences, depending on the circumstances and frequency of its use. Healthy persons normally use different defense mechanisms throughout life. Defense mechanisms become pathological when their persistent use leads to maladaptive behavior that adversely affects the physical or mental health of the individual. Although analysts disagree on the total number of defense mechanisms, most agree with Freud's assessment that defense mechanisms must possess the following properties:

1. They are unconscious.
2. They manage instincts, drives, and mood.
3. They are discrete.
4. They are dynamic and reversible.
5. They can be adaptive or pathological.

Classification of Defense Mechanisms

The list of defense mechanisms is long and there is no theoretical consensus on the number of defense mechanisms. Defense mechanisms could be classified according to some of their properties, e.g., underlying mechanisms, and similarities or connections with personality. Different theorists have different categorizations and conceptualizations of defense mechanisms. In adults, some authors suggest that defenses are hierarchically arranged according to their degree of maturity, with the most adaptive defenses ranked at the top of the hierarchy, and the less adaptive, most immature, defenses at the bottom. In children, defenses are arranged on a developmental continuum, with immature defenses emerging earlier than mature ones.

Robert Plutchik views defenses as derivatives of basic emotions. Plutchik proposed that eight defense mechanisms were related to eight core emotions: these eight defenses are:

1. reaction formation
2. denial
3. repression
4. regression
5. compensation
6. projection
7. displacement
8. intellectualization.

According to his theory, reaction formation relates to joy (and manic features), denial relates to acceptance (and histrionic features), repression to fear (and passivity), regression to surprise (and borderline traits), compensation to sadness (and depression), projection to disgust (and paranoia), displacement to anger (and hostility), and intellectualization to anticipation (and obsessionality) (Plutchik, Kellerman, & Conte, 1979).

Vaillant's Classification of Defense Mechanisms

George Eman Vaillant's categorization of defense mechanisms forms a continuum related to their psychoanalytical developmental level (Vaillant, 1977). Vaillant's levels are:

- Level 1: pathological defenses: delusional projection and psychotic denial.
- Level 2: immature defenses: fantasy, projection, passive aggression, and acting out.

- Level 3: neurotic defenses: intellectualization, reaction formation, dissociation, displacement, and repression.
- Level 4: mature defenses: humor, sublimation, suppression, altruism, and anticipation.

Pathological Defense Mechanisms

The defenses of this level prevent the individual from being able to cope with a real threat and obscure his or her ability to perceive reality. Thus, when mechanisms on this level predominate, it is almost always an indicator of severe psychopathology. The users of these mechanisms frequently appear irrational or insane to others. These defenses are common in psychosis, dreams, and throughout childhood as well. They include:

- *Delusional projection*: false thoughts, emotions, and impulses are attributed to others, i.e., genuine delusions about external reality that are attributed to others. These delusions are usually of a persecutory nature.
- *Denial*: refusing to acknowledge some painful aspect of external reality or subjective experience that is apparent to others, i.e., acting as if a painful event, thought, or feeling does not exist. This is considered one of the most primitive of the defense mechanisms because it is characteristic of early childhood development. Many people use denial in everyday life to avoid dealing with painful feelings or areas of their life they do not wish to admit, e.g., ignoring the physician's advice regarding taking medications and stopping smoking in a person who was told that he had myocardial infarction, assuming that he is quite well and does not need any treatment or precautions. Similarly, a person who was arrested several times because of drunk driving but denies having a problem with alcohol. In distinction from repression, which defends against bad affects, denial abolishes external reality. The term "psychotic denial" is usually used to denote a gross impairment in reality testing.
- *Distortion*: a gross reshaping of external reality to meet internal needs, e.g., blaming others for your emotional turmoil.
- *Splitting*: everything in the world is seen as all good or all bad with nothing in between, and there is no integration of positive and negative qualities into cohesive images. Splitting occurs when the ego attempts to evaluate a situation, an object, or people, but resorts to "black and white" or a "good versus bad" approach. This results in disturbance of self and object images that tend to alternate between polar opposites, e.g., a woman who believed her physician was god-like begins to think he is a terrible person after he is late for an appointment with her. These people reject others who do not live up to their expectations.

Immature Defense Mechanisms

Immature defense mechanisms are often present in adults and more commonly present in adolescents. These mechanisms minimize distress and anxiety provoked by threatening people or by uncomfortable and painful reality. People who excessively use immature defenses are not socially desirable in that they are immature and difficult to deal with. Overuse of these mechanisms almost always leads to problems in a person's ability to cope effectively. These defenses are often seen in severe depression and personality disorders. The occurrence of these defenses is considered normal in adolescence. Immature defenses include:

- *Acting out*: this refers to expressing emotional conflict and internal or external stressors in an extreme behavior, e.g., instead of saying "I am angry with you," a person may throw a book at the person, or punch a hole through a wall. A child's temper tantrum is a form of acting out when he or she does not get his or her own way with a parent. Self-injury may also be a form of acting out, expressing through physical pain what one cannot stand to feel emotionally. Acting out serves as a pressure release, and it often helps the individual feel calmer and peaceful once again. Acting out is related to emotional conflicts and is not synonymous with bad behavior.

- *Fantasy*: the person resorts to excessive daydreaming instead of effective problem-solving action or as a substitute for human relationships, in response to emotional conflict, and internal or external stressors. The person experiences an imaginary sequence of events which act to solve an emotional conflict, by affording unreal substitute satisfaction. The person may fantasize about winning the lottery or the idealized outcomes of his or her life changing for the better. Fantasy occurs normally in daydreaming. It is considered abnormal when it became excessive as it leads to losing touch with reality and prevents taking more practical actions to improve one's life.

- *Idealization*: this refers to ascribing magnified good qualities to a person, place, or object, by emphasizing their positive qualities and ignoring negative ones, as a way of dealing with emotional conflict and internal or external stressors. People often idealize the image they hold of others whom they admire (relatives, partners, or celebrities), making excuses for their failures and emphasizing their outstanding qualities. Idealization adjusts the way in which people perceive the world, and make judgments that supports their idealized concepts.

- *Passive aggression*: an overt display of aggression is considered unsociable and undesirable in most societies, so people tend to avoid aggressive or violent impulses if possible. Passive aggression refers to aggression toward others that is expressed indirectly through passivity and noncompliance or self-punishing behavior, as a way of dealing with emotional conflict or internal or external stressors. A passive aggressive person may be uncooperative in carrying out their duties or other tasks, or may deliberately ignore someone when spoken to.

- *Projection*: individuals attribute their own unacceptable thoughts, feelings, or impulses to another person. Projection reduces anxiety by allowing the expression of the undesirable thoughts, emotions, or impulses, through attributing it to others. This helps the individual to explain his or her emotional feeling toward that person. Thoughts most commonly projected onto others are those that would cause guilt, such as aggressive and sexual fantasies or thoughts, e.g., a person who hates someone assumes that the opposite is true.

- *Projective identification*: a person projects a thought or belief that they have onto a second person. Unlike simple projection, the projector induces the other person into thinking, feeling, and acting in accordance with the projection. The behavior of the person being projected onto may finally become altered so as to validate one's projection by making the projection real, e.g., if a person feels persecuted by others, the behavior of this person may appear suspicious to others. Others' suspicious looks additionally support the person's belief of being persecuted (Ogden, 1982).

- *Somatization*: internal conflicts between the drives of the ego, the id, and the superego adopt physical characteristics, e.g., negative feelings toward others are transformed into bodily symptoms, rather than psychic manifestations, e.g., distress arising from unacceptable aggressive impulses toward others is transformed into complaints of pain, somatic illness, and neurasthenia.

Neurotic Defense Mechanisms

These mechanisms are considered neurotic and are fairly common in adults. Such defenses have short-term advantages in coping, but can often cause long-term problems in relationships, work, and in enjoying life when used as one's primary style of coping with the world. They include:

- *Displacement*: dealing with emotional conflict or internal or external stressors by directing a feeling about, or a response to, one object onto another substitute object. The substitute object is usually less threatening or a more acceptable target, e.g., a mother may shout at her child because she is angry with her husband. An employee may displace his anger toward his boss onto a subordinate.

- *Dissociation*: this refers to disconnection in the usually integrated functions of consciousness, memory, self or environmental perception, or sensory/motor behavior, in response to emotional conflict or internal or external stressors. Dissociation often helps people to cope with uncomfortable situations by removing themselves from them. In extreme cases, dissociation can lead to a person having a multiple personality disorder.

- *Conversion*: anxiety caused by repressed impulses and feelings are converted into a physical complaint, such as a paralysis of a limb, or loss of sight.

- *Hypochondriasis*: an excessive preoccupation or worry about having a serious illness, e.g., cancer or brain tumor. In hypochondriasis, responsibility can be avoided, guilt may be bypassed, and instinctual impulses are avoided.

- *Isolation of affect*: separating conflicting or stressful thoughts and experiences from their accompanying emotions in dealing with emotional conflict or internal or external stressors. In other words, the person does not get in touch with the feelings associated with a given idea or event, while remaining aware of its cognitive details, e.g., a person with a stressful job may use isolation to separate their work life from their family life, to eliminate the effect of stress on family relationships.

- *Intellectualization*: in an attempt to control or minimize disturbing feelings resulting from emotional conflict or internal or external stressors, the person focuses on the intellectual components of a situation, by thinking about them in affectively bland terms and not acting on them, e.g., a person who has been dismissed after 20 years of service in a company may intellectualize it, acknowledging the management's view that terminations are essential for the company to survive. Intellectualization would not necessarily prevent the person's passionate feeling that they have been betrayed after committing to work for the company for so long. Similarly, instead of confronting the intense distress that a person feels after a roommate suddenly decides to move out, a detailed financial analysis is conducted about how much he or she can afford to spend now on his or her own. Although the person does not deny that the event occurred, this person is not thinking about its emotional consequences.

- *Rationalization*: a person conceals or justifies the true motivations of his or her own unacceptable or irrational thoughts, attitudes, feelings, or behavior, and gives seemingly reasonable, but untrue or partially true explanations, e.g., a student who fails a final examination says it was not an important course. If a favorite candidate does not win the election, one says that it is for the best anyway. If a student did not complete an assignment, he or she thinks the teacher is unfair to have given the assignment. The sour grapes syndrome is a classic example; if we do not get something we want, we will find it wrong and convince ourselves that we are better off without it. Rationalization may occur on a fairly conscious level when a person provides excuses. But for many people, with a sensitive ego, making excuses comes so easy that they are not truly aware of doing so.

- *Reaction formation*: adopting beliefs, attitudes, and feelings contrary to what a person really believe. Unacceptable or disapproved feelings and behavior are concealed and the opposite attitude and behavior are unconsciously adopted. This protects the conscious part of the mind from what the unconscious considers to be unsuitable, e.g., a person who behaves with excessive kindness and politeness with a workmate who hates him or her. Similarly, an employee who is very angry with his/her boss and would like to quit the job may instead be overly kind and generous toward this boss and express a desire to keep working there forever.

- *Regression*: this means returning to a more primitive mode of thinking and behavior that characterize a younger age, which they associate with more secure and happier times, rather than handling unacceptable impulses in a more adult way, e.g., retreating under the blankets during bad days, or refusing to talk to people who have made a person feel bad, or sad. An adult may regress when under a great deal of stress, refusing to leave their bed or to engage in normal everyday activities.

- *Repression*: this is the first defense mechanism that Freud discovered, and arguably the most important. It refers to expelling or restraining painful or threatening emotions, memories, impulses, or drives, from consciousness. The feeling component may remain conscious, detached from its accompanying thoughts. Repression involves simply forgetting something bad, e.g., an unpleasant experience. The repressed material is not really forgotten, it may appear in symbolic behavior, such as slips of the tongue.

- *Undoing*: a person tries to reverse or "undo" a thought or feeling by performing an action that signifies an opposite feeling to the original unacceptable, destructive or otherwise threatening thought or feeling, e.g., when someone deliberately hits another person, then hugs and kisses them. This counteraction is an attempt to convince himself or herself and the injured one that no harm has occurred.

Mature Defense Mechanisms

Mature defense mechanisms are usually found among emotionally healthy adults. They are considered mature, though many have their origin in an immature stage of development. The use of these defenses optimizes success in life and relationships, and enhances pleasure and feelings of control. These defenses help us to integrate conflicting emotions and thoughts, while still remaining effective. Those who use these mechanisms are usually considered honorable. They include:

- *Altruism*: unselfishly assisting others as a way to deal with emotional conflict or internal or external stressors. The person receives gratification either vicariously or from the response of others through doing helpful and gratifying service to others. This in distinction from self-sacrifice that may occur in reaction formation where one's personal interests are the goal.

- *Humor*: focusing on the funny aspect of the conflict or stressor as a way to deal with emotional conflict or external stressors. Humor helps to cope with these tense or stressful situations, and can even be an altruistic act in helping others to better cope as well, e.g., a person receiving treatment for cancer that makes him lose his hair may make jokes about being bald.

- *Identification*: unconsciously patterning of a behavior on that of one or a group of individuals, e.g., a person moving to a new country, starting a new job, or entering a new social circle might adopt the social norms or attitudes of neighbors, colleagues, or other people, from whom they seek acceptance, in order to avoid being rejected by their new peers. Identification may play a healthy role in child development, but this depends on those to whom the child is exposed. Anna Freud described a special type of identification and called it identification with an aggressor (a person whom we perceive to be a threat); the person imitates (identifies) aspects of the aggressor's behavior, in order to satisfy them. This may include adopting the aggressor's characteristic behavior, and phrases, or language patterns that they tend to use.

- *Introjection*: people incorporate positive qualities of another person into their own ego, and adopt them as their own, to reduce feelings of inferiority. This is the converse of projection. The person subconsciously "takes in" to their self an imprint of another person, including all their attitudes, messages, prejudices, expressions, even the sound of their voice, etc. Introjection may involve internalizing criticism from another person and believing the other person's points to be valid. A person may introject religious ideas or political opinions that friends adopt. Behavior can also be introjected, e.g., the mannerisms of a father may be observed by his son and then replicated. Introjection is healthy if the imprinted material is helpful advice, warnings, or other lessons from parents and respected others, but unhealthy if shaming messages from parents, or of hatred or aggression are turned inward on the self.

- *Sublimation*: An unconscious, unacceptable, or undesirable emotion, thought, instinctual drive and impulse are redirected into a socially approved behavior. Sublimation is the reverse of displacement, instead of displacing emotions in a destructive way, a person manages to displace emotions into a constructive activity. Sublimation allows instincts to be channeled, rather than blocked. A person diverts sexually inappropriate desires into socially approved creative work (e.g., art, literature, sciences or other activities that promote cultural development and a richer life, both for the individual and the social group). Many famous composers and poets are good examples of this defense mechanism. Their mental anguish is redirected into wonderful works of art. Similarly, intense rage is redirected in the form of participation in sports, such as boxing or football.

- *Suppression* (thought suppression): this involves intentionally avoiding thinking about disturbing problems, wishes, feelings, or experiences. Thus, it occurs on a conscious level, e.g., a person tries to think of another subject when a stressful thought enters their mind or they might preoccupy their minds by an unrelated task to distract themselves. A person suppresses feelings of dislike toward some person, behaving ordinarily toward them as though they felt dispassionate toward them.

- *Anticipation*: dealing with emotional conflict or internal or external stressors by experiencing prior emotional reactions or expecting possible future events and planning realistic alternative responses. Anticipation may involve rehearsing possible outcomes in one's mind, e.g., people with a phobia of dentists may anticipate an appointment to have a tooth filling and reassure themselves that the procedure will be over in just a few minutes, and remind themselves that the procedure has been safely accomplished previously.

- *Asceticism*: eliminating the pleasurable effects of experiences. There is a moral element in assigning values to specific pleasures. Gratification is derived from renunciation, and asceticism is directed against all base pleasures perceived consciously.

Clinical Notes

- Irrespective of theoretical psychological foundation, there is increasing evidence that defense mechanisms have important implications for everyone involved in the treatment of patients, either medical or psychiatric.
- Patients with serious medical conditions, such as cancer, diabetes, kidney failure, or obesity, who do not comply with medical advice, were found to show strong use of defense mechanisms. Although defenses protect these patients from anxiety about being ill, they do not allow them to acknowledge the importance of obtaining the needed treatment. Thus, in working with patients for whom continuing compliance with a therapeutic regimen is necessary, it is highly beneficial to know something about the patient's defenses—especially those that may interfere with treatment (Cramer, 2000).
- A psychodynamic psychotherapist tries to clarify and understand the defense mechanisms that keep painful emotions, thoughts, and fears outside of awareness as a way to help their clients, in their own method of therapy.

Summary

- Conflict is an internal struggle, often unconscious, that stems from the presence of antagonistic or reciprocally exclusive impulses, desires, or tendencies.
- The level of conflict is affected by the nature and strength of the opposing forces, the nature of the underlying motive, and the length of time during which conflict continues.
- Defense mechanisms are classically defined as automatic psychological processes adopted by the person in response to emotional conflicts and internal or external dangers or stressors. Individuals are usually unaware of these processes as they occur.
- Conscious coping strategies are strategies that are deliberately used to deal with stress. They are conscious, intentional, determined by the situation not a disposition, and are not hierarchically arranged.
- Pathological defenses include delusional projection, denial, distortion, and splitting.
- Immature defenses include acting out, fantasy, idealization, passive aggression, projection, projective identification, and somatization.
- Neurotic defenses include displacement, dissociation, conversion, hypochondriasis, isolation of affect, intellectualization, rationalization, reaction formation, regression, repression, and undoing.
- Mature defenses include altruism, humor, identification, introjection, sublimation, suppression, anticipation, and asceticism.

Test Your Knowledge

What is meant by each of the concepts in Table 4.1?

TABLE 4.1 Defense Mechanisms

1. Delusional projection	2. Denial	3. Distortion
4. Splitting	5. Acting out	6. Fantasy
7. Idealization	8. Passive aggression	9. Projection
10. Projective identification	11. Somatization	12. Displacement
13. Dissociation	14. Conversion	15. Hypochondriasis
16. Isolation of affect	17. Intellectualization	18. Rationalization
19. Reaction formation	20. Regression	21. Repression
22. Undoing	23. Altruism	24. Humor
25. Identification	26. Introjection	27. Sublimation
28. Suppression	29. Anticipation	30. Asceticism

Critical Thinking Questions

■ How has the concept of defense mechanisms changed since its emergence up to the present day?

■ How can defense mechanisms and coping strategies be compared to each other?

V. THE BEHAVIORAL SCHOOL

In spite of their differences in approach, structuralism, functionalism, and psychoanalysis were essentially studies of the mind; all of them shared an emphasis on mental processes that are unseen to the naked eye. John B. Watson strongly objected to this approach and prompted a revolution in psychological thinking, creating a new school of thought called behaviorism.

Behaviorism is based on the premise that psychologists should limit their attention to the study of behavior, because it is not possible to objectively study the mind itself. Thus, research was redirected from studying the mind to studying observable behavior. Watson was influenced by the work of the Russian physiologist, Ivan Pavlov (1849–1936), who had discovered that dogs would salivate at the sound of a tone that had previously been associated with the presentation of food. Watson and the other behaviorists began to use these ideas to explain how events that people and other organisms experienced in their environment (stimuli) could produce specific behaviors (responses), e.g., in Pavlov's research, the stimulus (either the food or, after learning, the tone) would produce the response of salivation in the dogs.

Behaviorism emphasizes the role of learning in explaining behavior; behaviorists believed that human behavior can be understood by examining the relationship between stimuli (events in the environment) and responses (observable behavior). They saw no need to employ subjective

PHOTO 4.26.   Ivan Pavlov.

techniques, such as introspection, to infer mental processes over which even trained subjects and researchers could not agree. Watson found that systematically exposing a child to fearful stimuli in the presence of innocent objects (that did not themselves elicit fear) could lead the child to develop a fearful behavior in the presence of those innocent objects.

Burrhus Frederick Skinner (1904–1990) expanded the principles of behaviorism and brought them to the attention of the public. Skinner used the ideas of stimulus and response, along with the application of rewards or reinforcements, to train pigeons and other animals. Also, he used the general principles of behaviorism to develop theories about how best to teach children and how to create societies that were peaceful

PHOTO 4.27.   Burrhus Frederick Skinner.

and productive. Additionally, Skinner developed a method for studying thoughts and feelings using the behavioral approach (Skinner, 1957, 1968, 1972).

Although behaviorism made substantial contributions to learning theories, many aspects of human experience (e.g., thinking, intrinsic motivation, creativity) lie outside the strict behavioral definition of psychology (Walters, 2002). Thus, the strict behaviorism view of Watson was in no way superior to the narrow emphasis of the structuralists and functionalists on mental life alone. Although the behaviorists are incorrect in their beliefs that it is not possible to measure thoughts and feelings, their ideas provided new ideas that helped our understanding regarding the nature-nurture debate, as well as the question of free will. More details on behaviorism are discussed in the learning section in Chapter 10.

Clinical Notes

- The ideas of behaviorism are fundamental to psychology and have been developed to help a better understanding about the role of prior experiences in many areas of psychology.
- Behaviorism made considerable contributions to learning theories.
- Behaviorism provided a simple useful explanation and a therapeutic technique of some mental disorders, such as specific phobia.
- An essential clinical application of behaviorism principles is its use in behavior modification programs and its integration with cognitive modification in cognitive behavior therapy.

Summary

- Behaviorism is interested only in the observed behavior, and emphasizes the role of learning in explaining behavior.
- Behaviorism made substantial contributions to learning theories.
- Behaviorism is useful in explaining and treating phobias.

Test Your Knowledge

- What is the advantage of behaviorism?
- What is the disadvantage of behaviorism?

Critical Thinking Question

How can behaviorism be used in behavior modification of a child with abnormal behavior?

VI. THE COGNITIVE SCHOOL

Although cognitive psychology has many roots, the analogy between the brain and the computer provided the energy to its development. In the 1960s, growing numbers of psychologists began to think about the brain and about human behavior in terms of the computer, which began its development at that time.

Ulric Neisser (1928–2012), the "father of cognitive psychology," defined it as "all processes by which the sensory input is transformed, reduced, elaborated, stored, recovered, and used." These processes include topics such as perception, attention, memory, knowledge, language, problem-solving, reasoning and decision-making, and aspects of intelligence, emotion, and consciousness (Neisser, 1967). Also, cognitive psychologists are interested in less cognitively oriented phenomena, such as emotion and motivation. In short, cognitive psychology is involved in nearly all human behavior and psychological phenomena, and almost any topic of psychological interest may be studied from a cognitive perspective. A lot of research studies derived from cognitive psychology have been integrated into various other modern disciplines of psychological study, including developmental psychology, educational psychology, personality psychology, and abnormal psychology. Some of these disciplines were developed into specific subdisciplines of cognitive psychology, such as developmental cognitive neuropsychology, cognitive neuropsychology, cognitive neuropsychiatry, and cognitive neuroscience.

Methods that are characteristically used in cognitive psychology include experimental studies of normal cognition, neuropsychological studies of normal and abnormal cognition, neuroimaging studies of brain activity, and computational models (Braisby & Gellatly, 2005).

Clinical Notes

- Cognitive psychology remains influential today, and it has guided research in such varied fields as language, problem-solving, memory, intelligence, education, and human development. Over the past decade, the cognitive revolution has made additional advances as a result of recent improvements in structural and functional brain neuroimaging techniques (Ilardi & Feldman, 2001).
- Knowledge of cognitive psychology can help people to better direct their life, e.g., to understand how best to study for tests, how to read effectively, and how to remember difficult-to-learn material.

Summary

- Cognitive psychology refers to all processes by which the sensory input is transformed, reduced, elaborated, stored, recovered, and used.

- Cognitive psychology is involved in nearly all human behavior and psychological phenomena.

Test Your Knowledge

- Define cognitive psychology.
- What is the value of the cognitive perspective in psychology?

Critical Thinking Questions

- How does the cognitive approach relate to neuropsychology?
- How does the cognitive approach relate to development?

VII. THE BIOLOGICAL SCHOOL

The biological school focuses on the biological processes that underlie behavior, which explore the mind-body connection through scientific research. It is the only approach in psychology that examines thoughts, feelings, and behaviors from the physical point of view. The biological school considers all that is psychological is at first physiological. It encompasses the study of genetics, neuroanatomy, physiology, neuroimaging, brain electrophysiology, and drug studies in relation to behavior. Several of the results of these studies are considered in Chapter 5 on brain organization and behavior, but, in brief, a biological perspective is relevant to the study of psychology in three ways:

1. *Physiology*: how the brain functions, how changes in structure and/or function can affect behavior, including the effect of different neurotransmitters and hormones, the function of different brain regions, and the effect of psychotropic drugs on behavior.
2. *Genetics*: what a person inherits from their parents, the mechanisms of inheritance, and the relationship of certain behavior to genetics.
3. *Comparative method*: different species of animals can be studied and compared. This can help in the search to understand human behavior.

Summary

All that is psychological is at first physiological. The biological school encompasses the study of genetics, neuroanatomy, physiology, neuroimaging, brain electrophysiology, and drug studies in relation to behavior.

VIII. SOCIAL-CULTURAL PSYCHOLOGY

By the late 1980s, cross-cultural psychology had emerged in full force as large numbers of psychologists began studying the diversity of human behavior in different cultural settings and countries (Berry & Triandis, 2006). Social-cultural psychology focuses on the study of how different social situations and cultures influence thinking and behavior. Social-cultural psychologists focus on how people perceive themselves and others, and how people influence each other's behavior, e.g., social psychologists found that

- people are attracted to others who are similar to them in terms of attitudes and interests (Byrne, 1969);

- people develop their own beliefs and attitudes by comparing these opinions to those of others (Festinger, 1954);
- people frequently change their beliefs and behaviors to be similar to those of other people they care about, a process known as conformity.

Research in social psychology focuses on topics, such as authority, obedience, and group behavior.

An important aspect of social-cultural psychology are social norms, i.e., the ways of thinking, feeling, or behaving that are shared by group members and perceived by them as appropriate (Cialdini, 2009). Norms include customs, traditions, standards, and rules, as well as the general values of the group. Many of the most important social norms are determined by the culture in which we live, and these cultures are studied by cross-cultural psychologists. A culture represents the common set of social norms, including religious and family values and other moral beliefs, shared by the people who live in a geographical region (Fiske, Kitayama, Markus, & Nisbett, 1998; Markus, Kitayama, & Heiman, 1996; Matsumoto, 2001). Culture influences every aspect of our lives, and it is appropriate to say that our culture defines our lives just as much as does our evolutionary experience (Mesoudi, 2009).

Psychologists have found that there is a difference in social norms between different cultures, e.g., Western cultures and East Asian cultures. Studies conducted with American and European subjects, in the 1970s, revealed that people exert more effort on a task when working alone than when working as part of a group, a phenomenon called social loafing. When similar studies were conducted with Chinese participants during the 1980s, the opposite was found to be true (Moghaddam, 2002). Chinese participants worked harder on a task when they were part of a group than when they were working alone.

Norms in Western cultures are primarily oriented toward individualism, which is about valuing the self and one's independence from others. Children in Western cultures are taught to develop and to value a sense of their personal self, and to see themselves in large part as separate from the other people around them. Children in Western cultures feel special about themselves, they enjoy getting gold stars for their projects and the best grade in the class. Adults in Western cultures are oriented toward promoting their own individual success, frequently in comparison

PHOTO 4.28.   Social Norms.

to (or even at the expense of) others (Stangor, 2010). On the other hand, norms in the East Asian culture are oriented toward interdependence or collectivism. In these cultures, children are taught to focus on developing harmonious social relationships with others. The predominant norms relate to group devotion and cohesion, and duty and responsibility to one's family and other groups. When asked to describe themselves, the members of East Asian cultures were more likely than those from Western cultures to indicate that they are particularly concerned about the interests of others, including their close friends and their colleagues (Stangor, 2010). Cultures also differ in terms of personal space, such as how closely individuals stand next to each other when talking, as well as the communication styles they employ.

The extent to which people in different cultures are bound to social norms and customs, rather than being free to express their own individuality without considering social norms is different (Chan, Gelfand, Triandis, & Tzeng, 1996).

Clinical Notes

Understanding the social and cultural perspective is essential in the assessment process of individuals, and it could set the boundary between normal and abnormal.

Summary

Social-cultural psychology focuses on the influence of social situations and the cultures on people's thinking and behavior.

Test Your Knowledge

How can social and cultural circumstances affect an individual's thinking and behavior?

Critical Thinking Questions

- Considering the influence of social and cultural circumstances on people, how can it be used to distinguish between normal and abnormal behavior?
- What do you know about culture-bound syndromes?

IX. THE GESTALT SCHOOL

The word "Gestalt" means a unified or meaningful whole. Gestalt psychology emerged as a rebellion against Wundt's structuralism. While Wundt was interested in breaking down psychological matters into their smallest possible part, the Gestalt psychologists were instead interested in looking at the whole mind and behavior. Gestalt psychologists believed that psychology should study human experience as a whole, not in terms of separate elements, as the structuralists assumed. Their slogan, "the whole is greater than the sum of its parts," conveyed the idea that meaning is often lost when psychological events are broken down. The whole pattern is visible, and we can find true meaning in our experiences when its components are analyzed together, e.g., the meaning of a phrase can be grasped only when the letters are properly combined to form words and structured into sentences, rather than breaking apart the words into individual letters and scattering them across the page, then it would be very difficult to recognize anything meaningful from them. Then, the whole becomes something different, something greater than the accumulation of its parts.

The fundamental formula of Gestalt theory can be expressed in Max Wertheimer's suggestion that there is a whole, the behavior of which is not determined by that of its individual elements, but where the part-processes are themselves determined by the intrinsic nature of the whole. Furthermore, Gestalt psychologists believe that people are built to experience the structured whole as well as the individual sensations. They not only have the ability to do so, but they have a strong tendency to do so. They even add structure to events which do not have Gestalt structural qualities.

Gestalt theory attempted to describe how people tend to organize perception into groups or unified wholes through certain principles. These organizing principles are called Gestalt laws. Gestalt laws of perception will be discussed later in Chapter 22.

Clinical Notes

Gestalt psychologists developed their principles into a method of therapy: Gestalt psychotherapy. More details of Gestalt therapy will be discussed in Chapter 22.

Summary

Gestalt psychology believed that psychology should study human experience as a whole, not in terms of separate elements, and adopted the slogan, the whole is greater than the sum of its parts.

Test Your Knowledge

Give an account of Gestalt psychology.

Critical Thinking Question

Comment on the Gestalt perceptual rules.

X. THE HUMANISTIC SCHOOL

During the 1950s, humanistic psychology began as a reaction to psychoanalysis and behaviorism, which dominated psychology at that time. The pioneer of humanistic psychology, Carl Rogers, was uncomfortable with the highly deterministic view of these two major forces in psychology. Humanist thinkers felt that both psychoanalysis and behaviorism were too pessimistic, failing to take into account the role of personal choice. Humanistic psychology acknowledges that the mind is strongly influenced by determining forces in society and the unconscious, but emphasizes the conscious capacity of individuals to develop personal competence and self-respect.

Humanism asserted a positive view of human nature, stressing that people are inherently good. It emphasizes that all individuals are unique and have an innate drive to achieve their maximum potential. This means that each

PHOTO 4.29.   Carl Rogers.

person, in different ways, seeks to grow psychologically and continuously enhance themselves. This has been captured by the term *self-actualization*, which refers to psychological growth, fulfillment, and satisfaction in life. Humanism is also characterized by unconditional positive regard, an attitude of acceptance and respect on the part of an observer, no matter what a person says or does.

Central to the humanistic theories of Rogers (1959) and Abraham Maslow (1943, 1968) are the subjective conscious experiences of the individual. Humanistic psychologists argue that objective reality is less important than a person's subjective perception and understanding of the world. Because of this, humanism rejects scientific methodology such as experiments (because they saw it as dehumanizing and unable to capture the richness of conscious experience) and typically uses qualitative research methods, e.g., diary accounts, open-ended questionnaires, unstructured interviews, and unstructured observations.

Clinical Notes

The humanistic approach is less influential today because its ideas are too subjective and difficult to test empirically. However, the humanist movement had an enormous influence on the course of psychology and contributed new ways of thinking about mental health. Major ideas and concepts emerged as a result of the humanist movement, including emphasis on the self-concept, the hierarchy of needs, unconditional positive regard, free will, self-actualization, the fully-functioning person, and peak experiences. Concepts central to humanistic psychology can be seen in many disciplines, including other branches of psychology, education, therapy, political movements, and other areas. Also, humanistic theories offered a new approach to understanding human behavior and motivations and led to developing new techniques and approaches to psychotherapy (e.g., client-centered therapy and Gestalt therapy). More details of humanistic therapies will be discussed in Chapter 22.

Summary

- The humanistic school was a new way of thinking contrary to the deterministic view of psychoanalysis and behaviorism schools.
- Humanistic psychology emphasizes that all individuals are unique and have an innate drive to achieve their maximum potential.

Test Your Knowledge

Give an account of humanistic psychology.

Critical Thinking Question

How does humanistic psychology relate to positive psychology?

Conclusion

Psychology is a science that involves a lot of fields that have developed during its history. It tries to understand behavior and mental processes and to apply that understanding in the service of human welfare. Though it has a relatively short history as a separate field of study, psychology is established as a rigorous science, with a broad human perspective. Each school of thought has provided an acknowledged hallmark on psychology, helping to shape it into the respected discipline that it now is. Many psychologists today adopt an eclectic approach; instead of clinging to one particular perspective, they carefully choose from each school of thought those ideas and methods they believe are most appropriate to achieve their objectives.

PART TWO
Biology, Consciousness, and Gender

five
Biological Basis of Behavior

Learning Goals

- This chapter is intended to provide the reader with an overview of the biological basis of human behavior. This will involve a thoughtful understanding of the effect of different paradigms of current basic neuroscience on human behavior, including genetics, structural and functional neuroanatomical changes, and different neurochemical changes on human behavior.

Introduction

PHOTO 5.1. DNA.

In humans, each cell normally contains 23 pairs of chromosomes which contain our genetic material, which is composed of double-stranded molecules called deoxyribonucleic acid (DNA).

Twenty-two of these pairs are called autosomes, which look the same in both males and females and contain pairs of genes. Corresponding forms of a gene are called alleles. Genotype refers to one's genes, but phenotype refers to one's expressed traits. An individual with identical alleles on the two chromosomes is called homozygous for that gene (e.g., blood group AA), whereas an individual with unmatched alleles is heterozygous for that gene (e.g., blood group AO). People with AA or AO have different genotypes but the same phenotype: blood group type A. The 23rd pair is called the sex chromosome, it differs between males and females. Females have two copies of the X chromosome, while males have one X and one Y chromosome.

Genes are the units of heredity that maintain their structural identity from one generation to another. A gene is classically defined as a portion of a chromosome. However, many genes do not have discrete locations, and several genes overlap on a stretch of chromosome (Bird, 2007).

A strand of DNA serves as a template for the synthesis of ribonucleic acid (RNA) molecules. There are four types of RNA, each encoded by its own type of gene. Messenger RNA serves as a template for the synthesis of protein molecules. DNA contains four bases (adenine, guanine, cytosine, and thymine). The order of those bases determines the order of corresponding bases along an RNA molecule (adenine, guanine, cytosine, and uracil). In turn, the order of bases along an RNA molecule determines the order of amino acids that compose a protein, e.g., if three RNA bases are, in order, cytosine, adenine, and guanine, then the protein adds the amino acid glutamine. If the next three RNA bases are uracil, guanine, and guanine, the next amino acid on the protein is tryptophan. In total, proteins consist of 20 amino acids, and the order of those amino acids depends on the order of DNA and RNA bases.

Genes may be dominant, recessive, or intermediate. When a gene is dominant, the feature it controls will appear every time the gene is present. When a gene is recessive, it must be paired with a second recessive gene (homozygous condition) before its effect can be expressed. In such situations, both parents, who did not show the abnormal trait, can have a child affected by a recessive trait. A classic example of recessive inheritance is phenylketonuria (PKU).

In some characteristics, multiple genes contribute to variations, e.g., eye color and height. Furthermore, it is also possible that a gene is expressed only partly in some cells and not others, or under some circumstances and not others. Genes affecting behavior are particularly subject to multiple influences. In many cases, part of a chromosome alters the expression of other genes without coding for any protein of its own.

The genes on the sex chromosomes are known as sex-linked genes. All other chromosomes are autosomal chromosomes, and their genes are known as autosomal genes. In humans, the Y chromosome is small, it has genes for only 27 proteins, while the X chromosome has genes for about 1,500 proteins (Arnold, 2004). Thus, when biologists speak of sex-linked genes, they usually mean X-linked genes. However, the Y chromosome also has many sites that influence the functioning of genes on other chromosomes. Distinct from sex-linked genes are the sex-limited genes, which are present in both sexes, generally on autosomal chromosomes, but active mainly in one sex, e.g., genes that control the amount of chest hair in men and breast size in women.

Science indicates that genes set the basis for many human traits. In a simple act like facial expressions, the role of genetic factors is suggested by finding that people who were born blind and therefore could not have learned to imitate facial expressions were remarkably similar in their use of facial expressions to those of their sighted relatives (Peleg et al., 2006). Behavior geneticists concluded that genetics plays a big role in personality, accounting for about half of the differences in personality test results and even more of the differences in IQ scores. The role of genetics in the causation of different psychiatric disorders (e.g., schizophrenia, mood disorders, personality disorders, and alcoholism) is well documented. Moreover, genetic predispositions are often important in determining the environments that people select for themselves. So, once again, biology and environment mutually influence each other. In other words, one's genes and one's experience influence the development of one's brain. Studies providing evidence of genetic contributions include:

1. *Pedigree studies*: a family tree is used to show the occurrence of behavior disorders and traits within a family.
2. *Family risk studies*: how frequently a behavioral disorder or a trait occurs in the relatives of the affected individual (proband) are compared with that of the general population.
3. *Twin studies*: identical and fraternal twins, both within the same familial environment and in different familial circumstances are compared, e.g., in adoption studies. Adoption studies using monozygotic twins (who are derived from a single fertilized ovum) or dizygotic twins (who are derived from two fertilized ova), reared in different homes, are used to differentiate the effects of genetic factors from environmental factors in the occurrence of psychiatric disorders. If there is a genetic component in the etiology, a disorder is expected to have a higher concordance rate in monozygotic twins than in dizygotic twins.
4. *Linkage studies*: new biochemical methods can identify specific genes linked to a behavior, e.g., genes that are more common than average among people with schizophrenia, depression, and bipolar disorder. In these cases, certain genetic defects are passed down from parental generations and increase an offspring's risk of inheriting a specific disorder. While neuropsychiatric disease susceptibility cannot be attributed exclusively to genetics, it is important to study how one's genetic makeup can affect various facets of human behavior. Uncovering this link between genes and behavior could lead to the discovery of new biological factors involved in the development of highly prevalent neurological responses and disorders.

Nowadays, genetic engineering and other techniques allow researchers to measure, analyze, and manipulate genetic material rapidly and easily. There are two general methods that are widely used by molecular behavioral and molecular psychiatric geneticists in their search for genes related to mental disorders: (1) linkage analysis; and (2) alleleic association. Linkage analysis is the traditional approach to gene identification, but it only works well when genes have reasonably large effects, which does not appear to be the case in normal human behavior or in psychiatry. Allelic association studies are more sensitive, but they require "candidate genes" to examine familial data. Studies in schizophrenia and Alzheimer's disease are illustrative of these approaches. Evidence has been accumulating for genes or gene regions of small effect related to schizophrenia on many chromosomes, including 1q, 2q, 3p, 5q, 6p, 8p, 11q, 13q, 20q, and 22q (Harrison & Owen, 2003). However, replication difficulties of these results in different populations of schizophrenics and their families have been a recurring problem.

Controversies arise when research moves beyond the generalization that both heredity and environment are important, where no one can ascertain the percentage of contribution of genetic and environmental factors in differences in human intelligence, sexual orientation, alcoholism, weight gain, and almost everything else that attracts psychologists. Genetic changes may occur in several ways:

1. *An extra or a missing chromosome*: e.g., Down syndrome is caused by an extra chromosome 21, and Klinefelter syndrome is caused by an extra X chromosome, or a missing chromosome, e.g., Turner syndrome is caused by a missing X chromosome.
2. *Gene mutation*: a permanent heritable change in a DNA molecule sequence. A change in just one base in DNA to any of the other three types means that the mutant gene will code for a protein with a different amino acid at one location in the molecule. A new mutation is rarely advantageous.
3. *Duplication or deletion*: during the process of reproduction, part of a chromosome that should appear once might instead appear twice or not at all, resulting in microduplication or microdeletion respectively. Many researchers believe that microduplications and microdeletions of brain-relevant genes are a possible explanation for schizophrenia (International Schizophrenia Consortium, 2008; Stefansson et al., 2008).
4. *Gene-environment interaction*: while the term genetics is typically used to describe how characteristics, such as height, hair color, and eye color are passed to offspring through inheritance, it also refers to the processes involved in turning genes "on" and "off." Research has shown that environmental factors can affect gene expression, i.e., a particular gene is turned on or off. Various experiences and environmental factors can turn a gene on or off. This is referred to as *epigenetics*, changes in gene expression without modification of the DNA sequence. The idea of epigenetic development contrasts sharply with that of preformism theory, according to which an ovum or sperm contains a preformed adult, i.e., everything is set in advance by genes. Epigenetics is a new, growing field that will improve our understanding of behavior, e.g., when monozygotic (identical) twins differ in their psychiatric or other medical conditions, epigenetic differences are a likely explanation (Poulsen, Esteller, Vaag, & Fraga, 2007), these are accomplished through *epigenomic modifications*.

Epigenome is the DNA modifications that do not change the DNA sequence and can affect gene activity. Chemical compounds that are added to single genes can regulate their activity; these modifications are known as epigenetic changes. The epigenome comprises all of the chemical compounds that have been added to one's DNA (genome) as a way to regulate the activity (expression) of all the genes within the genome. The chemical compounds of the epigenome are not part of the DNA sequence, but are on or attached to the DNA. Epigenomic modifications remain as cells divide and in some cases can be inherited down the generations. Environmental influences, such as a person's diet and exposure to pollutants, can also impact the epigenome. Epigenetic changes can help determine whether genes are turned on or off and can influence the production of proteins in certain cells, ensuring that only necessary proteins are produced. For example, proteins that promote bone growth are not produced in muscle cells. Patterns of epigenome modification vary among individuals, with different tissues within an individual, and even different cells. Common types of epigenomic modification include:

a. Histone modification: histones are spool-like proteins that enable the DNA's very long molecules to be wound up neatly into chromosomes inside the cell nucleus. A variety of chemical tags can grab hold of the tails of histones, changing how tightly or loosely they package DNA (Figure 5.1). If the wrapping is tight, a gene may be hidden from the cell's protein-making machinery, and consequently be switched off. In contrast, if the wrapping is loosened, a gene that was formerly hidden may be turned on. An experience such as maternal deprivation, new learning, or whatever brings new proteins into a cell or in other ways alters the chemical environment.

   In some cases, the outcome adds acetyl groups ($COCH_3$) to the histone tails near a gene, causing the histones to loosen their grip on the DNA, and facilitating the expression of that gene. Removal of the acetyl group causes the histones to tighten their grip on the DNA, and turns the gene off (see Figure 5.1).

b. DNA methylation: adding or removing methyl groups (CH_3) from DNA, usually at the promoter regions at the beginning of a gene. Adding methyl groups to promoters turns genes off, and removing them turns on a gene (Tsankova, Renthal, Kumar, & Nestler, 2007). The methyl groups turn genes off or on by affecting the interactions between the DNA and the cell's protein-making machinery. Actually, the result is more complicated, as attaching a methyl or acetyl group affects different genes in different ways (Alter et al., 2008) (see Figure 5.1).

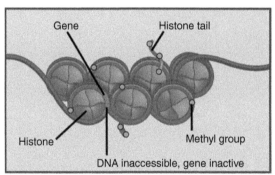

Methylation of DNA and histones causes nucelosomes to pack tightly together. Transcription factors cannot bind the DNA, and genes are not expressed.

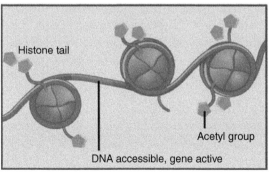

Histone acetylation results in loose packing of nucelosomes. Transcription factors can bind the DNA and genes are expressed.

FIGURE 5.1. Epigenetics.

Clinical Notes

Heredity or genetics play a well-established role in human behavior, in health and disease. However, their relative contribution is not well established.

Summary

- Each cell contains 23 pairs of chromosomes, which contain our genetic material, which is composed of a double-stranded molecule called DNA.
- Twenty-two of these pairs are called autosomes. The 23rd pair is called the sex chromosome.
- Genes are the units of heredity and are composed of portions of chromosomes. Genes may be dominant, recessive, or intermediate. In some characteristics, multiple genes contribute to its variations.
- Genes set the basis for many human traits.
- Studies providing evidence of genetic contributions include pedigree studies, family risk studies, twin studies, and linkage studies.
- Genetic change may occur in the form of an extra or a missing chromosome, gene mutation, duplication or deletion, or epigenomic changes.
- Epigenome is the DNA modifications that do not change the DNA sequence and can affect gene activity.
- Common types of epigenomic modification include histone modification, or DNA methylation.

Test Your Knowledge

- What types of studies provide evidence of genetic contributions?
- What is the difference between a gene and the epigenome?
- What are the types of epigenomic modification?

Critical Thinking Question

How do genetic factors and environmental factors interact to affect behavior?

Behavioral Neuroanatomy

Nervous tissue is composed of two types of cells: neurons and glial cells. Neurons are the primary type of cells whose function is to receive and transmit information. They are responsible for the computation and communication that the nervous system provides. Glial cells or glia play a supporting role for nervous tissue. Neurons are composed of: (1) a cell body that contains the nucleus and most of the cell's biosynthetic machinery and keeps the cell alive; (2) branching tree-like fibers called dendrites, which extend from the cell body, collect information from other cells and send the information to the cell body; (3) an axon, which transmits information away from the cell body to other neurons or to the muscles and glands; and (4) specialized regions, at the end of axons, called synaptic buttons or synaptic endings, where communication with other nerve cells or special effector tissues (such as gland or muscle cells) is carried out (Figure 5.2).

Neurons are differentiated according to their function into sensory and afferent neurons that carry information from the sensory receptors, and motor or efferent neurons that transmit

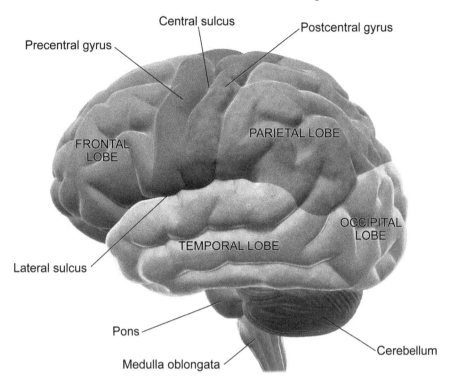

FIGURE 5.2. Lateral View of the Brain.

information to the muscles and glands. Interneurons are the most common type of neurons, and are located primarily within the central nervous system (CNS) and are responsible for communication among the neurons. Interneurons allow the brain to combine the multiple sources of available information to create a coherent picture of the sensory information being conveyed.

The human nervous system is organized into the CNS and the peripheral nervous system (PNS). The CNS includes the brain and the spinal cord. There are two general types of tissue in the CNS: gray matter and white matter. Gray matter consists of nerve cell bodies, dendrites, and axons. Neurons in gray matter organize either in layers, as in the cerebral cortex, or as clusters called nuclei. White matter consists mostly of axons, causing it to look white due to the myelin sheathing of the axons.

The three major components of the brain are the cerebrum, the cerebellum, and the brain stem. The cerebrum is divided into right and left hemispheres: each is composed of four major sections called lobes—the frontal, temporal, parietal, and occipital lobe—each separated by folds known as fissures. The cerebral cortex is the outside portion of the cerebrum. Deep in the cortex is the cerebral white matter. The white matter provides communication between the cortex and lower central nervous system centers. The two cerebral hemispheres are connected by the corpus callosum, the anterior commissure, the hippocampal commissure, and the habenular commissure. Studying the brain structure and functions can be achieved by the following means:

- Studying the brains of cadavers to discover brain structures. These studies are limited as the brain is no longer active.

- Lesion studies: the effects of lesions on different brain regions are informative about possible functions of those regions.
- Electrophysiological recording may be used in animals to directly measure brain activity. Measures of electrical activity in the brain, such as electroencephalography (EEG), are used to assess brain-wave patterns and activity (Figure 5.2).
- Computerized brain tomography (CT) and brain magnetic resonance imaging (MRI) may reveal structural brain abnormalities.
- Functional magnetic resonance imaging (fMRI) measures blood flow in the brain during different activities, providing information about the activity of neurons and thus the functions of brain regions.
- Transcranial magnetic stimulation (TMS) is used to temporarily and safely deactivate a small brain region, with the aim of testing the causal effects of the deactivation on behavior.

Brain Functions

The functions of the brain are lateralized. The right, or nondominant hemisphere, is associated primarily with perception, spatial relations, body image, recognition of faces and music, puzzle-solving, map-reading, and musical and artistic abilities. Damage to the right hemisphere has motor sequelae and indirect effects on behavior but does not usually affect intelligence or personality directly. The left, or dominant, hemisphere is associated with language function in about 96 percent of right-handed people and 70 percent of left-handed people. Damage to the left hemisphere results in impairment of skills such as speech, writing, and reading, in almost all right-handed people and most left-handed people. The following is a summary of the various functions of the different areas of the brain.

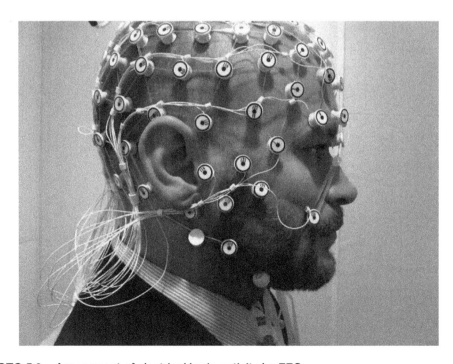

PHOTO 5.2.   Assessment of electrical brain activity by EEG.

The Cerebral Cortex

This is the outer layer of the cerebral hemispheres and gives the brain its distinctive wrinkled appearance. The cerebral cortex contains between 20 and 23 billion nerve cells and 300 trillion synaptic connections. The activity of the cortex can be classified functionally into sensory, motor, and association areas that act together to ultimately affect behavior. Each cerebral lobe has specialized areas that relate to particular functions.

The Frontal Lobe

The frontal lobe is the largest of the brain's structures. It is the main site of the higher cognitive functions. The frontal lobe is variably divided: one commonly used classification is to divide it into the precentral cortex, then the strip immediately anterior to the central or Sylvian fissure, and the prefrontal cortex, the section extending from the frontal poles to the precentral cortex, including the frontal operculum. The precentral cortex is composed of the primary motor cortex (Brodmann area 4), the premotor cortex, and the supplementary motor (Brodmann area 6). The precentral cortex is involved in voluntary movement, language, and posture and body orientation. The prefrontal cortex is subdivided into several regions, including the dorsolateral, orbitofrontal, ventrolateral, ventromedial, basal, orbital, and frontopolar areas. Each of these areas is suggested to have specialized behavioral functions and has widespread connectivity. Damage to these areas results in characteristic behavioral abnormalities.

The *dorsolateral prefrontal cortex* makes up the largest proportion of the frontal cortex. It is responsible for executive processes, which in a general sense involve the ability to use sensory input from multiple modalities (i.e., visual, auditory) in the generation of appropriate responses (decision-making, planning, problem-solving, and thinking). The dorsolateral prefrontal cortex has extensive connections with the rest of the brain, but input from the thalamus (primarily the ventral anterior and the mediodorsal nuclei) and output to the caudate nucleus of the basal ganglia form the circuit of considerable importance.

The *orbitofrontal cortex* has several functions, including control of response inhibition, and modulation of affective and social behavior. It is part of the dopamine-driven reward circuit of the brain and is activated by subjective pleasant or unpleasant taste, olfactory, visual, somatosensory, and auditory stimuli, and thus it is involved in emotion. The orbitofrontal cortex is also activated by abstract stimuli, such as winning or losing money, and its activation can be modulated by cognitive factors. Its cortex is also activated in addicts exposed to drug-related cues. Orbitofrontal lesions can impair reward-related learning, impair face and voice expression identification, and produce personality disorders, including impulsive and disinhibited emotional behavior.

Patients with orbitofrontal lesions are socially disabled, manifesting interpersonal disinhibition, poor social judgment, impulsive decision-making, lack of consideration for the impact of their behavior, absence of an appreciation for the effect of their behavior or comments on others, and lack of empathy for others. Other behaviors that frequently co-occur with the orbitofrontal disinhibition syndrome include apathy, restlessness, stereotypes, indifference, euphoria and impairment of emotional control, diminished attention, dependence or hyperdependence on stimuli in the physical environment, and planning disorders (Miller & Cummings, 2007).

The *ventrolateral prefrontal cortex* mediates response inhibition and goal-appropriate response selection. Depression seems to be associated with activation of the left ventrolateral prefrontal cortex, which in turn directs the individual to focus on a specific and consequential problem, minimizing distractions. On the other hand, anxiety seems to be associated with activation of the right ventrolateral prefrontal cortex, which enhances the vigilance of individuals to anticipated hazards.

The Parietal Lobe

The parietal lobe is located above the occipital lobe of the brain and behind the frontal lobe. The parietal lobe is divided into three parts: (1) the postcentral gyrus; (2) the superior parietal lobule; and (3) the inferior parietal lobule. The postcentral gyrus receives sensory input from the contralateral half of the body. The sequential representation is the same as in the primary motor area, with upside-down reversal of sensations: the head is represented in inferior parts of the gyrus and sensations from the lower extremities are represented in superior portions. The primary somatosensory cortex, located in the postcentral gyrus, integrates somesthetic stimuli for recognition and recall of form, texture, and weight. The primary somatosensory cortex on one side receives all the somatosensory input from the contralateral side of the body. Lesions of the postcentral gyrus can cause difficulty in recognizing objects by touch (astereognosis). The superior parietal lobule is regarded as an association cortex. The inferior parietal lobule (composed of the angular and supramarginal gyri) is a cortical region involved with the integration of multiple sensory signals (K. Rogers, 2011).

Areas posterolateral to the postcentral gyrus generate visual-spatial relationships and integrate these perceptions with other sensations to create awareness of trajectories of moving objects. These areas also mediate proprioception (awareness of the position of body parts in space).

Parts of the midparietal lobe of the dominant hemisphere are involved in abilities, such as calculation, writing, left-right orientation, and finger recognition. Lesions in the angular gyrus can cause deficits in writing, calculating, left-right disorientation, and finger-naming (Gerstmann syndrome).

The nondominant parietal lobe integrates the contralateral side of the body with its environment, enabling people to be aware of their environmental space, and is important for abilities such as drawing. Acute injury to the nondominant parietal lobe may cause neglect of the contralateral side (usually the left), resulting in decreased awareness of that part of the body, its environment, and any associated injury to that side (anosognosia), e.g., patients with large right parietal lesions may deny the existence of left-sided paralysis. Patients with smaller lesions may lose the ability to do learned motor tasks (e.g., dressing, other well-learned activities), this is a spatial-manual deficit called apraxia.

The Temporal Lobe

Only primates have temporal lobes, which are largest in man, accommodating about 25 percent of the cerebral cortex and including areas with auditory, olfactory, vestibular, visual, and linguistic functions. Important regions of the temporal lobe include Heschl's gyrus (primary auditory cortex) and the auditory association cortex, which includes the planum temporale in the temporal operculum, the superior, middle, and inferior temporal gyri, and the occipitotemporal (fusiform) gyrus. On the inferiomedial surface of the temporal lobe lies the parahippocampal gyrus, which contains the hippocampal formation. On the medial aspect of the anterior portion of the parahippocampal gyrus is the uncus, a small bulge on the surface of the brain that marks the general location of the amygdala lying beneath this surface feature. The temporal lobes are associated with the processing of auditory input and with the encoding of memory. The temporal lobes also may play a substantial role in the processing of affective information, language, and in certain aspects of visual perception. The left side of the temporal lobe deals with language and verbal memory, while the right side deals with the ability to process non-verbal sounds and non-verbal memory (Mendoza & Foundas, 2007).

The Occipital Lobe

The occipital cortex is the smallest of the four lobes of the brain. It is located posterior to the temporal lobe and parietal lobes. The occipital cortex is concerned with visual processing and is composed of primary visual cortex (Brodmann area 17), and secondary visual (association) cortex (Brodmann areas 18 and 19). It receives projections from the retina (via the thalamus) from where different groups of neurons separately encode different visual information, such as color, orientation, and motion. Two important pathways of information originate in the occipital lobes: the dorsal and ventral streams. The dorsal stream projects to the parietal lobes and processes *where* objects are located. The ventral stream projects to structures in the temporal lobes and processes *what* objects are.

Occipital lobe lesion may manifest as problems with or loss of vision. Blindness that is caused by damage to the visual area of the brain is called "central" or "cortical" blindness.

The Limbic System

The word "limbic" is a Latin word for "border," and this system serves as the border between the evolutionarily older parts of the brain (the brain stem and the cerebellum) and the evolutionarily newer part (the cerebral cortex). There is no universal agreement on the structures that comprise the limbic system. The brain regions that constitute the limbic system fall into two categories: cortical and subcortical structures. Cortical regions involved in the limbic system include the hippocampus as well as areas of the neocortex including the insular cortex, the orbital frontal cortex, the subcallosal gyrus, the cingulate gyrus, and the parahippocampal gyrus. This cortex is termed the "limbic lobe" because it makes a rim surrounding the corpus callosum, following the lateral ventricle. Subcortical portions of the limbic system include the amygdala, and the hippocampal formation (the dentate gyrus, the hippocampus proper, the subicular complex, and the septal area), the hypothalamus, and some thalamic nuclei, including the anterior nucleus and possibly the dorsomedial nucleus.

Functions of the Limbic System

The structures of the limbic system jointly control a variety of basic functions relating to emotions and self-preservation, such as eating, aggression, and reproduction. Injury to the limbic system can produce striking changes in behavior. The functions of the various structures of limbic system are summarized below (Rajmohan & Mohandas, 2007):

1. *Olfaction*: some of the limbic structures are closely related to the olfactory cortex and have a role in the processing of olfactory sensation. The olfactory bulb is the only area that has input into the amygdala and does not receive reciprocal projections from the amygdala. Olfactory cortex projections to the amygdala can influence emotional and endocrine response to smell, particularly via connections with the hypothalamus, while another limbic structure (the entorhinal cortex), is concerned with olfactory memories.

2. *Appetite and eating behaviors*: Some areas of the hypothalamus play a role in the regulation of appetite. The lateral hypothalamus is associated with feelings of hunger and compulsive craving to find food (the orexigenic effect). A lesion of the lateral hypothalamus leads to loss of appetite. The ventromedial nucleus of the hypothalamus is considered the center of satiety. Its stimulation of this center leads to the complete loss of interest in nourishment in experimental animals (the anorexigenic effect). Amygdala plays a role in food choice and the emotional modulation of food intake.

  Some studies have found that fat cells release a protein called leptin in proportion to fat mass, and one of leptin's tasks is to send signals regarding levels of fat mass (or changes in fat mass) to the hypothalamus, which in turn regulates both a decrease in energy intake and an increase in energy expenditure. However, present evidence suggests that leptin does not primarily protect the body against an increase in fat mass but instead defends the body against fat loss, thus operating in cases of negative energy balance only (Müller, Bosy-Westphal, & Heymsfield, 2010).

3. *Sleep and dreams*: the limbic system is one of the most active brain areas during the process of dreaming. The limbic system probably interweaves unconscious primal emotions with our conscious cognitive thoughts and perceptions and thereby ties together emotions and memory during rapid eye movement (REM) sleep to form the content of dreams. Details of mechanisms of sleep are discussed in Chapter 6.

4. *Emotional responses*: fear responses are produced by the stimulation of the hypothalamus and the amygdala. Destruction of the amygdala abolishes fear and its autonomic and endocrine responses. The amygdala is also involved in fear learning, which is blocked when long-term potentiation (LTP) is disrupted in pathways to the amygdala. Imaging studies have shown that viewing fearful faces activates the left amygdala. Rage responses to minor stimuli are observed after removal of the neocortex. The destruction of the ventromedial hypothalamic nuclei and septal nuclei in animals with intact cerebral cortices may induce rage. Rage may also be generated by the stimulation of an area extending back through the lateral hypothalamus to the central gray matter of the midbrain. Bilateral destruction of the amygdala results in placidity. However, when the ventromedian nucleus is destroyed after the destruction of the amygdala, the placidity generated is converted to rage.

5. *Autonomic and endocrine responses to emotion*: The hypothalamus strongly influences autonomic and endocrine functions. Autonomic functions are controlled via projections to the brain stem and the spinal cord. There are localized areas in the hypothalamus that will activate the sympathetic nervous system and some that will increase parasympathetic activity. Endocrine functions are controlled by direct axonal connections to the posterior pituitary gland (vasopressin and oxytocin control), and stimulation of anterior pituitary gland via releasing factors in the hypothalamic-hypophyseal portal system. There are also projections to the reticular formation that are involved in certain behaviors, particularly emotional reactions. Hypothalamic autonomic responses are triggered by a complex phenomenon mediated by the cortical and limbic structures processing drives and emotions. The fear and rage responses mediated by the limbic system cause stimulation of various parts of the hypothalamus, especially the lateral areas and produce diffuse sympathetic discharge. The massive sympathetic discharge during stress is called "the fight or flight response." Stress causes the release of the corticotropin-releasing hormone (CRH) from the paraventricular nuclei of the hypothalamus via cortical and limbic connections. CRH release mediates endocrine and immune responses.

6. *Sexual behavior*: the medial preoptic area of the hypothalamus is a key structure in the central control of male sexual behavior. Chemosensory efferents from the main and accessory olfactory systems project to the medial amygdala (MeA). The MeA sends direct and indirect innervations (through the bed nucleus of the stria terminalis) to the medial preoptic area (MPOA). The MPOA and the MeA receive genitosensory input from the spinal cord through the central tegmental field (CTF). The parvocellular portion of the CTF called the subparafascicular nucleus seems to be especially important for stimuli related to ejaculation. The MPOA sends efferents to the paraventricular nucleus (PVN) of the hypothalamus, the ventral tegmental area, the nucleus paragigantocellularis, and other autonomic and somatomotor areas.

The parvocellular part of the paraventricular nucleus of the hypothalamus contains neurons that send direct oxytocinergic and vasopressinergic projections to the lumbosacral cord. Dopamine can trigger penile erection by acting on oxytocinergic neurons located in the paraventricular nucleus of the hypothalamus. Activation of oxytocinergic neurons originating in the PVN and projecting to extrahypothalamic brain areas, by dopamine and its agonists-excitatory amino acids (N-methyl-D-aspartic acid) or oxytocin itself or by electrical stimulation, leads to penile erection. The inhibition of these neurons, on the other hand, by GABA and its agonists or by opioid peptides and opiate-like drugs, denies this sexual response. The activation of these neurons is secondary to the activation of nitric oxide synthase (NOS), which produces nitric oxide. At least some of the glutamatergic inputs to the MPOA are from the medial amygdala (MeA) and bed nucleus of the stria terminalis (BNST), which mediate the female-stimulated increase in dopamine, which in turn, enhances copulatory ability. Extracellular glutamate in the MPOA increases during copulation, especially during ejaculation and increased glutamate facilitates copulation and genital reflexes.

7. *Addiction and motivation*: the reward circuitry underlying addictive behavior includes the amygdala and the nucleus accumbens. The amygdala plays a central role in cue-induced relapse. Relapse associated with cues, stress, and a single dose of a drug of abuse results in release of excitatory neurotransmitters in brain areas such as the hippocampus and the amygdala. The pathway of motivated behavior involves the prefrontal cortex, the ventral tegmental area (VTA), the amygdala, especially the basolateral amygdala and extended amygdala, the nucleus accumbens core, and the ventral pallidum. This pathway

PHOTO 5.3. Drug Addiction Materials.

is involved in the motivation to take drugs of abuse (drug-seeking) and the compulsive nature of drug-taking (see ***Reward System and the Basal Ganglia***, p. 120).

8. *Memory*

   a. *Emotional memory*: the amygdala, in conjunction with the prefrontal cortex and the medial temporal lobe, is involved in the consolidation and retrieval of emotional memories. The amygdala, the prefrontal cortex, and the hippocampus are also involved in the acquisition, extinction, and recovery of fears to cues and contexts. The hippocampus is critical for long-term, declarative memory storage.

   b. *The medial temporal lobe memory system*: this includes the hippocampus and the adjacent cortex, the parahippocampal regions (PHG), and the entorhinal and perirhinal regions. This memory system is involved in the storage of new memories.

   c. *The diencephalic memory system*: the diencephalic memory circuit consists of the hypothalamus, the mammillary body, and the dorsomedial nucleus of thalamus. This circuit is important for the storage of recent memory; a dysfunction of this circuit results in Korsakoff's syndrome.

9. *Social cognition*: this refers to the thought processes involved in understanding and dealing with other people. Social cognition involves regions that mediate face perception, the emotional processing; theory of mind (TOM); self-reference, and working memory. Together, the functioning of these regions support the complex behaviors necessary for social interactions. The limbic structures involved are the cingulate gyrus and the amygdala.

Table 5.1 summarizes the basic functions of the limbic system.

TABLE 5.1 Summary of Functions of Specific Areas of the Limbic System

Areas	Functions
Cingulate gyrus	Autonomic functions regulating heart rate and blood pressure as well as cognitive, attentional and emotional processing.
Parahippocampal gyrus	Spatial memory
Hippocampus	Long-term memory
Amygdala	Anxiety, aggression, fear conditioning; emotional memory and social cognition.
Hypothalamus	Regulates the autonomic nervous system via hormone production and release. Secondarily affects and regulates blood pressure, heart rate, hunger, thirst, sexual arousal and the circadian rhythm sleep/wake cycle.
Mammilary body	Memory
Nucleus accumbens	Reward, addiction

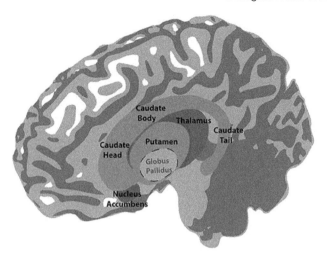

FIGURE 5.3.   The Basal Ganglia.

The Basal Ganglia

The basal ganglia or the basal nuclei are large masses of gray matter located within the white matter of the cerebral hemispheres. The basal ganglia are composed of the corpus striatum and related nuclei (the subthalamic nucleus, and the substantia nigra). The corpus striatum is the largest group of the basal ganglia nuclei. It consists of the caudate nucleus, the putamen, the nucleus accumbens, and the globus pallidus. The neostriatum refers to the caudate nucleus plus the putamen, while the lentiforme nucleus refers to the putamen plus the globus pallidus (Figure 5.3).

The basal ganglia and its related nuclei are characterized as one of three types of nuclei. (1) Input nuclei receive signals from the cerebral cortex and the thalamus. The caudate nucleus, the putamen, the nucleus accumbens, and the subthalamic nucleus are input nuclei. (2) Output nuclei send signals from the basal ganglia to the thalamus. The main output nuclei are the substantia nigra pars reticulata (SNr) and the medial globus pallidus/entopeduncular nucleus. The thalamus passes the information on to the cerebral cortex. (3) Intrinsic nuclei relay nerve signals and information between the input nuclei and output nuclei. The lateral globus pallidus (GP) is an intrinsic nucleus as most of its connections are with the input and output nuclei of the basal ganglia.

Connections of the Basal Ganglia

The basal ganglia form a collaborative system of connections between the cerebral cortex and the thalamus. The greatest input arises from the premotor cortex. This portion of the cortex is most involved in planning, patterning, and initiating movements.

There are two pathways for the transmission of signals through the basal ganglia, a direct and an indirect pathway; each has an opposite effect on thalamic target structures. The ultimate effect of the direct pathway is excitation of thalamic neurons, which results in a net facilitation of the cerebral cortex. In the case of the motor cortex, activation of the direct pathway would increase the ease of movement and of initiating movement. The indirect pathway has the opposite effects to the direct pathway. Excitation of the indirect pathway has a net effect of inhibiting thalamic neurons, making them unable to excite the motor cortical neurons. Ultimately, the indirect pathway is inhibitory to motor cortical activity. The basal ganglia output was thought to reflect a balance between these two pathways.

Functions of the Basal Ganglia

The basal ganglia are involved primarily in planning and programming of movements. They also process information related to emotions, motivations, cognitive functions, and eye movements. In humans, basal ganglia dysfunction has been associated with numerous conditions including Parkinson's disease, Huntington's disease, Tourette's syndrome, hemiballismus, athetosis, schizophrenia, attention deficit hyperactivity disorder, obsessive-compulsive disorder, and substance use disorders (addiction).

Reward System and the Basal Ganglia

The term reward system refers to a group of structures that are activated by rewarding or reinforcing stimuli. Food, water, and sex activate the reward system, this ensures our species survival. However, all addictive drugs and some activities also activate this system. The reward system is generally considered to be made up of the main dopamine pathways of the brain (especially the mesolimbic pathway) and structures like the VTA and nucleus accumbens, which are connected by these dopamine pathways.

When the brain's reward system is activated, dopamine is released, which creates a pleasing, enjoyable sensation. Thus, we are likely to repeat these behaviors that are necessary for survival. This is because dopamine rewards us with a pleasurable feeling. The mesolimbic dopamine pathway is thought to play a primary role in the reward system. It connects the ventral tegmental area (VTA), one of the principal dopamine-producing areas in the brain, with the nucleus accumbens, an area found in the ventral striatum that is strongly associated with motivation and reward. The mesocortical pathway travels from the VTA to the cerebral cortex and is also considered part of the reward system.

The Cerebellum

The cerebellum is the second largest part of the brain (about 11 percent of the brain's entire weight). It is located at the back of the brain under the cerebral hemisphere. It is attached to the brain stem with the help of pons. The cerebellum plays a vital role in the coordination of voluntary muscle activity, balance, and fine movements. Motor commands that originate in higher brain centers are processed in the cerebellum before transmission to the muscles. Damage to the cerebellum can cause hand tremors and ataxic gait. The cerebellum enables non-verbal learning and memory. Some studies have shown a correlation of the cerebellum with cognitive functions. The cerebellum also plays a role in vision and the auditory system. It can help in judging time, modulating emotions, and discriminating sounds and textures.

The Brain Stem

The brain stem connects the brain with the spinal cord and is composed of three structures: the midbrain, the pons, and the medulla oblongata. It plays an important role in maintaining homeostasis by controlling autonomic functions such as breathing, heart rate, and blood pressure. While the brain stem can organize motor movements such as reflexes, it coordinates with the motor cortex and associated areas to contribute to fine movements of limbs and the face. The brain stem play important role in alertness and sleep.

The Peripheral Nervous System

The peripheral nervous system (PNS) contains sensory, motor, and autonomic fibers outside of the CNS, including the spinal nerves, the cranial nerves, and the peripheral ganglia. The PNS carries sensory information to the CNS and motor information away from the CNS. The somatic nervous system (SNS) is the division of the PNS associated with skeletal muscle voluntary control of body movements and involuntary reflex arcs. The SNS consists of the efferent nerves responsible for stimulating muscle contractions, including all the non-sensory neurons connected with the skeletal muscles and skin. The somatic nervous system consists of three types of nerve fibers: (1) spinal nerves that carry motor commands and sensory information to the spinal cord; (2) cranial nerves that carry information into and out of the brain stem; and (3) association nerves that integrate sensory input and motor output.

The Autonomic Nervous System

The autonomic nervous system (ANS) is the division of the PNS that governs the internal activities of the human body, including the heart rate, breathing, digestion, salivation, perspiration, urination, and sexual arousal. Many of the actions of the ANS, such as heart rate and digestion, are automatic and outwit our conscious control, but others, such as breathing and sexual activity, can be controlled and influenced by conscious processes. The autonomic nervous system consists of sympathetic and parasympathetic divisions. The parasympathetic division of the ANS acts mainly to maintain homeostasis and conserve resources while the sympathetic division is closely involved in response to stress. Both divisions innervate the internal organs and coordinate emotions with visceral responses, such as heart rate, blood pressure, and peptic acid secretion. Exacerbation of these visceral responses as a result of psychological stress is implicated in the development and progression of physical illnesses, such as hypertension, peptic ulcer disease, and rheumatoid arthritis.

The autonomic nervous system is closely involved in behavior. The sympathetic division is involved in preparing the body's response to stress, by activating the organs and the glands in the endocrine system. The parasympathetic division of the ANS tends to calm the body by slowing the heart and breathing and by allowing the body to recover from the activities that the sympathetic system causes. The sympathetic and the parasympathetic divisions normally function in opposition to each other; the sympathetic division acts like the accelerator pedal on a car and the parasympathetic division acts like the brake.

Clinical Notes

Cortical and subcortical brain regions are specialized into different functions. This understanding helps in the assessment of the etiology of behavioral abnormalities, and hence better evaluation, and probably better management.

Summary

- Nervous tissue is composed of neurons and glial cells. Neurons are the primary cells, whose function is to receive and transmit information. Glial cells play a supporting role for the nervous tissue.
- The nervous system is organized into the central (CNS) and peripheral (PNS) nervous systems. The CNS includes the brain and the spinal cord.

- The brain is composed of the cerebrum, the cerebellum, and the brain stem.
- The cerebrum is divided into the right and left hemispheres; each is composed of four major sections called lobes: frontal, temporal, parietal, and occipital lobe, each separated by folds known as fissures.
- The right, or nondominant hemisphere, is associated primarily with perception, spatial relations, body image, recognition of faces and music, puzzle-solving, map-reading, and musical and artistic abilities.
- The left, or dominant, hemisphere is associated with language function in about 96 percent of right-handed people and 70 percent of left-handed people.
- The frontal lobe is divided into the precentral cortex, and the prefrontal cortex. Each of these areas is suggested to have specialized behavioral functions and has widespread connectivity.
- The parietal lobe is divided into three parts: the postcentral gyrus, the superior parietal lobule, and the inferior parietal lobule.
- Temporal lobes constitute about 25 percent of the human cerebral cortex and include areas associated with auditory, olfactory, vestibular, visual, and linguistic functions.
- The occipital cortex is concerned with visual processing and is composed of the primary visual cortex and the visual association cortex.
- The limbic system is composed of the cortical (the hippocampus as well as areas of neocortex) and the subcortical regions (the amygdala, the hippocampal formation, the hypothalamus, and some thalamic nuclei).
- The limbic system is involved in a variety of basic functions relating to emotions and self-preservation, such as eating, aggression, and reproduction.
- The basal ganglia are composed of the corpus striatum and related nuclei (the subthalamic nucleus, and the substantia nigra).
- The basal ganglia are involved primarily in planning and programming of movements. They also process information related to emotions, motivations, cognitive functions, and eye movements.
- The cerebellum is located at the back of the brain. It plays a vital role in the coordination of voluntary muscle activity, balance, and fine movements. Also, the cerebellum plays a role in non-verbal learning and memory, cognitive functions, vision and the auditory system, judging time, modulating emotions, and discriminating sounds and textures.
- The brain stem is composed of three structures: the midbrain, the pons, and the medulla oblongata. It plays an important role in maintaining homeostasis by controlling autonomic functions, such as breathing, heart rate, and blood pressure.
- The peripheral nervous system (PNS) contains the sensory, motor, and autonomic fibers outside of the CNS, including the spinal nerves, the cranial nerves, and the peripheral ganglia. The PNS carries sensory information to the CNS and motor information away from the CNS.
- The autonomic nervous system governs the internal activities of the human body, including heart rate, breathing, digestion, salivation, perspiration, urination, and sexual arousal.

Test Your Knowledge

- What are the methods of studying brain structure and its functions?
- What is the function of the frontal lobe?

■ What is the function of the parietal lobe?
■ What is the function of the temporal lobe?
■ What is the function of the limbic lobe?
■ What is the anatomical abnormality in Gerstmann syndrome?
■ Give an account of the reward system and basal ganglia.

Critical Thinking Question

How can understanding the functions of different brain regions help mental health professionals?

The Neurochemistry of Behavior

Operation of the nervous system is achieved through electrochemical processes. Within each neuron, when a signal is received by the dendrites, it is transmitted to the soma in the form of an electrical signal, and, if the signal is strong enough, it may then be passed on to the axon and then to the terminal buttons. If the signal reaches the terminal buttons, it triggers the release of chemical substances called "neurotransmitters" into the synapse. The binding of the neurotransmitter to the receptor molecules on the membrane of the postsynaptic cell gives rise, in turn, to a new class of signals called synaptic potentials. Thus, whereas the action potential is a purely electrical signal, the synaptic potential is an electrical signal initiated by a chemical one. The neurotransmitters fit into receptors on the receiving dendrites in a lock and key manner. More than 100 chemical substances produced in the body have been identified as neuro-transmitters, and these substances have a wide and profound effect on emotion, cognition, behavior, appetite, memory, as well as muscle action and movement. Neurotransmitters range from small molecules such as acetylcholine, noradrenaline, and serotonin to much larger molecules such as peptides.

Excess neurotransmitters that are not occupied by the receptor sites are removed from the synapse. This process occurs in part through the breaking down of the neurotransmitters by enzymes, and in part through reuptake into the transmitting terminal buttons, to be released again after the neuron fires.

The classic neurotransmitters include amino acids and biogenic amines, which are able to initiate synaptic transmission in the nervous system (Figure 5.4). A collection of criteria has

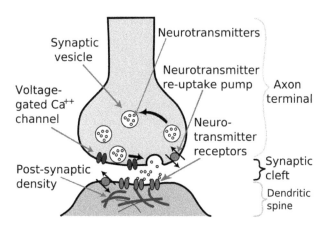

FIGURE 5.4.   Action of the Synapses.

been established to differentiate neurotransmitters from neuromodulators (Bohlen & Dermietzel, 2006):

1. The classic neurotransmitters are produced and stored within neurons and are released upon an adequate electrical signal.
2. Neurotransmitters are localized in the presynaptic terminals and are released into the synaptic cleft to mediate excitatory postsynaptic potentials (EPSP) or inhibitory postsynaptic potentials (IPSP).
3. Neurotransmitters are selectively released upon nerve stimulation in a calcium-dependent manner.
4. Neurotransmitters react with receptors on the postsynaptic or presynaptic sites. The effects can be prevented by specific antagonists and facilitated by specific agonists, which mimic the action of the transmitter.
5. Neurotransmitters are inactivated rapidly after release. This inactivation is mediated by specific enzymes or by re-uptake mechanisms.
6. Experimental application of a neurotransmitter at postsynaptic sites elicits effects identical to the endogenous substrate.

Presynaptic and postsynaptic receptors are proteins present in the membranes of neurons that can recognize specific neurotransmitters. When the presynaptic neuron is stimulated, the neurotransmitter is released, travels across the synaptic cleft (i.e., the space between the axon terminal of the presynaptic neuron and the dendrite of the postsynaptic neuron), and acts on receptors on the postsynaptic neuron. The effect of neurotransmitters on the receptors of the receiving neurons may be either excitatory or inhibitory. Neurotransmitters are excitatory if they increase the chance that a neuron will fire an action potential; major excitatory neurotransmitters include epinephrine and norepinephrine. Neurotransmitters are inhibitory if they have inhibitory effects on the neuron, i.e., they decrease the likelihood that the neuron will fire an action potential. Some of the major inhibitory neurotransmitters include serotonin and GABA. If the receiving neuron is the target of excitatory and inhibitory neurotransmitters, the neuron moves closer to its firing threshold if the excitatory effects of the neurotransmitters are greater than the inhibitory influences of the neurotransmitters.

Some neurotransmitters, such as acetylcholine and dopamine, can have both excitatory and inhibitory effects depending upon the type of receptors that are present. Neurotransmitters can be categorized as one of six types:

1. Acetylcholine.
2. Biogenic amines (monoamines): catecholamines (dopamine, norepinephrine), serotonin, and histamine.
3. Amino acids: gamma-aminobutyric acid (GABA), glycine, glutamate, and aspartate.
4. Neuropeptides: oxytocin, endorphins, vasopressin, etc.
5. Purines: adenosine, ATP.
6. Lipids and gases: nitric oxide, cannabinoids.

The Regulation of Neurotransmitters

Both passive and active mechanisms affect the concentration of neurotransmitters in the synaptic cleft. After release by the presynaptic neuron, neurotransmitters are removed from the synaptic cleft passively by simple diffusion into local tissue. Active removal is accomplished by reuptake by the presynaptic neuron or by degradation by enzymes, such as monoamine oxidase or acetylcholinesterase.

Regulation of neuron responsiveness is achieved not only by the lowered availability of the neurotransmitters, but also through changes in the number, or affinity (sensitivity) of the receptors for specific neurotransmitters (neuronal plasticity) and the efficiency with which a neurotransmitter signal is changed into a message.

When stimulated by neurotransmitters, postsynaptic receptors also may alter the metabolism of neurons by the use of second messengers, such as cyclic adenosine and guanosine monophosphate, lipids like diacylglycerol, and Ca^{2+}. The eicosanoid metabolites and gases, such as nitric oxide, also may act as second messengers as well as neurotransmitters.

Acetylcholine

Acetylcholine (ACh) was the first neurotransmitter to be discovered. The German biologist Otto Loewi isolated it in 1921, and won a Nobel Prize for this work. Acetylcholine is responsible for much of the stimulation of muscles, including the muscles of the gastro-intestinal system. It is also found in sensory neurons and in the autonomic nervous system, and has a part in scheduling REM sleep. Cholinergic neurons synthesize ACh from the acetyl coenzyme A and choline, using the enzyme choline acetyltransferase. The enzyme acetylcholinesterase (AChE) breaks ACh down into choline and acetate.

The ACh receptors consist of two major groups: the muscarinic (mAChRs) and the nicotinic receptors (nAChRs). These receptors are functionally different: muscarinic receptors are G-protein-coupled receptors (GPCRs), and hence responses to muscarinic agonists are slow, they may be either excitatory or inhibitory. On the other hand, nicotinic receptors are ligand-gated ion channels, which are permeable to sodium, potassium, and calcium ions, thus, these receptors show relatively fast responses (within milliseconds), and are excitatory.

The muscarinic receptors, M1, M4, and M5 receptors, are predominantly expressed in the CNS, whereas M2 and M3 receptors are found in both the peripheral nervous system and the CNS. M1, M3, and M5 receptors are found postsynaptically and they activate several effectors, including phospholipase C, intracellular calcium, inositol triphosphatase, and mitogen-activated protein kinase (MAPK). M2 and M4 receptors are found both pre- and postsynaptically, and inhibit adenylyl cyclase and voltage-operated calcium channels and activate MAPK and G-protein-activated inwardly rectifying potassium channels. Muscarinic receptors play a significant role in the side effects of psychoactive drugs, where blocking of muscarinic receptors by drugs, such as antipsychotics and tricyclic antidepressants, results in the classic anticholinergic side effects seen with use of these drugs, including dry mouth, blurred vision, urinary hesitancy, and constipation. Characteristics of different muscarinic receptors are summarized below (Toyohara, Sakata, & Ishiwata, 2010):

1. M1 receptors are widely expressed in the brain including the cerebral cortex, the hippo-campus, and the striatum. The M1 receptor has been implicated in learning and memory processes. Antagonism of the central M1 receptors with intrahippocampal pirenzepine impaired the spatial memory in a rat model. In addition, mice lacking the M1 receptor exhibit defects in a number of cognitive processes, and M1 receptor agonists ameliorate learning and memory impairment in animal models of Alzheimer's disease (AD).
2. M2 receptors are widely expressed in the CNS, and are located presynaptically and regulate the release of ACh and other neurotransmitters, including dopamine. Mice devoid of M2 receptor activity show cognitive deficits. Moreover, M2 knockout (KO)

mice showed deficits in behavioral flexibility, working memory, and hippocampal plasticity. M2 receptors are lost in the cerebral cortex in Alzheimer's disease and Parkinson's disease (PD). The M2 receptor is a potential treatment target for Alzheimer's disease and pain.

3. M3 receptors are sparsely distributed in the CNS, and their function has not been characterized in detail.

4. M4 receptors are found in the midbrain, the cortex, the hippocampus, and the striatum. M4 receptors are the most abundant in the striatum and preferentially coexpressed with dopamine D1 receptors in striatonigral projection neurons. M4 receptors are concentrated in postsynaptic sites and can be found in the postsynaptic density microdomain, and, therefore, this receptor is sensitive to synaptic input changes and plays a pivotal role in regulating synaptic strength and efficacy. Stimulation of M4 receptors is thought to reduce the activity of neurons in the dopaminergic ventral tegmental area (VTA), leading to reduced dopamine release in the nucleus accumbens. The M4 receptor is a potential treatment target for schizophrenia, Parkinson's disease, and possibly drug addiction..

5. M5 receptors are expressed on dopaminergic neurons in the substantia nigra and the VTA, suggesting that they may play a role in the modulation of dopaminergic transmission. Therefore, the M5 receptor is a potential treatment target for stimulant addiction, Parkinson's disease, and schizophrenia. In addition, M5 expression was shown to be unchanged in contrast to the marked reduction in M2 and upregulation of M4 in Alzheimer's disease patients.

Most nicotinic acetylcholine receptors (nAChRs) in the CNS are located presynaptically, and they modulate the release of ACh, dopamine, serotonin, glutamate, gamma-amino butyric acid, and norepinephrine. The nAChR can also be located postsynaptically, such as those on the dopaminergic neurons in the VTA. Nicotinic AChRs are composed of five types of subunits: alpha (2–6 and 9–19), beta (2–4), delta, epsilon, and gamma. These subunits are found in different combinations in different types of nAChRs. These subtypes are best characterized in terms of ligand selectivity (Dani, 2015; Toyohara et al., 2010).

Biogenic Amines (Monoamines)

The biogenic amines include catecholamines, indolamines, ethylamines, and quaternary amines. Dopamine, epinephrine, and norepinephrine constitute the main catecholamines family of neurotransmitters which are derived from the same precursor molecule (tyrosine). The monoamine theory of mood disorder hypothesizes that altered monoamine activity and related changes in monoamine receptors result in mood abnormalities.

Dopamine

Dopamine is the major catecholamine in the central nervous system that is produced in the dopaminergic neurons in the ventral tegmental area of the substantia nigra, and the ventral tegmental area in the midbrain. Dopamine is also a hormone released by the arcuate nucleus of the hypothalamus. Its main function as a hormone is to inhibit the release of prolactin from the anterior lobe of the pituitary. Dopamine has many functions in the brain, including motor activity, mood, memory, attention and cognition, learning, sleep, control of nausea and vomiting, and pain processing. Dopamine also is strongly associated with motivation and reward; drugs like cocaine, opium, heroin, alcohol, and nicotine increase the levels of dopamine. Dopamine is implicated in the pathophysiology of schizophrenia and other psychotic disorders. Dopamine has also been involved in the pathophysiology of Parkinson's disease, mood disorders, attention deficit hyperactivity disorder, and the conditioned fear response.

The various actions of dopamine are mediated by specific receptors. There are five subtypes of dopamine receptors, D1, D2, D3, D4, and D5, which are members of the large G-protein coupled receptor superfamily. The dopamine receptor subtypes are divided into two major subclasses: the D1-like group, which include types 1 and 5; and the D2-like group, which includes dopamine receptor types 2, 3, and 4. Whereas the D2 receptor subtype seems to be the major site of action for traditional antipsychotic agents, the D1 and D4 subtypes are implicated in the action of the newer, atypical antipsychotics like clozapine.

There are four dopaminergic pathways in the brain: (1) the nigrostriatal pathway; (2) the mesolimbic pathway; (3) the mesocortical pathway; and (4) the tuberoinfundibular pathway (Figure 5.5). *The nigrostriatal pathway* transmits dopamine from the substantia nigra to the neostriatum. This is achieved by neurons that have their soma in the substantia nigra projecting axons out to the caudate nucleus and the putamen. The nigrostriatal pathway is involved in the regulation of muscle tone and movement and its degeneration is seen in Parkinson's disease. Treatment with traditional antipsychotic drugs, which block postsynaptic dopamine receptors receiving input from the nigrostriatal tract, can result in Parkinsonism-like symptoms.

The mesolimbic pathway transmits dopamine from the ventral tegmental area to the nucleus accumbens, the amygdala, and the hippocampus. This is achieved by neurons that have their soma in the ventral tegmental area projecting axons out to the named areas. It is significantly involved with reward and pleasure and is hence of great interest in studies of depression, motivation and addition, where it has been linked with alcohol, nicotine, and cocaine.

The mesocortical pathway transmits dopamine from the ventral tegmental area to the frontal lobe of the pre-frontal cortex. This is achieved by neurons that have their soma in the ventral tegmental area projecting axons out to the frontal lobe. It is believed to be involved in motivational and emotional responses.

The tuberoinfundibular pathway transmits dopamine from the hypothalamus to the pituitary gland. Dopamine released here regulates secretion of prolactin from the anterior pituitary gland. Blockade of dopamine receptors by antipsychotic drugs prevents this inhibition, ultimately leading to elevated prolactin levels and side effects like breast enlargement, galactorrhea, and sexual dysfunction.

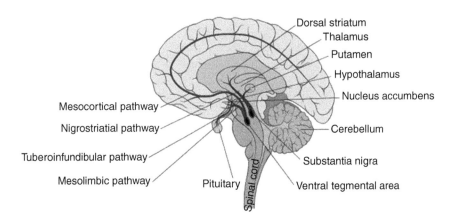

FIGURE 5.5. The Dopaminergic Pathways.

Norepinephrine

In 1946, the Swedish biologist Ulf von Euler identified norepinephrine as the adrenergic neurotransmitter. He won a Nobel Prize for this work. Norepinephrine is prevalent in the sympathetic nervous system. Also, adrenal glands release it into the bloodstream, along with its close relative, epinephrine. In contrast to epinephrine, which is mainly restricted to the peripheral nervous system, norepinephrine is a major transmitter in the central nervous system.

Norepinephrine interacts with specific receptors (adrenoceptors) that are located on the plasma membrane of neurons in the central and peripheral nervous system, and on peripheral glands and muscle cells. Adrenoreceptors have in common the property that they couple with G-proteins. There are two types of noradrenergic receptors (α and β). The α-adrenoreceptors have been further split into two different subcategories (α-1 and α-2). Each of the receptors can be further divided into several subtypes. Three different subtypes of the α-1 receptors (α-1A, α-1B, and α-1D) have been identified, as well as three different subtypes of α-2 receptors (α-2A, α-2B, and α-2C). Three further subtypes of β receptors (β-1, β-2, and β-3) complete the catecholamine receptor family. The distribution of the different subtypes of adrenoceptors is not homogeneous in the brain and each receptor subtype reveals a characteristic location (Bohlen & Dermietzel, 2006). The action of norepinephrine at a synapse is brought to an end primarily via reuptake. Norepinephrine may also be broken down by the MAO enzyme.

Results of activation of noradrenergic receptors can be either inhibitory or excitatory. In peripheral tissues, the activation of adrenoceptors of the α- and β-type exhibits inverse physiological effects; the activation of α-1 adrenoceptors causes vasoconstriction, enhances glycogenolysis, and more generally induces the contraction of smooth muscle cells, whereas activation of β adrenoceptors leads to vasodilatation, bronchodilatation, and positive ionotropic and chronotropic effects on heart tissue.

Most noradrenergic neurons are located in nuclei in the upper brainstem, the most important of these is the locus ceruleus. It is involved in nervous system arousal, hunger, and mood, anxiety, learning, and memory. The actions of norepinephrine are vital to the fight-or-flight response, whereby the body prepares to react to or retreat from an acute threat. The induction of stress is associated with an enhanced activity of the locus ceruleus which, because of its widespread projections into cortical and subcortical structures and lower brain stem areas, affects a variety of physiological functions (Bohlen & Dermietzel, 2006).

Serotonin

In 1948, Maurice Rapport et al. discovered a vasoconstrictor substance in blood serum; they named it serotonin, because it was a serum agent affecting vascular tone. Vittorio Erspamer in 1952 discovered that the substance which he identified in enterochromaffin cells of the gut (enteramine) in the 1930s, is the same as serotonin.

About 90 percent of serotonin (5-hydroxytryptamine; 5-HT) is found in the enterochromaffin cells of the gastrointestinal tract and 8–10 percent in platelets, 1–2 percent is present in the central nervous system. Serotonin cannot cross the blood-brain barrier and therefore neural 5-HT is synthesized in situ from the amino acid L-tryptophan in the nerve terminals, that is converted to serotonin by the enzyme tryptophan hydroxylase as well as by an amino acid decarboxylase. Anatomically, most serotonergic cell bodies in the brain are located in the dorsal raphe nucleus in the upper pons and lower midbrain, and send axons to almost every brain region. In the adult brain, the axons of 5-HT neurons innervate a large number of cortical areas, including the entorhinal and cingulate cortices, which contain a moderate to high density of

5-HT receptors. However, of all cortical regions, the frontal lobe is the area richest in serotonergic terminals and 5-HT receptors.

Serotonin is implicated in almost every physiological function (appetite and eating, reward, thermoregulation, cardiovascular regulation, locomotion, pain sensitivity, sexuality, sleep–wake cycle, memory, cognition, aggressiveness, responses to stressors, emotion, and mood, and impulse control) and in several human pathologies. Serotonergic dysfunction is thought to be associated with irritable bowel syndrome, restless legs syndrome, sudden infant death syndrome, autism, headache, insomnia, anxiety, depression, anorexia, schizophrenia, Parkinson's disease, and Alzheimer's disease. At the present time, most of the anxiolytic and antidepressant drugs such as tricyclic and tetracyclic antidepressants, selective serotonin reuptake inhibitors (SSRIs), azapirones, and triptans used to relieve migraine, all target the serotonergic systems. In addition, atypical antipsychotics, e.g., risperidone, olanzapine, clozapine, and quetiapine interact with serotonergic receptors (5-HT$_1$A, 5-HT$_2$A-2C, 5-HT$_6$, and 5-HT$_7$). Finally, hallucinogens such as LSD, mescaline, psilocybin, and ecstasy work by attaching to serotonin receptor sites and thereby blocking transmissions in perceptual pathways (Charnay & Léger, 2010).

Serotonin exerts its action via specific receptors which are identified as 5HT$_1$, 5HT$_2$, 5HT$_3$, 5HT$_4$, 5HT$_5$, 5HT$_6$, and 5HT$_7$. Various subpopulations for several of these receptors have been described. Most of these receptors are coupled to G-proteins that affect the activities of either adenylate cyclase or phospholipase Cβ. The 5HT$_3$ class of receptors are ion channels (ionotropic receptors). The diversity of 5-HT receptors should eventually allow a better understanding of the different and complex processes in which serotonin is involved. Characteristics of different subtypes serotonin receptors are summarized in Table 5.2 (Charnay & Léger, 2010).

Histamine

In the last quarter of the twentieth century, histamine was approved as a neuroactive substance within the central nervous system. Since histamine is unable to cross the blood-brain barrier, it was suggested that histamine is synthesized in brain tissues and represents a neurotransmitter per se. Both postsynaptic and presynaptic histaminergic receptors have been found in the brain as well as the precursor of histamine metabolism. Histamine has many features in common with the monoamines, such as catecholamines or indolamines (serotonin), with respect to release, metabolic pathway, and mode of action at the cellular level (Bohlen & Dermietzel, 2006).

Histamine is a major player in the control of sleep and wakefulness. Histamine is also involved in the regulation of the energetic balance of the body, by regulating glycogenolytic functions. The modulation of neuronal histamine, for instance, by blocking H3 receptors, reduces food intake. Furthermore, histamine exerts some endocrine functions because it influences the secretion of hormones from the pituitary. Blood pressure and body temperature are two further examples of a possible involvement of histamine in centrally regulated physiological processes. Histamine-receptor blockade with drugs such as antipsychotics and tricyclic antidepressants is responsible in part for common side effects of these agents, such as sedation and increased appetite leading to weight gain.

Amino Acids

Gamma-aminobutyric acid (GABA) is the principal inhibitory neurotransmitter in the CNS. GABA is synthesized from glutamic acid by glutamic acid decarboxylase (GAD), which catalyzes the removal of the α-carboxyl group. In the CNS, the expression of GAD appears to be

TABLE 5.2 Characteristics of Serotonin Receptor Subtypes

Receptor Subtype	Localization	Supposed Function	Effector Mechanism	Related Clinical Disorders
5-HT$_{1A}$	Limbic system (hippocampus, lateral septum, cortical areas), mesencephalic raphe nuclei	Neuronal hyperpolarization, inhibition of neurotransmitter release, thermoregulation, feeding, stress, pain, mood, emotion, cognition, learning, memory.	(–) AC, opening of K+ channels	Anxiety, depression, neurodegenerative disorders, schizophrenia
5-HT$_{1B}$	Basal ganglia, striatum, amygdala, trigeminal ganglion, vascular smooth muscle	Autoreceptor, modulation of neurotransmitter release, locomotion, mood, feeding, vasoconstriction.	(–) AC	Anxiety, depression, migraine
5-HT$_{1D}$	Basal ganglia, hippocampus, cortex, spinal cord, vascular smooth muscle	Autoreceptor, inhibition of neurotransmitter release, mood, feeding, vasoconstriction	(–) AC	Anxiety, depression, migraine
5-HT$_{1E}$	Cortex, caudate putamen, claustrum, hippocampus, amygdala	Unknown	(–) AC	Unknown
5-HT$_{1F}$	Hippocampus, cortex, dorsal raphe nucleus, uterus	Mood, emotion	(–) AC	Migraine
5-HT$_{2A}$	Forebrain, caudate nucleus, nucleus accumbens, hippocampus, olfactory tubercle, vascular smooth muscle, blood platelets	Neuronal depolarization, modulation of neurotransmitter release, Mood, smooth muscle contraction, platelet activation, feeding, nociception	(+) PLC, closing of K+ channels	Schizophrenia, anxiety, depression, Tourette's syndrome, Alzheimer's disease, anorexia/bulimia, drug abuse, pain
5-HT$_{2B}$	Brain, stomach fundus (rat), gut, heart, kidney, lung	Brain development (?), feeding (?)	(+) PLC	Drug abuse, anxiety (?)
5-HT$_{2C}$	Choroid plexus, cortex, limbic system, basal ganglia	Mood, impulsivity, feeding, penile erection, locomotor, activity	(+) PLC	Anxiety, depression, schizophrenia, drug abuse, obesity

5-HT$_3$	Dorsal vagal complex, hippocampus, amygdala, caudate, cerebral cortex, heart, intestines	Vomiting reflex, mood	Ligand-gated cation channel	Nausea, anxiety, depression
5-HT$_4$	Cerebral cortex, limbic areas, hippocampus, colliculus, intestines	Learning and memory, feeding, reward	(+) AC	Anorexia, drug abuse, Alzheimer's disease
5-HT$_{5A}$	Amygdala, hippocampus, caudate nucleus, cerebellum, hypothalamus, thalamus, substantia nigra, spinal cord	Circadian rhythm, sleep, mood, cognition	(−) AC	Schizophrenia (?), anxiety, depression (?)
5-HT$_6$	Striatum, olfactory tubercles, nucleus accumbens, hippocampus, stomach, adrenal glands	Memory and learning, feeding.	(+) AC	Alzheimer's disease, obesity
5-HT$_7$	Thalamus, hypothalamus, hippocampus, cerebral cortex, amygdala, GI and vascular smooth muscle, heart	Mood, sleep, cognition	(+) AC	Anxiety, depression, schizophrenia.

Notes

(−) AC = Inhibition of adenylyl cyclase.
(+) AC = Stimulation of adenylyl cyclase.
(+) PLC= Stimulation of phosphoinositide-specific phospholipase C.

restricted to GABAergic neurons, although in the periphery it is expressed in pancreatic islet cells. Two distinct but related genes encode GAD. GABA is widely distributed and utilized throughout the CNS. The GABA neurons are primarily the interneurons in the gray matter providing local constraint over cortical circuitry. Two distinct classes of GABA receptor were identified: GABA-A and GABA-B. They differ in their pharmacological, electrophysiological, and biochemical properties. GABA-A receptors are responsive to a wide variety of drugs, e.g., benzodiazepines, which are often used for their sedative/hypnotic and anxiolytic effects. GABA-B receptors are important for slow synaptic inhibition in the CNS. The efficacy of inhibition is directly related to the stability of the cell surface receptors.

Dysfunction of GABAergic neurotransmission has been implicated in a broad range of neuropsychiatric disorders, including anxiety disorders, schizophrenia, alcohol dependence, and seizure disorders. As would be expected, drugs that increase GABAergic activity can be an effective treatment for epilepsy. More recently, increasing GABAergic activity has been used to treat insomnia, pain, and anxiety, and to assist in the management of mania.

Glycine is an inhibitory neurotransmitter found primarily in the spinal cord. Glycine is a nonessential amino acid that is synthesized in the brain from L-serine by serine hydroxymethyltransferase. It works on its own and as a regulator of the excitatory neurotransmitter glutamate. Termination of the synaptic action of glycine is through reuptake into the presynaptic terminal by the glycine transporter II (GlyT2), which is quite distinct from GlyT1 that is expressed in astrocytes and modulates the NMDA receptor function.

Glutamate

Glutamate is the most common neurotransmitter in the central nervous system, with glutamate neurons making up more than half of the excitatory neurons. Glutamate and another excitatory transmitter aspartate are nonessential amino acids that do not cross the blood-brain barrier. Consequently, glutamate must be synthesized in the brain from glucose and other precursors. Glial cells assist in the reuptake, degradation, and resupply of glutamate for neurons.

Glutamate is toxic to neurons. Sometimes brain damage or a stroke will lead to glutamate excess and end with many more brain cells dying than from the original trauma. Glutamate itself has been associated with epilepsy, neurodegenerative illnesses, memory formation, mechanisms of cell death, and schizophrenia. Symptoms of schizophrenia have been linked specifically to alterations in the major glutamate receptor, N-Methyl-D-aspartate (NMDA). Drugs that block NMDA induce psychotic symptoms in healthy volunteers, and genes linked to the development of schizophrenia are associated with disruption of the NMDA-receptor pathway.

Neuropeptides

In the late 1960s and the early 1970s, it was established that many peptides initially discovered in a variety of regions, as well as the newly discovered endorphins and enkephalins, are also produced and are active in the brain. It appears that neuropeptides act as transmitters, hormones, or modulators depending on the tissue, synapse, and frequency of stimulation. The neuropeptides are small chains of amino acids, which are considerably larger than the classic neurotransmitters. Furthermore, the formation, release, and inactivation of the neuropeptides differ from that of the monoamines. Unlike the monoamines, neuropeptides are not recycled by the neuron, but are rather broken down by degradative enzymes (peptidases) on the receptor membrane.

Neuropeptides that act on behavior include the endogenous opioids, the enkephalins, and the endorphins. These neuropeptides are produced by the brain itself, serve to decrease pain and anxiety, and have a role in addiction and mood. Placebo effects (i.e., subjective responsiveness to inactive pharmacologic agents) may be mediated by the endogenous opioid and dopaminergic systems. Prior treatment with an opioid-receptor blocker like naloxone can inhibit the placebo effects. Placebo-induced release of endogenous dopamine in the striatum of patients with Parkinson's disease has also been demonstrated.

Hormones and other substances can also function as neurotransmitters. Neuropeptides with classic neurotransmitter effects are called neuromodulators. Additional classes of substances (neuromodulators) with neurotransmitter properties are gaseous molecules like nitric oxide (NO) or carbon monoxide (CO). These gaseous substances meet some criteria of neurotransmitters. Some essential neurotransmitter criteria, like receptor interaction and specific reuptake and degradation mechanisms, are not fulfilled by this group and thus they do not qualify as true neurotransmitters. Other neuropeptides associated with psychiatric disorders include:

- cholecystokinin (CCK) and neurotensin with schizophrenia
- somatostatin, substance P, vasopressin, oxytocin, and vasoactive intestinal peptide (VIP) with mood disorders
- somatostatin, and substance P with Huntington's disease
- somatostatin and VIP with dementia of the Alzheimer's type
- substance P and CCK with anxiety disorders
- substance P with pain and aggression

Clinical Notes

- Neurotransmitter abnormalities are proposed as an etiological factor in the development of mood and psychotic disorders. A role has been suggested in many other developmental disorders, and degenerative brain disease.
- Different drugs are developed based on the assumption of neurotransmitter dysregulation especially in mood and psychotic disorders.

Summary

- Operation of the nervous system is achieved through electrochemical processes. Signals received by the dendrites are transmitted to the soma in the form of an electrical signal, and, if the signal is strong enough, it may then be passed on to the axon and then to the terminal buttons. If the signal reaches the terminal buttons, it triggers the release of chemical substances called "neurotransmitters" into the synapse.
- Neurotransmitters include acetylcholine, biogenic amines, amino acids, and neuropeptides, purines, lipids, and gases.
- Neurotransmitters are excitatory if they increase the chance that a neuron will fire an action potential; major excitatory neurotransmitters include epinephrine and norepinephrine. Neurotransmitters are inhibitory if they decrease the likelihood that the neuron will fire an action potential. Some of the major inhibitory neurotransmitters include serotonin and GABA. Some neurotransmitters, such as acetylcholine and dopamine, can have both excitatory and inhibitory effects.

■ All neurotransmitters have specific pathways and sites of function. Different neurotransmitters are involved in the control of emotional and behavioral states.

Test Your Knowledge

■ What are the characteristics of classic neurotransmitters?
■ What is the function of acetylcholine as a neurotransmitter?
■ What is the function of serotonin as a neurotransmitter?
■ What is the function of dopamine as a neurotransmitter?
■ What is the function of norepinephrine as a neurotransmitter?
■ What is the function of amino acids as a neurotransmitter?

Critical Thinking Questions

Evaluate the role of neurotransmitters as an etiological factor in the development of:
■ major depression.
■ schizophrenia.

six

Consciousness, Sleep and Hypnosis, Meditation, and Psychoactive Drugs

Learning Goals

- This chapter is intended to provide the reader with an overview of consciousness, the causes of disturbed consciousness, and the phenomena associated with altered consciousness, including sleep, dreams, and their theories, induced conditions, such as hypnosis and meditation, and the effect of psychoactive drugs.
- The sleep section will include a review of the functions of sleep, the circadian rhythm, the neurobiology of sleep, the regulation of sleep, the stages of sleep, the effects of age on sleep, the effects of sleep deprivation, a clinical assessment of sleep, and a discussion of sleep disorders.
- The psychoactive drugs section will discuss depressants (alcohol, opiates, opioids, benzodiazepines, barbiturates, and inhalants), stimulants (caffeine, nicotine, amphetamines, and cocaine), hallucinogens, and other psychoactive drugs (cannabis and ecstasy).

Introduction

The nature of consciousness has been a topic of discussion and debate among philosophers and scientists since ancient times. Consciousness could be defined as the state of being awake, and being aware of one's own self, and what is going on around us. Consciousness is best understood as being composed of two dimensions: *vigilance* (wakefulness or arousal, i.e., the level of consciousness), and *awareness* (i.e., the content of consciousness). Awareness refers to conscious perception, which includes cognition, experiences from the past and the present, and intentions. It is supported by the cerebral cortex. Awareness can be divided into awareness of the self and of the environment:

1. *Awareness of self*: this is a mental process that does not require external stimuli, i.e., an ability to experience self, which is both immediate and complex, being aware of things inside us, aware of ourselves and our existence. Awareness of self includes internal stimuli, such as feeling pain, hunger, thirst, sleepiness, and being aware of our thoughts and emotions.
2. *Awareness of the environment*: this is the conscious perception of one's environment at a particular moment through the sensory modalities. It includes seeing the light of the sun, feeling the warmth of a room, and hearing the voice of a friend. It also refers to the knowledge of our own social and cultural history. This is called the lucidity-clouding dimension, as it may be clear or clouded. Obviously, lucidity is not unrelated to vigilance, unless the person is fully awake, their consciousness cannot be clear.

Vigilance is mainly supported by the brain stem and the thalami. Vigilance means the faculty of deliberately remaining alert, as opposed to feeling drowsy or being asleep. This is not uniform or unvarying, but fluctuating. Factors inside the individual that promote vigilance include interest, anxiety, extreme fear or enjoyment, whereas boredom encourages drowsiness. Environmental factors and the way the individual perceives them affect this dimension of consciousness (the vigilance-drowsiness/wakefulness–sleep dimension). Maintenance of vigilance or alertness depends on the interaction between the ascending reticular activating system (ARAS) and the cerebral hemispheres. ARAS extends from the lower border of the pons to the ventromedial thalamus and then projects to the whole of the cerebral cortex. It receives collaterals from the spinothalamic and trigeminal thalamic pathways. Disorders that distort the normal anatomical relationships of the midbrain, the thalamus, and the cortex can impair arousal. Alertness varies throughout the course of each day, and is regulated by the circadian rhythms.

A person who is awake and aware of external and internal stimuli can respond appropriately to the stimuli. So, to be conscious means being awake, being aware, and responding appropriately to stimuli. In the medical field, attention is usually given to any disturbance in wakefulness or arousal, which is a medical emergency, while psychologists always pay attention to awareness and its contents. The Freudian view of the levels of the mind was not an exception, he divided the mind into three different levels of awareness: (1) the conscious mind; (2) the preconscious mind; and (3) the unconscious mind, as discussed above.

Disturbed Consciousness

A disturbance of consciousness may entail either quantitative or qualitative changes, or both. Quantitative changes in consciousness affect essentially arousal or wakefulness of the patient, with subsequent changes in awareness.

Occasionally, a person may be overly alert, a state that is termed hypervigilance or hyper-arousal. Hypervigilant persons may restlessly scan the room and attend to every noticeable sound or change in visual stimuli, they may be easily startled. Hypervigilant persons appear anxiously attentive, and do not relax. This condition can be caused by mania, anxiety, paranoid delusions, as well as some medical conditions, such as hyperthyroidism. It may also be the effect of the ingestion of sympathomimetic drugs (cocaine, amphetamines, etc.). Quantitative lowering of consciousness may result from structural brain lesions, inflammatory brain diseases, metabolic disorders, an electrolyte imbalance, a postictal state, and the use of psychoactive drugs. A variety of adjectives are used to describe states of decreased arousal. In approximate order of increasing severity, these terms include drowsy, lethargic, obtunded, stuporous, and comatose. These states must be differentiated from normal sleep, from which patients can be fully aroused.

Qualitative changes in consciousness imply mainly changes in awareness without significant changes in arousal level. Qualitative changes of consciousness may occur during hypnosis and meditation, drug use, intense emotions, or during some religious experiences.

Clinical Notes

Evaluation of the level of consciousness is of the utmost clinical value. Quantitative lowering of consciousness usually stems from organic brain diseases or metabolic and toxic conditions affecting the brain. Urgent intervention is usually mandated. Qualitative lowering of consciousness may be induced in therapeutic situations, such as hypnosis and meditation, or it could result from drug use, intense emotions, or during religious experiences.

Summary

- Consciousness is the state of being awake, and being aware of one's own self, and what is going on around us. It is best understood as being composed of two dimensions: vigilance and awareness.
- Awareness refers to conscious perception, which includes cognition, experiences from the past and the present, and intentions.
- Vigilance means the faculty of deliberately remaining alert as opposed to being drowsy or asleep.
- A disturbance of consciousness may entail either quantitative or qualitative changes, or both.

Test Your Knowledge

- Define consciousness.
- What are the dimensions of consciousness?

Critical Thinking Question

Consciousness is an elusive concept, how is it understood from different psychological perspectives?

Sleep

PHOTO 6.1. Sleep.

Sleep is a complex combination of physiological and behavioral processes that occupies roughly one-third of human life. It can be defined as a state of reversible alteration of consciousness, and perceptual detachment from and unresponsiveness to the environment, that is associated with characteristic patterns of brain wave activities that include intervals of dreaming. Mental health clinicians acknowledge sleep as a fundamental human behavior, and state that inadequate sleep has adverse medical, psychiatric, and psychosocial consequences. On the other hand, sleep disturbances interact with common mental disorders; the two are mutually exacerbating, and both must be appropriately addressed to ensure optimal outcomes for patients. In some people, sleep disorders represent a primary condition that requires an intervention of its own.

Since the time of the early Greek philosophers, sleep has been a topic of discussion and research. Sleep studies essentially revolve about functions of sleep, the architecture of sleep, the mechanisms explaining the occurrence of sleep, dreams, and sleep disorders.

Functions of Sleep

A number of diverse theories have been proposed to explain the necessity of sleep as well as the functions and purposes of sleep. While there is some evidence to support each of these assumptions about sleep, there is no clear-cut support for any particular one. It is possible that each of these suppositions can be used to explain the impact of sleep on physiological processes, so it is very possible that sleep occurs for many reasons and purposes. Theories explaining sleep function include the following:

1. the repair and restoration theory of sleep;
2. the evolutionary theory of sleep;
3. the information consolidation theory of sleep;
4. sleep nourishes creative thinking;
5. the homeostatic function of sleep.

The Repair and Restoration Theory of Sleep

Sleep is supposed to play an essential role in restoring the physiological processes that keep body and mind healthy and properly functioning. This theory suggests that non-rapid eye movement (NREM) sleep is important for restoring physiological functions, while rapid eye movement (REM) sleep is essential in restoring mental functions. Sleeping gives a resting time to neurons to repair themselves, and to prune or weaken unused connections (Gilestro, Tononi, & Cirelli, 2009; Siegel, 2003; Vyazovskiy, Cirelli, Pfister-Genskow, Faraguna, & Tononi, 2008). Growth hormone production, which produces bodily protein synthesis, depends on uninterrupted stage 4 sleep. The release of this hormone decreases with aging (Kern, Dodt, Born, & Fehm, 1996). In support of this hypothesis is the finding that well-rested athletes have faster reaction times, more energy, and greater endurance, leading to improved performance (Maas & Robbins, 2010). Siegel (2003) states that, although most brain cells are at least as active during REM sleep as in waking, however, there is a specific group of cells that goes against this tendency. These cells produce the monoamine neurotransmitters (noradrenaline, serotonin, and histamine), inhibit body movement, reduce awareness of the environment, and play a part in rewiring the brain to respond to new experiences. These cells stop discharging completely during REM sleep. This interruption may allow the receptor systems to rest and regain full sensitivity (which may be crucial during waking for mood regulation), and may help in preventing changes in brain connections that might otherwise be accidentally created as a consequence of the activation of other neurons during REM sleep.

The Evolutionary Theory of Sleep

This theory assumes that the fundamental purpose of sleep is to keep an individual out of danger. Meddis (1975) proposed that the safer the animal from predators, the longer it is likely to sleep. Animals at risk from predators (those which cannot find a safe place to sleep, or which spend large parts of each day searching for and consuming food and water such as herd animals, e.g., zebras), sleep very little. On the other hand, predators that sleep in safe places, and can satisfy their food and water needs fairly quickly, such as lions, sleep much of the day. In a criticism of this theory, it is said that whatever the sleep pattern, it could be used as an indicator of safety; if an animal sleeps for shorter periods, it could be to guard against predators, while if an animal sleeps for longer periods, this could make it safer from predators.

The Information Consolidation Theory of Sleep

A number of sleep deprivation studies have demonstrated that lack of sleep has a serious impact on the ability to recall and remember information. Sleep is proposed to consolidate memories (Rasch & Born, 2008; Racsmány, Conway, & Demeter, 2010). This is supported by the finding that people could recall tasks after a night's sleep, or even after a short nap, better than after several hours awake (Stickgold & Ellenbogen, 2008). The mechanism by which memory is consolidated is not completely understood. Many researchers claim that recently formed memories are replayed during sleep and become consolidated in the process of synaptic potentiation; the synaptic connections that have been strengthened while the individual is awake are further reinforced while sleeping (Castro, 2012). Contrary to the synaptic potentiation assumption, Tononi and Cirelli (2014), in their synaptic homeostasis hypothesis, claimed that slow-wave activity is associated with synaptic weakening, which is tied to the beneficial effects of sleep on performance. Castro (2012) suggests that sleep serves as a reset button, loosening neural connections throughout the brain, and restoring it to a flexible state in which new learning can take place.

Sleep Nourishes Creative Thinking

REM sleep can aid problem-solving. Wamsley and Stickgold (2010) found that REM sleep sharpens the performance of participants navigating a virtual maze. When participants were awakened or interrupted during REM sleep, and asked what they were dreaming about, the theme was often the maze, and those people performed better the next time they began the maze.

The Homeostatic Function

Common experience suggests that the longer one is awake, the sleepier one feels. Conversely, sleep reverses sleepiness and the other consequences of wakefulness. Thus, sleep may represent a default state that has evolved from the circadian rest–activity cycle. Hence, sleep serves a homeostatic function, it is a time of rest and restoration that overcomes the consequences of wakefulness. Consistent with this hypothesis is that sleep deprivation usually decreases sleep latency and increases sleep efficiency and the amount of deep sleep on recovery nights.

The Circadian Rhythm

The circadian rhythm is a rhythmic alternation of various physiological and psychological processes, synchronized to the 24-hour cycle of light and dark. So, during a 24-hour period, there is a cycle of several physiological functions, e.g., rest–activity, heart rate, blood pressure, breathing rate, core body temperature, gastric activity, hormonal secretion, metabolic rate, urine excretion, immune function, and so on. Each of those examples represents a specific circadian rhythm.

Circadian rhythms can be characterized by three different measures: (1) cycle length (tau), e.g., the time between two peaks of the 24-hour temperature curve; (2) amplitude, e.g., the difference between the minimum value of the cycle (the nadir) and the maximum value, e.g., the difference between the lowest and highest points in the 24-hour temperature curve; and (3) the phase position of the rhythm (the acrophase), e.g., the time of day when the peak of the rhythm occurred. Different circadian rhythms are usually closely synchronized, e.g., the circadian rhythm of the growth hormone release is synchronized with the sleep–wake circadian rhythm, so that the growth hormone is released only during sleep. Similarly, sleep–wake rhythm, the core body temperature, and the melatonin cycles are usually very closely coordinated at about 3.00 a.m., the core body temperature dips to its lowest point just as the melatonin is reaching its highest level at deep sleep. Maximum sleepiness occurs when the core body temperature is at its lowest and the melatonin levels are at their highest.

In humans and mammals, the circadian rhythms are controlled by a tiny cluster of neurons in the medial hypothalamus called the suprachiasmatic nucleus (SCN), i.e., the master clock (Moore, 2007). Damage to the SCN in rats abolished their circadian rhythms of temperature, cortisol secretion, eating, drinking, and sleep–wakefulness. Keeping the circadian rhythms synchronized with one another and on a 24-hour schedule is also controlled by environmental time cues. The most important of these cues is bright light, especially sunlight. Light is detected by photoreceptors in the eye, and is communicated via the visual system to the SCN (which lies above the optic chiasm) in the hypothalamus (Berson, Dunn, & Takao, 2002; Drouyer, Rieux, Hut, & Cooper, 2007). A tuft of nerve fibers branches off from the main nerve and penetrates the hypothalamus above, forming synaptic connections with cells in the SCN. This pathway (the retinohypothalamic tract) allows a link between the outside world and the brain's own clock

(Blakemore, 1988). Information regarding light is also conveyed to the SCN indirectly through the intergeniculate leaflet of the lateral geniculate body.

As the sun sets each day, the decrease in available light is detected by the SCN through its connections with the visual system. In turn, the SCN triggers the pineal gland to increase the production of melatonin, peaking between 1.00 and 3.00 a.m. Increased blood level of melatonin helps sleep and reduces activity levels. As the sun rises, exposure to sunlight and other bright light suppresses melatonin levels, which remain very low throughout the day. In this way, sunlight regulates, or entrains the SCN, which in turn keeps the circadian cycles synchronized and operating on a 24-hour schedule.

In the absence of all environmental time cues, such as sunlight/darkness cues, clocks, and schedules, researchers found that our internal body clock drifts into its natural or intrinsic rhythm, which is about 24.2 hours, or slightly longer than a day (Czeisler et al., 1999). Also, when deprived of all environmental time cues, the sleep–wake, body temperature, and melatonin circadian rhythms become desynchronized so that they are no longer properly coordinated with one another (Dijk & Lockley, 2002). Thus, exposure to environmental time signals is necessary to stay precisely synchronized, or entrained, to a 24-hour day. Practically speaking, this has some important applications for people traveling to a new time zone, where the circadian rhythms adjust slowly and remain on their original biological schedule for several days. Those people experience a group of symptoms collectively called jet lag. The psychological and physiological effects of disruption of the circadian rhythms can be severe, these include difficulty in thinking, lack of concentration, and memory, fatigue, depression or irritability, and disrupted sleep (Eastman, Gazda, Burgess, Crowley, & Fogg, 2005).

Contrary to the view that the circadian system consists of a single pacemaker in the brain, other opinions postulate that many processes are autonomously rhythmic. Independent circadian rhythms are found in many organs and cells in the body outside the suprachiasmatic nuclei (SCN). These cells, called peripheral oscillators, are found in the esophagus, the heart, the skeletal muscles, the lungs, the liver, the endocrine tissues, the spleen, the thymus, and the skin. These peripheral oscillators respond not only to the master pacemaker in the SCN, but also respond to other zeitgebers (timegivers), specific to the function of the organ under consideration. Also at the level of the SCN itself, views that consider the SCN as a single circadian oscillator, operating as a single entity, have been replaced by the view that the SCN is composed of many pacemaker cells with their own intrinsic periods, the interaction of which determines aspects of the ultimate circadian signal (Bell-Pedersen et al., 2005).

The Neurobiology of Sleep and the Circadian Rhythm

The suprachiasmatic nucleus of the hypothalamus is the circadian rhythm generator controlling the sleep–wake cycle, presumably by modulating the sleep–wake regulatory system, including the ventrolateral preoptic nucleus (VLPO) of the hypothalamus. The VLPO sends projections to the histaminergic tuberomamillary nucleus (TMN), the serotonergic dorsal and median raphe nucleus, and the noradrenergic locus ceruleus. It also sends axons that terminate within the cholinergic basal forebrain, the pedunculopontine thalamic (PPT) nucleus and the lateral dorsal thalamic (LDT) nucleus. The VLPO projections to these areas are inhibitory in nature as they are γ-aminobutyric acid-ergic (GABAergic) and galaninergic. The VLPO, via its inhibition of the major arousal mechanisms, functions as a "sleep switch," promoting sleep. Its reciprocal relationship with the major arousal areas helps it to function as one half of a "flip-flop" circuit, which prevents intermediate states of sleep and wakefulness (Saper, Chou, & Scammell, 2001; Saper, Lu, Chou, & Gooley, 2005).

The lateral hypothalamic area (LHA) contains orexinergic neurons that promote wakefulness. The orexinergic neurons inhibit the sleep-promoting VLPO and the REM sleep-promoting neurons in the PPT-LDT. The orexinergic neurons also increase the firing of the locus ceruleus, the dorsal raphe and the TMN and, in a way, represent the other half of the "flip-flop" circuit, that switches it into the wakefulness position.

The Regulation of Sleep

There is no unifying theory that explains the mechanisms explaining the occurrence of sleep. Current theories of sleep–wake regulation include the *two processes model* and the *opponent process model.*

The two processes model postulates that sleep and wakefulness are regulated by a sleep-dependent homeostatic process (Process S), in which sleep propensity is dependent on the duration of prior sleep and waking; it increases during waking and decreases during sleep, and is entirely determined by the temporal sequence of behavioral states. As soon as S reaches the lower limit during sleep, subjects will wake up. If S reaches the upper limit during waking, sleep will be initiated. However, the type of physiological or psychological processes that require sleep and the time interval needed to experience the need for sleep (Process S) are controversial. The second component of the model is the circadian process (Process C), this entails that each person has an endogenous drive to fall asleep and awaken at a certain time regardless of the duration of prior sleep or wake. Process C is totally controlled by the circadian pacemaker, irrespective of behavioral state, and is proposed to set limits to Process S. Circadian factors confer additional levels of somnolence at certain times of the day, particularly at 3.00 p.m. and 4.00 a.m. This may explain the rise in sleep-related traffic accidents at these times. This process is under the control of an independent circadian oscillator, which determines the rhythmic propensity to sleep and awaken.

The two processes model is criticized as being deterministic: sleep is initiated when Process S reaches the upper threshold that triggers sleep, and awakening happens at another reverse threshold. The occurrence of short awakenings at night cannot be understood in this model, nor can the occurrence of short naps during the day. Also, the two processes model involves theoretical constructs: the need for sleep, expressed in Process S, does not refer to a specific quantifiable variable of a specific physiological process. The same applies to Process C, it is not clear where and how a circadian pacemaker influences the timing of sleep and wakefulness.

The opponent process model postulates that the sleep–wake cycle is a result of the opposition of the previous two forces (the Process S and the Process C). The duration of wakefulness (the sleep load) facilitates sleep, which is opposed by an alerting signal generated by the circadian pacemaker. The opponent process model is based on the findings that SCN lesions in squirrel monkeys lead to increasing need for sleep during waking that is counteracted by a circadian process that stimulates wakefulness during daytime for diurnal species. This is supplemented by the observation that the progressive decrease in the need for sleep is similarly mirrored by a circadian process that increasingly stimulates sleep in the other half of the day.

The explanation of the opponent processes model for the short waking bouts during sleep and the short duration of naps is that the circadian pacemaker draws the system toward wakefulness during the active period and pushes it toward sleep in the inactive interval. Intervals of waking during the sleep period are likely to end soon due to the influence of the pacemaker. The same applies to the naps, after initiation, they are apt to last only for a short time because of the opposing influence of the pacemaker. However, neither of the two models can explain why intermittent waking bouts occur during sleep and why naps occur during the day.

No specific "sleep neurotransmitter" has been identified as responsible for the induction or maintenance of sleep, but many different types of neurochemicals (neurotransmitters, neuro-modulators, neuropeptides, and immune modulators) have been implicated. Adenosine is a potential sleep-promoting neurotransmitter, its concentration in the basal forebrain increases with prolonged wakefulness. Caffeine probably promotes alertness by blocking the adenosine A1 receptor. Histamine and glutamine also appear to play important roles in promoting alertness and brain activation. Of particular importance to psychiatry, acetylcholine, released from neurons originating in the dorsal tegmentum, induces REM sleep and cortical activation. Serotonin and norepinephrine, on the other hand, inhibit REM sleep, possibly by inhibition of cholinergic neurons responsible for REM sleep. These physiological mechanisms may be involved in both depression and the sleep disturbances associated with depression and other neuropsychiatric disorders, such as short REM latency (see below). The suppression of REM sleep during treatment with antidepressants may reflect either enhanced serotoninergic or noradrenergic neurotransmission or anticholinergic effects.

The Stages of Sleep

The precise definition of the onset of sleep is a matter of debate; there is no single measure that is clear-cut all the time. The invention of the electroencephalograph allowed scientists to study sleep in ways that were not previously possible. Human sleep studies demonstrated that sleep follows a relatively consistent pattern of stages in which different brain wave patterns are displayed. A typical nocturnal sleep begins with non-rapid eye movement (NREM) sleep, followed 80 minutes or longer later by rapid eye movement (REM) sleep. Both NREM sleep and REM sleep continue to alternate through the night, with an average 90-minute cycle, but the duration of cycles may vary from 70–120 minutes. REM sleep episodes usually become longer across the night, while stages 3 and 4 NREM sleep occupy less time in the second cycle and might disappear altogether from later cycles, and NREM sleep becomes composed primarily of stage 2 sleep.

The typical sleep pattern highlights features of the two processes model of sleep. The preferential distribution of slow wave sleep at the beginning of a sleep episode is thought to be dependent on the length of prior wakefulness, and mediated by the homeostatic sleep system, highest at sleep onset and diminishing across the night as sleep pressure wanes (Weitzman et al., 1980). The preferential distribution of REM sleep toward the latter portion of the night is thought to be linked to a circadian oscillator, which can be gauged by the oscillation of the body temperature (Czeisler et al., 1980; Zulley, 1980). The absolute amount of deep slow wave sleep during the night may predict how refreshed a subject feels in the morning.

Non-Rapid Eye Movement (NREM) Sleep

NREM (also known as quiet sleep) consists of four distinctive stages, and each progressive NREM sleep stage is characterized by corresponding decreases in brain and body activity. On average, the progression through the first four stages of NREM sleep occupies the first 50–70 minutes of sleep. NREM sleep accounts for 75–80 percent of sleep time. The onset of sleep is ushered in by alpha waves (8–13 Hz), which begin to interpose the high frequency beta waves of active wakefulness. The transition from being awake to entering NREM stage 1 sleep is called the hypnagogic period, and is sometimes included in NREM stage 1.

NREM Stage 1: This stage of sleep lasts only a brief time (around 5–10 minutes), during which the brain produces high amplitude theta waves (4–8 Hz), accompanied by slow rolling eye movements, the slowing of the heart rate, and relaxation of the muscles. This is a relatively light stage of sleep, and if you awaken someone in this stage, they might report that they were not really asleep. During this stage the person may experience strange and extremely vivid sensations known as hypnagogic hallucinations, e.g., feeling like you are falling or hearing someone call your name. Myoclonic jerks are common during this stage.

NREM Stage 2: Stage 2 sleep lasts for approximately 15–20 minutes. It is defined by the appearance of sleep spindles (bursts of 12–14 Hz waves, lasting at least 0.5 second, and having a spindle-shaped appearance), and K complexes (single high-voltage spikes of the whole EEG, that have two components: a negative wave followed by a positive wave, both lasting more than 0.5 second), which last up to 2 seconds. Brain activity continues to slow down considerably during stage 2; theta waves become predominant in stage 2, and slower delta waves (0.5–4 Hz) begin to emerge, but are present in small amounts.

During stage 2, the body temperature starts to decrease and the heart rate slows down, breathing becomes rhythmic, slight muscle twitches may occur, but the EMG activity is diminished compared to wakefulness. A more intense stimulus is required to produce arousal from this stage; the same stimulus that produced arousal from stage 1 sleep often results in an evoked K-complex but not awakening.

NREM Stage 3 and Stage 4: Stages 3 and 4 are often referred to in combination as slow-wave sleep (SWS), delta sleep, or deep sleep. The amount of delta brain-wave activity delineates each stage; delta waves represent more than 20 percent of total brain activity in stage 3 NREM, but exceed 50 percent of total brain activity in stage 4 NREM. Stage 3 sleep usually lasts only a few minutes in the first cycle and is transitional to stage 4. During SWS, sleep becomes deeper and the sleeper becomes less responsive to noises and activity in the environment. When people are briefly awakened by sleep researchers during stage 4 NREM and asked to perform some simple task, they often do not remember it the next morning. Heart rate, blood pressure, and body temperature all continue to drop. Bed-wetting and sleepwalking are most likely to occur at the end of stage 3 and typically occur in stage 4 of sleep. In a typical night's sleep, the sleeper spends approximately 70 minutes in deeply relaxed stage 4 NREM sleep. At that point, the sequence reverses in minutes, the sleep cycles back from stage 4 to stage 3 to stage 2 and enters the night's first episode of REM sleep.

Rapid Eye Movement Sleep (REM)

This phase of sleep is accompanied by considerable physiological arousal. Eyes move back and forth behind closed eyelids (the rapid eye movements), the heart rate, blood pressure, and respirations can fluctuate up and down. This phase is also known as paradoxical sleep, because while the brain and other body systems become more active, the muscles become more relaxed, which prevents the dreaming sleeper from acting out his or her dreams. Sexual arousal may occur in both sexes in this stage unrelated to dreams. Dreams usually occur during REM sleep. Stoppage of drugs that suppress REM sleep after prolonged intake lead to rebound symptoms, including vivid dreaming or even visual hallucinations. On average, we enter the REM stage approximately 90 minutes after falling asleep. The first cycle of REM sleep might last only 5–15 minutes, but each cycle becomes longer as sleep progress.

The Effects of Age on Sleep

PHOTO 6.2. Newborn Sleep.

The quantity and the quality of sleep change markedly across the lifespan. The newborn spends more than 16 hours asleep a day, but intermittently sleeps and awakens throughout the 24-hour period. Babies usually spend about 50 percent of the sleep time in REM sleep. The rest is spent in quiet sleep that is very similar to NREM stages 1 and 2. Slow-wave NREM sleep appears in the third month of life. The infant's sleep during the first months of life is characterized by shorter 50–60 minutes sleep cycles, producing up to 13 sleep cycles per day. At the age of 3 months, infants become able to sleep through the course of the night and take two or more daytime naps. By age 2 years, toddlers develop 75-minute sleep cycles. The typical 90-minute sleep cycles of alternating REM and NREM sleep develop at age 5 years (Grigg-Damberger, 2007; Jenni, Borbély, & Achermann, 2004). REM sleep decreases from more than 50 percent at birth to 20–25 percent during adolescence and middle age.

During teenage years, sleep onset becomes progressively later. Lifestyle factors and habits may fuel this tendency, however, there is evidence that most teenagers have internal clock mechanisms that predispose them to become "night owls." This sleep pattern leads to difficulty in rising at a conventional hour for educational purposes. The increased depth of non-REM sleep in younger subjects accounts for the extreme difficulty often encountered if children need to be awakened from deep sleep in the first third of the night. Forced arousals frequently produce apparent confusion or "sleep drunkenness," a phenomenon also frequently observed in sleep-deprived adults (Reading, 2013).

Beyond adolescence, the brain's internal clock tends to advance. The natural desire to sleep typically occurs around 30 minutes earlier with each subsequent decade. The National Sleep Foundation concluded that most adults need about 7–9 hours of sleep per night to function optimally, although those over 65 years might only require 7–8 hours. However, there are also short sleepers who appear to function adequately with less than 6 hours per night as well as long sleepers who may need 12 or more hours per night (Hirshkowitz et al., 2015).

Sleep consolidation progressively deteriorates with age. Several minor arousals, usually later in the night, might be considered normal in early middle age. In the healthy elderly, sleep fragmentation is very common. The depth of slow wave sleep (non-REM stages 3 and 4) is also reduced dramatically with age, with the earliest changes evident in males as young as 25 (Reading, 2013). The percentage of REM sleep increases during childhood and adolescence, remains stable throughout adulthood, and then decreases during late adulthood (Ohayon, Carskadon, Guilleminault, & Vitiello, 2004). Healthy older individuals may experience twice as much time awake during a night's sleep episode than young adults, suggesting that impaired sleep consolidation is associated with aging per se, rather than being a by-product of concurrent ailments linked to aging (Schmidt, Peigneux, & Cajochen, 2012).

Effects of Sleep Deprivation

Researchers found that sleep deprivation for one night led to episodes of sleep lasting only a few seconds (microsleeps) that occur during wakefulness among research subjects. Both total and partial sleep deprivation induce adverse changes in cognitive performance. First and foremost, total sleep deprivation impairs attention and working memory, long-term memory, and decision-making. Partial sleep deprivation is found to influence attention, especially vigilance (Alhola & Polo-Kantola, 2007). Sleeping as little as 4 hours per night produces diminished concentration, vigilance, reaction time, and memory skills, and reduces the ability to gauge risks. It also reduces motor skills, including driving skills, producing a greater risk of accidents. As sleep restriction continues, the abilities and reaction time are greatly diminished (Choudhary, Kishanrao, Dadarao Dhanvijay, & Alam, 2016). Mood, especially negative mood, becomes increased, especially feelings of fatigue, and loss of vigor (Durmer & Dinges, 2005). Metabolic and hormonal disruptions occur, including harmful changes in levels of stress hormones (Van Cauter, 2005). The immune system's effectiveness is diminished by sleep deprivation, making the person more susceptible to colds and infections (Motivala & Irwin, 2007). When infections set in, we typically sleep more, boosting our immune cells. No remarkable changes were observed in heart and breathing rates, blood pressure, skin conduction, body temperature, EMG or EEG, even when sleep deprivation continues for up to 200 hours (Pinel, 1993).

After several nights of selectively depriving REM sleep, when those subjects are allowed to sleep uninterrupted, they experience REM rebound, the amount of time spent in REM sleep increases by as much as 50 percent. Similarly, when people are selectively deprived of NREM stages 3 and 4, they experience NREM rebound, spending more time in NREM sleep (Borbély & Achermann, 2005; Tobler, 2005). Thus, it seems that the brain needs to experience the full range of sleep states, making up for missing sleep components when given the chance.

Clinical Assessment of Sleep

Sleep is clinically assessed using the following methods:

- a sleep history is taken;
- a sleep diary is compiled;
- actigraphy
- polysomnography
- the multiple sleep latency test.

These tests are performed by medical professionals.

- *Sleep history*: an accurate clinical history is the basis of proper diagnosis and treatment of a sleep disorder. It includes:
  - *Current sleep problem*: nature, severity, duration, frequency, time course, exacerbating and reliving factors, effect on daily life and/or impairments.

- *24-hour history*: the circumstances of sleep and wakefulness. Sleep-related questions may include activities prior to bedtime that may be incompatible with restful sleep, sleep latency (the time to fall asleep), number/duration/timing of night-time awakenings, snoring, limb movements, and other behaviors during sleep.
- *Daytime-related questions* may include naps, difficulty staying awake, inadvertent sleep episodes, use of alarm clocks, periods of confusion, and amount of time needed to fully awaken.
- *Regularity and timing* of sleep–wake behaviors over time.
- *Bed partner history*: the reporting of breathing problems (choking, snoring, gasping), limb or muscle movement during sleep as well as complex behaviors, such as sleep walking/talking, changes in mood, substance use.
- *Family history* of sleep disorders.
- *Medication use*, including timing and recent changes.
- *Substance use*, including the timing and use of caffeine, nicotine, alcohol, and illicit substances.
- *Previous treatments* and their effects on sleep disorders.
- *Keeping a sleep diary*: this is a record created by the patient detailing his or her sleep–wake pattern over a period of weeks. Information in the diary includes: daily activities, sleep/wake times, naps, exercise, mealtimes, and use of caffeine/nicotine/alcohol/other substances.
- *Actigraphy*: this is a method to measure motor activity, usually through an activity meter worn on the wrist. Data collected by this device may reveal general patterns of sleep and wakefulness.
- Polysomnography (PSG)
  - A polysomnogram includes at least one channel of electroencephalography (EEG) to measure brain activity, electrooculography (EOG) to measure eye movements, and electromyography (EMG) to measure muscle tone, usually in the submentalis muscles.
  - Additional channels of PSG may measure nasal-oral airflow or nasal pressure, chest and abdominal movement to measure breathing, oximetry to measure oxygen desaturation, and additional EMG channels of the anterior tibialis muscles to evaluate for movements before or during sleep.
  - Polysomnography is indicated for the evaluation of patients with suspected sleep apnea and in some cases of parasomnia. It is not routinely indicated for restless legs syndrome, circadian rhythm sleep disorders, and insomnia; in these disorders, the diagnosis relies on the clinical history.
- Multiple Sleep Latency Test (MSLT)
  - The MSLT is a variant of polysomnography used to evaluate daytime sleepiness. EEG, EOG, and EMG data are recorded while the patient is allowed to nap four to five times at two-hour intervals throughout the day. The sleep latency and presence or absence of rapid eye movement sleep for each nap are noted.
  - Mean sleep latency values >10 minutes are considered normal, while values <8 minutes suggest clinically significant sleepiness. The presence of REM sleep in at least two naps may indicate the presence of narcolepsy.

Sleep Disorders

The fifth revision of the APA's *Diagnostic and Statistical Manual* (DSM-5) (American Psychiatric Association, 2013) classifies sleep–wake disorders into 10 disorders: insomnia disorder, hypersomnolence disorder, narcolepsy, breathing-related sleep disorders, circadian rhythm sleep disorders, non-REM (NREM) sleep arousal disorders, nightmare disorder, REM sleep behavior disorder, restless legs syndrome, and substance- or medication-induced sleep disorder. The core features of each of these disorders relate to the patient's dissatisfaction regarding the quality, timing, and amount of sleep with resulting daytime distress and impairment. The DSM-5 sleep–wake classification provides both categorical and dimensional approaches to diagnosis and severity in order to facilitate measurement-based care in general mental health and medical or pediatric settings. The focus on measurement-based care is fundamental to the goals of the sleep–wake disorders classification.

Dreams

Dreams are the blend of images, emotions, sensations, and ideas that occur during sleep. Since ancient times, dreams have been a source of interest and discussion among philosophers and scientists, and interpretation of dreams has been practiced in many cultures for centuries. The formal study of dreaming is called oneirology. Dreaming is a universal human phenomenon. Studies of REM sleep suggest that even people who insist that they have never dreamed often dream as much as those who report dreaming. However, some studies suggest that preschool children do not dream and young children dream much less than adults (Foulkes, 1999). In addition, adults with certain types of brain damage also do not appear to dream (Solms, 1997).

William Domhoff stated that dreams are usually coherent, patterned, and thoughtful, rather than bizarre, dreams are generally a realistic simulation of waking life. Some aspects of dream content are unusual and perhaps nonsensical, but bizarre dream stories tend to be the exception, not the rule. Themes of dreams usually revolve about everyday settings, people, activities, and events, with only a relatively small amount of bizarreness. When emotions are experienced in dreams, they are usually appropriate in the context of the dream story. According to Domhoff (2003, 2007), patterns and themes dream are usually characterized as follows:

- Women report males and females in equal proportion as other dream story characters. However, men are more likely to report other males as the dream story characters.
- Women are more likely than men to report emotions in their dreams. Negative feelings and events are more common than positive ones, and instances of aggression are more common than are instances of friendliness, especially among people under the age of 30. Men are much more likely than women to report dreams involving physical aggression. Dreamers, especially women, are more likely to be victims of aggression than aggressors in their dreams.
- Sex or sexual behaviors seldom occur as elements of the dream story.

The content of dreams varies according to age, gender, and culture, leading some theorists to propose that dreaming is a cognitive process (Antrobus, 1991; Domhoff, 1996; Foulkes, 1985). Dream content may reflect personal conflicts, but dreams do not necessarily function to resolve those conflicts (Levin & Nielsen, 2007). In general, dreams cannot be viewed as simple extensions of the previous day's activities. A dream usually contains fragments related to the events of the previous day, but not full memories of episodes in the day (Nielsen & Stenstrom, 2005). In addition, there are more negative than positive emotions in dreams.

Domhoff (1996) found that the concerns and contents people express in their dreams are the concerns when they are awake. Domhoff and others refer to this as the "continuity theory" of dreaming, in which dreaming is an imaginative process that reflects the individual's conceptions, concerns, and emotional preoccupations. However, dreaming differs from waking thoughts in that it lacks intentionality and reflectiveness (Blagrove, 1992, 1996; Foulkes, 1985), and it is unlikely that dreaming has a problem-solving function, as most people remember only a small number of their many night dreams. More importantly, dreams collected inside and outside the sleep laboratory rarely have even a hint of a solution to a problem, and most of the anecdotal examples that are provided by proponents of the theory actually involve daydreams, drug-induced states, or thoughts while falling asleep or waking up (Domhoff, 2003).

The emotional content varies widely; it includes nightmares and terrors, social dreams with significant others that arouse happiness, dreams of loss of a loved one that provoke intense sadness, and bizarre dreams that arouse confusion and strangeness (Busink & Kuiken, 1996; Kuiken & Sikora, 1993). Apprehension or fear is the most frequently reported dream emotion for both sexes, followed by happiness and confusion. A nightmare is a vivid and disturbing dream that often awakens the sleeper. During a nightmare, the disturbing and emotionally charged dream imagery rapidly accelerates, often causing the person to awaken, and the person can immediately recall the exact, frightening dream details. Nightmares occur most commonly during middle and late childhood, and become less during adolescence and young adulthood. About 25 percent of children in the 5–11 age group report having at least one nightmare per week (Mindell & Barrett, 2002). In adults, occasional nightmares are reported by about 85 percent of people, while weekly nightmares are reported by 5–10 percent. Females at all ages report more frequent nightmares. Daytime stress, anxiety, and emotional difficulties are often associated with nightmares. As a general rule, nightmares are not indicative of a psychological or sleep disorder unless they occur frequently, cause difficulties returning to sleep, or cause daytime distress (Levin & Nielsen, 2007; Nielsen, Stenstrom, & Levin, 2006).

Theories of Dreaming

Why people dream and why they have certain dream content are not completely understood. There are many theories of dream function, which are highly speculative and difficult to disprove in a definitive way, therefore, they remain despite lack of evidence for any of them. Proposed explanations of dreams include wish fulfillment, memory consolidation, emotional regulation, and regulation and analysis of everyday life events.

In his (1900) book, *The Interpretation of Dreams*, Freud proposed that dreams provide a royal road to understand the unconscious activities of the mind. Freud believed that wish fulfillment is the meaning of each and every dream; dreams are a disguised attempt at wish fulfillment, in which dreams symbolize wishes, needs, or ideas that the individual finds unacceptable and have been repressed to the unconscious. Freud believed that dreams have two components: the *manifest content* or the dream images themselves, and the *latent content*, the disguised psychological meaning of the dream, e.g., Freud believed that dream images of sticks, swords, brooms, and other elongated objects were phallic symbols, representing the penis. Dream images of cupboards, boxes, and ovens supposedly symbolized the vagina. These wishes and ideas are the latent content of the dream (Freud, 1900). According to Freud, dreams function as a sort of psychological safety valve for the release of unconscious and unacceptable urges, and are seen as an important source of information about psychological conflicts in psychoanalytic psychotherapy (Pesant & Zadra, 2004).

Subsequent research has challenged several aspects of Freud's theory. Fisher and Greenberg (1977, 1996) stated that there is no evidence to support Freud's distinction between manifest and latent content, and they challenged Freud's view suggesting that the content of dreams has a psychological meaning. Evans (1983) assumed that our brain, like a computer, has programs for dealing with survival. Evans suggested that dreams are the means by which we both practice and update our programs of survival. Without the reprogramming occurring in dreams, we would be stuck at one level of behavioral maturity. As we gain in experience, we modify our programs rather than replacing them with a completely new set.

The evolutionary explanation of dreams proposes that it may act as mental simulation of potential real-life threatening events that allows for safe trials, and permits testing and analysis of possible responses. Thus, dreams may use past experiences to anticipate possible future experiences, and permit the testing of possibilities and scenarios which might help in dealing with those experiences whenever they occur. Some of the scenarios may be nonsensical, while others may be useful in providing some insights, and thus have at least a partial function.

Dreams may also help in resolving emotional problems and inconsistencies arising from our daily activities, and aid in mood regulation. Some studies revealed that people tend to report more negative emotions when awakened during REM sleep than during non-REM sleep, suggesting that REM dreams and non-REM dreams may have different, yet complementary, functions in this regard. The selective mood regulatory theory of dreaming assumes that the first main dream of the night is likely to be the most upsetting, while subsequent dreams become gradually better adjusted, in a continuing, and largely automatic process of emotional resolution. Dreams recur when this process becomes blocked at an early stage, and the emotional issues remain unresolved.

Although it is difficult to be sure that REM sleep in very young children is accompanied by dreams, some researchers assume that dreams play an important role in brain development in young children; this is based on the findings that REM sleep in the premature and full-term babies represents as much as 80 percent and 50 percent, respectively, of their total sleep time. This percentage continues to fall as the child grows, to around 35 percent at 1 year, and 20–25 percent in older children and adults.

The *activation–synthesis model* of dreaming, proposed by Allan Hobson and Robert McCarley in 1977, maintains that dreaming results from the forebrain's attempt to make sense of the random activation of the thalamocortical networks by the upper brainstem, like the music produced by unmusical fingers wandering over the keys of a piano (Hobson & McCarley, 1977). This model suggests that dreams are a physiological process that results from activation of the brain stem circuits during REM sleep, and the resulting activation of areas of the limbic system involved in emotions, sensations, and memories, including the amygdala and the hippocampus. Dreams result from attempts by the forebrain to synthesize the meaningless, apparently random images, thoughts, and feelings that are randomly thrown up by the brainstem, and interprets this internal activity and attempts to create meaning from these signals. Hence, dreams are epiphenomena or by-products of the REM state and are inherently meaningless (Solms & Turnbull, 2007). The dream story is derived from memories, emotions, and sensations that are triggered by the brain's activation and chemical changes during sleep. The activation–synthesis theory does not emphasize that dreams are completely meaningless, but if there is a meaning to dreams, it is not reached by decoding the dream symbols, but by analyzing the way the dreamer makes sense of the progression of chaotic dream images. The meaning lies in the personal way in which the images are organized, or synthesized (Hobson & McCarley, 1977).

Clinical Notes

Sleep is a fundamental human behavior. Inadequate sleep has adverse medical, psychiatric, and psychosocial consequences. On the other hand, sleep disturbances and disorders interact with common mental disorders, the two are mutually exacerbating. So, a good understanding of sleep across lifespan and in health and disease is of important clinical value, and ensures optimal outcomes for patients. In some people, sleep disorders represent a primary condition that needs an intervention of its own.

Summary

- A number of diverse theories have been proposed to explain the necessity of sleep as well as the functions and purposes of sleep. These include the repair and restoration theory, the evolutionary theory, the information consolidation theory, nourishing creative thinking, and the homeostatic regulation of sleep–wakefulness.
- A circadian rhythm is a rhythmic alternation of various physiological and psychological processes, synchronized to the 24-hour cycle of light and dark.
- Circadian rhythms are controlled by the suprachiasmatic nucleus (SCN), and environmental time cues.
- Current theories of sleep–wake regulation include the two processes model and the opponent process model.
- A typical nocturnal sleep begins with non-rapid eye movement (NREM) sleep, followed 80 minutes or longer later by rapid eye movement (REM) sleep. Both NREM sleep and REM sleep continue to alternate through the night, with an average 90-minute cycle, but the duration of cycles may vary from 70–120 minutes.
- The quantity and the quality of sleep change across lifespan.
- Sleep deprivation has a variable deleterious effect on mental and physical health.
- Clinical assessment of sleep could be achieved by taking a sleep history, keeping a sleep diary, actigraphy, polysomnography, and the multiple sleep latency test.
- The fifth revision of the APA *Diagnostic and Statistical Manual* (American Psychiatric Association, 2013) classifies sleep–wake disorders into 10 disorders.
- Dreaming is a universal human phenomenon. Studies of REM sleep suggest that even people, who insist that they have never dreamed, often dream as much as those who report dreaming.
- The content of dreams varies according to age, gender, and culture, leading some theorists to propose that dreaming is a cognitive process.
- The continuity theory of dreaming suggests that dreaming is an imaginative process that reflects the individual's conceptions, concerns, and emotional preoccupations.

Test Your Knowledge

- What are the functions of sleep?
- Give an account of the circadian rhythm.
- What is the effect of the circadian rhythm on sleep?
- Give an account of the regulation of sleep.
- What are the different stages of sleep?
- What are the effects of age on sleep?
- What are the effects of sleep deprivation?

- How can one assess sleep clinically?
- Describe Domhoff's patterns and themes of dreams.
- What are the theories of dreaming?
- What is the activation-synthesis model of dreaming?

Critical Thinking Questions

- How could understanding the neurobiology of sleep help in evaluating the effect of different psychoactive drugs on sleep?
- How were dreams considered in the different psychological schools?

Hypnosis

Hypnosis is a sleep-like trance in which those under hypnosis are open to the suggestions of the hypnotist but are not under the hypnotist's control. It is not a form of mind control, the subject is nearly always fully aware of what is happening and cannot be forced to do anything against his or her will. The hypnotist suggests to hypnotized individuals changes in their feelings, perceptions, thoughts, or behavior.

People vary in degrees of hypnotic responsiveness, only some people can be hypnotized. Even the best of hypnotists cannot hypnotize a subject who does not want to be hypnotized. In other words, whether or not a subject enters a hypnotic state is dependent upon the subject more than on the hypnotist. Those who are able to lose themselves in books and movies, or have active imaginations, are good candidates for hypnosis. Those who are content with the real world at all times are not likely to be nearly as responsive to hypnosis. This susceptibility is in no way tied to personality traits such as gullibility or submissiveness.

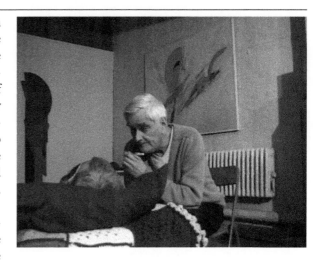

PHOTO 6.3.   Undergoing Hypnosis.

The core feature of hypnosis is suggestibility, the person displays a state of greatly enhanced receptiveness and responsiveness to suggestions and stimuli presented by the hypnotist. A wide range of psychological, sensory, and motor responses from persons who are deeply hypnotized can be induced by appropriate suggestions from the hypnotist; the subject can be induced to behave as if deaf, blind, paralyzed, hallucinated, delusional, amnesic, or impervious to pain or to uncomfortable body postures. In addition, the subject can display various behavioral responses that he or she regards as a reasonable or desirable response to the situation that has been suggested by the hypnotist.

Contrary to popular belief, hypnosis is not a guaranteed way to bring to the surface suppressed memories. Because the subject is highly responsive to the hypnotist's suggestions, answers to questions or recall of memories may be led in a particular way depending on how the suggestion is given. Also, the subject may have a vivid imagination and play out a role from that imagined state that leads the subject to believe that the experience is real, when it is merely a product of imagination.

Studies have shown that hypnosis can be quite effective in medical practice. Hypnosis has been used to alleviate chronic pain, stress, and anxiety, to reduce nausea in chemotherapy patients, and to help women manage pain during childbirth. It has even been used to anesthetize patients who are undergoing surgery. Some psychologists are able to use hypnosis to break unwanted habits, such as nail biting, or to increase self-esteem by boosting a subject's self-confidence in self and belief in their abilities.

Meditation

Meditation refers to an altered state of consciousness or focused attention and heightened awareness induced by a variety of techniques. These techniques include rituals and exercises, such as controlling breathing, restricting one's attention, eliminating external stimuli, assuming yogic body positions, and forming mental images of an event or a symbol. Though meditation is usually practiced independent of any religious tradition or spiritual context, it is essentially based on practices present in virtually all major religions, especially religions in India. Goals of meditation vary from the development of wisdom to a general well-being state in which the individual feels mentally and physically relaxed (Walsh & Shapiro, 2006).

PHOTO 6.4.   **Meditation.**

Meditation techniques can be divided into two general categories: *concentration techniques* and *opening-up techniques*. Concentration techniques include focusing awareness on a visual image, breathing, a word, or a phrase, e.g., while concentrating on a single image, repeating a simple sound, or repeating a short religious statement; meditators observe their own thoughts, attempt to modify them, or distance themselves from certain thoughts. In opening-up techniques, people attend uncritically to all potential stimuli; they clear their mind in order to receive new experiences. Rather than concentrating on an object, sound, or activity, the meditator engages in quiet awareness of the "here and now" without distracting thoughts.

Meditation can increase relaxation, decrease pain, decrease anxiety, and alleviate problems related to anxiety (Wachholtz & Pargament, 2008; Yunesian Aslani, Vash, & Yazdi, 2008). The medical and psychological benefits appear attributable to relaxation. However, few studies used double-blind procedures, and most studies fail to control for participants' expectations of benefits (Holmes, 1987). Many studies have shown that regular meditation can enhance physical and psychological functioning beyond that provided by relaxation alone (Andresen, 2000; Wittmann & Schmidt, 2014).

Clinical Notes

- Hypnosis can be used to alleviate chronic pain, stress, anxiety, to reduce nausea in chemotherapy patients, and to help women manage pain during childbirth.

- Meditation can increase relaxation, decrease pain, decrease anxiety, and alleviate problems related to anxiety.

Summary

- Hypnosis is a sleep-like trance in which those under hypnosis are open to the suggestions of the hypnotist but are not under the hypnotist's control.
- The core feature of hypnosis is suggestibility; the person displays a state of greatly enhanced receptiveness and responsiveness to suggestions and stimuli presented by the hypnotist.
- Meditation refers to an altered state of consciousness or focused attention and heightened awareness induced by a variety of techniques.
- Meditation techniques include concentration techniques and opening-up techniques.

Test Your Knowledge

- What is the core feature of hypnosis?
- How is hypnosis useful in clinical practice?
- What is meant by meditation?
- What use is meditation in clinical practice?

Critical Thinking Questions

- How could you evaluate hypnosis as a technique of therapy?
- How could you evaluate the usefulness of meditation in the management of anxiety?

Psychoactive Drugs

Some substances can chemically alter arousal, mood, thinking, sensation, and perception, these substances are called psychoactive drugs. These substances or drugs can be legal, such as tranquilizers and stimulant drugs, or illegal drugs, such as heroin and marijuana. Psychoactive drugs have been used by people since ancient times to stimulate or relax them, to improve sleep or prevent it, to enhance ordinary perceptions, or to produce hallucinations. The repeated use of psychoactive drugs is usually accompanied by:

- *Tolerance*: with continued use of a psychoactive drug, individuals need to take more of the drug to obtain the same effect.
- *Withdrawal symptoms*: when blood or tissue concentrations of a substance are reduced after prolonged use, the person experiences unpleasant physical and psychological responses, plus an intense craving for it. Withdrawal symptoms are usually opposite to the drug's action, e.g., withdrawal from a stimulant drug, like the caffeine in coffee, may produce depression and fatigue, while withdrawal from a depressant drug like alcohol may produce excitability.
- *Compulsive use*: the individual feels compelled to take these drugs to avoid withdrawal symptoms or to achieve the desired goal.

The degree of tolerance and the severity of withdrawal symptoms vary from one drug to another, e.g., tolerance for opiates develops quickly, and heavy users can tolerate high dosages that would be lethal to a non-user. In contrast, marijuana smokers occasionally develop a high level of tolerance. Withdrawal symptoms are common following heavy and sustained use of alcohol, opiates, and sedatives. Withdrawal symptoms are also common but less apparent for stimulants, and non-existent after repeated use of hallucinogens (American Psychiatric Association, 2013).

Psychoactive drugs typically activate dopamine receptors in the reward pathway of the brain, particularly the ventral tegmental area (VTA), and the nucleus accumbens. Psychoactive drugs can be categorized into four broad categories:

1. *Depressants* (also known as hypnotics or sedatives): drugs that decrease alertness by slowing down the activity of the brain. Depressant drugs include alcohol, opiates and opioids, benzodiazepines, barbiturates, and inhalants (volatile solvents and aerosols). Opiates and opioids (also known as narcotics) are sometimes separated as a distinct category due to their specific action on opiate receptors in the brain, through it they mediate relief from pain.
2. *Stimulants*: drugs that increase the body's state of arousal by increasing the activity of the brain (e.g., caffeine, nicotine, amphetamines, and cocaine).
3. *Hallucinogens* (also known as dissociative drugs or psychedelics): drugs that distort sensory perceptions (e.g., mescaline and LSD).
4. *Others*: some drugs may have properties of more than one of the above categories (e.g., cannabis has depressive, hallucinogenic and some stimulant properties).

Alcohol

Since ancient times people in most societies have consumed alcohol and synthesized it by fermenting grains and fruit. Alcohol is usually a part of social life to ease tension, release inhibitions, and generally to increase the fun. The prevalence of alcohol use varies greatly across nations and cultures. The alcohol used in beverages is called ethanol and consists of relatively small molecules that are readily absorbed and evenly distributed through the whole body. Even when used on an occasional basis in social situations, drinking can lead to loss of work time, poor performance the next morning, and arguments or accidents while intoxicated. In 2012, 5.1 percent of the burden of disease and injury worldwide (139 million disability-adjusted life-years) was attributable to alcohol consumption. In 2012, 3.3 million deaths, or 5.9 percent of all global deaths (7.6 percent for men and 4.0 percent for women), were attributable to alcohol consumption. In 2014, the World Health Organization reported that alcohol contributed to more than 200 diseases and injury-related health conditions, most notably DSM-IV alcohol dependence, liver cirrhosis, cancers, and injuries (World Health Organization, 2014).

According to the National Survey on Drug Use and Health (NSDUH) (SAMHSA, 2015), 33.1 percent of youths aged 15 years

PHOTO 6.5. A Variety of Alcoholic Drinks.

report that they have had at least one drink in their lives; about 20.3 percent of youths aged 12–20 reported drinking alcohol in the past month (19.8 percent of males and 20.8 percent of females). According to the NSDUH in 2015, 86.4 percent of people aged 18 or older reported that they have drunk alcohol at some point in their lifetime; 70.1 percent reported that they drank in the past year; 56.0 percent reported that they drank in the past month. In 2015, 26.9 percent of people aged 18 or older reported that they had engaged in binge drinking in the past month; 7.0 percent reported that they had engaged in heavy alcohol use in the past month.

Alcohol intoxication is often a factor in domestic and partner violence, child abuse, and public violent behavior (Easton, Mandel, & Babuscio, 2007; Shepherd, 2007). Alcohol is involved in more than half of all assaults, homicides, and motor vehicle accidents (Julien, 2008). An estimated 88,000 people (approximately 62,000 men and 26,000 women) die from alcohol-related causes annually, making alcohol the fourth leading preventable cause of death in the United States (Mokdad, Marks, Stroup, & Gerberding, 2004). In 2014, alcohol-impaired driving fatalities accounted for 9,967 deaths (31 percent of overall driving fatalities). Drinking during pregnancy is a leading cause of mental retardation and birth defects, it causes fetal alcohol syndrome.

Measuring the amount of alcohol in the expiratory air gives a reliable index of the amount of alcohol in the blood. Although the relationship between alcohol intake and blood alcohol concentrations is not simple but depends on multiple other factors, such as age, a person's sex, body weight, individual metabolism, experience with drinking, and speed of consumption, there is a clear correlation in the relationship between blood alcohol concentration and behavior:

- At concentrations of 0.03–0.05 percent in the blood (30–50 milligrams of alcohol per 100 milliliters of blood), alcohol produces light-headedness, relaxation, and disinhibition (the person loses control over things that they might not ordinarily say and tends to become more sociable and expansive). Self-confidence may increase, but motor reactions begin to slow, and fine tremors are observed. These effects make it dangerous for the drinker to drive after drinking.
- At concentrations of 0.10 percent, there is noticeable impairment in sensory and motor functions. Speech becomes slurred, and people have difficulty coordinating their movements with ataxic gait and poor balance. Some people become angry and aggressive, others grow silent and gloomy.
- At concentrations of 0.20 percent the drinker is seriously incapacitated with lethargy and has difficulty in sitting upright, difficulty in memory, and feels nausea and vomiting. Levels above 0.40 percent may cause coma and death.

Stoppage of alcohol consumption after heavy prolonged use usually leads to withdrawal symptoms. The severity of the withdrawal symptoms ranges from disrupted sleep, anxiety, and mild tremors (in mild cases), to confusion, hallucinations, and severe tremors or seizures in severe cases (delirium tremens). This is a serious condition that needs urgent medical interventions.

Opiates

Opiates are substances derived from the opium poppy that exert a strong pain-relieving effect and produce feelings of euphoria, e.g., morphine and codeine. Opiates act on specific receptors: mu (μ), kappa (κ), and sigma (σ). Mu receptors appear most important in analgesia (μ1), and respiratory depression and physical dependence (μ2) effects. These findings have led to the development of drugs that operate by modulating the opioid receptors. There are two basic

PHOTO 6.6.   The Poppy as a Source of Opiates.

types of drugs acting on opiate receptors: *agonists* and *antagonists*. Agonist drugs bind to the opioid receptors to produce a feeling of pleasure and thereby reduce the craving for opiates, but they cause less psychological and physiological impairment than the opiates. Antagonists block the receptors so that the opiates cannot gain access to them.

Synthetic and semi-synthetic drugs acting as agonists on opiate receptors are called opioids, e.g., heroin, methadone, oxycodone, and many of the prescription painkillers. The differences between opioid drugs depend on their potency, how quickly they reach the receptors and how much it takes to activate them. Illicit use of prescription painkillers is second only to use of marijuana (SAMHSA, 2009). Most illegal opiate use involves heroin because it is more concentrated and can be concealed and smuggled more easily than morphine.

The level of opiates in the body depends on the route of administration. When opiates are smoked or injected, they reach peak levels in the brain within minutes, creating an intense rush of euphoria that is followed by feelings of contentment, peacefulness, and warmth. When opiates are snorted, they are absorbed more slowly because they must pass through the mucous membranes of the nose to the blood vessels beneath. The faster this occurs, the greater the danger of death by overdose. The sense of well-being (euphoria and reduced anxiety) produced by opiates prompts people to repeat using these drugs. Tolerance and physical dependence develop after a brief period of usage. Experienced users report a special thrill, or rush, within a minute or two of intravenous injection of heroin. Some describe this sensation as intensely pleasurable, similar to an orgasm. Young people who sniff heroin report that they forget everything that troubles them. Following this, the user feels fixed, or gratified, and has no awareness of hunger, pain, or sexual urges.

Withdrawal from opiates produces uncomfortable drug rebound symptoms, including an intense drug craving, fever, chills, muscle cramps, and gastrointestinal problems, but it is not usually life-threatening for healthy adults. Nevertheless, reducing withdrawal symptoms may help to engage an addict in a treatment program or facilitate the management of another medical condition.

Because maintaining the habit is costly, the user often becomes involved in illegal activities to acquire money to purchase the drug. Death is caused by suffocation resulting from depression of the brain's respiratory center. Heroin use is generally associated with a serious deterioration of personal and social life. Sharing needles used to inject heroin increases the risk of HIV, hepatitis C, and other infections associated with nonsterile injections. A partial agonist, e.g., buprenorphine, activates mu-opioid receptors to a certain limit. So, buprenorphine intake produces analgesia and euphoria. However, increasing the dosage of buprenorphine does not lead to additional euphoric effects (the ceiling effect).

Methadone is an opioid agonist drug that is used in the treatment of heroin dependence. When taken orally in low doses, it suppresses the craving for heroin and prevents withdrawal symptoms. Although it is addictive in its own right, it produces less psychological impairment than heroin and has few disruptive physical effects.

Naltrexone is an opioid antagonist drug that blocks the action of heroin because it has a greater affinity for the opioid receptors than does heroin itself. It is often used in hospital emergency rooms to reverse the effects of a heroin overdose.

Benzodiazepines

Benzodiazepines are a group of drugs that are anxiolytic, hypnotic, anticonvulsant, and used as muscle relaxants. Benzodiazepines enhance GABA transmission and produce a marked anxiolytic and euphoriant effect. All benzodiazepines have similar effects and are distinguished by their length of action: short-acting (e.g., temazepam, oxazepam), medium-acting (e.g., lorazepam, alprazolam), long-acting (e.g., diazepam, nitrazepam, chlordiazepoxide). Benzodiazepines are usually taken orally, or less commonly by injection. Tolerance develops rapidly to benzodiazepine, with cross-tolerance to the whole group. Long-term use results in drug dependence. When stopped, withdrawal symptoms are experienced, and these can be complicated by seizures and delirium.

Barbiturates

Barbiturates are a group of drugs that were used as hypnotics/anxiolytics prior to the introduction of the benzodiazepines. They act by facilitating GABA neurotransmission. Barbiturates depress activity in the brain centers that control arousal, wakefulness, and alertness. They also depress the brain's respiratory centers. Like alcohol, barbiturates at low doses cause relaxation, mild euphoria, and reduced inhibitions. Larger doses produce a loss of coordination, impaired mental functioning, and depression. High doses can produce unconsciousness, coma, and death. Barbiturates produce a very deep but abnormal sleep in which REM sleep is greatly reduced.

Tolerance develops rapidly to their anxiolytic effects in regular use but not to the associated respiratory depression. Because of the additive effect of depressants, barbiturates combined with alcohol are particularly dangerous. Common barbiturates include the prescription sedatives secobarbital and pentobarbital. Barbiturates produce both physical and psychological dependence. Withdrawal from low doses of barbiturates produces irritability and REM rebound nightmares. Withdrawal from high doses of barbiturates can produce hallucinations, disorientation, restlessness, and life-threatening convulsions.

Inhalants

Inhalants are chemical substances that are inhaled to produce an alteration in consciousness, e.g., paint solvents, spray paint and paint thinner, gasoline, nitrous oxide, and aerosol sprays. Inhalants do not have a common chemical structure, but they generally act as central nervous system depressants. Inhalants are inexpensive and readily available, and are most prevalent among adolescent and young adult males.

At low doses, they may cause relaxation, giddiness, and reduced inhibition. The effects of inhalants usually last only a few minutes, leading

PHOTO 6.7.   Inhalants.

to repeated inhalation to prolong the high. At higher doses, inhalants can lead to hallucinations and a loss of consciousness. Chronic abuse leads to brain damage, MRI scans showed that the inhalant users had more extensive brain damage than cocaine users (Rosenberg, Grigsby, Dreisbach, Busenbark, & Grigsby, 2002). Inhalants users also scored below the cocaine abusers on problem-solving and memory tests, and both groups scored well below the normal population.

Stimulant drugs

Caffeine

Caffeine is the most widely used psychoactive drug in the world. It is found in drinks like coffee, tea, cola drinks, and in chocolate and certain over-the-counter medications. Caffeine is usually used to promote wakefulness, mental alertness, and vigilance. Excess caffeine can produce anxiety, restlessness, and increased heart rate and can disrupt normal sleep patterns and can also contribute to the incidence of sleep disorders, including the NREM parasomnias, like sleepwalking (Cartwright, 2004). There is clear scientific evidence that caffeine is physically addictive. If caffeine intake is abruptly stopped, withdrawal symptoms are experienced: headaches, irritability, drowsiness, and fatigue can last a week or longer (Juliano & Griffiths, 2004; Reissig, Strain, & Griffiths, 2009).

PHOTO 6.8.   Caffeine.

Nicotine

Nicotine is highly addictive, both physically and psychologically (Laviolette & van der Kooy, 2004). Nicotine is found in all tobacco products, including pipe tobacco, cigars, cigarettes, and smokeless tobacco. About 19.4 percent of American adults are cigarette smokers (Substance Abuse and Mental Health Services Administration, 2015). The proportion of smokers is much higher in Japan, many European countries, and developing countries. Nicotine increases mental alertness and reduces fatigue or drowsiness. Brain-imaging studies show that nicotine increases neural activity in many brain areas, including the frontal lobes, the thalamus, the hippocampus, and the amygdala (Rose et al., 2003). Thus, it is not surprising that smokers report that tobacco enhances mood, attention, arousal, and vigilance. When cigarette smoke is inhaled, nicotine reaches the brain in seconds. But over the next hour or two, nicotine's desired effects diminish. For the addicted person, smoking becomes a finely tuned and regulated behavior so that steady brain levels of nicotine are maintained. At regular intervals ranging from about 30–90 minutes, the smoker lights up to avoid the occurrence of withdrawal symptoms.

PHOTO 6.9.   Nicotine.

People who start smoking for nicotine's stimulating properties often continue smoking to avoid the withdrawal symptoms. Withdrawal symptoms include irritability, tremors, headaches, impaired concentration, and light-headedness.

Amphetamines

Amphetamines are synthetic substances that act primarily by increasing the release of dopamine. In addition, they inhibit the dopamine metabolism and its reuptake, and increase the release of noradrenaline and serotonin. Amphetamines are frequently prescribed for attention deficit hyperactivity disorder (ADHD), and to treat narcolepsy, treatment-resistant depression, and obesity.

The immediate effects of non-medical use of amphetamines are increased concentration and alertness, euphoria, mood elevation, and a sense of well-being, and an increase in energy and a reduction in fatigue. Amphetamines can be used orally, snorted, or injected intravenously. Tolerance develops quickly, and the user needs increasingly larger doses to produce the desired effect. Symptoms of use will show up immediately if it is injected, within 3–5 minutes if it is snorted and within 15–20 minutes if it is ingested. When tolerance develops to oral doses to the point at which they are no longer effective, intravenous amphetamines are used to produce an immediate pleasant experience (a "flash" or "rush"). This sensation is followed by irritability and discomfort, which can be overcome only by an additional injection.

Long-term use of amphetamines is accompanied by psychotic symptoms, including persecutory delusions and visual or auditory hallucinations. The delusions may lead to unprovoked violence. Chronic amphetamine abusers are likely to be severely malnourished and suffering serious mental effects from the drug use. Withdrawal symptoms include depression, anxiety, and extreme fatigue.

Cocaine

Cocaine or coke is a substance obtained from the dried leaves of the coca plant, which is found in South America. Cocaine produces intense euphoria, mental alertness, and self-confidence, mostly because of blocking the reuptake of three different neurotransmitters: dopamine, serotonin, and norepinephrine. Cocaine is a highly addictive substance that can be inhaled or snorted, or made into a solution and injected intravenously. It can also be converted into a flammable compound, "crack," which is smoked. Tolerance develops with repeated use, and withdrawal effects include restless irritability and a feeling of depressed anguish.

PHOTO 6.10.   Cocaine.

The effects of cocaine depend on whether it is snorted, swallowed, smoked, or injected. When smoked or injected, cocaine reaches the brain in seconds and its effects peak in about 5 minutes. Crack cocaine, a more concentrated form of cocaine, is smoked. (The name crack refers to the sound of the cocaine crystals popping and cracking when smoked.) When snorted, the nasal membranes absorb cocaine more slowly, with peak blood levels occurring some 30–60 minutes later.

Prolonged use of cocaine can result in stimulant-induced psychosis (also called cocaine-induced psychosis), manifest as visual hallucinations (commonly flashes of light, "snow lights," or moving lights), and less common tactile hallucination (feeling that bugs—"cocaine bugs"—are crawling under one's skin) that may be so strong that the individual tries to use a knife to cut out the bugs. In response to imagined threats, the psychotic person can become highly aggressive and dangerous.

Hallucinogens

Hallucinogens are drugs taken recreationally to alter thoughts, perceptions, and emotions. Hallucinogens may be natural, like mescaline, psilocin, and psilocybin, or synthetic, like lysergic acid diethylamide (LSD).

Hallucinogens can be classified into two subcategories: the *classic hallucinogens* and the *dissociative drugs*, but they are typically classified pharmacologically according to the affected neurotransmitter system. Cholinergic hallucinogens (drugs altering acetylcholine transmission) include physostigmine, scopolamine, and atropine. Drugs that alter norepinephrine transmission include mescaline and ecstasy. Drugs that alter serotonin transmission include LSD and psilocin. Drugs that alter glutamate transmission include phencyclidine (PCP) and ketamine. Marijuana is often classified as a hallucinogen substance, though it produces sensory distortions only at high doses.

Hallucinogens produce visual, tactile, and auditory hallucinations. Euphoria may occur, but these drugs also commonly cause confusion, agitation, paranoid delusions, loss of social inhibitions, and wildly labile emotions. Large doses of hallucinogens can cause ruptured blood vessels in the brain, seizures, and potentially fatal respiratory and heart failure.

The effects of hallucinogens vary greatly, depending on an individual's personality, current emotional state, surroundings, and the other people present. Tolerance to hallucinogens may occur after heavy use. However, even heavy users of LSD do not develop physical dependence, nor do they experience withdrawal symptoms. Adverse reactions to LSD include flashbacks (recurrences of the drug's effects), extreme anxiety, panic, depression, and even psychotic episodes (Seymour & Smith, 1998). In a psychologically unstable or susceptible person, even a single dose of LSD can precipitate a psychotic reaction.

Dissociative anesthetics include phencyclidine (PCP) and ketamine. These drugs were originally developed for surgical use as anesthetics in the late 1950s, before being abandoned due to their psychological effects. PCP can be eaten, snorted, or injected, but it is most often smoked or sprinkled on tobacco or marijuana. The effects are unpredictable, and a PCP effect can last for several days.

Phencyclidine and ketamine produce marked feelings of dissociation and depersonalization. Feelings of detachment from reality, including distortions of space, time, and body image are common. PCP users can become severely disoriented, violent, aggressive, or suicidal. High doses of PCP can cause hyperthermia, convulsions, and death. PCP affects the levels of the neurotransmitter glutamate, indirectly stimulating the release of dopamine in the brain. Thus, PCP is highly addictive. Memory problems and depression are common effects of long-term use.

Other Drugs

Some drugs do not properly fit into a specific category, these essentially are cannabis and ecstasy.

Cannabis

The cannabis plant has been cultivated since ancient times for its psychoactive properties. It creates a high feeling, cognitive and motor impairment, and sometimes hallucinations. The dried leaves, stems, flowers, and seeds are used to produce marijuana, while the resin of the plant is used to produce hashish. Marijuana and hashish are usually smoked but may be taken orally, mixed with tea or food. The active ingredient in both substances is tetrahydrocannabinol (THC). When marijuana is smoked, THC reaches the

PHOTO 6.11. The Cannabis Plant.

brain in less than 30 seconds. Low doses of THC (5–10 milligrams) typically produce a sense of well-being, mild euphoria, and a dreamy state of relaxation. At high doses (30–70 milligrams), marijuana may produce sensory distortions that resemble those of hallucinogenic drugs.

The method of smoking can affect the amount of THC reaching the body; a cigarette allows the transfer of 10–20 percent of the THC in the marijuana, whereas a pipe allows the transfer of about 40–50 percent of the THC in the marijuana. A water pipe traps the smoke until it is inhaled and therefore is a highly efficient means of transferring THC. Once in the brain, the THC binds to cannabinoid receptors, which are especially numerous in the hippocampus. Because the hippocampus is involved in the formation of new memories, it is not surprising that marijuana use inhibits memory formation, people under the influence of marijuana may lose the thread of a conversation or forget what they are saying in the middle of a sentence because of momentary distractions.

Marijuana use is not always pleasurable: 16 percent of regular users report anxiety, fearfulness, and confusion as a usual occurrence, and about one-third report that they occasionally experience such symptoms as acute panic, hallucinations, and unpleasant distortions in body image. Individuals who use marijuana regularly (daily or almost daily) often report both physical and mental lethargy, and about a third show mild forms of depression, anxiety, or irritability (American Psychiatric Association, 2013).

Motor coordination is significantly impaired, and reaction time for car braking and the ability to drive in a twisting road course are adversely affected by low to moderate doses of marijuana. The effects of marijuana may persist long after the subjective feelings of euphoria or sleepiness have passed. However, THC declines rapidly in the blood, quickly going to the fatty tissues and organs of the body. A blood analysis performed 2 hours after a heavy dose of marijuana may show no signs of THC, even though an observer would judge the person to be clearly impaired. Urine tests do not detect the psychoactive component in marijuana (THC), and therefore in no way measure impairment, rather, they detect the non-psychoactive marijuana metabolite THC-COOH, which can remain in the body for days and weeks with no impairing effects.

Chronic use of high doses of marijuana can lead to tolerance to THC and development of withdrawal symptoms when its use is discontinued (Budney, Roffman, Stephens, & Walker, 2007; Nocon, Wittchen, Pfister, Zimmermann, & Lieb, 2006). Such symptoms include irritability, restlessness, insomnia, tremors, and decreased appetite.

Ecstasy

Ecstasy (methylenedioxymethamphetamine, MDMA) was developed in 1912 for possible use as an appetite suppressant, but it was not tested on humans until the 1970s.

Structurally similar to both mescaline and amphetamine, MDMA has stimulant and psychedelic (hallucinogenic) effects. Ecstasy act through enhancing the release of serotonin, blocking the serotonin reuptake, amplifying and prolonging the serotonin effects (Braun, 2001). At low doses, MDMA acts as a stimulant, but at high doses it has mild psychedelic effects.

The popularity of ecstasy stems from its emotional effects: feelings of euphoria and increased well-being are common. Users experience increased energy and restlessness,

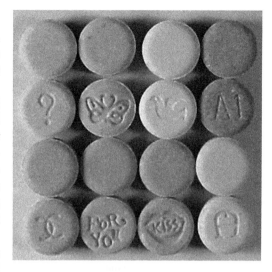

PHOTO 6.12.   A Range of Ecstasy Pills.

and feel their affection for others being increased, open, and more close, while their social inhibitions decrease, effects that led to its use in psychotherapy for a brief time until its adverse effects became apparent (Braun, 2001).

While flooding the brain with serotonin initially enhances feelings of emotional well-being, this is followed by depression when the drug wears off. Serotonin levels become severely depleted after long-term use, possibly causing the depression that follows when the drug wears off (Kuhn & Wilson, 2001). Several studies show that moderate or heavy use of ecstasy can damage serotonin neurons in the brain (Croft, Klugman, Baldeweg, & Gruzelier, 2001; Reneman, Schilt, & de Win, 2006).

Frequent use of ecstasy can lead to a broad range of cognitive problems, such as impaired memory and decision-making (Kalechstein, De La Garza, Mahoney, Fantegrossi, & Newton, 2007; Montgomery & Fisk, 2008). Even occasional use of ecstasy may produce memory problems (Schilt et al., 2007). Memory and verbal reasoning problems may persist up to a year after the last dose of ecstasy (Reneman et al., 2001).

Clinical Notes

Owing to the effect of psychoactive substances on arousal, mood, thinking, sensation, and perception, a good understanding of the effect of the use of these substances on these psychological functions is of utmost importance in clinical practice. Knowledge of symptoms and management of intoxication and withdrawal of these substances provides the basis of the necessary interventions in emergency departments.

Summary

- Psychoactive drugs can chemically alter arousal, mood, thinking, sensation, and perception.
- The repeated use of psychoactive drugs is usually accompanied by tolerance, withdrawal symptoms, and compulsive use.

- Psychoactive drugs typically activate dopamine receptors in the reward pathway of the brain.
- Psychoactive drugs can be categorized into four broad categories: depressants (alcohol, opiates and opioids, benzodiazepines, barbiturates, and inhalants); stimulants (caffeine, nicotine, amphetamines, and cocaine); hallucinogens (mescaline and LSD); and others (cannabis, ecstasy, ketamine, and PCP).

Test Your Knowledge

- What is the effect of alcohol consumption and stoppage?
- What are the types of opiates?
- What is the effect of using inhalants?
- What is the effect of using amphetamines?
- What is the effect of using cocaine?
- What is the effect of using hallucinogens ?
- What is the effect of using dissociative anesthetics?

Critical Thinking Questions

- How could you evaluate the possible risk factors of drug dependence?
- How could you explain the development of transient or persistent drug-induced psychosis?

seven
Gender and Sexuality

Learning Goals

■ This chapter is intended to provide the reader with an overview of the different components of sexuality, the development of sexual identity, the development of gender identity, sexual development, the factors that influence the timing of puberty, the sexual response cycle, sexual changes through the life cycle, sexuality across cultures, and sexual dysfunction.

Introduction

Sexuality is fundamental to the well-being of humanity on many levels: individual, interpersonal, societal, and global. It has been a consistent focus of curiosity, interest, and analysis to humankind. Depictions of sexual behavior have existed from the time of prehistoric cave drawings through da Vinci's anatomical illustrations of intercourse to current pornographic sites available on the internet. Sexual behavior—solitary and partnered, normal and abnormal—is multi-determined, being simultaneously influenced by biological, personal, interpersonal, and cultural forces. Sexuality slowly develops over decades and rapidly oscillates during short periods of time. Biological and psychological maturation creates different sexual challenges at each life era. Short-term fluctuations are produced by the inevitable changes of our biological, psychological, and interpersonal states. Each of us has a dynamic potential to change: from normal to dysfunctional, from dysfunctional to normal, and from ordinary to remarkable.

Components of Sexuality

An adult's sexuality has several components, this includes gender identity, sexual orientation, sexual intention, sexual desire, sexual arousal, orgasm, and emotional satisfaction. The first three components constitute our *sexual identity*, while the second three comprise our *sexual function*. The seventh component, emotional satisfaction, is based on our personal reflections on the first six. Box 7.1 presents a glossary of terms used.

BOX 7.1 Definition of Terms

Gender   refers to the attitudes, feelings, and behaviors that a given culture associates with a person's biological sex.

Gender expression   refers to the way in which a person acts to communicate gender within a given culture, e.g., clothing, communication patterns, and interests. A person's gender expression may or may not be consistent with socially prescribed gender roles, and may or may not reflect their gender identity.

Gender identity   refers to one's feeling like a man, woman, nonbinary, gender non-conforming, and/or transgender. When one's gender identity and biological sex are not congruent, the individual may identify as outside of the male/female gender binary.

PHOTO 7.1.   Gender Identity.

Gender role   includes all the things that a person says or does to disclose himself or herself as having the status of a boy or a man, a girl or a woman, respectively. A gender role is not established at birth but is built up cumulatively through experiences encountered and transacted through casual and unplanned learning, and explicit instruction. The usual outcome is a congruence of gender identity and gender role. Although biological attributes are significant, the major factor in identifying with socially accepted gender roles is through learning.

Culturally acceptable gender roles exist: boys are not expected to be effeminate, and girls are not expected to be masculine.

PHOTO 7.2.   Girl as Feminine Gender Identity.

There are boys' games (e.g., cops and robbers) and girls' toys (e.g., dolls and dollhouses). Although these roles are learned, some investigators believe that some boys are temperamentally delicate and sensitive and that some girls are aggressive and have traits that are stereotypically known in today's culture as feminine and masculine, respectively. In the past few decades, greater tolerance has been developed for mild cross-gender activity in children.

Research on sex differences in children's behavior reveals more psychological similarities than differences. Girls, however, are found to be less susceptible to tantrums after the age of 18 months than are boys, and boys generally are more physically and verbally aggressive than are girls from age 2 onward. Little girls and little boys are similarly active, but boys are more easily stimulated to sudden bursts of activity when they are in groups. Some researchers speculate that, although aggression is a learned behavior, male hormones may have sensitized boys' neural organizations to absorb these lessons more easily than do girls.

Sexual identity   refers to the pattern of a person's biological sexual characteristics: chromosomes, external genitalia, internal genitalia, hormonal composition, gonads, and secondary sex characteristics. Typically, these characteristics form a cohesive pattern that leaves a person in no doubt about his or her sex. Sexual identity and gender identity are interactive. Genetic influences and hormones affect behavior and the environment affects hormonal production and gene expression.

Sexual orientation   refers to the sex of those to whom one is sexually and romantically attracted. Categories of sexual orientation typically include attraction to members of the opposite sex (heterosexual), to members of one's own sex (homosexual), to members of both sexes (bisexual). While these categories continue to be widely used, research has suggested that sexual orientation does not always appear in such definable categories and instead occurs on a continuum. In addition, some research indicates that sexual orientation is fluid for some people.

For centuries, homosexuality was considered to be either a mental illness or a sexual abnormality related to hormonal imbalance, that designation was removed from the DSM in the 1980s. While the exact cause of homosexuality is unknown, it is now widely accepted in the health professions that the two most commonly repeated myths about sexual orientation—that homosexuality is caused by childhood sexual abuse or by an abnormal relationship with a parental figure—are both false.

Considering that biological factors play a strong role in motivating sexual behavior, it is only natural that there has been considerable interest in the possible biological causes of sexual orientation. However, experiments involving hormonal manipulation seemed to affect only the person's sex drive and not his or her sexual preference. Bailey and Pillard's (1991) twins study suggested that there may be a genetic component involved in determining sexual orientation: 52 percent of identical twins shared the same sex orientation, while the number drops to 22 percent among fraternal twins. However, the conclusions of this, and other genetic studies are limited by their reliance on self-selected volunteers and associated ascertainment biases. No candidate genes have been identified.

Development of Sexual Identity

Embryological studies show that all mammalian embryos, whether genetically male (XY genotype) or genetically female (XX genotype), are anatomically female during the early stages of fetal life. Differentiation of the male from the female results from the action of fetal androgens, the action begins about the sixth week of embryonic life and is completed by the end of the third month.

So, a male is produced only if the Y chromosome initiates androgen production (which is responsible for testicular development). Without testes and androgen, female external genitalia develop. Thus, maleness and masculinity depend on fetal and perinatal androgens. The expression of sexual behavior in mature men or women is influenced by sex steroids, that is, testosterone can increase libido and aggressiveness in women, and estrogen can decrease libido and aggressiveness in men. However, postnatal life events influence masculinity, femininity, and gender identity more than prenatal hormonal organization (Sadock, Sadock, & Ruiz, 2015).

Development of Gender Identity

By 2 or 3 years of age, most children can correctly label their own gender, and the stereotypical behaviors that go with them.

Children usually develop a gender identity that is consistent with their sex of rearing. The formation of gender identity is complex, and is influenced by the interaction of an infinite series

PHOTO 7.3.   Boy as Masculine Gender Identity.

of cues and expectations derived from experiences with family members, teachers, and friends. Physical characteristics derived from a person's biological sex, such as physique, and body shape interact with a complex system of stimuli, including rewards and punishment and parental gender labels, to establish gender identity. How parents raise their children might play an important role in the fostering and development of a child's sense of gender identity. According to some experts, kids who are raised more in line with socially and culturally accepted notions of gender may be more likely to identify with their assigned sex. Conversely, kids who are raised outside of socially and culturally accepted gender norms may grow to experiment more with their gender identity and identify outside of the gender binary. Of course, this is by no means true of all kids; those who are raised more in line with socially and culturally accepted notions of gender may also grow up to identify outside of the gender binary, and conversely, kids who are raised outside of socially and culturally accepted gender norms may continue to identify in line with their assigned sex. In addition, the absence of parents also has an influence on the development of gender identity (Sadock, Sadock, & Ruiz, 2015).

Sexual Development

Adolescence is the period of time between late childhood and adulthood. It is a time of important physical development as well as social, emotional, and psychological growth. Human adolescence officially begins with the onset of puberty, when a person becomes physically able to reproduce. A huge rush of hormones marks the beginning of puberty and rapid physical development ensues. Puberty usually begins in a girl around age 11 and around age 13 in boys, though the age of onset can vary.

The physical changes associated with puberty include the development of primary and secondary sex characteristics. Primary sexual characteristics are those needed for reproduction, these involve development of the uterus in girls, and testicles in boys. Girls begin their menstrual cycle. Boys might experience their first ejaculation. Secondary sexual characteristics are not necessary for reproduction but appear during sexual maturation, these include breast development and widening of the hips in girls and voice changes and facial hair in boys.

Factors that Influence the Timing of Puberty

Both biological and environmental factors play a role in controlling the timing of puberty, e.g., girls typically begin to menstruate around the same age that their mothers did (Ersoy, Sadock, & Ruiz, 2005). Similarly, the timing of pubertal changes tends to be closer for identical twins than for non-twin siblings (Mustanski, Viken, Kaprio, Pulkkinen, & Rose, 2004), suggesting that heredity plays an important role. Environmental factors, such as nutrition and overall health, also determine when puberty begins. Generally, well-nourished and healthy children begin puberty earlier than do children who have experienced serious health problems or inadequate nutrition. As living standards and health care have improved, the average age of puberty has steadily been decreasing in many countries over the past century. The average age of menarche in the United States and other developed countries 150 years ago was about 17 years old. Today it is about 13 years old. Similarly, boys develop the physical changes of puberty about a year earlier today than they did in the 1960s (Irwin, 2005).

Girls who develop early maturation tend to have negative feelings about their body image and pubertal changes, such as menarche, compared with late-maturing girls (Ge et al., 2003). This may be due to receiving less information about development, or being embarrassed by unwanted attention from older males (Brooks-Gunn & Reiter, 1990). On the other hand, early-maturing girls have higher rates of sexual risk-taking, drug and alcohol use, and delinquent behavior, and are at greater risk of unhealthy weight gain later in life (Adair & Gordon-Larsen, 2001; Belsky, Steinberg, Houts, & Halpern-Felsher, 2010). Early maturation can be advantageous for boys, but it is also associated with risks. Those boys tend to be popular with their peers. However, early-maturing boys are more prone to feelings of depression, problems at school, and engaging in drug or alcohol use (Ge et al., 2003; Hayatbakhsh, Najman, McGee, Bor, & O'Callaghan, 2009).

Sexual Response Cycle

Sexual response is a true psychophysiological experience. Normally, men and women experience a sequence of physiological responses to sexual stimulation. In the first detailed description of these responses, William Masters and Virginia Johnson observed that the physiological process involves increasing levels of vasocongestion and myotonia (tumescence) and the subsequent release of the vascular activity and muscle tone as a result of orgasm (detumescence). The phases of response cycle include: phase 1, desire; phase 2, arousal; phase 3, orgasm; phase 4, resolution. It is important to remember that the sequence of responses can overlap and fluctuate. Psychosexual development, psychological attitudes toward sexuality, and attitudes toward one's sexual partner are directly involved with, and affect, the physiology of human sexual response.

1. *Desire phase*: this phase consists of fantasies about sexual activity and the desire to have sexual activity. In this phase, one or more stimuli (e.g., visual, olfactory, tactile, fantasies) stimulate a desire to engage in sexual activity.
2. *Arousal phase*: this phase consists of a subjective sense of physical pleasure and accompanying changes. The major changes in the male consist of penile tumescence and erection. The major changes in female consist of vasocongestion in the pelvis, vaginal lubrication and expansion, and swelling of the external genitalia. The arousal phase, brought on by psychological stimulation (fantasy or the presence of a love object) or physiological stimulation (stroking or kissing) or a combination of the two, consists in a subjective sense of pleasure.

3. *Orgasmic phase*: this phase consists of a peaking of sexual pleasure, with release of sexual tension and rhythmic contraction of perineal muscles and reproductive organs. In the male, there is the sensation of ejaculatory inevitability, which is followed by ejaculation of semen. In the female there are contractions of the wall of the outer third of the vagina. In both genders, the anal sphincter rhythmically contracts.

4. *Resolution phase*: this phase consists of a sense of muscular relaxation and general well-being. During this phase, males are physiologically refractory to further erection and orgasm for a variable period of time. In contrast, females may be able to respond to additional stimulation almost immediately.

Sexual Changes through the Life Cycle

While the psychological foundations for a healthy sexual life are laid down during childhood through parent-child relationships, each subsequent phase of life (adolescence, young adulthood, middle life, and older age) has inherent developmental challenges and potentials. The normal tasks of sexual development at each phase provide the clinician with an understanding of age-related etiologies of sexual disorders.

Changes in Sexuality in the Elderly

Many people think that once one reaches a certain age, sex is no longer an important part of life. This is simply not true. Elderly people may not be like young adults when it comes to sexual practice, but they do still have the desire to have sex, even into their late eighties. Sex is an important part of any relationship and does not exclude itself from the relationships of older people. However, men and women do undergo changes in their sexuality as they age.

Changes in Sexuality in Elderly Men

One of the main concerns of men as they age is their ability to achieve erection. In some men, it may take longer and require more stimulation to achieve erection, and even then it may not be as it was in their young adult years. Some men are unable to achieve erection at all. This is referred to as erectile dysfunction or "impotence."

Impotence can result from psychological or emotional issues, including excessive stress, worry, fatigue, anger, or depression. Impotence is also linked to certain physical causes or diseases including reduced testosterone levels, heart disease, diabetes, drug use, or as a side effect of taking certain medications. An inability to perform is rather embarrassing and frightening for a man.

Changes in Sexuality in Elderly Women

The menopause is the most common cause for sexual changes in women as they age. As estrogen diminishes with age, women may see some changes that affect their sexual response. Some of these changes are because hormones are waning, and some of them could be psychological or emotional in nature. These changes include vaginal dryness, pain during sex, lower sexual desire, difficulty becoming aroused, more vaginal or bladder infections, or less sensation in the genital area. However, many women do not have any of these symptoms, but at least half of women have one or more of them. For many women, a lowering in the priority of sexual activities means more room for other things that they value, like putting that time and energy into their job or a hobby. For others, any change in their ability to have or enjoy sex is a major threat to their self-esteem.

Sexuality across Cultures

Researchers of sexuality focus their attention on sexual attitudes and practices, not on physiology or anatomy. Throughout time and place, the vast majority of human beings have participated in sexual relationships. Each society, however, interprets sexuality and sexual activity in different ways. Many societies around the world have different attitudes to premarital sex, the age of sexual consent, homosexuality, masturbation, and other sexual behaviors that are not consistent with the universal cultural. At the same time, researchers have learned that certain norms (like disapproval of incest) are shared among most societies. Likewise, societies generally have norms that reinforce their accepted social system of sexuality.

What is considered normal in terms of sexual behavior is determined by the customs and values of the society, e.g., societies that value monogamy are more likely to oppose extramarital sex. Individuals are socialized to these mores and values by their family, the education system, peers, the media, and religion. Historically, religion has been the greatest influence on sexual behavior in most societies, but in more recent years, peers and the media have emerged as two of the strongest influences, particularly for American teens.

Sexual Dysfunctions

Sexual dysfunctions are a heterogeneous group of disorders that are typically characterized by a clinically significant disturbance in a person's ability to respond sexually or to experience sexual pleasure. An individual may have several sexual dysfunctions at the same time. In such cases, all of the dysfunctions should be diagnosed.

According to DSM-5, sexual dysfunctions include delayed ejaculation, erectile disorder, female orgasmic disorder, female sexual interest/arousal disorder, genito-pelvic pain/penetration disorder, male hypoactive sexual desire disorder, premature (early) ejaculation, substance/medication-induced sexual dysfunction, other specified sexual dysfunction, and unspecified sexual dysfunction.

- *Delayed ejaculation*: there is either marked delay in or marked infrequency or absence of ejaculation that is experienced on almost all or all occasions (approximately 75–100 percent) of partnered sexual activity (in identified situational contexts or, if generalized, in all contexts), and without the individual desiring delay.
- *Erectile disorder*: where a man is unable to achieve or maintain a firm erection during intercourse or other sexual stimulation (e.g., oral copulation) or there is marked decrease in erectile rigidity.
- *Female orgasmic disorder*: this occurs when a woman has marked delay in, marked infrequency of, reduced intensity, or absence of orgasm. Symptoms must be experienced on almost all or all (approximately 75–100 percent) occasions of sexual activity (in identified situational contexts or, if generalized, in all contexts).
- *Female sexual interest/arousal disorder*: refers to lack of, or significantly reduced, sexual interest/arousal, as manifested by at least three of the following:
  - absent or reduced interest in sexual activity;
  - absent or reduced sexual or erotic thoughts or fantasies;
  - no or reduced initiation of sexual activity, and typically unreceptive to a partner's attempts to initiate;

- absent or reduced sexual excitement or pleasure during sexual activity in almost all or all sexual encounters (in identified situational contexts or, if generalized, in all contexts);
- absent or reduced sexual interest/arousal in response to any internal or external sexual/erotic cues (e.g., written, verbal, visual);
- absent or reduced genital or non-genital sensations during sexual activity in almost all or all sexual encounters (in identified situational contexts or, if generalized, in all contexts).
- *Genito-pelvic pain/penetration disorder*: refers to persistent or recurrent difficulties with one (or more) of the following:
  - vaginal penetration during intercourse;
  - marked vulvovaginal or pelvic pain during vaginal intercourse or penetration attempts;
  - marked fear or anxiety about vulvovaginal or pelvic pain in anticipation of, during, or as a result of vaginal penetration;
  - marked tensing or tightening of the pelvic floor muscles during attempted vaginal penetration.
- *Male hypoactive sexual desire disorder*: refers to persistently or recurrently deficient or absent sexual or erotic thoughts or fantasies and desire for sexual activity. The judgment of deficiency is made by the clinician, taking into account factors that affect sexual functioning, such as age and general and sociocultural contexts of the individual's life.
- *Premature ejaculation*: a persistent or recurrent pattern of ejaculation occurring during partnered sexual activity within approximately 1 minute following vaginal penetration and before the individual wishes it. However, perceptions of the average length of time before a man should ejaculate vary widely across the cultures.

Clinical Notes

Sexual dysfunctions represent a clinically significant heterogeneous group of disorders that affect the individual's well-being and quality of life. Inability to detect and manage these disorders will lead to significant personal implications.

Summary

- Components of an adult's sexuality include sexual identity (gender identity, orientation), sexual function (intention, desire, arousal, orgasm), and emotional satisfaction.
- Differentiation of the male from the female begins about the sixth week of embryonic life and is completed by the end of the third month, from the action of fetal androgens.
- Hormone changes mark the beginning of puberty and its associated physical changes. Both biological and environmental factors play a role in controlling the timing of puberty.
- Sexual response is a true psychophysiological experience. Normally, men and women experience a sequence of physiological responses to sexual stimulation. The phases of the response cycle include: desire, arousal, orgasm, and resolution.
- Sexual life changes across lifespan; each phase of life (adolescence, young adulthood, middle life, and older age) has developmental challenges and potentials.
- According to DSM-5, sexual dysfunctions include delayed ejaculation, erectile disorder, female orgasmic disorder, female sexual interest/arousal disorder, genito-pelvic pain/

penetration disorder, male hypoactive sexual desire disorder, premature (early) ejaculation, substance/medication-induced sexual dysfunction, other specified sexual dysfunction, and unspecified sexual dysfunction.

Test Your Knowledge

- What are the components of sexuality?
- What is gender identity?
- What is gender role?
- What is sexual orientation?
- Discuss sexual identity and its development.
- What is the sexual response cycle?
- How does sexuality change across the lifespan?
- How does sexuality change across cultures?

Critical Thinking Questions

- How do cultural values affect sexual practices?
- How could you evaluate the biological underpinnings of sexual orientation?

PART THREE
Basic Psychological Processes

eight
Emotions

Learning Goals

- This chapter is intended to provide the reader with an overview of the functions of emotions, the components of emotions, theories explaining emotions, the neurobiological basis of emotions, the classification of emotions, measuring emotions, culture and emotions, gender differences in emotions, and the effect of emotions on health.

Introduction

PHOTO 8.1. Emotional Excitement.

Emotions are a complex psychological state that are easily recognized, though difficult to define, in part, because our emotional experiences are so varied and complex. However, emotion researchers define an emotion as *a pattern of response subjectively experienced as strong feeling, usually directed toward a specific object*. The responses include physiological arousal, impulses to action, thoughts, and expression of all these. The specific objects are the goals and needs which could be fundamental, such as food, shelter, and survival, or could be more complex like searching for love, ambition to win a prize, or to build self-respect.

Emotions are usually intense, transitory, with relatively well-defined beginnings and endings, and they are about something or someone. This is in contrast to mood, which involves a milder emotional state that is more general and pervasive, such as sadness or happiness. Mood has less specific causes and may last for a few hours or days (Gendolla, 2000).

The Functions of Emotions

Psychologists have identified several important functions that emotions may play in our daily lives. The following is a summary of the importance of those functions:

1. *Making life interesting*: life would be considerably less satisfying, and even dull, if we lacked the capacity to feel and express emotion. Thus, emotions make life interesting. Imagine that your favorite team winning a football game is like them losing it, that success in an exam is like failing it; variability in emotion gives life its flavor.
2. *Preparing us for action*: human survival depends on being able to recognize and respond quickly to the emotional state of others, e.g., if you saw an angry dog charging toward you, your emotional reaction (fear) would be associated with the physiological arousal of the sympathetic nervous system and activation of the "fight or flight" response. This will help you to do the best response, either to stand and fight (if you can) or run away and hide.
3. *Feelings modify attention and learning*: we tend to pay more attention to events that fit our current feelings than to events that do not. Current feelings guide attention automatically, by producing faster reaction times to feeling-congruent events (Derryberry & Tucker, 1994). As a consequence, we learn more about the events that fit, or are congruent with, our feelings.

4. *Modifying evaluations and judgments*: feelings can affect evaluations of other people and inanimate objects and circumstances, e.g., a feeling of fear leads us to appraise subsequent situations as uncertain and uncontrollable and thus causes us to overestimate future risk. In contrast, feelings of being angry or happy, although of different valence, lead us to appraise subsequent circumstances as certain and controllable, leading to underestimation of future risks (Johnson & Tversky, 1983; Lerner & Keltner, 2001).

5. *Shaping our future behavior*: emotional response to unpleasant events may represent an alarm that pushes an individual to avoid similar circumstances in the future, e.g., exposure to a stressful situation, like an exam, may lead you to decide to study hard in the future to avoid a similar situation. Similarly, seeing the scene of a terrible car accident may push you to drive safely in the future to avoid a similar fate.

6. *Helping people to interact more effectively with others*: emotions serve an adaptive function through communicating internal states to friends and enemies. People often communicate their emotional experience through verbal and non-verbal behaviors. These behaviors can act as a signal to observers, allowing them to understand better what we are experiencing and to help them to predict our future behavior.

7. *Cognitive functions*: psychologists generally acknowledge that it is unrealistic to try to separate emotion from cognition (Phelps, 2006). Everyday cognition is far from cold and rational, decisions and judgments are affected by emotions and moods, e.g., when people are in good moods, they tend to be persistent and to find creative, elaborate responses to challenging problems (Isen, 1993).

8. *Modification of performance*: performance is optimal at a moderate level of emotional arousal, while low and high levels of arousal are associated with poor performance. Moderate levels of arousal increase efficiency levels by making people more alert. However, intense emotions, either positive or negative, interfere with performance because the central nervous system responses are channeled in too many directions at once. The effects of arousal on performance also depend on the difficulty of the task at hand, emotions interfere more with complicated tasks than with simple ones.

Components of Emotions

Emotions are multifaceted, with each distinct emotion having multiple components (Frijda, 1986; Lazarus, 1991).

Cognitive Appraisal

Typically, an emotion begins with an assessment of the personal meaning or significance of current circumstances. All appraisal theories suggest that people's appraisals of situations (not their appraisals of physiological arousal) lead to the subjective experience of emotion, which in turn triggers the arousal associated with it, and other components of the emotional response. Factors or dimensions that govern personal cognitive appraisal of an emotion may be reduced to a limited number of core themes, that represent a personal meaning of specific person-environment relationship, or it may involve numerous dimensions. Examples of these dimensions include: (1) the desirability of the situation (pleasant or unpleasant); (2) the amount of effort the person anticipates spending on the situation; (3) the certainty of the situation; (4) the amount of attention the person wants to devote to the situation; (5) the degree of control the person has over the situation; and (6) the degree of control the person attributes to nonhuman forces in the situation (Smith & Ellsworth, 1985, 1987). Cognitive control of emotion includes altering our goals and desires, altering our appraisal by re-evaluating events or situations, and religious training or therapy.

Conscious and Unconscious Appraisals

Whether the appraisal process occurs consciously and deliberately is debatable. Some have argued that emotions can occur automatically at unconscious levels, without any preceding conscious thought (Zajonc, 1984), making people experience emotions for reasons unknown to them. It is debatable how much of the appraisal process can occur unconsciously. In summary, the cognitive appraisals within the emotion processes are similar to other forms of cognition, they result in part from automatic processing, outside conscious awareness, and in part from controlled processing, of which we are aware. To illustrate, if you glimpse something that looks like a snake, an automatic and unconscious appraisal process may make you jump before a more controlled and deliberate appraisal process can determine that the object in question is, in fact, a harmless piece of rope.

Physiological Changes (Arousal)

Intense emotions are usually associated with the activation of the sympathetic nervous system, this leads to a series of rapidly occurring automatic physical reactions (the fight-or-flight response), which may not occur all at once. These include acceleration of breathing and heart rate, elevation of blood pressure, blood sugar level increases to provide more energy, trembling hands and feet, perspiration, dry mouth, erection of hairs on skin giving the familiar sensation of goose pimples, pupils dilate to allow taking in a wider visual field, digestion stops as blood is diverted from the stomach and intestines to the brain and skeletal muscles. The autonomic nervous system activities are triggered by activity in certain regions of the brain, including the hypothalamus and the amygdala. Impulses from these areas are transmitted to nuclei in the brain stem that control the functioning of the autonomic nervous system. The hypothalamus also secretes a corticotropin-releasing hormone that induces the adrenocorticotropic hormone from the pituitary to stimulate the release of cortisol from the adrenal cortex to increase blood sugar levels. Simultaneously, the adrenal gland also releases catecholamines, such as adrenaline or noradrenaline, into the bloodstream.

Not all emotions involve intense physical reactions, and some emotions, such as contentment, are characterized by decreased physical arousal and the slowing of some body processes (Levenson, Ekman, & Friesen, 1990; Levenson, Ekman, Heider, & Friesen, 1992). Also, research has shown that different emotions are associated with different patterns of physiological arousal. Levenson (1992) found that fear, anger, and sadness are associated with increased heart rate. But anger produces greater increases in blood pressure than fear. While anger produces an increase in skin temperature, fear produces a decrease in skin temperature.

Subjective Experience (Affective Aspect)

Subjective experience of the emotions refers to the affective state or feeling tone the emotion brings, e.g., being afraid, angry, sad, happy, etc. Many studies suggest that visceral perception plays a role in the experience of the intensity of emotions (Schachter, 1964). In a study of army veterans with spinal cord injuries to determine their feelings in situations of fear, anger, grief, and sexual excitement, it was found that the higher the lesion on the spinal cord, the less feedback of the autonomic nervous system to the brain, the greater the decrease in emotionality following injury. The same relationship was true for states of sexual excitement and grief. A reduction in autonomic arousal resulted in a reduction in the intensity of experienced emotion (Hohmann, 1962). Comments by veterans with the highest spinal cord lesions suggested that they could react emotionally to arousing situations but that they did not really feel emotional, e.g., being afraid is not associated with feeling tense or being shaky.

PHOTO 8.2.   Sadness.

Other studies among healthy individuals showed that people who are classified as good at visceral perception (e.g., good at detecting their own heartbeat) report more intense subjective experiences of emotions (Barrett, Quigley, Bliss-Moreau, & Aronson, 2004), more intense facial expressions (Ferguson & Katkin, 1996), and more pronounced emotion-related brain activity (Pollatos, Kirsch, & Schandry, 2005). Thus, autonomic arousal contributes to the intensity of emotional experience.

Expressive Behavior

People express emotions through verbal or non-verbal behavior (body language). Facial expressions are one of the most important ways that we express emotions. Smiling, crying, running, shouting, a change in facial expression, various body gestures, and vocal qualities usually convey the person's emotions. Body language, such as a stooped posture or crossed arms, can be used to send different emotional signals.

Psychologists agree that there are a limited number of basic emotions that all humans, in every culture, experience. Ekman identified the most common six basic emotions: fear, disgust, surprise, happiness, anger, and sadness (Ekman, 1992a, 1992b). Robert Plutchik grouped basic emotions into four pairs of polar opposites (joy-sadness, anger-fear, trust-distrust, and surprise-anticipation). These basic emotions are thought to be biologically determined, the products of evolution, automatic, fast, and trigger behavior with a high survival value. However, emotional experience is not limited to pure forms of each basic emotion. Rather, emotional experience can be complex and multifaceted (Cacioppo, Gardner, & Berntson, 1999). In complex situations, people may experience a blend of emotions, in which different emotions are experienced simultaneously or in rapid succession.

The Facial Feedback Hypothesis

In addition to its communicative function, the facial feedback hypothesis assumes that facial expression also contributes to our experience of emotions (Tomkins, 1962), i.e., expressing a specific emotion facially causes us to subjectively experience that emotion. Some studies found that when people mimic the facial expressions characteristic of a given emotion, such as anger or fear, they tend to report feeling that emotion (Duclos et al., 1989; Flack, Laird, & Cavallaro, 1999; Schnall & Laird, 2003). In one such experiment, participants rated cartoons for funniness while holding a pen either in their teeth (to smile without knowing it) or in their lips (to prevent a smile). Participants who held the pen in their teeth rated the cartoons as funnier than those who held the pen in their lips (Strack, Martin, & Stepper, 1988). Similar studies show an effect for body postures as well (Flack, 2006). The basic explanation for this phenomenon is that the facial muscles send feedback signals to the brain. In turn, the brain uses this information to activate and regulate emotional experience, intensifying or lessening emotion (Izard, 1990a, 1990b). Ekman and Davidson (1993) demonstrated that deliberately creating a happy smile produces brain-activity changes similar to those caused by spontaneously producing a happy smile in response to a real event. The facial feedback hypothesis supports the notion that our bodily responses affect our subjective experience, and adds support for aspects of the James–Lange theory (see p. 183). However, even supposing that an emotion can be produced by changing facial expression, this does not mean that this is the typical way that emotions are experienced. In daily life, appraisals of our current circumstances are still the most likely trigger of emotions.

PHOTO 8.3.   Facial Expressions.

Thought and Action Tendencies

Emotions usually urge someone to think and act in certain ways. Being angry may lead one to act aggressively, either physically or verbally. Liking something may push one to explore it and learn more about it.

Emotional Regulation

Emotional regulation refers to attempts to influence emotions that one has, when one has them, and how one experiences or expresses these emotions (Gross, 1998a, 1998b). A considerable part of the socialization process is directed toward teaching children how and when to regulate their emotions. Parents teach their children when certain emotions are appropriate and when they are not. Evidence suggests that children's success in learning these lessons about emotion regulation generally predicts their social success (Eisenberg, Cumberland, & Spinrad, 1998).

People control or regulate their emotions in many different ways, including cognitively and behaviorally (either by diversion or engagement) strategies (Parkinson & Totterdell, 1999). An angry person can disengage from anger through mental effort, by trying to stop thinking, or can distract himself or herself by doing something fun or demanding, like playing the guitar or doing a calculus assignment. Alternatively, he or she can confront the feelings or the situation by reappraising the situation as being better than he or she thought, trying to solve the underlying problem, or by talking through the issues with a friend. These tactics are not mutually exclusive. With repeated use of these strategies, they can become automatic responses, outside of conscious awareness.

Theories Explaining Emotions

Psychologists have proposed several theories to explain emotional behavior. The focus of one theory differs from another theory, but all seem to contribute to the understanding of emotional situations. Major theories explaining emotion include the following:

- evolutionary theories;
- the James–Lange theory;
- the Cannon–Bard theory;
- the Schachter–Singer theory (the two-factor theory).

Evolutionary Theories

Charles Darwin proposed that emotions evolved because they had an adaptive value, e.g., fear evolved because it helped people to act in ways that enhanced their chances of survival. Darwin believed that facial expressions of emotion are innate responses to stimuli that allow people to quickly judge someone's hostility or friendliness and to communicate intentions to others. Evolutionary theories of emotion tend to underestimate the influence of thought and learning on emotion, although they acknowledge that both can have an effect. Evolutionary theorists believe that all human cultures share several primary emotions, including happiness, surprise, disgust, anger, fear, contempt, and sadness. They believe that all other emotions result from blends and different intensities of these primary emotions, e.g., terror is a more intense form of the primary emotion of fear.

The James–Lange Theory

Contrary to common-sense thinking that our bodies respond to emotions, William James (1884) suggested that a person's interpretation of physical changes leads a person to feel an emotion. A similar theory was independently proposed by the physician and psychologist, Carl Lange.

James and Lange arrived at the view that body reactions itself are interpreted as emotions, i.e., the perception of stimulus leads to the activation of visceral and skeletal responses, which will result in the experience of emotion in the brain. The brain responds to a threatening situation by activating peripheral responses, but we do not consciously experience the emotion until these responses are activated. Thus, the central nervous system itself does not actually produce the emotion. Emotional expression (response) precedes emotional experience (feelings). So, we feel sad because we cry, angry because we strike, afraid because we tremble, and we neither cry, strike, nor tremble because we are sad, angry, or fearful, as the case may be.

PHOTO 8.4.   Carl Lange.

Some research supports the James–Lange theory. Brain imaging studies found that different primary emotions produce different patterns of brain activation (Vytal & Hamann, 2010). These results suggest that different experiences that generate emotion are associated with different physiological reactions (Levenson, 2014).

One implication of the James–Lange theory is that if you modify your facial muscles to mimic an emotional state, you activate the associated emotion. In other words, facial expressions trigger the experience of emotions, not the reverse. In 1963, Silvan Tomkins proposed this idea as the facial feedback hypothesis (Davis, Senghas, & Ochsner, 2009), see p. 181.

Criticism of the James–Lange Theory

- Artificially inducing the bodily changes associated with an emotion through injecting a drug such as epinephrine does not produce the experience of a true emotion.
- The patterns of autonomic arousal are often not specific enough and may not differ much from one emotional state to another, e.g., anger accelerates heart rate as does the sight of a loved one.
- Internal changes occur too slowly to be the primary source of emotional feeling.
- Emotions remain intact after cutting sensory tracks.
- Removal of the cerebral cortex leads to disorganized emotion.

The Cannon–Bard Theory

In 1927, Walter B. Cannon came up with some objections to James's theory. These objections were later expanded by Philip Bard (1934). They proposed what is called the Cannon–Bard theory of emotion. They assumed that emotional response arises from the thalamic processes first, then turns to the hypothalamus for emotional expression and to the cerebral cortex for emotional experience, both occur at the same time (Figure 8.1).

This theory suggests that an emotion-producing stimulus is processed in the subcortical structures. Cannon originally focused on the thalamus, but it is now known that many limbic system structures are involved in producing emotion. The subcortical structures then send information separately to the cortex and the body (the external muscles and the internal organs). The muscles and organs make the physiological reactions to the emotion. As a result, people experience two separate things at roughly the same time: an emotion, produced in the cortex, and the relevant physical reactions, produced in the body. Cannon and Bard thought that the brain is quick to experience, while the autonomic nervous system was too slow to account for the subjective feelings of emotions, taking at least a second or two to react, e.g., you may feel embarrassed before you blush. Cannon and Bard also noted that many emotions produce similar bodily responses. The similarities make it too difficult for people to determine quickly which emotion they

PHOTO 8.5.   William B. Cannon.

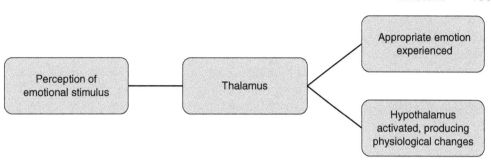

FIGURE 8.1. The Cannon–Bard Theory.

are experiencing, e.g., anger, excitement, and sexual interest all produce similar changes in heart rate and blood pressure. Exercise also produces the same changes, and it may affect your emotional state, but it does not generate a specific emotion.

Criticism of the Cannon–Bard Theory

- Cannon's and Bard's studies were based on animal and case studies as evidence for their theory. This may be unreliable as it can be doubtful whether findings generated by these methods can be generalized to human behavior.
- Cannon and Bard assumed that bodily responses have no influence on emotion, but this contradicts the findings of other studies. Visceral responses can induce an emotional state in the absence of any obvious eliciting stimuli, e.g., a racing heartbeat and increased respiration can produce a feeling of fear in the absence of eliciting stimuli.
- The Cannon–Bard theory overestimated the function of the thalamus in emotional processes, as there are other parts of the brain that are involved in emotions.

The Schachter–Singer Theory (Two-Factor Theory)

Stanley Schachter and Jerome Singer saw some merit in the previous two theories. According to their theory, emotions were thought to result from the combination of two factors: an initial state of unexplained arousal plus a cognitive explanation (or appraisal) for that arousal. They agreed with James that physiological arousal is a central element in emotion. But they also agreed with Cannon that physiological arousal is very similar for different emotions. Thus, arousal would not produce an emotional response on its own. Instead, Schachter and Singer proposed that cognitive evaluation of what caused the responses is an essential part necessary for its occurrence. The Schachter–Singer theory stressed the interaction of cognitive (intellectual) and physiological (bodily) influences, where physiological arousal was considered as the first component and the interpretation of that arousal as the second one. According to this theory, when people experience arousal, they search for its source. The cognitive explanation, or label, is often quick and straightforward, since a person generally recognizes the event that led to his or her emotional state. When the situation is more ambiguous, the emotion will be determined by the person's beliefs about the cause of such emotion. This theory thus contradicts James's assertion that emotion is communicated only on the basis of physical feedback, asserting that this feedback by itself is not clear enough to specify a particular emotion. Rather, the brain chooses one of many possible interpretations and determines the feedback pattern, resulting in the experiencing of a particular emotion (Schachter & Singer, 1962).

To prove their proposal that subjects can have different emotional reactions despite being placed into the same physiological state; Schachter-Singer injected male volunteers with epine-phrine, to produces sympathetic nervous system arousal. One group was informed that their symptoms were caused by the injection, but the other group was not given this explanation. The subjects who were not informed tended to report feeling either happier or angrier than the informed subjects. Participants were left in a waiting room with another person, allegedly another participant but actually an assistant of the experimenter. The assistant created either a happy situation (by making paper airplanes, playing basketball with wads of paper, and so on) or an angry situation (by complaining about the experiment, tearing up a questionnaire, and so on). The uninformed participants placed in the happy situation rated their feelings as happier than did the informed participants in that same situation. Although the data were less clear for the angry situation, Schachter and Singer claimed that the uninformed participants were angrier than the informed participants. Subjects expressed either anger or happiness, depending on whether another person in the experiment displayed that emotion. Participants who had a phys-iological explanation for their arousal appeared to be less influenced by the situation than those who did not have an explanation. Hence, the combination of the appraisal of the situation (cog-nitive) and the participants' reception of epinephrine or a placebo together determined the response.

Schachter and Singer's theory has two implications: the first is that emotions are not entirely defined by the bodily changes that often accompany them, i.e., we do not recognize an instance of anger or happiness simply by turning our attention inwards and checking off internal symp-toms. The second is that emotions and our interpretations of them are closely associated with what other people say and do.

Schachter and Singer's theory stimulated research on the importance of cognition in emotion. Craig Smith and Richard Lazarus (1993) developed the Schachter–Singer theory into the cognitive appraisal theory of emotion. This theory asserts that the most important aspect of an emotional experience is the cognitive interpretation, or appraisal, of the situation or stimulus. That is, emo-tions result from our appraisal of the personal meaning of events and experiences. Although both theories emphasize the importance of cognitive appraisal, the Schachter–Singer theory assumes that emotion results from physiological arousal plus a cognitive label. In contrast, cognitive appraisal theorists stress that cognitive appraisal is the essential trigger for an emotional response (Lazarus, 1995). Critics of the cognitive appraisal approach state that emotional reactions to events are virtually instantaneous, too rapid to allow for the process of cognitive appraisal. In conclusion, emotional responses can be triggered in multiple ways; some emotional responses are instantan-eous, bypassing conscious consideration, while complex stimuli like social situations or personal interactions are cognitively appraised before an emotion is generated (Forgas, 2008; Kihlstrom, Tobias, & Tobis, 2000; Scherer & Ellgring, 2007).

The Neurobiological Basis of Emotions

The experience of emotion is accompanied by the activation of two major parts of the nervous system: the brain and the autonomic nervous system. Early research focused on the role of auto-nomic nervous system in triggering physiological arousal, as discussed before. More recently, brain-imaging techniques have identified specific brain regions involved in emotions. Many brain areas are implicated in emotional responses, particularly the amygdala, the reticular for-mation, the limbic system, and the cerebral cortex.

The reticular formation is a group of nuclei found throughout the brain stem. The dorsal teg-mental nuclei are in the midbrain, the central tegmental nuclei are in the pons, and the central nuclei and inferior nuclei are found in the medulla. The reticular formation receives and filters sensory information before passing it on the limbic system and cortex.

The limbic system includes the hypothalamus, which produces most of the peripheral responses to emotion through its control of the endocrine and autonomic nervous systems, the amygdala, which is associated with fear and aggressive behavior; the hippocampus, and parts of the thalamus.

The frontal lobes of the cerebral cortex receive nerve impulses from the thalamus and play an active role in the experience and expression of emotions. fMRI has revealed that the lateral aspects of the frontal lobes are most associated with positive emotions, whereas the medial aspects of the frontal lobes are most associated with negative emotions. The right hemisphere is more involved in perception of emotion, specifically facial expression and prosody (the melody of speech that conveys sincerity, sarcasm, etc.). Although lesions of the right and left frontal lobes equally disrupt perception of emotion from facial features, lesions of the right but not the left temporal lobe disrupt it. In addition, PET studies indicate that the right amygdala and prefrontal cortex are more active in prosody, whereas the right temporal lobe is less responsive than the left.

The amygdala is a key brain structure in the emotional response of fear in humans (Davis & Whalen, 2001). The amygdala appears to be very involved in the perception (as opposed to the expression) of fear. Brain imaging techniques have demonstrated that the amygdala is activated when viewing threatening or fearful faces or hearing people make non-verbal sounds expressing fear (Morris, Ohman, & Dolan, 1999; Ohman, Carlsson, Lundqvist, & Ingvar, 2007). Even when people simply anticipate a threatening stimulus, the amygdala is activated as part of the fear circuit in the brain (Phelps et al., 2001). In humans, damage to the amygdala disrupts elements of the fear response, e.g., a lesion of the amygdala leaves a person unable to perceive fearful emotions from others, although these patients have no problems matching the appropriate emotion with a sentence or in expressing various emotions using facial expressions upon request. Interestingly, criminals with antisocial personality disorder show less activation in the amygdala during emotional processing than non-antisocial persons (Kiehl et al., 2001), providing neurological evidence for an emotion-related deficit.

With the exception of olfactory sensations, all incoming sensory information is processed in the thalamus before being relayed to sensory centers in the cerebral cortex. However, LeDoux (1996, 2000) suggested that there are two neural pathways for sensory information that project from the thalamus. An indirect pathway in which external stimuli pass to the cortex (where they are consciously appraised) before going to the amygdala. Meanwhile, there is a direct connection between the sensory channels and the amygdala, bypassing the cortex. This direct pathway responds to an alarming situation before the cortex, and explains why we can experience an emotion before we know why, due to the unconscious appraisal of emotion (Phelps & LeDoux, 2000). The direct thalamus-amygdala pathway rapidly triggers an emotional response to threats that, through evolution, we are biologically prepared to fear, such as snakes, wild animals, or rapidly moving vague (shadowy) objects. In contrast, the indirect pathway allows more complex stimuli to be evaluated in the cortex before triggering the amygdala's alarm system.

The amygdala sends information along neural pathways that project to other brain regions that make up the rest of the brain's fear circuit. One pathway leads to an area of the hypothalamus, then on to the medulla at the base of the brain. In combination, the hypothalamus and medulla trigger arousal of the sympathetic nervous system. Another pathway projects from the amygdala to a different hypothalamus area that, in concert with the pituitary gland, triggers the release of stress hormones (LeDoux, 1995, 2000).

The thalamus sends information to the visual cortex, which creates a detailed and more accurate representation of the visual stimulus. This allows the signal that prompted the initial instinctive response to be re-evaluated. But information traveling along the thalamus-cortex-amygdala route takes about twice as long to reach the amygdala as the information traveling along the direct thalamus-amygdala route. Thus, the alarm reaction is already in full swing before signals from the cortex reach the amygdala.

Classification of Emotions

Emotions are described in terms of feeling, e.g., fear, anger, joy, grief, and sadness. Most languages contain many words and descriptive phrases associated with emotions. However, no consensus has been reached on attempts to classify emotions into basic categories. This may be due to cultural differences. However, all accounts of emotion agree that emotions can be classified along two broad dimensions: the degree of pleasantness and the degree of arousal:

- the pleasant-unpleasant dimension: some emotions, such as fear, are clearly unpleasant (also called negative), and others, such as joy, are clearly pleasant (also called positive);
- the degree of arousal dimension: some emotions, such as anger and joy, are associated with high level of arousal; others, such as sadness, are associated with decreased energy (low level of arousal).

Measuring Emotions

The judgment of emotion is largely a subjective matter (this is true both for a person experiencing an emotion and for someone else who is judging that personal experience). However, several different indicators can be used to identify the emotion expressed and the level of arousal and feelings being experienced. These indicators include:

1. *Observation of behavior*: observed behavior such as facial expression, gestures, and postures can be used to understand the emotion being expressed. Most people can detect subtle emotional expressions. It is difficult to fool an expert, because microexpressions of genuine emotion often come out with the false one. Movements of the facial muscles are hard to control, and can reveal signs of emotions one may be trying to conceal. For example, genuine smiles (Duchenne smiles) involve contraction of both the zygomaticus major and the orbicularis oculi, whereas false smiles only involve the zygomaticus major. Lifting just the inner part of eyebrows, which few people do consciously, reveals distress or worry. However, whatever one's emotion-detecting skill, it may be difficult to detect deceiving expressions (Porter & ten Brinke, 2008). The behavioral differences between liars and truth tellers are too minute for most people to detect (Hartwig & Bond, 2011).
2. *Recording physiologic changes*: changes in heart rate, blood pressure, breathing pattern, pupillary dilation, blood flow to the periphery, and electrodermal activity are often interpreted as indicators of emotions. Electromyography (EMG) recordings can also detect emotional changes even when the motor output to the facial muscles is too slight to change them. Detecting and recording these physiologic changes are the basis behind lie-detectors.
3. *Self-reports of emotional experience*: this could be achieved through direct inquiry about emotional experience or through the administration of formal scales, such as the Hamilton depression rating scale. Personal reports often include written or spoken descriptions of feelings.
4. *The projective technique*, e.g., the Rorschach test (see p. 389).

Culture and Emotions

The ways of expressing emotion may be either innate or culturally acquired. Certain facial expressions, such as smiling, have been found to be universal, even among blind persons, who have no means of imitating them. Other expressions vary across cultures. Cultural messages, received by people since early childhood, influence the emotions that people attempt to feel, e.g., children's storybooks in the United States emphasize excited states, whereas similar books in Taiwan emphasize calm states (Tsai, Louie, Chen, & Uchida, 2007).

There is general agreement that the subjective experience and meaning of emotions vary in different cultures (Scherer & Wallbott, 1994). However, facial expressions for the basic emotions seem to be universal across different cultures (Waller, Cray, & Burrows. 2008). Some specific non-verbal gestures vary across cultures, e.g., the Chinese may stick out their tongues to register surprise, in contrast to Americans and other Westerners, who raise their eyebrows and widen their eyes. Shaking one's head means "no" in the United States but "yes" in southern India and Bulgaria. Nodding one's head means "yes" in the United States, but in Japan it could mean "maybe" or even "no way." Nevertheless, some body language seems to be universal. Some cultures do not distinguish between anger and sadness, e.g., Tahitians, have no word for either sadness or guilt, but have 46 words for various types of anger.

People usually adjust their emotional expressions to suit a particular social context. How, when, and where they display emotional expressions are strongly influenced by cultural norms. Cultural differences in the management of facial expressions are called display rules. Display rules can vary for different groups within a given culture. In some countries like Japan, an important display rule is that you should not reveal negative emotions in the presence of an authority figure so as not to offend the higher-status individual. Cultures which value interdependence among people differ in their emotional reaction to situations from cultures that emphasize independence of individuals, due to a different perception of situations.

James Russell (1991) found that different cultures commonly classify emotions according to two dimensions: (1) the degree to which the emotion is pleasant or unpleasant; and (2) the level of activation, or arousal, associated with the emotion, e.g., joy and contentment are both pleasant emotions, but joy is associated with a higher degree of activation (Barrett & Russell, 1999). Japanese people add a third dimension: interpersonal engagement. This dimension reflects the idea that some emotions result from your connections and interactions with other people (Kitayama, Markus, & Kurokawa, 2000). Japanese subjects rate anger and shame as being about the same in terms of unpleasantness and activation, but they rated shame as being much higher than anger on the dimension of interpersonal engagement.

Gender Differences in Emotions

Gender variation in display rules is noticed in many cultures, women are allowed a wider range of emotional expressiveness and responsiveness than men, while expressing certain emotions, such as sadness openly or crying, is considered unmasculine (Fischer, Rodriguez, van Vianen, & Manstead, 2004; Plant, Kling, & Smith, 2004).

Gender differences in emotion may stem primarily from the ways in which men and women regulate and express their emotions. These differences, in turn, most likely stem from gender differences in the way males and females are socialized (by parents and culture) to conform to gender stereotypes. Such differences may set the stage for the emergence of gender differences in emotion regulation habits in later life. In other words, gender-specific lessons about appropriate emotion regulation are one way that boys and girls learn to be masculine or feminine, powerful or powerless.

Some psychologists have attributed observed gender differences in emotion to a gender hierarchy, in which women, who have relatively less power and status than men, express the powerless emotions of sadness, anxiety, and fear (emotions that work to make one appear weak and helpless). Men, as higher status beings, express the "powerful" emotions of anger, pride, and contempt (emotions that work to maintain control and dominance) (Fischer, 2000).

Emotions and Health

The effect of emotions on health is complex, it can be briefly summarized into two claims: (1) positive emotions promote positive health and a longer and more satisfying life; and (2) negative emotions can impair health and place individuals at risk for poor health outcomes, ranging from depression to heart disease.

Prospective evidence connecting positive emotions to physical health and longevity has steadily accumulated. Experiencing positive emotions is frequently associated with having fewer colds (Cohen, Alper, Doyle, Treanor, & Turner 2006), reduced inflammation (Steptoe, O'Donnell, Badrick, Kumari, & Marmot, 2008), and lower likelihood of cardiovascular disease (Boehm & Kubzansky, 2012). However, the causal link between positive emotions and physical health may run in the opposite direction as well: Physical health appears to promote positive emotions.

However, this conclusion about the effect of emotions on health is not absolute. Researchers have found that happiness and positive emotions may negatively affect health, perhaps by promoting denial or underestimation of the likelihood that illness will happen. In support of this view, unrealistically high levels of optimism have sometimes been related to a diminished likelihood of engaging in health-protective behaviors. On the other hand, negative emotion is not harmful per se and can be an adaptive response to a situation. Grief, for example, is not associated with the negative immunological changes that characterize depression. So, grief is an adaptive response to loss, whereas depression is maladaptive.

Frustration

Frustration is an emotional state that occurs when a person is faced with an obstacle that interferes with satisfaction of a desire, need, or a goal. Certain situations may be frustrating to some people but not to others, this is because of differences in people's desires and goals. Frustration

PHOTO 8.6.   Frustration.

can occur not only in a human being but also in other animals, e.g., a rat in a maze subjected to electric shock when he tries to eat a piece of cheese will finally be frustrated and stop attempts to eat it.

Causes of Frustration

In everyday life, we are subjected to a lot of obstacles which may interfere with satisfying our wishes. These obstacles could be summarized as follows:

- *Physical environment*: bad weather, floods, rough unpaved roads are examples of physical factors that could limit the person's ambitions with resultant frustration.
- *Social factors*: every society has its norms and standards which ought to be followed by persons living in that society. The limits imposed by these norms and standards lead to interference with the needs and desires of some people, resulting in frustration in those people.
- *Psychical personal factors*: psychical handicaps (e.g., blindness or deafness, limb paralysis, or speech difficulties) may represent a barrier to goal satisfaction.
- *The person's choices*: making decisions may reveal bad choices which lead to choosing bad options or leaving a good one. This situation could lead to frustration.

Factors determining behavior following frustration include the following:

- *Motive strength*: the interference of a highly motivated person results in a stronger reaction than a mildly motivated one.
- *Previous learning*: previous experience helps the person to learn alternative ways of responding to frustration, resulting in low frustration. On the contrary, a particular situation may be considered not acceptable and result in a high level of frustration.
- *Frustration tolerance*: people vary in their reaction to a frustrating situation. Some people cope easily with frustrating situations while others become disorganized in a frustrating situation.
- *Specific situations*: when there is a chance to escape or avoid a problem, and when an alternative is available, frustration will be less than that which will develop in reverse situations.

Reactions to frustration include the following:

- *Physiological responses*: stress, especially chronic stress, has been accused of being the result of or sharing in the occurrence of many physical symptoms, e.g., peptic ulcer, bronchial asthma, hypertension, and skin eruptions.
- *Psychomotor hyperactivity*: the person develops an increase in inner tension associated with restlessness, trembling, clenching fists.
- *Aggression*: Any response made with the intention of harming a person, animal, or object. Aggression may be direct or displaced:
  - direct aggression: aggression is directed at the individual or object which is the source of the frustration;
  - displaced aggression: redirecting aggression to a target other than the source of one's frustration, i.e., rather than aggression directed to the individual or object which is the source of frustration, aggression is directed to another individual or

object, which acts as a scapegoat. This usually occurs because of the inability to react directly against the source of frustration. Breaking a cup or glass whenever frustrated is an example.

- *Stereotypical behavior*: instead of flexibility and striking out in new directions to solve problems, people tend to exhibit a repetitive fixed pattern of behavior, if the way to their goal is blocked.
- *Fantasy*: when people find it difficult to solve their problems in the real world, they resort to imagination and day-dreaming.
- *Regression*: a return to a more primitive mode of behavior that characterizes younger age.
- *Social withdrawal*: sometimes people withdraw from their social surroundings as a reaction to frustrating situations. This passive reaction may result from the failure of an aggressive reaction to satisfy their needs or the inability to express frustration aggressively due to any reason.

Clinical Notes

Assessment of the affect and mood is one of the key clinical skills. Affect refers to the prevailing emotional tone during the interview as observed by the clinician. Mood is the emotional state prevailing over a given period of time. Assessment of affect and mood is essential to establish a proper evaluation and diagnosis in a significant number of patients asking for psychiatric advice. Affect is usually assessed by describing its content or type, depth or intensity, range, change pattern (lability), and appropriateness to mood/context. Mood is assessed by describing the predominant mood, its intensity, its duration, reactivity, and the presence of diurnal variation.

Summary

- Emotion is a pattern of response subjectively experienced as a strong feeling, usually directed toward a specific object.
- Psychologists have identified several important functions for emotion that include making life interesting, preparing us for action, feelings modify attention and learning, modifying evaluations and judgments, shaping our future behavior, helping people to interact more effectively with others, cognitive functions, and modification of performance.
- Emotions are multifaceted; each distinct emotion has its own cognitive appraisal, physiological changes, subjective experience, and expressive behavior.
- People control or regulate their emotions in many different ways including cognitive and behavioral (either diversion or engagement) strategies.
- Psychologists have proposed several theories to explain emotional behavior, these include evolutionary theories, the James–Lange theory, the Cannon–Bard theory, and the Schachter–Singer theory.
- Emotions can be classified along two broad dimensions: the degree of pleasantness and the degree of arousal.
- Indicators that can be used to identify emotions include observation of behavior, recording physiologic changes, self-reports of emotional experience, and the projective technique.
- The effect of emotions on health is complex; it can briefly be summarized in two claims. Positive emotions promote positive health and a longer and more satisfying

life. Negative emotions can impair health and place individuals at risk for poor health outcomes, ranging from depression to heart disease.

■ Frustration is an emotional state that occurs when a person is faced with an obstacle that interferes with the satisfaction of a desire, need, or a goal.

■ Frustration may result from obstacles due to physical environment, social factors, psychical personal factors, and the person's choices.

■ The behavior following frustration is determined by motive strength, previous learning, frustration tolerance, and specific situations.

■ Reactions to frustration include physiological responses, psychomotor hyperactivity, aggression, stereotyped behavior, fantasy, regression, and social withdrawal.

Test Your Knowledge

■ What are the functions of emotions?
■ What are the components of emotions?
■ Give an account of the conscious and unconscious appraisals of emotion.
■ What is the facial feedback hypothesis?
■ Discuss emotional regulation.
■ What are the theories explaining emotions?
■ Discuss the James–Lange theory.
■ Discuss the Cannon–Bard theory.
■ What are the neurobiological bases of emotion?
■ How can emotions be classified?
■ How can emotions be measured?
■ What is the effect of culture on emotion?
■ What are the causes of frustration?
■ What are the factors determining behavior following frustration?
■ Describe the reactions to frustration.

Critical Thinking Questions

■ How does thinking relate to emotions?
■ How can you explain that people feel more enjoyment when sharing watching movies and attending music parties than when doing this alone?

nine
Motivation

Learning Goals

- This chapter is intended to provide the reader with an overview of the concept of motivation and the theories explaining it. The conflict of motives and the types and factors affecting the level of conflict are discussed.

Introduction

PHOTO 9.1.   Motivation.

What stimulates someone to get up in the morning to go to school or work? Why do you choose to eat certain foods or to buy a certain dress? Questions like these are about why people do what they do. These behaviors are strongly influenced by motivation. All human behaviors, whatever they do or refuse to do, are powered by motivation. A motive is an internal state (physiological or psychological) that arouses, directs, and maintains behavior toward a goal. Motivation can significantly influence our ability to learn, our memory, and our perception.

Explaining Motivation

Human behavior is varied and complex. It is difficult to find a single explanation for its occurrence. Many psychological theories have attempted to explain why a person is motivated to follow a certain behavior. Theories of motivation focus on either the internal processes that prompt people to behave in certain ways (e.g., instinct, drive reduction, and arousal theories), or emphasize the role of external stimuli that motivate behavior (incentive theory). The different theories include:

- the instinct theory
- the drive reduction theory
- the incentive theory
- the arousal theory
- cognitive approaches
- the needs satisfaction theory (Maslow's hierarchy of needs)
- the achievement motivation theory.

The Instinct Theory

According to instinct theory of motivation, people and animals are born pre-programmed with sets of behaviors essential to their survival. Animals display automatic and innate instinctual behavior patterns that are needed for their survival (called fixed action patterns), such as migration or mating rituals, avoiding danger, and building nests by birds, or spinning webs by spiders. Even if the spider never saw a web before, never witnessed its creation, it would know how to create one.

Humans were thought to have the same types of innate tendencies, and their behavior was motivated by inborn instinctual behavior patterns. Babies are born with a unique ability that allows them to survive; they are born with the ability to cry to signal attention of their mother to feed, to know when they need changing, or when they want attention and affection. Thus, crying allows a human infant to survive. Also, we are born with particular reflexes which promote survival. The most important of these include sucking, swallowing, coughing, blinking. Newborns can perform physical movements to avoid pain; they will turn their head if touched on their cheek and search for a nipple (rooting reflex); and they will grasp an object that touches the palm of their hands (grasping reflex). Thus, instincts were thought to provide the energy that channels behavior in appropriate directions.

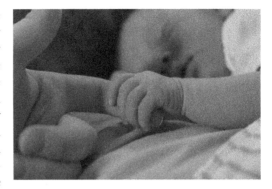

PHOTO 9.2. The Grasping Reflex.

However, controversy emerged over the exact definition of instinct, and many lists were proposed as representing instincts. By the 1920s, instinct theories had fallen out of favor as an explanation of human motivation, because of their lack of explanatory power, and more acknowledgment of the role of learning in shaping of human behavior. But the general idea that some human behaviors are innate and genetically influenced remained an important element in the overall understanding of motivation.

The Drive Reduction Theory

According to Clark Hull (1943), humans have internal biological needs which motivate them to perform in a certain way. These needs, or drives, are defined by Hull as internal states of arousal or tension which must be reduced. A key example is the internal feelings of hunger or thirst, which motivates us to eat and drink. According to this theory, we are driven to reduce the unpleasant state of tension in the body and to return the body to a state of homeostasis. Homeostasis is the tendency to maintain a balance, or an optimal level, within a biological system.

The original Clark Hull drive reduction theory was modified by other psychologists to include acquired (secondary) drives. Thus, drives can generally be divided into primary and secondary drives. Primary drives are mainly physiological/biological and unlearned, and are necessary for survival. They include need for food, water, clothing and shelter, sleep, sex, and other material concerns. Secondary drives are mainly psychological and learned, and are not necessary for survival. Secondary drives are usually associated with primary drives because the satisfaction of secondary drives indirectly satisfies primary drives, e.g., the desire for wealth is not necessary for survival, however, wealth provides you with money that can be used to acquire

PHOTO 9.3. The Drive Reduction Theory.

food, shelter, and other basic needs, thereby indirectly satisfying these primary drives. Secondary drives become associated with primary drives through conditioning.

Today, the drive concept remains useful in explaining motivated behaviors that clearly have biological components, such as hunger, thirst, and sexuality. However, drive theories also have limitations:

- Pleasure-seeking behaviors seem to be contradictory to the theory's precepts, e.g., why individuals eat when they are not hungry.
- Why would an individual actively seek out more stimulation if he/she is already in a state of relaxation and fulfillment? Proponents of the drive reduction theory would argue that one is never in a state of complete fulfillment, and, thus, there are always drives that need to be satisfied.
- Needs can arise without specific drives, as in learning what and how much to eat, e.g., a person may eat foods containing vitamin C after knowing of its value, but we would not normally talk of a vitamin C drive.
- Drives can occur in the absence of any obvious physiological need, e.g., a non-homeostatic drive in rats is electrical self-stimulation of the brain or intracranial self-stimulation (Toates, 2001).

The Incentive Theory

The incentive theory of motivation suggests that a behavior is motivated by the desire to obtain valued external goals, or incentives. In this view, people are more motivated to perform activities if they receive a reward afterward (extrinsic sources), rather than simply because they enjoy the activities themselves. The desirable properties of external stimuli account for a person's motivation, e.g., when a delicious dessert appears on the table after a filling meal, its appeal has little or nothing to do with drive theory. If we choose to eat the dessert, such behavior is motivated by the properties of the dessert itself, which acts as an anticipated reward. From this perspective, incentives may sound like operant conditioning, where reinforcement governs the occurrence of learned behavior.

Some incentives are primary reinforcers, i.e., they are able to act as rewards independently of prior learning, e.g., a sweet taste or a sexual sensation may be pleasant the first time it is experienced. Other incentives are secondary reinforcers, i.e., they have gained their status as rewards at least partly through learning about their relationship to other events, e.g., money or good grades can be effective incentives, based on our cultural experience with them and with the status and success they represent. Learning is crucial to the formation of secondary reinforcers, and plays a part in modulating the effectiveness of some primary reinforcers, e.g., people are born without an idea about which foods are their favorites.

However, the drive reduction and the incentive theories provide different perspectives on the control of motivation; the difference is primarily in their points of view, and there is no actual conflict between the two. It is widely acknowledged that both types of

PHOTO 9.4.   The Incentive Theory.

processes exist for almost every kind of motivation (Toates, 1986). When combined, drive and incentive theories account for a broad range of the forces motivating certain behavior. However, in some situations, such as playing a rapid-response video game, our behavior seems to be directed toward increasing tension and physiological arousal, a behavior that is not motivated by either an internal, biological drive or an external incentive.

The Arousal Theory

The arousal theory expands upon the drive reduction theory by considering levels of arousal as potential motivators. Arousal refers to a state of emotional, intellectual, and physical activity. Arousal theory does not rely on only a reduction of tension, but also we wish to maintain a balanced amount of arousal. If we are under-aroused, we experience boredom and become motivated to increase arousal by seeking out stimulating experiences, but when arousal is too high, we seek to reduce our arousal (Berlyne, 1960). Thus, people are motivated to maintain an optimal level of arousal, one that is neither too high nor too low.

The optimal level of arousal varies from person to person, from time to time, and from one situation to another. People who rank high on the dimension of sensation-seeking have a need for varied, complex, and unique sensory experiences (Zuckerman, 1979, 2007). People who participate in risky sports, high stakes gamblers, and criminals who perform high-risk robberies may be exhibiting a particularly high need for arousal. Research shows that moderate arousal is generally best; when arousal is very high or very low, performance tends to suffer. The optimal arousal level depends on the complexity and difficulty of the task to be performed. The Yerkes-Dodson Law states that performance on tasks is best when the arousal level is appropriate to the difficulty of the task (Yerkes & Dodson, 1908). It is generally accepted that higher arousal is needed for simple tasks, moderate arousal for tasks of moderate difficulty, and lower arousal for complex tasks. Too high or too low arousal for the task can affect performance.

PHOTO 9.5. The Arousal Theory.

Cognitive Approaches

Cognitive theories of motivation stress the active processing and understanding of information. These theories view individuals as thinking about, planning, and exercising control over their behavior. Cognitive theories are based on two basic factors: (1) information available to the individual; and (2) the individual's past experience, which the person refers to when trying to make sense of the available information and to determine how to respond or relate to the current situation. Cognitive theories of motivation draw a key distinction between intrinsic and extrinsic motivation. *Intrinsic motivation* is the force that compels a person to fulfill his or her inner potential and interests, it causes us to participate in an activity for our own enjoyment rather than for any concrete reward that it will bring us. It corresponds to the inherent desire of an individual to express his or her actual self through selected actions and behavior, across different settings, whether at work or at play. In contrast, *extrinsic motivation* is experienced when a person's actions are influenced by the desire to attain goal objects or rewards. Rewards may be material, such as food or money, or intangible, such as pride and recognition. Among the most prominent cognitive theories are cognitive consistency theories, goal-setting theory, expectancy theory, and frustration theory.

Cognitive Consistency Theories

Cognitive consistency theories refer to the tendency of individuals to seek consistency among their cognitions (i.e., beliefs, opinions). Cognitive consistency theories gained tremendous popularity in the social sciences in the 1950s, and generated hundreds of studies. This research interest waned toward the end of the 1960s. The term cognitive refers to almost anything that humans can hold consciously (thoughts, beliefs, knowledge, opinions, attitudes, and intents). The term consistency refers to consistency across cognitions, meaning that cognitions should be in agreement, symmetrical, balanced, or congruent. Conflicting cognitions place individuals in an unpleasant psychological state. The basic premise of cognitive consistency theories is that humans are motivated by inconsistencies and a desire to change them. This theory states that people anticipate consistency. Cognitive inconsistencies arise when thoughts conflict with each other, and cause imbalance and dissonance in individuals. The tension from this imbalance motivates people to alter these inconsistencies. When this tension is reduced, balance is achieved in the individual.

The major theories of cognitive consistency that have had the most impact on the behavioral sciences include cognitive dissonance theory (Festinger, 1957), balance theory (Heider, 1946, 1958), the strain toward symmetry (Newcomb, 1953, 1968), congruency theory (Osgood & Tannenbaum, 1955), and, finally, the affective-cognitive consistency model (Rosenberg, 1956).

Cognitive Dissonance Theory

Cognitive dissonance theory is a phenomenon in which people experience psychological distress when they have contradictory attitudes or when their behavior contradicts their stated attitudes. That is, people have a need for consistency in their thoughts, perceptions, and images of their selves (Cooper, Mirabile, Scher, Brock, & Green, 2005; Festinger, 1957). Leon Festinger proposed that people have a motivational drive to reduce dissonance in their cognitions by either changing or justifying their attitudes, beliefs, and behaviors, e.g., smokers who are told that cigarettes increase the risk of cancer, may resolve the tension between this information and their actions, by deciding to quit smoking. However, it is usually easier for smokers to reject the causal link between cigarettes and cancer, and convince themselves that smoking is not really so dangerous. To do this, smokers seek examples of heavy smokers who have lived long happy lives. Sometimes, a smoker may reduce the tension between information and their actions by making excuses for themselves, such as "I am going to die anyway, so it does not matter." The number of dissonant beliefs, and the importance attached to each belief affect the strength of the dissonance. Dissonance theory is especially relevant to decision-making and problem-solving, but it applies to all situations involving attitude formation and change (Wicklund & Brehm, 1976).

Balance Theory

Balance theory refers to the idea that we want to maintain psychological stability, and we form relationships that balance our likes and dislikes. Fritz Heider developed the P-O-X triangle to examine these relationships. Each corner of the triangle represents a different element: P is the person, O is the object of the analysis (some other person), while X is a physical object, idea, or conflict. In this triangular relationship, two types of relationship dynamics are taking place. First, is unit relationship, or how much the different elements of the triangle belong together. The more similarities that exist between each element, the more likely psychological balance will occur. The second type of relationship is sentiment relationship, or how we feel about something. The attitudes in the structure are designated as either positive or negative. Heider categorizes all feelings into one of two areas: liking or disliking. In most situations, if a positive unit relationship exists, a positive sentiment relationship will exist as well. Likewise, negative unit relationships and negative sentiment relationships tend to go together. The goal of assessing the structure of a triad is to ascertain whether the relationships (attitudes) between the actors and the other elements are balanced, or consistent. Heider assumed that people prefer balanced states to unbalanced ones, because an imbalance results in tension and feelings of unpleasantness.

According to Heider (1958), a balanced triad occurs when all the relationships are positive, or two are negative and one is positive (i.e., two people have a negative attitude toward an issue, but they like each other), and the elements in the triad fit together with no stress. Imbalance occurs when these outcomes are not achieved (i.e., all three relationships are negative, or you have a negative attitude toward an issue that your friend favors). According to balance theory, there are three ways to restore balance to an unbalanced state: (1) changing one's attitude toward either the object or the other person, in order to restore balance (e.g., one may take a side in the argument between friends); (2) distorting reality to perceive that the relationships are balanced (e.g., your friends actually like each other); and (3) one may cognitively differentiate the relationship one has with a friend, so that the friend's opposing attitude toward something one favors is separated from one's positive attitude toward the friend as a person (e.g., you may separate a friend's opposite views as apart from your attitude, in order to maintain your friendship and maintain balance) (Eagly & Chaiken, 1993), or a situation that causes psychological discomfort. Cartwright and Harary (1956) generalized Heider's theory to account for structures of any size.

Strain Toward Symmetry

Systems of relationships that are in equilibrium tend to be stable. This would be the case when professor and student like each other and share a similar attitude toward certain topic. It would also be true if they had opposing attitudes toward that topic, but they really did not like each other very much. In contrast, incompatibility provides an impulse toward resolving the tension, what Newcomb designated as strain toward symmetry. Newcomb (1953, 1968) suggested that there are three types of balance relationships in a triad: (1) an unbalanced structure, which refers to a structure that does not motivate modification or acceptance. These situations are characterized by indifference. Here, disagreement with another individual about an issue or object does not arouse tension if that other individual is devalued (or otherwise not important; (2) a positively balanced structure: when the other person is valued (i.e., a friend or significant other), then agreement with him or her about an object results in a positively balanced structure; and (3) a positively imbalanced structure occurs when there is disagreement with the other person. The term positive in the latter two types of structure denotes the valence of the relationship between P and O, who is a valued other. The important focus in Newcomb's approach is the relationship of O to P, and P's view of O as a valued person, and suitability as a source of information, or support, or of influence concerning the object (Newcomb, 1968). Newcomb found that positively balanced situations are the preferred structures, followed by unbalanced structures, with the positively unbalanced situations being the least preferred.

Congruency Theory

Congruency theory deals specifically with the attitudes a person holds toward sources of information and the objects of the source's assertions. Osgood and Tannenbaum reframe the Heider triad into the P-S-O triangle, where P is the person, O is the attitude (called the "assertion") toward another object or concept, and S is the source of such an attitude. Distinct from balance theory, congruency theory refers to the ability to make predictions about the direction and degree of attitude change: a change is always toward greater congruity. According to the theory, attitudes can be quantified along a seven-unit evaluative scale, from extremely negative (-3) to neutral (0) to extremely positive ($+3$). When P's attitude toward S and O are positive, and S's assertion is equally strong and of the same valence, there is a congruous structure to the triad, and there will be no motivation to change one's attitude toward the object or toward the source. When P's attitude toward S is positive and P has an equally positive attitude toward O that S later negatively evaluates, an incongruous structure is established. In this situation, P is motivated to change his or her attitude toward S, or O, or both, in the direction of congruity, e.g., if P's attitude toward S is a $+2$, and P's attitude toward O is a -2, the structure would be congruent if S's assessment is a -2. If, however, the assessment is a $+2$, the structure is imbalanced. In this case, P's attitude toward either O or S needs to change by four units to make the triad congruent (Tannenbaum, 1968).

The Affective-Cognitive Consistency Model

Rosenberg's approach is called the affective-cognitive consistency model because it proposes that inconsistency results when one's feelings are inconsistent with one's beliefs. That is, when the way we think and feel about an object or person are at odds, we will modify one or both to make the attitude consistent. Thus, this model attempts to address consistency within one's own attitudes toward other people and objects, but also consistency in how one's value system relates to other people and objects. The model is also unique in suggesting that people experience more tension as a result of one's own inconsistency (Rosenberg, 1956, 1968).

The theory suggests that the affective component of the attitude system may be altered by changing the cognitive component through providing new information. It does not matter how the new cognition is produced, only that it occurs. Providing an individual with new information that changes the cognitive component of attitude will tend to cause that individual to change their overall attitudes toward an object and to bring the knowledge and affect into harmony.

Expectancy Theory

Vroom's expectancy theory assumes that behavior results from conscious choices among alternatives whose purpose is to maximize pleasure and to minimize pain. Selection of a specific behavior over other behaviors is directed by one's expectation about what the result of the selected behavior will be (Vroom, 1964). The relationship between people's behavior at work and their goals was not as simple as was first imagined by other scientists. Vroom suggested that an employee's performance is based on different factors such as personality, skills, knowledge, experience, and abilities. Vroom proposed that factors which play an important role while selecting one element over another include an employee's beliefs about expectancy, instrumentality, and valence. These factors interact psychologically to create a motivational force such that the employee acts in ways that bring pleasure and avoid pain. The three elements are:

- *Expectancy*: is the likelihood that a behavior will lead to a certain goal, i.e., it is the belief that increased effort will lead to improved outcome. This depends on having self-efficacy (the belief of an individual about their own efficiency and ability to perform a particular behavior effectively), goal difficulty (if the desired performance goal is higher than expected, it might cause lack of high expectancy perception), and control (the degree of perceived control of a person over performance).
- *Valence*: refers to attractiveness or the value of the goal, the importance that the individual places upon the expected outcome. For a positive valence, the person must prefer attaining the outcome over not attaining it, e.g., if someone is mainly motivated by money, it will not be of value to them to offer additional time off.
- *Instrumentality*: is the belief that if you perform well, the valued outcome will be received. This depends on a clear relationship between performance and outcomes, e.g., the rules of the reward game, trust in the people who will take the decisions on who gets which outcome, and transparency of the process that decides who gets what.

Thus, Vroom's expectancy theory of motivation is not about self-interest in rewards but about the associations people make toward expected outcomes and the contribution they feel they can make toward those outcomes. According to expectancy theory, motivational force is the product of three variables of expectancy theory, i.e., expectancy, valence, and instrumentality.

$$\text{Motivational Force} = \text{Expectancy} \times \text{Instrumentality} \times \text{Valence}$$

Goal-Setting Theory

Goal-setting theory was introduced by Edwin Locke. The primary factor explained by the theory is that the goal-setting comprises direct and enough impact on the task performance. A set of specific and hard-to-achieve goals will lead to a greater accomplishment of tasks and possibly will motivate an individual additionally. On the other hand, easy-to-achieve goals may result in poor or very low task performance. When challenging goals are set for an employee, the proper tools are provided to accomplish those goals and positive feedback is given, the employee feels satisfaction with the performance and the reward. This makes the employee want to strive to accomplish an even more challenging goal. The set goals must be Specific, Measurable, Attainable, Realistic, and Time-bound (SMART). Goals need to be precise so that the individual knows exactly what is expected, and the type and amount of effort/actions needed in order to attain the goal. A goal that is neither too easy nor too difficult to accomplish is the most attractive and appealing to an individual. Goals that are too easy fail to provide self-satisfaction while goals that are too difficult to achieve can discourage a person from making an effort in trying to accomplish them. Also, the shorter the time between the initiation of action toward a goal and the time of goal achievement, the greater are the chances of success (Locke & Latham, 1990).

Frustration Theory

Abram Amsel formulated the frustration hypothesis to explain how the motivation to perform some behaviors can be so strong and long-lasting, despite lack of rewards or even harsh punishments. The basic assumption behind Amsel's theory is that an expectancy of reinforcement can cause frustration when it is not fulfilled. According to Amsel, frustration is an unpleasant drive that can motivate animals to avoid what has been frustrating them (due to the negative reinforcement of a decrease in frustration). At the same time, because it is a drive, it increases the overall activity level of the animal, which can result in new responses, and thus, the possibility of learning responses to complete those that led to the frustration (Amsel, 1992).

Need Satisfaction Theory (Maslow's Hierarchy of Needs)

Abraham Maslow outlined a general theory of motivation, based mainly on humanistic psychology and clinical experience. Maslow arranged motivational needs into a hierarchy composed of five levels of needs. The five levels in Maslow's hierarchy are presented in a pyramidal form, with the more basic needs at the bottom and the higher-level needs at the top of the pyramid (Figure 9.1). Maslow suggested that people tend to satisfy their needs systematically starting

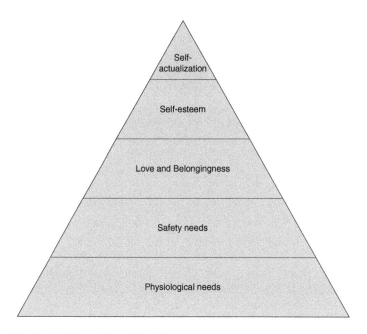

FIGURE 9.1.   Maslow's Hierarchy of Needs.

with basic physiological needs and then move up the hierarchy. Needs of a particular level should be satisfied, at least partially, before moving up to the next level. Thus, a person who is hungry will not be motivated by safety or affection needs. Maslow later modified this argument by stating that there was an exception to this rule in respect to self-actualization, for that level, satisfaction of one need gives rise to a further need to realize one's potential (Maslow, 1954, 1970).

Maslow's hierarchy of needs is:

- *Basic or physiological needs*: these are the needs which must be satisfied to maintain life, such as the need for food, water, air, and shelter. When one is very hungry, behavior will be motivated by the need to find food. Once one eats, the search for food ceases, and the need for food is no longer a current motivator.
- *Safety needs*: once physiological needs are satisfied, people tend to become concerned about safety needs. This includes emotional as well as physical safety. Safety needs include the desire for protection from physical danger, the search for economic security, and the desire for an orderly predictable world.
- *Love and belonging*: when physiological and safety needs have been met, social needs for love/belonging become important. This can include the need to bond with other human beings, the need to be loved and accepted, and the need to form lasting attachments.
- *Esteem needs*: self-esteem needs can be broken down into two categories: (1) the need for competence and achievement or success, which can be satisfied intrinsically; and (2) the desire for reputation, prestige, and recognition from others. People will often look for ways to achieve a sense of mastery, and they may seek validation and praise from others in order to fulfill these needs.
- *Self-actualization or self-fulfillment needs*: self-actualization or self-fulfillment is the highest level in the hierarchy. Individuals seek to realize their own potential for continued self-development and creativity. At this level, people have feelings of accomplishment and of being satisfied with their selves. This can be seen in acquiring new skills, taking on new challenges, and behaving in a way that will help to achieve life goals. Maslow suggested that this is an ongoing, lifelong process and that only a small percentage of people actually achieve a self-actualized state.

Clayton Alderfer modified Maslow's hierarchy by categorizing the needs into three groups (E.R.G. theory):

- *Existence needs*: provide basic physical requirements.
- *Relatedness needs*: provide requirements of interpersonal relationships.
- *Growth needs*: provide requirements of personal development.

Alderfer proposed that people can move up the hierarchy when needs are satisfied, or move down the hierarchy when a need is frustrated (Alderfer, 1969).

The Achievement Motivation Theory

The achievement motivation theory assumes that people are motivated to succeed by seeking achievement and the associated competitive drive to meet standards of excellence. Achievement motivation is influenced by a combination of internal factors, including personal drives, and external or environmental factors, including pressures and expectations of relevant organizations and society. David McClelland believed that the need for achievement is a distinct human motive that can be distinguished from other needs. He believed that people seeking achievement do not reject rewards but the rewards are not as essential as the accomplishment itself. In addition to an individual's need for achievement, David McClelland assumed that human motivation is also driven by the individual's need for power and need for affiliation as motivators of human behavior. All people have the three motivating drives, and one of these will be the dominant motivating drive. This dominant motivator is largely dependent on our culture and life experiences.

People who have strong achievement needs take responsibility for their actions, take calculated risks, set moderate achievement goals that they are more likely to succeed at, favor non-routine tasks over routine assignments, and welcome comments about their behavior. Achievement motivation is often distinguished from failure avoidance, in which the person is motivated to simply avoid failure. People motivated by failure avoidance do not put as much work into what they do and focus on passing rather than exceeding expectations.

People who have a strong need for power focus on how to influence and control the behavior of other people, and the means to do this. People who have strong affiliation needs focus on establishing, maintaining, and restoring good relations with others. They usually search for the approval of others, need other people to like them, and, finally, to be in the company of others.

Conflict of Motives

PHOTO 9.6.   A State of Conflict.

Conflict is an internal struggle, often unconscious, that stems from the presence of antagonistic or reciprocally exclusive impulses, desires, or tendencies. Choosing one option prevents choosing the other one, at least temporarily. Conflicts can be classified according to whether the goal is needed or rejected:

- *Approach versus approach conflict*: this is one of the mildest and easily resolved conflicts. The person is faced with two or more favorable options, e.g., two job offers, both with good salaries and positions.
- *Approach versus avoidance conflict*: the person is faced with an option which has both good and bad aspects, e.g., studying medicine requires a lot of money and time. Living in big cities need good tolerance to crowding and noise.
- *Avoidance versus avoidance conflict*: the person is faced with two or more unfavorable options. The person here tries to choose the option with least deleterious effect.
- *Multiple approach avoidance conflict*: this arises in situations when the person is faced with more than one stimulus and each has positive and negative aspects.

Conflicts could also be classified according to the driving force (needs or motives) into:

- *Conflict between two incompatible biological needs*: e.g., the sex motive may conflict with harm avoidance motives due to fear from infection with venereal diseases.
- *Conflict between two incompatible self-constructive needs*: e.g., the motive to be famous in sports may conflict with excelling in scientific study.
- *Conflict between two duties to different affairs*: a physician may find conflict between his private and work duties.
- *Conflict between motives and conscience*: social standards usually put limits to excess revenge or indulgence in pleasurable activities (sex, drinking, money).

Factors affecting the level of conflict include:

- The nature of the opposing forces: conflict between agreeable goals is easier to solve than that between disagreeable ones.
- The strength of the opposing forces: the more equal the conflicting forces, the stronger the conflict.
- The nature of the underlying motive: biological needs, especially life preservation and sex motives, are associated with stronger motives.
- The length of time during which conflict continues.

Clinical Notes

Applying different approaches of motivation to understand certain behaviors enables the clinician to more appropriately recognize the real causes. Understanding motivation can be of value in evaluating and management cases of obesity and eating disorders, gambling, drug abuse, and sexual disorders.

Summary

- A motive is an internal state (physiological or psychological) that arouses, directs, and maintains behavior toward a goal.
- The instinct theory of motivation suggests that people and animals are born pre-programmed with sets of behaviors essential to their survival.
- The drive reduction theory suggests that humans have internal biological needs which motivate them to perform in a certain way.
- The incentive theory of motivation suggests that a behavior is motivated by the desire to obtain valued external goals, or incentives.
- The arousal theory of motivation considers levels of arousal as potential motivators.
- Cognitive theories of motivation stress the active processing and understanding of information.
- Maslow arranged motivational needs into a hierarchy presented in a pyramidal form, with the more basic needs at the bottom and the higher-level needs at the top of the pyramid. Maslow suggested that people tend to satisfy their needs systematically, starting with basic physiological needs and then moving up the hierarchy.
- Conflict of motives is an internal struggle, often unconscious, that stems from the presence of antagonistic or reciprocally exclusive impulses, desires, or tendencies.

Test Your Knowledge

- Define the instinct theory of motivation.
- Explain the drive reduction theory of motivation.
- Describe the incentive theory of motivation.
- Define the arousal theory of motivation.
- What are the cognitive approaches to motivation?
- Describe Maslow's hierarchy of needs.
- Define conflict and its types.

Critical Thinking Questions

- How can motivation play a role in obesity and weight reduction?
- What types of motivation theories can explain drug dependence?

ten
Learning

- This chapter is intended to provide the reader with an overview of the concepts of learning, the general laws of learning, associative learning (conditioning), observational learning (modeling), the cognitive learning theory, and the constructivist learning theory.

Introduction

Learning is a hypothetical concept that cannot be directly observed, but only inferred from observable behaviors. It is formally defined as an enduring change in the mechanisms of behavior resulting from prior experience with particular stimuli and responses. Learning manifests as acquisition of skills, values, or preferences, and as acquiring new or modifying existing knowledge. This definition has many important consequences:

PHOTO 10.1.   Early Learning.

1. Learning is defined as a change in the mechanisms of behavior to emphasize the distinction between learning and performance. The performance of a new response or the suppression of a response that occurred previously is not enough as evidence of learning. This is because performance of behavior is determined by many factors in addition to learning, e.g., jumping into a swimming pool cannot be automatically considered to reflect learning, as it is determined by multiple factors including the depth of the pool, the temperature of the water, the physical ability to spring away from the side of the pool, and so forth.
2. Behavioral changes in learning should be enduring to rule out changes resulting from transient or temporary states, such as alterations in the physiological or motivational state.
3. Behavioral changes in learning should result from experience with environmental events, to rule out behavioral changes resulting from causes unrelated to learning, such as the effects of brain damage on behavior, and changes associated with puberty and other maturational processes (J. R. Anderson, 1995; Coon, 1983).

Learning is not restricted to classrooms, but occurs in all settings, and at every age. The ability to learn is not restricted to humans, but includes animals and may involve some machines. Learning may take different forms; the simple forms of learning, such as habituation and sensitization, occur in all species through repeated presentation of one stimulus, i.e., learning is non-associative.

Habituation

A person first responds to a stimulus, but if it is neither rewarding nor harmful, the person reduces subsequent responses, i.e., there is a progressive diminution of behavioral response probability with repetition stimulus, e.g., the sound of fireworks may be startling at first; after feeling safe, the amount of surprise will progressively decrease by each sound.

Sensitization

Contrary to habituation, sensitization refers to progressive amplification of a response following repeated administrations of a stimulus, e.g., a person who rubs his arm continuously. After a while, this stimulation will create a warm sensation that will eventually turn painful. The pain is the result of the progressively amplified synaptic response of the peripheral nerves warning the person that the stimulation is harmful. Although habituation and sensitization are simple types of learning, they are important for directing attention of the individual.

Transfer of Learning

Transfer of learning refers to the ability to apply information learned in one situation to another and different situation, e.g., applying mathematic procedures learned in a classroom when going to the grocery store to determine the best prices. Some kinds of transfer take the form of simple stimulus generalization, while in more complex learning situations transfer may depend on the acquisition of rules or principles that apply to a variety of different circumstances. Learning sets can be viewed as intermediate between simple generalization, and the more complex transfer phenomena involved in hierarchically organized skills (Howe, 1980).

General Laws of Learning

The general process approach of learning is based on the work of the behaviorists, they assume that there are some principles called laws of learning (Domjan, 2006). Ivan Pavlov and John B. Watson believed the basic laws of learning were essentially similar in all animals. In his doctoral dissertation, Edward L. Thorndike (1911) introduced a theory of learning based on his experiments in the field of animal psychology, named connectionism. This theory of learning emphasizes that the behavior begins with conditioned reflexes and natural responses and new behaviors result from the acquisition of new bonds through experience. Thorndike proposed the first three learning laws to explain the learning process: (1) readiness; (2) exercise; and (3) effect, while other laws of learning were added later on by other psychologists. The following is a summary of the general learning laws:

1. *Law of readiness*: learning cannot be automatically instilled in a learner; learning can only take place when an individual is ready to learn. This readiness results from a combination of growth and experience. Children cannot learn to read until their nervous systems are mature enough, and have a sufficient background of spoken words and pre-reading experience with letters and pictures. When students are ready to learn, they act or learn more effectively and with greater satisfaction than when not ready.
2. *Law of exercise*: this law is similar to the law of use and disuse, doing something regularly makes one perfect. In other words, the more a person repeats something, the better he or she is able to retain that knowledge. On the other hand, knowledge that is not used becomes weakened and disappears from memory.
3. *Law of effect*: learning is strengthened when the learner feels a pleasant or satisfying feeling, and is rewarded for learning. Learning is weakened when associated with an unpleasant feeling. Therefore, students are more likely to learn when they feel satisfied or are rewarded for learning, rather than punished for not learning. They need to feel good in order to retain motivation. However, in certain cases the law of effect fails, i.e., criticism or punishment may yield better learning.
4. *Law of multiple responses*: when a response fails to elicit a desired effect, the learner will try a new response (trial and error) until the goal is reached.
5. *The law of set or attitude*: learning is guided by a total mental set or attitude of the learner, which determines not only what the person will do but what will satisfy or annoy him or her, e.g., unless a student determines to get first position and has the attitude of being at the top, the student will not learn much.

6. *Law of prepotency of elements*: the learner reacts selectively to the important or the salient elements of the problem or situation and neglects irrelevant or non-essential elements.

7. *Law of response by analogy*: the individual compares a new situation to the previously learned one and gives a response according to similarity, where common elements of a new situation and a similar past situation are usually used, e.g., driving a new car is usually facilitated by previous experience of driving different type of cars.

8. *Law of associative shifting*: according to this law, a response may occur if it becomes associated with another situation to which the learner is sensitive, e.g., after a number of trials, a cat can be taught to stand up at a command, if a fish was swayed before the cat while saying "stand up." This law represents the basis of operant conditioning.

Theories of Learning
Associative Learning (Conditioning)

Associative learning refers to the process by which an element is taught through association with another separate, pre-occurring element, that is, learning that occurs when certain events go together. If one associates a sound with a frightening consequence, hearing the sound alone may trigger fear. Learned associations feed our habitual response (Wood & Neal, 2007). Two major types of associative learning are described: classic and operant conditioning.

Classic Conditioning (Respondent Conditioning)

Based on Ivan Pavlov's experiments, John B. Watson proposed that classical conditioning can explain all aspects of human behavior. Watson believed that all individual differences in behavior result from different experiences of learning, and that everything "from speech to emotional responses" is simply patterns of stimulus and response. In classic conditioning, learning is a form of making an association between a stimulus and another event, the response. In the experiments with the dogs described by Pavlov, he paired a bell sound with the meat powder and found that a dog would eventually begin to salivate after hearing the bell, even in the absence of the meat powder. In this case, since the meat powder naturally results in salivation, these two variables are called the unconditioned stimulus (UCS) and the unconditioned response (UCR), respectively. In the experiment, the bell and salivation are not naturally occurring, the dog is conditioned to respond to the bell. Therefore, the bell is considered the conditioned stimulus (CS), and the salivation to the bell, the conditioned response (CR). Thus, classic conditioning includes the following variables (Figure 10.1):

- *Neutral stimulus* is a stimulus that currently does not produce the response of interest when it is presented.
- *Unconditioned stimulus* (UCS) is any stimulus that automatically (without being learned) produces a response (e.g., the odor of food).
- *Unconditioned response* (UCR) is the response made to the unconditioned stimulus (e.g., salivation in response to the odor of food).
- *Conditioned stimulus* (CS) is a previously neutral stimulus that has now been conditioned to produce a response (e.g., the sound of the bell).
- *Conditioned response* (CR) is the response made to the conditioned stimulus (e.g., salivation in response to the sound of bell).

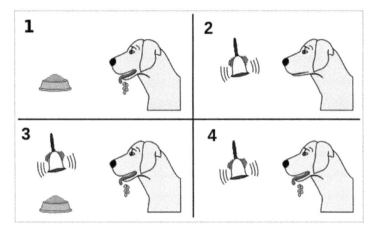

FIGURE 10.1.   Pavlov's Classic Conditioning.

Further concepts that apply to classical conditioning are:

■ *Generalization*: the tendency to respond similarly to stimuli resembling the conditioned stimulus. Generalization can be adaptive, e.g., when toddlers taught to fear
moving cars also become afraid of moving trucks and motorcycles, or non-adaptive
when it occurs in response to similar disgusting, distressing, or undesirable stimuli.
■ *Discrimination*: the ability to distinguish between a conditioned stimulus and other
irrelevant stimuli, thus, a conditioned response is not given to stimuli that are dissimi-
lar to the conditioned stimulus.
■ *Extinction*: the diminution of a conditioned response. This occurs in classical conditioning when the conditioned stimulus is presented repeatedly without being followed
by the unconditioned stimulus, and occurs in operant conditioning when a response is
no longer reinforced.
■ *Spontaneous recovery*: the reappearance of conditioned response, after a pause, following extinction.
■ *Second-order conditioning* (also known as higher-order conditioning): refers to a situation in which a neutral stimulus (e.g., a light) is paired with a conditioned stimulus
(e.g., a tone that was conditioned with food to produce salivation "this is the first
order") to produce the same conditioned response as the conditioned stimulus.
■ *Counter-conditioning*: a previously conditioned response is replaced by a more desirable response. It is used in behavior modification.

Classic conditioning is criticized for underestimating the complexity of human behavior by
emphasizing the role of the environment in learning, and supports nurture over nature. Classic
conditioning is also reductionist in its explanation of behavior, it reduces complex behavior into
smaller units of stimulus-response behavior. Although breaking complicated behaviors down
into small parts facilitates its scientific testing, it can lead to incomplete explanations. Classic
conditioning is also criticized for being deterministic, a person has no control over what is
learned from classical conditioning, such as a phobia.

Operant Conditioning (Instrumental Conditioning)

In operant conditioning, learning occurs because of the consequences to the individual of a previous behavior. Although a behavior may occur randomly at first, the consequences that occur immediately after the behavior determine whether the behavior continues, i.e., operant conditioning is a type of learning in which a voluntary response is strengthened or weakened, depending on its favorable or unfavorable consequences. The likelihood that a behavior will occur is increased by reinforcement and decreased by punishment.

Operant conditioning is distinguished from classic conditioning in that operant conditioning uses reinforcement/punishment to alter an action outcome association. In contrast, classic conditioning involves strengthening of the stimulus-outcome association. So when teaching an individual a response, you need to find the most potent reinforcer for that person. This may be a larger reinforcer at a later time or a smaller immediate reinforcer.

Principles of operant conditioning are useful in explaining and managing behavioral problems. Parents asking children to go to bed and then yielding to protests or defiance reinforce such behaviors (Wierson & Forehand, 1994). Also, high-frequency behavior (eating dessert) can be used to reward or reinforce low-frequency behavior (eating greens), this is called Premack's principle (Grandma's rule).

At school, reinforcement of bright kids may lead the slower ones to be frustrated and fail, this illustrates the need to tailor educational and reinforcement programs to allow all students to achieve their potentials and ideals. Principles of operant conditioning are used effectively to produce behavioral changes in behavior modification techniques, e.g., reduce public smoking by teenagers (Jason, Pokorny, Sanem, & Adams, 2006), improve student behavior in school (Fabiano, Schatz, Aloe, Chacko, & Chronis-Tuscano, 2015), reduce tantrums in preschool children (Wilder, Chen, Atwell, Pritchard, & Weinstein, 2006), and improve social skills and reduce self-destructive behaviors in people with autism and related disorders (Matson & LoVullo, 2008; Matson & Smith, 2007).

The reinforcement of successive behaviors to some final goal is called shaping. It allows behavior to be molded from simple behavior already present in the organism to a relatively complex one (not part of the animal's natural repertoire). Most human skills are learned in this step-by-step manner. Shaping is used to teach language to children with intellectual disability or autism, teach them to use the toilet, to feed and dress themselves, and other social skills.

The factors operating in operant conditioning are reinforcement or punishment.

Reinforcement is the stimulus that increases the probability that a prior behavior will occur again. It can be positive or negative:

■ *Positive reinforcement*: this is the introduction of a rewarding or positive stimulus that results in an increase in a preceding response, e.g., rewarding a child will increase the chances of him or her cleaning his or her bedroom. Positive reinforcers are typically classified into primary and secondary ones. Primary reinforcers are characterized by being natural reinforcers, and reinforcing in themselves, such as food, water, sex. Secondary reinforcers are not rewarding in themselves, but acquire their reinforcing properties through association with primary reinforcers, e.g., money, grades, trophies, and praise from others. Secondary reinforcers play an important role in bridging the gap between the response and the primary reinforcer. Using an imagined pleasant event (such as imagining a graduation event to reinforce studying hard) rather than any material pleasure is called covert reinforcement. It should be noted that a stimulus that functions as a positive reinforcer at one time or in one context may have a different effect at another time or place, e.g., food may serve as a positive reinforcer when you are hungry, but not when you are ill or just after you finished a large meal. Also, due to individual differences, a stimulus that functions as a positive reinforcer for one person may fail to operate in a similar manner for another person.

■ *Negative reinforcement*: this is the removal of an aversive stimulus that led to an increase in the probability that a preceding response will occur again in the future, e.g., while sleeping soundly in a warm, comfortable bed, hearing the alarm clock will get a person out of bed to turn off the alarm, on subsequent mornings, the person will get up early to avoid hearing the sound of the alarm altogether, getting up early has been negatively reinforced by the alarm clock. In agoraphobia, the patient avoids places in which panic occurs and may eventually become housebound, this is called escape conditioning.

Punishment is the use of an aversive stimulus to decrease the probability that a prior behavior will occur again, e.g., using time outs for a child misbehaving leads to stoppage of that behavior to avoid punishment. The reduction of the preceding behavior is the main differentiating point between reinforcement and punishment. Punishment can be positive or negative:

■ *Positive punishment*: this refers to the application of an unpleasant stimulus, e.g., paying fines when exceeding the driving speed limit leads to obeying the posted speed limit next time. Similarly, the use of disulfiram can reduce the frequency of drinking alcohol. The use of positive punishment to reduce the frequency of the target behavior is called aversive conditioning.
■ *Negative punishment*: this consists of the removal of something pleasant, e.g., in an attempt to decrease the frequency of certain behaviors of their teenagers (e.g., hitting younger siblings or talking back to parents), parents may temporarily deny them access to positive reinforcers, such as going to cinema on weekend dates. A common form of negative punishment is "time out."

Punishment can be effective, when applied immediately and consistently following the unwanted behavior. However, punishment can provoke negative responses, such as anger and resentment. Punishment studies of parenting practices support nonviolent parenting. These studies highlighted four major drawbacks of physical punishment (Gershoff, 2002; Marshall, 2002):

■ Punishment of behavior leads to its suppression, but it is not forgotten. This temporary state of successfully stopping of unwanted behavior may negatively reinforce parents' punishing behavior.
■ Punishment teaches discrimination among situations; punishment will lead the person to learn to avoid situations associated with punishment.
■ Punishment can teach fear: generalization to similar stimuli is reinforced. A punished child may associate fear not only with the undesirable behavior but also with the person who delivered the punishment or the place where it occurred. Thus, children may learn to fear a punishing teacher and try to avoid school, or may become more anxious (Gershoff, 2013; Gershoff et al., 2010).
■ Physical punishment may increase aggression by modeling aggression as a way to cope with problems. Many aggressive delinquents and abusive parents come from abusive families (Larzelere, 2000; Larzelere & Kuhn, 2005; Straus, Sugarman, & Giles-Sims, 1997). However, some researchers argue that increased aggression among parents of aggressive delinquents is a way of coping which triggered the delinquents' behavior.

Reinforcement could be continuous (where every correct response is followed by a reinforcer), or partial (where only some correct responses are followed by reinforcement). Continuous reinforcement is the best choice for rapid mastering of a behavior; however, real life rarely provides continuous reinforcement, and extinction also occurs rapidly, when reinforcement stops. With partial reinforcement schedules, learning is slower to appear, but resistance to extinction is greater than with continuous reinforcement. Skinner (1956) found that different arrangements of partial reinforcement produced different patterns and rates of responding. Collectively, these different reinforcement arrangements are called schedules of reinforcement. Skinner identified four basic schedules of reinforcement, these include:

- *Fixed-ratio schedule*: reinforcement occurs after a certain number of responses. A behavior on a 3-to-1 fixed-ratio schedule (abbreviated FR-3) should be repeated three times in order to receive reinforcement. In everyday life, the fixed-ratio schedule is reflected in any activity that requires a precise number of responses in order to obtain reinforcement, e.g., a shop may reward customers with a free product after every two purchased items, or taking a break, drinking coffee or eating chocolate after completing a book chapter. This usually produces a high rate of responding that follows a burst–pause–burst pattern.
- *Variable-ratio schedule*: reinforcement occurs after an average number of responses, which varies from trial to trial, rather than after a fixed number, e.g., a behavior on a variable-ratio-15 schedule (abbreviated VR-15) should be repeated 20 times on the first trial before being reinforced and repeated 11 times on the second trial before reinforcement. Although the number of responses required on any specific trial is unpredictable, variable-ratio schedules of reinforcement produce high, steady rates of responding with hardly any pausing between trials or after reinforcement. Over repeated trials, the ratio of responses to reinforcers works out to the predetermined average. Gambling is the classic example of a variable-ratio schedule.

PHOTO 10.2.   Gambling.

- *Fixed-interval (FI) schedule*: reinforcement is given only after a fixed time has elapsed, overall rates of response are relatively low. On a fixed-interval schedule, a behavior on a 2-minute fixed interval schedule (abbreviated FI-2 minutes) would receive enforcement after 2 minutes. The number of responses tends to increase as the time for the next reinforcer draws near, producing a scallop-shaped pattern of responding, e.g., receiving a salary at the end of month. Observing the studying behavior over a semester reveals an increase near the end of the semester and drops off at its end.

- *Variable-interval (VI) schedule*: the time between reinforcements varies around some average amount of time, but the interval varies from trial to trial. A behavior on a VI-10 minutes schedule might be reinforced after 5 minutes have elapsed on the first trial, then, after 15 minutes have elapsed on the second trial, and after 10 minutes have elapsed on the third trial. This works out to an average of one reinforcer every 10 minutes. Generally, the unpredictable nature of variable-interval schedules tends to produce moderate but steady rates of responding, especially when the average interval is relatively short. In daily life, we experience variable-interval schedules when we have to wait for events that follow an approximate, rather than a precise, schedule, e.g., parents often unintentionally reinforce a challenging child on a variable-interval schedule. From the child's perspective, the challenging behavior usually results in the desired request, but how long the child has to behave before getting reinforced can vary. Thus, the child learns that persistent challenging behaviors will eventually succeed in getting desired goals.

Observational Learning (Modeling)

The social learning theory (observational learning, or modeling) proposed by Albert Bandura has become perhaps the most influential theory of learning and development. This theory suggests that the learning process takes place by observing the behavior of other people, and how they handle everyday life events. Observational learning is used to teach appropriate behaviors in a wide variety of everyday life, including education, vocational and job training, psychotherapy, and counseling. The skills and rituals acquired by each generation are passed on this way, not through deliberate training. At school, a child learns science concepts by demonstration from the teacher, and learns not to cheat by watching another student be punished for cheating. In everyday life, a new customer in a store learns the procedure for trying on clothes by watching others, and learns the process for lining up and checking out by watching other customers. Persons are likely to learn from people they perceive as similar to them, or as successful, or as admirable.

While rooted in many of the basic concepts of traditional learning theory, Bandura believed that direct reinforcement could not account for all types of learning. His theory added a social element, arguing that people can learn new information and behaviors by watching other people. By observing others, one forms an idea of how new behaviors are performed, and on later occasions this coded information serves as a guide for action. This type of learning can be used to explain a wide variety of behaviors.

Unlike behavioral theories, Bandura believed that external reinforcement was not the only way that people learned new things. Instead, intrinsic reinforcements such as a sense of pride, satisfaction, and accomplishment could also lead to learning. By observing the actions of others, including parents and peers, children develop new skills and acquire new information. The core concepts of social learning theory include the following:

People Can Learn Through Observation

In his famous Bobo doll experiment, Bandura demonstrated that children learn and imitate behaviors they have observed in other people. The children in Bandura's studies observed an adult acting violently toward a Bobo doll. When the children were later allowed to play in a room with the Bobo doll, they began to imitate the aggressive actions they had previously observed. Bandura identified three basic models of observational learning:

- a live model, which involves an actual individual demonstrating or acting out a behavior;
- a verbal instructional model, which involves descriptions and explanations of a behavior;
- a symbolic model, which involves real or fictional characters displaying behaviors, such as books, films, television programs, or online media.

Behavior is Strengthened by Reinforcement

A child who relates to the father in a particular way and is rewarded either by a gift, a comment such as "thank you" or "well done," or freedom from punishment is likely to continue behaving in the same way. When behavior is reinforced on an irregular basis, it tends to persist. The point is that, for several reasons, we fail to reward good or punish bad behavior all the time.

Mental States Are Important to Learning (Intrinsic Reinforcement)

Bandura noted that external environmental reinforcement was not the only factor to influence learning and behavior. He described intrinsic reinforcement as an essential form of internal reward, such as pride, satisfaction, and a sense of accomplishment. This emphasis on internal thoughts and cognitions helps connect learning theories to cognitive developmental theories. While many textbooks place social learning theory with behavioral theories, Bandura himself describes his approach as a social cognitive theory.

Learning Does Not Necessarily Lead to a Change in Behavior

While behaviorists believed that learning led to a permanent change in behavior, observational learning theory demonstrates that people can learn new information without demonstrating new behaviors.

Albert Bandura (1974) suggested that observational learning is not mechanical copying, but result from cognitive processes that are actively judgmental and constructive. Not all observed behaviors are effectively learned. Factors involving both the model and the learner can play a role in whether social learning is successful. Because it encompasses attention, memory, and motivation, social learning theory spans both cognitive and behavioral frameworks. Bandura (1986) suggested that observational learning is controlled by four interacting cognitive processes. These include:

- *Attention to the other person's behavior*: in order to learn, you need to pay attention, this includes modeled events (distinctiveness, affective valence, complexity, prevalence, functional value) and observer characteristics (sensory capacities, arousal level, perceptual set, and past reinforcement). Anything that detracts attention can yield a negative effect on observational learning. Full attention is usually committed to learning in the case of interesting models or novel situations.
- *Retention*: the ability to form and store a mental representation of the other person's behavior to be imitated, so that it can be remembered and performed at a later time is vital to observational learning. This includes symbolic coding, cognitive organization, symbolic rehearsal, motor rehearsal. Retention can be affected by a number of factors.

■ *Reproduction*: this necessitates having the motor skills that can transform mental representation into actions and reproduce the other person's behavior. Motor skills include physical capabilities, self-observation of reproduction, and accuracy of feedback. Further practice of the learned behavior leads to improvement and skill advancement.

■ *Motivation*: the previous factors (attention, memory, and motor skills) lead to learning of the other person's behavior, but the actual performance of the learned behavior will depend on the presence of some motivation to imitate that behavior. A person is likely to imitate a behavior if there is some expectation that doing so will produce reinforcement or reward, including external, vicarious, and self-reinforcement. Bandura suggested that by watching a model, we experience vicarious reinforcement or vicarious punishment, and we learn to anticipate a behavior's consequences in situations like those we are observing, e.g., if you see another student rewarded with extra credit for getting to class on time, you might start to show up a few minutes early each day.

Currently, a group of neurons called mirror neurons were supposed to provide the neural basis for everyday imitation and observational learning. A mirror neuron fires when one performs an action or sees someone doing the same action, e.g., these neurons will fire when one picks up a ball, or sees someone else picking up a ball.

Application of Social Learning Theory

Bandura was interested in studying the effect of exposure to aggressive models on behavior. To test the effect of observational learning on the development of aggressive behavior, Bandura (1965) examined 4-year-old children who separately watched a short film displaying an adult playing aggressively with a Bobo doll (a large inflated balloon doll that stands upright because the bottom is weighted with sand). All the children saw the adult hit, kick, and punch the Bobo doll in the film. The film had three different versions, each with a different end. In the first version, the adult was reinforced with soft drinks, candy, and snacks after performing the aggressive actions. In the second version, the aggressive adult was punished for the actions with a scolding and a spanking by another adult. In the third version, the aggressive adult experienced no consequences. When children were allowed to play alone in a room with several toys, including a Bobo doll, Bandura found that children who watched the film in which the adult was punished were much less likely to imitate the aggressive behaviors than were children who watched either of the other two film endings. In a further extension of the experiment, each child was asked to show the experimenter what the adult did in the film, and rewarded with snacks and stickers for every behavior they could imitate. As a result, virtually all the children imitated the adult's behaviors they had observed in the film, including the aggressive behaviors, without regard to the particular version of the film the children had seen (Bandura, 1965).

Collins et al. (2004) examined the impact of television presentation of sexual activity on the behavior of US adolescents between the ages of 12 and 17. Although other factors contributed to the likelihood that adolescents would become sexually active, the impact of television shows was substantial. Adolescents who watched sexual content for a longer time were twice as likely to begin engaging in sexual intercourse in the following year, compared to adolescents at the same age but who watched the least amount of sexually oriented shows. The 12-year-olds who watched a lot of television shows with sexual content behaved like the 14- or 15-year-olds who watched the least amount of sexual shows. Researchers found that exposure to television shows that simply talked about sex were associated with the same risks as exposure to television that portrayed sexual behavior.

Prosocial models can have prosocial effects; principles of observational learning were used to produce serial dramas in different countries to motivate individuals to adopt new attitudes and behavior by modeling behaviors that promote family health (e.g., family planning and reproductive health), and improve the environment (e.g., improve sanitation, adopt fuel-conservation practices to reduce pollution, and launch a tree-planting campaign) (Papa et al., 2000). The dramatic intensity, involving complex plot lines and engaging characters, ensured that viewers would become involved in the dramas and pay attention. To ensure that the modeled messages were remembered, conclusive statements at the end of each episode were used to summarize the key points and issues of the episode. To enhance the viewers' ability to carry out the modeled behaviors, a variety of support programs and groups were put in place at the time of broadcasting the series. Research studies have confirmed the highly successful impact of these extremely popular dramas (Singhal, Cody, Rogers, & Sabido, 2004; Sood, SenGupta, Mishra, & Jacoby, 2004).

Studies have shown that modeling can be used to ease fear in people undergoing medical procedures, e.g., before having an endoscopy, a patient is instructed to view a videotape of another patient comfortably undergoing the same procedure while successfully using relaxation and other coping strategies. When the patient then undergoes the procedure, he or she is relaxed and comfortable.

Cognitive Learning Theory

Behaviorists were unable to explain why children do not imitate all behavior that has been reinforced. Furthermore, new behavior may arise without having been reinforced. Brewer (1974) suggested that there is no convincing evidence for unconscious, automatic mechanisms in the conditioning of adult human beings, and that higher mental processes influence conditioning process. Later reviews replicated Brewer's conclusions regarding the failure of research to support mechanistic views of conditioning (Kirsch, Lynn, Vigorito, & Miller, 2004). Cognitive theorists view learning as involving the acquisition or reorganization of the cognitive structures through which people process and store information (Good & Brophy, 1990). In cognitive learning theory, the mind is conceptualized as an information processor rather than a blank store to be filled.

The Cognitive View of Other Theories

Edward Tolman developed a cognitive view of learning that proposed individuals do more than merely respond to stimuli, they act on beliefs, attitudes, changing conditions, and they strive toward goals. Tolman (1932, 1948) suggested that the stimulus-response theory (conditioning) is unacceptable, because reinforcement is not necessary for learning to occur. Tolman argued that reinforcement may be important in relation to performance of learned behavior, but that it is not necessary for the learning itself. Tolman suggested that people and animals are active information processors and not passive learners as behaviorism had presumed. In his study of rats in mazes, Tolman (1948) found that rats which explored a maze without obvious rewards seemed to develop a cognitive map, the rats learned expectations as to which part of the maze will be followed by which other part of the maze. Tolman called these expectations cognitive maps, a primitive kind of perceptual map of the maze, an understanding of its spatial relationships (much like the mental map people have of familiar streets leading to home or college). When an experimenter then places food in the maze's goal box, these rats run the maze as quickly and efficiently as other rats that were previously reinforced with food for this result. The exploring rats seemingly experienced latent learning during their earlier tours. This learning became apparent only when there was some incentive to demonstrate it.

Considering the cognitive behavioral views of learning, operant conditioning could be seen to fall into one of the following explanations:

1. Conditioning is a stimulus-response (S–R) mechanistic process in which expectancy and other cognitive factors are, at best, epiphenomena. From this perspective, conditioning trials produce conditional responses and perhaps expectancies, but there is no causal relation between expectancy and response (the behavioral view).
2. Expectancy is a future-oriented belief, it is a belief that something will happen. Expectancy is hypothesized to mediate the effects of conditioning, thus, conditioning trials produce expectancies, and it is the expectancy that produces the response (the cognitive view).

Constructivist Learning Theory

Jerome Bruner (the founder of constructivist theory) suggested that learning is an active process in which learning takes place when the learners combine prior knowledge and experience with the information being offered; these should be personally interpreted, and lead to changing of internal representations. Learners construct their own reality or at least interpret it based upon their perceptions of experiences, so an individual's knowledge is a function of one's prior experiences, mental structures, and beliefs that are used to interpret objects and events (Jonassen, 1991). According to this theory, learning requires teachers and students to engage in an active dialog (i.e., Socratic learning). Teachers should encourage students to discover principles by themselves, through presenting topics in a way that can be efficiently processed by the students (e.g., meaningfully organized, clearly in the context of what they already know, attention grabbing so that the information is processed in the first place).

Clinical Notes

- Understanding different learning theories enables the promotion of the learning process of children. This is more important for children with a learning disorder.
- Learning theories help our understanding of the etiology of some behavioral and emotional disorders, and hence provide the scientific background for changing these disorders. Specifically, operant conditioning represents the scientific base of biofeedback training, and most behavior modification programs.

Summary

- Learning is defined as an enduring change in the mechanisms of behavior resulting from prior experience with particular stimuli and responses.
- Simple forms of learning, such as habituation and sensitization, occur in all species through repeated presentation of a stimulus.
- Associative learning is the process by which an element is taught through association with another separate, pre-occurring element. In classic conditioning, learning is a form of making association between one stimulus and a response. In operant conditioning, learning occurs because of the consequences to the individual of a previous behavior.

- In observational learning, the learning process takes place by observing the behavior of other people, and how they handle everyday life events.
- Cognitive theorists view learning as involving the acquisition or reorganization of the cognitive structures through which people process and store information. In cognitive learning theory, the mind is conceptualized as an information processor rather than a blank store to be filled.
- Constructivist learning theory suggests that learning is an active process in which learning takes place when the learners combine prior knowledge and experience with the information being offered; these should be personally interpreted, and lead to change in internal representations.

Test Your Knowledge

- Describe the general laws of learning.
- What is associative learning?
- What is observational learning?
- Give an account of the cognitive learning theory.
- Describe the constructivist learning theory.

Critical Thinking Questions

- How can learning theories be integrated with each other?
- What is the clinical application of observational learning in psychiatry?
- How can psychology improve the process of learning?

eleven
Sensation and Perception

Learning Goals

■ This chapter is intended to provide the reader with an overview of the concepts of sensation and perception, the bottom-up processing and top-down processing of percepts, the factors affecting perception, perceptual constancy, and the disorders of perception.

Introduction

In order to survive and function well in the world, an animal or human needs to know what is present and what is going on in the environment. The main processes involved in our exploration of the world are sensation and perception. Though some researchers regard sensation and perception as a single process, each topic will be discussed separately in this chapter.

Sensation

Sensation is the process through which the senses detect visual, auditory, and other sensory stimuli and transmit them to the brain. In other words, sensation refers to how our sensory receptors respond to stimulation and transmit that information in a usable form to the brain. There are some common processes that govern sensation, these include:

- All sensations result from stimulation of specialized cells, called sensory receptors, via a certain form of energy. Each sensory system has its receptor cells designed to detect a particular form of energy.
- Human beings can receive auditory, visual, olfactory (smell), gustatory (taste), tactile, vestibular (sense of balance), and kinesthetic (the sense that provides information about body movement and position) stimuli.
- Transduction refers to the process by which a form of physical energy is converted into a neural signal that can be processed by the nervous system. These neural signals are sent to the brain, where the perceptual processes start.
- The weakest stimulus that our senses can reliably detect varies across individuals. Because of these variations, researchers have arbitrarily set the limit as the minimum level of stimulation that can be detected half the time, they called this the *absolute threshold*. Stimuli that are below the absolute threshold, and hence below the threshold of conscious perception or awareness, are called subliminal stimuli, this results in what is called subliminal perception. Such stimuli might be rapidly flashed visual images, sounds, or odors that are too faint to be consciously detected. Although not consciously perceived, subliminal stimuli can still evoke a brain response (Bahrami, Lavie, & Rees, 2007). Whether people's behavior could be manipulated by subliminal messages is an issue that lacks scientific evidence.
- Subliminal stimuli effect may be experienced through the mere exposure effect, which means that repeated exposure to a particular stimulus (including subliminally presented stimuli) leads to increased liking for that stimulus (Zajonc, 2001). Thus, people exposed to subliminal images of a particular geometric shape are more likely to choose the subliminally presented shape when they are asked to pick the shape they prefer from a group of shapes later on. Attitudes and emotions similarly can be influenced by subliminal stimuli (P. K. Smith, Dijksterhuis, & Chaiken, 2008; Westen, Weinberger, & Bradley, 2007).
- The smallest change in a stimulus that produces a noticeable change in sensation is known as the *difference threshold* (or just noticeable difference); it varies depending on its relation to the original stimulus (Weber's law). This law emphasizes that our psychological experience of sensation is relative, i.e., there is no simple, one-to-one correspondence between the objective characteristics of a physical stimulus, and our psychological experience of it, e.g., if you hold a small stone, you will notice an increase in weight if another one is placed in your hand. But if you initially hold a very heavy rock, you probably would not detect an increase in weight when the same stone is added on top of it.

■ Sensory adaptation: this refers to a gradual decline in sensitivity to a constant stimulus, e.g., we do not feel our clothes or the smell of food after a period of exposure. This process shows again that our experience of sensation is relative, in this case, it is relative to the duration of the exposure.

Perception

Perception is the process by which sensory information is actively organized and interpreted by the brain, i.e., it is the process of giving a meaning to a sensation. There is no clear boundary line that distinguishes where the process of sensation leaves off and the process of perception begin.

All external stimuli are not necessarily processed into perceptions, because the reticular activating system has an inhibitory function on many incoming stimuli. Processing of stimuli proceeds in two ways that often occur simultaneously: bottom-up processing and top-down processing.

Bottom-Up Processing

Bottom-up processing was proposed by James Gibson (1972). The brain assembles individual components of stimuli, such as lines and angles to form patterns that are compared with the stored images, hence it is also known as data-driven processing, e.g., the brain combines discrete lines and angles to form a pattern characteristic of the letter "A" or the number "2." Combining the individual letters and words into recognizable patterns is also an example of bottom-up processing.

Top-Down Processing

Top-down processing was proposed by Richard Gregory (1970), who argued that perception is a constructive process which relies on top-down processing. Stimulus information is frequently ambiguous in its interpretation; we need higher cognitive information either from past experiences, stored knowledge, expectations, and other cognitive processes in order to make inferences about what we perceive. In this way we are actively constructing our perception of reality based on our environment and stored information. We often proceed in accordance with what our past experience tells us to expect, and therefore we do not always analyze every feature of most stimuli we encounter. Tulving and Gold (1963) suggested that if stimulus information is high, then the need to use other sources of information is reduced.

Although top-down processing can be extremely efficient, it can also lead to errors. Nearly everyone has had the experience of rushing over to greet another person who appears to be an old friend, before realizing that he or she is actually a stranger.

Combined Bottom-Up and Top-Down Processing

Bottom-up and top-down processing theories do not seem capable of explaining all perceptions all the time. Neisser (1967) advanced a model (the perceptual cycle model) that attempted to integrate bottom-up and top-down processing models. Both sets of processing are allowed for and one set is not emphasized to the exclusion of the other, as in the previous two theories. Neisser considered perception to be a cyclical activity, a continuous process that has no definite starting or finishing point. Internally held mental schemata are triged by environmental conditions and direct perception and behavior, thus, our interactions with the world. The environmental experience can result in the modification of cognitive schema, and this in turn influences further interaction with the environment. Though it seems plausible, Neisser's perceptual cycle model is vague as it lacks reference to the neural mechanisms that underlie this interaction, or how stored schemas interact with incoming sensory information.

Perceptual interpretation may be influenced by many factors which may enhance or impair our perception:

Factors in the Stimulus (External Cues)

Figure-Background Relationship

The placement or arrangement of stimuli can affect how one attends to and understands them. The relationship between the main stimulus and any surrounding stimuli is called the figure-background relationship. This relationship determines how distinct the main stimulus (the figure) is within the total context (the background).

In general, the greater the intensity of the stimulus is, the more likely a subject will attend to it. In addition, a stimulus that differs noticeably from the background surround is more likely to be noticed. This is the principle of contrast. The figure-background relationship is called unstable if the figure sometimes can be perceived as the background and the background can be perceived as the figure. Figures may be described as ambiguous if they can be correctly interpreted in more than one way (see Figure 11.1). This figure may be seen as either a vase or as two faces.

FIGURE 11.1.   The Figure–Background Relationship.

Laws of Perceptual Grouping (Gestalt Laws of Organization)

Many of the forms perceived by people are composed of a number of different elements that seem to go together (Prinzmetal, 1995). People organize the diverse elements in an attempt to produce a stable perception of well-defined whole objects. This is what perceptual psychologists refer to as "the urge to organize." Gestalt principles are examples of bottom-up processing. Gestalt psychologists proposed a number of laws derived from our tendency to organize stimuli into coherent groups, these include:

- *Law of similarity*: there is tendency to perceive similar items or stimuli as one group (see Figure 11.2). It may be based on color or shape, etc.

X	O	X	O	X
X	O	X	O	X
X	O	X	O	X
X	O	X	O	X
X	O	X	O	X
X	O	X	O	X
X	O	X	O	X

FIGURE 11.2.   The Law of Similarity.

■ *Law of proximity*: there is tendency to perceive nearby objects as one figure (see Figure 11.3).

XXX   XXX   XXX   XXX   XXX   XXX

FIGURE 11.3.   The Law of Proximity.

■ *Law of closure*: there is tendency to perceive incomplete, unclosed, interrupted figures as complete and closed figures. Depending on previous knowledge, the person fills in the gaps of information to complete the stimulus (see Figure 11.4).

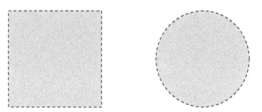

FIGURE 11.4.   The Law of Closure.

■ *Law of symmetry*: despite the pressure of proximity to group the brackets nearest each other together, symmetry overwhelms our perception and makes us see them as pairs of symmetrical brackets (see Figure 11.5).

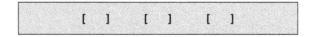

FIGURE 11.5.   The Law of Symmetry.

■ *Law of common region*: the tendency to perceive objects as a group if they occupy the same place within a plane.

- *Law of good continuity*: a subject is likely to perceive continuous items as one object, rather than a combination of irregular or discontinuous stimuli.
- *Law of simplicity*: reality is organized or reduced to the simplest form possible, e.g., you see the image in Figure 11.6 as a series of circles rather than a mixture of curved, more complicated shapes.

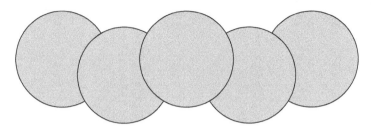

FIGURE 11.6.   The Law of Simplicity.

- *Common fate*: objects moving together are perceived as one object.
- *Part–whole relationship*: the tendency to see a form as a part of a whole. As well as illustrating continuity and proximity, the two shapes illustrate the principle that "the whole is other than the sum of its parts." Despite the similarity of the parts (each pattern is composed of five crosses), their perception is different (see Figure 11.7).

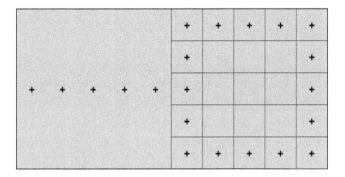

FIGURE 11.7.   The Part–whole Relationship.

Perceptual Set

A set of mental tendencies and assumptions can affect readiness to perceive selected features as an object (top-down). It may alter perception of the true stimulus, e.g., if someone is waiting for an important telephone call, they may perceive the ringing of the bell of the door as a telephone ring. It has been found that a number of factors influence the perceptual set, and this in turn influences perception. The factors include:

- *Emotions*: can color perceptions, e.g., a loving spouse perceives less threat in stressful marital events.
- *Motivation*: may intensify or reduce the acuity of perception; desired objects appear more clear to a motivated person.
- *Experience*: perception of present events is strongly influenced by past experiences; it may help or hinder perception.

- *Context effects*: a given stimulus may trigger radically different perceptions, because of the immediate context, e.g., hearing a noise interrupted by the words "eel is on the wagon," the first word is likely to be perceived as wheel. Given "eel is on the orange," the first word is likely to be perceived as peel. This phenomenon, discovered by Richard Warren, suggests that the brain can work backward in time to allow a later stimulus to determine how we perceive an earlier one. The context creates an expectation, that is, top-down processing influences our perception (Grossberg, 1995).
- *Level of fatigue*: fatigue may negatively affect perception, e.g., a distance to walk looks farther to a fatigued person.
- *Culture*: our perception may vary due to our cultural beliefs and traditions, e.g., during choosing our clothes we consider the opinion of our friends and the society in general about the style and suitability of that clothes, that is, we usually buy what others consider good.

Perceptual Constancy

Perceptual constancy refers to the tendency to perceive objects, especially familiar objects, as constant and unchanging in spite of changes in sensory input, an ability that promotes a stable view of the world. Without perceptual constancy, our perception would fluctuate continually, e.g., if we simply responded to retinal images, our perceptions of objects would change as lighting, viewing angle, and distance from the object changed from one moment to another. However, perceptual constancy does not always work. Perceptual constancy is the result of size, shape, location, and color and brightness constancy.

- *Size constancy*: refers to the perception of an object as being the same size despite its changing image on the retina. This occurs because the perceptual system takes into account an object's distance from the perceiver, e.g., we perceive an object to be the same size in spite of changes in our distance from that object. If the retinal image of an object does not change but the perception of its distance increases, the object is perceived as larger.
- *Shape constancy*: the tendency to perceive familiar objects as having a fixed shape, regardless of its image on the retina, e.g., when looking at a familiar object (the rectangular shape of a door) from different angles, the perception of that object remains constant despite changes in its retinal image.
- *Location constancy*: though moving our heads around produces a constantly changing pattern of retinal images, we do not perceive the world as spinning around. This is because kinesthetic feedback from the muscles and balance organs in the ear are integrated with the changing retinal stimulation in the brain to inhibit perception of movement. The brain subtracts the eye-movement commands from the resulting changes on the retina, to keep objects in a constant location.
- *Color and brightness constancy*: under a variety of lighting conditions, familiar objects retain their hue, provided there is sufficient contrast and shadow. Also, brightness of objects seems to be a more or less constant, even though the amount of light which objects reflect can change according to the level of illumination. Perceived brightness depends on the relative luminance of objects (how much light an object reflects relative to its surroundings).

Disorders of Perception

A person may experience unreal perception that may or may not be in response to external stimuli, this includes illusions or hallucinations (respectively).

Illusions

Illusions mean misinterpretations of a real stimulus, such as seeing a rope as a snake. The perceptual stimulus arises from an actual object and the illusion is formed by the perception's transformation. Illusions are most likely to occur due to the following states:

- The general level of stimulation is reduced, thus, at dusk a common illusion is to misperceive the outline of a bush as that of a man.
- Expectations may facilitate the occurrence of illusions, e.g., if someone is waiting for an important telephone call, they may perceive the ringing of the bell of the door as a telephone ring.
- Intense emotions: a strong affective state e.g., in a dark lane, a frightened person is more likely to misperceive the outline of a bush as that of an attacker.
- Impaired consciousness may be associated with illusions especially in acute cases, e.g., alcohol intoxication or withdrawal.
- Epilepsy: aura or psychomotor epilepsy may present with illusions of familiarity or unfamiliarity.

Optical Illusions

An optical or visual illusion is an illusion caused by the visual system and characterized by visually perceived images that differ from objective reality. Optical illusions are a normal phenomenon that results from tricking the brain into misunderstanding what is seen in various ways. There are currently three types of optical illusions: literal illusions, cognitive illusions, and physiological illusions.

- *A cognitive illusion*: the brain perceives an object based on prior knowledge or assumptions. The vase/face image in Figure 11.1 is a good example of a cognitive illusion. The brain analyzes this picture, looking for something familiar, which ended up being either two faces or a vase.
- *A literal illusion* occurs when the brain describes an image that is completely different than the objects that create it. One of the best-known literal illusions is the painting by Charles Allan Gilbert entitled *All Is Vanity*. In this painting, a young girl sits in front of a mirror that appears to be a skull (Figure 11.8). There is no actual skull, however, the objects in the painting come together to create that effect.
- *Physiological illusions* that are the effects of excessive stimulation of a specific type (brightness, color, size, position, tilt, movement).

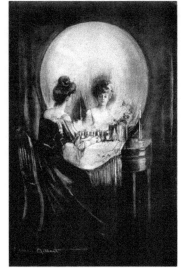

FIGURE 11.8. Literal Illusion: *All Is Vanity.*

Hallucinations

Hallucinations mean false perception in the absence of an external stimulus. They may be visual, auditory, olfactory, gustatory, or tactile (Figure 11.9).

FIGURE 11.9.   Hallucination.

Proper hallucinations are actual false perceptions, not distortions of real perceptions. They are experienced as occurring in the real world and as inhabiting objective space.

Causes of Hallucinations

- Hypnagogic and hypnopompic hallucinations occur when one is going to sleep or awakening from sleep respectively, they are considered normal.
- Psychotic disorders, e.g., schizophrenia (commonly auditory hallucinations) and psychotic depression.
- Medical conditions, e.g.,
  - metabolic encephalopathy, e.g., hepatic encephalopathy
  - intoxication: either accidental (pesticides) or recreational substances (e.g., LSD)
  - febrile illness, e.g., typhoid
  - brain diseases, e.g., encephalitis and brain tumors
  - epilepsy.

Clinical Notes

Persistent perceptual abnormalities are among the key symptoms in psychiatry that need proper evaluation. The causes of illusions and hallucinations vary greatly, encompassing normal to organic and psychiatric disorders. Proper assessment ensures better diagnosis and management.

Summary

- Sensation is the process through which the senses detect visual, auditory, and other sensory stimuli and transmit them to the brain.
- Perception is the process of giving a meaning to a sensation. Perception proceeds in two manners that often occur simultaneously: bottom-up and top-down processing.
- In bottom-up processing, the brain assembles individual components of stimuli such as lines and angles, to form patterns that are compared with the stored images.

- Top-down processing proposes that stimulus information is frequently ambiguous to interpret; it needs higher cognitive information either from past experiences, stored knowledge, expectations, and other cognitive processes in order to make inferences about what we perceive.
- Perception may be influenced by external cues such as figure background relationship and Gestalt laws of organization, or perceptual sets such as emotions, motivation, experience, context effects, level of fatigue, and culture.
- Perceptual constancy refers to the tendency to perceive objects, especially familiar objects, as constant and unchanging in spite of changes in sensory input, an ability that promotes a stable view of the world.
- Illusions mean misinterpretations of a real stimulus, such as seeing a rope as a snake.
- Hallucinations mean false perception in the absence of an external stimulus. They may be visual, auditory, olfactory, gustatory, or tactile.

Test Your Knowledge

- Define sensation.
- Define perception.
- What are the types of processing of stimuli that may be involved in perception?
- What are the factors affecting perception?
- Define perceptual constancy.
- What is the difference between illusions and hallucinations?

Critical Thinking Question

Considering Gestalt principles of perceptual organization, how is perception different from a photographic image?

twelve
Attention

- This chapter is intended to provide the reader with an overview of different forms of attention, types of voluntary attention, the neural correlates of attention, the theories of attention, and causes of impaired attention.

Introduction

It is difficult to define attention or to determine its precise nature, however, it could be considered an umbrella term for a number of processes and abilities. These include the ability to focus consciousness or awareness on a single aspect of the environment or activity (voluntary attentional vigilance) at any given time, on one hand, and automatic, uncontrollable responses to unusual or unexpected events (involuntary attentional capture), on the other. Attention helps to direct sensory and perceptual systems toward certain stimuli, to select specific information for further processing, to ignore unwanted stimuli, to allocate the mental energy required to process selected stimuli, and to regulate the flow of resources necessary for performing a task or coordinating several tasks at once (Wickens & Carswell, 2006). Attention is not just a cognitive factor but is also determined by emotions, interest, attitude, and memory.

Forms of Attention

Probably the most fundamental division of attentive processes, and certainly one of the oldest classification of attention, is its division into active and passive, or, as they are better termed, voluntary (or controlled) and involuntary (or automatic) attention.

- *Active or voluntary attention* is precisely what the name implies, attention resulting from self-initiated activity. Voluntary attention is assumed to make heavy demands on processing resources. In its clearest form, it always involves mental strain and effort. Whenever we attend to anything, we are experiencing active attention.
- *Passive or involuntary attention* makes no demands on attentional resources, i.e., it does not draw on attentional capacity or processing resources and occurs without conscious awareness. People attend in an effortless way to many things to which they have no clear purpose to direct their thought, and therefore they cannot be said to attend voluntarily in the full sense of the word, but they certainly do not attend against their will.

Interrelations of the Forms of Attention

The Stroop effect is a simple yet elegant demonstration of the interaction between automatic and controlled processes. In Stroop tasks, one dimension of stimulus should be recognized while another, more well-learned dimension is ignored. The reaction time difference between the two conditions is calculated, and is called Stroop interference (SI).

In visual color word Stroop task, participants are asked to name the color of a word, irrespective of the word itself, e.g., naming the color of word green written in blue ink. Since word reading has prepotent response than color naming, and naming colors requires more attention than reading words, word reading interfere with color naming. The difference in reaction time (RT) between color naming in the two situations is taken as a measure of inhibitory ability (SI).

Also, auditory tasks can be used to assess stroop effect, where a person is asked to respond to one perceptual feature of a word (e.g., speaker gender, voice pitch, stimulus location) while ignoring an irrelevant or conflicting semantic information, (e.g., man spoken by a woman, low in a high pitched voice, right heard in the left ear).

Types of Voluntary Attention

Sohlberg and Mateer (1987, 1989) proposed a clinical model of attention that incorporated many of these theoretical concepts and was based upon the symptoms of attentional difficulty reported or observed in individuals with traumatic brain injury. This model involves five different kinds of activities of growing difficulty:

1. *Focused attention*: is the ability to respond discretely to specific visual, auditory or tactile stimuli.
2. *Sustained attention (vigilance)*: is the ability to maintain a consistent behavioral response during continuous and repetitive activity.
3. *Selective attention*: is the ability to select from various stimuli that are presented and to focus only on the one that you want. Selective attention basically allows people to select what they want to pay attention to.
4. *Alternating attention*: is the mental flexibility that allows individuals to shift their focus of attention and move between tasks having different cognitive requirements. In other words, it is alternating attention back and forth between two or more different tasks that requires the use of different areas of brain.
5. *Divided attention*: this is the highest level of attention that refers to the ability to respond simultaneously to two or more tasks or task demands. It is often referred to as multitasking, e.g., checking email while listening in a meeting, talking with friends while making dinner, or talking on the phone while getting dressed. Unlike alternating attention, you do not change from one task to another completely different task during divided attention. Instead, you attempt to perform them at the same time. So you are really splitting your attention, and focusing part of attention on each task, instead of alternating it. However, it seems impossible to concentrate on two different tasks simultaneously, as the brain can only process one task at a time. So you are really not "focused" on one task at a time, you are really continuously alternating your attention between tasks. That is why it is so difficult and dangerous to text and drive or talk and drive. Good memory and habit allow you to perform two or more tasks seemingly simultaneously, such as talking to a person while typing, or driving your car while listening to the radio. In these situations, you are really not concentrating on the individual acts of driving, for example. You are able to do the task without conscious effort or actually paying attention.

Neuroanatomical Correlates of Attention and Arousal

Three systems are involved in the physiology of attention: (1) the ascending reticular activating system (ARAS); (2) the intralaminar thalamic nuclei; and (3) the cerebral cortex. The ARAS projects to the intralaminar nuclei of the thalamus that project widely throughout the cortex. A small lesion in the ARAS results in coma. However, a bilateral extensive lesion of the cortex is needed to disturb arousal; it does not result in coma, but leads to a vegetative state in which the sleep/wake cycle and eye movement are preserved without evidence of conscious thought.

Theories Explaining Attention

A lot of models have been proposed to explain attention. The capacity theory and the mental bottleneck theories are the most famous of these models. Knudsen (2007) described a general model of attention that identifies four core processes of attention, with working memory at the center:

1. Working memory temporarily stores information for detailed analysis.
2. Competitive selection is the process that determines which information gains access to working memory.

3. Top-down sensitivity control: the momentary content of working memory can influence the selection of new information, and thus mediate voluntary control of attention in a recurrent loop (endogenous attention).
4. Bottom-up saliency filters automatically enhance the response to infrequent stimuli, or stimuli of instinctive or learned biological relevance (exogenous attention) (Pattyn, Neyt, Henderickx, & Soetens, 2008).

The Capacity Model of Attention

The capacity model of attention was proposed by Kahneman (1973), and entails the following:

- People can only handle a limited amount of sensory information because competing information from different sources can overwhelm the higher cortical centers of the brain by giving more information than they can cope with.
- We do not perceive a large amount of what our senses pick up, possibly because we have only limited processing resources to handle incoming sensory information. Kahneman suggested that in the brain there is some sort of limited-capacity central processor. This processor is responsible for analyzing incoming information and integrating it with information already held in memory. As the processor is of limited capacity, some information cannot be processed.
- Kahneman suggests that arousal may influence the capacity of the processor: the higher the level of arousal, the more information can be taken in and processed.
- Contradictory studies to Kahneman's view demonstrated that it is possible to do two or more tasks at the same time without any mutual interference. This implies that either one or more of the tasks is not drawing on the central processor at all or that each task is accessing a separate pool of resources. This idea has been embodied in multiple-resource theories of attention, which suggest that different pools of resources are available for different types of tasks.

Bottleneck Theories

As resources are limited, at some point in the attentional system, incoming information must be reduced to a manageable level, leading to a bottleneck. The bottleneck theories describe a process that uses a filter to temporarily block one channel while the other channel processes information. A number of theories suggest that somewhere in the system there is a bottleneck limiting the amount of information that can be processed. These theories differ on the issue of where the bottleneck occurs in the system and what happens to information that fails to get through this bottleneck. The following is a summary of these theories.

Broadbent's Filter Model (1958)

This theory was first proposed by Donald Broadbent. Information is selected on the basis of physical characteristics (e.g., location of sound, pitch, etc.) at the level of our senses, so that most of the incoming sensory information receives no conscious processing at all. The selected information is allowed to pass to later stages where it undergoes further processing. Unselected information is blocked completely (see Figure 12.2).

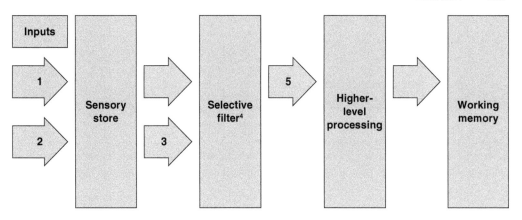

FIGURE 12.1.   Broadbent's Filter Model.

Notes: 1 = attended messages; 2 = unattended messages; 3 = unattended messages are completely blocked at this stage; 4 = based on physical properties such as pitch and loudness; 5 = bottleneck.

Against this model is the idea that filtering information only on the basis of physical characteristics would suggest that one knows nothing about the meaning of the information. Also, it seems unreasonable that information is filtered out without knowing anything about the rest of it, or that one decides it is time to switch attention to something else after knowing only a small amount of information one has already selected.

The Attenuation Model

This was formulated by Anne Treisman (1964) as a revision of Donald Broadbent's filter model. Unattended stimuli are not blocked completely but attenuated. The attenuation of unattended stimuli would make it difficult, but not impossible to extract meaningful content from irrelevant inputs, if stimuli possessed sufficient strength after attenuation to make it through a hierarchical analysis process. So it is possible to switch attention if unattended information was meaningful to the person in the current situation, e.g., if you were at a party and somebody in a conversation in

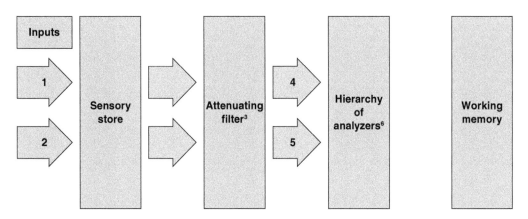

FIGURE 12.2.   The Attenuation Model.

Notes: 1 = attended messages; 2 = unattended messages; 3 = based on physical properties such as pitch and loudness; 4 = bottleneck; 5 = attenuated messages; 6 = hierarchy of analyzers (syllables, words, grammar, semantics); whether or not attenuated messages get processed at this stage, and to what degree is determined by its threshold.

which you were not involved mentioned your name, you might switch attention to monitor that conversation) (see Figure 12.3).

The Deutsch–Norman Selection Model

This model is attributed to Deutsch and Deutsch (1963) and Norman (1968). Selection happens later in the attentional processing sequence. It is therefore an example of a late selection model. The contents are analyzed semantically, and no signal is filtered out, but all are processed to the point of activating their stored representations in memory. The point at which attention becomes selective is when one of the memory representations is selected for further processing. At any time, only one can be selected, resulting in the attentional bottleneck.

The Multimode Model of Attention

The multimode model of attention adds a new dimension called "mode of selection." Mode of selection can be viewed on a continuum with "early mode" on one end and "late mode" on the other. The filter is moveable and can take place at various stages of processing based on the observer's needs. A couple of things happen as you move from early to late mode of selection: the bottleneck shifts to filter input after pattern recognition, and attention capacity decreases. Both of these events can inhibit the performance of secondary tasks. Selection can be based on physical or semantic characteristics.

The Attentional Spotlight Model

One approach that explains how incoming information might be filtered suggests that attention resemble a spotlight. This attentional spotlight illuminates only a small part of the visual field (i.e., only a small proportion of everything that is registered by the eyes) and any items that lie within that spotlight receive priority for processing. Any information lying outside the beam of the attentional spotlight receives far less processing, and so saves on valuable resources.

A modification of this theory suggests that attention resembles a zoom lens; attention can be focused tightly on a narrow area, or broadened to cover a wider area, so one can either put a lot of effort into processing a small area, or spread that effort at a lower concentration over a larger area.

Causes of Impaired Attention

1. *Normal causes*: sleep, dreams, hypnosis, transcendental meditation, trance, fatigue and boredom.
2. *Neurological causes*: all causes of impaired consciousness whether due to organic brain diseases (head injury, epilepsy or increased intracranial pressure) or metabolic disorders (hepatic or renal impairment).
3. *Intoxication*: acute intoxication by drugs or alcohol.
4. *Psychiatric disorders*: as in cases of attention deficit hyperactivity disorder, dissociative disorders, depression, and in mania which causes distractibility (the patient gives attention to every passing stimulus).

Clinical Notes

Attentional difficulties are a common symptom in normal people and among psychiatric patients. These may be the primary problem as in attention deficit hyperactivity disorder, or it may be one of the features of a disorder, as in major depressive disorder. Distinguishing significant attentional impairment is of utmost clinical importance. A lot of psychometric tests have been constructed to evaluate different aspects of attention, e.g., the Stroop test, the Wisconsin card sorting test, and the continuous performance test.

Summary

- Attention is an umbrella term for a number of processes and abilities that include the ability to focus awareness on a single aspect of the environment at any given time, on the one hand, and automatic responses to unexpected events, on the other.
- Attention is divided into voluntary and involuntary attention.
- Types of voluntary attention are focused attention, sustained attention, selective attention, alternating attention, and divided attention.
- Three brain areas are involved in attention: the ascending reticular activating system (ARAS), the intralaminar thalamic nuclei, and the cerebral cortex.
- Theories explaining attention include the capacity theory and the mental bottleneck theories.
- Impaired attention may result from normal, neurological, and psychiatric causes. It may also be caused by intoxication.

Test Your Knowledge

- Identify the different forms of attention.
- Describe the clinical models of voluntary attention.
- What are the neural correlates of attention?
- Give an account of the theories of attention.
- What are the causes of impaired attention?

Critical Thinking Question

Evaluate the usefulness of the available psychometric tests in the evaluation of different aspects of attention.

thirteen
Memory

Learning Goals

- This chapter is intended to provide the reader with an overview of the definition of memory, the theories that explain our understanding of memory, types of memory, memory processes, the biological bases of memory, memory measurement, the mechanisms of forgetting, and how to improve memory.

Introduction

PHOTO 13.1.   Memory.

It is difficult to imagine what life would be like without being able to remember. Without memory, we would rely on our innate reflexes to deal with the world. Learning and memory represent two sides of the same coin: learning depends on memory for its permanence, and memory would have no content without learning. In a broad sense, learning is the acquisition of knowledge and memory is the storage of an internal representation of that knowledge. Hence, we could define memory as the retention of learning and experience. In other words, memory is the capacity to take in information, retain it over time, and retrieve that information later on. It involves the encoding, storage, and retrieval of information. However, there is some disagreement as to the precise nature of the human memory system. Theories that explain our understanding of memory include the multi-store model and the levels of processing theory.

The Multi-Store Model

The multi-store model was proposed by Richard Atkinson and Richard Shiffrin in 1968. This model suggested that information exists in one of three states of memory: the sensory, the short-term (STM), and the long-term (LTM) stores. Each store can be characterized by a specific duration, capacity, and coding. With the rehearsal of information, it passes from one stage to the next, but it can fade away if we do not pay enough attention to it (Atkinson & Shiffrin, 1968).

The stream of information entering our senses is held in the sensory memory store. Because it is a huge amount, most of the sensory information decays and is forgotten after a short period of time. Only important data attract our attention, and are promoted to the short-term memory store, where it will be held for less than 30 seconds.

Because of the limited capacity of short-term memory, rehearsal of information is essential to remember it for longer, so it promotes this significant information to the long-term memory store, where Atkinson and Shiffrin believed that it could survive for years, decades, or even a lifetime. Key information regarding other people and important life events are achieved through passing through the sensory and short-term memory stores to reach the long-term memory.

The multi-store model has fairly high face validity, as it offers a plausible explanation as to how information passes through memory and is either stored or forgotten. This model is supported by a large base of research that supports the distinction between the STM and LTM systems, e.g., brain-damaged patients with anterograde amnesia. However, the assumption that both short-term and long-term memory can operate in a single uniform fashion is too simplistic. Evidence suggests that there are multiple short- and long-term memory stores. LTM can be split into episodic, procedural, and semantic memory, while STM is more than a simple unitary store that includes diverse components. The linear nature of the Atkinson-Shiffrin model was criticized as being passive and a one-way model, where there are rare occasions when STM is damaged but LTM is not. According to the Atkinson-Shiffrin model, this is not possible.

The Levels of Processing Theory

Fergus Craik and Robert Lockhart proposed the levels of processing theory as an alternative to the multi-store model. They proposed that memories do not reside in three stores, instead, the strength of a memory trace depends upon the depth of mental processing of a stimulus, and there is no clear distinction between short-term and long-term memory, i.e., there is only one kind of memory (Craik & Lockhart, 1972). Instead of focusing on the memory stores, the levels of processing theory focuses on the processes involved in memory. Craik and Lockhart classified the level of processing into shallow and deep processing. Deeply processed memories will remain in memory for a long time, while superficial and shallow processed memories will decay easily. Shallow processing only involves maintenance rehearsal and leads to fairly short-term retention of information. Deep processing involves elaboration rehearsal which involves a more meaningful analysis of information and leads to better recall.

Verbal data are processed at three levels: structural, phonetic, and semantic. The level of processing progresses, from the most shallow (structural) to the deepest level (semantic). Each level allows a person to make sense of the information and relate it to past memories, determining if the information should be transferred from the short-term memory to the long-term memory.

- Structural processing examines the physical qualities of something (appearance), e.g., the font of the typed word or the letters within it.
- Phonemic processing is meant to process or encode how words sound, i.e., the sounds it makes when the letters are read together. We compare the sound of a word to other words we have heard in order to retain some level of meaning in our memory.
- Semantic processing is when we encode meaning of words and relate it to words with similar meanings.

The strength of levels of processing theory stems from its suggestion that memory is improved when it undergoes deeper processing, this helps to explain why certain things are better remembered than others. The levels of processing theory highlighted that encoding is not a simple process. Also, brain imaging studies showed that higher levels of processing lead to greater activity levels in different parts of the brain which gives the theory some credibility.

Criticism of the levels of processing theory was that it was a simplistic explanation of a complex subject. The suggestion that shallow processing led to memories that decay easily is not accurate in all cases. Those with illnesses that affect memory cannot be explained by the levels of processing theory. On the contrary, various neuropsychological studies have suggested that there are specific systems of storage and structures contained in our memory.

Types of Memory

Memory is usually classified into sensory memory, short-term memory, and long-term memory.

Sensory Memory

Sensory memory is a system for retaining a brief impression of a sensory stimulus after the stimulus has ceased. The vast majority of information that are grasped by our senses cannot be processed correctly due to the limitations of our memory. The role of sensory memory is to provide a detailed representation of our entire sensory experience from which relevant pieces of information are extracted by short-term memory and processed by working memory. Sensory memory is not involved in higher cognitive functions like short- and long-term memory, it is not consciously controlled. Information from the different sensory modalities is stored in separate sensory memories for a very short period of time. All of our senses have sensory memory systems but the systems focused on by the Atkinson–Shiffrin model relate to visual (iconic) and auditory (echoic) stores.

- Iconic memory is a visual sensory store with a short duration of less than 1 second.
- Echoic memory is an auditory sensory store that lasts about 2 or 3 seconds.

Short-Term Memory

Short-term memory (STM) allows a person to recall something after a short period of time without practicing or rehearsing. Peterson and Peterson (1959) showed that STM lasts for less than 30 seconds unless the information is rehearsed in that 30-second period, e.g., when someone gives you a phone number verbally and you say it to yourself repeatedly until you can write it down. If someone interrupts your rehearsal by asking a question, you can easily forget the number, since it is only being held in your short-term memory. George Miller (1956) concluded from his experiments that one could retain from five to nine items in short-term memory. Yet this has been disputed, with the belief that STM varies depending on conditions. The capacity of the short-term memory can be increased by grouping items into meaningful wholes called chunks; most people remember phone numbers in three chunked sets, the area code, the first three numbers, and the last four numbers.

Long-Term Memory

All the memories that can be remembered after a period of about a minute are usually classified as being stored in the long-term memory (LTM). It has an incredibly limitless storage capacity, and some memories can last from the time they are created until the end of life. Long-term memory consists of several distinct subtypes, each of which is named according to the type of information it handles.

- *Procedural* (implicit) memory consists of motor skills learning, habits learning, simple classically conditioned responses, and a phenomenon called priming. It is demonstrated by doing, and occurs without conscious recall, e.g., when riding a bike or driving a car, you do not need to consciously remember how to ride a bike or drive a car.
- *Declarative* (explicit) memory keeps information that can be consciously retained or retrieved. It holds memory for facts and events. Declarative long-term memory consists of two types:
  - Semantic memory retains general knowledge that is not linked to a particular time or place (memories of facts, concepts, names, and other objective facts and information). None of these tasks requires recall of where or when the information was learned, e.g., Cairo is the capital of Egypt.

- Episodic memory stores personal experiences linked to specific times and places, e.g., what do you see when you were in Paris? What happened on your first day of college. What you did on your wedding day.

PHOTO 13.2.   Episodic Memory.

NB: autobiographical memory contains memories of events that have occurred during the course of our lifetime. It can be divided into episodic and semantic memories. Our episodic memories help us recollect times, locations, and people while semantic memories deal with general facts.

Working Memory

The term working memory was introduced by Miller, Galanter, and Pribram (1960) to refer to memory as it is used to plan and carry out behavior. Sometimes working memory is used interchangeably with short-term memory. But these two terms are different. Working memory holds transitory information and processes which allows this information to be manipulated, e.g., when one walks into a new building, the direction to turn at each hall is stored in short-term memory. Processing that information to reverse to get back out is working memory. The ability to manipulate information is essentially the theoretical difference between short-term memory and working memory. Thus, short-term memory is a part of working memory, but both short-term memory and long-term memory hold information available for working memory usage. Other processes that working memory holds are reasoning and comprehension. The prefrontal cortex seems to play a fundamental role in both short-term and working memory. It serves as a temporary storage facility for short-term memory while at the same time making the memory available for recall and manipulation.

Memory Processes

Memory processing involves three cognitive processes: encoding, storage, and retrieval of information.

- *Encoding (or registration)*: this refers to the process of receiving a sensory input and transforming it into a form or a code which can be stored in memory. Encoding may be intentional or incidental. The main ways in which information can be encoded are visual (images), acoustic (sound), tactile (touch), and semantic (meaning). It is believed that encoding for short-term memory storage in the brain relies primarily on acoustic encoding. When a person is presented with a list of numbers and letters, they will try to hold them in STM by rehearsing them (verbally). Rehearsal is a verbal process regardless of whether the list of items is presented acoustically (someone reads them out), or visually (on a sheet of paper). Encoding for long-term storage is suggested to be more reliant (although not exclusively) on semantic encoding (understanding of meaning). Information in LTM can also be coded both visually and acoustically.

■ *Storage*: this is the second memory stage or process in which we maintain information over periods of time. It refers to the creation of a permanent record of the encoded information. Most adults can store between five and nine items in their short-term memory for a brief duration (15–30 seconds). In contrast, the capacity of LTM is thought to be unlimited, and can last a lifetime.

■ *Retrieval*: this refers to the process of getting information out of storage when it is needed. Inability to retrieve certain information leads to its forgetfulness. STM is stored and retrieved sequentially, while LTM is stored and retrieved by association. Retrieval can be evidenced through recall and recognition. Recall refers to direct retrieval of facts or information (free recall, ordered recall, and cued recall). Recognition refers to correctly identifying previously learned material. It is usually superior to recall.

The factors affecting retrieval are:

■ *Context-dependent memory*: information is easier to recall when people are in the same environmental context they were in when they learned it.

■ *State-dependent memory*: what we learn in one state may be more easily recalled when we are again in that state, i.e., there is tendency to recall experiences that are consistent with one's current good or bad mood.

■ *Serial position effect*: there is the tendency to recall best the last and first items in a list, but it is more difficult to recall items in the middle of a list. This is explained by the primacy and recency effects:

  ■ Primacy effect: information at the beginning of a sequence is likely to be recalled because it has already been placed in the long-term memory.

  ■ Recency effect: information at the end of a sequence has a higher probability of being recalled because it is still in the short-term memory.

■ *Presence of a cue*: retrieval cues come from associations we form at the time we encode a memory. It may be a word, an emotion, a sound, smells, tastes, or sights, that can evoke our memory of the associated person or event. Associations are usually activated without our awareness. Whatever the specific cue, a memory will suddenly come to mind when the retrieval cue is present. The process of facilitation of the ability to detect or identify a particular stimulus that is based on a previous experience or exposure to another stimulus is called priming. It is related to implicit memory. A specific cue can be used to elicit specific behavior (cueing or prompting), e.g., when a teacher puts a finger on lips in a classroom to reduce chatter and elicit silence. The process of unlearning cue associations is called fading.

The Biological Basis of Memory

The formation of long-term memories is a vital function for adaptive survival. In the last two decades, great progress has been made in the understanding of the biological basis of memory formation (Bisaz, Travaglia, & Alberini, 2014). Though the cellular and molecular basis of memory formation it is not yet clearly understood, simple forms of procedural memory, such as habituation, and sensitization were used to identify neuronal changes associated with memory formation.

Studies of the synaptic connections between the sensory and motor neurons that control the gill-withdrawal reflex in the sea slug Aplysia revealed that a single sensitizing stimulus to the tail increases the strength of the synaptic connections between the sensory and motor neurons. The stimulus leads to the activation of modulatory neurons that release serotonin onto the sensory neuron. Serotonin, in turn, increases the concentration of cyclic adenosine monophosphate (cAMP) in the sensory cell. The cAMP molecules signal the sensory neuron to release more glutamate into the synaptic cleft, thus temporarily strengthening the connection between the sensory and motor neuron. Directly injecting cAMP into the sensory neuron produces temporary strengthening of the sensory-motor connection (Bisaz et al., 2014). Short-term memory and intermediate-term memory parallel synaptic strengthening that lasts from minutes to hours, and long-term memory parallels synaptic strengthening that lasts from days to weeks (Carew, Castellucci, & Kandel, 1979; Castellucci, Carew, & Kandel, 1978).

Long-term potentiation (LTP) is operationally defined as a long-lasting increase in synaptic efficacy following high-frequency stimulation of the afferent fibers (Shors & Matzel, 1997). Changes in synaptic efficacy are thought to play a key role in the formation of long-lasting memories. LTP has a number of properties that make it suitable as a physiological substrate of memory: (1) *synapse specificity*: it occurs only at potentiated synapses that are activated by the tetanic stimulation; (2) *cooperativity*: multiple inputs must be activated simultaneously to produce sufficient postsynaptic depolarization to induce LTP; and (3) *it is associative*: when a

PHOTO 13.3.   The Sea Slug Aplysia.

weak input that is normally insufficient to induce LTP is paired with a strong input, the weak input will become potentiated (Mayford, Siegelbaum, & Kandel, 2012). LTP occurs prominently in the hippocampus, a structure important for memory. Long-term depression (LTD) of synaptic transmission is the opposite of LTP, i.e., a decrease in the strength of synaptic connections. The encoding of long-term memories is suggested to involve modification of synaptic connections through LTP and LTD.

Researchers have suggested that several brain parts are involved in the memory processes including the hippocampus, the thalamus, and the amygdala. The hippocampus appears to be involved in the recollection of recent events, it is active during the initial storage of information. Damage to the hippocampus is associated with the inability to store new information, however, the person can still remember things stored before the occurrence of the damage.

Declarative memory depends on the medial temporal and midline diencephalic structures, along with large portions of the neocortex. Procedural memory depends on several different brain systems. Habits depend on the neocortex and the neostriatum, the cerebellum is important for conditioning of skeletal musculature, the amygdala for emotional learning, and the neocortex for priming. The frontal lobes are fundamentally important for declarative memory. Patients with frontal lesions have poor memory for the context in which information was acquired, they have difficulty in uncued recall, and they may even have some mild difficulty on tests of item recognition. More generally, frontal lesions may lead to difficulty in implementing memory retrieval strategies, and evaluating and monitoring memory performance.

Positron emission tomography (PET) scans and functional magnetic resonance imaging (MRI) studies have shown that posterior prefrontal regions are involved in strategic processing during retrieval, as well as in working memory. Anterior frontal regions near the frontal poles have been linked with functions such as evaluating the products of retrieval. Frontal connections with posterior neocortical regions support the organization of retrieval and the manipulation of information in working memory. Consistent with the evidence from patients with frontal lesions, frontal-posterior networks can be viewed as instrumental in the retrieval of declarative memories and in the online processing of new information. Neuroimaging has also identified contributions to memory made by the parietal cortex. Multiple parietal regions (including the inferior and superior parietal lobules, the precuneus, the posterior cingulate, and the retrosplenial cortex) are activated in conjunction with remembering recent experiences (Sadock, Sadock, & Ruiz, 2017).

The thalamus is a relay station that receives signals from the senses and then passes the signals to its corresponding area in the cerebral cortex. The thalamic midline nuclei serve as a hub linking the hippocampus, the medial prefrontal cortex, and the posterior representational areas during memory retrieval at an early (2 hours) stage of consolidation (Thielen, Takashima, Rutters, Tendolkar, & Fernández, 2015).

The amygdalae are associated with both emotional learning and memory, as they respond strongly to emotional stimuli, especially fear. These neurons assist in encoding emotional memories and enhancing them. This process results in emotional events being more deeply and accurately encoded into memory. Lesions to the amygdalae in monkeys have been shown to impair motivation, as well as the processing of emotions (Robbins, Ersche, & Everitt, 2008).

Mechanisms of Forgetting

If new information is not rapidly encoded, or rehearsed, it is forgotten. If it is transferred to long-term memory, it becomes relatively permanent, although retrieving it may be a problem. Forgetting may result for different reasons, such as encoding failure, consolidation failure, storage decay, or retrieval failure.

- *Encoding failure*: failure to encode information leads to the inability to put materials into long-term memory. Age-related memory decline could be explained by the effects of age on encoding efficiency.
- *Consolidation failure*: disruption to the consolidation process prevents a permanent memory formation, e.g., in cases of head trauma with retrograde amnesia, loss of memory affects experiences that occurred shortly before a loss of consciousness which were not consolidated.
- *Storage decay*: memory traces that are not used disappear with the passage of time.
- *Retrieval failure*: forgetting may result from retrieval failure. It may be caused by a lack of retrieval cues, proactive or retroactive interference, or it may be motivated forgetting. Motivated forgetting refers to states, in which information is forgotten through suppression or repression in order to protect oneself from painful materials that produce anxiety or guilt.

Interference Theory

This theory suggests that memory loss may occur because information or associations stored either before or after a given memory hinder the ability to remember it. Interference may be either proactive or retroactive.

- Proactive interference occurs when information or experiences already stored in long-term memory hinder the ability to remember newer information.
- Retroactive interference happens when new learning interferes with the ability to remember previously learned information.

How Can You Improve Your Memory?

Memory may not work well all the time, but a number of factors could help to improve memory performance. Here are some suggestions one can readily use:

- *Chunking*: organizing items into familiar, manageable units, which usually occurs automatically. It is evident that sentences are remembered easily than random and incoherent words. Thus, how information is organized strongly influences the acquisition and retrieval of information.
- *Mnemonics*: develop your own shorthand codes, e.g., the first-letter technique could be used to learn the names of the nine planets, the first letter of each word in a phrase stands for an item to be remembered. In this case, the phrase was "Mary's Violet Eyes Make John Stay Up Nights Pondering" (for Mercury, Venus, Earth, Mars, Jupiter, Saturn, Uranus, Neptune, and Pluto). This can be a useful technique if you need to remember lists of items.
- *Spacing effect*: learning in short sessions yields better long-term retention than is achieved through one long study session. Long periods of memorizing make materials subject to interference and often result in fatigue and lowered concentration
- *Hierarchies*: dividing and subdividing broad concepts into narrower concepts and facts.
- *Rehearsal*: reviewing information and practice or trial performance allow the consolidation of information into the long-term memory storages. Memory is enhanced after rehearsal, rather than simply rereading information.
- *Making associations between new and existing knowledge*: this could be achieved by asking questions about it, considering its meaning, and examining its relationship to existent information.

- *Imagery*: it is often easier to remember information associated with a vivid mental image than abstract information; a picture is worth a thousand words.
- *Overlearning*: overlearned materials are remembered better and longer.
- *Minimize interference*: the more similar materials are, the more likely they will produce interference. In practical terms, interference could be minimized by arranging to study unrelated subjects rather than similar subjects one after the other.
- *Good sleep*: sleep aids consolidation of memory, and its lack decreases retention.
- *Satiety*: hunger decreases retention, so satiety may help in good retention.

Memory Disorders

Memory may be the subject to loss (amnesia) or distortion (dysmnesia). Amnesia refers to the inability to memorize information or recall information that is stored in memory, to a greater extent than simple everyday forgetting. Amnesia is usually classified into:

- *Anterograde amnesia*: refers to impairment or inability to memorize new things; the person cannot recall or recognize new information or events that occurred after an amnesia-inducing event, e.g., not remembering or the inability to learn retain new names, faces, events, or sequences after an accident.
- *Retrograde amnesia*: refers to the inability to recall or recognize information or events that occurred before an amnesia-inducing event.
- *Total or global amnesia*: loss of memory of all events.
- *Localized or circumscribed amnesia*: loss of memory for a discrete period of time (amnesic gap). It typically occurs after a traumatic event, e.g., loss of memory how a mother left her office and went to hospital after learning that her child had an accident.
- *Selective amnesia*: inability to recall certain aspects of an event.

Causes of Amnesia

Amnesia may result from organic or neurological disorders affecting the brain function or integrity, or from functional or psychogenic causes:

- *Normal forgetfulness*: Healthy people can experience memory loss or memory distortion, but they are not extreme, persistent nor impairing.
- *Dementias*: e.g., Alzheimer's disease, frontotemporal lobe degeneration, and Lewy body disease. Memory is specifically affected in all types of dementias in addition to other cognitive functions.
- *Other neurological disorders*: a variety of neurological diseases, including cerebral vascular disorders, encephalitis due to viral infection, or as an autoimmune reaction, some brain tumors, anoxic brain damage due to a heart attack, respiratory distress or carbon monoxide poisoning, and long-term alcohol abuse leading to thiamin (vitamin B-1) deficiency, and Korsakoff syndrome.
- *Head injuries* that cause a concussion, due to a car accident or sports accident, can lead to problems remembering new information. This is especially common in the early stages of recovery.
- *Electroconvulsive therapy*: may lead to transient retrograde amnesia. Anterograde amnesia may also occur, but usually resolves within 2–6 weeks of the treatment.
- Psychiatric disorders:

- Dissociative amnesia: severe trauma or stress can cause dissociative amnesia that may be total, circumscribed to certain periods, or selective to certain aspects of an event. A specific type of dissociative amnesia, called fugue, can lead to unexpected traveling away from one's customary environment, with the inability to recall one's past and assumption of a new identity, which may be partial or complete. Dissociative identity disorder is characterized by the presence of two or more distinct personality states or an experience of possession, associated with recurrent episodes of amnesia. Individuals may experience discontinuities in identity and memory that may not be immediately evident to others or are obscured by attempts to hide the dysfunction.
- Depressive disorders may be associated with memory complaints, and differential recall of unhappy memories. Memory impairment may be so severe that it accounts for what is called "depressive pseudodementia."
- Severe anxiety disorders can interfere with memory functions due to a lack of attention.

Distortion of memory (dysmnesia) encompasses distortion of recall or recognition. Distortion of recall (paramnesia): may be in the form of:

- *Confabulation*: this is a detailed false description of an event. The patient gives imaginary accounts of his or her activities which may be influenced by suggestion. This usually occurs in organic brain syndromes (e.g., Korsakoff syndrome), and occurs unconsciously.
- *Retrospective falsification*: the subject modifies his or her memories according to his or her general attitudes. The patient adds false details and meaning to a true memory. We all falsify the past to some degree. Excessive retrospective falsification is common in depressive illnesses and histrionic personality. The depressed patient looks back over the past and see only failures, insist that he or she was a useless or worthless person. Histrionic personalities may produce a complete falsified set of memories of the past.
- *Delusional memory*: primary delusional experiences may take the form of memories; the subject suddenly remembers that the Queen greeted him when he was a child because she recognized him as a member of the royal family.
- *Retrospective delusions*: in some schizophrenic patients, the subject back-dates delusions, getting fragments of true memories interwoven with delusional reminiscences.

Distortion of recognition includes:

- *Déjà vu*: a new situation is incorrectly regarded as a repetition of a previous memory.
- *Jamais vu*: a false feeling of unfamiliarity with a real situation one has experienced.
- *Misidentification*: this can be positive or negative. In positive misidentification strangers are recognized as friends or relatives. It occurs in an acute confusional state and in schizophrenia. In negative misidentification, friends and relatives are recognized as strangers. Capgras syndrome is a form of a negative misidentification.

Clinical Notes

A variety of quantitative methods are available and useful in evaluating the current status of memory function and following patients longitudinally. The Wechsler Memory Scale-Revised is the single most useful measure of memory. A complete assessment of memory usually involves the assessment of other intellectual functions, new learning capacity, remote memory, and memory self-report. Information about intellectual functions provides both information about a patient's general test-taking ability and a way to assess the selectivity of memory impairment.

Summary

- Memory is defined as the capacity to take in information, retain it over time and retrieve that information later. It involves the encoding, storage, and retrieval of information.
- Theories that explain our understanding of memory include the multi-store model, and the levels of processing theory.
- The multi-store model suggests that information exists in one of three states of memory: the sensory, short-term (STM), and long-term (LTM) stores.
- The levels of processing theory proposes that there is only one kind of memory, and there is no clear distinction between short-term and long-term memory. The strength of a memory trace depends upon the depth of the processing of the information.
- Memory is usually classified into sensory memory, short-term memory, and long-term memory.
- Long-term memory consists of procedural and declarative memories. Declarative memory is subdivided into semantic and episodic memories.
- Memory processing involves three cognitive processes: encoding, storage, and retrieval of information.
- Retrieval of information is influenced by context, state, serial position effect, and presence of a cue.
- The cellular and molecular basis of memory formation includes two basic processes: sensitization and long-term potentiation (LTP).
- Forgetting may result from encoding failure, consolidation failure, storage decay, retrieval failure, and interference.
- Memory performance could be improved by chunking, mnemonics, spacing effect, hierarchies, rehearsal, making associations, imagery, overlearning, minimizing interference, good sleep, and satiety.
- Amnesia is usually classified into anterograde amnesia, retrograde amnesia, total or global amnesia, circumscribed, and selective amnesia.

Test Your Knowledge

- Define memory.
- Describe the multi-store model of memory.
- What is the levels of processing theory?
- Describe the types of memory.
- Describe memory processes.
- What are the biological bases of memory?
- How can memory be measured?
- What are the mechanisms of forgetting?
- How can you improve your memory?

Critical Thinking Question

How has your understanding of memory helped in your evaluation of the reliability of a witness in court?

fourteen
Thinking and Problem-Solving

Learning Goals

- This chapter is intended to provide the reader with an overview of the definition of thinking, the building blocks of thinking, types of concepts, types of thinking, problem-solving, decision-making, and errors of thinking, including cognitive distortions and cognitive biases.

Introduction

For generations, philosophers have debated the meaning of thinking, with some placing it at the core of human beings' understanding of their own existence. Thinking could be defined as the cognitive activities that one uses to process information, to solve problems, to make decisions, and to create new ideas. Thus, thinking is a constructive process that leads to the formation of a new representation of any object or event by transforming the available information. Thinking involves a number of mental activities, such as inferring, abstracting, reasoning, imagining, judging, problem-solving, and creative thinking. The essential building blocks involved in the thinking process include language, symbols and signs, mental images, and concepts.

PHOTO 14.1.   Thinking.

- *Symbols and signs*: symbols and signs represent substitutes for the actual objects, experiences, and activities, e.g., numbers, letters, words, traffic lights, railway signals, school bells, badges, flags, and slogans; all are symbolic expressions that stimulate thinking because they tell us what to do or how to act.
- *Language*: language is the system of symbols that allows a person to communicate ideas to others. It is the most efficient and developed vehicle used for carrying out the process of thinking. A person is stimulated to think when he or she reads, writes or hears words or sentences, or observes gestures in any language. Thus, reading and writing documents or literature help in stimulating and promoting the thinking process.
- *Mental images*: these are the mental representations of objects, persons, and situations, heard or experienced. The mental images have some features in common with actual visual images, but they are not exact duplicates of our actual sensory experience. Shepard and Metzler (1971) discovered that participants in their experiment rotated one image of one of a pair of images in their minds to determine if the objects in each pair were identical or different.
- *Concepts*: a concept is a general idea that stands for a general class and represents the common characteristics of all objects or events of this general class. Concepts economize the cognitive effort required for thinking and communicating, e.g., when we hear the word horse, it reminds us not only about the nature and qualities of horse as a class but also reminds us about our own experiences and understanding of them. Using concepts makes it easier to communicate with others, remember information, and learn new information.

    Concepts are usually organized into orderly hierarchies composed of main categories and subcategories. Thus, a very general concept, such as animals, can be mentally divided into a variety of subcategories: invertebrates and vertebrates, each subcategory is further subdivided into different sub-groups, e.g., vertebrates are divided into reptiles, birds, amphibians, and mammals. As we learn the key properties that define general concepts, we also learn how members of the concept are related to one another.

Types of Concepts

- *Artificial (formal) concepts* are defined by a set of characteristics that all members have and nonmembers do not have. If the defining features are present, then the object is included as a member or example of that concept, e.g., geometric shapes, disease, normal, intelligent.

- *Natural concepts*: this refers to a mental category that is derived from everyday perceptions and experience, rather than by logically determining whether an object or event fits a specific set of rules. Its members have some of the characteristics that define the concept (e.g., birds, mammals). Some members are better representatives of a natural concept than are others. The best or most typical example of a particular concept is called a prototype. People tend to determine whether an object is an example of a natural concept by comparing it to prototypes that they have stored in memory to determine whether it belongs to that category, rather than by logically evaluating whether the defining features are present or absent. So, if you are trying to decide whether a coconut is a fruit, you compare it to your memories of other items that you know to be fruits, not to a single fruit. The more closely an item matches the prototype, the more quickly we can identify it as being an example of that concept.

- *Rules* are statements of relation between concepts, e.g., a person cannot be in two places at the same time, or mass remains constant despite changes in appearance.

Types of Thinking

There are several types of thinking or ways to think, which may overlap and are not exclusive. These include:

1. *Concrete thinking*: this form of thinking considers the literal meaning of objects or ideas of specific items, rather than as a theoretical representation of a more general concept.
2. *Abstract thinking*: this refers to the ability to use and to understand concepts, relating or connecting them to other items, events, or experiences, and to make generalizations. It involves paying attention to the hidden meanings, thus allowing a person to observe and understand the underlying purpose.
3. *Analytical thinking*: this refers to the ability to break information down into its basic parts in order to examine the parts and their relationships. It involves thinking in a logical, step-by-step manner in order to analyze data, solve problems, make decisions, and/or use information.
4. *Critical thinking*: this refers to the process of independently analyzing, synthesizing, and evaluating information as a guide to behavior and beliefs. Key critical thinking skills include observation and description, critical reading, verifying and interpreting data, weighing up evidence, assessing relevance, and applying the principles of logic. The process of using critical thinking to guide writing is called critical writing. Critical thinking helps a person to step back from their own personal beliefs, prejudices and opinions to sort out the faiths and discover the truth, even at the expense of their basic belief system. Critical thinking and reflective thinking are often used synonymously, but reflective thinking is specifically used to refer to the processes of analyzing and making judgments about what has happened.
5. *Divergent thinking*: thinking is creative, open-ended thinking aimed at generating fresh views and novel solutions. Divergent thinking refers to breaking a topic into its various components, to gain insight about the various aspects of the topic, and then

generate new ideas and solutions. It starts from a common point and moves outward in diverging directions to involve a variety of aspects or perspectives. In other words, in divergent thinking, an idea is followed in several directions to lead to one or more new ideas, which in turn lead to more ideas.

6. *Convergent thinking*: this refers to the ability to put a number of different pieces or perspectives of a topic together in some organized, logical manner to find a single answer. It involves focusing on a finite number of solutions rather than proposing multiple solutions. The deductive reasoning that Sherlock Holmes used in solving mysteries is a good example of convergent thinking. By gathering various bits of observations or premises, he was able to put the pieces of a puzzle together and come up with a logical answer to the question of who done it.

7. *Sequential (linear) thinking*: this refers to the ability to process information in an orderly prescribed manner. It involves a step-by-step progression where a response to a step needs to be completed before a second step occurs.

8. *Holistic (nonlinear) thinking*: this refers to the ability to see the big picture and recognize the interconnection of various components that form the larger system. It involves expanding the thought process in multiple directions, rather than in just one direction, to understand how everything connects. Holistic thinking aims at understanding the patterns and how things connect to each other.

9. *Creative thinking*: this refers to thinking which involves reaching out to the solution of a problem in a unique, original, and novel way that others have not thought of before. Creative thinking is often referred to as "thinking outside the box." The creative solutions or productions may come suddenly, but are the outcome of a lot of work and preparation already done consciously and unconsciously. The sudden appearance of new ideas is called "insight." The creative thinker may be an artist, musician, writer, scientist, or sports person. Graham Wallas proposed that creative thinking passes through five stages: preparation, incubation, illumination, evaluation, and revision (Wallas, 1926).

    a. Preparation: the thinker formulates the problem and collects data and materials necessary for the solution. At this stage of problem-solving, it is important to overcome negative consequences of any kind of mental set or bias.

    b. Incubation: the thinker deliberately or involuntarily turns away from the problem, when he or she is unable to solve the problem. The negative effects of mental set, functional fixedness, and other ideas that interfere with the solution tend to fade, while fatigue and concern about the problem increase during this period. Further, the unconscious thought processes involved in creative thinking are at work during this stage.

    c. Illumination: this refers to having the insight about the possible solution. Illumination occurs when a sudden solution to the problem seems to be realized.

    d. Evaluation: the obtained solution is verified or tested to see if it works. The insight may turn out to be unsatisfactory, and may need some modification in the strategy of approaching the problem.

    e. Revision: this is required if a solution is not satisfactory.

Creativity is affected by both individual and group or organizational factors. individual factors include motivation of the individual to innovate, autonomy, and control over work and ideas, clarity of the problem and the goal, and adequacy of resources including time, and training. Organizational factors include: *group characteristics*: such as norms, group cohesiveness, size, diversity, roles, task characteristics, and the problem-solving approaches used. Internal strife, conservatism, rigid and formal management structures impede creativity, while diversity of team members' background, mutual openness to ideas, constructive challenging of ideas, and shared commitment help creativity. *Management practices*: freedom in conduct of work, provision of challenging and interesting work, specification of clear strategic goals, formation of work teams with diverse skills and perspectives, a focus on technology, and reward and incentive structures. Encouraging risk taking and idea generation at all levels, and supportive evaluation of new ideas help creativity, while excessive workload pressure impair creativity.

10. *Magical thinking*: this is a clinical term used to describe a wide variety of nonscientific and sometimes irrational beliefs, that are characterized by the belief that thinking or wishing something can cause its occurrence. These beliefs are generally centered on correlations between events, e.g., a belief in the power of magic rituals and spells. Magical thinking need to be considered in context, e.g., while a belief in the paranormal could be seen as magical thinking, many religious and cultural traditions believe in the existence of spirits, demons, and other entities. A person with such a background should not be diagnosed with magical thinking based only on a belief in such entities. Furthermore, it is important to distinguish between scientific hypothesis, which is normal, and a belief in a situation, which may demonstrate magical thinking. Many people enjoy thinking of improbable possibilities and situations. Thus, it is not magical thinking to propose a theory, provided that the person expresses understanding that the theory is not necessarily rational by today's scientific logic. Various points in the history of science told us that the Earth is flat and man cannot fly. Once considered radical and even magical thinking, the opposite of these ideas now forms some of the basic concepts for our world, e.g., the Earth is round. Magical thinking is sometimes symptomatic of a mental disorder. Obsessive compulsive disorder, depression, schizotypal personality disorder, and psychosis are just a few diagnoses that include magical thinking as a possible symptom.

11. *Non-directed or associative thinking*: this lacks leading ideas and the sense of direction and goals stemming from them. One no longer compels thoughts along a definite track. This type of thinking is reflected in dreaming and other free-flowing uncontrolled activities. Psychologically, these forms of thought are termed associative thinking.

Thinking Skills

Thinking skills are the mental activities one uses to process information, make connections, make decisions, and create new ideas. There are several core thinking skills including gathering, focusing, connecting, organizing, compiling, integrating, analyzing, evaluating, and generating.

- *Gathering*: means bringing to the conscious mind the relative information needed for cognitive processing.
- *Focusing*: means attending to selected pieces of information while ignoring other stimuli.
- *Connecting*: means making connections between related items or pieces of information.
- *Organizing*: means arranging information in a way that it can be used more effectively.
- *Compiling*: means putting parts together to form a whole or building a structure or pattern from diverse elements.
- *Integrating*: means connecting and combining information to better understand the relationship between the information.

- *Analyzing*: means breaking down information by examining parts and relationships, so that its organizational structure may be understood.
- *Evaluating*: means assessing the reasonableness and quality of ideas or materials in order to present and defend opinions.
- *Generating*: means producing new information, ideas, products, or ways of viewing things.

Problem-Solving

Problem-solving refers to the process of arriving at a solution to a given problem, in which one employs mental strategies directed toward attaining a goal that is not readily available. Problem-solving strategies include a wide variety of scientific, nonscientific, and sometimes irrational beliefs that are influenced by the nature of the problem and degree of experience, familiarity, and knowledge about the problem.

Once people discover a solution to a problem, they continue to use it even when it is less efficient. Tracking the eye movements of

PHOTO 14.2.   Problem-Solving.

highly skilled chess players revealed that they are literally blind to certain areas of the chess board that could provide clues to faster checkmate positions. They tend to stick to a well-known sequence of moves that has proved successful in the past. Failure to see other functions of an object than what one experiences in everyday practice is another type of mental set that leads to fixity in problem-solving. Common strategies used in problem-solving include:

- *Trial and error*: the person tries a variety of solutions, and eliminates those that do not work. Trial and error can be a useful problem-solving strategy, when there is a limited range of possible solutions. However, when the range of possible answers or solutions is large, trial and error can be very time-consuming.
- *Algorithms*: an algorithm is a defined set of step-by-step procedures that provides the correct answer to a particular problem, e.g., mathematical and scientific formulas. Such a step-by-step approach is useful in situations where each decision must be made following the same process and where accuracy is critical, e.g., a physician making a decision about how to treat a patient. By following the instructions correctly, one is supposed to arrive at the right answer each time. However, using an algorithm is not always practical.
- *Insight*: sometimes, an abrupt, true-seeming, and often satisfying solution comes into the mind, usually after a period of thinking deeply about a problem. Insights rarely occur through the conscious manipulation of concepts or information, but are often generated through unconscious processes that finally deposit their results in awareness.
- *Intuition*: this means our fast, automatic, unreasoned feelings and thoughts. One influential model of intuition is the two-stage model. In the first stage, called the guiding stage, you unconsciously perceive a pattern in the information you are considering. The perception of such patterns is based on your expertise in a given area and your

memories of related information. In the second stage, the integrative stage, a representation of the pattern becomes conscious, usually in the form of an impression or hypothesis. At this point, conscious analytic thought processes take over. Later on, a person systematically may attempt to prove or disprove this impression or hypothesis, e.g., an experienced physician may integrate both obvious and subtle cues to recognize a pattern in a patient's symptoms, which takes the form of a preliminary diagnosis. Then, the physician may order lab tests to confirm or refute the tentative diagnosis. Some intuitions are likely to be accurate only in contexts in which you already have a broad base of knowledge and experience.

Decision-Making

PHOTO 14.3.   Decision-Making.

Decision-making is a special case of problem-solving in which one selects an appropriate alternative from a number of available alternatives. Some decisions are relatively trivial and easy to make, such as deciding what to wear or what to have at breakfast, while others are more important and have a major influence on the course of our life, such as deciding which university to attend, or whether or not to have children. Some decisions take time while others must be made immediately.

Decision-Making Strategies

Different cognitive strategies are used when making decisions, depending on the type and number of available options. When a decision is important or complex, we are more likely to invest time, effort, and resources in considering different options. The decision-making process becomes complicated when each option involves the consideration of several features. It is unusual for one alternative to be superior in every category, each alternative usually has its pros and cons. In decision-making we usually use one of the following models.

The Single-Feature Model

Choice among alternatives is based on a single feature. When the decision is a minor one, the single-feature model can be a good decision-making strategy, e.g., buying a laundry detergent, you may simplify your decision by deciding to buy the cheapest brand. When a decision is important or complex, making decisions on the basis of a single feature is not the best strategy and can result in risky decisions.

Compensatory Models

All desirable and undesirable potential outcomes of a particular decision are evaluated. Then one of the following models can be used:

- *The additive compensatory model*: this method involves taking into account all the important features of the possible choices and then systematically evaluating each option. Each feature of an alternative is rated using an arbitrary scale, such as from –5 to +5, e.g., when you are interested in buying a new car, you create a list of important features of the car that you want to have, then you rate each possible feature on a scale of –5 to +5. A car that has many advantages or a lot of appeal is given the maximum rating (+5), while those that have major drawbacks might get a –5 rating. Once you have looked at each feature, you can verify the results to determine which car has the highest rating. This strategy can often reveal the best overall choice. If the decision involves a situation in which some factors are more important than others, you can emphasize the more important factors by multiplying the rating. Taking the time to apply the additive model to important decisions can greatly improve your decision-making. This approach tends to be a good method when making complex decisions.
- *The utility-probability model*: decisions are made by weighting the desirability of each expected outcome according to its utility (the value placed on expected positive or negative outcomes) and probability (the likelihood that the choice will actually produce the potential outcome).

Non-Compensatory Models

We may not consider every feature of each alternative and features do not compensate for each other. There are at least four such models:

- *Elimination by aspects model*: this was first proposed by psychologist Amos Tversky in 1972. In this approach, a person facing complex decisions evaluates one characteristic of an option at a time, beginning with whatever feature one believes to be the most important. When an item fails to meet the established criteria, one removes the item from the list of options. The list of possible choices gets smaller and smaller as you discard items until you eventually arrive at just one alternative (Tversky, 1972).
- *Maximax strategy*: one looks at the best features of each option and then selects the one with the best features. People using this strategy assume that they will get the "best of the best."
- *Minimax strategy*: the person will attempt to minimize their loss by considering the weakest feature of each option, and then selecting the option with the least drawbacks among those alternatives. People using this strategy assume that they will get the best of the worst.
- *Conjunctive strategy*: this involves setting a minimum acceptable value on each option. Any option which does not meet this value is discarded. The chosen option is the one that meets or exceeds the minimum acceptable value on each criterion.

The Heuristics Model

A heuristic is a mental shortcut or rule of thumb that allows one to make a judgment or conclusion quickly and efficiently. These rule-of-thumb strategies shorten decision-making time and allow people to function without constantly stopping to think about their next course of action. While heuristics are helpful in many situations and can speed up our problem-solving and decision-making process, they can lead to cognitive biases. This is because if something has worked in the past, it does not mean it will work again. Also, relying on an existing heuristic can make it difficult to see alternative solutions or new ideas. Heuristics can also contribute to stereotypes and prejudice. The two common types of heuristics include:

- *The availability heuristic*: the likelihood of an event is estimated on the basis of how quickly one can call similar events to mind. The key point here is that our memory may not accurately reflect the actual frequency of an event, leading to an inaccurate estimate of the event's likelihood of occurring. When instances of an event are easily recalled, one tends to consider the event as being more likely to occur. So, exceeding the speed limit is less likely if one can readily recall that a friend recently got a speeding ticket. However, when a rare event makes a vivid impression on us, e.g., a plane crash, one may overestimate its likelihood, and may feel air travel is too dangerous and decide to travel by car instead.
- *The representativeness heuristic*: the likelihood of an event is estimated by comparing how similar its essential features are to our prototype of a particular event or behavior. A prototype is the most typical example of a particular object or event. Making decisions based on prototypes is likely to make more errors and to overestimate or underestimate the likelihood that something will occur. The representativeness heuristic can lead to inaccurate judgments, e.g., comparing the number of registered nurses (which is very large) to the number of successful female fiction writers (which is very small), may lead to the conclusion that Maria is likely to be a nurse. Thus, the representativeness heuristic can produce faulty appraisals, if (1) we fail to consider possible variations from the prototype or (2) we fail to consider the approximate number of prototypes that actually exist.

Barriers to Problem-Solving

A successful solution to a problem could be compromised by a wide range of types of barriers, including perceptual, emotional, intellectual, as well as by social and physical barriers, or a combination of these. The following is a summary of important barriers to problem-solving.

- *Functional fixedness*: this refers to the tendency to view problems only in their habitual manner. Functional fixedness comes from people thinking that an object has only one function, e.g., a jug can only be used to pour fluids. Functional fixedness prevents people from fully seeing all the different options that might be available to find a solution.
- *Irrelevant or misleading information*: when solving a problem, it is important to distinguish between information that is relevant to the issue and irrelevant data that can lead to misunderstandings and faulty solutions. A brainstorming session can be impaired because people go off topic. This is why many brainstorming sessions have a facilitator to get things back on track.
- *Mental set*: this is the tendency of people to rely on solutions and experiences that have been successful in the past to guide problem-solving, rather than assessing and

evaluating the current problem and looking for alternative ideas, that is, a particular strategy becomes a habit. Although a mental set can work as a heuristic, that speeds up problem-solving, it can lead to inflexibility, making it difficult to find effective solutions.

- *Learned helplessness*: a condition in which repeated failure to control a situation results in the belief that the situation is uncontrollable and stopping further attempts.
- *Emotional barriers*: certain feelings may hinder problem-solving accurately, e.g., fear of change, or feeling guilty that the problem occurred.
- *Intellectual barriers*: lack of adequate training, skills or knowledge to solve a problem, e.g., lack of skills in evaluation or research, etc.
- *Perspective*: certain perspectives may lead us to see the world in different ways. It may cause a potential solution to be ignored or marked as unworkable based on our beliefs, attitudes, and opinions. A marketing executive is likely to see a problem in a different way to a service manager.
- *Culture*: cultural expectations about good behavior may encourage or inhibit certain behaviors. If a culture is reserved, one may have issues regarding sharing ideas. If a culture encourages discussion, one may diverge from the topic. Similarly, all forms of discrimination and cultural bias can hinder problem-solving.
- *Physical environment*: this may affect our ability to think clearly or to perform a task, e.g., a noisy office prevents the problem-solver from being able to concentrate on the task, while the lack of access to the internet will deprive the problem-solver of a useful tool.

Errors of Thinking

Errors of thinking are irrational patterns of thinking that are commonly divided into cognitive distortions or cognitive biases. However, this distinction or categorization looks ambiguous, not based on scientific background. Common cognitive distortions and biases will be described.

Cognitive Distortions

Cognitive distortions refer to biased patterns or ways of thinking that one possesses about oneself and the world, and lead to misrepresentation or distortion of a person's perception of reality. Cognitive distortions can feed negative emotions and lead to an overall negative outlook of the world and consequently a depressive or anxious mental state. The term cognitive distortion was originally used by Beck to describe idiosyncratic thought content in patients suffering from depression (Beck, 1963). In his work with depressed patients, Beck defined six systematic errors in thinking which were extended by his followers to include other types of cognitive distortions.

Cognitive distortions are common, may be difficult to recognize, and may occur as automatic thoughts. If left unchecked, these automatic thought patterns may negatively influence the rational, logical way you make decisions. People who suffer from depression, anxiety disorders and personality disorders often exhibit these negative thought patterns. One of the goals of cognitive-behavioral therapy is to identify unhelpful thinking styles and modify the thinking process. A number of these cognitive distortions are described below:

- *Black-and-white thinking (polarized/dichotomous thinking)*: this means seeing everything in extremes, everything is seen as all or none. In this type of faulty thinking, people cannot see the alternatives in a situation or solutions to a problem. Whatever the issue, there are no shades of gray when thinking this way, e.g., people are right or wrong, situations are good or bad. People who have this type of polarized thinking believe that they are either successful or unsuccessful in life. To correct dichotomous thinking, notice the possibility of gray areas, consider the complexity of most people and situations, and avoid unconditional terms, such as nothing or never.

- *Mental filtering*: this occurs when a person selects (filters) negative details, so that perception of reality becomes darkened, e.g., someone may leave a party because of forgetting someone's name or because he spilled a drink.

- *Discounting the positive*: this refers to rejecting positive experiences by insisting that they "do not count" for some reason. In this way a person can maintain a negative belief that is contradicted by his or her everyday experiences, e.g., a person may look at his or her feedback on an assignment in school or at work and ignore the positive notes to focus on one critical comment.

- *Overgeneralization*: this refers to coming to a general conclusion based on a single or two incidents or a single piece of evidence, despite the fact that reality is too complex to make such generalizations, e.g., a single bad incident is expected to happen over and over again; a friend who missed a lunch date will be supposed to continue missing commitments. A person may see a single, unpleasant event as part of a never-ending pattern of defeat. Overgeneralizing statements often include the words always, never, every, or all.

- *Jumping to conclusions*: this refers to making a negative interpretation even though there are no definite facts that convincingly support that conclusion. This may occur through:
  - *Mind reading*: believing that one knows what others are thinking, e.g., arbitrarily concluding that someone is reacting negatively to him or her, without checking this assumption.
  - *Fortune-telling*: predicting the future, e.g., when one anticipates that things will turn out badly, and feels convinced that this prediction is an already established fact, without evidence.

- *Catastrophizing*: this means turning small problems into big ones. Someone might think that giving a poor presentation at work will mean that co-workers will dislike her and that she may lose her job, or that failing an exam means failing the entire course. A person may even believe he or she will fail an exam, assuming the worst, because of a trivial incident of not understanding a topic.

- *Magnification and minimization*: people magnify or minimize the positive attributes of self or others. When magnifying, things are exaggerated out of proportion, though not quite to the extent of catastrophizing. When minimizing, the person distorts reality by minimizing positive events, and think something like, "Yes, I got a promotion, but it was not very big and I am still not very good at my job."

- *Emotional reasoning*: this is the belief that if you feel something, it must be true. Someone might believe that because he or she feels anxious, there is something in the situation to be feared. Emotional reasoning is irrational, and feelings can have many causes, and do not always reflect reality.

- *Shoulding and musting*: this is a type of black-and-white thinking. It involves thoughts such as "I should arrive for the meeting early" or "I must lose weight to be more attractive." When statements are directed toward self, this type of thinking may induce feelings of guilt or shame, but if they are directed toward others, one often feels anger, frustration, and resentment, when others fail to meet unrealistic expectations.

- *Labeling*: this is a more severe form of overgeneralization that occurs when a person labels someone or something based on a limited amount of experience or limited number of events. Instead of describing an error in the context of a specific situation, a person will attach an unhealthy label to himself or others, e.g., instead of believing that one had made a mistake, a person may automatically label himself a failure, e.g., one may say, "I am a loser" in a situation where they failed at a specific task.
- *Personalizing*: this involves blaming oneself, either partly or fully, for external events outside one's personal control. Those external events are believed to be one's own fault. A musician might consider a poor musical group performance to be due to his own mistakes. Similarly, if one sees that being late to arrive at the dinner party is the reason why the hostess overcooked the meal, and that would not have happened if one had arrived on time.

Cognitive Biases

A cognitive bias is a systematic (non-random) error in thinking, in which an error in reasoning, evaluating, remembering, or other cognitive process often occurs, leading to systematic deviations from a standard of rationality or good judgment (Ariely, 2008). A cognitive bias is a mind set that sees something in a certain preconceived way. It is a matter of one's perceptions of something conforming to one's prejudged expectations (like any bias) and therefore influences how and what one hears, sees, or experiences. Cognitive biases distort thinking, influence beliefs, and affect everyday decisions. These biases may be fairly obvious, and one is able to recognize them, or they may be subtle so that they are almost impossible to notice. Cognitive biases are not to be confused with logical fallacies, which are errors in logical argument.

Cognitive biases may serve an adaptive purpose, as they allow us to reach decisions quickly. This can be vital if we are facing a situation that seems so be dangerous or threatening, e.g., if you are walking down a dark street and spot a dark shadow that seems to be following you, a cognitive bias might lead you to assume that it is an assailant and that you need to get out of that street as quickly as possible. The dark shadow may have simply been caused by a flag waving in the breeze, but relying on mental shortcuts can often get you out of the way of danger in situations where decisions need to be made quickly.

Though there are controversies about how to classify biases or how to explain them, the following are the common cognitive biases that have a powerful influence on thinking, many of which have overlapping characteristics.

1. *The confirmation bias*: this is the tendency to search for information and evidence that confirm our preconceived beliefs, hypotheses, or desires, while simultaneously undervaluing, ignoring, dismissing, or giving disproportionately less consideration to information or alternatives that do not confirm to our preconceived beliefs, hypotheses, or desires, no matter how valid, e.g., we tend to visit websites that support our own perspectives and read blogs and editorial columns written by people who interpret events from our perspective, while avoiding websites, blogs, and columns written by people who do not share our way of thinking. This bias is sometimes called the wishful thinking bias. This inherent flaw in cognitive reasoning leads to misinterpretations of information, errors in judgment, and poor decision-making. The effects of confirmation bias have been shown to be much stronger for emotionally charged issues or beliefs that are deeply ingrained. In addition to overvaluing information that confirms our pre-existing beliefs, confirmation bias also includes our tendency to

interpret ambiguous evidence as supporting existing positions, even if no true relationship exists. In short, this concept says that individuals are biased toward information that confirms their existing beliefs and biased against information that disproves their existing beliefs, leading to overconfidence in their opinions and decisions, even in the face of strong contrary evidence.

2. *Illusory correlation (clustering illusion)*: this refers to seeing a pattern in what is actually a random sequence of numbers or events, e.g., gamblers who desperately try to beat the system by seeing patterns of events in cards and other games of chance. Similarly, a person may believe that two unrelated events have some type of relationship simply because they occurred around the same time. This bias is more or less related to confirmation bias.

3. *The hindsight bias*: this is the tendency to look back retrospectively, after an event has occurred, to see the event as having been predictable, even if there had been little to no objective basis for predicting it. It is sometimes referred to as the "I-knew-it-all-along" phenomenon, e.g., a gambler might mistakenly believe that they can accurately predict the outcome of a game of cards. In reality, there is no way that one can know what will happen since the game is based upon probability. Similarly investors may look back and believe that they could have predicted which tech companies would become dominant forces. This tendency can lead individuals to believe that they can actually predict consequences in situations that are really dependent upon chance.

4. *The anchoring bias (the relativity trap)*: the tendency to be overly influenced by the first piece of information that one hears, this is a phenomenon referred to as the anchoring bias or anchoring effect, e.g., the first number stated during a price negotiation usually becomes the anchoring point from which all further negotiations are based, e.g., one tends to see and value the difference in price of an item at the store that is on sale, but not the overall price itself. This is why some restaurant menus feature very expensive entrees, while also including more apparently reasonable priced ones. Similarly, when given a choice, people tend to pick the middle option, not too expensive, and not too cheap. Also, the physician's first impressions of a patient often create an anchoring point that can sometimes incorrectly influence all subsequent diagnostic assessments.

5. *The misinformation effect*: memories of particular events tend to be heavily influenced by things that happened after the actual event itself. Persons who witness a car accident or a crime may believe that their recollection is crystal clear, but memory is surprisingly susceptible to subtle influences. When questions are changed in a small degree, it may lead them to recall things that they did not actually witness, e.g., when witnesses to a car accident were questioned a week later, they were more likely to incorrectly report events that they had not seen.

6. *The self-serving bias*: this refers to the tendency to attribute positive events to personal characteristics, but lay the blame for failures on external causes outside one's control, e.g., when you do well on a project, you probably assume that it is because you worked hard, but when things turn out badly, you are more likely to blame circumstances or bad luck. This bias helps protect our self-esteem. However, this pattern of thinking may cause a person to refuse to admit mistakes or flaws and to live in a distorted reality where he or she can do no wrong.

7. *The actor observer bias*: the way we perceive an event or behavior is heavily influenced by whether we are the actor or the observer in a situation. When it comes to our own actions, we are often more likely to attribute things to external influences, e.g., when we fail an important meeting, we attribute that to having jet lag or when we fail an

exam, it is due to the teacher who posed too many trick questions. However, when it comes to explaining other people's actions, we are more likely to attribute their behavior to internal causes, e.g., they are lazy, or stupid.

8. *Projection bias*: people assume that their way of thinking or doing things is typical, and therefore other people should respond in a similar manner. Thus, people expect that other people think, feel, believe, and behave much like they do. This cognitive shortcoming often leads to a related effect known as the false consensus bias.

9. *The false consensus bias*: this is the tendency to overestimate how much other people agree with one's own beliefs, behaviors, attitudes, and values, and assume that a consensus exists on matters when there may be none. This can lead people not only to incorrectly think that everyone else agrees with them, but it can also lead them to overvalue their own opinions, and think that this way of thinking is the majority opinion. This cognitive bias allows us to feel normal and maintain a positive view of ourselves in relation to other people. Believing that other people are just like us is good for our self-esteem.

10. *The halo effect*: a tendency to generalize our overall impression of a person to unrelated personal characteristics. Thus, our overall impression of a person influences how one feels and thinks about this person's character (nice, attractive, and successful), e.g., celebrities and attractive individuals are rated more favorably for their characteristics than those who are less attractive. Since one perceives celebrities as attractive, successful, and likable, one also tends to see them as intelligent, kind, and funny. Similarly, good-looking teachers or job applicants who are perceived as attractive and likable are more liable to be viewed as competent, smart, and qualified for the job.

11. *The availability heuristic*: the tendency to estimate the probability of something happening based on how many examples readily come to mind. This is essentially a mental shortcut that serves to save time when one is trying to determine risk, e.g., after hearing several news reports of car thefts in your neighborhood, one may start to believe that such crimes are more common than they are. The problem with relying on this way of thinking is that it often leads to poor estimates and bad decisions, e.g., smokers who do not know someone who died of a smoking-related illness may underestimate the health risks of smoking.

12. *The optimism bias*: the tendency to overestimate the likelihood that good things will happen to us while underestimating the probability that negative events will impact our lives. This tendency toward optimism helps create a sense of hope about the future, giving people the motivation they need to follow their goals, though it can distort thinking and sometimes lead to poor decisions. Unrealistic optimism can lead people to take health risks like smoking, eating poorly, or not wearing a seat belt.

13. *Control fallacies*: a person may have an external or internal control fallacy. Someone who sees things as internally controlled may see one's self at fault for events that are truly outwith the person's control, such as another person's happiness or behavior. Persons who see things as externally controlled might blame their boss or their workmates for poor work performance.

14. *The belief-bias effect*: this refers to the tendency to accept any and all conclusions that fit in with person's systems of belief, without challenge or any deep consideration of what they are actually agreeing with. The reverse is also true, and people will tend to reject assertions that do not fit in with their belief systems, even though these statements may be perfectly logical and arguably possible.

15. *The fallacy of positive instances*: this is the tendency to remember uncommon events that seem to confirm our beliefs and to forget events that disconfirm our beliefs.

Often, the occurrence is really nothing more than coincidence, e.g., when you find yourself thinking of a friend, then the phone rings and it is him. You remember this seemingly telepathic event, but forget all the times that you have thought of this friend and he did not call. In other words, you remember the positive instance but fail to notice the negative instances when the anticipated event did not occur.

16. *Negativity bias*: this is the tendency to pay more attention or to over-emphasize negative information and experiences over neutral or positive ones. This bias probably evolved as a survival technique. Assuming the worst of a situation that turns out not to be dangerous is much safer than not expecting danger that turns out to be present.

17. *The gambler's fallacy*: the tendency to believe that if something happens more frequently than "usual" during a period of time, it must happen less frequently in the future, or that, if something happens less frequently than "usual" during a period of time, it must happen more frequently in the future. This tendency presumably arises out of an ingrained human desire for nature to be constantly balanced or averaged, e.g., gamblers believe that subsequent events will cancel out previous events to produce a representative sequence, and that the probability of winning will increase with the length of an ongoing run of losses, this pushes them to continue buying lottery tickets while experiencing losses. In coin-tossing, after flipping heads five consecutive times, for example, one's inclination is to predict an increase in likelihood that the next coin toss will be tails, that the odds must certainly be in the favor of heads. But in reality, the odds are still 50/50, as the outcomes in different tosses are statistically independent and the probability of any outcome is still 50 percent.

PHOTO 14.4.   The Gambler's Fallacy.

Closely related bias is the *positive expectation bias*, which often fuels gambling addictions. This is the sense that our luck has to eventually change and that good fortune is on the way. Similarly, it is the same feeling we get when we start a new relationship that leads us to believe it will be better than the last one.

18. *The hot-hand fallacy*: this is the belief that an individual who experienced success with a random event has a greater chance of continuing that success in subsequent attempts. This cognitive bias is most frequently applied to gambling, where individuals believe that the luck they have is actually a "hot hand" and will continue indefinitely. Similarly, in sports such as basketball, where "hot" shooters see a spike in confidence after making multiple shots in a row, fueling a belief that the trend will continue throughout the rest of the game. While previous success at a skill-based athletic task, such as making a shot in basketball, can change the psychological behavior and future success rate of a player, there is little evidence for a true "hot hand" in practice. As an investor, a series of winning deals can induce risky overconfidence of one's "hot hand," leading to errors in judgment and poor decision-making.

19. *The overestimation effect*: this is the tendency to overestimate the rarity of events. Suppose a "psychic" comes to a classroom of 23 students. Using his psychic abilities, the visitor "senses" that two people in the class were born on the same day. A quick survey finds that, indeed, two people share the same month and day of birth. Though many may consider this as an evidence of clairvoyance, because they may estimate that it is very unlikely that two people in a class of 23 will share a birthday, in reality, the odds are 1 in 2, or 50–50.

20. *Fallacy of fairness*: this fallacy assumes that things have to be measured based on fairness and equality; things do not always work that way in reality, e.g., a person who justifies infidelity if the person's partner has cheated.

21. *Selective observational bias*: this is the tendency to suddenly notice things that we did not notice much before, and wrongly assuming that its frequency has increased, e.g., after buying a new car, we start to see the same car virtually everywhere. A similar effect may happen to pregnant women who suddenly notice a lot of other pregnant women around them. The frequent observation of these things appears to be due to selecting those items in our mind, and in turn, noticing them more often.

22. *Neglecting probability*: this is the tendency to disregard probability when making a decision under uncertainty. Some people have difficulty coping with the concept of probability, making an absolute yes or no decision, and assigning either 100 percent or 0 percent to the likelihood of future events. This leads to a black-and-white decision-making process. Small risks are typically either neglected entirely or hugely overrated; the continuum between the extremes is ignored, e.g., being worried about getting killed in an act of terrorism as opposed to more probable causes such as traffic accidents.

23. *Post-purchase rationalization*: this is a cognitive bias whereby someone who has purchased an expensive product or service overlooks any faults or defects in order to justify their purchase. It is a special case of choice-supportive bias, e.g., when one buys a totally unnecessary, faulty, or over-priced product, and then tries to rationalize the purchase to convince oneself it was a good idea. Similarly, if a person chooses option "A" instead of option "B," they are likely to ignore or nullify the faults of option "A" while amplifying those of option "B." Conversely, they are also likely to notice and amplify the advantages of option "A" and not notice or de-emphasize those of option "B." Post-purchase rationalization is a kind of built-in mechanism that makes us feel better after making poor decisions, because it helps us to stay committed and consistent.

24. *Status quo bias*: people tend to be apprehensive of change, this often leads to making choices that guarantee that things will remain the same, or making as few changes as possible. This bias has a wide ramifications, from politics to economics, where people are more likely to stick to routines, political parties, and favorite meals at restaurants. Part of this bias is the unjustified assumption that another choice will be inferior or will make things worse.

25. *Bandwagon effect*: the tendency to conclude that something must be desirable because other people desire it. The bandwagon effect usually leads to a wide range of behavior and social norms among groups of individuals, regardless of the evidence or motives supporting them.

26. *The framing effect*: the tendency to react, to judge, to interpret or to arrive at different conclusions when reviewing the same information, depending upon how the information is presented or framed, i.e., whether the information is framed as a loss

or as a gain (Tversky & Kahneman, 1981). Prospect theory helps to develop an understanding of the frame effect. This theory proposes that a loss is more significant than the equivalent gain, a sure gain (either real or pseudo certainty) is favored over a probabilistic gain, a probabilistic loss is preferred to a definite loss, and loss aversion drives people to be risk averse when evaluating outcomes that involve similar gains and losses, e.g., the bad feelings from losing $20 are stronger than the happy feelings of finding $20, thus people tend to avoid choosing options that might result in loss. Many studies on loss aversion commonly suggest that the human perception of loss is twice as powerful as that of gain. One of the dangers of framing effects is that people are often provided with options within the context of only one of the two frames.

Fixing Cognitive Distortions

People can recognize another person's bias easily, but are blind to their own. This can cause bad consequences if not checked, because biases can distort the perception of reality, leading to faulty thinking and bad decisions. Thought patterns can be changed through a process referred to as cognitive restructuring that involves influencing one's emotions and behaviors by adjusting automatic thoughts. This is the basis of several popular forms of therapy, including cognitive-behavioral therapy (CBT) and rational emotive behavioral therapy (REBT). The core features of cognitive-behavioral therapy will be discussed later.

Clinical Notes

- Every clinician should be trained in decision-making strategies that enable him or her to deal with different clinical situations, and how to deal with complex situations in a scientific way. This helps avoid inappropriate practices and aids patients.
- Cognitive distortions are a common accompaniment to depression and anxiety disorders. Correction of these distortions is helpful in the management of these disorders, and is the core feature of cognitive behavior therapy.
- Cognitive biases may share in the development of many behavioral problems such as drinking, gambling, and reckless driving. These necessitate cognitive restructuring to correct these behaviors.

Summary

- Thinking is the cognitive activities that one uses to process information, to solve problems, to make decisions, and to create new ideas.
- The essential building blocks involved in the thinking process include language, symbols and signs, mental images, and concepts.
- There are several types of thinking or ways to think, which may overlap and are not exclusive. These include concrete thinking, abstract, analytical, critical, divergent, convergent, sequential, holistic, creative, magical, and non-directed or associative thinking.
- There are several core thinking skills including gathering, focusing, connecting, organizing, compiling, integrating, analyzing, evaluating, and generating.
- Problem-solving refers to the process of arriving at a solution to a given problem, in which one employs mental strategies directed toward attaining a goal that is not readily available.

- Common strategies used in problem-solving include trial and error, algorithms, insight, and intuition.
- Decision-making is a special case of problem-solving in which one selects an appropriate alternative from a number of available alternatives.
- Decision-making strategies include the single-feature model, compensatory models, non-compensatory models, and heuristics model.
- Important barriers to problem-solving include functional fixedness, irrelevant or misleading information, the mental set, learned helplessness, emotional barriers, intellectual barriers, perspective, culture, physical environment, and errors of thinking.
- Cognitive distortions refer to biased patterns or ways of thinking that an individual possesses about self and the world, and lead to misrepresentation or distortion of a person's perception of reality.
- Common cognitive distortions include black-and-white thinking, mental filtering, discounting the positive, overgeneralization, jumping to conclusions, catastrophizing, magnification and minimization, emotional reasoning, shoulding and musting, labeling, and personalizing.
- A cognitive bias is a systematic (non-random) error in thinking, in which an error in reasoning, evaluating, remembering, or other cognitive processes often occurs, leading to systematic deviations from a standard of rationality or good judgment.
- Common cognitive biases include the confirmation bias, illusory correlation, hindsight bias, the anchoring bias, the misinformation effect, the self-serving bias, the actor observer bias, the projection bias, the false consensus bias, the halo effect, the availability heuristic, the optimism bias, control fallacies, the belief-bias effect, the fallacy of positive instances, the negative impression bias, the negativity bias, the gambler's fallacy, the hot-hand fallacy, the overestimation effect, the fallacy of fairness, the selective observational bias, neglecting probability, post-purchase rationalization, the status quo bias, the bandwagon effect, and the framing effect.

Test Your Knowledge

- What is meant by language, symbols and signs, mental images, and concepts?
- Describe types of concepts.
- Define different types of thinking.
- What are problem-solving strategies?
- Define decision-making, and describe its main strategies.
- What are the common cognitive distortions?
- What are the common cognitive biases?

Critical Thinking Questions

- How could one promote creativity in an organization?
- How may cognitive distortions contribute to depressed mood?
- What are the types of cognitive biases a gambler has?

PART FOUR
Development, Social Factors, Personality, and Intelligence

fifteen
Human Development and Its Theories

Learning Goals

- This chapter is intended to provide the reader with an overview of controversial issues in developmental psychology, the factors affecting development and growth, the domains of development, the stages of physical development, theories of development with stress on Piaget and other cognitive development theories, the behavioral theories of child development, and moral development.

Introduction

Development refers to the dynamic process which leads to quantitative and qualitative changes taking place from conception to death. In this way, development is a broad term and deals with all the areas of life, including physical, motor, cognitive, physiological, social, emotional, and moral development. The scientific study of human development seeks to understand, describe, predict, and explain how and why people change throughout life. Studying development can help to recognize significant departures from the typical or average, and to better support the needs and rights of children. Studying development is important not only to psychology, but also to sociology, education, and health care professionals.

Genetic, environmental, and psychological factors, and diseases can affect development. This is why parents, teachers, and health care professionals should routinely assess patterns of development throughout the years. Study of human development makes it easier to spot possible signs of physical or cognitive developmental problems in early childhood, making it possible to overcome it, and help people achieve their expected developmental milestones. The earlier developmental problems are detected, the sooner interventions can begin.

Controversial Issues in Developmental Psychology

There are a number of important issues that have been debated throughout the history of developmental psychology. The major questions include the following.

Is Development More Due to Genetics or Environment Factors? (Nature vs. Nurture)

The debate over the relative contributions of inheritance and the environment is one of the oldest issues in both philosophy and psychology. Philosophers such as Plato and Descartes supported the idea that some human characteristics are inborn. On the other hand, thinkers such as John Locke argued that the mind is a blank slate at birth, with experience determining our knowledge. Today, most psychologists believe that both nature and nurture contribute to specific aspects of development, but their influences on all human characteristics are intertwined and are mutually influential.

Early Experience vs. Later Experience

The effect of early childhood events and the role that later events play are controversial. Psychoanalytic theorists tend to focus upon events that occur in early childhood. According to Freud, much of a child's personality is completely established by the age of 5. If this is the case, those who have experienced deprived or abusive childhoods might never adjust or develop normally. In contrast to this view, researchers have found that the influence of childhood events does not necessarily have a dominating effect over behavior throughout the life. Many people who had experienced problems during childhood go on to develop normally into well-adjusted adults.

Continuity vs. Discontinuity

Whether developmental changes occur smoothly over time, or through a series of predetermined steps is debated. Some theories of development argue that changes are simply a matter of quantity, children display more of certain skills as they grow older. Other theories outline a series of sequential stages in which skills emerge at certain points of development. Psychoanalytic theories proposed that development occurs through a series of psychosexual stages, and Erik Erikson proposed a stage theory of psychosocial development. Learning theories proposed that behavior is a continuous dynamic process that is shaped by the interaction between the individual and the environment.

Abnormal Behavior vs. Individual Differences

Developmental milestones offer guidelines for the ages at which certain skills and abilities typically emerge, but concerns usually arise when a child falls slightly behind the norm. While developmental theories have historically focused upon deficits in behavior, focus on individual differences in development is becoming an important component of different psychological theories. Psychoanalytic theories are traditionally focused upon abnormal behavior, so developmental differences in these theories are described as a deficit in behavior. Learning theories rely more on the environment's unique impact on an individual. Today, psychologists look at both norms and individual differences when describing child development.

Factors Affecting Development and Growth

Development and growth are influenced by several factors including genetic and environmental factors. The following is a summary of possible factors that can affect development.

Genetic Factors

A child is born with a unique set of genetic endowments that influence his or her physical growth. Genetics have a strong effect on rate of growth, the size of body parts, and the onset of growth events. Genes are a biological risk factor that cannot be changed. However, early interventions can improve the outcome of these risk factors on a child's physical and cognitive growth and development. This is especially crucial when dealing with genetic conditions that are preventable, e.g., phenylketonuria (PKU), which is a recessive genetic disorder that leads to the inability to metabolize the amino acid phenylalanine, which accumulates to toxic levels, impairing brain development and leaving children mentally retarded, restless, and irritable. Although PKU is a hereditary condition, an early strict low-phenylalanine diet can prevent brain damage (Waisbren, Brown, de Sonneville, & Levy, 1994). A more detailed account of genetics was presented on pp. 106–109.

Environmental Influences

The effect of environmental factors on development starts at conception. Malnutrition and intake of medications, tobacco, alcohol, recreational drugs or other chemical agents during pregnancy can affect the growth of a fetus either directly or indirectly. These substances can cause birth defects, and can also affect a child's cognitive growth in the later developmental stages. The effect of these risk factors on a child's learning and behavior may not become obvious for years. After birth, malnutrition, poor housing, pollution and lack of appropriate toys and activities may have detrimental effects on human growth.

Medical Diseases

Serious and chronic illnesses often put a child at an increased risk of developing additional health problems along with emotional and behavioral problems. Physical disabilities can also lead to social isolation, which may have a significant impact on a child's educational outcome and in turn affect an individual's ability to secure long-term employment in adulthood. The child's ability to communicate and interact socially with peers can be further impeded by the physical and cognitive limitations caused by a medical illness. This may eventually lead to the child becoming socially stigmatized, resulting in further negative effects on the individual's physical health.

Social Influences

Social relationships play a vital role in a child's cognitive development. Play is one of the first social interactions that contribute to a child's ability to learn. Later, as a child becomes involved in different social activities with other children, he or she learns how to solve problems. Cultural influences also affect a child's cognitive development, with one of the most persistent cultural influences being the school system. Much of what children learn is the particular ways their culture views reality, the roles of different people and different sexes, and the rules and norms that govern social relationships in their particular culture. In these areas there are no universally valid facts or correct views of reality.

Psychological Factors

The quality of caregiving, especially maternal, is a strong indicator of a child's cognitive abilities and social competence. Families provide a nurturing environment in which security, protection, satisfaction, and love are given. Physical needs for food and clothing are met. In this environment, family members grow to maturity. Parenting style is another factor that affects a child's cognitive development. A parent's values and beliefs influence how a child understands what goes on around him. Some parenting styles may be unresponsive to a child's needs; others encourage academic achievement, self-confidence, independence, and maturity. However, finding actual cause-and-effect links between specific actions of parents and later behavior of children is very difficult. Some children raised in dramatically different environments can later grow up to have remarkably similar personalities. Conversely, children who share the same home and are raised in the same environment can grow up to have astonishingly different personalities to one another.

Despite these challenges, researchers have uncovered convincing links between parenting styles and the effects these styles have on children. However, there is no universally "best" style of parenting. It is probably the fit between the particular style and the particular child that affects the child. Parenting styles must be evaluated in terms of their cultural context. Researchers have identified four basic parenting styles:

PHOTO 15.1.   Parenting Styles.

1. *Authoritarian parents* are strict, punishing, and unsympathetic. They value obedience from their children, do not encourage independence, and seldom praise their children. Children raised in this way tend to be unfriendly, distrustful, and withdrawn.
2. *Permissive parents* give their children complete freedom with little discipline. Children raised in this way tend to be immature, dependent, and unhappy.
3. *Authoritative parents* reason with their children, and them give greater responsibilities with age. They set firm limits but also remain understanding and encourage independence. Their demands are reasonable, rational, and consistent. Children raised in this way tend to be friendly, cooperative, self-reliant, and socially responsible. They are also more successful in school and better tolerate the divorce of their parents, if it should occur.
4. *Uninvolved parents* invest as little time, money, and effort in their children as possible, focusing on their own needs before their children's.

Domains of Development

The study of development is often divided into the domains of physical, cognitive, and social-emotional development. Dividing development into these areas makes it easier to study. However, all the areas of development are linked to one another; achievements in one area can strongly influence another area, e.g., writing requires both fine motor skills and cognitive development. Thus, it is not surprising that typically developing 1-year-old children learn to walk and use their first words at approximately the same time. Similarly, the effects of delay in one area can be profound on other areas, e.g., a child with cerebral palsy does not start walking until approximately the second birthday.

Physical Development

Physical development refers to physical body changes across time. This occurs in a relatively stable, predictable sequence. It is orderly, not random. Changes in bone thickness, vision, hearing, and muscle are all included. Changes in size and weight are also part of physical development. Physical skills, such as crawling, walking, and writing result from physical development. These skills fall into gross and fine motor development. Gross motor development involves improvement of skills using the large muscles in the legs and arms. Activities such as running, skipping, and bike riding fall into this category. Fine motor development involves the small muscles of the hands and fingers. Grasping, holding, cutting, and drawing are examples of activities that require fine motor development.

Physical development tends to proceed from the head downward (cephalocaudal principle). Accordingly, the child first gains control of the head, then the arms, then the legs. Development also proceeds from the center of the body outward according to the proximodistal principle. Accordingly, the spinal cord develops before other parts of the body. The child's arms develop before the hands, and the hands and feet develop before the fingers and toes. Fingers and toes are the last to develop.

Stages of Physical Development

Human beings usually physically grow and mature at about the same periods during their life span. Most psychologists identify the following stages of development: the prenatal period, infancy and toddlerhood, childhood, adolescence, and adulthood.

1. *Prenatal period*: this begins at conception and lasts till birth. In this period, the single-celled organism changes into a human baby within the uterus.

2. *Infancy and toddlerhood*: this begins at birth and lasts to about 24 months. Infancy represents the first year of life, while toddlerhood represents the second year of life. The first four weeks of life are called the neonatal period. The baby develops rapid changes in the body and brain that lead to the emergence of several sensory, motor, social and cognitive capacities.

3. *Childhood*: this begins at the end of infancy and lasts until somewhere between ages 11 and 14. This period may be subdivided into early (2–6 years) and middle childhood (7–11 years). Early childhood period include the preschool years where the child learns through play: motor skills are refined, language develops, and ties are formed with peers. Middle childhood period include the school years when the child acquires literacy skills, thought processes are refined, friendships emerge, and self-concept is formed. Adolescence is sometimes called late childhood.

4. *Adolescence*: this begins at the end of childhood and lasts until somewhere between 18 and 21 years. This period is marked by puberty which signals the onset of rapid physical and hormonal changes, the emergence of abstract thinking, sexual maturity, stronger peer ties, a sense of self, and autonomy from parental control.

5. *Adulthood*: this begins at the end of adolescence and lasts until death. It is further subdivided into *early adulthood* in which the adolescent leaves home for the sake of education, or to find a career, and to form intimate relationships leading to marriage and having children. *Middle adulthood* (40–60 years) is the period in which the person is at the peak of his or her career, helps his or her children to begin independent lives and to look after their own parents who are aging. *Late adulthood* (60 years till death): this period is marked by retirement from work, decrease in stamina and physical health, bonding with grandchildren, and dealing with impending old age and death of self and spouse.

Characteristics of the Prenatal Period

Prenatal development involves changes that occur during pregnancy, starting from the time of fertilization of an ovum to time of birth. Pregnancy is divided into three equal periods called "trimesters" that constitute the nine-month period from conception to birth. However, prenatal development is commonly divided into the germinal period, the embryonic period, and the fetal period.

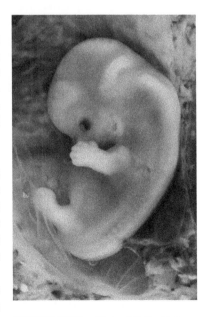

1. The germinal period (the zygotic period) lasts about two weeks. The fertilized ovum (zygote) that is formed by union of an ovum and a sperm (each has to have only one set of 23 chromosomes, called the gamete) undergoes rapid cell division to form a blastocyst, that implants itself in the wall of the mother's uterus.

2. The embryonic period extends from week three to week eight. The embryo undergoes rapid growth and extensive cell differentiation, where body parts,

PHOTO 15.2.   Prenatal Period.

e.g., eyes, arms, and the organs and major systems of the body form, e.g., the respiratory system, the skeletal system, the circulatory system, the nervous system; the tiny heart starts beating, and brain development begins and continues through the fetal period. The developing brain cells multiply, differentiate, and migrate to their final destination (neuronal migration), where they develop further connections with other neurons (Balbernie, 2001, Bystron, Blakemore, & Rakic, 2008). They join with other developing neurons and begin forming the structures of the developing nervous system. Also, the initial development of the sex organs is triggered by genes on the sex chromosomes and hormonal influences.

The embryo forms a protective sac (the amniotic sac) in which the embryo floats, and the umbilical cord through which nourishment, oxygen, and water flow to the embryo, and it carries away carbon dioxide and other wastes. The placenta is a vascular organ, disk-shaped, that prevents the mother's blood from directly mixing with that of the developing embryo. It acts as a filter that prevents many, but not all harmful substances that might be present in the mother's blood from reaching the embryo. Harmful substances that can cause birth defects or abnormal development are called teratogens. The vulnerability to teratogens is greatest during the embryonic stage, when the major body systems are forming. Known teratogens include exposure to radiation or toxic substances (e.g., mercury and lead), infection by viruses and bacteria (e.g., German measles, genital herpes, and human immunodeficiency virus), use of addictive drugs (e.g., heroin and cocaine), and some prescription drugs. Alcohol drinking during pregnancy can cause several disorders that are collectively referred to as fetal alcohol spectrum disorders (FASD), which include mental retardation, heart problems, and a number of distinctive facial features (Sokol et al., 2003). It is interesting to know that the mother's psychological state can affect the fetus. Chronic stress, depression, and anxiety are associated with low birth weight and premature birth (Dunkel Schetter, 2011), while poor maternal nutrition, lack of sleep, and other unhealthy behaviors can affect the fetal growth and development.

3. The fetal period begins at eight weeks after conception and ends with the birth of the baby. The main task during this period is to grow the body systems to reach maturity in preparation for life outside the mother's body. By the end of 12 weeks, the fetus can move its arms, legs, mouth, and head. The fetus becomes capable of reflexive responses, such as fanning its toes if the sole of the foot is stroked and squinting if its eyelids are touched. The fetal brain is constantly changing, forming as many as 2 million synaptic connections per second.

At 16 weeks, teeth buds have formed and fingernails are forming. By 18–20 weeks, an ultrasound scan should be able to identify the sex if the baby is in a position that allows the genitals to be seen. At 20 weeks, bone is forming from cartilage. Hair and eyelashes are also present. The mother can feel the baby moving. At six months, the fetus's brain activity becomes similar to that of a newborn baby, and the baby's skin is covered by a protective paste called vernix. In the eighth and ninth months, the baby stores fat and approximately doubles in weight. This additional body fat will help the newborn adjust to changing temperatures outside the womb. It also contributes to the newborn's chubby appearance. As birth approaches, growth slows and the fetus's body systems become more active.

Characteristics of Infancy and Childhood Development

Infants are born with a set of reflexes that enable them to survive. These include:

- *Rooting*: newborns turn their head and open their mouths toward a stimulus that strokes the cheek, chin, or corner of mouth. This reflex facilitates finding the mother's nipple for sucking.
- *Sucking*: babies suck nearly anything that touches the lips. Later on, this is replaced by voluntary sucking.
- *Moro or startle reflex*: this is produced by suddenly changes of baby's position and when startled or neck support is lost. Infants arch their backs and legs and arms are flung out and then brought back toward chest into a hugging motion. It usually disappears at 6–7 months of birth.
- *Grasping reflex*: infants grip whatever is placed in their palms using four fingers. This usually disappears at 3 or 4 months, and is replaced by voluntary grasping at 5–6 months.
- *Stepping reflex*: when held up under the arms, the baby's feet can make a stepping motion. This usually disappears by 3 or 4 months.
- *Tonic-neck reflex*: while lying on the back, the baby turns the head to one side and extends the arm and leg on that side, while flexing limbs on the opposite side.
- *Babinski reflex*: When the side of foot is stroked, from heel to toes, toes fan (spread) and the foot twists. This usually disappears at the end of the first year.

At birth, the brain is about 25 percent of its adult weight. After birth, the neurons grow in size and continue to develop new dendrites and interconnections with other neurons. Myelin forms on axons in key areas of the brain, such as those involved in motor control (Jakovcevski, Filipovic, Mo, Rakic, & Zecevic, 2009). Axons also grow longer, and the branching becomes more dense at the ends of the axons, a process that continues throughout the lifespan. During infancy, the brain will grow to about 75 percent of its adult weight. By the end of the second year, the brain reaches about 80 percent of its adult weight. By puberty, the brain reaches its adult weight.

Brain development enables motor development and physical coordination. The sequence of motor development is mostly universal; babies roll over before they sit unsupported, and they usually crawl before they walk. Though there are substantial individual differences, children can hold their heads up at about 6 weeks, roll over at 3 months, sit at 6 months, stand at 11 months, and walk at 12 months. The typical ages to reach these milestones are referred to as developmental norms. In the United States, 25 percent of all babies walk by 11 months of age, 50 percent within a week after their first birthday, and 90 percent by age 15 months (Frankenburg, Dodds, Archer, Shapiro, & Bresnick 1992).

Newborns are responsive to touch, temperature changes, and pain. They have generally good hearing

PHOTO 15.3.   Motor Development.

and smell. Newborns are less sensitive to soft sounds than an adult, but turn in the direction of sounds and can discriminate sounds according to their loudness, direction, and frequency. Newborns turn away from unpleasant sounds and can identify a variety of odors, such as the odor of the mother's breast. Newborns can distinguish between sweet, salty, and bitter tastes, and favor sweet tastes. At birth, vision is the least developed sense. Though babies are sensitive to brightness, can discriminate some colors, and track moving targets; they show little or no visual accommodation with the optimal viewing distance, which is about 15–30 cm. Convergence does not occur until 7 or 8 weeks. Visual acuity improves during infancy to reach adult levels at the end of the preschool years.

Dramatic changes occur in weight and height during infancy and childhood. A typical infant usually doubles their birthweight by six months and triples it by the first birthday. Infants are about 45–60 cm long at birth, but they reach about approximately half their adult height by their second birthday (Levine & Munsch, 2018). The baby's head will grow at its fastest rate during the first four months after birth than at any other time. This increase is due to rapid brain growth. The average head circumference at birth is about 34.5 cm. By the end of the first month, it increases to about 37.5 cm. However, the head size decreases in proportion to the entire body from 1/3 at birth, to ¼ at age 2, to 1/8 by adulthood.

Language development is probably the most noticeable accomplishment in infancy and childhood. At birth, infants can distinguish among the speech sounds of all the world's languages (Kuhl, 2004; Werker & Desjardins, 1995). This ability is lost by 10–12 months of age, where infants can distinguish only among speech sounds that are present in the language to which they have been exposed (Kuhl, Williams, Lacerda, Stevens, & Lindblom, 1992; Yoshida, Pons, Maye, & Werker, 2010). Thus, infants begin to master the sound structure of their own native language during the first year of their life. By 2–3 months, infants can make vowel-like noises called cooing, repeating vowel sounds such as *ahhhhh* or *ooooo*, varying the pitch up or down. At about 5 months of age, infants begin to *babble*. They combine consonants to the vowels and string the sounds together in sometimes long-winded productions of babbling, such as *ba-ba-ba-ba*, *de-de-de-de*, or *ma-ma-ma-ma*. Babbling is not simply imitation of adult speech. Infants all over the world use the *same* sounds when they babble, including sounds that do not occur in the language of their parents and other caregivers. At around 9 months of age, babies begin to babble more in the sounds specific to their language. Babbling, then, seems to be a biologically programmed stage of language development (Gentilucci & Dalla Volta, 2007; Petitto, Holowka, Sergio, Levy, & Ostry, 2004).

Before they are a year old, most infants can understand simple commands, such as "Bring Mom the key," even though they cannot *say* the words *bring*, *Mom*, or *key*. Generally, infants acquire comprehension of words more than twice as fast as they learn to speak new words. Somewhere around their first birthday, infants produce their first real words. First words usually refer to concrete objects or people that are important to the child, such as *mama*, *daddy*, or *ba-ba* (bottle). First words are also often made up of the syllables that were used in babbling. During the *one-word stage*, babies use a single word and vocal intonation to stand for an entire sentence. With the proper intonation and context, *baba* can mean "I want my bottle" or "where is my bottle?"

Around their second birthday, toddlers begin putting words together. During the *two-word stage*, they combine two words to construct a simple sentence, such as "Mama go," "Where kitty?," and "No potty." During this stage, the words used are primarily content words: nouns, verbs, and sometimes adjectives or adverbs. Articles (*a*, *an*, *the*) and prepositions (such as *in*, *under*, *on*) are omitted. Two-word sentences reflect the first understandings of grammar. Although these utterances include only the most essential words, they basically follow a grammatically correct sequence.

At around 2.5 years of age, children move beyond the two-word stage. They rapidly increase the length and grammatical complexity of their sentences. There is a dramatic increase in the number of words they can comprehend and produce. By the time a child reaches 3 years of age, he or she will have learned thousands of words and the complex rules of language. By the age of 3, the typical child has a production vocabulary of more than 3,000 words. Acquiring about a dozen new words per day, a child may have a production vocabulary of more than 10,000 words by school age (Bjorklund, 1995).

Characteristics of Adolescence

Adolescence is the transitional stage between childhood and the beginning of adulthood, which is marked by physical, social, and cognitive changes. Although it can vary by individual, culture, and gender, it usually begins around age 11 or 12. Adolescence starts with the physical signs of sexual maturity (puberty) and ends with the social achievement of independence and adult responsibilities. Puberty follows a surge of hormones which trigger a series of bodily changes outlined in Chapter 7 on gender and sexuality.

The body changes in adolescents are accompanied by changes in their social interactions, most notably with parents and peers. Contrary to what many people think, parent–adolescent relationships are generally positive. Most teenagers report that they admire their parents and turn to them for advice (Steinberg, 1990, 2001). As a general rule, when parent–child relationships have been good before adolescence, they continue to be relatively smooth during adolescence. Adolescents who perceive their relationships with their parents as being warm and supportive have higher self-esteem and are most likely to follow their parents' guidance (McElhaney, Porter, Thompson, & Allen, 2008). However, some friction seems to be inevitable as children make the transition to adolescence.

Although parents have an influential role throughout adolescence, relationships with friends and peers become increasingly important (Albert. Chein, & Steinberg, 2013; Somerville, 2013). Adolescents usually encounter greater diversity among their peers as they make the transitions to middle school and high school, a matter that influences their values, norms, and expectations. Susceptibility to peer influence peaks during early adolescence (Dishion & Tipsord, 2011). Though parents frequently worry that negative peer influence may lead to undesirable behavior, researchers found that peer relationships tend to reinforce the traits and goals that parents fostered during childhood (Steinberg, 2001), and adolescents tend to form friendships with peers who are similar in age, social class, race, beliefs, and educational goals. As they grow older, adolescents develop resilience against peer influences and increasingly rely on parents' influences regarding appropriate behaviors (E.C. Cook Buehler, & Henson, 2009; Sumter, Bokhorst, Steinberg, & Westenberg, 2009). On the other hand, peers can influence one another in positive ways. Friends often exert pressure on one another to study, make good grades, attend college, and engage in prosocial behaviors. This positive influence is especially true for peers who are strong students (Allen, McHugh, & Barlow, 2008; T.D. Cook, Deng, & Morgano, 2007).

Romantic and sexual relationships become increasingly important throughout the adolescent years. One national survey in the USA showed that by the age of 12, about one-quarter of adolescents reported having had a "special romantic relationship," although not necessarily a relationship that included sexual intimacy. By age 15, that percentage increased to 50 percent, and reached 70 percent by the age of 18 (Connolly & McIsaac, 2009). Social and cultural factors influence when, why, and how adolescents engage in romantic and sexual behaviors, e.g., the beginning of dating coincides with cultural and social expectations and norms, such as when friends begin to date, more than with an adolescent's degree of physical maturation (Collins, 2003).

Characteristics of Adulthood

On one's 18th birthday, one becomes an adult according to the law. However, there is no clear-cut mark that defines the transition from adolescence to adulthood. In some cultures there are some rituals that mark the transition from adolescence to adulthood, but in most countries it is not so clear what defines adulthood. A lot of occasions may be supposed as the start of adult-hood: graduation from high school, starting a real job, marriage. Arnett (e.g., Arnett, 2007) sug-gests that the late teens to mid-twenties should be viewed as a period of emerging adulthood, where people are negotiating the transition to adulthood. According to Arnett (2011), emerging adulthood exists only in cultures in which adult responsibilities and roles are postponed until the twenties. This pattern occurs most typically in industrialized or post-industrialized coun-tries. Even in industrialized countries, emerging adulthood may not characterize the develop-mental trajectory of all young adults, e.g., members of minority groups, immigrants, and young adults who enter directly into the workforce rather than seeking college or university education are less likely to experience emerging adulthood as a distinct period of exploration and change.

Genetic heritage greatly influences the unfolding of certain physical changes during adult-hood, such as when hair starts graying. However, lifestyle choices that people make in adult-hood influence the aging process, e.g., staying physically and mentally active, avoiding tobacco products and other harmful substances, and eating a healthy diet can both slow and minimize the physical decline that is typically associated with aging.

Physical strength typically peaks in early adulthood (the twenties and thirties). Young adults are stronger than older adults, including hand strength (Ranganathan, Siemionow, Sahgal, & Yue, 2001) and finger strength (Oliveira, Hsu, Park, Clark, & Shim, 2008). Young adults also have faster reaction time (Fozard, Vercruyssen, Reynolds, & Hancock, 1994) and better vision (Kline, Kline, Fozard, & Kosnik, 1992). Young adults rarely have life-threatening diseases such as coronary heart disease, rather, accidents, such as automobile accidents, are the most common cause of death (Park, Mulye, Adams, Brindis, & Irwin, 2006).

By middle adulthood, most people begin to see a physical decline. Perhaps the most obvious declines are those related to appearance. One begins to gain weight around the middle, hair begins to turn gray or fall out, and wrinkles appear. People also begin to show declines in sensory acuity, and physical and mental reaction times also begin to slow during middle adult-hood. During late adulthood, from the mid-sixties on, physical stamina and reaction time tend to decline further and faster.

Significant reproductive and hormonal changes occur during middle adulthood. In women, the cessation of menstruation (the *menopause*) signals the end of reproductive capacity and occurs any time from the late thirties to the early fifties. Women have differing reactions to menopause; some women focus on unpleasant symptoms of menopause, e.g., *hot flushes* or *flashes*, which are a feeling of warmth, sometimes associated with flushing that spreads over the body and sometimes is followed by perspiration (Umland, 2008), night sweats, and disturbances in sex drive, sleep, eating, weight, and motivation. Emotional symptoms may include depres-sion, sadness, and emotional instability (Freeman, 2010). However, many women experience what is called "postmenopausal zest." Many women feel a renewed sense of energy, freedom, and happiness due to feeling freed of menstruation, childbearing, and worries about becoming pregnant. Postmenopausal women often develop a new sense of identity, become more asser-tive, and pursue new aspirations (Fahs, 2007). In many cultures, postmenopausal women are valued for their experience and wisdom (Robinson, 2002).

Middle-aged men experience changes that accompany a decline in testosterone, such as reduced sperm production, but these changes are less noticeable than those experienced by

women. Decreased levels of testosterone may cause loss of lean muscle,
increased body fat, weakened bones,
reduced sexual motivation and function, and cognitive decline (Harman,
2005). Emotional problems such as
depression and irritability may also
occur.

During late adulthood, there are
continued changes in appearance
(e.g., gray hair, wrinkles). There is
also a continued decline in sensory
ability, e.g., older people typically
experience a decline in the ability to
adjust to dim light (dark adaptation)

PHOTO 15.4.   Elderly Couple.

(Jackson, Owsley, & McGwin, 1999; Jackson, Felix, & Owsley, 2006). Other eye diseases, such as
cataracts and glaucoma, are also more common among elderly people (Klein, 1991). Aging is
also associated with a decline in hearing, especially at higher frequencies, referred to as presby-
cusis (Raynor et al., 2009).

Although older people experience many physical and sensory changes, *most* of them live
healthy, active, and self-sufficient lives (National Institute on Aging, 2007).

Even adults 85 years and older report good health and functioning, and well-being despite
increasing prevalence of disease and impairment (Collerton et al., 2009; Charles & Carstensen,
2010).

Salthouse (2009) suggests that physiological functioning of the brain begins to slow with age.
Neurons appear to become less efficient at communicating with one another, and this seems to
result in slowed and sometimes inhibited cognitive performance (Bucur et al., 2008). However,
Schaie K. Warner (1995, 2005) and his colleagues have shown that mental abilities remain relatively stable until about the age of 60. After age 60, slight declines begin to appear on tests of
general intellectual abilities, such as logical reasoning, math skills, word recall, and the ability to
mentally manipulate images (Alwin, 2009; Siegler et al., 2009). But even after age 60, most older
adults maintain their previous levels of ability. A longitudinal study of adults in their seventies,
eighties, and nineties found that there were slight but significant declines in memory, perceptual
speed, and fluency. However, measures of knowledge, such as vocabulary, remained stable up to
age 90 (Singer, Felix, & Owsley, 2003; Zelinski & Kennison, 2007).

Cognitive Development

This refers to the development of cognitive and intellectual processes including attention,
perception, memory, language, acquiring, organizing, and using knowledge, reasoning, problem-
solving, imagination, and creativity. With time, these attributes change from being simple to more
complex and integrated ones. Many theories have been proposed to explained cognitive
development. The best-known of them is Jean Piaget's theory of cognitive development.

Piaget's Cognitive Development Theory

Cognitive theory focuses on the structure and development of the individual's thought processes
and their effect on one's understanding of the world. Piaget did not view children's intellectual

development as a quantitative process in which children just add more information and knowledge to their existing knowledge as they get older, but he suggested that there is a qualitative change in how children think as they gradually process through four stages of cognitive development. Thus, a child at age 7 not only has more information about the world than he or she did at age 2, but there is a fundamental change in how he or she thinks about the world.

Piaget viewed cognitive development as a process that follows a universal sequence of age-related periods: sensorimotor, preoperational, concrete operational, and formal operational. He suggested that adaptation and organization are the two major processes that guide intellectual growth and biological development. Individuals should adjust to the environment through a process called adaptation that results from both assimilation and accommodation (discussed later). Organization refers to how experiences are sorted and related to each other. Piaget suggested that the mind is organized in a logical, complex, and integrated way. The following is a brief discussion of the key concepts of Piaget's theory:

PHOTO 15.5.   Jean Piaget.

- *Schemas*: these are categories of knowledge that help us to interpret and understand the world. A schema describes both the mental and physical actions involved in understanding and knowing. In Piaget's view, a schema includes both a category of knowledge and the process of obtaining that knowledge. As experiences happen, this new information is used to modify, add to, or change previously existing schemas, e.g., a child may have a schema about a type of animal, such as a dog. If the child's experience is limited to small dogs, a child may believe that all dogs are small, furry, and have four legs. When this child encounters a large dog, the child will take in this new information, and modifies the previously existing schema to include this new information.
- *Assimilation*: the process of taking in new information into existing schemas is known as assimilation. The process is somewhat subjective, because we tend to modify experience or information to conform with our pre-existing beliefs. In the example above, seeing a dog and labeling it "dog" is an example of assimilating the animal into the child's dog schema.
- *Accommodation*: this is another part of adaptation that occurs in the light of new information and the constantly changing aspects of the external environment. When a child faces a new stimulus (such as a cat) that does not fit into existing cognitive schema of dogs, the child may initially try to incorporate this new animal into his or her cognitive schema for dogs. As cats are a different type of animal and cannot be integrated into the dog schema, a new schema is created.
- *Equilibration*: As cognitive development progresses, it is important to maintain a balance between applying previous knowledge (assimilation) and changing schemas to account for new knowledge (accommodation). With continued adaptations of cognition, the child maintains equilibrium with the environment. Piaget called the balance process between assimilation and accommodation, "equilibration." Equilibration helps in integrating new information, and explains how children are able to move from one stage to the next one of cognitive development.

Piaget viewed cognitive development as a process of restructuring knowledge through interaction with the environment. It begins with sensorimotor activity and progressively transforms into complex, abstract thought (Piaget, 1954). Piaget suggested children of similar ages responded in noticeably similar ways and yet were noticeably different from adult responses. He suggested the following stages of cognitive development:

1. the sensorimotor stage
2. the preoperational stage
3. the concrete operations stage
4. the formal operational stage.

The Sensorimotor Stage

This stage extends from birth to approximately age 2 and is centered on the infant trying to make sense of the world. During this stage, infants and toddlers acquire knowledge through sensory experiences and motor activity without the use of symbols, thus, an infant's knowledge of the world is limited to his or her sensory perceptions and motor activities. Behaviors are limited to simple motor responses caused by sensory stimuli. Children use the skills and abilities they were born with (such as looking, sucking, grasping, and listening) to learn more about the environment.

The development of *object permanence*, at about 7 months of age, is one of the most important accomplishments at the sensorimotor stage of development. It requires the ability to form a mental representation (i.e., a schema) of the object. Object permanence is the child's understanding that objects continue to exist even though they cannot be seen or heard, in a game like peek-a-boo, a very young infant will believe that the other person or object has actually vanished and will act shocked or startled when the person reappears. Some symbolic abilities (language) are developed at the end of this stage. The sensorimotor stage can be divided into six separate substages that are characterized by the development of a new skill.

1. *Simple reflexes (0–1 month)*: this corresponds to the first month after birth. The neonate responds to external stimulation with innate reflex actions. Neonates show the aforementioned reflexes at birth. These reflexes eventually disappear as the infant's brain develops over the first 6–12 months of life.

PHOTO 15.6.   Object Permanence.

2. *Primary circular reactions*: this stage develops between 1–4 months of age. A primary circular reaction refers to the infant's attempt to reproduce chance pleasurable actions, centered on the body, e.g., when a child accidentally sucks his or her thumb and enjoy the sensation; later on, the child repeats bringing thumb to mouth and sucks it.

3. *Secondary circular reactions*: this stage develops between 4–8 months of age. The child becomes more focused on the world, notices the effect of his or her behavior on external objects, and begins to repeat chance pleasurable actions in the environment in order to trigger a response, e.g., a child will shake a rattle to hear its pleasurable sound, and pick up a toy in order to put it in the mouth.

4. *Coordination of secondary circular reactions*: this stage develops between 8–12 months of age. Actions are even more outwardly directed. The child can combine previously learned schemes or secondary circular reactions together in a coordinated way to solve new problems, e.g., uncover, and then grasp. The child will not just shake the rattle, but will reach out and remove an object that stands in the way of holding of the rattle.

5. *Tertiary circular reactions*: this stage develops between 12–18 months of age. Children begin a period of trial-and-error experimentation. They deliberately try an action pattern, to purposely discover the consequences, and to explore new possibilities, e.g., dropping ball from different heights, or the child may knock over a container to get something inside. Piaget called these purposive exploration or experimentation to bring desirable consequences "tertiary circular reactions." This leads to a better understanding of object permanence.

6. *Internalization of schemes (early symbolic representation)*: this stage develops between 18–24 months. The infant's mental functioning shifts from a purely sensorimotor paradigm to a symbolic one. The infant develops the ability to use primitive symbols (internalized sensory images or words that represent events) and talk about events and things that are not present using words, e.g., a child can request cookies when none are in sight. Primitive symbols permit infants to think about concrete events without directly acting out or perceiving them.

The Preoperational Stage

The preoperational stage occurs roughly between the ages of 2 and 7 years. Language development is one of the hallmarks of this period. During the preoperational stage, children also become increasingly skillful at using symbols, as evidenced by the increase in playing and pretending, e.g., a child is able to use an object to represent something else, such as pretending a broom is a horse. Role playing also becomes important during the preoperational stage. Children often play the roles of "mommy," "daddy," "doctor," and many other characters.

In this stage of development, Piaget focused more on what children could not yet do than what they can do. Piaget noted that children in this stage do not yet understand concrete logic, cannot mentally manipulate information, cannot understand conservation, and are unable to take the point of view of other people, which he termed egocentrism.

Egocentrism: Piaget demonstrated egocentrism through using a three-dimensional display of a mountain scene (the Three Mountain Task). Children are asked to choose a picture that showed the scene they had observed. Most children are able to do this with little difficulty. Next, children are asked to select a picture showing what someone else would have observed when looking at the mountain from a different viewpoint. Invariably, children almost always choose the scene showing their own view of the mountain scene. According to Piaget, children experience this difficulty because they are unable to take on another person's perspective.

However, recent theory of mind research has found that children aged 4 and 5 years old have a sophisticated understanding of their own mental processes as well as those of other people, e.g., children of this age have some ability to take the perspective of another person, meaning they are far less egocentric than Piaget believed.

PHOTO 15.7.   Conservation.

Conservation: this refers to the ability of children to realize that the properties of objects, such as mass, volume, and amount, remain the same, in spite of a change in the form of objects. To demonstrate a child's understanding of conservation, Piaget poured equal amounts of liquid into two identical containers. The liquid in one container is then poured into a different shaped cup, such as a tall and thin cup or a short and wide cup. Children are then asked which cup holds the most liquid. Despite seeing that the liquid amounts were equal, children always choose the cup that appears fuller. Piaget conducted a number of similar experiments on conservation of number, length, mass, weight, volume, and quantity. He found that few children showed any understanding of conservation prior to the age of 5. However, some researchers argued that the reason that children failed at tasks was simply because they did not understand it.

Concrete Operations

This stage begins around age of 7 years and continues until approximately the age of 11 years. The concrete operational period marks the beginning of logical or operational thought. Children begin thinking logically about concrete events, but have difficulty understanding abstract or hypothetical concepts, that is, the child can understand concepts, such as time, space, and quantity. Compared with preoperational children who can focus on only one dimension of a problem at a time, concrete-operational children can focus on multiple aspects of a problem at once (decentration), a point that has its implications on understanding conservation and other intellectual accomplishments.

The egocentrism of the previous stage begins to disappear as children can think better about how other people might view a situation. The child turns into being *sociocentric* (as opposed to egocentric), being aware that others have their own perspectives on the world, and that those perspectives are different from the child's own. However, the concrete operational child may not be aware of the content of others' perspectives (this awareness comes during the next stage of cognitive development).

One of the most important developments in this stage is an understanding of different types of conservation: number, length, liquid, mass, weight, area, and volume. In addition, children become aware that actions can be reversed, i.e., the child can reverse the order of relationships between mental categories, e.g., a child might be able to recognize that his or her dog is a chihuahua, that a chihuahua is a dog, and that a dog is an animal.

While thinking becomes much more logical at this stage of development, it tends to be rigid and children struggle with abstract and hypothetical concepts. Piaget suggested that children in the concrete operational stage were fairly good at the use of inductive logic (going from a specific experience to a general principle), but have difficulty using deductive logic, which involves using a general principle to get a logically probable conclusion. Deductive logic requires the ability to use a set of observations or propositions (premises) to reach a logically certain conclusion. This type of thinking involves hypothetical situations that are usually required in science and mathematics.

The Formal Operational Stage

The formal operational stage begins at approximately age 12 and lasts into adulthood. The ability to think about abstract ideas and situations is the key hallmark of this stage. Actual (concrete) objects are no longer required and mental operations can be undertaken in the head using abstract terms. During this stage, children develop an increase in logic, the ability to use deductive reasoning, and systematic planning for the future and reason about hypothetical situations.

Piaget believed that deductive logic becomes important during the formal operational stage. An operational thinker also has the ability to consider multiple potential solutions to problems and think more scientifically about the world around them before acting. This greatly increases the individual's efficiency, because the individual can avoid potentially unsuccessful attempts at solving a problem. The formal operational person considers past experiences, present demands, and future consequences while attempting to maximize the success of his or her adaptation to the world.

Evaluation of Piaget's Theory

Piaget's theory is much appreciated among psychologists, and has generated a great deal of interest in education and developmental psychology. While he did not specifically apply his theory in education, many educational programs are built upon the belief that children should be taught at the level to which they are developmentally prepared. In addition, a number of instructional strategies have been derived from Piaget's work. These strategies include providing a supportive environment, using social interactions and peer teaching, and helping children see fallacies and inconsistencies in their thinking.

Although it is presented in a series of progressive stages, even Piaget believed that development does not always follow such a smooth and predictable path. Developmental psychologists believe that cognitive abilities develop at different ages in different areas, and in small rather than in large all-or-none steps or stages.

Most researchers agree that children possess many of the abilities at an earlier age than Piaget suspected. People displaying features of more than one stage led some researchers to suppose that, in addition to their general level of development, children's reasoning depends on the ease of the task, familiarity with the objects involved, understanding of the language being used, and previous experiences they had in similar situations.

Although heredity is an important factor, experience (the environment) also plays a role in cognitive development, leading to individual differences. Research has disputed Piaget's argument that all children will automatically move to the next stage of development as they mature, as evidenced by:

- Cognitive development can be slowed by conditions of deprivation, such as those resulting from abuse, neglect, poverty, and poor nutrition.

- Parents can aid a child's cognitive development by exposing him or her to a variety of interesting materials and experiences, supportive conversation, and loving interactions with family members or others, as well as by encouraging the child to take on challenges actively.
- Special programs for poor preschool children can enhance children's cognitive abilities. Music lessons and electronic games can also promote children's cognitive development.

Information-Processing Model of Cognitive Development

The information-processing model of cognitive development refers to the acquisition of separate specific information-processing skills used in gathering and analyzing information from the environment, these include attention, memory, reasoning, and problem-solving. The information-processing model studies how information is received, encoded, stored, organized, retrieved, and used by people at different ages.

Information processing skills improve as children grow, e.g., the ability to focus attention and to shift attentional focus, and processing speed increase with age (Nettelbeck & Burns, 2010; Rebok et al., 1997). With age, children also show improvements in working memory span (Bayliss, Jarrold, Baddeley, Gunn, & Leigh, 2005), visual working memory (Riggs, McTaggart, Simpson, & Freeman, 2006), and conceptual explicit memory (Perez, Peynircioglu, & Blaxton, 1998). However, theorists of this approach did not agree on whether development is best understood as a series of qualitatively distinct stages or as a continuous process of change. Some theorists suggest separate skills develop smoothly and continuously rather than in a series of discrete stages. Others agree with Piaget about the presence of stages but only in more narrow domains, e.g., language skills, mathematical understanding, and social reasoning may develop in a stage-like fashion, but each domain proceeds relatively independently of the others and at its own speed. The later theorists are called "neo-Piagetians."

The Sociocultural Theory of Cognitive Development

The sociocultural theory stresses the dynamic interaction between developing people and the surrounding social and cultural forces, rather than considering the individual in isolation. Although Piaget emphasized the child's interactions with the environment, the environment he had in mind was the immediate physical environment. The social and cultural context plays virtually no role in Piaget's theory. This in distinction from sociocultural theory, which suggests that parents, caregivers, peers, and the culture at large are responsible for the development of higher-order functions. Lev Vygotsky (1934–1986) emphasized the social aspect of cognitive development, pointing out that children learn best when they have a teacher or mentor to aid them (Vygotsky, 1962, 1978). According to Vygotsky, every function in the child's cultural development appears twice: first, on the social level between people (interpsychological), and later, on the individual level inside the child (intrapsychological). This applies equally to voluntary attention, to logical memory, and to the formation of concepts. All the higher functions originate as actual relationships between individuals. Vygotsky introduced several important ideas:

1. *The zone of proximal development*: Vygotsky distinguished between two levels of cognitive development: the child's actual level of development, as expressed in problem-solving ability, and the child's level of potential development, which is determined by the kind of problem-solving the child can do when guided by an adult or a more knowledgeable peer. Thus, whether we are trying to solve a mathematic

problem, learning how to ride a bike, or learning how to make a cake, an educator can help in the achievement of what we cannot do alone. The zone of proximal development refers to the difference between what a child can do independently and what a child can do with the assistance of a parent or teacher. Essentially, it includes all of the knowledge and skills that a person cannot yet understand or perform on their own, but is capable of learning with guidance.

2. *Scaffolding*: this refers to providing a child with the needed assistance to accomplish a task. The help is proportionate to the child's needs, it is less when the child can do something alone and more when the child needs it.

3. *Private speech*: Vygotsky viewed language development as central to cognitive development. Children speak to themselves to give themselves guidance and direction as they practice new skills, e.g., a child gives instructions to self about how to tie shoes, which were previously heard from an adult. Vygotsky called this kind of self-instruction "private speech." In Vygotsky's view, private speech is a good thing that offers helpful and encouraging comments, and acts as one's own mentor (Berk, 2001; Gaskill & Díaz, 1991; Montero & De Dios, 2006).

Social-Emotional Development

Social development refers to learning how to relate to other people, while emotional development involves feelings and expression of feelings. Trust, fear, confidence, pride, friendship, and humor are all part of social-emotional development. The initial smiles of infants expressed after birth are called reflexive smiles (like a reflex), presumably they do not reflect happiness and appear to be due to internal states. Social smiles begin at about 2 months, in response to external events (e.g., face or voice of mother). Infants often express fear of strangers (stranger anxiety) and display distress when separated from their primary caregiver (separation anxiety) at about 6–9 months, with peak at about 9–15 months and decline in the second year. The degree of stranger anxiety varies from one baby to another. Learning to express emotions in appropriate ways begins early in life. Caregivers can promote this learning when they positively model these skills. A person's self-concept and self-esteem are also part of this area. Early social development is recognized in close emotional bond, or attachment, that infants form with their primary caregivers (see pp. 72–76). Also, Erikson's psychosocial theory was discussed above (pp. 65–70).

Urie Bronfenbrenner's ecological theory is one of the few systematic analyses that addresses children's socio-emotional development. It focuses primarily on the social contexts in which children and the people who influence their development live. The theory consists of five environmental systems that range from close interpersonal interactions to broad-based influences of culture (Figure 15.1): (1) the micro-system; (2) the meso-system; (3) the exo-system; (4) the macro-system; and (5) the chrono-system.

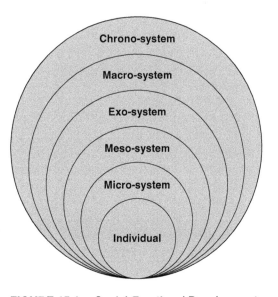

FIGURE 15.1. Social-Emotional Development.

1. *The micro-system*: this is a setting in which the individual spends considerable time. Some of these contexts are the child's family, peers, the school, and the neighborhood. The child reciprocally interacts with others and helps to construct these settings.

2. *The meso-system*: this involves linkages between micro-systems, e.g., the connections between family and school experiences, and between family and peers, etc. Experiences from one micro-system may affect experiences from another micro-system, e.g., a rejected child from a broken home may not relate well to the teacher in the school.

3. *The exo-system*: this contains settings or events in which the child is not directly involved, though they have a profound effect on a child's development. The exo-system influences the child indirectly, through its effect on other individuals who have an influence on the child's life. Exo-systems may be temporary, like a parent being dismissed from a job, or long-term, like the death of a family member.

4. *The macro-system*: this involves the broader culture in which the child lives, including the societal values, customs and norms e.g., some cultural practices are known to promote gender differences and stereotyping, while others do not. The roles of ethnicity, religion, and socio-economic factors in children's personality development are also significant.

5. *The chrono-system*: this refers to the socio-historical conditions of thechild's development, e.g., children today are expected to develop differently from children 30 years ago, for example. The easy availability of information will affect the present-day children's personality development.

Critics of Bronfenbrenner's ecological theory say it lacks attention to biological and cognitive factors, and it does not address the step-by-step developmental changes of children.

Moral Development

Moral development is a major topic of interest in both psychology and education. It refers to the formation of a system of values, that help us to arrive at appropriate decisions concerning right and wrong, or good and bad. Moral development is shaped by multiple factors including children's interpersonal experiences with family, peers, and other adults, in addition to physical, cognitive, emotional, and social skills development.

There are several approaches to the study of how children develop a sense of morality through adulthood. The social learning theory claims that humans develop morality by learning the rules of acceptable behavior from their external environment. Psychoanalytic theory proposes that morality develops through humans' conflict between their instinctual drives and the demands of society. Cognitive development theories view morality as an outgrowth of cognition, or reasoning.

Determining the limits of moral behavior is difficult, and controversies exist over what is or is not moral, including the morality of warfare (especially nuclear), ecological conservation, genetic research and manipulation, alternative fertility and childbearing methods, abortion, sexuality, pornography, drug use, euthanasia, racism, and sexism. Each society develops its own set of norms and standards for acceptable behavior, leading many to assume that morality is entirely culturally conditioned. There is a relatively small number of theories that specifically address moral development, these include theories by Jean Piaget, Lawrence Kohlberg, and Carol Gilligan.

Piaget's View of Moral Judgment

Piaget was the first psychologist to specifically outline a theory of moral development. Piaget's view of moral development was influenced by his cognitive theory, though he does not make an explicit cross-mapping between stages of moral development and his stages of cognitive development. Piaget believed that children's overall level of cognitive development determine their understanding of moral judgment and social conventions. Piaget

PHOTO 15.8.   Children's Marbles.

views the maturing morality as the result of cognitive development and interactions with the environment. Piaget's staging was based on his observations of children at different ages playing games with rules, such as marbles, and their querying about the rules.

According to Piaget's theory, there are three broad stages of moral development. Although Piaget proposed that these stages as exclusively distinct from one another, movement from one stage to another may go on a continuum. These stages are:

1. *Premoral judgment*: it extends from birth until about 5 years of age. In this stage, children do not understand the concept of rules and have no idea of morality, either internal or external. Children follow a private set of idiosyncratic rules. These rules give the child's play some regularity, but they are frequently changed and serve no collective purpose such as cooperation or competition, e.g., a child may sort marbles according to their colors or size.
2. *Moral realism (heteronomous morality)*: this extends from age of 5 until 10 years of age. The child in this stage understands the concept of rules, and can make moral decisions based on what an authority figure believes as right. The young child believes that rules are always externally given, cannot be altered, and must be literally obeyed. Thus, rules from parents or teachers are unchangeable, and the child follows them out of fear of consequences associated with breaking them. Hence, moral realist children evaluate wrongdoing in terms of its consequences, not the intentions of the wrongdoer, e.g., a person who accidentally damaged a large number of cups is judged as worse than another one who intentionally damaged one cup.
3. *Moral relativity*: this begins at age of 11 years. As children develop the ability to put themselves into someone else's shoes, their appreciation of morality becomes more autonomous (self-directed) and less black and white in nature. Children in this stage recognize that rules are not fixed, but can be changed with group consensus, and they start to develop their own internal morality which is no longer the same as external rules. A major development is that the morality of an action is evaluated in terms of the intentions of an actor, rather than just the consequences of the action. Children also develop a firm concept of the necessity that punishment should be proportionate to the wrongdoing, and they see punishment as a human choice rather than as inevitable, divine penalty (Piaget, 1965).

Kohlberg's Moral Theory

The American psychologist Lawrence Kohlberg modified and expanded upon Jean Piaget's work about moral reasoning, proposing that moral development is a continuous process that occurs throughout the lifespan (Kohlberg, 1969, 1976). Kohlberg based his theory upon research and interviews with groups of young children. A series of moral dilemmas were presented to those children and they were also interviewed to determine the reasoning behind their judgments of each scenario. The following is one example of the dilemmas presented by Kohlberg.

Heinz's wife was dying from a particular type of cancer. Doctors said a new drug might save her. The drug had been discovered by a local chemist and Heinz tried desperately to buy some, but the chemist was charging ten times the money it costs to make the drug and this was much more than what Heinz could afford. Heinz could only raise half the money, even after help from family and friends. He explained to the chemist that his wife was dying and asked if he could have the drug cheaper or pay the rest of the money later. The chemist refused, saying that he had discovered the drug and was going to make money from it. Heinz was desperate to save his wife, so later that night he broke into the chemist's and stole the drug.

Kohlberg asked a series of questions such as:

1. Should Heinz have stolen the drug?
2. Would it change anything if Heinz did not love his wife?
3. What if the person dying was a stranger, would it make any difference?
4. Should the police arrest the chemist for murder if the wife died?

Kohlberg was not interested so much in the answer to the question of whether Heinz was wrong or right, but in the reasoning for each participant's decision. The responses were then classified into various stages of reasoning in his theory of moral development. Kohlberg proposed six universal stages in the development of moral judgments, which he grouped into three levels: preconventional, conventional, and postconventional.

Level 1: preconventional morality: moral values reside in external, quasi-physical events, or bad acts. The child is responsive to rules and evaluative labels, but views them in terms of pleasant or unpleasant consequences of actions, or in terms of the physical power of those who impose the rules.

Stage 1: Punishment and Obedience Orientation: in this stage, children obey authority in order to avoid punishment. Thus, the physical consequences of an action determine its goodness or badness regardless of the human meaning or value of these consequences. At this stage, children see rules as fixed and absolute. Avoidance of punishment and complete regard to power are valued in their own right, not in terms of respect for an underlying moral order.

Stage 2: Instrumental and Exchange Orientation: in this stage children obey authority and conform to rules to gain rewards or satisfy their needs. Right action is that which satisfies one's own needs and occasionally the needs of others. Human relations are viewed in terms like those of the marketplace with elements of fairness, sharing, and reciprocity present, but always interpreted in a physical or pragmatic way. In the Heinz dilemma, children argued that the best course of action was the choice that best served

Heinz's needs. Reciprocity is possible at this point in moral development, but only if it serves one's own interests.

Level 2: conventional morality: Moral values reside in performing the right role, in maintaining the conventional order and expectancies of others as a value in its own right. This is based on an acquisition of the importance of rules or keeping to it just for the sake of society. Children begin to evaluate actions in terms of other people's opinions. It begins at about age 10, and most youngsters can reason at this level by age 13.

Stage 3: Mutual Interpersonal Expectations, Relationships, and Interpersonal Conformity (good-boy, nice-girl orientation): this stage of moral development is focused on living up to social expectations and roles. The concern is "what will people think of me?" and the desire is for group approval. Moral behavior is that which helps, impresses, pleases, or is approved by others. There is an emphasis on conformity, being "nice," and consideration of how choices influence relationships. Behavior is frequently judged by intention (he means well). One earns approval by being nice.

Stage 4: Social System and Conscience Orientation): at this stage, people begin to consider society as a whole when making judgments. The focus is on maintaining law and order by following the rules, doing one's duty and respecting authority, owing to a belief that rules and laws are necessary for order which is perceived as good and moral. Right behavior consists of doing one's duty, showing respect for authority, and maintaining the given social order for its own sake. The concern goes beyond one's immediate groups to the larger society, to maintain law and order. One's obligation to the law overrides one's obligations to family or friends. No one group is above the law.

Level 3: postconventional morality: morality is defined in terms of conformity to shared standards, rights, or duties apart from supporting authority. The standards conformed to are internal, and decisions are based on an inner process of thought and judgment concerning right and wrong. Postconventional morality becomes evident when the person does the same thing when present among people, the same way when alone and there is no chance of anybody will hear about or see what is done.

Stage 5: Social Contract or Individual Right Orientation: moral action is that which protects the rights of the individual according to rules agreed on by the whole society. There is flexibility in moral reasoning, in which there is a sense of having to abide by the law, concurrent with an understanding that laws can be wrong. The individual becomes aware that while rules/laws might exist for the good of the greatest number, there are times when they will work against the interest of particular individuals, e.g., in Heinz's dilemma, the protection of life is more important than breaking the law against stealing. When conflict arises between individual needs and law or contract, though sympathetic to the former, the individual believes the latter must prevail because of its greater functional rationality for society, and the majority welfare. It is not a strict "law and order" approach. While rules are needed to maintain social order, they should not be blindly obeyed but should be evaluated or changed for the good of society.

Stage 6: universal ethical principles orientation: people at this stage are oriented not only toward existing social rules, but also toward right and wrong defined on a personal belief or self-chosen ethics. People develop their own set of moral guidelines which may or may not fit the law. The principles apply to everyone, e.g., justice, equal rights, and respect for the dignity of human beings as individual persons. The person will be prepared to act to defend these principles even if it means going against the rest of society and having to pay the consequences of disapproval and/or imprisonment.

Kohlberg doubted few people reached this stage. Kohlberg reported that fewer than 10 percent of adult participants in his studies showed the kind of "clear-principled" Stage 6 thinking. Before he died, Kohlberg eliminated Stage 6 from his theory; Level III is now sometimes simply referred to as high-stage principled reasoning.

Criticisms of Kohlberg's Theory of Moral Development

1. Kohlberg's dilemmas were criticized for being artificial and unfamiliar to most people, while the sample used in the study was criticized for being biased as it was based on males only.

2. In practice, the reasoning about right and wrong usually depends more upon the situation than upon general rules. There is evidence that people use different rules for different situations and that the stages are not sequential (Kurtines & Greif, 1974). Thus, there is little evidence to support the presence of distinct stages of moral development, e.g., a person who justified a decision on a certain basis in one situation (e.g., post-conventional morality stage 5 or 6) may fall back on conventional reasoning (stage 3 or 4) in another situation.

3. Kohlberg's theory overemphasized western individualistic cultures which emphasize personal rights, while collectivist cultures stress the importance of society and community. Eastern cultures may have different moral outlooks that are ignored by Kohlberg's theory.

4. The theory was been criticized as being "male-centered" because it places a "masculine" style of abstract reasoning, based on justice and rights, higher on the moral scale than a "feminine" style of reasoning, based on caring and concern for the integrity and continuation of relationships (Gilligan, 1982). Gilligan suggested that traits that traditionally define the goodness of women, and their care for and sensitivity to the needs of others, are those that discriminate them as deficient in moral development, hence, girls are usually found at stage 3 whereas boys are more at stage 4 in Kohlberg's theory.

5. Moral judgment does not always match moral behavior; Kohlberg never claimed that there would be a one-to-one correspondence between thinking and acting (what we say and what we do) but he suggested that the two are linked. On the other hand, Bee (1994) pointed out that moral behavior is only partly a question of moral reasoning, and suggested that we need to take account of:
   a. habits that people have developed over time;
   b. whether people see situations as demanding their participation;
   c. the costs and benefits of behaving in a particular way;
   d. competing motives, such as peer pressure, self-interest, and so on.

Gilligan's Theory Moral Development

Carol Gilligan criticized Kohlberg's ideas about moral dilemmas which mirrored his own experiences and were ultimately biased against women. Gilligan asserts that women have different moral and psychological tendencies from men. According to Gilligan, men think in terms of rules and justice while women are more inclined to think in terms of caring, responsibility, and welfare of others. According to Gilligan, these differences place women at a lower level of moral reasoning than where Kohlberg places men. Gilligan outlined three stages of moral development: the transitions between the stages are fueled by changes in the sense of self rather than by changes in cognitive capability. These stages include:

1. Preconventional (self-oriented): persons are oriented only toward care for themselves in order to ensure survival. In this phase, the person's attitude is considered selfish, and the person sees the connection between themselves and others. The transition to next level begins with the recognition of the conflict between one's own needs and the needs of others.
2. Conventional (others-oriented): more care is shown for the needs of other people. The person adopts the traditional conception of feminine goodness, the maternal morality of self-sacrifice, whereby the good is equated with caring for others. Consequently, one's own needs become devalued. Gilligan says this is shown in the role of mother and wife. Needs of self may be ignored in some situations. In the transitional stage to the next post-conventional stage, tensions between responsibility of caring for others and caring for self are faced.
3. Post-conventional (universal-oriented): care for self and care for others are shown as intertwined (do not hurt others or self), because the self and others are recognized as interdependent. Some people never reach this level.

Clinical Notes

Understanding normal developmental sequences and variations are important issues in clinical practice, education, and in everyday life interactions. In clinical practice, it is important to know the limits of normal variations to deal effectively with young persons and to detect abnormal variations and thence to search for possible factors and to intervene appropriately. In education, it is important to implement programs that consider the developmental age and to consider those with developmental delay. In everyday life, parents and families should deal with their children in an appropriate manner that provides a nurturing environment that promotes development.

Summary

- Development refers to the dynamic process which leads to quantitative and qualitative changes taking place from conception to death. In this way, development is a broad term and deals with all areas including physical, motor, cognitive, physiological, social, emotional, and moral development.
- Development and growth are influenced by several factors, including genetic, environmental factors, medical diseases, social influences, and psychological factors.
- There are four basic parenting styles: authoritarian parents, permissive parents, authoritative parents, and uninvolved parents.
- Human beings usually physically grow and mature at about the same periods during their life span. Most psychologists identify the following stages of development: the prenatal period, childhood, adolescence, and adulthood.
- Piaget suggested four stages of cognitive development: the sensorimotor stage, the preoperational stage, the concrete operations stage, and the formal operational stage.
- Moral development refers to the formation of a system of values that help us to arrive at appropriate decisions concerning right and wrong, or good and bad.

- Moral development is shaped by multiple factors, including children's interpersonal experiences with family, peers, and other adults, in addition to physical, cognitive, emotional, and social skills development.
- Major theories concerned with moral development include the moral theories of Piaget, Kohlberg, and Gilligan.

Test Your Knowledge

- What are the factors that may influence development?
- Describe the basic parenting styles.
- What are the characteristics of the prenatal period of development?
- Describe the characteristics of the childhood period of development.
- What are the characteristics of the adolescence period of development?
- Describe the characteristics of the adulthood period of development.
- What are the characteristics of the sensorimotor stage of cognitive development?
- Describe the characteristics of the preoperational stage of cognitive development.
- What are the characteristics of the concrete operations of cognitive development?
- What are the characteristics of the formal operational stage of cognitive development?
- Give an account of Vygotsky's sociocultural theory.
- Describe Piaget's view of moral development.
- Give an account of Kohlberg's moral development theory.

Critical Thinking Questions

- How are developmental theories useful in schools?
- How is adulthood distinguished in different cultures?
- How could you evaluate moral development theories?

sixteen
Social Psychology

Learning Goals

This chapter is intended to provide the reader with an overview of several important concepts:

1. Social cognition and social perception: this will include definition and components of social cognition, and an idea about social perception, self-concept, social schemas, first impressions, and stereotypes.
2. Attribution: this will include definition and types of attribution, factors influencing the formation of an attribution, and attributional biases.
3. Attitudes and attitude change: this will include definition and components of attitude, theories of attitude formation and change, factors moderating attitude change, and types of persuasion strategies.
4. Aggression: this will include definition and types of aggression, gender difference in aggression, theories explaining aggression, provocation of aggressive behavior, and how to reduce aggression.
5. Prosocial behavior: this will include the definition and theories that explain why people care about others, and how we can increase helping.
6. Interpersonal attraction: this will include factors that influence an individual's attraction, and give an idea about intimate relationships and love.
7. Groups and social influence: this will include the importance of social categorization, group structure and cohesion, social roles, group interactions and social influence, and an overview of the main areas of group interaction and social influence including conformity, obedience, reactance, minority influence, social facilitation, social loafing, deindividuation, group polarization, and groupthink.
8. Prejudice: this will include the definition and components of prejudice, theories of intergroup prejudice, group conflict, and how to reduce prejudice.

Introduction

PHOTO 16.1.   Social Psychology.

According to Gordon Allport, social psychology is the scientific study of how people's thoughts, feelings, and behaviors are influenced by the actual, imagined, or implied presence of others (Allport, 1985). Therefore, social psychologists are interested in factors that lead people to behave in a given way in social circumstances, and look at the conditions under which certain behaviors/actions and feelings occur.

Social Cognition

Social cognition is an area of social psychology that studies mental processes associated with how people perceive and react to others. Research in social cognition investigates how people make sense of themselves and others to make judgments, form attitudes, and predict the future, e.g., when going on a date or to a job interview, one is concerned with the impression and signals sent to the other person, as well as interpreting the signals given by the other person.

PHOTO 16.2.   Perceiving and Reacting to Others.

Social cognition includes a group of skills: (1) emotion processing; (2) theory of mind (ToM); (3) social perception; and (4) attributional style.

Emotion processing denotes the perception and the application of emotion information. Salovey and Sluyter (1997) suggested that emotion perception has four components: (1) identifying emotions, either through facial affect or vocal prosody; (2) understanding the effect of emotions on performance of different tasks; (3) understanding emotions; and (4) regulation of emotional states of self and others.

Theory of Mind (also called mentalizing, mind reading, or perspective taking) refers to the ability to infer the thoughts, beliefs, hints, metaphor, and sarcasm, and intentions of others. It develops around age 3½–4 years.

Social Perception

Social perception is the process by which individuals form impressions of and make inferences about other individuals or social groups. It is one of the components of social cognition. Social perception includes knowledge about social roles, rules, norms, and schemas surrounding social situations and interactions. Social perceptions can obviously be flawed, even skilled observers can misperceive, misjudge, and reach wrong conclusions. Aside from the available information, observers with different moods and temperament can account for a variety of perceptions. The importance of social perception is derived from the fact that people's impressions and judgments about others, whether accurate or not, can have profound effects on their own and others' behavior. Social perception is formed through observation, attribution, integration, and confirmation:

- *Observations of available data*: the raw data of social perception include the interplay of three sources: persons, situations, and behavior. These sources are used as evidence in supporting a person's impression or inference about others.
- *Attribution*: the process through which people infer the link of events or behaviors and its possible causes (see p. 306).
- *Integration*: all available information is incorporated into a unified impression.
- *Confirmation of impressions*: individuals form final impressions that are subject to confirmation biases and the threat of a self-fulfilling prophecy. Confirmation is also shaped by an individual's current motivations, emotions, and cognitive load capacity. Cognitive load is the complete amount of mental effort used in the working memory.

Self-Concept

The whole sum of beliefs that people have about themselves is called self-concept. It plays an influential role in social psychology.

Self-concept is often divided into a cognitive component, known as the self-schema, and an evaluative component, the self-esteem. Self-schemas refer to beliefs that people have about themselves and guide the processing of self-reliant information, e.g., when you see a job advertisement for a teacher, you can evaluate the match between your teacher schema and your self-schema to decide whether you should apply for the job. Every person has more than one self-schema, e.g., an athletic university student may have multiple self-schemas that process different information related to each self: the student-self processes information related to a student, e.g., taking notes in class, completing a homework assignment, etc., and the athlete-self processes information about things related to being an athlete e.g., recognizing an incoming pass, aiming a shot, etc. (Markus, 1977). If a self is not part of one's identity, then it will be difficult for one to behave accordingly, e.g., a civilian may not be familiar with how to handle a hostile threat as a trained Marine. In contrast to civilians, Marines have a self that enables them to process information about hostile threats and react accordingly.

Some self-schemas may represent a significant part of self-concept, e.g., everyday events such as grocery shopping, new clothes, eating out, or going to the beach can trigger thoughts about the self among people who regard themselves as over- or under-weight and those

PHOTO 16.3. Self-Concept.

for whom body image is a significant self-concept aspect. In contrast, people who do not regard their weight as an important part of their lives are a-schematic on such an attribute.

People develop their self-concepts by varied means, including introspection, feedback from others, self-perception, and social comparison. According to Leon Festinger's social comparison theory (Festinger, 1954), people usually gain insight about themselves by comparing themselves to others. Daryl Bem's self-perception theory (Bem, 1967) suggested that people use their behavior and the circumstances in which it occurs to infer their own beliefs and attitudes. Bem's self-perception theory assumes that people know their own attitudes, beliefs, and other internal states through (1) inferring from their own behavior and the circumstances under which they occur, e.g., students who observe that they constantly read psychology books may infer an interest in psychology; (2) when internal cues are weak, the individual adopts the same position of an outside observer, and relies upon the external cues to infer their own inner characteristics, e.g., other people's conclusion such as having high grades in psychology will reinforce the inference of interest in psychology.

Culture also affects self-concept; individualist cultures emphasize the individual by assuring personal freedom and personal responsibility. In contrast, collectivist cultures emphasize the group. In such cultures, one should fulfill one's role within one's group, support the group, and maintain group harmony (Hofstede, 1983).

Self-esteem refers to the value one places on one's self (Baumeister, Campbell, Krueger, & Vohs, 2003). People with high esteem think more favorably of themselves, and people with low esteem think less favorably. According to *Tesser's self-evaluation maintenance model*, people maintain or enhance their self-esteem through comparison and reflection processes (Tesser, Millar, & Moore, 1988). Comparing ourselves to others helps to understand our strengths and weaknesses. Social comparisons also influence self-esteem; comparison with others who are more capable (upward social comparison) tends to decline esteem, while comparison with others who are less capable (downward social comparison) tends to increase esteem.

The reflection process denotes enhancing our self-esteem by sharing in the talents or accomplishments and success of others, e.g., students are more likely to wear school dress when their school football team wins. Also, they are more likely to describe results of their football team with the pronoun we, e.g., we won, thereby participating in the victory (Cialdini et al., 1976). On the contrary, people try to distance their selves from someone who has done something bad. When comparison and reflection processes are in conflict, the choice will depend on the self-relevance of the comparison. The comparison process will have priority if its theme is important to the person, if not, the reflection process will take precedence.

Social Schemas

Schemas are mental representation or shortcuts that a person makes about objects, situations, and events they encounter. Instead of spending time learning about each new individual object, people rely on schemas to tell them about the newly encountered object or subject, e.g., when you meet a new teacher, the "teacher schema" is activated, and automatically you will associate this person with wisdom and authority if this is your experience of past teachers. In this way, schemas greatly reduce the amount of cognitive work we need to do, and allow us to go beyond the information given (Bruner, 1957). Social perception is usually guided by schemas, or mental representations, of knowledge. Schemas often operate automatically and unintentionally, and can lead to biases in perception and memory. People can hold schemas about almost anything: individual people (person schemas or social perception), ourselves (self-schemas), and recurring events (event schemas or scripts). People also develop associations between related schemas, which play an important role in the thought process and social behavior.

An accessible schema is more quickly activated and used in a particular situation. Two cognitive processes can increase the accessibility of schemas: salience and priming. Salience is the degree to which a particular social object stands out relative to other social objects in a situation. The higher the salience of an object, the more likely the schema for that object will be made accessible, e.g., if there is one female in a group of seven males, female gender schemas may be more accessible and influence the group's thinking and behavior toward the female group member. Priming refers to situational contexts that immediately precede a situation and cause a schema to be more accessible, e.g., watching a scary movie late at night might increase the accessibility of frightening schemas, increasing the likelihood that a person will perceive shadows and background noises as potential threats.

Expectations from schemas may lead us to see something that is not there. One experiment found that people are more likely to misperceive a weapon in the hands of a black man than a white man (Correll et al., 2002). This type of schema is actually a stereotype. A stereotype is a generalized set of beliefs about a particular group of people, which, when incorrect, is called the ultimate attribution error. Stereotypes are often related to negative or preferential attitudes (prejudice) and behavior (discrimination). Schemas for behaviors (e.g., going to a restaurant, doing laundry) are known as scripts. Perceptions of people follow many of the same laws that govern the perception of objects (Macrae & Quadflieg, 2010). As a result, our prior knowledge and our schemas about people can have a significant influence on our perceptions of them. The roles that schemas play are summarized in the following:

- *Schemas influence what to attend to and what to ignore.* Characteristics that are consistent with our schema about another person usually get more attention than those that are inconsistent with that schema. As a result, we tend to process information about other people more quickly if it confirms our beliefs about them, than if it violates those beliefs (Smith & Queller, 2001).
- *Schemas influence what to remember about others*, e.g., if people thought a woman they saw in a video was a waitress, they later recalled that she had a beer with dinner. If they thought she was a librarian, they remembered that she was wearing glasses and liked classical music (Macrae, Quinn, Mason, & Quadflieg 2005; Quadflieg & Macrae, 2011).

■ *Schemas affect judgment about other people's behavior*, e.g., participants' ratings of male and female friends' sadness were influenced not only by the friends' actual behavior but also by the participants' general schemas about whether men or women experience more sadness (Hill, Smith, & Lewicki, 1989).

First Impressions

The schemas about people lead people to make judgments and infer much about a person on the basis of limited information, e.g., after seeing a person's face for only a tenth of a second (Willis & Todorov, 2006). A few number of those assumptions may turn out to be true. Those impressions in turn influence both perceptions of others' behaviors and our reactions to those behaviors. The first impressions we learn about someone influence us more than later information does (Jones. Goethals, Kennington, & Severance, 1972), this tendency is called the primacy effect, e.g., hearing both favorable and unfavorable reports about a restaurant, the influence of the first report one hears is usually more than that of reports one may hear later on (Russo, Carlson, & Meloy, 2006). The first impressions are formed quickly, usually change slowly, and typically have a long-lasting influence, and hence their importance in the development of social relations.

The reason that first impressions change slowly is that negative first impressions may cause us to avoid certain people and locations, thus reducing our exposure to new information that might change our view of them (Denrell, 2005). In addition, we adhere to our beliefs about the world by giving a meaning to new information that leads to holding on to existing impressions (Kenrick, Neuberg, & Cialdini, 2010). Further, people often do things that push others to confirm their impressions, e.g., assuming that members of a certain ethnic group are unfriendly, one may be defensive or even hostile when meeting a member of that group. If the person reacts to this behavior with hostility, one's prediction will be fulfilled and one may even have a stronger impression that all those people are unfriendly, this is called a *self-fulfilling prophecy* (Kenrick et al., 2010; Madon, Guyll, Spoth, & Willard, 2004). Thus, in a self-fulfilling prophecy, actions toward others influence their beliefs about us, which directs their actions toward us, which then reinforces our beliefs about ourselves. This, in turn, influences our actions toward others, which brings us back to the beginning of the cycle. In one study regarding self-fulfilling prophecies, psychologists led some male college students to believe that a female student was attracted to them and not attracted to another group. Later on, the social psychologists observed interactions between the men and the female in question. The woman was much more likely to act as if she was attracted to the first set of men, because those men behaved in a way that led her to actually be attracted to them.

Stereotypes

Stereotypes are schemas or a set of beliefs about a group or subtypes of people. This includes perceptions, beliefs, and expectations that a person has about members of a group. People usually do not process available information in an unbiased manner, but filter incoming information through pre-existing stereotypes and motives and actively construct perceptions, memories, and inferences. The effects of stereotypes on perception and thinking are usually invisible.

Stereotypes usually assume that all members of a group share the same positive or negative characteristics. The most common categories upon which most stereotypes are grounded are sex, age, race, and religion (Fiske, 1993; Fiske, Cuddy, Glick, & Xu, 2002). The stereotypes can be so ingrained that their effects on behavior can be habitual and automatic and operating outside conscious awareness, e.g., young black males are hostile, women are passive, or old people are slow (Dovidio et al., 2010). In one study, American participants of European and African ethnicity played a video game in which white or black men suddenly appeared on a screen holding objects that might be weapons (Correll, Park, Judd, & Wittenbrink, 2002). The participants were instructed to immediately shoot an armed man but not an unarmed one. Under time pressure, the participants' errors were not random. If they shot an unarmed man, he was significantly more likely to be black than white. If they failed to shoot an armed man, he was more likely to be white than black. These differences occurred among both European American and African American participants but were most pronounced among those who held the strongest cultural stereotypes about blacks. In another study, police officers showed a similar pattern of results, except that the officers were not as quick as civilians to shoot an unarmed black man (Correll et al., 2007).

Stereotypes persist in society, even they are false due to a lot of reasons, these include perceptual assimilation, self-fulfilling prophecy, and subtyping. Subtyping refers to a process whereby people come to view individuals who do not fit a stereotype as exceptions or as poor members of a group. It explains why people often do not change their stereotypes in the face of disconfirming information; people who have prejudice do not change their view about the group in general because they assign different people to a subcategory; essentially they label them as exceptions to the rule, leaving the overall stereotype intact.

Stereotype threat refers to how being identified with a stereotype can raise an individual's anxiety level, which in turn worsens his or her performance (Steele, 1997). That is, targets of stereotypes experience undue stress, actively monitor their performance, and try to suppress negative thoughts and feelings, processes that combine to reduce working memory capacity, and derail test performance (Schmader & Johns, 2003; Schmader, Johns, & Forbes, 2008), e.g., in an attempt to fight the stereotype that men are better than women in math and science, the anxiety and distraction caused by the stereotype may actually lead a woman to get a lower score on the exam than her true potential. Thus, women's performance in math may not be due to lower ability compared to men but to negative stereotypes.

Studies have shown that the influence of stereotypes can be consciously overridden when one becomes aware of the potential negative influence of stereotypes, is motivated to reduce prejudice, and gets sufficient attentional resources to engage in controlled and deliberate thinking.

Clinical Notes

- Social cognition involves a wide variety of skills, including affect recognition, facial memory and recognition, appropriate interpretation of affect and prosody, and theory of mind.
- Neurological, psychiatric, and developmental conditions (e.g., autistic disorder, schizophrenia) often impact social ability or include them as diagnostic criteria.
- Deficits in social cognition directly impact an examinee's ability to function in most environments.
- In addition to specific deficits in social cognition, general cognitive deficits often produce difficulties in aspects of social cognition.

Summary

- Social cognition refers to mental processes associated with how people perceive and react to others. It includes emotion processing, theory of mind, social perception, and attributional style.

- Social perception is the process by which individuals form impressions of and make inferences about other individuals or social groups.
- Social perception is formed through observation, attribution, integration, and confirmation
- The whole sum of beliefs that people have about themselves is called the self-concept. It is often divided into a cognitive component, known as the self-schema, and an evaluative component, self-esteem.
- Schemas influence what to attend to and what to ignore, what to remember about others, and judgment about other people's behavior.
- First impressions are formed quickly, usually change slowly, and typically have a long-lasting influence, and hence their importance in the development of social relations.
- Stereotypes are schemas or a set of beliefs about a group or subtypes of people.

Test Your Knowledge

- Define social cognition.
- What is meant by social perception?
- Define self-concept.
- How do schemas influence social perception?
- How do stereotypes influence social relationships?

Critical Thinking Questions

- How can an understanding of social psychology be of benefit in evaluating personal ideas and behavior?
- How do you explain the lasting effect of first impressions?

Attribution

In their attempt to predict, understand, and control their social atmosphere, people constantly try to explain others' motives, preferences, and behavior. Each individual has a unique set of personal perspectives on a situation, leading people to act differently in the same situation. Also, each situation brings a unique set of features, leading an individual to act differently in different situations. Attribution or attributional style is the process through which people infer the possible causes of events or behaviors. Fritz Heider (1958) proposed that people try to identify stable causes of behavior because this helps them to understand and control their social worlds, e.g., students usually expect that if they study for an exam, they will do well in it. Heider suggested that people observe others, analyze their behavior, and come up with their own explanations for such actions. If someone fails an exam, it is important to decide if one should study harder or if the reason is that he or she cannot succeed in an exam. Heider grouped these explanations into either external attributions or internal attributions. When some people do not leave tips in restaurants, one may consider them misers, or attribute this to bad service. Similarly, when some people are late, one may consider them irresponsible, or attribute this to an event that is beyond their control. Thus, attribution summarizes how we think about ourselves and others.

In external attribution (situational attribution), the cause of an event is ascribed to an external factor, i.e., ascribing the behavior of people to the situation that they are in, e.g., a star football player may consistently underestimate his athletic talent, emphasizing instead the support and love of his family as key to his success, another star football player may ascribe his poor performance in a game to bad weather. Internal attribution (dispositional attributions) refers to assuming that personal factors (personality traits, abilities, feelings, and attitudes) are the cause of an event or behavior. People usually make internal attributions when someone does something they consider surprising, e.g., if someone wants to visit Hawaii, people usually draw no conclusions about him. However, when this person wants to visit northern Norway in winter, they wonder about this special interest, and suggest an internal attributional factor. Similarly, when a man gets angry in public, most people assume he had a reason. When a woman gets equally angry in public, her behavior is more surprising, and people may attribute it to her personality (Brescoll & Uhlmann, 2008).

Kelley (1967) proposed a logical model (Kelley's Covariation Model) for judging whether a particular action should be attributed to some characteristic (internal) of the person or to the environment (external). He argues that people (called observers) rely on three key types of information when making an attribution for someone's behavior (called actors): consensus, consistency, and distinctiveness:

■ *Consensus information*: consensus looks for generalization across actors. In other words, the degree to which one person's behavior compares with other people's behavior. If someone behaves the same way you believe other people would behave in the same situation, this behavior has high consensus, and you can suggest that an external attribution led to the behavior. When someone's behavior seems unusual, this behavior has low consensus, and you can suggest that an internal attribution relating to the person led to the behavior.

■ *Consistency information*: this is the degree to which the person responds in the same way across time. If someone almost always seems friendly (high consistency), one make an internal attribution: this is a friendly person. If someone's friendliness varies (low consistency), one make an external attribution, e.g., ascribing such fluctuations to an event that elicited a good or bad mood.

■ *Distinctiveness*: this is the degree to which the person's behavior varies from one situation to another. If your friend is pleasant to everyone except one individual, this behavior has high distinctiveness; you assume that this person has done something to irritate your friend (an external attribution).

In summary, Kelley's theory suggests that people are most likely to make internal attributions about an actor's behavior when there is low consensus, high consistency, and low distinctiveness. External attribution about an actor's behavior is inferred when there is high consensus, low consistency, and high distinctiveness.

In another attempt to define conditions under which we make internal or dispositional attributes to behavior we perceive as intentional, Edward Jones and Keith Davis proposed the correspondent inference theory. This theory refers to assuming that people's behaviors match or correspond with their motives, dispositions, or personality, e.g., correspondence between behaving in a friendly way and being a friendly person (Jones & Davis, 1965). The inferences people will make are based on the following factors:

■ *Personal choice*: if a behavior is considered voluntary and freely chosen, it is believed to be due to internal (dispositional) factors.

■ *Accidental vs. intentional behavior*: behavior that is intentional is likely to be attributed to the person's personality, and behavior which is accidental is likely to be attributed to situational/external causes. If perceived environmental forces are strong, people are not likely to make dispositional attributions, e.g., if a student always comes late to class, as the class is on the other side of campus, teacher is less likely to make a dispositional attribution.

■ *Normativeness*: the greater the degree to which an action conforms to social norms, the less information it yields about the intentions and dispositions of actors. Actions which violate norms are more likely to be attributed to dispositions than to environmental forces, e.g., teachers behaving in a standard way do not tell us anything about how they really are. However, if a teacher behaves unusually harsh to his/her students, then it may be more expressive of their personal attributes.

■ *Hedonic relevance*: this is the net result of the positive or negative outcomes of an action for the observer. That is, hedonic relevance occurs whenever the action is gratifying or punishing to the observer. Thus, hedonic relevance seems to consist of two components: (1) the degree to which the observer's goal attainment is facilitated or interfered with as a result of the action; and (2) the positive or negative emotional response of the observer's as a result of the first component. When hedonic relevance is high, the observer should make more dispositional attributions as to the cause of an action than when hedonic relevance is low, even if the situation is completely outwith the control of the actor.

■ *Personalism*: the extent to which the actor's behavior is perceived as intended to affect or influence the observer in some way. High personalism needs two prerequisites: (1) the observer must believe that the actor had some personal knowledge of him or her prior to the performance of the actions; and (2) the observer must perceive the action as being specifically directed toward him or her and not toward people in general or a subclass of people (e.g., Blacks, agriculture students). If the two requirements are met, the act is considered high in personalism, and thus the observer will make a dispositional attribution of that behavior.

■ *Non-common effects*: inference about dispositional attributes of a person is done by comparing the action chosen by the actor in relation to the possible alternatives. The inference becomes harder if choices have little differences. Increasing the number of non-common effects makes inference easier, e.g., when a person chooses to drink Coca-Cola instead of Pepsi Cola, the choice here is quite similar, as both are soft drinks and both have little or no non-common effects. It will be difficult for a perceiver to infer the dispositional attributes of the person behind his or her reasons to drink Coca-Cola. However, if a person chooses vodka instead of Pepsi Cola, then inference becomes significantly easier. The two drinks are completely different, and it can be concluded that the actor prefers alcoholic beverages rather than soft drinks.

Attributional Biases

When making judgments and decisions about the world around us, people like to think that they are objective and logical in their evaluation of available information. However, the reality is that their judgments and decisions are often violated with errors and influenced by a wide variety of biases. Attributional biases are systematic errors that distort perceptions and attributions. There are a number of attributional biases; common examples are described below.

The fundamental attribution error (Ross, 1977) refers to the tendency of people to attribute the behavior of others to internal personal characteristics, while ignoring or underestimating the role of situational factors (correspondence bias) (Van Boven, Kamada, & Gilovich, 1999; Zimbardo, 2007). On the contrary, people tend to be biased in the opposite direction, when it comes to explaining their own behavior, through using external or situational attributions (self-serving bias). *Self-serving bias* is the tendency to attribute dispositional causes for successes, and situational causes for failure, particularly when self-esteem is threatened (Kruger & Gilovich, 2004). This leads to assuming one's successes are from innate traits, and one's failures are due to situations, including other people, e.g., when students do well on a test, they tend to attribute their success to their hard study, their intelligence, and so forth (internal attributions). But when students fail a test, they try to find every possible external cause, e.g., all questions were tricky, or difficulty in concentration because of the behavior of some students. Self-serving bias is an attempt to protect self-esteem in the face of failure (Dunning, Leuenberger, & Sherman, 1995).

The fundamental attribution error plays a role in blaming the innocent victim of a crime, disaster, or serious illness, e.g., many people blame the sick for bringing on their illnesses, and battered women and rape survivors for somehow provoking their attackers. Blaming the victim is reinforced by another common cognitive bias, *hindsight bias*, which refers to the tendency to overestimate one's ability to have foreseen or predicted the outcome, after an event has occurred. Hindsight bias makes it seem as if the victim was able to predict and prevent what happened (Goldinger, Kleider, Azuma, & Beike, 2003). Blaming the victim reflects the belief that the world is fair, and people deserve what they get and the victim must have done something to deserve his or her fate (just-world hypothesis) (M. Lerner, 1980).

The ultimate attribution error is a cognitive bias that is closely related to the fundamental attribution error: when members of a social group whom we see as different (the outgroup) do something positive, we attribute their behavior to luck or some other external cause. But we attribute their negative behavior, such as dishonesty, to an internal cause (Pettigrew, 1979). At the same time, when members of a similar group (the ingroup) do good deeds, we attribute the behavior to integrity or other internal factors. If they do something bad, we attribute it to some external cause. As result of this bias, members of the outgroup receive little credit for their positive actions, and members of the ingroup get little blame for their negative actions (Khan & Liu, 2008).

Clinical Notes

- Several attributional styles have reliable associations with depression scores, e.g., internal attributions to negative events, and external attributions to positive events had a reliable and significant association with depression (Sweeney, Anderson, & Bailey, 1986).

- Patients with persecutory delusions are likely to show bias toward blaming others for negative outcomes, and there was a linear association between persecutory ideation and a self-serving attributional style (Martin & Penn, 2002). However, Sanford, and Woodwarda (2017) found that disorganization and manic symptoms correlate with situation attributions and self-blame, while depression and anxiety correlated with other person and self-attributions, regardless of the diagnosis in patients with schizophrenia and bipolar disorder.

- Research revealed an association between social anxiety and internal attributions for negative expectations about social events, but no significant correlations were found between negative or positive attributions and students' ability to issue romantic invitations (Chyrelle, 2006).

Summary

- Attribution or attributional style is the process through which people infer the possible causes of events or behaviors. People may have either external or internal attributions.
- In external attribution, the cause of an event is ascribed to an external factor.
- Internal attribution refers to assuming that personal factors are the cause of an event or reason for a behavior.
- Kelley argues that people rely consensus, consistency, and distinctiveness of information, when making an attribution about someone's behavior.
- Correspondent inference theory refers to assuming that people's behaviors match or correspond with their motives, dispositions, or personality.
- Attributional biases are systematic errors that distort perceptions and attributions.
- The fundamental attribution error refers to the tendency of people to attribute the behavior of others to internal personal characteristics, but when it comes to explaining their own behavior, they use external or situational attributions (self-serving bias).
- Ultimate attribution error is attributing positive behavior of members of an outgroup to luck or some other external cause, while attributing their negative behavior to an internal cause. The reverse occurs with one's own ingroup.

Test Your Knowledge

- Give an account of attribution or attributional style.
- Define the fundamental attribution.
- What is self-serving bias?
- Explain the ultimate attribution error.

Critical Thinking Questions

- How can attributional style help or prevent learning from mistakes?
- How do you view attributional style in different mental disorders, is it a transient state or a permanent trait?

Attitudes and Attitude Change

Attitude is a learned tendency to evaluate some object, person, event, or issue in a particular way (Krosnick, Judd, & Wittenbrink, 2005; Olson & Zanna, 1993). Such evaluations may be positive or negative, but they can be ambivalent, e.g., one might have mixed feelings and thoughts about a particular person or issue (Ajzen, 2001). Attitudes can be explicit or implicit. Explicit attitudes are those that people are consciously aware of and that clearly influence their behaviors and beliefs. Implicit attitudes are unconscious, but still have an effect on people's beliefs and behaviors. Attitudes are suggested to have cognitive, affective, and behavioral components (Banaji & Heiphetz, 2010):

- *Cognitive component*: this is the set of thoughts and beliefs about a person, group or object.
- *Affective component*: feelings toward the person, object, issue or object.
- *Behavioral component*: how the attitude influences behavior. Contrary to the intuition that attitudes tend to guide behavior, social psychologists have consistently found that

people do not always act in accordance with their attitudes, e.g., a student who disapproves of cheating, may glance at a classmate's exam paper when the opportunity presents itself. Attitudes are likely to influence behavior when:

- One anticipates a favorable outcome or response from others for behaving that way.
- The attitudes are extreme or are frequently expressed (Ajzen, 2001).
- The attitudes were formed through personal experience (Fazio, 1990).
- Being an expert in the subject and having extensive working knowledge (Wood, Rhodes, & Bick, 1995).
- People act in a consistent way on important issues of high hedonic relevance (Lehman & Crano, 2002).

Factors other than attitudes that may influence behavior include: personality traits, personal abilities, motivation, habits, needs, and social pressure.

Theories of Attitude Formation and Change

A lot of theories have been put forward to explain the development and acquisition of attitudes and consequently may also be considered in attitude change:

- *Functional theory*: this is proposed by Daniel Katz and suggests that attitudes are determined by the functions they serve for us (Katz, 1960). People hold given attitudes because these attitudes help them to achieve certain goals. Katz distinguishes four types of psychological functions that attitudes perform:
  - Instrumental: people develop favorable attitudes toward things that aid or reward them. Katz suggests that people develop attitudes that help them to maximize rewards and minimize penalties. People are more likely to change their attitudes if doing so allows them to fulfill their goals or avoid undesirable consequences.
  - Knowledge: people usually seek some degree of order, clarity, and stability that provides a personal frame of reference in their life. Attitudes provide people with such standards of evaluation. Via attitudes, such as stereotypes, people can bring order and clarity to the complexities of human life.
  - Value-expressive: attitudes help to express basic values, and to reinforce self-image, e.g., if you view yourself as liberal, you can reinforce that image by adopting liberals' beliefs and values.
  - Ego-defensive: Some attitudes serve to protect people from acknowledging basic truths about themselves or the harsh realities of life. Thus, attitudes serve as defense mechanisms, e.g., those who have feelings of inferiority may develop an attitude of superiority.

  According to Katz, an attitude changes when it no longer serves its function and the individual feels blocked or frustrated. That is, according to Katz, attitude change may not be achieved by changing a person's information or perception about an object, but rather by changing the person's underlying motivational and personality needs.
- *Learning theory*: attitudes are acquired by learning, which can occur through:
  - Classical conditioning: advertisers usually use classical conditioning to influence customers' attitude toward a particular product. In a television commercial, an attractive and appealing imagery of young beautiful people having fun on a tropical beach while enjoying a soft drink is used to develop a positive association with this particular beverage.

- Operant conditioning: behaviors or attitudes that are followed by positive consequences are reinforced and are more likely to be repeated than behaviors and attitudes that are followed by negative consequences, e.g., asking a young man who has just started smoking to stop smoking or to leave their vicinity whenever he lights up a cigarette, this negative feedback from those around him may eventually cause him to develop an unfavorable opinion about smoking and give up the habit.
- Observational learning: some people adopt a particular attitude because it is modeled by a person they love, e.g., children spend a great deal of time observing the attitudes of their parents and usually begin to demonstrate similar positions.

- *Cognitive consistency theories*: these hypothesize that, if inconsistencies develop among cognitions, people are motivated to restore harmony. To minimize cognitive dissonance, people tend to emphasize positive aspects of what they choose, while downgrading other alternatives (as discussed on pp. 200–203).
- *Self-perception theory*: Daryl Bem (1967) suggested that while people are not quite sure about their attitudes, they look at their own behavior under particular circumstances and then infer what attitude they should adopt. This process makes their attitudes consistent with their behavior, but the process is not driven by tension or discomfort, e.g., if you prefer Coca-Cola, while you are drinking Pepsi, this self-perception may drive an attitude change toward Pepsi even when you did not experience much dissonance. However, when attitudes are strong and clearly defined and the inconsistency between attitudes and behaviors is greater and more important to a person's self-concept, attitude change appears to occur mainly because of cognitive dissonance (Dunning, 2001).

Attitude Change

People usually unconsciously resist personal and environmental change because of uncertainty and fear about the safety and well-being of the consequences of change. Attitude changes can occur suddenly or slowly. Some are predicted, and others come without warning. People have a better chance of adjusting to changes if they know what will change in advance, and how changes will affect them. This suggests the value of planning voluntary changes and discussing the plan with all the people affected. Even planned change causes temporary anxiety and stress, while unplanned change can cause more stress. However, attitude changes affect different people differently, some people can adapt to change and resume their balance faster than others. This may be linked to differences in age, gender, values, personality, and prior experience.

Attitude change can be voluntary (intentional) or imposed. Voluntary changes usually aim to reduce or prevent discomfort, and to gain security and pleasure. Some changes require grieving, and others do not. The former involve losing physical or virtual things to which one is bonded or attached. Some changes occur in clusters, and others happen alone. Buying a new car or TV has fewer effects on family than changing jobs or careers, conceiving a baby, or moving to a new home or city. Adults and kids are at the highest risk of significant stress if they are subjected to unplanned major changes. Multiple small concurrent changes or losses can be as stressful as a major change. Too many losses at once can overwhelm even the most resilient, grounded child or adult. Also, immaterial changes can cause just as much stress as physical ones.

The effects of personal and family changes vary between predictable and unexpected. The effects of unexpected shifts usually take longer to adapt to than predictable changes like choosing a new school or family church. This is partly because adapting can start before the actual change. There is a difference between freely chosen changes, and those that are imposed by others. The latter can add hurt, resentment, and anger to the normal mix of emotional changes that need to be felt, expressed, and released. There are two levels of personal change: superficial changes, and deep changes. Superficial changes involve behavioral shifts, and represent transient adjustment to a situation to achieve a desired result. Deep changes occur after changes of core values or attitudes.

Factors Moderating Attitude Change

Attitude change is not always an easy process. Although factors that influence attitude formation, particularly cognitive dissonance and self-perception can contribute to attitude change, these factors are not very effective at changing existing ones, e.g., if someone is strongly against using a seat belt during driving, that attitude is unlikely to change, no matter how often this person sees others using it (Crano & Prislin, 2006). Attitude change usually necessitates external persuasion (Gass & Seiter, 2007). Persuasion is any active and deliberate attempt to change attitudes or beliefs through information and arguments (Brock & Green, 2005). Persuasion can change an attitude through transmission of a specific message. In most cases, the success or failure of persuasion depends on the person communicating the message, the content of the message, and the audience who receives it (Albarracin & Vargas, 2010):

- *The person communicating the message*: people who are attractive and expressive, trustworthy, and expert on the topic are the most persuasive. Thus, television advertisements for medicines and medical services often present very attractive people playing the roles of physicians, and much better if they are both attractive and an actual doctor. Credibility and persuasiveness may be heightened when the receiver perceives the source as similar to himself or herself, and if the communicator appears to have nothing to gain if the audience accepts the message.
- *The content of the message*: the arguments in the message are important for persuasion (Greenwald, 1968). Strong arguments that appeal to emotions are the most persuasive. Other characteristics of effective messages include its effect on emotions, particularly on fear or anxiety: asserting clear-cut conclusions, providing a clear course of action that reduces fear or produces personally desirable results, and being backed up by facts and statistics (Aronson, 2008; Oskamp & Schultz, 2005). Advertisers usually use the mere exposure effect, that is, repeating the message over and over in the hope that multiple exposures will lead to increased persuasiveness. For this reason, politicians often make the same statements over and over during campaigns. It is also important to decide whether to deliver one-sided arguments or to consider both sides of particular issues. One-sided arguments work best when the audience is on the speaker's side or is naïve.
- *The receiver of the message*: According to the elaboration likelihood model, persuasiveness leads to attitude change in two fundamental ways: the central and the peripheral routes (Cacioppo & Petty, 1986). The central route is used when people are both motivated and able to process information. That is, the central route is used by people who can pay attention to arguments, consider information, and use rational cognitive processes. This route leads to strong attitudes that last over time and people actively defend. The peripheral route is used when people are unmotivated or unable to process information or the message. Peripheral cues, such as the attractiveness or status of the person making the argument, influence which attitude will be adopted. This route may lead to impulsive actions, as when a person decides to purchase a product because a celebrity has recommended it or because of an advert for that product. Attitudes

adopted through the peripheral route are weaker and more likely to change over time. Several factors may play a role whether choosing either central or peripheral route, e.g.,

■ Personal involvement with the content of the message is one important factor; the more a topic is personally related, the more likely it is that the central route will be activated (Bohner, Erb, & Siebler, 2008).

■ Cognitive preoccupation: If you are preoccupied about other things while a message is being delivered, you will be unable to pay much attention to its content. In this case, activation of the peripheral route becomes more likely.

■ Personality characteristics: people who like to engage in thoughtful mental activities are more likely to use the central route to attitude change (Suedfeld & Tetlock, 2001). In contrast, people whose discomfort with uncertainty creates a need for conclusion are more likely to use the peripheral route (Cacioppo, Petty, Feinstein, Jarvis, & Blair, 1996).

Types of Persuasion Strategies

Choosing a persuasive strategy depends on the purpose of the argument, and the characteristics of the audience, including the audience's core values, beliefs, and the level of knowledge they already have about the subject you are addressing. The following is a summary of some common strategies.

For people using the central route, the use of logic is the most suitable strategy, where reasoning is used to convince the audience of a certain perspective. Arguments based on logic usually employ deductive and/or inductive reasoning. Deductive (or top-down) reasoning applies a general rule to draw a conclusion about a specific case or cases. In other words, deductive reasoning starts with applying a theory to a hypothesis and collects observations to confirm or dispute such a hypothesis. Inductive (or bottom-up) reasoning constructs a premise or rule by generalizing and inferring from a specific case or cases. In other words, inductive reasoning starts by collecting observations to formulate a hypothesis that is explored before forming a theory. Statistics are sometimes used to support an argument with a different sort of evidence.

For people using the peripheral route, Robert Cialdini (2009) described ethos, pathos, and many other strategies:

1. *Ethos*: this relies on the power and authority of the speaker. Ethos stresses the personal credibility and reputation of the speaker/writer, or citing reliable authors or sources. The most effective ethos develops from what is stated, whether it is in spoken or written form. Writers and speakers who employ ethos to strengthen their argument should avoid attacking or insulting an opponent or an opposing viewpoint. Ethos is usually used, not to convince, but to fasten the already established rightness of their cause in the minds of their listeners.

2. *Pathos*: this relies on evoking an emotional reaction from the audience, e.g., describing the difficult situation of people affected by certain issue. Thus, the success of the argument depends on a good understanding of the audience's values and beliefs, and manipulating them. This necessitates carefully choosing words and suggestions that have a subconscious effect on the reader or listener.

3. *Liking and similarity*: people are more successful at persuading you if you like them or see them as similar to yourself. Knowing this, salespeople, politicians, and others try to emphasize the ways in which they are similar to you.

4. *Social proof or social validation*: people tend to do what others are doing, so significant influencing is to show people that many others are doing what you want them

to do, e.g., some hotels try to influence guests to agree to use towels more than once instead of replacing them daily. A typical message in the room points out that reusing towels saves energy, reduces the use of detergents, and contributes to protecting the environment. Researchers found that more guests agree to reuse their towels if the message adds that most other guests using this room have agreed to reuse their towels (Goldstein, Cialdini, & Griskevicius, 2008). Informational influence, social comparison theory, and pluralistic ignorance explain this tendency to use other people as a standard.

5. *Reciprocation*: the reciprocity principle suggests that our behavior toward others tends to be similar to their behavior toward us. In other words, if you do me a favor, then I owe you one, e.g., if you are walking across campus and some people give you a cookie and then ask you to donate to their campus group, you may donate because you have received a cookie, even if you did not ask for it. Similarly, many companies donate free samples, confident that many of those who accept the samples will feel obliged to do something in return.

6. *The door-in-the-face effect*: Robert Cialdini coined the term the door-in-the face effect to describe the tendency for a person who has refused a major request to agree to a smaller request. In other words, after a person has refused a major request, he or she may be more willing to comply with a lesser request. This strategy works because a person who refuses a large request appears to have given up something. In response, many people feel that they must repay by giving in to the smaller request (Cialdini & Goldstein, 2004), e.g., when a neighbor asks you to pick up his mail, feed his dogs, water his plants, and trim his yard while he is out of town for a month. This is quite a major request, one that most people will refuse. If the same neighbor returns the next day and asks if you could pick up his mail while he is gone, there is more chance that you will accept this request, even if you have originally refused.

7. *That is not all technique*: this involves improving the terms of an initial request without even waiting for a refusal. In this technique, someone makes an offer and then improves the offer before you have a chance to reply. People who hear the first offer followed by the improved offer are more likely to comply than are people who hear the improved offer from the start (Burger, 1986).

8. *The foot-in-the-door technique*: this involves making a small request and then making a related larger request; a person who first agrees to a small request is later more likely to comply with a larger demand (Pascual & Guéguen, 2005). The foot-in-the-door technique is based on the commitment and consistency principle which suggests that people do not like to be self-contradictory. Once they commit to an idea or behavior, they are averse to changing their minds without good reason. However, cultural differences revealed that this tendency was strong for Americans, but weak for Chinese (Petrova, Cialdini, & Sills, 2007).

9. *The bait-and-switch technique*: this technique involves attracting people with a desirable offer and then switching them to a related offer that has additional demands and is more profitable, e.g., a car dealer offers you an exceptionally good price on a new car and a considerable price for the exchange of your old car, which is too good to resist. After committing yourself to buying this car, the dealer checks with his boss, who rejects the deal. The salesperson asks you to excuse that he forgot that this car has some special features that raise the price, and they will lose money if you buy it at the first specified price. When you agree to the higher price, the company corrects the trade-in value of your old car to a lower amount after inspection by a used car spe-

cialist. Still, you feel committed to buying the car, so you do not back out. Finally, you leave with a new deal that you might not have accepted if you had known it at the start. Similarly, a salesperson may offer a product at a very low price to get customers into the store but then claim to be out of stock and try to sell them something else.

10. *The lowball technique*: an actual agreement is made, but then hidden costs are revealed. A good example is the car dealer who convinces a customer to buy a car by offering an unrealistically low estimate that challenges the competition, then, once the customer is committed, the salesperson reveals that there is a processing fee and an inspection fee, and the car does not have a spare tire but you can buy a spare.

11. *The role of fear*: a fear message is an effective strategy of persuasion if people believe that their actions will be effective, e.g., a message about the dangers of influenza motivates people to get immunized. However, messages about global warming are very frightening, so people doubt that one person's behavior can have a significant effect, or the problem is hopeless, thus the message is ineffective (Cialdini, 2003).

12. *The scarcity principle*: a perceived limitation of resources will generate demand, and people tend to want them more. Advertisers usually use the scarcity principle during sales, where only limited number of a product is offered or the sale is for a limited period only. Such strategies make people eager to buy before they miss out.

13. *Delayed influence*: Some messages have little influence at first but more later, e.g.,
   a. The sleeper effect: this refers to delayed persuasion by an initially rejected message, e.g., if you reject an idea after hearing it from someone with poor qualifications. Weeks later, you may forget its source and remember only the idea itself. At that point, its influential impact may increase, and you may even claim it as your own idea if you completely forget its source (Kumkale & Albarracín, 2004).
   b. Minority influence: this occurs when a minority group proposes a valuable idea; the majority may reject the idea at first but reconsiders it later. If the minority continually repeats a single simple message and its members seem united, it has a good chance of eventually influencing the majority. The minority's influence often increases gradually, even if the majority hesitates to admit that the minority has influenced them (Wood, Lundgren, Ouellette, Busceme, & Blackstone, 1994). By expressing its views, the minority also prompts the majority to generate new ideas of its own and opens the way for other people to offer additional views (Nemeth, 1986).

Clinical Notes

Attitudes and beliefs about symptoms of mental health issues, perceived causes, and preferred treatment and help-seeking behavior differ among people and societies. Thus, a good understanding of personal and cultural points of view is an important issue in clinical practice.

Summary

- Attitude is a learned tendency to evaluate some object, person, event, or issue in a particular way. It is suggested that attitudes have a cognitive, an affective, and a behavioral component.
- Many theories attempt to explain the development and acquisition of attitudes. These include the functional theory, the learning theory, cognitive consistency theories, and the self-perception theory.

- Attitude change can be voluntary or imposed. Some changes require grieving, and others do not.
- Attitude change usually necessitates an active and deliberate attempt to change beliefs through information and arguments (external persuasion). Success or failure of persuasion depends on the person communicating the message, the content of the message, and the audience who receives it.
- Choosing a persuasive strategy depends on the purpose of the argument, and characteristics of the audience. the use of logic is the most suitable strategy for people using the central route, while ethos, pathos, and many other strategies are suitable for people using peripheral route.

Test Your Knowledge

- Define the concept of attitude and describe its components.
- Give an account of the theories of attitude formation and change.
- What are the factors moderating attitude change?
- Describe the types of persuasion strategies for people using the central route.
- Describe the types of persuasion strategies for people using the peripheral route.

Critical Thinking Question

How can you implement a strategy to change attitudes about mental illness?

Aggression

Aggression refers to any behavior whose intent is to harm another person (Bushman & Huesmann, 2010). Aggression is expressed in a countless number of behaviors that involve the intention to harm another, whether physical or verbal in nature. Thus, although significant pain and distress may be caused by extracting a tooth, this is not aggressive behavior, as there is no intent to harm.

PHOTO 16.4. Aggression.

Aggression is increasing worldwide, and murders have become a leading cause of death in some countries. In the USA, 31.5 percent of women and 27.5 percent of men have experienced physical violence by an intimate partner in their lifetime; of those, 22.3 percent of women, and 14 percent of men experience an act of severe violence (Breiding, Smith, Basile, Walters, & Chen, 2014). Among children aged 2–17 years old, the minimum prevalence of past-year violence approached or exceeded 50 percent for Africa, Asia, and Northern America, and exceeded 30 percent for Latin America (Hillis et al., 2016). Aggression is generally divided into instrumental and hostile aggression:

- *Instrumental aggression*: this is often referred to as "predatory or goal-oriented aggression" and is characterized by being goal-oriented, planned, or controlled behavior. In instrumental aggression, harming the person is used to obtain some other goal, such as money, e.g., killing someone to steal money, or a soldier killing a suspect. Instrumental aggression often involves systematic thinking about the situation, as opposed to an immediate emotional reaction.
- *Hostile aggression* (also known as affective or retaliatory aggression): this is accompanied by strong emotions, particularly anger, e.g., hitting or shouting at someone who has upset you, or murdering out of rage. It is characterized by being impulsive, unplanned, and uncontrolled. Harming the other person is the goal. Hostile aggression can involve both immediate reactions in blind rage, or carefully planned and deliberate acts.

Gender Differences in Aggression

Males are historically believed to be generally more physically aggressive than females, and men commit the majority of murders in the United States. This is one of the most evidenced behavioral gender differences, and it has been found across many different age groups and cultures. Males are quicker to feel aggression and more likely than females to express their aggression physically. When considering indirect forms of aggression, such as relational aggression and social rejection, some scientists argue that females can be quite aggressive, although female aggression is often expressed less physically. The approaches that women use to express aggression vary from culture to culture. Whether this gender difference in aggression is a result of nature (such as biology, genetics, or hormonal differences) or nurture (such as gender roles and socialization) continues to be debated.

Theories Explaining Aggression

The emergence of aggressive behavior is thought to reflect the interplay of nature and nurture (Bushman & Huesmann, 2010). No equation can predict when people will be aggressive, but studies suggest a number of biological, psychological, and social-cultural and environmental factors combine in various ways to produce aggressive behavior.

Instinctive and Evolutionary Theories

After World War I, Sigmund Freud recognized aggression as an instinct distinct from sexuality (libido) (see p. 38). He distinguished between the Eros (the life instinct), including sexuality, and the Thanatos (the death instinct). Freud proposed that aggression is an instinctive biological urge that builds up in everyone and must be released, either in the form of physical or verbal aggression against others. Sometimes, the aggressive impulse is turned inward and leads to suicide or other self-injuries. The aim of aggression (as with all instincts, in Freud's view) is to reduce tension or excitation to a minimum and, ultimately, to eliminate it completely.

Evolutionary psychologists argue that humans are naturally aggressive beings, having inherited a killer instinct from our animal ancestors, and that aggressive tendencies have been passed on through successive generations (Ferguson & Beaver, 2009). They consider aggression to be instinctive in all mammalian species and important in the evolutionary development of the species, as it allows individuals to survive and adapt to their environments. Aggression is clearly important in competing successfully for limited resources, in defending territory, and for basic survival. However, evolutionary theorists themselves realize that nature alone cannot fully account for aggression.

Biological Mechanisms of Aggression

Genetic Influences

There is strong evidence of hereditary influences on aggression, especially in animals (Bushman & Huesmann, 2010). In one study, interbreeding the most aggressive members of a large group of mice for 25 generations led to breeding of animals that immediately attacked any mouse put in their cage, while continuous inbreeding of the least aggressive members of the original group produced animals that were so docile that they did not fight, even when attacked (Lagerspetz & Lagerspetz, 1983). Similarly, follow-up of human twins reared together or apart suggests that there is a genetic component of aggression in people (Vierikko, Pulkkinen, Kaprio, & Rose, 2006). However, other studies suggest the tendency to be aggressive is not necessarily inherited, instead, a person may inherit certain temperaments, such as impulsiveness or emotional over-sensitivity in social situations, that in turn make aggression more likely (Alia-Klein et al., 2009; Eisenberger, Way, Taylor, Welch, & Lieberman, 2007). Having a family history of antisocial personality disorder has been shown to increase the risk of development of conduct disorder, aggression, and antisocial behavior in children (Green & Kowalick, 1997).

The monoamine oxidase A (MAOA) gene controls the amount of the monoamine oxidase (MAO) enzyme that regulates the activity of a number of neurotransmitters, including serotonin and norepinephrine. People who have low MAOA gene expression tend to behave aggressively when provoked (McDermott, Tingley, Cowden, Frazzetto, & Johnson, 2009). Nielson et al. (1994) found preliminary evidence that a disturbance in coding for tryptophan hydroxylase, the rate-limiting enzyme in serotonin synthesis, correlates with impulsive aggressive behavior. However, there is no evidence that there is a specific genetic locus, and it is unknown whether a family history of violence signifies genetic transmission or learned behavior. Violence is likely a polygenetic phenomenon, with many genes acting in a coordinated fashion to produce an aggressive phenotype (Cadoret, Leve, & Devor, 1997).

Biochemical Influences

Both animal and human studies have linked lower levels of serotonin with higher levels of impulsive aggression (Carver, Johnson, & Joormann, 2008). People who commit impulsive violent crimes tend to have lower levels of serotonin than those whose crimes are premeditated (Bushman & Huesmann, 2010). Brown et al. (1982) recognized an inverse correlation between 5-hydroxyindoleacetic acid (5-HIAA) concentrations and a lifetime history of aggression, in patients with personality disorder. In one study, participants who were randomly selected to receive a selective serotonin reuptake inhibitor drug behaved much less aggressively in a competitive game than those whose serotonin level remained unchanged (Berman, McCloskey, Fanning, Schumacher, & Coccaro, 2009).

Subjects receiving drugs that increase norepinephrine activity in the central nervous system showed increased aggression. Additionally, beta (β)-blockade in rats, decreasing norepinephrine availability, initially decreased fighting behavior. When the β-receptors were up-regulated, fighting behavior returned. Gamma-amino butyric acid (GABA) may also have an inhibitory effect on aggressive behavior, although the evidence is inconclusive (Oquendo & Mann, 2000).

High testosterone correlates with irritability, assertiveness, impulsiveness, and low tolerance for frustration, qualities that predispose somewhat to more aggressive responses to provocation or competition for status (Dabbs, Riad, & Chance, 2001; Harris, 1999; McAndrew, 2009). Some studies showed criminals who committed violent crimes had higher levels of testosterone than those whose crimes were nonviolent. Murderers with higher levels of testosterone are more likely than others to have planned their crimes (Dabbs et al., 2001; Klinesmith, Kasser, & McAndrew, 2006). Among both teenage boys and adult men, high testosterone levels correlate with delinquency, drug use, and aggressive-bullying responses to frustration (Berman et al., 1993; Dabbs & Morris, 1990; Olweus, Mattsson, Schalling, & Low, 1988). Drugs that sharply reduce testosterone levels reduce men's aggressive tendencies. The effect of testosterone on aggression may have its significant and durable influence through its impact on early brain development. Children who were exposed to high doses of testosterone during prenatal development show more aggressive behavior than their non-exposed same-sex siblings (Cohen-Bendahan, van de Beek, & Berenbaum, 2005; Reinisch, Ziemba-Davis, & Sanders, 1991). However, testosterone changes may be the result rather than the cause of aggressive behavior. That is, the aggressive situation may change the testosterone levels. A number of studies have shown that testosterone rises just before athletic competition (Mazur & Booth, 1998). Testosterone remains high for the winners of competitive matches and drops in the losers (Booth, Shelley, Mazur, Tharp, & Kittok, 1989).

Drugs that alter brain functioning can affect the likelihood of aggressive behavior. Alcohol can substantially increase some people's aggression (Giancola, Duke, & Ritz, 2011; Giancola, Josephs, Parrott, & Duke, 2010). Police data, prison surveys, and experiments show that aggression-prone people are more likely to drink, and to become violent when intoxicated (White, Brick, & Hansell, 1993). The degree of aggression correlates with the amount of alcohol consumed (Wells, Graham, & West, 2000). Research on the effects of other drugs on aggression revealed that amphetamine stimulants do not usually make people more aggressive, but opiates (e.g., heroin and morphine) and some tranquilizers may do so (Taylor & Hulsizer, 1998).

Neural Influences

Imaging studies in violent individuals demonstrated a dysfunction in the temporal lobe activity, especially in the subcortical structures such as the amygdala, the hippocampus, and the basal ganglia. These regions are involved in fear and danger responsiveness, and they are dense in serotonin receptors, indicating that dysfunction in these regions may disrupt serotonin activity (Bufkin & Luttrell, 2005). Damage to the amygdala is suggested to produce defensive aggression, which includes heightened aggressiveness to stimuli that are not usually threatening or a decrease in the responses that normally inhibit aggression (Coccaro, 1989; Siever, 2008).

Studies of violent criminals revealed diminished activity in the frontal cortex, which plays an important role in controlling impulses. If the frontal lobes are damaged, inactive, disconnected, or not yet fully mature, aggression may be more likely (Amen, Stubblefield, Carmichael, & Thisted, 1996; Raine, 2005). Single-photon emission computed tomography (SPECT) and positron emission tomography (PET) imaging in violent individuals show deficits in either prefrontal or frontal functioning, suggesting problems in executive functions and interpreting environmental stimuli as threatening or safe (Bufkin & Luttrell, 2005). PET scanning of 41 subjects charged for homicide found significantly lower levels of glucose metabolism in the prefrontal cortex and corpus callosum, as compared to matched controls, also suggesting that the ventral prefrontal cortex plays an important role in the control of impulsive urges, including aggression (Raine, Buchsbaum, & LaCasse, 1997). Studies of people with personality disorder identified a significant decrease in glucose metabolism in the frontal cortex among those with aggressive tendencies (Oquendo & Mann, 2000).

Physiological Influences

Resting heart rate in young outpatients with antisocial personality disorder was significantly lower than controls (Scarpa & Raine, 1997), a finding that suggests under-arousal state among antisocial subjects. Also, abnormalities on electroencephalography (EEG) were found in 25–50 percent of violent criminals studied (Mednick et al., 1981).

Social Learning Theory

Social learning theory implies that aggression begets aggression. Thus, people growing up in nonaggressive cultures will be nonaggressive, while people who grow up in aggressive cultures, where aggressive models prevail, will develop aggressive responses, e.g., children who are physically abused, those who suffer severe physical punishment, and those who witness violence in the community, are more likely to be involved in fighting, aggressive play, and antisocial behavior at school (Bartholow, Sestir, & Davis, 2005; Margolin & Gordis, 2000).

Young adolescents who play a lot of violent video games see the world as more hostile, and are more likely to get into more arguments and fights, and get worse grades compared with nongaming kids (Gentile, 2009; Gentile et al., 2009). In addition to teaching new antisocial actions, media such as TV and video games may lower sensitivity to violent acts and disinhibit dangerous impulses that viewers already have, e.g., many TV programs give the message that violence is correct and acceptable behavior that can lead to success and popularity. This message can lower inhibitions against acting out hostile feelings (C.A. Anderson et al., 2003). Evidence consistently disconfirms the catharsis idea that expressing an emotion can keep it from "building up." Aggressing or witnessing aggression does not make people feel calmer, but may even make them more angry. People with extensive experience in violent video gaming display desensitization to violence, as shown by blunted brain responses, they also are less likely to help an injured victim (Bartholow, Bushman, & Sestir, 2006; Bushman & Anderson, 2009). In summary, social learning theorists assume that aggression is aggravated by watching it through short-term and long-term processes:

- Short-term effects include priming of already existing cognitions or scripts for behavior, immediate imitation of observed behaviors, changes in emotional arousal, and the misattribution of that arousal (excitation transfer).
- Long-term effects include modeling of behavioral scripts, world schemas, and normative beliefs, activation and desensitization of emotional processes, and educational processes.

Provocation of Aggressive Behavior

Social norms can either promote or restrain aggression. Because aggression is a potentially destructive force, almost all societies and groups have norms that regulate it. Group norms often promote aggressive behavior rather than restrain it. Models can reduce aggression, but can also send the message that an aggressive response is acceptable. A person's accumulated experiences, including culturally transmitted teachings, combine with daily rewards and punishments to influence whether, when, and how aggressive acts occur (Baron & Richardson, 1994; Bettencourt, Talley, Benjamin, & Valentine, 2006). In general, people are more likely to be aggressive when they are both physiologically aroused and experiencing angry or hostile thoughts and feelings (C. A. Anderson & Bushman, 2002). Factors provoking aggression include: the following.

1. *The frustration-aggression hypothesis* was originally developed by Dollard and his colleagues (1939). They proposed that aggression will not occur unless a person is frustrated. However, this hypothesis is too simple and too general, and ignores that frustration may produce depression and withdrawal rather than aggression. Leonard Berkowitz modified the frustration-aggression hypothesis by proposing that stress produces a readiness to respond aggressively, but aggression is displayed only if there are environmental cues associated with an aggressive response. The cues might be guns or knives, people arguing on TV, or other triggers. Neither stress alone nor the cues alone are sufficient to provoke aggression, it is the combination of both (Berkowitz, 1994, 1998).

2. *Aversive stimuli*: these produce discomfort or displeasure which can heighten hostility and aggression (C. A. Anderson et al., 1996; Morgan, 2005). These include insults, high temperatures, noise, crowding, pain, and even disgusting scenes or odors. Such stimuli probably raise overall arousal levels so that one becomes more sensitive to aggression cues (signals that are associated with aggression) (Carlson, Marcus-Newhall, & Miller, 1990). Aversive stimuli also tend to activate ideas, memories, and expressions associated with anger and aggression (Morgan, 2005). Cues for aggression may be internal (e.g., angry thoughts), or external (e.g., certain words, actions, and gestures made by others), e.g., a raised middle finger is an almost universal invitation to aggression in North America. Weapons serve as particularly strong cues for aggressive behavior (Morgan, 2005).

3. *Heightened arousal*: emotional arousal due to threat, trauma, and intense emotions can reduce people's capacity to process information carefully. It diminishes the ability to interpret social cues correctly, and to generate imaginative responses to conflict situations. These deficits increase the tendency to turn to aggression. Also, physiological arousal may increase the probability that one may act aggressively (Zillmann, 1988). This is explained by excitation transfer (i.e., arousal from one experience may carry over to an independent situation). Heightened arousal does not lead to aggression by itself; it is most likely to produce aggression when the situation contains some reason, opportunity, or target for aggression (Zillmann, 2003).

4. *Alcohol use*: this can diminish people's ability to think systematically. Alcohol plus anger or threat is a formula for aggression. Also, alcohol lessens people's concern for factors that normally restrain aggression.

5. *Time pressure*: when a decision has to be made quickly, an initial tendency to be aggressive may precede other alternatives.

6. *Social rejection*: throughout evolutionary history, rejection by the group has been analogous to a death merit, and therefore signs of rejection can activate defensive

mechanisms that include attacking those who are perceived to be responsible for the rejection (MacDonald & Leary, 2005). Feeling rejected and the desire for revenge have been identified as factors in many school shootings (Fox & DeLateur, 2014).

7. *Realistic conflict theory* argues that intergroup hostility, conflict, and aggression arise from competition among groups for mastery of scarce but valued material resources. Group aggression is facilitated by diffusion of responsibility, social contagion, social identity, and collective mentality leading to genocide.

8. *Threats to self-esteem* may lead people to act aggressively without thinking about the consequences. People who react aggressively to threats to self-esteem usually have low self-esteem, and probably have low resources to cope with frustrations. Thus, narcissists usually have a higher than average likelihood of committing aggression, because they have very high, but insecure and fluctuating, self-esteem. Also, children who have a cognitive bias that leads them to interpret ambiguous acts as intentional disrespect, are prone to become chronically aggressive.

Approaches to reduce aggression involve the following.

1. *Minimizing or removing the cues* that often cause individuals to commit aggressive acts. Some cues activate aggressive thoughts and feelings, making overt acts of aggression more likely, whereas other cues can decrease aggression.

2. *Avoiding provoking factors*: avoiding those that make it difficult for people to think carefully and can increase aggressive behavior, such as alcohol use, high emotion, or limited time to think.

3. *Promoting empathy with others*: empathy is incompatible with aggression. Aggression is easiest when victims are distanced and dehumanized. To avoid this, people should intentionally think about the fact that victims are still human beings, because similarity is a barrier to aggression.

4. *Reducing aggression in society*: school-based programs aimed at reducing aggression are generally effective, and the effects endure over time. It is useful to encourage cooperation; encourage careful interpretation and identification with others; try to find mutually acceptable solutions; and work together toward a shared goal.

5. *Reducing exposure to violent media*: elementary school children show less aggression when they decrease the amount of time they spend watching TV and playing video games (Robinson, Wilde, Navracruz, Haydel, & Varady, 2001). Parents can make a big difference if they limit total media time, closely monitor what children experience, show disapproval to imitating violent TV and computer game heroes, and discuss the social conflicts and violent solutions shown in the media, and actively seek media that model positive behavior and social attitudes and entertain children at the same time (Frydman, 1999; Gentile, Reimer, Nathanson, & Walsh, 2014). TV could be used to promote helping, cooperation, charity, and brotherhood in the same way that it has tended to stereotype and encourage aggression (Penner, Dovidio, Piliavin, & Schroeder, 2005). Many studies have shown that prosocial behavior on TV increases prosocial behavior by viewers (Hearold, 1987).

6. *Anger control*: teaching people to control their anger and aggressive impulses can help to lessen tendencies toward child abuse, family violence, and other destructive outbursts (Meichenbaum, Henshaw, & Himel, 1982). Anger control refers to personal strategies for reducing anger. A person is taught to define the problem and its possible solutions, and to select the best solution and assess its success.

Clinical Notes

Aggression or violence is not always associated with mental disorder. However, violent behavior is always a critical issue in clinical mental health services. It is difficult to reach a conclusive answer on whether psychiatric patients are more likely to be aggressive, or whether certain diagnoses can predict violent behavior. Whatever, early recognition of potentially dangerous situations is the most efficient way to avoid violence. Thus, routine assessment of violence potential is part of good clinical practice. The clinician must take into consideration the demographic, historical, environmental factors, and the clinical aspects of psychopathology that may relate to increased risk of violence. Risk factors for violence among psychiatric patients include the individual's history of violence, active paranoid delusions, hallucinations associated with negative affect, manic states, non-compliance with treatment, neurologic abnormalities, alcohol or drug intoxication and withdrawal states, history of abuse, and family violence.

Summary

- Aggression refers to any behavior whose intent is to harm another person. It is generally divided into instrumental and hostile aggression.
- Instrumental aggression is "predatory or goal-oriented" aggression and is characterized by being goal-oriented, planned, or controlled behavior.
- Hostile aggression is accompanied by strong emotions, particularly anger.
- A number of biological, psychological, and social-cultural, and environmental factors combine in various ways to produce aggressive behavior.
- Factors provoking aggression include the frustration-aggression hypothesis, aversive stimuli, heightened arousal, alcohol use, time pressure, social rejection, realistic conflict theory, and threats to self-esteem.
- Approaches to reduce aggression involve minimizing or removing the cues, avoiding provoking factors, promoting empathy with others, reducing aggression in society, reducing exposure to violent media, and anger control.

Test Your Knowledge

- Define aggression.
- Give an account of theories explaining aggression.
- Describe the factors that can provoke aggression.
- Identify the factors that may play a role in reducing aggression.

Critical Thinking Question

Is it possible to prevent aggression in the world?

Prosocial Behavior

Prosocial behavior is defined as any act that is intended to benefit another person. Helping can range from picking up dropped packages to donating a kidney. Closely related to helping is altruism, which means an unselfish concern for another person's welfare (Penner et al., 2005). Altruism is generally understood to be an intentional and voluntary act performed to benefit another person at a personal cost to the behaving individual (A. Smith, 2009; Staub, 1978). It involves doing things simply due to a desire to help, not because one feels obliged because of duty, loyalty, or religious reasons. Psychological altruism is contrasted with psychological egoism, in which helping others arises from a conscious or unconscious motivation to increase one's own welfare (pseudo-altruism). Thus, the underlying motivation is what separates altruism from pseudo-altruism. There has been some debate on whether or not humans are truly capable of psychological altruism. However, one could imagine a spectrum that ranges from genuine altruistic behavior to truly egoistic behavior.

Psychology helps us to understand the motivation behind helping behavior, and to recognize the core and peripheral mechanisms in altruistic helping. Also, psychology allows the identification of factors involved in promoting a truly caring society. Daniel Batson (2011) identified four major motives for altruism: (1) altruism to ultimately benefit the self (egoism); (2) altruism to ultimately benefit the other person (altruism); (3) altruism to benefit a group (collectivism); or (4) altruism to uphold a moral principle (principilism). The following is a summary of theories that explain why people care about others.

- *Evolutionary theories*: It may not seem reasonable to apply the evolutionary theory concept "the survival of the fittest" to helping and altruism because helping others at the risk of one's own well-being does not seem to be adaptive. If one dies while trying to help others, it is their genes that will survive. However, contemporary evolutionary theorists have introduced the concept of "inclusive fitness" to refer to the survival of one's genes in future generations (Hamilton, 1964; Kruger, 2003; West & Gardner, 2010). Because we share genes with our relatives, helping or even dying for our own child, a sibling, or a cousin potentially increases the likelihood that at least some of our genetic characteristics will be passed on to the next generation through the beneficiary's future reproduction (Rachlin & Jones, 2008). Group and kin selection theories have argued that natural selection favored groups over individuals through an increased likelihood of passing on genes successfully. So, kin selection or helping a relative survive may produce genetic benefits, in spite of the absence of personal benefits for the helper (Brown & Brown, 2006). Reciprocal altruism theory argues that natural selection favors altruism even among non-kin because of its long-term benefits.
- *Arousal-reduction model*: this suggests that the distress of another person creates unpleasant empathic arousal in the observer that motivates helping behavior to reduce the unpleasant arousal. The experience of guilt in response to suffering of others can be a powerful motivator to help. Several studies have shown that all other things being equal, the more physiologically aroused the bystanders are, the more likely to help someone in an emergency (Dovidio, Piliavin, Schroeder, & Penner, 2006).
- *Cost-reward theory*: in distinction from the arousal-reduction model, where empathic arousal motivates someone to help, the cost-reward analysis provides direction for the observer's actions. That is, people weigh the costs of helping versus not helping. If the costs of helping are low and the costs of not helping are high, the bystander will almost certainly help. However, if the costs of helping are high and the costs of not helping are low, the bystander is unlikely to offer help. This theory provides a framework for explaining research findings on the factors that affect helping. A number of factors influence the cost-reward decision for helping: these include, personality characteristics, environmental factors, and the bystander effect:
    - Personality of the helper: this plays an influential role in helping, some people are more likely to help than others. Those were found to have more empathy, more

concern about others, a greater sense of responsibility for their own actions, and a greater sense of self-efficacy. Empathic individuals usually estimate the costs of not helping as high, and people with a sense of self-efficacy usually rate the costs of helping as low (Penner et al., 1995). These patterns of cost estimation may partially explain why such people tend to be especially helpful.

- Environmental factors affect helping: people in urban areas are generally less helpful than those in rural areas (Dovidio et al., 2006). One study of 24 US cities found that the larger a city's size and density (the number of people per square mile), the less likely people were to help others. Helping was also much less likely in cities where stressful economic conditions were greatest (Levine, Reysen, & Ganz, 2008). Similar results have been found in cities in the United Kingdom, the Middle East, and Africa (Hedge & Yousif, 1992; Yousif & Korte, 1995). Stress makes people less helpful, as stressful environments create bad moods which make people less likely to help (Salovey, Mayer, & Rosenhan, 1991). A study of department store clerks found that those in a good mood were much more likely to help customers than those who were feeling bad-tempered (Forgas, Dunn, & Granland, 2008). A second possibility is that noise, crowding, and other urban stressors create too much stimulation. To reduce this excessive stimulation, people may pay less attention to their surroundings, which might include individuals who need help.

- *Social responsibility theory*: people feel personal responsibility for reducing others' distress. They are most likely to help if they identify a negative change in the victim's circumstance, and that this person is in need for help. The clearer the need for help, the more likely people are to help. This is basis for the social responsibility theory of altruism. Internal emotional states and external influences (such as aspects of the physical and social environment) can influence whether a situation is interpreted as negative. Positive internal mood states are more facilitating for helping behavior than negative mood states. Research suggests that the number of bystanders witnessing an individual's distress adversely affects the likelihood of someone helping the person in need. This is commonly referred to as the bystander effect. This phenomenon could be attributed to:
  - Pluralistic ignorance: each bystander looks to the others to see how they behave, lack of action by others is interpreted as it not being an emergency and no help is needed.
  - Audience inhibition: people do not want to look foolish in public by over-reacting to potentially safe situations.
  - Diffusion of responsibility: the greater numbers of bystanders decrease individual feelings of responsibility. When other people are present, people assume someone else will deal with the situation.

- *Empathy-altruism theory*: this states that psychological altruism does exist and it is evoked by the empathic desire to help someone who is suffering. People are more likely to help others in distress when they feel empathy toward them, even when the cost of helping is high or when exposure to the situation could be easily avoided, whereas those lacking in empathic concern avoid helping unless it is difficult or impossible to avoid (Batson, 2011).

- *Neurological reasons*: altruism activates reward centers in the brain. Neurobiologists have found that when engaged in an altruistic act, the pleasure centers of the brain become active.

- *Cognitive reasons*: while the definition of altruism involves doing something for others without reward, there may be cognitive incentives that are not obvious, e.g., we might help others to relieve our own distress or because being kind to others upholds our view of ourselves as kind and empathetic people. According to the negative-state relief model, all helping behaviors are motivated by the desire to relieve personal distress, whether or not it is caused by the presence of someone in need of help. But help will only be given if the personal distress cannot be relieved by anything else, such as walking away. This means there is no altruism, only egoism.

■ *Social learning*: altruistic behavior is facilitated by observational learning. Parental models have been proposed to exert the strongest and most prolonged influences on the development of altruistic behavior during childhood and this in turn serves as an internal reinforcement.

■ *Reciprocity norm*: the reciprocity norm refers to the expectation that we should return help to those who have helped us. Research shows that helping others is more likely to occur if there is a chance that they will reciprocate the help. People tend to be less cooperative if they perceive that the frequency of helpers in the population is lower. On the other hand, people will avoid or even react against those perceived to be uncooperative.

How Can We Increase Helping?

There is no absolute way to increase helping behavior, but a lot of steps derived from the theories explaining this behavior may pave this way, these include:

1. Increase models of helpfulness e.g., positive models in the media.
2. Reduce ambiguity and make the need for help more obvious.
3. Reduce concerns about competence to help, and reduce uncertainties of obstacles.
4. Teach moral inclusion: reduce the distinction of people as inside/outside our bounds of moral or ethical concern.
5. Educate about bystander indifference: this could reduce pluralistic ignorance and audience inhibitions, and increase personal responsibility and reduce diffusion of responsibility, e.g., reduce anonymity.

Clinical Notes

Research has revealed a link between prosocial behavior in children and adolescents, and outcomes in positive socio-emotional, health, and educational domains. From a preventive perspective, improving prosocial behavior may play a protective factor against behaviors that pose a risk for adverse health and educational outcomes.

Summary

■ Prosocial behavior is defined as any act that is intended to benefit another person, which can range from picking up dropped packages to donating a kidney.
■ Theories that explain why people care about others include evolutionary theories, the arousal-reduction model, the cost-reward theory, the social responsibility theory, the empathy-altruism theory, neurological reasons, cognitive reasons, social learning, and the reciprocity norm.
■ There is no absolute way to increase helping behavior, but a lot of steps derived from the theories explaining this behavior may pave the way.

Test Your Knowledge

- Define prosocial behavior.
- Describe the theories that explain why people care about others.
- How can we increase helping?

Critical Thinking Question

How can prosocial behavior be promoted in society?

Interpersonal Attraction

Interpersonal attraction refers to affinity with and liking for another person, e.g., friendship and romantic attraction. It is the basis for most voluntary social relationships (Berscheid & Regan, 2005). People like others who like them, this makes them feel good and respond to others warmly, which in turn leads others to like them even more (Curtis & Miller, 1986). Several factors influence an individual's attraction, these include reward, transference, physical proximity, familiarity, attractiveness, and similarity.

PHOTO 16.5.   Interpersonal Attraction.

- *Reward theory of attraction*: people like those whose behavior is rewarding to them, and they will continue relationships that offer more rewards than costs. When people are attractive, they are aesthetically pleasing, and their proximity can be socially rewarding. When people share our views, they reward us by validating our own.
- *Transference*: this refers to the tendency of clients to transfer their feelings and assumptions about a particular significant other, like their parent or spouse, onto their therapist. In a broader sense, it may be used to refer to the tendency to transfer feelings and assumptions about a particular significant other onto another one. In this sense, any time we meet a new person who reminds us of someone who has been important to us in our past, this may influence our perceptions and liking of the new person (Chen & Andersen, 1999). Thus, being reminded of someone who has been significant to us in the past automatically activates stored knowledge or schemas about that significant other. This, in turn, leads us to process information about the newly encountered person in ways consistent with the activated schema.
- *Physical proximity*: this means geographic nearness. It influences our choice of friends and even lovers; the closer people live to each other, the more likely they are to become friends or lovers. Marriages are not made in heaven, they are made in neighborhoods, businesses, churches, bars, and clubs. One reason proximity is important in promoting attraction is that it allows people to discover what they have in common. Another reason

is the mere exposure effect: the more often we come in contact with someone or something, the more we tend to like that person or object (Saegert, Swap, & Zajonc, 1973; Zajonc, 1968).

Nowadays, it is increasingly easier to stay in constant virtual contact through the internet, leading to more and more long-distance friendships and romances (Lawson & Leck, 2006; Ridings & Gefen, 2004). However, when researchers ask people who are about to go on a first date arranged by an online dating service, how much each person expected to like the person they are about to date and how much

PHOTO 16.6.   Physical Proximity.

the two of them seem to have in common, a few people's ratings go up, but more go down, and some go all the way to the bottom (Norton, Frost, & Ariely, 2007).

- *Familiarity*: People tend to like people who are familiar, a phenomenon referred to as mere exposure. This applies both to people and to things, such as products used in advertising (Matthes, Schemer, & Wirth, 2007). When listening to a particular song, eating a particular food, or reading a book several times, you often come to like it more. Research also suggests that mere exposure can cause people who are White to like Asian and Black faces more, even when the faces are presented subliminally (Zebrowitz, White, & Wieneke, 2008).

- *Physical attractiveness*: Being physically attractive can be an advantage for both males and females (Mehrabian & Blum, 2003). People who are physically attractive are generally rated as more attractive than average. This is a halo effect bias which is referred to as the beautiful-is-good stereotype. Basically, people act as if what is beautiful is good. Even characters in Hollywood movies tend to be portrayed more favorably if they are beautiful. An analysis of 100 top-grossing films from 1940 to the 1990s found that attractive characters were portrayed as morally superior to unattractive characters (S. M. Smith, McIntosh, & Bazzini, 1999). In addition, the matching hypothesis suggests that people tend to become matched with those who are similar in attractiveness. Thus, physically attractive people will tend to get paired up with other physically attractive people (Montoya, 2008; L.S. Taylor, Fiore, Mendelsohn, & Cheshire, 2011).

Physical attractiveness is an important basis for romantic attraction (Byrne, Ervin, & Lamberth, 1970; Sprecher & Duck, 1994), even at an implicit (unconscious) level (Eastwick et al., 2011). In a study of dating choices, physically attractive men and women were more popular (Green et al., 1984). In a study of speed dating, physical attractiveness was the strongest predictor of attraction for both men and

PHOTO 16.7.   Physical Attractiveness.

women (Luo & Zhang, 2009). However, the appraisal of physical attractiveness changes as you get to know someone, the reaction to his or her personality alters it. Someone whom you respect and admire seems more attractive than before, while others whom you find deceitful and cruel look unattractive (Kniffin & Wilson, 2004). Also, there are limits to the traits people associate with beauty, e.g., people do not expect beautiful people to be more honest or concerned about others (Johnson, 1991).

- *Similarity*: this includes aspects such as age, interests, attitudes, beliefs, and so forth. It is reinforcing to see our beliefs and attitudes shared by others. In everything from casual social contact to marriage, similar people are attracted to each other (Figueredo, Sefcek, & Jones, 2006; R. S. Miller, Perlman, & Brehm, 2007). Age, sex, and ethnicity are the usual similarity dimensions affecting friendships. Most romantic partners and close friends resemble each other in age, physical attractiveness, political and religious beliefs, intelligence, education, and attitudes (Eastwick et al., 2007; Laumann, 1969; Lee, Loewenstein, Ariely, Hong, & Young, 2008; Montoya, 2008; Rushton & Bons, 2005).

Intimate Relationships and Love

People who are attracted to each other usually become interdependent, i.e., the thoughts, emotions, and behaviors of one person affect the thoughts, emotions, and behavior of the other (Clark & Lemay, 2010). Interdependence is one of the defining characteristics of intimate relationships. Another key component of successful intimate relationships is commitment, which is the extent to which each party is psychologically attached to the relationship and wants to remain in it (Amodio & Showers, 2005). People feel com-

PHOTO 16.8.   Intimate Relationships and Love.

mitted to a relationship when they are satisfied with the rewards they receive from it, when they have invested significant tangible and intangible resources in it, and when there are few attractive alternative relationships available to them (Bui, Peplau, & Hill, 1996; Lydon, Fitzsimons, & Naidoo, 2003).

Love is more than just strong liking; many people like someone very much but they do not love them, and some feel passionate attraction for someone whom they do not particularly like. Research suggests that romantic love and liking are quite separate emotions, at least in the sense that they are associated with differing patterns of brain chemistry and brain activity (Aron et al., 2005; Emanuele et al., 2006). Although romantic love and sexual desire are often experienced together, they are associated with different patterns of physiological arousal (Diamond, 2004). Further, most theorists agree that there are several different types of love (Berscheid, 2010).

Cultural factors have a strong influence on the value that people place on love. In some cultures, marriage is a contractual or financial arrangement that does not always mean love. In the United States, the link between love and marriage has actually become stronger over time, and the vast majority of people believe that they should love the person they marry (Levine et al., 1995; Simpson, Campbell, & Berscheid, 1986).

Love is widely differentiated into romantic or passionate love and companionate love (Berscheid, 2011). Passionate love is an intense emotional state, marked by strong physical arousal, physical attraction, and deep emotional attachment. Sexual feelings are strong, and thoughts of the loved one intrude frequently on a person's awareness. The desire and attachment of romantic love often endure, but the intense absorption in the other and the intense feelings that characterize passionate love, typically fade. Companionate love is less arousing but psychologically more intimate. It is marked by mutual concern for the welfare of the other (Berscheid, 2010). The characteristics of companionate love are trust, caring, tolerance of the partner's flaws and idiosyncrasies, and an emotional tone of warmth and affection rather than high-pitched emotional passion. As a relationship continues over time, interdependence grows, and the potential for strong emotion actually increases. This can be seen when long-time partners experience intense feelings of loneliness and desire when temporarily separated or in the emotional hurt typically experienced by someone who loses a long-time partner. But, paradoxically, because companionate couples become so compatible and coordinated in their daily routines, the actual frequency of strong emotions is usually fairly low (Kelley et al., 1983).

In his triangular theory, Robert Sternberg (1997) suggested that love has three basic components: passion, intimacy, and commitment. Intimacy is the emotional component and involves closeness and sharing of feelings. Passion, the motivational component, consists of sexual attraction and the romantic feeling of being in love. Commitment is the cognitive component that reflects the intention to remain in the relationship. Sternberg suggests that combining these three components in different ways yields eight kinds of relationships. These include: (1) consummate love, the most complete and satisfying. This is the most complete because it includes a high level of all three components, and it is the most satisfying because the relationship is likely to fulfill many of the needs of each partner. (2) Romantic love involves a high degree of passion and intimacy but lacks substantial commitment to the other person. (3) Conjugal love is marked by intimacy and commitment without passion. (4) Fatuous love is marked by passion and commitment without intimacy. (5) Companionate love is marked by a great deal of intimacy and commitment but little passion. (6) Empty love is marked by commitment without passion and intimacy.

Sternberg advanced a duplex theory of love by pairing his triangular theory with a second one that focuses on love as a story. This second theory focuses on the idea that, at least in Western cultures, the success of a relationship appears to depend not just on its perceived characteristics but also on the degree to which those characteristics fit each partner's ideal story of love, whether it is that of a prince and princess or a pair of business partners. Vital ingredients of gratifying and enduring love relationships include:

- *Equity*: At the core of every type of loving relationship are mutually sharing self and possessions, making decisions together, giving and getting emotional support, promoting and caring about each other's welfare (Sternberg & Grajek, 1984). It's true for lovers, for parents and children, and for close friends. When both partners receive the equal proportion of what they give, their chances for sustained and satisfying companionate love are good (Gray-Little & Burks, 1983; Van Yperen & Buunk, 1990).
- *Self-disclosure*: the revealing of intimate details about ourselves: likes and dislikes, dreams and worries, and proud and shameful moments. Self-disclosure breeds liking, and liking breeds self-disclosure (Collins & Miller, 1994).
- *Positive support*: relationship conflicts are inevitable, but happy couples in enduring relationships moderate these conflicts through positive interactions (compliments, touches, laughing) rather than negative interactions (sarcasm, disapproval, insults)

(Gottman, 2007; K. T. Sullivan, Pasch, Johnson, & Bradbury, 2010). For unhappy couples, disagreements, criticisms, and insults are routine.

Clinical Notes

- Psychiatrists and clinical psychologists should be aware of the role of transference and countertransference in establishing and sustaining a therapeutic alliance. In clinical practice, transference refers to the way patients "transfer" their feelings from important persons in their early lives onto the psychoanalyst or therapist, while countertransference refers to the therapist's or clinician's attitude or reactions toward the patient.
- The purpose of a doctor-patient relationship should be strictly a therapeutic one. If this relationship deviates from its basic goal of treatment, it is called boundary violation and becomes non-therapeutic. In psychiatry, there is a likelihood of developing strong emotional bonds, as the therapeutic relationship is prolonged and many confidential personal matters are discussed. This may lead to non-therapeutic activity (Gutheil & Gabbard, 1993). It is unethical for a psychiatrist to have a romantic relationship with a patient or a key third party associated with a patient. A romantic relationship may discourage the patient and other family members from pursuing treatment with a trustworthy psychiatrist.

Summary

Interpersonal attraction refers to affinity to and liking for another person, e.g., friendship and romantic attraction. Several factors influence an individual's attraction, these include reward, transference, physical proximity, familiarity, attractiveness, and similarity.

Test Your Knowledge

- Give an account of factors that can influence an individual's attraction.
- Describe the factors involved in intimate relationships and love.

Critical Thinking Questions

- Evaluate the role of the internet in interpersonal attraction.
- Evaluate the effect of personal attraction and aversion in the clinical settings.

Groups and Social Influence

A group can be defined as two or more individuals that are connected to each other by social relationships. Social categorization helps people to do the following:

1. Simplify perception by grouping together similar experiences, thus one can pay attention to some stimuli while ignoring others, e.g., if one perceives a neighborhood as friendly, one can walk down the street without attending carefully to every look from bystanders.
2. Allow people to go beyond the available information, by inferring additional ones, e.g., recognizing a discussion as a bargaining session helps to infer that the participants

PHOTO 16.9.   Groups.

represent groups with conflicting interests, and that anger and verbal attacks do not necessarily signify personal hostility.

3. Help people know how to relate to other people and objects, e.g., one can tell secrets to people who are trustworthy, and remain tight-lipped in the presence of gossips.
4. Allow us to predict others' behavior, e.g., a friend will help us to change a flat tire.
5. Groups offer social support, resources, a feeling of belonging, and supplement an individual's self-concept.

The mental processes involved in categorizing other people are conscious in many social situations. However, social perceptions and evaluations are not always completely conscious or deliberate. In many situations, reaction to other people occurs spontaneously, with automatic social perceptions, categorizations, and attitudes. At least initially, these automatic evaluations tend to occur implicitly or outside conscious awareness. The term implicit cognition describes the mental processes associated with automatic, unconscious social evaluations, while explicit cognition refers to deliberate, conscious mental processes involved in perceptions, judgments, decisions, and reasoning (McConnell, Rydell, Strain, & Mackie, 2008). Groups tend to interact, influence each other, and share a common identity. Groups have a number of qualities that distinguish them from other aggregates, such as people waiting in line to get on a bus, these include:

■ *Norms*: groups are usually influenced by a number of unspoken rules of conduct that represent the standard for appropriate behaviors that are to be followed by the whole group members, called norms, e.g., saying thank you, shaking hands. The broadest norms established by society as a whole help in defining the normal or acceptable behavior in most situations. Comparing hairstyles, habits of speech, dress, eating habits, and social customs in two or more cultures illustrates how people conform to social norms. A degree of uniformity is necessary to interact comfortably; being totally unable to anticipate the actions of others in stores, schools, or homes would be frustrating and disturbing, and it would be lethal while driving on the highways.
■ *Roles*: implicit roles and expectations for specific members within the group, e.g., the oldest sibling, who may have additional responsibilities in the family.
■ *Relations*: patterns of liking, and differences in prestige or status within the group, e.g., family members, leaders.

Group Structure and Cohesion

Any group has two important dimensions: structure and cohesiveness (Forsyth, 2010). Group structure consists of the network of roles, communication pathways, and power in a group. Some groups are organized and have a high degree of structure, such as an army or an athletic team, while some groups may or may not be very structured, e.g., friendship. Group cohesiveness refers to the degree of attraction or the strength of desire to remain in among group members. Members of cohesive groups usually stand or sit together, pay more attention to one another, show more signs of mutual affection, and their behavior tends to be coordinated (Chansler, Swamidass, & Cammann, 2003). Cohesiveness is the basis of much of the power that groups exert over their members, e.g., therapy groups, businesses, or sports teams seek to increase cohesion because it helps people work better when together (Craig & Kelly, 1999; Marmarosh, Holtz, & Schottenbauer, 2005). Cohesiveness is particularly strong for groups with which a person mainly identifies (in-groups). In-groups are usually defined by a combination of prominent social dimensions, such as nationality, ethnicity, age, education, religion, income, political values, gender, sexual orientation, and so forth. People tend to exaggerate differences between members of out-groups and their own groups. They tend to attribute positive characteristics to their in-group and negative qualities to out-groups.

Social Roles

Social roles are patterns of behavior expected of persons in various social positions (Breckler, Olson, & Wiggins, 2006), e.g., the role of mother, boss, or student. Some assigned roles are not under personal control, e.g., being male or female, son, adolescent, or inmate. Achieved roles are voluntarily attained by special effort, e.g., spouse, teacher, or scientist.

Social roles allow people to expect certain behaviors, e.g., doctor, mother, clerk, or police officer. However, people may experience role conflicts, in which two or more roles make conflicting demands on them, e.g., a mother who has a full-time job. Similarly, the clashing demands of work, family, and school create role conflicts for many students (Hammer, Grigsby, & Woods, 1998; Senécal, Julien, & Guay, 2003).

Group Interactions and Social Influence

Many decisions are not made by individuals but by groups: members of a family jointly decide where to spend their vacation, and a jury judges a defendant to be guilty. Psychology is interested in studying how such decisions compare with those that may be adopted by individual decision-making. Social influence refers to change in an individual's thoughts, feelings, attitudes, or behaviors that result from interaction with another individual or a group. Gordon Allport suggests that the social influence affects people even when they are alone, such as when watching television. A lot of factors were found to govern decisions of a group and the individual in a group. The

PHOTO 16.10.   Group Interactions.

main areas of group interaction and social influence include conformity, obedience, reactance, minority influence, social facilitation, social loafing, deindividuation, group polarization, and groupthink.

Conformity

This is the tendency of an individual to adopt beliefs, attitudes, and behaviors of other members of the group, in an attempt to fit into this group. This is also known as majority influence. Conformity can occur in the presence of others, or when an individual is alone, regardless of whether others are present e.g., people usually follow social norms when eating or watching television. The identity of members within a group, i.e., status, similarity, expertise, as well as cohesion, prior commitment, and accountability to the group help to determine the level of conformity of an individual. Individual variation among group members plays a key role in the dynamic of how willingly people will conform. Conformity is usually viewed as a negative tendency in American culture, but a certain amount of conformity is adaptive in some situations, as is nonconformity in other situations. Kelman (1958) identified three broad varieties of social conformity:

- *Compliance*: this refers to public conformity, while possibly keeping one's own original beliefs independent, e.g., one may laugh at a joke because one's group of friends find it funny, but the individual does not find the joke funny. Thus, compliance is a change in behavior but not necessarily in attitude. It is motivated by the need for approval and the fear of being rejected. According to Kelman, the satisfaction derived from compliance is due to the social effect of accepting influence (i.e., people comply for an expected reward or punishment-aversion).
- *Identification*: this is conforming to someone who is liked and respected, such as a celebrity or a favorite relative. Advertisements that depend on a celebrity to market products are taking advantage of this phenomenon. However, there is no change in internal personal opinions.
- *Internalization*: this is the deepest level of conformity, where the beliefs or behaviors of the group become part of the individual's own belief or behavioral system, an internal (private) and external (public) change of behavior occurs. The individual accepts the influence because the accepted content is rewarding, e.g., when someone lives with a vegetarian and decides to become a vegetarian, because he or she agrees with their view.

A classic study of conformity conducted by Solomon E. Asch showed that people usually conform to the obviously wrong opinion of the group. Eight to ten college students were placed around a table, with the seating plan carefully constructed to prevent any suspicion. Only one student was actually a genuine subject for the experiment, the rest were confederates who were instructed to unanimously give the wrong answer. Asch arranged for the real subject to be the next-to-the-last person in each group to announce his answer so that he would hear most of the confederates' incorrect responses before giving his own. Most real students (37 of the 50) conformed to the clearly wrong answers given by the other group members at least once, and 14 of them conformed on more than 6 of the trials.

Factors Affecting Conformity to a Group

Asch conducted further experiments in order to determine which factor affecting conformity within groups, and he found that the following applied:

- *Size of the opposing majority*: in a series of studies he varied the number of confederates who gave incorrect answers from 1 to 15. He found that when just one other confederate was present, there was virtually no impact on participants' answers. The presence of two confederates had only a tiny effect. The level of conformity seen with three or more confederates was far more significant. Follow-ups to the experiments showed that, even if only one other participant disagreed with the confederates, the subject was more likely to resist peer effect; in this situation, only 5–10 percent of the participants conformed to the rest of the group.
- *Informational social influence*: driven by the desire to be right, people see others as valid sources of information. In situations when they are unsure of the situation or lack knowledge, people look to others for confirmation, assuming that others may have more information than them and it seems right to follow their lead, e.g., when someone goes to a party for the first time, where he or she does not know about its protocol, he or she may look at people nearby to see what they are doing. The more difficult the task, the greater the conformity.
- *Consensus*: a person is more likely to conform when there is agreement among all the members of the groups. The presence of just one person that goes against the majority choice can reduce conformity (Asch, 1951).
- *Normative social influence*: driven by the desire to be liked and accepted by the group, people conform because they want to fit in and be accepted. People conform even when they know the group is wrong, e.g., a person may feel pressure to smoke or drink like the rest of their friends. But normative social influence is not simply pressure to conform; the group usually provides a frame of reference for its members, a context within which they can re-evaluate their positions.
- *Conformity to social roles*: there is considerable pressure to conform to the expectations of a social role played as members of a social group (e.g., student, teacher, policeman, etc.).
- *Emotion and disposition*: these may affect an individual's likelihood of conformity or non-conformity. Fear increases the chance of agreeing with a group, while romance or lust increases the chance of going against the group (Griskevicius et al., 2009).
- *Social status*: conformity increases when other members of the group are of a higher social status. When people view the others in the group as more powerful, influential, or knowledgeable than themselves, they are more likely to go along with the group.

Obedience

This is a change in behavior that is the result of a direct order or command from another person. While conformity focuses on changing to fit into a group, obedience is a response to authority. Individuals are more likely to respond and comply with the requests of people who are perceived to be in charge or are seen as an authoritarian. While this is in part because of the dictatorial nature of those people, it could also be due to fear of punishments if compliance is not achieved (Fiske, 2010). The Milgram experiment, Zimbardo's Stanford prison experiment, and the Hofling hospital experiment are three particularly well-known experiments on obedience: all conclude that humans are surprisingly obedient in the presence of perceived legitimate authority figures. In the Milgram experiment, participants were told they were going to contribute to a study about punishment and learning, but the actual focus was on how long they would listen to and obey orders from the experimenter. The real participant was assigned to be the teacher and the confederate of the experimenter was assigned to be the learner. The real participants were instructed to give an electric shock to a person in another room for every wrong answer on a learning task, and the shocks increased with intensity for each wrong answer, although shocks were not actually given. If participants questioned the procedure, the researcher would encourage them to continue. All the subjects continued to obey the experimenter and to administer shocks even at shock intensities they believed to be 300 volts, while 65 percent continued to the highest level of 450 volts.

Factors Affecting Obedience to Authority Figures

Milgram's and other researchers' experiments revealed variable factors that affect the level of obedience, these include:

- *Agency theory*: this proposes that people obey an authority when they believe that the authority will take responsibility for the consequences of their actions. In Milgram's experiment, when participants were told that they had responsibility for their own actions, almost none of them were ready to obey. In contrast, many participants who initially refused to obey did so if the experimenter said that he would take responsibility.
- *Legitimacy of authority figure*: people tend to obey others if they recognize their authority as morally right and/or legally based. This response to legitimate authority is learned in a variety of situations, e.g., in the family, school, and the workplace.
- *Status and prestige*: to test the effects of reduced status and prestige, Milgram rented an office in a rundown building in Bridgeport, Connecticut, without mentioning Yale University, and placed a newspaper ad for people to participate in research sponsored by a private institution. Otherwise, all the other experimental procedures were identical to the original, that was had been performed at Yale University. Under these less impressive circumstances, the level of obedience dropped: 48 percent of the participants continued to the maximum level of shock, compared to 65 percent in the original study.
- *The behavior of other people*: in a variation of Milgram's study, two other participants (confederates) were also teachers but refused to obey. Confederate 1 stopped at 150 volts and confederate 2 stopped at 210 volts. The presence of others who are seen to disobey the authority figure reduced the level of obedience to deliver shocks all the way up to 450 volts to 10 percent (compared to 65 percent in the original study).
- *The behavior of the learner*: a reanalysis of data from Milgram's obedience studies (Packer, 2008) found that the learner's increasingly intense expressions of pain did not affect whether the participants disobeyed the experimenter, while the learner's request to be released from the experiment reduced obedience to authority.
- *Personality characteristics*: most of the participants in Milgram's original experiment were nice people who were influenced by experimental situations to behave in apparently antisocial ways. In a later demonstration of the same phenomenon, college students playing the role of prison guards behaved with aggressive heartlessness toward other students who were playing the role of prisoners (Haney, Banks, & Zimbardo, 1973). Students high in authoritarianism are more likely than others to comply with an experimenter's request to shock the learner (Blass, 1991).

- *Locus of control*: this refers to how much control persons feel they have over their own behavior. A person can either have an internal locus of control or an external locus of control. Persons with a high internal locus of control perceive themselves as having a great deal of personal control over their behavior and are therefore more likely to take responsibility for the way they behave. Research has shown that people with an internal locus of control tend to be less conforming and less obedient (i.e., more independent). Rotter (1966) suggests that people with internal locus of control are better at resisting social pressure to conform or obey, perhaps because they feel responsible for their actions.
- *Situational factors*: The Milgram experiment was carried out many times whereby Milgram varied the basic procedure. By doing this Milgram could identify which situational factors affected obedience.
  - Authority figure wearing a uniform: the uniform of the authority figure can give them status.
  - Status of location: the status of a location affects obedience. The high status of a location gave credibility and respect in the eyes of people, making them more likely to obey.
  - Proximity of authority figure: people are more likely to obey an authority figure who is nearby. If the authority figure is distant (e.g., ordering by telephone), it is easier to resist their orders.

Minority influence

Minority influence takes place when a majority is influenced to accept the beliefs or behaviors of a minority. Minority influence can be affected by the size of the majority and the minority groups, the level of consistency of the minority group, and situational factors (such as the luxury or social importance of the minority). Minority influence most often operates through informational social influence (as opposed to normative social influence) because the majority may be indifferent to the liking of the minority (Moscovici & Nemeth, 1974; Wood et al., 1994). Minority influence occurs when the minority behaves in the following ways.

- *Consistency*: Moscovici and Nemeth stated that consistent view of a minority is more likely to influence the majority than if a minority is inconsistent and changes their mind. Consistency should be synchronic (all members agree and back each other up), and diachronic (consistency over time).
- *Flexibility*: A number of researchers have questioned whether consistency alone is sufficient for a minority to influence a majority. They argue that the key is how the majority interprets consistency. If the consistent minority are seen as inflexible, rigid, uncompromising and dogmatic, they will be unlikely to change the views of the majority. However, if they are flexible and compromising, they are likely to be seen as less extreme, as moderate, cooperative and reasonable. As a result, they will have a better chance of changing majority views.
- *Commitment*: When the majority is confronted with someone with self-confidence and dedication to take a popular stand or view, they may accept his or her opinion.

Reactance

This is the adoption of a view contrary to the view that a person is being pressured to accept, perhaps due to a perceived threat to behavioral freedoms. This phenomenon has also been called anticonformity. While the results are the opposite of what the influencer intended, reactance is a result of social pressure (Brehm, 1966). It is notable that anticonformity does not necessarily mean independence. In many studies, reactance manifests itself in a deliberate rejection of an influence, even if the influence is clearly correct (Frager, 1970).

Social facilitation

This refers to an improvement in the performance of a task produced by the mere presence of others, e.g., the presence of an audience may facilitate a subject's multiplication performance. Social psychologists offered a number of explanations to social facilitation, these include:

■ *Activation theory*: Robert Zajonc found that in the presence of others, people can perform simple tasks with greater accuracy than when they were alone. However, when people attempt to perform more complex tasks or tasks which they are not familiar with, they complete it with less accuracy in the presence of others than when alone. Zajonc proposed that the presence of others serves as a source of arousal, which increases the likelihood of an organism to do better on simple, well-learned or habitual responses, but impairs performance on complex, or not well-learned tasks. Zajonc's explanation is based on Yerkes-Dodson's law, which holds that arousal enhances performance within limits. Once arousal exceeds the optimal level, performance begins to diminish. The presence of other people arouses and increases drive level, and so an individual's performance will be enhanced if a task is simple but degenerates if the task is complex.

■ *Evaluation approach*: this assumes that it is not the presence of other people that is important for social facilitation to occur but the apprehension about being evaluated by them (Cottrell et al., 1968; Henchy & Glass, 1968). Groups who feel their performance is being evaluated show more dominant responses than groups who do not feel being evaluated in the presence of others or those who are alone.

■ *Attention approach*: attention theories imply that withdrawal from some things is necessary in order to deal effectively with others. This approach takes into account the effect of distractions on social facilitation. Attention theories that explain social facilitation include:

  ■ Distraction-conflict hypothesis: Robert Baron proposed that distraction leads to arousal, so the presence of others always impedes performance on difficult tasks, but the number of distractions in the environment either improves or impedes the performance on simple tasks.

  ■ Overload hypothesis: this suggests that distractors lead to cognitive overload. When an individual is bombarded with excessive information in their working memory, individuals will do worse on complex tasks and better on more simple tasks. Performance increases on simple tasks because the performers focus their attention on the new stimuli. Performance decreases in complex tasks because the performers focus on the distracters, but also need to focus on the relevant stimuli that are characteristic of complex tasks, and they cannot handle all of the information they are being presented with.

  ■ The feedback-loop model: this postulates that when people feel they are being observed, they focus attention on themselves. In this state, individuals become aware of the differences between their actual behavior and the anticipated behavior. So, by the feedback-loop model, people do better in the presence of others because of this increased awareness about their behavior.

■ Capacity model: the presence of others does not cause problems in tasks that require automatic information processing, because the short-term memory is not required for automatic information processing, this leads to an improvement in performance quality. However, for tasks that require controlled information processing, the presence of others impedes the level of performance because the short-term memory is necessary to focus attention on both the audience, as well as the task at hand.

Social loafing

This is the tendency for people to exert less effort to achieve a goal when they are in a group, e.g., in a simple rope-pulling competition, participants are likely to exert less effort when pulling the rope in a group than when they are asked to pull the rope individually. Social loafing is typically absent when the group's task is personally meaningful or challenging or when the members of the group value each other. A group of close-knit friends who are working together are unlikely to experience social loafing because they do not want to let each other down. Social loafing is likely to occur due to the following:

■ *The free-rider effect*: this refers to the tendency of people to reduce their efforts when they believe that it will not affect the final performance of the group. Thus, individuals decrease their effort and contributions when they feel that their contributions do not matter, e.g., most citizens agree that voting in election is important, however, only a small percentage participate in voting and elections. An individual can feel insignificant in such a massive population, so people may not think it is worthwhile voting.

■ *Uncoordinated effort*: lack of coordination of individual activities and contributions to reach the maximum level of efficiency, e.g., people in a rope-pulling competition, invariably pull and pause at slightly different times, so their efforts are uncoordinated (Diehl & Stroebe, 1987).

■ *The sucker effect*: this refers to the tendency of people to try and avoid feeling like a sucker by waiting to see how much effort others will put into a group first, to estimate the possible effort to be done and to avoid doing all the work. If all the group members try to avoid being the sucker, then each person's effort will be significantly diminished.

Deindividuation

This refers to the point at which people lose their sense of individual identity or differentiation. Deindividuation includes a sense of belonging and friendship, and causes people to follow group norms instead of personal norms. When a person deindividuates within a non-destructive group, the benefits can be positive. However, deindividuation can be extremely emotional, which sometimes leads individuals to display aggressive behavior, and contribute to destructive group behavior. Most individuals would normally refrain from aggression because they do not want to be blamed for their actions. In situations, such as crowds, social restraints and personal responsibility are perceived to be lessened, leading to displays of aggressive behavior. Political oppression, mass violence, and bullying can all stem from deindividuation. The three most important factors for deindividuation in a group of people are:

■ Anonymity: being anonymous within the group leads to the feeling that one will not be found out.

- Diffusion of responsibility: diminished sense of responsibility for actions, and diminished fear of punishment.
- Group size: The bigger the crowd, the more deindividuation there will be, as a larger group increases the above two factors.

Group Polarization

This refers to the tendency of people in a group to polarize their views in a more extreme direction after group discussion. With group discussion, people make attitudes or decisions that are more extreme than the initial preference of its members, but in the same direction as the average of individual judgments made prior to discussion (Myers & Lamm, 1976). If the majority of members feel that taking risks is more acceptable than exercising caution, the group will become riskier after a discussion, e.g., prejudiced people who discussed racial issues with other prejudiced individuals became even more negative, but those who were relatively unprejudiced exhibited even more acceptance of diversity when in groups (Myers & Bishop, 1970). The group polarization effect is usually explained by informational and normative social influence (Isenberg, 1986).

- *Informational social influence*: members of a group are most likely to present points in support of the position they initially favor and to discuss information they already share (Stasser, Taylor, & Hanna, 1989; Stasser & Titus, 1985). Accordingly, the discussion will be biased in favor of the group's initial position, and the group will move toward that position as more of the group members become convinced. Interestingly, the polarization effect may occur, even when all participants are given an extensive list of arguments before the experiment begins, a finding that cannot be explained by informational social influence (Zuber, Crott, & Werner, 1992).
- *Normative social influence*: people compare their own views with the norms of the group. During the discussion, they may learn that others have similar or even more attitudes than they have. If they are motivated to be seen positively by the group, they may conform to the group's position or even express a position that is more extreme than the group, to be different from the mean, in the right direction and to the right degree (Brown, 1974).

Groupthink

This is a term coined by social psychologist Irving Janis. The desire of people in a group to keep harmony or conformity in the group, creates a pressure on its members to put their ideas and beliefs aside and adopt the group decisions and conclusions, regardless of their irrationality and personal inconvenience. Groupthink not only occurs due to negative reasoning, but results from the desire for a more cohesive group dynamic by avoiding conflict or controversy. Individuals consider that expressing loyalty to the group requires avoiding views which may be out of harmony with what the group has achieved consensus on. This is in distinction from group polarization in which the emphasis is on enhancing an opinion within a group.

Groups affected by groupthink ignore alternatives and tend to take irrational actions that dehumanize other groups. Information held by most members of a group exert a stronger impact on the group's final decision, while information or data that is only in the hands of a few members with novel viewpoints are ignored or rejected. Groups tend to mention and discuss information that is common to and known by all the group members. As a result, a group will likely spend most of its time reviewing the factors that favor the option supported by the majority, and will never discover any of its drawbacks, this is called the common knowledge effect (Stasser & Titus, 1987).

A group is especially vulnerable to groupthink when its members form a cohesive group, its leader is biased and exerts too much authority over group members, when the group is isolated from outside opinions, when there are no systematic procedures for considering both the pros and cons of different courses of action or clear rules for decision-making, and high stress, e.g., due to an external threat, recent failures, moral dilemmas, and an apparent lack of viable alternatives. Groupthink is especially dangerous when it comes to designing a project that is focused on creating an innovative solution to combat a tricky problem. With groupthink, the team may suppress nonconforming viewpoints and be less critical when evaluating ideas (Janis, 1972, 1982). Classic real examples of group thinking are:

- *The Bay of Pigs invasion (1961)*: soldiers trained and equipped by the US attempted to overthrow Fidel Castro's Cuban government. The Kennedy administration accepted Eisenhower administration invasion plan, but ignored questions and accepted stereotypes about the Cubans without questioning whether the Central Intelligence Agency information made sense.
- *The bombing of Pearl Harbor (1941)*: despite the fact that Japanese messages about the attack had been intercepted, many of the senior officers at Pearl Harbor did not take warnings from Washington, DC, about the potential invasion seriously. Those who did not take action believed that the Japanese would not dare to attempt an assault against the US because they would recognize the futility of war with the United States.

Clinical Notes

The influence of a group on the individual is used to induce a therapeutic change. The beneficial effect of support groups among people who share common problems, life transitions, or chronic medical diseases is widely declared. Different psychotherapeutic views can be followed to construct a group, including psychodynamic, cognitive behavioral, and interpersonal perspectives.

Summary

- A group is two or more individuals who are connected to each other by social relationships.
- Groups have a number of qualities that distinguish them from other aggregates. These include norms, roles, and relations.
- Social roles are patterns of behavior expected of persons in various social positions.
- The main areas of group interaction and social influence include conformity, obedience, reactance, minority influence, social facilitation, social loafing, deindividuation, group polarization, and groupthink.
- Conformity is the tendency of an individual to adopt beliefs, attitudes, and behaviors of other members of the group, in an attempt to fit into this group.
- Obedience is a change in behavior that is the result of a direct order or command from another person.
- Minority influence takes place when a majority is influenced to accept the beliefs or behavior of a minority.

- Reactance is the adoption of a view contrary to the view that a person is being pressured to accept, perhaps due to a perceived threat to behavioral freedom.
- Social facilitation refers to improvement in the performance of a task produced by the mere presence of others.
- Social loafing is the tendency for people to exert less effort to achieve a goal when they are in a group.
- Deindividuation refers to the point at which people lose their sense of individual identity.
- Group polarization refers to the tendency of people in a group to polarize their views in a more extreme direction after group discussion.
- Groupthink refers to the desire of people in a group to keep harmony or conformity in the group, creating pressure on its members to put their ideas and beliefs aside and adopt the group decisions and conclusions, regardless of their irrationality and personal inconvenience.

Test Your Knowledge

- Identify the value of social categorization.
- Describe the dimensions of a group.
- What are social roles?
- Define conformity and the factors affecting it within a group.
- Define obedience and the factors affecting it within a group.
- What is minority influence?
- Explain what is meant by reactance, social facilitation, social loafing, and deindividuation.
- What is the difference between group polarization and groupthink?

Critical Thinking Question

Knowing the processes that may influence a group, how can this knowledge be used beneficially or harmfully to influence people?

Prejudice

Prejudice is a common part of everyday life. The literal meaning of the word prejudice is prejudgment, this refers to any belief, whether positive or negative, that people hold about someone before they really know them, but in practice the term prejudice usually refers to negative attitude toward a person or a group, often of a different gender, cultural, or ethnic background.

Though overt prejudice has waned in most countries, symbolic or subtle prejudice remains. Although many people realize that crude and obvious prejudice is socially unacceptable; this does not stop them from expressing prejudice in disguised forms when they state their opinions. Consequently, modern prejudices find ways to rationalize their prejudice to seem justified and based on sensible arguments rather than raw prejudice. Prejudice comprises the three components common to all attitudes:

1. *Cognitive component*: stereotypes often lead to a positive or negative attitude toward an individual that are based only on membership of some group, i.e., prejudice (Maio, Haddock, Manstead, & Spears, 2010).

2. *Affective component* such as feelings of disgust, anger, hatred, hostility, and other feelings. The influence of affective component is shown by finding that (a) individual differences in emotional prejudice correlate with discrimination more than stereotypes do (Dovidio et al., 1996); and (b) affective reactions to gay men predict discrimination more than stereotypes do (Talaska, Fiske, & Chaiken, 2008).

3. *Behavioral component*: there is moderate relationship between prejudice and discrimination, which is comparable to the general attitude–behavior relationship (Fiske, 2004). Allport (1954) proposed five stages of discrimination:

   a. Antilocution: negative verbal remarks such as hostile and insulting talk, and racial jokes.
   b. Avoidance: keeping a distance but without actively inflicting harm.
   c. Discrimination: exclusion from housing, civil rights, and employment.
   d. Physical attack: violence against the person and property.
   e. Extermination: indiscriminate violence against an entire group (including genocide).

Though prejudice usually focuses on race and ethnicity, it can occur with respect to many different kinds of social groups. Prejudice can be based on sexual orientation, religion, gender, or age (Herek & McLemore, 2013; Newheiser et al., 2013; North & Fiske, 2013). Despite gender equality in intelligence scores, people tend to perceive their fathers as more intelligent than their mothers (Furnham & Wu, 2008). Worldwide, women are more likely to live in poverty (Lips, 2016), and they represent two-thirds of illiterate adults (UNESCO, 2013). In many places, sons are valued more than daughters. With testing that enables sex-selective abortions, several South Asian countries have experienced a deficit in female births. Although China has declared that sex-selective abortions (gender genocide) are now a criminal offense, the country's newborn sex ratio is still 118 boys for every 100 girls, and 95 percent of the children in Chinese orphanages are girls (Myers, 2008). Also, males under the age of 20 exceed females by 32 million, and many Chinese bachelors will be unable to find partners (Zhu, Lu, & Hesketh, 2009).

Older people were perceived more negatively than middle-aged or younger people when they act in unexpected ways, such as listening to old singers. Although younger people and middle-aged people could act in ways that were unexpected for their age, older people could not do so without consequences (North & Fiske, 2013). Older people do not have the same freedom to have the same range of interests that younger people have.

Theories of Intergroup Prejudice

Gordon Allport proposed that there are two important sources of prejudice: personal and group prejudice (Allport, 1954). Personal prejudice occurs when members of another social group are perceived as a threat to one's own interests, e.g., members of another group may be viewed as competitors for jobs. Group prejudice occurs when a person conforms to group stereotypes, e.g., you have no personal reason for disliking out-group members, but your friends, acquaintances, or co-workers expect it from you. There are several explanatory theories of prejudice, and each approach provides an important perspective to a better understanding of the causes of intergroup conflict and prejudice. The following are some possible explanations to prejudice:

Scapegoating

Scapegoating is a type of displaced aggression in which hostilities triggered by frustration are redirected at "safer" targets (Nelson, 2006). Prejudice may be a form of scapegoating, blaming a person or a group for the actions of others or for difficulties experienced in everyday life. Evidence for the scapegoat theory of prejudice comes from finding high level of prejudice among economically frustrated people, and from experiments in which a temporary frustration intensifies prejudice, e.g., when a group of young European Americans men at a summer camp failed in a difficult test and missed their weekly entertainment, attitudes toward Mexicans and Japanese ethnic groups were rated lower after being frustrated (Miller & Bugelski, 1970). Similarly, students who experienced failure or were made to feel insecure often restored their self-esteem by derogating an opposing or competing person (Crocker, Thompson, McGraw, & Ingerman, 1987). This is why a rival's misfortune sometimes provides a feeling of pleasure. By contrast, those made to feel loved and supported have become more open to and accepting of others who differ (Mikulincer & Shaver, 2001). Scapegoating was also observed following the 9/11 attacks in the United States, some outraged people attacked innocent Arab-Americans.

Personality Variables

The authoritarian personality is marked by rigidity, inhibition, prejudice, and oversimplification (black-and-white thinking). Authoritarianism is composed of three elements: (1) acceptance of conventional or traditional values; (2) willingness to unquestioningly follow the orders of authority figures; and (3) inclination to act aggressively toward individuals or groups identified by these authority figures as threatening the values held by one's in-group (Altemeyer, 2004; Altemeyer & Hunsberger, 2005).

Some researchers suggest that prejudice is more likely among people who display authoritarian personality trait. Adorno et al. (1950) proposed that people with an authoritarian personality are prejudiced and are likely to be hostile towards ethnic, racial, and other minority or out-groups. People with an authoritarian orientation tend to view the world as a dangerous place (Cohrs & Ibler, 2009), and one way to protect themselves is to identify strongly with their in-group and to dislike, reject, and perhaps even punish anyone who belongs to an out-group (Thomsen, Green, & Sidanius, 2008). Authoritarians also tend to highly value social conformity (Feldman, 2003) and hence to consider their own ethnic group superior to others, and place their own group at the center (ethnocentric), usually by rejecting other groups. In fact, authoritarians think they are superior to everyone who is different, not just other ethnic groups (Altemeyer, 2004; Whitley, 1999).

While authoritarians consciously and strikingly express the opinions held by their parents, they often reveal considerable latent (unconscious) hostility toward them, stemming from the extreme frustration they experienced as children. Adorno et al. (1950) proposed that such unconscious hostility may be displaced onto minority groups. Authoritarians may also project their own unacceptable, antisocial impulses (especially sexual and aggressive) onto these groups, so that they feel threatened by members of these groups. They have very little self-understanding and their prejudice can serve a vital ego-defensive function, as it protects them from the unacceptable parts of themselves.

Learning Theories

Like other attitudes, prejudice can be learned, thus the development of prejudice can be traced to direct experiences with members of the rejected group. A child who is repeatedly bullied by members of a particular ethnic group might develop a lifelong dislike for all members of this group. In addition, learning theories suggest that children can develop prejudices just by watching and listening to parents, peers, and others (Castelli, Zogmaister, & Tomelleri, 2009; Rutland,

Killen, & Abrams, 2010; Taylor et al., 2006). Subtle influences such as parents' attitudes, books, movies, and television programs that portray ethnic or other groups in ways that teach stereotypes and prejudice can have a significant influence (Jost & Hamilton, 2005). Many children show signs of race bias at age of three years (Katz, 2003). Unfortunately, once prejudices are established, they prevent us from accepting more positive experiences that could reverse the damage (Wilder, Simon, & Faith, 1996).

Group Membership

Dividing the world into groups can provide public harmony and cohesion, people cheer for their groups, kill for them, die for them. People define who they are partly in terms of their groups. However, dividing people into groups, into us and them, can cause prejudice. People tend to make favorable, positive attributions for behaviors of their in-group members and unfavorable, negative attributions for behaviors of out-groups members (this is called in-group bias). Members of in-group were typically seen as being fairly varied, despite having enough features in common to belong to the same group, i.e., people notice the diversity within their own group. On the other hand, people tend to see out-group members as nearly similar to one another, even in areas where they are obviously different from other members of the group. This tendency is called the out-group homogeneity effect.

An inevitable by-product of group membership is that it often limits contact with people in other groups. In addition, groups themselves may come into conflict. Both occasions tend to foster hate and prejudice toward the out-group. Daily news is full of tragic conflicts between political, religious, or ethnic groups. People are often prejudiced against groups that are perceived as an important threat to in-group norms and values (Esses, Jackson, Dovidio, & Hodson, 2005; Stephan, Renfro, Esses, Stephan, & Martin, 2005), e.g., a person might be extremely prejudiced against gays and lesbians because he feels that they threaten his in-group's precious values, such as a strong commitment to traditional sex roles and family structure.

Group Conflict

Shared beliefs concerning superiority, injustice, vulnerability, and distrust are common triggers for hostility between groups. People in a conflict with those in another group usually think they are superior to other group, but they have been unjustly exploited, wronged, or humiliated (superiority and injustice), and that other group is a threat to them (vulnerability). They consider the other group as dishonest and repeatedly deceive them (distrust). Hence, people are hostile toward them, and think that they do not deserve respect or cooperation (Eidelson & Eidelson, 2003). Victims of discrimination may react with either self-blame or anger (Allport, 1954). Either reaction can feed prejudice through the classic blame-the-victim dynamic. Theories that explain intergroup conflict include:

■ *Realistic group conflict theory*: this suggests that prejudice is caused by the perception of conflict between groups, e.g., competing for limited resources, such as food, jobs, or a championship. In a classic study, Sherif et al. (1961) arranged a summer camp for two groups of adolescent boys at Robber's Cave State Park. The two groups (the Eagles and the Rattlers) participated in a series of competitions (e.g., baseball, rope-pulling), with prizes (e.g., knives, medals) to be awarded to the winning group. Soon, the Eagles and the Rattlers began to dislike one another. They called each other insulting nicknames (e.g., stinkers, sissies), got into fights, and threw food at one another. The rivalry became increasingly hostile, the Eagles burned the Rattlers' flag. In response, the Rattlers damaged the Eagles' cabin. A matter that clearly demonstrates that intergroup competition can have negative consequences.

■ *Integrated threat theory*: this was originally introduced by Walter G. Stephan. It suggests that prejudice and negative attitudes toward immigrants and out-groups are explained by four types of threats: realistic threat, symbolic threat, negative stereotype, and intergroup anxiety. Realistic threats are concerned with the physical well-being and the economic and political power of the in-group; symbolic threats arise due to cultural differences in values, morals, and worldview of the out-group; the in-group has negative stereotypes about the out-group; and intergroup anxiety refers to anxiety experienced by the in-group in the process of interaction with members of the out-group, especially when both groups had a history of antagonism (Croucher, 2017). Riek et al. (2006) found that multiple types of threats predicted prejudice. Stephan et al. (2002) found that the most important predictor of perceived threats was negative experiences with the other group.

■ *Tajfel's social identity theory*: this explains intergroup behavior on the basis of perceived group status differences, perceived legitimacy and stability of those status differences, and the perceived ability to move from one group to another (Tajfel & Turner, 1979). It is closely related to our desire for self-esteem. Because part of our collective self-esteem derives from our group memberships, we want to see our groups favorably. In-group favor can enhance self-esteem (Verkuyten & De Wolf, 2007).

■ *Social inequalities*: the just-world phenomenon refers to the idea that goodness is rewarded and evil is punished. Accordingly, when some people have money, power, and prestige and others do not, they usually develop attitudes that those who succeed must be good and those who suffer must be bad. Such reasoning enables the rich to see both their own wealth and the poor's misfortune as justly deserved.

Reducing Prejudice

There is no single way or hypothesis that could lead to prejudice reduction. Multiple hypotheses have been postulated:

1. *Cooperative and on an equal status contact*: Allport (1954) proposed that prejudice can be reduced by equal status contact between majority and minority groups in the pursuit of common goals. Equal status contact refers to interacting on an equal footing, without obvious differences in power or status. The effect is greatly enhanced if this contact is guided by institutional supports (i.e., by law, custom, or local atmosphere). bringing groups into contact will reduce prejudice, however, certain conditions need to be met for contact to be most effective. When people are segregated, they are likely to experience hostility, because ignorance of others can result in failure to understand the reasons of their actions. Lack of contact means there is no "reality testing" against which we can check our own interpretations of others' behavior, and this in turn is likely to reinforce negative stereotypes. Bringing people into contact with each other should make them seem more familiar and offers the possibility that the negative cycle can be interrupted and even reversed.

   In one early study of equal status contact, Deutsch and Collins (1951) compared two kinds of housing project, one group was thoroughly integrated (black people and white people were assigned houses regardless of race) and the other group was segregated. Those in the integrated project showed a favorable shift in attitudes toward members of the other racial group. Those in the segregated project showed no change or actually became more prejudiced than before. Other studies concluded that personal contact with a disliked group will induce friendly behavior, respect, and liking. However, these benefits occur only when personal contact is cooperative and on an equal status (Grack & Richman, 1996).

In Sherif et al.'s (1961) study (discussed on p. 346), bringing the two groups of adolescent boys into contact without having them compete (e.g., going to the movies together, eating in the same dining hall, and so forth) failed to alleviate the hostility. It appears that once prejudice exists, simply removing competition is not enough. Sherif arranged circumstances where boys should cooperate to achieve common goals that are referred to as superordinate goals, e.g., working together to fix a problem with the water supply. On another occasion they requested a movie, but they were told that the camp could not afford it, then both groups contributed to get a movie. After a series of such joint efforts, the rivalry diminished and the intergroup hostility was reduced and the boys began to make friends. Thus, it seems that conflict between groups can increase prejudice, but cooperation can reduce it. However, other researchers questioned whether these results would apply to other intergroup situations, especially heterogeneous groups. A meta-analysis on the contact hypothesis suggests that contact is effective in reducing prejudice, especially when the groups have common goals, have equal status, and when the contact is guaranteed by authorities (Pettigrew, Tropp, Wagner, & Christ, 2011).

Elliot Aronson found that integrating public schools often has little positive effect on racial prejudice, and prejudice may even be worse, and the self-esteem of minority students frequently decreases (Aronson, 2008). The competitive nature of schools almost guarantees that children will not learn to like and understand each other. Aronson pioneered a way to apply superordinate goals in ordinary classrooms to create mutual interdependence. Aronson has successfully created "jigsaw" classrooms that emphasize cooperation rather than competition. Each child is given a "piece" of the information needed to complete a project or prepare for a test. In a typical session, children are divided into groups of five or six and given a topic to study for a later exam. Each child is given his or her "piece" of information and asked to learn it, e.g., one child had information on Thomas Edison's invention of the light bulb; another, facts about his invention of the long-playing phonograph record; and a third, information about Edison's childhood. After the children had learned their parts, they taught them to others in the group. Even the most competitive children quickly realize that they cannot do well without the aid of everyone in the group. Each child makes a unique and essential contribution, so the children learn to listen to and respect each other. Children in jigsaw groups are less prejudiced compared with children in traditional classrooms; they like their classmates more, they have more positive attitudes toward school, their grades improve, and their self-esteem increases (Aronson, 2008; Walker & Crogan, 1998). However, the imposition of superordinate goals may increase antagonism toward the out-group, if the cooperation fails to achieve its aims. When this does not happen, liking for the other group may actually decrease, perhaps because group members are concerned with the integrity of the in-group (Brown, 1988).

2. *Inhibiting stereotypes*: prejudice-reduction techniques have traditionally been concerned with changing conscious attitudes (overt racism) and obvious expressions of bias. However, because of its pervasiveness, subtlety, and complexity, conventional interventions and legal practices for eliminating racial bias are often ineffective for combating aversive racism. A major challenge is how to encourage and educate people to

be motivated to control their implicit biases. Patricia Devine (1989) suggested that people can override the stereotypes they hold and act in nondiscriminatory ways. Numerous studies have shown that people can consciously alter their automatic stereotyping (Blair, 2002), e.g., Dasgupta and Greenwald (2001) found that presenting positive examples of admired black individuals (e.g., Denzel Washington) produced more-favorable responses toward African Americans. In another study, training people to oppose stereotypes, as in pressing a "no" key when they see an elderly person paired with a stereotype of the elderly, led to a reduction of automatic stereotyping in subsequent tasks (Kawakami, Dovidio, Moll, Hermsen, & Russin, 2000). However, in everyday life, inhibiting stereotyped thinking is difficult and requires self-control (Monteith, Ashburn-Nardo, Voils, & Czopp, 2002). The following strategies may be effective in reducing stereotypes:

a. Learning: counter-stereotypic associations can be learned in a way that is similar to how stereotypic associations were learned. One can practice favorable associations with stereotyped groups (e.g., Black people are friendly), which is a more effective strategy than attempting to refute stereotypes (e.g., Black people are not violent), which can actually promote bias rather than reduce it (Gawronski, Deutsch, Mbirkou, Seibt, & Strack, 2008).

b. Implicit inhibition: just as stereotypes can be implicitly activated, they can also be implicitly inhibited. Egalitarian goals can actually inhibit the activation of stereotypes, because when one encounters a member of a stereotyped group, the egalitarian goal is activated rather than the stereotype (Moskowitz, 2010). This can occur whether egalitarian goals are long-term (Moskowitz, Salomon, & Taylor, 2000) or temporary (Moskowitz & Ignarri, 2009).

c. Self-regulation: even if people dispute, as is likely to occur sooner or later, self-regulation can reduce future prejudice. The self-regulation of prejudice model suggests that when people catch themselves being prejudiced, such as wrongly assuming that a Black man shown on the news is a criminal, this tends to elicit guilt and associations are formed about the event. Then, when a similar situation occurs, the activation of these associations encourages unbiased responses (Monteith et al., 2002; Monteith, Lybarger, & Woodcock, 2009).

3. *Perspective taking and perspective giving*: The perspective taking approach involves actively considering the psychological experiences of other people. Such an approach can reduce racial bias and help to smooth potentially awkward interracial interactions (Todd, Bodenhausen, Richeson, & Galinsky, 2011). Taking another group's perspective appears to reduce negative or positive stereotypes. In one study, participants who used perspective taking rated a typical construction worker to be smarter and more passionate and a typical doctor to be less intelligent and less passionate than did participants in the control group who did not engage in perspective taking and used their stereotypes to rate a typical construction worker and doctor (Wang, Kenneth, Ku, & Galinsky, 2014).

4. *The common in-group identity model*: Dovidio et al. (2010) suggest that aversive racism and in-group preference can be reduced by emphasizing a common identity (e.g., we are all university students) rather than a divided "us" and "them." This change from viewing people as "us" and "them" to categorizing them as a unified group is referred to as recategorization. Gaertner and colleagues (1989) found that when members of two groups were encouraged to view themselves as a single group, in-group preference was reduced, and the former out-group members were rated like in-group members. Using a similar procedure, Dovidio and colleagues (1997) found that participants assigned to two groups showed the typical in-group bias in that they were much more

helpful to in-group members than to out-group members. However, members of two groups who were encouraged to view themselves as a single group helped former in-group members and former out-group members equally. The beneficial effects of recategorization can work even for implicit bias. Van Bavel and Cunningham (2009) assigned participants to either of two groups (the Lions and the Tigers), each of which had six White members and six Black members, or to neither group. Whereas participants who were assigned to neither group showed implicit racial bias, members of the mixed-race groups showed implicit racial bias for out-group faces but not for in-group faces.

Clinical Notes

Prejudice against mental illness and mentally ill people is well known and is a principal cause of the stigma of mental illness. This prejudicial attitude leads to social distance, and discriminatory behavior toward persons with mental illness, which adds to their suffering. Stigma may involve also psychiatrists and mental health professionals, and may affect recruitment into psychiatry and mental health services.

Summary

- Prejudice usually refers to a negative attitude toward a person or a group, often of a different gender, cultural, or ethnic background.
- Prejudice comprises cognitive, affective, and behavioral components.
- Personal prejudice occurs when members of another social group are perceived as a threat to one's own interests, while group prejudice occurs when a person conforms to group stereotypes.
- Possible explanations to prejudice include scapegoating, personality variables, learning, and group membership.
- Shared beliefs concerning superiority, injustice, vulnerability, and distrust are common triggers for hostility between groups.
- Theories that explain intergroup conflict include the realistic group conflict theory, the integrated threat theory, Tajfel's social identity theory, and social inequalities.
- There is no single way or hypothesis that could lead to prejudice reduction. Multiple hypotheses have been postulated including cooperative and on an equal status contact, inhibiting stereotypes, perspective taking and perspective giving, and creating a common in-group identity model.

Test Your Knowledge

- Define prejudice and describe its components.
- What are the possible explanations for prejudice?
- Explain the reasons for hostility between groups.
- Describe the theories that explain intergroup conflict.
- How can one reduce prejudice?

Critical Thinking Question

Considering the stigma of mental illness, how is it possible to improve the public's and other health professionals' opinion and attitude?

seventeen
Intelligence

Learning Goals

- This chapter is intended to provide the reader with an overview of the concept of intelligence, theories of intelligence, factors determining intelligence, group differences in intelligence, assessment of intelligence, and a brief account of emotional intelligence.

Introduction

The origin of the term "intelligence" has its roots in the derivation of the Latin verb *intelligere*, which literally means "to understand." There is no standard definition of what exactly constitutes intelligence. Some researchers have suggested that intelligence is a single general ability, while others believe that intelligence encompasses a range of aptitudes, skills, and talents, and knowledge, which is simply an accumulated collection of facts derived from the environment. Intelligence is also defined as the ability to understand complex ideas, learn from experience, engage in various forms of reasoning and deal with difficulties by original thought, solve problems, and adapt effectively to the environment. Combining various concepts of intelligence together, intelligence could be defined as the composite ability to do the following:

- Learn: this includes all kinds of formal and informal learning via any combination of experience, education, and training.
- Explore problems: this includes recognizing problem situations and transforming them into more clearly defined problems.
- Solve problems: this includes the ability to reason, plan, solve problems, accomplish tasks, and do complex projects.

Theories of Intelligence

There are several different theories about intelligence, none of which have received complete agreement. Each theory has its own perspective and assumptions. The following are some of the major theories of intelligence that have been formulated during the past 100 years.

Spearman's Two-Factor Theory

British psychologist Charles Spearman (1927) proposed a theory of two factors (general ability "g" and a group of specific abilities known as the "s" factor). The "g" factor is the universal inborn ability that influences the performance on all mental tasks, as it is constant in all intellectual activity. It varies among individuals, and the greater the "g" an individual has, the more success in life. Thus, people who are smart in one area are usually smart in other areas. The "s" factor is acquired from the environment. Individuals differ in the amount of "s" ability, and it varies from activity to activity in the same individual. This theory was widely accepted for practical use. The tests directly measuring Spearman's "g" are in a wide practice nowadays, e.g., the Raven Standard Progressive Matrices, developed by J.C. Raven.

Thorndike's Multifactor Theory

Thorndike believed that there is nothing like general ability. Each mental activity requires a combination of numerous separate elements or factors, each one being a minute element of one's ability. Thorndike assumed that intelligence involves three mutually independent abilities:

- *Abstract intelligence*: the ability to perform verbal and symbolic thinking.
- *Mechanical intelligence*: the ability to effectively control your body and manipulate objects.
- *Social intelligence*: the ability to communicate with people, understand, and perform in social relations.

Thorndike proposed four general dimensions of intelligence:

- *Altitude*: the complexity or difficulty of tasks one can accomplish.
- *Range*: the number of tasks of a given degree of difficulty that one can do.
- *Area*: the total number of situations at each level of complexity to which the individual is able to respond. It is a function of range and altitude.
- *Speed*: the number of tasks one can complete in a given time.

Thurstone's Theory: Primary Mental Abilities Theory

Louis L. Thurstone (1887–1955) rejected the general theory of intelligence and instead theorized that intelligence was composed of seven parallel primary mental abilities. Each of these primary factors is said to be relatively independent of the others. Thurstone identified seven, which he considered would describe intelligence more specifically. Based on these factors, Thurstone constructed a new test of intelligence known as the Test of Primary Mental Abilities (PMA). Though this theory is accepted, it is not widely used for practical assessment because of difficulties with analysis and applications. Thurstone's primary mental abilities include:

- Associative memory (M): the ability to memorize and recall.
- Numerical ability (N): ability to do numerical calculations rapidly and accurately.
- Perceptual speed (P): the ability to rapidly and accurately detect differences and similarities among objects.
- Reasoning (R): the ability to find rules. It is found in tasks that require a subject to discover a rule or principle involved in a series or groups of letters.
- Spatial visualization (S): the ability to visualize relationships. It is involved in any task in which the subject manipulates the imaginary object in space.
- Verbal comprehension (V): the ability to define and understand words.
- Word fluency (W): the ability to produce words rapidly. It is involved whenever the subject is asked to think of isolated words at a rapid rate.

Guilford's Model of Structure of Intellect

Guilford (1967, 1985, 1988) proposed an extension of Thurstone's theory that incorporates Thurstone's abilities while adding new ones, so that the total number of abilities is increased from 7 to 120 abilities, arranged along three dimensions. According to Guilford's structure-of-intellect theory: each mental task requires three elements: (1) content (visual, auditory, symbolic, semantic and behavioral); (2) the mental operation involved (cognition, memory, divergent thinking, convergent thinking, and evaluation); and (3) the cognitive product resulting from the operation (units, classes, relations, systems, transformations, and implications).

The Cattell–Horn–Carroll Theory

Raymond B. Cattell and John L. Horn proposed that Spearman's "g" and Thurstone's primary mental abilities can be reduced to two major dimensions that interact together to produce overall individual intelligence: Fluid and Crystallized intelligence.

The Cattell–Horn–Carroll (CHC) theory of cognitive abilities is a composite of Cattell–Horn's fluid-crystallized intelligence (Gf-Gc) and Carroll's three-stratum theory. It is one of the most researched and widely accepted theories of the composition of intellectual abilities.

In his three-stratum theory, Carroll proposed that there are a fairly large number of distinct individual differences in cognitive ability, and that the relationships among them can be derived by classifying them into three different strata: stratum I, "narrow" abilities; stratum II, "broad" abilities; and stratum III, consisting of a single "general" ability.

■ *Stratum I, narrow abilities*: this represents greater specializations of abilities, often in quite specific ways that reflect the effects of experience and learning, or the adoption of particular strategies of performance (Carroll, 1993).

■ *Stratum II, broad abilities*: this represents basic constitutional and long-standing characteristics of individuals that can govern or influence a great variety of behaviors in a given domain. They vary in their emphasis on process, content, and manner of response.

PHOTO 17.1.   Raymond B. Cattell.

■ *Stratum III*: this is the broadest or most general level of ability in the Gf-Gc model, it is located at the apex of Carroll's (1993) hierarchy. This single cognitive ability, which includes both broad (stratum II) and narrow (stratum I) abilities, is interpreted as representing a general factor (i.e., g) that is involved in complex higher-order cognitive processes (Gustaffson & Undheim, 1996; Jensen, 1998).

Carroll's three-stratum theory is used extensively as the foundation for selecting, organizing, and interpreting tests of intelligence and cognitive abilities. The current model of CHC theory includes 16 broad cognitive abilities, and over 80 narrow abilities, with the broad abilities described as follows (Flanagan & Dixon, 2013; McGrew, 2009; Newton & McGrew, 2010; Schneider & McGrew, 2012):

1. *Fluid intelligence/fluid reasoning (Gf)*: this denotes being able to think and reason abstractly and solve problems, e.g., solving puzzles and coming up with problem-solving strategies. It includes mental operations that are used to solve novel instant problems that cannot be performed by relying exclusively on previously learned information. This ability is considered independent of learning, experience, and education. It includes, among others, spatial and visual imagery, rote memory, the ability to notice visual details, inferential reasoning, concept formation, classification of unfamiliar stimuli, hypothesis generation and testing, generalization of old solutions to new problems, and inferring of reasonable

PHOTO 17.2.   Solving puzzles.

estimates in equivocal situations. Quantitative, inductive (making broad generalizations from specific observations), and sequential (ability to reason logically, to apply rules) reasoning are part of this construct.

2. *Crystallized intelligence/comprehension knowledge (Gc)*: this denotes the depth and breadth of acquired knowledge regarding the language, information, and concepts that are valued in one's culture. It involves knowledge that comes from prior learning and past experiences. Situations that require crystallized intelligence include reading comprehension and vocabulary exams. This type of intelligence is based upon facts and rooted in experiences. While many people claim that intelligence seems to decline with age, research suggests that while fluid intelligence begins to decrease after adolescence, crystallized intelligence continues to increase throughout adulthood due to accumulation of new knowledge and understanding.

3. *General (domain-specific) knowledge (Gkn)*: the depth, breadth, and mastery of specialized knowledge that typically does not represent the general universal experiences of individuals in a culture.

4. *Quantitative knowledge (Gq)*: the depth and breadth of quantitative, numerical, and mathematical knowledge.

5. *Reading and writing ability (Grw)*: the depth and breadth of reading and writing skills and knowledge.

6. *Short-term memory (Gsm)*: this is the ability to encode, maintain, and manipulate information in one's immediate awareness. It refers to both the size of primary memory and to the efficiency of attentional control mechanisms that manipulate information within primary memory.

7. *Long-term storage and retrieval (Glr)*: this refers to the ability to store and consolidate new information in long-term memory and fluently retrieve it later on.

8. *Visual processing (Gv)*: the ability to perceive, store, retrieve, and transform visual input.

9. *Auditory processing (Ga)*: the ability to detect and process meaningful auditory information.

10. *Olfactory abilities (Go)*: the ability to detect and process meaningful olfactory information.

11. *Tactile abilities (Gh)*: the ability to detect and process meaningful tactile information.

12. *Psychomotor abilities (Gp)*: the ability to perform physical body motor movements with precision, coordination, or strength.

13. *Kinesthetic abilities (Gk)*: the ability to detect and process meaningful information in proprioceptive sensations.

14. *Processing speed (Gs)*: this refers to the ability to quickly perform automatic, routine cognitive tasks, particularly when pressured to maintain focused attention. It is the speed with which we process rote information.

15. *Decision speed/reaction time (Gt)*: this is the ability to make elementary decisions and/or responses, or one of several elementary decisions and/or responses, at the onset of simple stimuli.

16. *Psychomotor speed (Gps)*: the ability to rapidly and fluently perform physical body motor movements largely independent of cognitive control.

Sternberg's Triarchic Theory

This theory is noteworthy due to making a shift of concepts toward understanding the nature of intelligence by identifying the underlying cognitive processing involved in intelligence.

Psychologist Robert Sternberg proposed a triarchic model of three intelligences, namely: analytical (A), creative (C), and practical (P).

- *Analytical intelligence*: this is how an individual thinks abstractly, evaluates, compares, and analyzes information. It is what we generally think of as academic ability. It enables us to solve problems and to acquire new knowledge. Problem-solving skills include encoding information, combining and comparing pieces of information, and generating a solution.
- *Creative intelligence*: this is defined as the abilities to react and cope with novel stimuli and situations and to profit from experience. This includes the ability to quickly relate novel situations to familiar situations, that is, to perceive similarities and differences. Moreover, as a result of experience, people become able to solve problems more rapidly.
- *Practical intelligence*: this refers to solving real-life problems in everyday life. It enables people to adapt to the demands of their environment, e.g., keeping a job by adapting one's behavior to the employer's requirements is adaptive. But if the employer is making unreasonable demands, reshaping the environment (by changing the employer's attitudes) or selecting an alternate environment (by finding a more suitable job) is also adaptive.

The existence of P and C in this theory shows that intelligence is wider than it is assumed to be in Spearman's "g" theory and, in part, explains why some people, who have high IQ, may fail to succeed in life. Sternberg developed the Sternberg Triarchic Abilities Test (STAT), a battery of multiple-choice questions that measures all three intelligences on separate scales.

Howard Gardner's Multiple Intelligences

Howard Gardner (1983) proposed that numerical expressions of human intelligence are not a comprehensive or accurate representation of people's abilities. Gardner's theory describes eight distinct intelligences that are based on skills and abilities that are valued within different cultures. This requires multiple tests for every intelligence:

1. *Linguistic intelligence*: this involves the ability to learn languages and use language. This includes the ability to effectively use language to express oneself rhetorically or poetically. Writers, poets, lawyers, and public speakers are among those whom Howard Gardner sees as having high linguistic intelligence.

2. *Logical-mathematical intelligence*: this consists of the capacity to analyze problems logically, carry out mathematical operations, and investigate issues scientifically. In Howard Gardner's words, it entails the ability to detect patterns, reason deductively, and think logically. This intelligence is most often associated with scientific and mathematical thinking and professions.

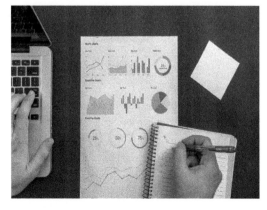

PHOTO 17.3. Mathematical.

3. *Musical intelligence*: this involves skill in the performance, composition, and recognition of musical patterns, pitches, tones, and rhythms. According to Howard Gardner, musical intelligence runs in an almost structural parallel to linguistic intelligence.

PHOTO 17.4.   Musical intelligence.

4. *Bodily-kinesthetic intelligence*: this is the ability to use mental abilities to coordinate bodily movements. It entails the potential of using one's whole body or parts of the body to solve problems. Howard Gardner sees mental and physical ability as related. Mechanics, athletes, and dancers have high bodily-kinesthetic intelligence.

PHOTO 17.5.   Bodily-Kinesthetic intelligence.

5. *Spatial intelligence*: this involves ability to perceive spatial relationships, arrange objects, and use patterns of wide and more confined areas. Painters, sculptors, and designers are characterized by this type of intelligence.

PHOTO 17.6.   Spatial intelligence.

6. *Interpersonal intelligence*: this is concerned with the capacity to understand the intentions, motivations, and desires of other people. It allows people to work effectively with each other. Educators, salespeople, religious and political leaders, and counselors all need to excel in this type of intelligence.

PHOTO 17.7. Interpersonal intelligence.

7. *Intrapersonal intelligence*: this entails the capacity to understand oneself, to appreciate one's feelings, fears, and motivations. In Howard Gardner's view, it involves having an effective working model of ourselves, and to be able to use such information to regulate our lives.
8. *Naturalistic intelligence*: this enables people to recognize, categorize, and discriminate between similar objects in the environment. Botanists, biologists, and naturalists are among those who have high naturalistic intelligence

Applying Gardner's theory to improve classroom activities necessitates enhancing all seven intelligences rather than relying solely on development and use of verbal and mathematical intelligences. Hence, teachers should organize the educational material in a manner that arouses most or all components of intelligences.

Burt and Vernon's Hierarchical Theory

Burt (a student of Spearman) agreed that there is a "g" factor common to all intelligence tests, but he thought that the two-factor model was too simple. He and Vernon elaborated and extended Spearman's model by identifying a series of group factors (major and minor) in between the "g" and "s" factors.

Burt and Vernon's theory of different levels of intelligence fills the gaps between two extreme theories, the two-factor theory of Spearman, which did not allow for the existence of group factors, and the multiple-factor theory of Thurstone, which did not allow a "g" factor. Vernon and Burt proposed a hierarchical model composed of abilities at varying levels of generality, where Spearman's general intelligence "g" takes the top position, and then it is broken down into major group factors, which are subdivided into minor group factors. This model is widely accepted nowadays and is in constant development. The four levels of theory of intelligence include:

1. The "g" factor (general intelligence): this is the highest level, with the largest source of variance between individuals.
2. Major group factors such as verbal-numerical-educational and practical-mechanical-spatial-physical ability.
3. Minor group factors are divided from major group factors.
4. The "s" (specific) factor: this is the bottom level.

Factors Determining Intelligence

Today, nearly all psychologists recognize that both genetics and environmental factors play a role in determining intelligence. However, the relative contribution of each factor cannot be estimated. Both genetics and environmental factors interact to determine exactly how inherited genes are expressed, e.g., if a person has tall parents, it is likely that the individual will grow to be tall. However, the exact height that the person reaches can be influenced by environmental factors such as nutrition and disease. Research has revealed that personal life experiences can cause physiological brain changes. Thus, the influence of environment and biology on intelligence is a bi-directional one, and hence intelligence is more fluid than previously believed.

Environmental factors include prenatal environment, postnatal environment, home environment, parent-child interaction, social and environmental deprivation, education, physiological conditions, such as nutrition, health, drugs, disease, and physical injury.

Twin studies suggest that identical twins' IQs are more similar than those of fraternal twins. However, identical twins reared apart have IQs that are less similar than identical twins reared in the same environment. Also, siblings reared together in the same home have IQs that are more similar than those of adopted children raised together in the same environment. Children who are breastfed during the first three to five months of life score higher on IQ tests at age 6 than same-age children who were not breastfed. School attendance has an impact on IQ scores.

Group Differences in Intelligence

Debates over the existence of racial and ethnic differences in intelligence emerged as the first intelligence tests came into widespread use. The debate concerns the interpretation of research findings that the average scores on IQ tests of White American test takers tend to be higher than test takers of African ancestry, and subsequent findings that test takers of East Asian background tend to score higher than whites. The relation, if any, between group differences in IQ and race, is an unsolved issue. Several environmental factors have been shown to affect group differences in intelligence, however, they cannot explain the entire disparity. On the other hand, no genetic factor has been conclusively shown to have a causal relation with group difference in intelligence test scores.

Effect of Socio-economic Status on Intelligence

Children of the upper socio-economic class of the society are exposed to more intellectual stimulation, get better social opportunities, and have better nutrition. All these are believed to influence their intellectual development in a positive direction. The index of socio-economic status (SES) is based on parental education, occupation, and income. The higher the socio-economic status of the parents, the higher the average IQ of the children.

The children of low socio-economic status score approximately 10–15 IQ points below the middle-class and higher-class children. These differences are present by the first grade and are sustained throughout the school years. Parental occupation is closely related to the IQ level of children.

Effect of Gender on Intelligence

The overall IQ scores of boys and girls are very similar. There is some evidence that sex differences exist for particular kinds of cognitive abilities. Review of a number of studies has shown that females are superior in language skills, verbal fluency, and reading, while males are superior in mathematical reasoning and spatial abilities (Oetzel, 1966).

The Flynn Effect

In industrialized countries, people's performance on IQ tests has improved over time, this improvement is called the Flynn effect. The precise cause of the Flynn effect is unclear. Researchers speculate that it may be due to environmental factors such as improvement of nutritional status among children, enhancement of skills through television and video games, improved schools, smaller family sizes, higher level of parental education, or improvements in parenting.

Assessment of Intelligence

Intelligence can be assessed individually or in groups of people. The best-known individual intelligence tests are the Stanford–Binet Intelligence Scale, and the Wechsler Intelligence Scales.

During the early 1900s, the French government had passed laws requiring that all French children attend school, so it was important to find a way to identify children who would need specialized assistance. The French government asked psychologist Alfred Binet to help in identifying which students were mostly likely to experience difficulty in schools. Faced with this task, Binet and his colleague Theodore Simon developed a number of questions that focused on things that had not been taught in school such as attention, memory, problem-solving skills, comprehension, imagination, aesthetic sentiment, moral sentiment, motor ability, and hand-eye coordination (Roid, 2003). The original scale involved 30 pass/fail items. Using these questions, Binet determined which ones served as the best predictors of school success. He quickly realized that some children were able to answer more advanced questions that older children were generally able to answer, while other children of the same age were only able to answer questions that younger children could typically answer. Based on this observation, Binet suggested the concept of a mental age, or a measure of intelligence based on the average abilities of children of a certain age group.

PHOTO 17.8. Alfred Binet.

This first intelligence test, referred to today as the Binet–Simon Scale, became the basis for current intelligence tests. However, Binet himself did not believe that his psychometric instruments could be used to measure a single, permanent and inborn level of intelligence. Binet stressed the limitations of the test, suggesting that intelligence is too broad a concept to quantify with a single number.

The Stanford–Binet Intelligence Test

After the development of the Binet–Simon scale, the test was soon brought to the United States where it generated considerable interest. Stanford University psychologist Lewis Terman standardized Binet's original test using a sample of American participants. Over one-third of new items were added, and old items were revised and reorganized to different age levels. This adapted test, first published in 1916, was called the Stanford–Binet Intelligence Scale and soon became the standard intelligence test used in the US. Terman used the classic intelligence quotient formula by the German psychologist William Stern to calculate the level of a person's intelligence:

$$IQ = (\text{mental age}/\text{chronological age}) \times 100$$

A score of 100 is considered average. Thus, when the mental age of a child as assessed by the test as greater than the child's chronological age, the child's IQ will be greater than average (100). Currently, the IQ formula is no longer used, and is replaced by deviation IQ. The Stanford–Binet test has undergone a number of revisions over the years since its foundation, that kept it a popular assessment tool today. The current edition of the test (SB5) combines many insights implicitly considered in the early editions of the test, but presents them in a way that offers practical improvements in content coverage and psychometric characteristics (Table 17.1). Factors assessed by the SB5 include fluid reasoning, quantitative reasoning, knowledge, visual-spatial processing, and working memory. Each is assessed through verbal and nonverbal items.

The Wechsler Intelligence Scales

The next development in the history of intelligence testing was the creation of a new measurement instrument by American psychologist, David Wechsler. The assessment of adult intelligence using the Stanford–Binet Test was particularly problematic, because it was essentially

TABLE 17.1 Stanford–Binet Fifth Edition (SB5) IQ Classification

IQ Range	IQ Classification
145–160	Very gifted or highly advanced
130–144	Gifted or very advanced
120–129	Superior
110–119	High average
90–109	Average
80–89	Low average
70–79	Borderline impaired or delayed
55–69	Mildly impaired or delayed
40–54	Moderately impaired or delayed

developed to assess children, and at some point the mental age levels, but the chronological age keeps increasing, hence, a person's IQ declines owing to natural aging. Wechsler introduced the Deviation IQ score that is calculated by comparing how far the person's raw score is from the mean raw score in terms of standard deviation units from the mean. Wechsler set the mean to 100 and the standard deviation to 15 to make the deviation scores similar to the IQ formula.

Much like Binet, Wechsler believed that intelligence involved a number of different mental abilities, describing intelligence as "the global capacity of a person to act purposefully, to think rationally, and to deal effectively with his environment." Wechsler felt Spearman's "g" ignored such factors as motivation and personality. Wechsler (1939) believed that general intelligence is a separate entity and that a combination of the abilities that comprise general intelligence was necessary.

Wechsler published his new intelligence test, known as the Wechsler Adult Intelligence Scale (WAIS), in 1955. Later on, Wechsler developed two different tests specifically for use with children: The Wechsler Intelligence Scale for Children (WISC) and the Wechsler Preschool and Primary Scale of Intelligence (WPPSI). The adult version of the test has been revised since its original publication and is now known as the WAIS-IV (Table 17.2).

The WAIS-IV contains 10 sub-tests along with five supplementary tests. The test provides scores in four major areas of intelligence: a Verbal Comprehension Index, a Perceptual Reasoning Index, a Working Memory Index, and a Processing Speed Index. The test also provides two broad scores that can be used as a summary of overall intelligence: a full-scale IQ score that combines performance on all four index scores and a General Ability Index based on six subtest scores. Sub-test scores on the WAIS-IV can be useful in identifying learning disabilities, such as cases where a low score on some areas combined with a high score in other areas may indicate that the individual has a specific learning difficulty (Kaufman, 1990).

Group Intelligence Tests

Individual intelligence tests can be given only by specially trained psychologists. Such tests are expensive and time-consuming to administer, and so educational institutions often use tests that can be given to a group of people at the same time. Group tests are primarily used for screening purposes. Commonly used group intelligence tests include the Otis–Lennon School Ability Test and the Lorge–Thorndike Intelligence Test.

TABLE 17.2 Current Wechsler[1] IQ Classification

IQ Range	IQ Classification
130 and above	Very Superior
120–129	Superior
110–119	High Average
90–109	Average
80–89	Low Average
70–79	Borderline
69 and below	Extremely Low

Note
[1]WAIS–IV, WISC–IV, WPPSI–IV.

The Distribution of IQ Scores

Historically, the IQ assessment was based on the "ratio IQ," which depends on estimating the "mental age" of the test-taker (measured in years and months), divided by the test-taker's "chronological age" (measured in years and months), e.g., a student who is 10 years and zero months (chronological age) had a mental age score of 13 years and zero months, therefore, the IQ of this student will be $13/10 \times 100 = 130$.

The current scoring method for all IQ tests is the "deviation IQ." In this method, IQ is scored by comparing an individual's score to the scores of others in the same age group. The median level of performance of population on IQ measurement equals 100, and one standard deviation equals 15. Approximately half of the population have IQ scores between 90–110, while one quarter have higher or lower IQ scores. It should be noted that IQ scores do not have a linear relationship with mental ability, so a person with a score of 50 does not have half the mental ability of a person with a score of 100.

Emotional Intelligence

Emotional intelligence (EI) refers to the ability to perceive, control, and evaluate emotions. Some researchers suggest that emotional intelligence can be learned and strengthened, while others claim it is an inborn characteristic. Table 17.3 presents a brief history of emotional intelligence.

TABLE 17.3 A Brief History of Emotional Intelligence.

Date	Event
1930s	Edward Thorndike described the concept of "social intelligence" as the ability to get along with other people.
1940s	David Wechsler suggested that affective components of intelligence may be essential to success in life.
1950s	Humanistic psychologists such as Abraham Maslow described how people can build emotional strength.
1975	Howard Gardner published *The Shattered Mind*, which introduces the concept of multiple intelligences.
1985	Wayne Payne introduced the term "emotional intelligence" in his doctoral dissertation entitled "A study of emotion: developing emotional intelligence; self-integration; relating to fear, pain and desire (theory, structure of reality, problem-solving, contraction/expansion, tuning in/coming out/letting go)."
1987	In an article published in *Mensa Magazine*, Keith Beasley used the term "emotional quotient." It had been suggested that this was the first published use of the term, although Reuven Bar-On claimed to have used the term in an unpublished version of his graduate thesis.
1990	Psychologists Peter Salovey and John Mayer published their landmark article, "Emotional Intelligence," in *Imagination, Cognition, and Personality* journal.
1995	The concept of emotional intelligence was popularized after publication of Daniel Goleman's book *Emotional Intelligence: Why It Can Matter More than IQ*.

Components of Emotional Intelligence

Salovey and Mayer proposed a model that identified four different factors of emotional intelligence: (1) the perception of emotion; (2) the ability to reason using emotions; (3) the ability to understand emotion; and (4) the ability to manage emotions. These factors are arranged from more basic psychological processes to higher, more psychologically integrated processes.

- *Perceiving emotions*: the first step in understanding emotions is to accurately perceive them. In many cases, this might involve understanding of non-verbal signals such as body language and facial expressions.
- *Reasoning with emotions*: this involves using emotions to promote thinking and cognitive activity. Emotions help prioritize what we should pay attention and react to, we respond emotionally to things that get our attention.
- *Understanding emotions*: the emotions that we perceive can carry a wide variety of meanings. If someone is expressing angry emotions, the observer must interpret the possible causes of their anger and what it might mean.
- *Managing emotions*: the ability to manage emotions effectively is the highest level of emotional intelligence. Conscious, reflective regulation of emotion and responding appropriately to the emotions of others are all important aspects of emotional management.

Clinical Notes

- Though intelligence testing still has its shortcomings, assessment of intelligence is of great value in schools, clinical settings, courts, and research. The purpose of assessment is to gain insight into an individual that will facilitate the decision-making process regarding screening, diagnosis, rehabilitation, and progress monitoring.
- In a school setting, intelligence assessment is useful in evaluating children with academic difficulties, and it could help in differentiating specific learning disorders from intellectual disability. It can also be of help in determining deficit cognitive functions among those students, and benefit in constructing helpful remedial educational programs.
- Intelligence tests such as Binet–Simon tests are useful in predicting school success in both primary and secondary educational level. However, their predictive power in post-secondary academic and occupational domains is less successful.
- In clinical settings, intelligence tests are usually used, in combination with other forms of cognitive and behavioral testing, to evaluate traumatic brain injury, learning disabilities, and neuropsychological disorders. They are also beneficial in assessing and monitoring the progress of individuals with such disorders.

Summary

- Intelligence is the composite ability to learn, explore problems, and solve problems.
- Spearman proposed that intelligence is made up of two factors: general ability, "g," and a group of specific abilities known as the "s" factor.
- Thorndike assumed that intelligence involves three mutually independent abilities: abstract intelligence, mechanical intelligence, and social intelligence.
- Thurstone theorized intelligence as composed of seven primary mental abilities: associative memory, numerical ability, perceptual speed, reasoning, spatial visualization, verbal comprehension, and word fluency.

- Guilford assumed that every intellectual task can be classified according to: (1) its content; (2) the mental operation involved; and (3) the product resulting from the operation. He further classified content into five categories, namely, visual, auditory, symbolic, semantic, and behavioral.
- The Cattell–Horn theory of fluid and crystallized intelligence suggests that intelligence is composed of a number of different abilities that interact and work together to produce overall individual intelligence.
- Carroll's three-stratum theory states cognitive abilities can be classified into three strata: stratum I, "narrow" abilities; stratum II, "broad" abilities; and stratum III, consisting of a single "general" ability.
- Fluid intelligence (Gf) denotes being able to think and reason abstractly and solve problems.
- Crystallized intelligence (Gc) denotes the depth and breadth of acquired knowledge regarding the language, information, and concepts that are valued in one's culture.
- Sternberg proposed a triarchic model of three intelligences, namely, analytical (A), creative (C), and practical (P).
- Approximately half of the population have IQ scores between 90–110, while one quarter have higher or lower IQ scores.
- Emotional intelligence (EI) refers to the ability to perceive, control, and evaluate emotions.
- Salovey and Mayer proposed a model that identified four different factors of emotional intelligence: (1) the perception of emotion; (2) the ability to reason using emotions; (3) the ability to understand emotion; and (4) the ability to manage emotions.

Test Your Knowledge

- Define intelligence.
- Describe Spearman's view of intelligence.
- Give an account of the triarchic model of intelligence.
- Describe Carroll's three-stratum theory.
- Give an account of Thurstone's theory of intelligence
- What are the factors affecting intelligence?
- Give an account of intelligence testing.
- What is the effect of gender, culture, and socio-economic status on intelligence?
- Give an account of emotional intelligence.

Critical Thinking Questions

- Intelligence testing is a matter of controversy, how could you discuss this topic?
- How does general intelligence correlate with a person's typical daily functioning, their potential maximum performance, and their functioning under unusual circumstances, such as extreme emotional disturbance or in an attempt to avoid consequences of certain actions?
- How could intelligence testing be used to improve scholastic achievement and activities?
- Evaluate the possible role of emotional intelligence in a school.

eighteen
Personality

Learning Goals

- This chapter is intended to provide the reader with an overview of what is meant by personality, the different personality theories, the factors affecting the development of personality, the methods of personality assessment, and the different types of personality disorders.

Introduction

The diversity of human characteristics is reflected in trials to define personality; no single definition is accepted by all personality theorists. However, personality can be defined as the enduring patterns of cognition, emotion, motivation, and behaviors that make a person unique, which remains fairly consistent throughout life. Several theories have been proposed to explain different aspects of personality. Some theories focus on explaining how personality develops while others are concerned with individual differences in personality. The following is a summary of the major theories of personality proposed by different psychologists.

Theories of Personality

Type Approach of Personality

Perhaps the earliest known theory of personality is that of the Greek physician Hippocrates (400 BC), who characterized human behavior in terms of four temperaments, each associated with a different bodily fluid, or "humor." The sanguine, or optimistic, type was associated with blood; the phlegmatic type (slow and lethargic) with phlegm; the melancholic type (sad, depressed) with black bile; and the choleric (angry) type with yellow bile. Individual personality was determined by the amount of each of the four humors an individual possessed.

William Sheldon, an American psychologist, classified personality according to body physique into three categories: the endomorph (heavy and easy-going), mesomorph (muscular and aggressive), and ectomorph (thin and intellectual or artistic) (Sheldon. Stevens, & Tucker, 1940).

During the 1950s, Meyer Friedman and his co-workers defined what they called Type A and Type B behavior patterns. Type A individuals tend to be very competitive and self-critical. They strive toward goals without feeling a sense of joy in their efforts or accomplishments and have high work involvement. They theorized that type A personalities had a higher risk of hypertension and coronary disease because they are stress-seeking. Type B people, on the other hand, tend to be more tolerant of others, are more relaxed than Type A individuals, more reflective, experience lower levels of anxiety, are less competitive, and display higher levels of imagination and creativity (Friedman & Ulmer, 1985; Rosenman et al., 1970).

A major weakness of the typological classification system is the oversimplification inherent in placing individuals into one of a limited number of categories, which ignores the fact that every personality represents a unique combination of qualities.

Trait Approach of Personality

Traits are enduring personality characteristics and behaviors displayed in different situations. Traits are usually described by two opposite adjectives referring to the extremes of these traits, but people are distributed over the range of the spectrum e.g., cheerful–depressed, friendly–suspicious, excitable–tolerant. The trait approach has three basic assumptions:

- Personality traits are relatively stable over time.
- Personality traits are consistent in diverse situations.
- Each person has a different set or degree of particular traits.

Trait theorists do not assume that some people have a trait and others do not; rather, they propose that all people possess certain traits, but the degree to which a particular trait applies to a specific person varies and can be quantified, e.g., considering a "sociability" trait, one person may be relatively sociable, whereas another may be relatively unsociable, but both of them have the trait, although the degree of "sociability" is higher in the first person than the other one. The major challenge for trait theorists in assuming this approach is to identify the specific primary traits necessary to describe personality. Different theorists have proposed different sets of traits. The following is a summary of important trait approach theories.

Allport's Trait Theory

Gordon Allport (1897–1967) extensively investigated the ways in which traits combine to form normal personalities. He sorted over 18,000 traits over a period of 30 years. He proposed that each person has one cardinal trait and about seven central traits that dominate his or her behavior. Secondary traits are specific to certain situations and have less control over behavior. Allport proposed the following main types of traits:

1. *Common traits*: these are characteristics shared by most members of a culture.
2. *Cardinal trait*: this is the single pervasive characteristic that dominates an individual's whole life. It influences most of a person's behavior in most situations, usually frequently to the point that the person is characteristically known by these traits, e.g., selflessness and devotion toward humanitarian activities, honesty, and justice. Allport suggested that not all people possess cardinal traits.
3. *Central traits*: the small group of characteristics that form the most descriptive features of an individual's personality. While these traits are less pervasive and are not as dominating as cardinal traits, they influence behavior in various situations, and are characteristic of a person. Terms such as intelligent, independent, sociable, honest, arrogant, shy and fearful are considered central traits.
4. *Secondary traits*: these are superficial characteristics that occasionally contribute to attitudes or preferences. These often appear in certain situations or specific circumstances, e.g., styles of clothing, food preferences, political opinions, or favored music.

Cattell's Sixteen Personality Factors

Raymond Cattell believed that there are two basic levels of traits: surface traits and source traits. Surface traits are characteristics of personality that lie on the surface of personality, and can be inferred from the observed behavior, e.g., sociable, shy, and stubborn. Source traits constitute a deeper level of personality traits. Using factor analysis among surface traits, Cattell identified closely related terms and reduced the number of main personality traits to 16 key personality traits. According to Cattell, these 16 traits are the source of all human personality. He developed one of the most widely used personality assessments known as the Sixteen Personality Factor (16PF) Questionnaire. According to Cattell, there is a continuum of personality traits. In other words, all people have all these 16 traits to a certain degree, but each person might be high in some traits and low in others. The following personality trait list describes the terms used for each of the 16 personality dimensions described by Cattell.

1. Abstractedness: imaginative versus practical.
2. Apprehension: worried versus confident.
3. Dominance: forceful versus submissive.
4. Emotional stability: calm versus nervous.

5. Liveliness: spontaneous versus restrained.
6. Openness to change: flexible versus attached to the familiar.
7. Perfectionism: controlled versus undisciplined.
8. Privateness: discreet versus open.
9. Reasoning: abstract versus concrete.
10. Rule consciousness: conforming versus non-conforming.
11. Self-reliance: self-sufficient versus dependent.
12. Sensitivity: tender-hearted versus tough-minded.
13. Social boldness: uninhibited versus shy.
14. Tension: impatient versus relaxed.
15. Vigilance: suspicious versus trusting.
16. Warmth: outgoing versus reserved.

Eysenck's Three Dimensions of Personality

British psychologist Hans Eysenck used factor analysis to identify three basic personality factors: (1) introversion-extraversion; (2) neuroticism-emotional stability; and (3) psychoticism.

1. *Introversion/Extraversion*: introversion involves directing attention to inner experiences, while extraversion relates to focusing attention outward on other people and the environment. So, a person high in introversion might be quiet and reserved, while an individual high in extraversion might be sociable and outgoing.
2. *Neuroticism/Emotional Stability*: this dimension is related to moodiness versus even temperament. Neuroticism refers to an individual's tendency to become upset or emotional, while stability refers to the tendency to remain relaxed, calm, emotionally stable, and even-tempered.

PHOTO 18.1. Hans Eysenck.

3. *Psychoticism*: individuals who are high on this trait tend to be cold, non-empathetic, impulsive, antisocial, hostile, and manipulative. Persons who are low on psychoticism are warm, sensitive, and concerned about others.

The "Big-Five" Model of Personality

Lewis Goldberg proposed basic differences in personality can be reduced to five dimensions. He proposed a five-dimension personality model, called the "Big Five." These include:

1. *Openness to experience*: the tendency to be imaginative, independent, and interested in variety, versus practical, conforming, and interested in routine, respectively.
2. *Conscientiousness*: the tendency to be organized, careful, and disciplined versus disorganized, careless, and impulsive, respectively.
3. *Extraversion*: the tendency to be outgoing, fun-loving, active, and talkative versus solitary, reserved, passive, and quiet, respectively.
4. *Agreeableness*: the tendency to be soft-hearted, trusting, and concerned with other's feelings and needs, versus cold, suspicious, and unfriendly, respectively.
5. *Neuroticism*: the tendency to be calm, secure, and emotionally stable versus worried, insecure, and emotionally tense and unstable, respectively.

Some personality researchers argue that the Big Five list of major traits is not exhaustive. Some support has been found for two additional factors: excellent/ordinary and evil/decent. However, no definitive conclusions have been established. Other theorists have proposed additional factors.

Evaluation of the Trait Approach

Trait approaches provide a clear, straightforward explanation of people's behavioral consistencies. Traits allow us to readily compare one person with another, so they were influential in the development of several useful personality measures. However, various trait theories debate the number of basic traits that frame human personality. The difficulty in determining which of the theories is the most accurate has led some personality psychologists to question the validity of trait conceptions of personality in general.

Also, trait models have been criticized as being purely descriptive and offering little explanation of the underlying causes of personality. If someone donates money to charity because he or she has the trait of generosity, it is still unknown why that person became generous in the first place or the reasons for displaying generosity in a specific situation. Also, trait approaches may lead some people to accept oversimplified classifications, or to offer advice based on a superficial analysis of personality. Finally, trait models often underestimate the effect of specific situations on people's behavior.

The Psychodynamic Approach

The psychodynamic approach to personality proposes that active forces within the personality that motivate behavior stem from the unconscious conflict between the id, the ego and the superego. Freud believed that conflict within the personality is unavoidable, because the ego is being pulled in two opposing directions by the id and the superego. The ego's solution comes in the form of three forms of compromise, namely, dreams, neurotic symptoms. and defense mechanisms.

Freud's View of Structure and Development of Personality

- Personality is composed of three structures: the id, the ego, and the superego (see psychoanalytic theory, pp. 38–41).
- Stages of personality development: Freud believed that personality develops in stages (psychosexual stages); in each stage a part of the body becomes the child's main source of pleasure. Failure to resolve conflicts at any stage can cause fixation (an unconscious preoccupation with the pleasure area associated with that stage) (see human development, pp. 41–44).
- Personality characteristics results from:
  - Fixation: this refers to conflicts or concerns that persist beyond the developmental period in which they first occur.
  - Defense mechanisms: these are unconscious strategies that people use to reduce anxiety by concealing its source from themselves and others.

Evaluation of the Freudian Approach

Freud's theory was criticized for being based on an unrepresentative sample: his own patients were predominantly upper-class Viennese women with psychological problems. Freud never examined patients from, or examined his theory with regard to, other cultures. Also, the belief that humans are driven mainly by instincts and the unconscious ignores the role of conscious drives and learning as important determinants of behavior, a matter that was inappropriate and markedly criticized.

Jung's View of the Structure of the Personality

Jung believed that the mind has inherited characteristics that determine how a person will react to life experiences. For Jung, the person is a whole being almost from the moment of birth. Personality is not acquired piece by piece (the "jigsaw" concept) through learning and experience, but is already there. So, instead of striving to achieve wholeness, our aim in life is to maintain it and to prevent the splitting (or dissociation) of the psyche into separate and conflicting parts. Jung saw the role of therapy as helping the patient recover this lost wholeness, and to strengthen the psyche so as to resist future dissociation. The details of Jung's view were described (see pp. 58–59).

Horney's Perspective of Personality

Karen Horney suggested that personality develops in the context of social relationships and depends mainly on the relationship between parents and child and how well the child's needs are met. Horney stressed the importance of cultural factors in the determination of personality, e.g., she suggested that society's rigid gender roles for women lead them to experience ambivalence about success because they fear they will make enemies if they are too successful (for more details, see pp. 78–80).

Adler's Perspective

Alfred Adler proposed that the primary human motivation is a striving for superiority, not in terms of superiority over others but in a search for self-improvement and perfection. Adler used the term inferiority complex to describe adults who have not been able to overcome the feelings of inadequacy they developed as children. Early social relationships with parents have an important effect on children's ability to outgrow feelings of personal inferiority. If children have positive experiences, they can orient themselves toward attaining socially useful goals (for more details, see pp. 46–50).

The Learning Approach to Personality

This approach views personality as a collection of learned behavior patterns. Similarities in responses across different situations are caused by similar patterns of reinforcement that have been received in such situations in the past. If one is sociable both at parties and at meetings, it is because one has been reinforced for displaying social behaviors, not because one is fulfilling an unconscious wish based on past experiences during childhood or because of an internal trait of sociability.

Learning theorists such as Skinner are less interested in the consistencies in behavior across situations than in ways of modifying behavior. To a learning theorist who adopts Skinner's view, humans are infinitely changeable through learning new behavior patterns. If we are able to control and modify the patterns of reinforcement in a situation, behavior that other theorists views as stable can be changed and improved. Learning theorists are optimistic in their attitudes about the potential for resolving personal and societal problems through treatment strategies based on learning theory.

Evaluation of the Learning Approach

This approach is objective, experimentally oriented, defined by operational concepts, and based on empirical data. However, behaviorists restricted their focus on behavior, the environment, and even cognitive factors, but ignore other potential influences on behavior (subjective experiences, genetic and physiological factors).

Social Cognitive Approaches to Personality

According to social cognitive approaches, personality develops through repeated observation of others' behavior, e.g., children who view a model behaving in an aggressive manner tend to copy the behavior if the consequences of the model's behavior are seen as positive. If the model's aggressive behavior has resulted in no consequences or negative consequences, children are considerably less likely to act aggressively. Social learning theory emphasizes the influence of cognition "thoughts, feelings, expectations, and values" as well as observation of others' behavior on personality. According to Albert Bandura, people can foresee the possible outcomes of certain behaviors in a specific setting without actually having to carry them out.

Bandura places particular emphasis on the role played by self-efficacy, the belief that we can master a situation and produce positive outcomes. People with high self-efficacy have higher aspirations and greater persistence in working to attain goals, and they ultimately achieve greater success than those with lower self-efficacy. Self-efficacy develops by paying attention to our prior successes and failures. Direct reinforcement and encouragement from others also play a role in developing self-efficacy (for more details, see social learning theory, pp. 217–220).

The Humanistic Approach to Personality

The humanistic approach defines personality as the unique way in which each individual perceives and interprets the world. The primary human motivator is an innate drive toward growth that prompts people to fulfill their unique and natural potential. Humanistic theories emphasize the importance of free will and individual experience in the development of personality. Humanistic theorists Carl Rogers and Abraham Maslow emphasized a view of the person as an active, creative, experiencing human being who lives in the present and subjectively responds to current perceptions, relationships, and encounters, and stressed the tendency of the human personality toward growth and self-actualization. Characteristics of self-actualizers, according to Maslow, include the four key dimensions:

1. *Awareness*: maintaining constant enjoyment and admiration of life. These individuals often experienced a "peak experience." He defined a peak experience as an "intensification of experience to the degree there is transcendence of self." The individual perceives an expansion of his or herself, and detects a unity and meaningfulness in life. Intense concentration on an activity that one is involved in, such as running a marathon, may result in a peak experience.
2. *Reality- and problem-centered*: having a tendency to be concerned with problems in surroundings.
3. *Acceptance/Spontaneity*: accepting surroundings and what cannot be changed.
4. *Unhostile sense of humor/democratic*: have friends of all backgrounds and religions and hold very close friendships. They do not joke about others, which can be viewed as offensive.

Evolutionary and Biological Approaches to Personality

Although there is an increasing number of personality theorists who are taking evolutionary and biological factors into account, no comprehensive unified theory that considers biological and evolutionary factors is widely accepted. Evolutionary and biological approaches suggest that personality is determined at least in part by genes in much the same way that genetics affect human height. The evolutionary perspective assumes that personality traits that led to survival and reproductive success of our ancestors are more likely to be preserved and passed on to subsequent generations.

Research studies conducted on monozygotic twins who are raised apart illustrate the importance of genetic factors in personality. Personality tests indicate that in major aspects, genetically identical twins raised apart are quite similar in personality, despite having been separated at an early age. Moreover, certain traits are more heavily influenced by heredity than others, e.g., social potency (the degree to which a person assumes mastery and leadership roles in social situations) and traditionalism (the tendency to follow authority) had particularly strong genetic components, whereas achievement and social closeness had relatively weak genetic components. Some researchers argue that specific genes are related to personality, e.g., people with a longer dopamine-4 receptor gene are more likely to be thrill-seekers than those without such a gene. Those thrill-seekers tend to be extroverted, impulsive, quick-tempered, and always in search of excitement and novel situations. Furthermore, the structure of their brains may reflect their thrill-seeking tendencies.

Infants are born with a specific temperament that influences their behavioral style and characteristic way of expressing needs and emotions. Temperament encompasses several dimensions, including the general activity level and mood, e.g., some individuals are quite active, while others are relatively calm. Similarly, some are relatively easy-going, whereas others are irritable, easily upset, and difficult to soothe. Temperament is quite consistent, with significant stability from infancy into adolescence. Innate and cultural factors play an adaptive role in the development of temperament. Also, the match between an infant's temperament and parental expectations or personal style affects the stability of a child's temperamental qualities. The following types of temperament are usually described in the majority of infants:

- *Easy temperament*: the most common; babies are usually predictable, react to new situations cheerfully, and seldom bother.
- *Difficult temperament*: babies usually have intense reactions to situations, inflexible, have irregular biological rhythms, and impulsive activities, and intense mood swings.
- *Slow-to-warm-up temperament*: babies usually react cautiously to new situations but slowly come to enjoy them.
- *Combinations*: some infants show a combination of the three types depending on the situation.

Factors Affecting the Development of Personality

Regardless of the theory proposed to explain personality, two main general factors are supposed to influence personality development: genetic factors and a person's experience within the environment:

- *The particular genetic pattern* established at the time of conception influences the personality characteristics of the person. This is evidenced by the higher concordance of personality traits in monozygotic than dizygotic twins. Also, one study found that personality traits, temperament, and occupational and leisure time interests, in monozygotic twins reared apart are nearly similar to monozygotic twins reared together.
- *Environmental factors*: a person's experiences in the surrounding environment may have significant effects on the development of personality characteristics. These experiences may be unique to one person or common to many people. Environmental factors include:
  - Social factors: there are many factors in the society which shape the individual's personality, e.g., the value system in the society, the degree of social support, socio-economic state, norms, and traditions.
  - Physical factors: some physical environmental factors may shape the personality, e.g., the weather or living in an isolated place.
- *Interaction of heredity and environment*: the combined effect of heredity and environment appear to influence many personality characteristics. It is clear that certain personality traits have substantial genetic components and that heredity and environment interact to determine personality. In most cases, it is difficult or impossible to assign percentages of importance to heredity and environmental influences, but it is easy to see that the two interact.

Assessment of Personality

Aspects of personality can be assessed by interviews, observational methods, and personality tests. Personality tests are more standardized and economic than either observations or interviews. In evaluating a person, the clinician should be aware of the halo effect. Personality assessment includes an interview of the person, direct observation, personality inventories, and projective tests (see psychological assessment).

- *Personality inventories*: these consist of questionnaires in which people report their feelings or reactions in certain situations. Inventories may assess a particular trait, such as anxiety, or a group of traits. They may also measure either a single dimension of personality, e.g., the introversion–extroversion dimension in Eysenck's personality inventory, or a group of personality traits simultaneously, e.g., the Minnesota Multiphasic Personality Inventory (MMPI), which is one of the most comprehensive personality inventories.
- *Minnesota Multiphasic Personality Inventory-2 (MMPI-2)*: this consists of a series of 567 questions used to assess a number of personality traits and psychological disturbances for people over the age of 16. While initially designed to aid in the diagnosis of serious personality disorders, the MMPI-2 is now widely used for persons with less severe problems, as enough data has been collected to allow for reliable interpretation of test results. MMPI-2 consists of eight basic syndrome scales "schizophrenia, mania, depression, paranoia, psychasthenia, hypochondriasis, psychopathic deviation, hysteria," and two additional basic clinical scales "masculine and feminine characters, and social introversion-extroversion." The test contains three validity scales which to large extent show how far it is accurate and reliable. The validity scales are lie scale, infrequency scale, and correction/defectiveness scale. Many additional subscales were developed on the basis of clusters of item contents. This helps to determine the characteristic symptomatic trends contributing to the full scale.

One problem with personality inventories is that people may try to twist their answers in the direction they think it will help them to obtain their objective in taking the test. Validity scales and other methods are commonly used to help determining whether an individual has answered the test items carefully and honestly.

Personality Disorders

According to the *Diagnostic and Statistical Manual*, fifth edition (DSM-5) (American Psychiatric Association, 2013), a personality disorder is an enduring pattern of inner experience and behavior that deviates markedly from the expectation of the individual's culture, that is pervasive and inflexible, has an onset in adolescence or early adulthood, is stable over time, and leads to distress or significant impairment in social functioning. Personality disorders may manifest as problems in cognition (ways of perceiving and thinking about self and others), affect (range, intensity, and appropriateness of emotional response), and/or behavior (interpersonal functioning, occupational and social functioning, and impulse control). To diagnose personality disorders, the observed manifestations should not be part of social and cultural norms, and should not be due to other conditions (such as psychosis, mood disorder, substance abuse, or general medical condition). The symptoms that characterize personality disorders are often similar to those of other disorders and illnesses.

Some types of personality disorder (especially, antisocial and borderline personality disorders) tend to become less evident with age, whereas this is less evident with some types (e.g., obsessive compulsive and schizotypal personality disorders). It is noteworthy that a personality disorder may worsen, following loss of significant supporting persons (e.g., a spouse) or previously stabilizing social situations (e.g., a job). However, the development of a change in personality in middle adulthood or later life warrants a thorough evaluation to determine the possible presence of a personality change due to mental disorder, another medical condition, or an unrecognized substance use disorder.

Clinical Types of Personality

The features of a personality disorder are usually recognizable during adolescence or early adult life. Personality disorders are classified in different ways. DSM-5 divides personality into three clusters based on descriptive similarities:

- *Cluster A personality disorders (odd eccentric cluster)*: this includes paranoid, schizoid, and schizotypal personality disorders. Individuals with cluster A personality disorders rarely seek psychiatric treatment. Core clinical features of cluster A disorders are: (1) profound problems in interpersonal relationships, characterized by severe mistrust or lack of interest in others; and (2) a tendency toward paranoid or idiosyncratic thinking in the absence of frank psychosis.
- *Cluster B personality disorders (erratic or dramatic personalities)*: this includes borderline, antisocial, histrionic, and narcissistic personality disorders. Core features of cluster B disorders include: (1) emotional reactivity, (2) poor impulse control, and (3) an unclear sense of identity, and (4) high levels of aggression (in persons with borderline, narcissistic, and antisocial personality disorders).
- *Cluster C personality disorders (the anxious/fearful group)*: this includes avoidant, dependent, and obsessive-compulsive disorder. The core feature of cluster C disorders is a propensity toward anxiety. Avoidant patients are fearful of other people in general and of criticism and ridicule in particular. Dependent patients are fearful of losing others or having to function autonomously. Obsessive-compulsive individuals fear loss of control.

DSM-5 added a general type called General Personality Disorder. This is characterized by an enduring pattern of inner experience and behavior that deviates markedly from the expectations of the individual's culture. This pattern is manifested in two or more of the following areas: cognition (i.e., ways of perceiving and interpreting self, other people, and events), affectivity (i.e., the range, intensity, lability, and appropriateness of emotional response), interpersonal functioning, and impulse control. The enduring pattern is inflexible and pervasive across a broad range of personal and social situations, and it leads to clinically significant distress or impairment in social, occupational, or other important areas of functioning.

Individuals frequently present with co-occurring personality disorders from different clusters. Prevalence estimates for the different clusters suggest 5.7 percent for disorders in Cluster A, 1.5 percent for disorders in Cluster B, 6.0 percent for disorders in Cluster C, and 9.1 percent for any personality disorder, indicating the frequent co-occurrence of disorders from different clusters. Personality disorders also commonly co-occur with other illnesses (American Psychiatric Association, 2013). Substance abuse and mental disorders are potential differentials that must be ruled out before diagnosing an individual with a personality disorder.

Paranoid Personality Disorder

Persons with paranoid personality disorder are characterized by long-standing suspicion and mistrust of people in general. Prevalence estimates for paranoid personality disorder in the US suggest a prevalence of 2.3–4.4 percent of the general population, and it is more common in men than women. Persons with this disorder have difficulties with bosses and co-workers and may become socially isolated because of their suspiciousness. Those individuals incorrectly interpret the motives of others to be malevolent, suspecting that others are exploiting, deceiving, or harming them. They endlessly question the trustworthiness and fidelity of friends and romantic partners, and they are reluctant to confide in others for fear the information will be used against them. So, they frequently scan their environments for clues of possible attack, deception, or betrayal. They often misinterpret benign events as evidence of malevolence, demeaning, or threatening. In response to perceived or actual insults or infidelities, these individuals overreact quickly, becoming excessively angry and responding with counterattacking behavior. They are unable to forgive or forget such incidents and instead bear long-term grudges against their supposed betrayers.

Schizoid Personality Disorder

Schizoid personality disorder is characterized by a profound impairment in the ability to relate to others in a meaningful way. It is rare in clinical settings, with an estimated prevalence of 3.1–4.9 percent in the general population. It is more common among men than women. The hallmark of schizoid personality disorder is a lack of interest in and an inability to establish meaningful relationships with others and, as a result, they have few or no close friends or confidants, and are extremely socially isolated. They date infrequently, typically do not marry, and have little interest in sex. They prefer to engage in solitary, often intellectual, activities, such as computer and web-based games, and choose professions that require little interpersonal interaction (e.g., as a night watchman). They often develop elaborate fantasy lives that substitute for engagement in the real world. Affective experience of individuals with schizoid personality disorder is flattened, with a general lack of pleasure and chronic anhedonia. They usually appear cold, detached, aloof, and constricted, and they have particular discomfort with warm feelings.

Schizotypal Personality Disorder

These individuals display a pervasive pattern of social and interpersonal deficits marked by discomfort with and reduced capacity for close relationships, and are socially withdrawn and anxious, similar to persons with schizoid personality. The hallmark of schizotypal personality disorder is the presence of eccentricities of behavior and cognitive or perceptual distortions in the absence of frank psychotic symptoms, beginning by early adulthood and present in a variety of contexts. The prevalence of schizotypal personality disorder ranges from 0.6 percent to 4.6 percent in community settings, and 0–1.9 percent in clinical populations. It is equally common among men and women.

Common cognitive and perceptual distortions include ideas of reference, persecutory beliefs, bodily illusions, and unusual telepathic experiences. These distortions, which are inconsistent with cultural norms, occur frequently and represent an important and pervasive component of the person's experience. The distortions may be used by the person to explain the odd and eccentric behavior characteristic of this disorder. Individuals with schizotypal personality disorder may talk to themselves in public, gesture for no apparent reason, or dress in a peculiar or unkempt fashion. Their speech is often odd and idiosyncratic, e.g., circumstantial, metaphorical, vague, overinclusive, or difficult to follow, and their affect is constricted or inappropriate. Such a person may laugh inappropriately when discussing his or her problems. Interpersonally, those individuals appear eccentric or odd and emotionally constricted. Persons with schizotypal personality disorder are socially uncomfortable and isolated, with few friends. This isolation is often due to their eccentric cognitions and behavior, as well as their lack of desire for relationships, which stems in part from their suspicion of others. If they develop relationships, they tend to remain distant or may end them because of their persistent social anxiety and paranoia.

Schizotypal personality disorder is not associated with gradual deterioration of social and cognitive functioning, though some of these individuals may be subject to brief psychotic decompensation.

Antisocial Personality Disorder

Antisocial personality is characterized by a pervasive pattern of disregard and violations of the rights of others. It is more common in men than in women, with about 3 percent of men and 1 percent of women having this disorder at some time in their lives (Kraus & Reynolds, 2001). Etiologic factors of antisocial behavior include membership in a delinquent gang or a criminal subculture, the need for attention and status, and inability to control impulses. People who have antisocial personality disorder have little sense of responsibility, morality, or concern for others. Individuals who have antisocial personalities consider only their own desires and rarely consider others' desires. They behave impulsively, seek immediate gratification of their needs, and cannot tolerate frustration. People with antisocial personalities have little feeling for anyone except themselves and seem to experience little guilt or remorse, regardless of the degree of suffering caused by their behavior. In contrast, most juvenile delinquents and adult criminals show some concern for others (for example, family or gang members) and adhere to some code of moral conduct (never betray a friend). Other characteristics of the antisocial personality include a marked ability for lying, a need for thrills and excitement with little concern for possible injury, and inability to alter behavior as a consequence of punishment. Such individuals are sometimes attractive, intelligent, charming people who are skilled at manipulating others. When they are caught, their declarations of regret are so convincing that they often escape punishment and are given another chance, but what they say has little relation to what they feel or do. Deceitfulness is one of the defining characteristics of antisocial personality (Kraus & Reynolds, 2001).

Borderline Personality Disorder

Borderline personality is characterized by a pervasive pattern of significant instability of interpersonal relationships, mood, and self-image, and marked impulsivity. About 1–2 percent of the population will develop borderline personality disorder at some time in their lives (Weissman, 1993). The disorder is diagnosed much more often in women than in men. People with this disorder tend to have more difficulties in marital relationships and job, and a higher rate of physical disability than average.

Instability is a key feature of borderline personality disorder. The mood of those individuals is unstable, with frequent bouts of severe depression, anxiety, or anger, often without good reason. The self-concept is unstable, with periods of extreme self-doubt and others of grandiose self-importance. Interpersonal relationships are extremely unstable, and the person can switch from idealizing other people to hating them with little or no rationale. People with borderline personality disorder often feel crucially empty, so they cling to a new contact to fill the large void they feel in themselves. At the same time, they may misinterpret other people's innocent actions as signs of neglect or rejection. People with borderline personality disorder have also a tendency toward impulsive self-damaging behaviors, including self-mutilation and suicidal behavior. Self-mutilation often takes the form of burning or cutting. Longitudinal studies of people with this disorder indicate that about 10 percent die by suicide. On average, each person with borderline personality disorder attempts suicide 3.3 times in his or her life (Soloff & Chiappetta, 2012). The greatest risk of suicide appears to be in the first or second year after receiving a diagnosis of borderline personality disorder. Substance abuse, depression, generalized anxiety disorder, specific phobia, agoraphobia, post-traumatic stress disorder, and panic disorder are likely to co-occur in people with borderline personality disorder (Kraus & Reynolds, 2001). Finally, people with borderline personality disorder are prone to episodes of transient stress-related psychosis or severe dissociative symptoms.

Histrionic Personality Disorder

Histrionic personality disorder occurs in about 1.8 percent of the general population and is more common among women than men. The hallmark of histrionic personality disorder is excessive attention-seeking and rapidly shifting, dramatic, and superficial expression of emotion. Persons with this disorder spend an excessive amount of time seeking attention and making themselves attractive. They characteristically use their physical appearance to gain attention, often in a sexually provocative or seductive fashion. People with histrionic personality disorder are impressionistic in their speech and cognition, do not attend to details or facts, and they are reluctant or unable to make reasoned critical analyses of problems or situations. Those persons exaggerate their own qualities, role, situation, and feelings. They often consider relationships to be more intimate than they are. Interpersonally those individuals tend to be engaging initially, but over time they often seem superficial and excessively demanding of attention. Persons with this disorder often present with complaints of depression, somatic problems of unclear origin, and a history of disappointing romantic relationships. Compared with the other cluster B personality disorders, histrionic personality disorder is associated with a greater capacity to establish stable and meaningful relationships and with better work functioning.

Narcissistic Personality Disorder

The core features of narcissistic personality disorder are a grandiose sense of self, fantasies of unlimited success and power, and excessive need for admiration from others.

Interpersonally, individuals with narcissistic personality disorder appear self-centered and arrogant, and they can be exploitative and strikingly lacking empathy in their relationships with others. Because their sense of self depends on their feeling of being superior to others, failure, slights, and criticism are poorly tolerated, often leading to emotional collapse and depression, or alternatively, rage and devaluation of others. In general, those individuals do not tolerate being in need of help or relying on others. Seeking help stimulates painful feelings of envy and inferiority. These individuals usually present with chronic, treatment-refractory depression.

PHOTO 18.2.   Self love.

Avoidant Personality Disorder

The key features of avoidant personality disorder are excessive and pervasive anxiety and discomfort in social situations and in intimate relationships, feelings of inadequacy, and hypersensitivity to criticism. Although strongly desiring relationships, they avoid them because they fear being ridiculed, criticized, rejected, or humiliated. These fears reflect their low self-esteem and hypersensitivity to negative evaluation by others. As a result, they tend to avoid social or intimate settings, and are unwilling to become involved with others unless they are certain of being liked. They avoid occupational activities that involve significant interpersonal contact, because of fear of humiliating themselves or being criticized. There is a high co-occurrence of avoidant personality disorder with social phobia, as well as with a broad spectrum of other anxiety disorders. The avoidant behavior often starts in infancy or childhood with shyness, isolation, and fear of strangers or new situations. Patients with avoidant personality disorder may engage in deliberate self-harm (Klonsky, Oltmanns, & Turkheimer, 2003) and experience disability in social, educational, and physical fields (Kessler, 2003).

Dependent Personality Disorder

Dependent personality is characterized by an excessive need to be taken care of that leads to submissive and clinging behavior and excessive fears of separation. It is estimated to have a prevalence of between 0.49 percent and 0.6 percent in the general population. Although these individuals are able to care for themselves, they tend to devalue their own abilities and decision-making, and to view others as much stronger and more capable than they are. As a result, they depend on others to make decisions and take care of them, and excessively seek to develop and maintain dependent relationships with partners whom they feel can provide nurturance and guidance. Interpersonally, people with dependent personality disorder often seem appealing. In the setting of a dependent relationship, they often become submissive and childlike, while experiencing a desperate need to maintain the relationship in the face of fear of losing their partner. They feel panicked at the prospect of being left to care for themselves, and if a relationship ends, they may quickly indiscriminately begin another relationship so that they can be provided with direction and nurturance; an unfulfilling or even abusive relationship may seem better than being on their own. Low self-esteem and doubts about their effectiveness lead those people to avoid positions of responsibility.

Obsessive Compulsive Personality Disorder

The hallmarks of this personality are a preoccupation with orderliness, perfectionism, control, and emotional constriction. These individuals are excessively devoted to work, to the exclusion of friendships and leisure activity, so that they may avoid vacations. People with obsessive-compulsive personality disorder often experience themselves as robots, their emotional lives are constricted and flattened, and they value self-control above all else. Lack of control can lead to an increase in anxiety. They have a marked attention to details and can frequently be successful in methodical, detail-oriented jobs. They are overly conscientious in their morals, and they are miserly with regard to spending money. They also tend to be controlling of others, and they have difficulty delegating tasks, feeling that no one can do the task the way they want it done. Interpersonally, obsessive-compulsive individuals appear stiff, excessively controlled, and emotionally distant and constricted. Some individuals with obsessive-compulsive personality disorder are functioning relatively well, especially in their professional lives, while others suffer significant impairment in all domains of functioning.

Clinical Notes

- Assessment of personality disturbances is usually limited by diagnostic categories to secure against over-diagnosis. In clinical practice, people show a wide range of personality pathology which needs careful attention.
- Some of the personality traits are dysfunctional and maladaptive so as to warrant a diagnosis of personality disorder. In clinical practice, it is of particular importance when diagnosing personality disorders to differentiate them from other mental disorders, from general personality functioning, and from each other (Widiger, 2003).
- Personality disorder is associated with high service use and excess medical morbidity and mortality (Gask, Evans, & Kessler, 2013). Labeling people with personality disorder can influence their care when they come into contact with services, including mental health providers.

Summary

- Personality is the enduring patterns of cognition, emotion, motivation, and behaviors that make a person unique, which remain fairly consistent throughout life.
- Several theories have been proposed to explain different aspects of personality. These include: the type approach, the trait approach, the psychodynamic approach, the learning approach, social cognitive approaches, the humanistic approach, and evolutionary and biological approaches.
- Two main general factors are supposed to influence personality development: genetic factors and a person's experience in the environment.
- Personality disorder is an enduring pattern of inner experience and behavior that deviates markedly from the expectation of the individual's culture, that is pervasive and inflexible, has an onset in adolescence or early adulthood, is stable over time, and leads to distress or significant impairment in social functioning.
- The features of a personality disorder are usually recognizable during adolescence or early adult life.
- Aspects of personality can be assessed by interviews, observational methods, and personality tests.
- DSM-5 divides personality into three clusters based on descriptive similarities: Cluster A personality disorders (odd, eccentric cluster) that includes paranoid, schizoid, and schizotypal personality disorders. Cluster B personality disorders (erratic or dramatic personalities) that includes borderline, antisocial, histrionic, and narcissistic personality disorders. Cluster C personality disorders (the anxious/fearful group) that includes avoidant, dependent, and obsessive-compulsive disorder.

Test Your Knowledge

- Outline the type approach to personality.
- Define the trait approach.
- Describe the psychodynamic approach.
- Summarize the learning approach.
- Outline social cognitive approaches.
- Define the humanistic approach.

- Describe the evolutionary and biological approaches.
- Define the differentiating features between Cluster A personality disorders.
- Describe the differentiating features between Cluster B personality disorders.
- Outline the differentiating features between Cluster C personality disorders.

Critical Thinking Questions

- How can different approaches to personality help in a real understanding of personality?
- Evaluate the problems inherent in personality classification and diagnosis.
- What are the implications of linking certain personality traits to certain brain structures?
- What is the harm or benefit of assigning certain personality traits to a person, is it just descriptive?
- What is the value of classifying personality disorders?

nineteen
Psychological Testing

Learning Goals

- This chapter is intended to provide the reader with an overview of the characteristics of a good psychological test, the common uses of psychological tests, and the methods and techniques of psychological assessment.

Introduction

One of the first applications of psychological principles is the development of psychological testing to predict things, such as school success and mental fitness. Psychologists are the only professionals who, as part of their education and the licensing process, receive extensive training and supervision in psychometrics (the theory and technique of psychological measurement), how to select and administer tests appropriately, as well as the ethnic, racial, cultural, and other important factors that affect the interpretation of psychological tests (American Psychological Association, 2010). Psychologists use assessment tools to better understand the possible causes of behavioral, emotional, or cognitive symptoms. Psychological tests can also describe capacities and treatment needs, and predict outcomes and subsequent functioning in a way that is sometimes better than medical tests, including Pap smears, magnetic resonance imaging (MRI), and electrocardiograms (Meyer et al., 2001). The psychological assessments encompass a wide range of individuals and institutions, including medical patients, students, individuals with disabilities, parents, teachers, and job applicants.

Psychological assessment uses a variety of methods: interview, observation, self-reports, and projective techniques. Some of these methods have standard sets of stimuli, administration procedures, and ways of measuring subjects' responses and transforming them into standard scores. All assessment methods have particular sources of error, thus, the use of multiple methods is highly recommended.

Characteristics of a Good Psychological Test

- *Reliability*: the extent to which the scores for a test are consistently obtained when the test or supposedly equivalent forms of a test are used. It is impossible to make accurate or meaningful predictions from the results of an unreliable test. The common methods used for assessing reliability are:
  - Parallel form reliability: this calculates the correlation between the results from two forms of a test that are supposed to be equal in difficulty.
  - Split-half reliability: when only one form is available, the items are divided into two halves. Correlation is made between the results of the two halves.
  - Test-retest: the test is given twice to the same sample, and the correlation coefficient for the two sets of scores is computed.
- *Validity*: this means the extent to which a test actually assesses what it intends to measure or to predict. Thus, it is very important to identify what a test measures or predict. Content validity denotes the extent to which the content of the test measures all of the knowledge or skills that are supposed to be included in the test according to the experts' opinion (face validity is the same but according to the test takers' opinion), while predictive validity denotes that the test predicts behavior being measured by the test. Construct validity is the ability of the test to measure the specific construct/behavior that is supposed to measure. A test may have several validities, e.g., a high validity for prediction of scholastic success in literature courses but much lower validity for predicting success in mathematics course. Improper use of tests may lead to inaccurate predictions and therefore faulty counseling and advice.

  It is noteworthy that a test may be highly reliable but invalid, and this occurs when a test measures something consistently does not measure what it claims to measure. However, a valid test must be reliable, that is, it measures what it claims to measure, and it has to do so consistently.

■ *Standardization*: all aspects of the testing process, including the administration, the scoring, and the evaluation of the results should follow the same pattern each time. This helps to avoid differences in test results as a consequence of variation of test procedures. An essential step to standardize a test is to establish norms, which are scores obtained from groups of people who have taken the test. Once norms have been determined, the performances of others taking the test in the same manner can be compared to the norms.

■ *Objectivity*: this means that measurements are made in a neutral fashion, and the assessment tool is not prejudiced to affect the results of measurement.

Ethics of Testing

The increasing use of psychological tests is associated with increased concern about ethical administration, scoring, interpretation, and reporting the results. Perhaps the most serious has been the concern for privacy, that is, to whom the results should be made available. Test results should not be revealed without the test taker's knowledge or consent.

Test Fairness

Attempts have been made to develop culture-free or culture-fair tests, but success was limited. Thus, psychological tests may be misused if they are administered to a subcultural group for which they are inappropriate. Also, psychologists must realize the limitations of test scores and not rely on them exclusively when making decisions about individuals.

Uses of Psychological Tests

1. Selection of people who fit into certain situation, e.g., children who need special education or workers suitable for certain jobs.
2. Guidance of persons with certain deficits, e.g., children with learning disabilities.
3. Diagnosis of psychological and behavioral disturbance. Some psychological tests may be useful in the diagnosis of certain psychological and behavioral problems, e.g., the Connor scale in diagnosing attention deficit hyperactivity disorder, and the Hamilton scale in diagnosing depression.
4. Evaluation of treatment: comparing the initial results of a test with that obtained during follow-up can be used as a guide of the efficacy of treatment modality used in the management of the condition.

Methods and Techniques of Psychological Assessment

Most assessment methods fall into one of four categories: (1) interview; (2) observational methods; (3) self-reports; or (4) projective techniques.

Interview

Interviewing is a face-to-face meeting designed to gain information about personal history, current psychological state, or someone's personality. It is the most commonly used method in psychological assessment in all basic and applied fields: clinical, educational, work and organizations, forensic, laboratory, and so on. It has the broadest scope, so it can be used for assessing any psychological event (subjective or objective, motor, cognitive or physiological). For assessment purposes, an interview is basically an interactional process between two people, in which one person (the interviewer) elicits and collects information with a given purpose, and the other person (the interviewee, client, or subject) responds or answers questions. The information collected can refer to the interviewee (their motor, cognitive, or emotional responses) or to relevant others. Interviews may be either structured with a standard agenda, or unstructured, allowing the subject to determine much of what is discussed and in what order.

- *Unstructured interview*: the conversation is informal, and topics are discussed as they arise. It helps the patient to express himself or herself without shame or embarrassment; however, it is personal and depends on the experience and impression of the interviewer and his or her own conflicts and difficulties.
- *Structured interview*: this follows a prearranged plan, using a series of planned questions.

Observational Methods

This refers to direct measurement of an individual's behavior through a set of data collection procedures containing a protocol with a predefined list of behavioral categories in which subjects' behaviors are coded or registered during various structured and unstructured tasks. Observational assessment is performed by a trained professional, either in the subject's natural setting (such as a classroom), an experimental setting, or during an interview. Observational methods have been classified according to the following:

- *The observer*: participant versus non-participant observer.
- *The target or observed event*: overt event (motor response or stimuli parameter) versus subject's attribute or moral characteristic of the observed person.
- *The situation in which observations take place*: natural versus artificial or standardized situations.
- *The protocol*: coding system versus open description of the spectrum of behavior.

Self-Reports

Self-reporting is a method for collecting data whose source is the subject's verbal statement about him/herself. This is the most common assessment procedures for collecting data in psychology and psychological assessment. Self-reports provide information about thousands of targets including historical events, motor behaviors in the present situation, or even in future plans.

Self-reports can be obtained through questionnaires, inventories, or scales containing a set of relevant verbal statements. The individual can respond with answers such as yes, maybe, true, false, or cannot say. Self-reports have several sources of bias. Several internal and external conditions can affect the fidelity of self-reports, e.g., the length of the questionnaire, the formulation of the questions, the type of answer and the response requested, and the subject's characteristics. The best example of these tests is the Minnesota Multiphasic Personality Inventory-2 (MMPI-2) (see personality section, p. 376).

Projective Techniques

These are tests that consist of a series of unstructured ambiguous stimuli which can be perceived and responded to in many ways. Individuals are asked for a description or a story about each, thus projecting their own characteristics onto those stimuli. The best-known projective tests are the *Rorschach test* and the *Thematic Apperception Test (TAT)*. Responses to projective tests reflect many aspects of an individual's personality. These tests are relatively difficult to score and tend to be less reliable and valid than objective tests.

In the Rorschach test, the subject describes his or her reactions to 10 elaborate inkblots presented on a series of ten cards. Responses are interpreted with attention to three factors: (1) which parts of each inkblot the subject responds to; (2) which aspects of the inkblot are stressed (color, shape, etc.); and (3) content (what the inkblot represents to the subject).

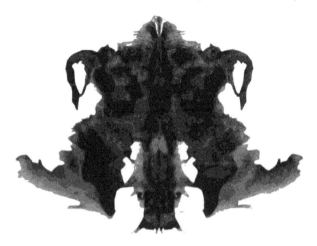

FIGURE 19.1.   A Rorschach Test Inkblot.

In the Thematic Apperception Test (TAT), the subject is shown a series of 20 pictures, each of which can be interpreted in a variety of ways, and is asked to construct a story based on each one. Responses tend to reflect a person's problems, motives, preoccupations, and interpersonal skills.

FIGURE 19.2.   A TAT Example.

Clinical Notes

- Psychological assessments can offer great benefit for clinicians and patients. They cover a wide and specific area that may need special elaboration. Test results can be useful in elucidating management needed as in cases of intellectual disability, in predicting outcome, and in follow-up of patients. Also, the test process communicates a genuine respect for the patient as an integral part of the process rather than just the "subject" of an assessment. The test process promotes rapport with patients in the form of a mutual understanding and decisions about the type of interventions.
- Test bias can over-estimate or over-predict minority examinees' performance, so that its social consequences may be very different from those typically ascribed to it, and appropriate responses to it may differ from those typically made. However, bias cannot be understood in isolation from other possible influences, and research findings suggest that in a standardized test, bias is not a major source of discrimination. Rigorous examination of possible test bias and inaccuracy should continue, employing the latest and most diverse techniques. However, one should be cautious against labeling tests biased in the absence of, or in opposition to, reliable evidence (Reynolds & Suzuki, 2013).

Summary

- Psychologists use assessment tools to better understand possible causes of behavioral, emotional, or cognitive symptoms. Psychological tests can also describe capacities, and treatment needs, and predict outcomes and subsequent functioning.
- Psychological assessment uses a variety of methods: interview, observation, self-reports, and projective techniques.
- Reliability: the consistency with which a result will be obtained when identical or supposedly equivalent forms of a test are used.
- Validity means that a test actually assesses what it intends to measure. A test may have several validities, e.g., a high validity for prediction of scholastic success in literature courses but much lower validity for predicting success in mathematics courses.
- In a standardized test, all aspects of the testing process, including the administration, the scoring, and the evaluation of the results should follow the same pattern each time.
- Most assessment methods fall into one of four categories: interview, observational methods, self-reports, or projective techniques.
- Interviewing is a face-to-face meeting designed to gain information about personal history, current psychological state, or someone's personality. Interviews may be either structured with a standard agenda, or unstructured, allowing the subject to determine much of what is discussed and in what order.
- Observational methods refer to direct measurement of an individual's behavior through a set of data collection procedures containing a protocol with a predefined list of behavioral categories in which subjects' behaviors are coded or registered during various structured and unstructured tasks.
- Self-report is a method of collecting data whose source is the subject's verbal statement about him/herself.

■ Projective techniques are tests that consist of a series of unstructured ambiguous stimuli which can be perceived and responded to in many ways. Individuals are asked for a description or a story about each, thus projecting their own characteristics onto those stimuli.

Test Your Knowledge

■ What is meant by validity, reliability, and standardization?
■ Define a psychological interview.
■ Describe observational methods in psychological assessment.
■ Outline a self-report.
■ Define projective techniques.

Critical Thinking Questions

■ Give your own opinion about the pros and cons of psychological testing.
■ Evaluate the ethical issues versus the practical value of the predictive value of psychological testing.

PART FIVE
Clinical and Health Psychology

twenty
Stress, Health, and Coping

Learning Goals

This chapter is intended to provide the reader with an overview of: (1) stress and stressors; (2) the psychological reaction to having a serious or chronic illness; and (3) the reaction to dying and death.

This will include an idea about what is meant by stress and stressors, general adaptation syndrome (GAS), explaining the effect of stress on the endocrine system and the immune system, describing types of stressors, identifying stress outcomes, describing the relation between stress and mental health, describing the relation between stress and health behaviors, identifying factors that influence the response to stress, coping resources, and coping strategies.

In the overview of psychological reaction to having a serious or chronic illness, the factors affecting this reaction, coping tasks in the face of illness, and how to manage maladaptive responses are discussed.

Also, this chapter is intended to provide an overview or reaction to death and dying. This involves Bowlby's view and phases of grief, Elisabeth Kübler-Ross's stages of grief, how children cope with the death of a parent or sibling, the physician's response to death, and cultural influences on bereavement.

Introduction

PHOTO 20.1.   Work Stress.

The term stress was coined by Hans Selye in 1936, to refer to the nonspecific response of the body, whether biological and psychological, to challenging or threatening events. Stress can be caused by both good and bad experiences. However, it is reasonable to assume that positive life events are generally less disruptive than negative life events, e.g., marriage tends to be less stressful than divorce or separation. Because most people viewed stress as an unpleasant threat, Selye introduced the term, stressor, to distinguish stimulus from response. A stressor refers to any environmental, social, biological, or psychological demand that requires a person to adjust his or her usual patterns of behavior, e.g., exam, moving house, loss of job, or death of loved one. Selye also pointed out that human perception of and response to stress are highly variable: a job or sport that one person considers anxiety-provoking or exhausting might be quite appealing and enjoyable to someone else.

Stress
The General Adaptation Syndrome (GAS)

Hans Selye observed that human bodies respond to many kinds of unpleasant stressors in a similar way, whether the source of stress is an invasion of body by a tiny infectious organism, divorce, or the consequences of flood. Selye called the body's short-term and long-term reactions to stress, the general adaptation syndrome. Selye supposed that adaptation passes through three stages (Selye, 1952):

1. *Alarm reaction*: this is the immediate reaction to a stressor that mobilizes the body's resources to prepare for a challenge or stress, through what is called the fight-or-flight response. The body responds in a complex, integrated manner, including the central nervous system, the immune system, and the endocrine system (Ellis, Jackson, & Boyce, 2006). When exposed to a stressor, the body labels it as a threat or danger, and immediately activates the sympathetic autonomic nervous system, and releases the stress hormones, such as adrenaline, noradrenaline, and cortisol. These hormones enable the body to perform the recommended reactions.

2. *Adaptation (resistance) stage*: when a stressor is persistent, the parasympathetic nervous system counteracts the changes that are produced by the stressful stimulus,

and attempts to restore a state of homeostasis (the default state in which the body functions normally). During this stage, the results of the hormonal changes which occurred in the previous stage are still apparent, including increased glucose levels in the blood and higher blood pressure, but the stress hormones level begin to return to normal, enabling the body's focus to shift from alertness to repair. If stress is overcome, the body continues to repair itself until the hormone levels, the heart rate, and the blood pressure return to the pre-stress state. If the adaptation stage continues for a long period without pauses to counterbalance the effects of stress, this can lead to the exhaustion stage. Signs of the adaptation stage include irritability, frustration, poor concentration, and that things seem harder than they used to be.

3. *Exhaustion stage*: although there are individual differences in the capacity to resist stress, struggling with stress for long periods can drain a person's physical, emotional, and mental resources to the point where their body no longer has the strength to fight stress. The exhaustion stage is characterized by the dominance of the parasympathetic activity. Consequently, our heart and respiration rates slow down. Signs of exhaustion include fatigue, burnout, depression, anxiety, and decreased stress tolerance. The physical effects of this stage impair the immune system and put a person at risk for stress-related illnesses, and unexplained medical symptoms, such as hair loss.

Although Selye's model refers to the general response pattern of the body under stress, different biological processes may specifically respond to certain kinds of stressors, e.g., persistent exposure to loud noise may cause different bodily processes than other sources of stress, such as overcrowding; or psychological stress, such as divorce or separation. The general adaptation syndrome is influenced by a variety of factors, including overall health and nutritional status, sex, age, ethnic or racial background, level of education, socio-economic status, genetic make-up, etc.

Stress and the Endocrine System

Stress produces a cascade of changes in the endocrine system. The hypothalamus releases a hormone that stimulates the pituitary gland to secrete adrenocorticotrophic hormone (ACTH), which in turn stimulates the adrenal glands to release a group of hormones called corticosteroids. The sympathetic branch of the autonomic nervous system stimulates the adrenal medulla to release a mixture of epinephrine and norepinephrine. The stress hormones produced by the adrenal glands help the body prepare to cope with stressors. They increase the heart rate and stimulate the liver to release stored glucose, making energy necessary for responding to a stressor. Once the stressor has passed, the body returns to its normal state. However, when stress is enduring or recurring, the body regularly pumps out stress hormones and activates other systems, which over time can drain the body's resources and impair health (Kemeny, 2003). Chronic or repetitive stress can damage many bodily systems, including the cardiovascular system and the immune system.

Stress and the Immune System

Occasional stress may not harm one's health, however, chronic or repetitive stress can ultimately impair the body's immune system (Kemeny, 2003; Segerstrom & Miller, 2004). Impairment of the immune system increases susceptibility to many illnesses, e.g., the common cold, and may increase the risk of developing chronic diseases, e.g., cancer. Life stressors that can affect the immune system and leave people more vulnerable to disease include marital conflict, divorce, and chronic unemployment (e.g., Kiecolt-Glaser, McGuire, Robles, & Glaser, 2002). Traumatic stress, such as exposure to earthquakes, hurricanes, or other natural or technological disasters, and terrorist attacks or other forms of violence, can also impair immunological functioning (Solomon, Segerstrom, Grohr, Kemeny, & Fahey, 1997). Kiecolt-Glaser et al. (1984) found that immune responses were especially weak in students who reported more loneliness, as well as those who were experiencing other stressful life events and psychiatric symptoms such as depression or anxiety.

Even relatively brief periods of stress, such as final exam time, can weaken the immune system, although these effects are more limited than those associated with chronic or prolonged stress. One way that chronic stress may damage the body's immune system is by increasing levels of interleukin-6 (Kiecolt-Glaser et al., 2003). Sustained high levels of this substance are linked to inflammation, which in turn can contribute to the development of many disorders, including cardiovascular disease, cancer, and arthritis. In their meta-analytic study, Segerstrom and Miller (2004) found that acute stressors (lasting minutes) were associated with potentially adaptive up-regulation of some parameters of natural immunity and down-regulation of some functions of specific immunity. Brief naturalistic stressors (such as exams) tended to suppress cellular immunity while preserving humoral immunity. Chronic stressors were associated with suppression of both cellular and humoral immunity. In some cases, physical vulnerability as a function of age or disease increases vulnerability to immune change during stressors.

Social support appears to moderate the harmful effects of stress on the immune system; medical and dental students with large numbers of friends showed better immune functioning than students with fewer friends (Jemmott et al., 1983; Kiecolt-Glaser et al., 1984). On the other hand, lonely students showed greater suppression of immune responses than did students with more social support (Glaser, Kiecolt-Glaser, Speicher, & Holliday, 1985).

Types of Stressors

The types of stressors to which one is most susceptible vary widely by one's social location, reflecting patterns of race, gender, age, and class stratification. Stressors are empirically classified into three major categories: life events, chronic strains, and daily hassles (Carr & Umberson, 2013). Although the three types of stressors are described as distinctive and discrete experiences, stressors rarely occur in isolation. A life event may create new and multiple chronic strains (e.g., a job loss may create financial problems), and chronic strains may give rise to a stressful life event (e.g., workplace strains may precede involuntary job loss).

- *Life events*: these refer to acute changes that require people to adjust. They include both positive events, such as getting married, and negative events, such as getting divorced. The impact of a stressful life event depends on its magnitude, desirability, expectedness, and timing. Events that are severe, undesirable, or unexpected (e.g., sudden death of son) are particularly distressing (George, 1999).
- *Chronic strains*: these are persistent and recurring demands that require adaptation over sustained periods, such as a strained marriage, a stressful job, or living in a hazardous district. With the exception of traumatic events, chronic strains are generally found to be more powerful predictors of health than acute events, due to their persistent nature (Turner, Wheaton, & Lloyd, 1995). Chronic strains typically fall into three subcategories:

- Status strain: this occurs as a result of challenges to one's position in the social structure, such as belonging to an ethnic or racial minority, or living in poverty.
- Role strains: these are conflicts or demands related to social roles, such as handling work and family demands.
- Ambient strains: these refer to stressful aspects of the physical environment, such as noise or pollution (Pearlin, 1999).

- *Daily hassles*: these are minor events that require adjustment throughout the day, such as traffic jams, or an argument with a spouse (Lazarus & Folkman, 1984). This is the most neglected type in stress research. The emotional effects of daily hassles are generally found to recede in a day or two. However, the frequency and type of daily hassles experienced can better explain associated psychological and somatic outcomes than do recent life events or chronic role-related stressors (Bolger, DeLongis, Kessler, & Schilling, 1989). Moreover, daily hassles that recur over long periods of time may become chronic strains and have cumulative effects on health.

Stress Outcomes

People who experience greater numbers of life changes are more likely to suffer from psychological and physical health problems (Dohrenwend, 2006). However, these links are correlational, so that a causal relationship could not be established. Such relationships are open to other interpretations. It could be that physical symptoms are sources of stress in themselves and lead to more life changes. Physical illness may cause disruptions of sleep or financial burdens, and so forth. Hence, at least in some cases, the causal direction may be reversed. Selye suggested that the stressors themselves are less dangerous to health than people's maladaptive responses to them.

Multiple rather than single stress outcomes should be considered when comparing stress effects, particularly across social groups (Aneshensel, Rutter, & Lachenbruch, 1991), to avoid bias resulting from a general vulnerability within certain groups to specific health threats even in the absence of a stressor, e.g., women are more prone to depression and men more likely to use alcohol in the general population, even when stress exposure is held constant. Thus, studies focusing only on depressive symptoms following divorce may erroneously conclude that divorce affects the well-being of women only, such a study could conceal the fact that men may be more likely to respond to divorce by turning to alcohol, rather than becoming depressed (Horwitz, White, & Howell-White, 1996).

Stress and Mental Health

Studies of mental health outcomes of stress usually focus on data that can be easily and accurately measured using self- or telephone-administered instruments, e.g., the measurement of depressive symptoms using the Center for Epidemiological Studies Depression scale (Radloff, 1977), or assessment of major depressive disorders using the Composite International Diagnostic Interview (Robins et al., 1988). Psychological outcomes include positive and negative affect, and anxiety. Studies of bereavement usually focus on symptoms of grief and loss-related distress. It is interesting to note that, not experiencing an event that one had expected, such as marrying or having a baby, can also harm one's mental health (Carlson, 2010). Also, the impact of an event may depend on the context in which it occurs, e.g., divorce from an abusive spouse, or being fired from an intolerable job may enhance well-being. On the other hand, loss of particularly salient and valued roles may compromise well-being.

Stress and Physical Health

Most studies of stress and physical health focus on general outcomes such as self-rated health, number of current illnesses or health symptoms, and all-cause mortality. Among the most commonly used specific health outcomes are heart disease, and high blood pressure. Exposure to stress is linked to greater risk of developing the common cold, and people who reported the most stressful life events and highest levels of perceived stress and negative affect had the greatest probability of developing cold symptoms (Cohen, Tyrrell, & Smith, 1991). In a subsequent study of volunteers inoculated with a cold virus, it was found that people enduring chronic, stressful life events (i.e., events lasting a month or longer, including unemployment, chronic underemployment, or continued interpersonal difficulties) had a high likelihood of catching cold, whereas people subjected to stressful events lasting less than a month did not (Cohen et al., 1998). Laboratory studies of marital strain consistently show that stressful conflict can impair immune response, slow wound healing, heighten susceptibility to infectious agents, increase cardiovascular reactivity, and ultimately compromise physical health (Robles & Kiecolt-Glaser, 2003).

The stress process beginning in childhood has cumulative physiological effects over the life course (Repetti, Robles, & Reynolds, 2011). Exposure to stressors including child abuse (Slopen et al., 2010), discrimination (Friedman, Williams, Singer, & Ryff, 2009), and marital strain (Whisman & Sbarra, 2012) are linked to elevated inflammation levels at midlife; inflammation is a well-documented correlate of cardiovascular disease and cancer. Both current stressors as well as those dating back to prenatal conditions may speed up cellular aging, operationalized as shortened telomere length. More rapid cellular aging has been detected among young adult mothers who were exposed to prenatal stress (Entringer et al., 2011) and persons who anticipate stressful events in the near future (O'Donovan et al., 2012).

Stress and Health Behaviors

Health behaviors are important stress outcomes in their own right, and are a critical pathway linking stress to physical and mental health outcomes. Stress exposure has been associated with unhealthy diets and physical inactivity (Ng & Jeffery, 2003), smoking and alcohol consumption (Steptoe, Wardle, Pollard, Canaan, & Davies, 1996), and poor sleep quality (Burgard & Ailshire, 2009). Some health behaviors reflect coping strategies: overeating, smoking, and drinking may alleviate psychological/physiological arousal and regulate mood state, at least temporarily (Kassel, Stroud, & Paronis, 2003). Health behaviors, in turn, are associated with negative health outcomes, including heart disease, depression, and cancer. Recent work emphasizes that stress affects the health behavior of children and adolescents, contributing to cumulative disadvantage in health over the life course (Repetti, Robles, & Reynolds, 2011).

Factors that Influence the Response to Stress

Several theoretical perspectives were developed to explain the ways by which stress affects health. The most influential perspectives include role theory, fundamental cause theory, cumulative advantage/disadvantage theory, life course frameworks, and the stress process model (Carr & Umberson, 2013).

Role Theory

Everyday activities involve carrying out different social roles, that are accompanied by a set of expectations and norms that guide one's performance. Holding multiple roles that burden one's coping resources (role overload) or that are viewed as conflicting, such as devoted mother and competent worker, are used as an explanation of the experience of more depressive symptoms among women (Biddle, 1979; Gove & Tudor, 1973). However, managing multiple roles is not necessarily stressful, nor is it consistently harmful effects on health. A role has a significant effect only when it is highly important and one is highly committed to it, when it is involuntary, or when difficulties in one role are not counterbalanced by other roles (Simon, 1992; Mirowsky & Ross, 2003; Thoits, 1983)

Fundamental Cause Theory

Socio-economic status (SES), operationalized as education, income, occupational status, or assets, is inversely associated with nearly all indicators of health, including mortality, self-rated health, disability (i.e., functional limitations), most major diseases, and mental health (e.g., Schnittker & McLeod, 2005). Fundamental cause theory (FCT) suggests that the effects of SES persist across a range of health outcomes because SES encompasses an extensive collection of resources, including money, knowledge, power, and beneficial social connections that may affect health, regardless of which mechanisms are relevant in a particular context (Phelan, Link, & Tehranifar, 2010).

Low SES increases one's risk of stressful life events ranging from divorce to job loss to early onset of health problems (Turner et al., 1995), and chronic stressors including poor, overcrowded and unsanitary living conditions (Krieger & Higgins, 2002), persistent economic strain (Kahn & Pearlin, 2006), and discrimination (Kessler, Mickelson, & Williams, 1999). SES also is inversely associated with coping resources including supportive social ties (Krause & Borawski-Clark, 1995), the use of adaptive coping strategies (Kristenson, Eriksen, Sluiter, Starke, & Ursin, 2004), and self-esteem (Pearlin Schieman, Fazio, & Meersman, 2005). These stressors, in turn, affect health.

Cumulative Disadvantage Theory

Cumulative disadvantage theory proposes that adversity gives rise to subsequent adversities, and health-depleting social stressors, whereas advantage gives rise to advantage, e.g., children who grow up in financially and emotionally secure families have better educational outcomes, which give rise to more stable professional and family lives in adulthood, thus minimizing risk of divorce, job loss, and other health-depleting stressors in adulthood. Consequently, an event that has adverse effects in the short term may lead to increasingly enormous implications over the life course (Dannefer, 2003; Gotlib & Wheaton, 1997; Merton, 1968).

The Life Course Perspective

This perspective was developed by Glen Elder to explain the origins and impacts of stress. This perspective has four main themes: (1) human lives are shaped by historical context; (2) individuals construct their own life course through their choices and actions, within the constraints of historical and social circumstances; (3) life domains, including work, family, and social background are interdependent and reciprocally connected on several levels; and (4) the developmental impact of a life transition is dependent on when it occurs; periods of life, such as childhood, adolescence, and old age, influence positions, roles, and rights in society. These periods may be based on culturally shared age definitions (Elder, 1995). Transitions that happen earlier than the typical age are viewed as particularly stressful because one may lack the peer support, maturity, life experience, or education essential to manage the stressor.

The life course paradigm is influential in emphasizing the importance of childhood events and conditions for later life health and well-being. Childhood and adolescent experiences, including parental death (Slavich, Monroe, & Gotlib, 2011), parental divorce (Amato, 2000), child abuse (Slopen et al., 2010), poverty (Duncan, Ziol-Guest, &, Kalil, 2010), and living in a hazardous neighborhood (Vartanian & Houser, 2010) have deleterious implications on adult health. One pathway linking early adversity to adult health is the cumulative disadvantage processes (as discussed above). Also, early life adversities may trigger physiological responses that impede health in both the short and longer term.

The Stress Process Model

The stress process model is the most influential perspective in contemporary research exploring stress, coping, and health (Pearlin, Menaghan, Lieberman, & Mullan, 1981). This incorporates key themes of fundamental cause theory, cumulative disadvantage, and life course theories. The model holds that most stressors are rooted in roles that link individuals to social structures, and that stressors are partly determined on the basis of characteristics such as age, race, and gender. Exposure to stress is not randomly distributed throughout the population, but is highly structured and reflects patterns of inequality. The impact of a stressor on health is not universal in magnitude; it varies widely based on one's other risk factors and resources, such as social support, self-esteem, and mastery.

Coping
Coping Resources

Studies of stress and health focus on two main resources for coping: social support, and the sense of mastery or perceived control over one's environment. Social support refers to the functions performed for an individual by significant others, including family, friends, and colleagues. The types of support provided may be instrumental (e.g., financial), emotional (e.g., listening to one's problems), or informational (e.g., providing advice). Early studies focused on structural aspects of potential support, such as the number of persons in one's social network, rather than the nature of such relationships. Although the two are highly correlated (House, Kahn, McLeod, & Williams, 1985), most research agrees that subjective aspects of social support are more protective than simple counts of significant others (Wethington & Kessler, 1986). Having a person with whom one can share their private thoughts has proven to be a powerful predictor of health (Cohen & Wills, 1985). Multi-item scales (e.g., the Multidimensional Scale of Perceived Social Support; Zimet, Dahlem, Zimet, & Farley, 1988) capturing positive and negative relationship characteristics also are widely used (Rook, 1998). Positive aspects include feeling loved and understood, and negative aspects include criticism and conflict. Ambivalence, which refers to having both positive and negative sentiments toward a single person or relationship, also carries health implications (Pillemer & Suitor, 2008).

An equally important coping resource is a sense of mastery, or control over one's environment. An early intervention, locus of control, captured one's attributions for the events in his or her life (Rotter, 1966). An individual could attribute a personal experience to his or her own actions or characteristics (internal) or to situational factors (external). Commonly used measures of self-efficacy include Ryff's scales of psychological well-being (1989) that include autonomy, environmental mastery, personal growth, positive relations with others, purpose in life, and self-acceptance, and Bandura's (1977) self-efficacy.

In conclusion, coping resources are usually treated as either a mediator of the stress impact on health, or a moderator that buffers against its health-depleting effects. However, researchers also acknowledge that coping may affect stress; coping resources may prevent a stressor from occurring in the first place or from escalation into secondary stressors (Wheaton, 1999).

Coping Strategies

Coping strategies are the changes people make to their behaviors, thoughts, or emotions in response to the stressors they encounter (Lazarus & Folkman, 1984). The two main strategies are problem-focused coping, and emotion-focused coping. In problem-focused coping, one tries to alter the situation that is causing the stressor (e.g., exiting an unhealthy relationship) or preventing the stressor from recurring. In emotion-focused coping, one alters their reactions and feelings regarding the impact of the stressor, such as finding the humor in the situation, denying its existence, or withdrawing from the situation. However, emotion-focused coping does not eliminate the stressor (e.g., a serious illness) or help the individual to develop better ways of managing it (Carver, Johnson, & Joormann, 1989).

Most studies agree that problem-focused strategies are more effective than emotion-focused coping in protecting against distress. Problem-focused strategies are associated with lower levels of psychological disorders, whereas emotion-focused strategies are related to higher levels of distress and hopelessness (Billings & Moos, 1981). However, emotion-focused coping may be particularly effective when the stressor cannot be altered, and in the immediate aftermath of the stressor (e.g., P. Reynolds et al., 2000).

The selection and efficacy of a particular coping strategy are shaped partly by one's coping resources as well as one's preferred coping style. Coping style refers to one's general orientation and preferences for addressing problems, such as confronting versus denying (Menaghan, 1983). However, coping styles and strategies alone do not fully determine the health consequences of stress, where structural, demographic, and psychosocial factors, such as education, social, and economic resources, and cognitive flexibility also may moderate whether and how stress affects health (Thoits, 1995, 2010).

Clinical Notes

- Research has confirmed that stress has many implications on health, emotion, and behavior. Effects on the immune and endocrinal systems may mediate the link between stress and its consequences.
- Empowering people with effective coping strategies can help them to develop appropriate behavior, thoughts, or emotions in response to the stressors they encounter.

Summary

- Stress is the nonspecific response of the body, whether biological and psychological, to challenging or threatening events.
- A stressor refers to any environmental, social, biological, or psychological demand that requires a person to adjust his or her usual patterns of behavior.
- The general adaptation syndrome is the body's short-term and long-term reactions to stress. This encompasses alarm reaction, the adaptation (resistance) stage, and the exhaustion stage.

- Stress produces a cascade of changes in the endocrine system. It involves the hypothalamus, the pituitary gland, and the adrenal glands.
- Chronic or repetitive stress can ultimately impair the body's immune system.
- The types of stressors to which one is most susceptible vary widely by one's social location, reflecting patterns of race, gender, age, and class stratification. Stressors are empirically classified into three major categories: life events, chronic strains, and daily hassles.
- Multiple rather than single stress outcomes should be considered when comparing stress effects, particularly across social groups.
- Theoretical perspectives that explain the ways in which stress affects health include role theory, fundamental cause theory, cumulative advantage/disadvantage theory, life course frameworks, and the stress process model.
- Coping resources involve essentially social support, and the sense of mastery or perceived control over one's environment.
- Coping strategies are the changes people make to their behavior, thoughts, or emotions in response to the stressors they encounter. The two main strategies are problem-focused coping, and emotion-focused coping.

Test Your Knowledge

- What is the difference between stress and a stressor?
- Give an account of the general adaptation syndrome.
- Outline the effects of stress on the endocrine system.
- Outline the effects of stress on the body's immune system.
- Describe the types of stressors.
- Give an account of stress outcomes.
- What are the theoretical perspectives that explain the effect of stress on health?
- Give an account of coping resources and coping strategies.

Critical Thinking Question

Discuss how reaction to stressors may vary among people.

Psychological Reaction to Illness

It is normal to experience a range of emotions in the wake of being diagnosed with a serious or chronic illness that can be shocking to patients such as cancer, or diabetes and arthritis. Coping with medical illness is usually a pattern of learned response to stressful events, which the individual develops through a trial and error process over their life span. Thus, coping is a process rather than an event.

Ill adults may have many reactions to illness. Careful attention to the patient's opinion is essential to identify catastrophic thinking, core beliefs, and associated core

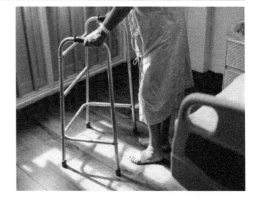

PHOTO 20.2.   Reaction to Illness.

emotions. Either acute or chronic medical illness is likely to trigger anxiety and depression in patients with mood or anxiety disorders. Lazarus (1995) lists some core emotions in coping with medical illness including anger, anxiety, guilt, fright, shame, sadness, happiness, envy, relief, and hope. Psychological variables are often more powerful predictors of poor quality of life than physical symptoms. Three major categories of reactions are frequently seen in hospitalized individuals:

1. *Anger*: this is often a reaction to perceived weakness and disability. Patients may behave in an angry manner with staff in an unconscious attempt to externalize their uncomfortable inner experience. Their angry style may also be an indirect expression that others are responsible for their internal discomfort. Such patients may be loud, demanding, rude, time-consuming and very frustrating to staff. Successful interventions may include admitting the patient's individuality and unique situation; keeping them informed; or responding to their realistic needs while setting firm limits.

2. *Agitation and hypervigilance*: This response presents its own set of challenges to the caregiver. The anxiety underlying the agitation is often a response to the individual's feelings of helplessness or decreased control due to their illness. These uncomfortable perceptions cause anxiety, which in turn, increases the uncomfortable feelings. The hypervigilance represents an attempt to regain a sense of control by asking questions to obtain information but the anxiety may prevent the ill adult from adequately processing and integrating the information received. Some successful interventions might include consistency in staff assignment; suggesting relaxation interventions; teaching patients while a family member is present and encouraging the individual to make notes to review later; and offering the patient sufficient pain control.

3. *Withdrawal*: this reaction is serious for a number of reasons. A withdrawn patient can be overlooked. This patient may not receive the appropriate assessment and intervention, and can be ignored emotionally and even physically in a busy practice setting. Some patients are habitually isolated and have a minimal support system because of their personality style. Other patients may express this reaction in relation to a clinical depression which needs further assessment. Some helpful interventions include identifying the behavior as a problem and interviewing the patient as well as significant others to establish whether this behavior is the typical coping response of this person or if it is an unusual response to stress; monitoring the intensity of the withdrawal behavior from day to day; and communicating concerns to other caregivers including the patient's physician. Finally, nurses need to have a basic knowledge of assessing suicidal risk, and the ability to ask the appropriate questions when circumstances indicate this intervention is appropriate.

Concurrent with these emotional events in the ill individual, significant others may also experience their own emotional responses to their loved one's illness. Whatever their response, the initial situation is one of emotional instability in a situation that needs more stability and support than usual. Friends and family members may feel overwhelmed, uncertain, doubting, uncomfortable, sad, upset, angry, or other strong reactions. Their responses may vary and fluctuate. Significant others may feel unable to comfort the ill individual or may over-react to the illness.

Factors Affecting Reaction to Illness

People react differently to being ill, this result from personal differences, the interrelated conditions in which the illness occurs, the disease, or the pathophysiology, and the style of medical care. Response to medical illness is also governed to a large degree by the meaning of the illness to the patient. The belief that a diagnosis of cancer is synonymous with death or that diabetes signals inevitable blindness can trigger anxiety, depression, panic, or anger. In summary, factors affecting how one reacts to illness include:

- the nature and severity of the illness;
- the special meaning that illness or hospitalization has for the patient;
- the personality traits of the patient;
- the defense mechanisms the patient commonly uses;
- the patient's past experience with illness/hospitalization/physicians;
- the patient's relationship with physicians/nurses.

Coping Tasks of Ill Adults

Patients suffering an illness may need to adapt to one of several variables, as shown below.

Change in Body Image

This is obvious in surgical patients who suffer an incision and often removal of a body part. Even in non-surgical situations, most patients experience a change in their self-image when a disease relates to body image, e.g., people who cannot perform basic bodily functions if unassisted, such as using a catheter to replace going to the bathroom. Cardiac patients may experience their illness as having a deficit at the core of their physical being. Changes in body image may cause individuals to feel they are less than their previous self or to question if others still perceive them as adequate as before their illness.

Reality of Their Own Mortality

Illnesses are frequently characterized by a sense of vulnerability. A hospitalized patient may be surrounded by seriously ill individuals, the atmosphere may be tense, the staff are busy, and the array of technology is impressive, if not frightening. In many instances, such as critical care units, defenses which usually protect individuals from awareness of serious thought about their own mortality are swept away. This provokes the ill adult to think about spiritual, psychological, or philosophical issues on a personal level. Often such concerns are on the minds of close family members or friends as well. A family communication system which supports expression of these feelings and concerns may provide the most helpful coping mechanism for dealing with this issue.

Coping with Altered Relationships with Others in Their Social/Support System

The illness of an adult often affects their relationships with significant others. The patient typically experiences more need for support and nurturance from others in reaction to their health impairment; they may feel more dependent, less in control, more anxious, or less decisive as they enter the health care system. Their self-esteem and self-image may suffer in adjusting to the routine of assessment, diagnosis, and treatment, e.g., in a parent with CVA, the son may take a parental role and cause the patient to be downgraded to a childlike position in the family. Also, a serious illness of a middle-aged adult can push a comfortably retired grandparent into role of housekeeper/parent to young grandchildren. Each scenario would require significant family adaptation on emotional, physical, and financial levels at a time when all are severely stressed by the presenting problem of the illness.

Dealing with an Altered Level of Dependency

Being dependent and needing the care of others as in serious physical illness create uncomfortable feelings. The illness interrupts and disrupts an individual's lifestyle either suddenly or over a brief period. In many situations, care and assistance may be required for the most basic daily functions: hygiene, eating, ambulation, and elimination. In serious illness, this issue may be sustained for a long period as life at home becomes oriented around physicians' visits, lab tests, physical therapy, etc. These changes are a serious challenge to an individual's self-image and self-esteem.

Adjusting to Physiological Changes

While the emotional tasks seem to predominate, adjustment to changes in body physiology is also a significant demand. This area includes changes in the lifestyle and self-care that patients should do to adjust to illness. Typical changes include dietary restrictions, medication usage, alterations in sexual abilities, alteration in physical abilities such as after an amputation, alterations in sensory abilities or sensitivity. These physiological changes may become a central theme, even a battleground in the patient's everyday life. The individual can use non-compliance as a way to express their anger and frustration, or rejection of their altered life situation, e.g., non-compliance can be a big issue in newly diagnosed diabetic or recovering cardiac patients.

Grieving for Their Losses (Self or Lifestyle)

This grief may be expressed in an overt, direct manner or more indirectly through a sad mood. The individual may verbalize wishes for the wholeness, vigor, strength or well-being they enjoyed prior to the onset of their condition. Also, they may experience guilt or regret that they did not adequately value their well-being. Affording acceptance, empathy, and understanding of the patient's perceived loss by the caregiver can provide needed support and role model the appropriate response for other family members. Some patients may experience themselves as a new person, who is unfamiliar with the "new self" and practice it with uncertainty. Other patients may undergo the well-known stages of grieving as described by Kübler-Ross as the individual gives up their former self and self-image.

Fear of Recurrent Problems

The individual may experience fears about possible future health problems. Many individuals will verbalize fears and a general pessimism regarding their health status and their future. These fears may be supported by misunderstandings or deficits in the patient's knowledge regarding their illness. It is noteworthy that patient education proceeds slowly when an individual (and possibly significant others, as well) is impaired, due to anxiety or depression.

Illness Occurs with Other Stressors

Many premorbid stressors may be aggravated by the consequences of health problems. Financial stressors may be severely complicated by reduced income and increased health care costs. Premorbid marital and familial stressors can be complicated by the role changes and the physiologic/emotional changes that arise from serious illness. Everyday stressors, housing and car problems, raising children problems, and work problems, can all be aggravated by illness. The patient's illness usually takes priority, at least for a time, over other concurrent stressors. This shift can cause increased stress on other family members who must take on additional coping and problem-solving responsibilities.

Management of Maladaptive Responses

The initial goals of management strategies include exploring the patient's understanding of their current medical problems and how the patient is using available support. Inquire about the emotional reaction and cognitive interpretations of the illness to identify the patient's strengths and to detect ways the patient has handled stressful situations in the past. Determine available sources of support, and examine how the family is coping with the medical illness. Assess how spirituality or religion plays a role in the patient's life.

Intervention strategies include minimizing uncomfortable emotional responses such as anxiety, fear, guilt, etc.; enhancement of self-esteem; maintenance of positive/supportive relationships; and generation of hope. Physicians of all specialties can learn the motivational interviewing technique to change feelings of hopelessness into significant rewards for patients. Self-regulation interventions help patients balance the problem-focused input with emotional regulation to cope with illness-related distress. It is interesting that pure problem-focused interventions have not always been successful and even occasionally have had negative outcomes. Patients can be taught to regulate their emotions through writing, talking, or thinking, conferring benefits on their physical health conditions.

For most chronic medical conditions, a healthy lifestyle would benefit patients physically and mentally, e.g., weight reduction, cessation of smoking, reducing alcohol, exercising, and others.

Clinical Notes

In their way to develop an understanding empathetic position, clinicians need to be aware of the range of emotional reactions frequently displayed by patients, factors affecting reaction to illness, and coping tasks of ill adults. This understanding will help clinicians develop and manage maladaptive responses.

Summary

- Ill adults may have many reactions to illness. Careful attention to the patient's opinion is essential to identify catastrophic thinking, core beliefs, and associated core emotions.
- Three major categories of reactions are frequently seen in hospitalized individuals: anger, agitation and hypervigilance, and withdrawal.
- People react differently to being ill; this results from personal differences, the interrelated conditions in which the illness occurs, the disease, or the pathophysiology, and the style of medical care.

■ Patients suffering an illness may need to adapt to one of several variables: change in body image, reality of their own mortality, coping with altered relationships with others in their social/support system, dealing with an altered level of dependency, adjusting to physiological changes, grieving for their losses (self or lifestyle), and fear of recurrent problems.

Test Your Knowledge

■ Describe the reactions that ill adults may have to illness.
■ Outline the categories of reactions frequently seen in hospitalized individuals.
■ Give an account of the factors affecting patients' reaction to illness.
■ Describe the coping tasks of ill adults.
■ Give an account of the management of the maladaptive responses that adults may have to illness.

Critical Thinking Question

How do you understand the psychological reactions to a medical illness as a part of the mind-body relationship?

Reaction to Dying and Death

There is a widely held assumption that grief proceeds through an orderly series of stages or phases, with distinct features. While different accounts vary in the details of particular stages, the two most commonly cited views are those of Bowlby (1980) and Kübler-Ross (1969). According to John Bowlby (1980), adult grief is an extension of a general distress response to separation commonly observed in young children, i.e., adult grief is a form of separation anxiety response to the disruption of an attachment bond. It includes the following phases:

■ *Phase of numbing*: numbness and disbelief, which can last from a few hours up to a week, may be punctuated by outbursts of extremely intense distress and/or anger.
■ *Yearning and searching*: these are accompanied by anxiety and intermittent periods of anger, and can last for months or even years.
■ *Disorganization and despair*: feelings of depression and apathy occur when old patterns have been discarded.
■ *Reorganization*: there is a greater/lesser degree of recovery from bereavement and acceptance of what has occurred.

In 1969, Elisabeth Kübler-Ross identified five stages of patient's reaction to death and dying. These stages could take place within hours, or it could take weeks or months to move through the stages. Coping with loss of one's life is ultimately a deeply personal and singular experience. The person may experience all the stages in a linear fashion and it is quite possible to experience more than one emotion simultaneously. The person may also move back and forth through the stages, depending on the progress of the disease or illness and how treatment goes. It is possible to get stuck at a stage for weeks, months, or even the rest of one's life. Elisabeth Kübler-Ross's stages include:

1. *Denial*: the patient refuses to believe that he or she is dying. It may take the form of seeking a second opinion. It is a normal reaction to rationalize overwhelming

emotions. It is a defense mechanism that buffers the immediate shock. This is a temporary response that carries patients through the first wave of pain.

2. *Anger*: the patient may become angry at the physician and hospital staff. Physicians must learn not to take such comments personally. As the effects of denial and isolation begin to wear, reality and its pain re-emerge. The anger may be aimed at inanimate objects, complete strangers, friends, or family.

3. *Bargaining*: the patient may try to bargain with God or some higher being to regain his or her health and stay alive, e.g., I will give half of my money to charity if I get rid of this disease.

4. *Depression*: the patient becomes preoccupied with death and may become hopeless, and emotionally detached and distant from others. Two types of depression are associated with mourning. The first one is a reaction to practical implications relating to the loss. Sadness and regret predominate this type of depression. This may be eased by simple clarification and helpful cooperation and a few kind words. The second type of depression is subtler and perhaps more private. It is our quiet preparation to depart and to leave our loved ones.

5. *Acceptance*: the patient is calm and accepts fate. This stage of mourning is not reached by everyone. This phase is marked by withdrawal and peace. It is not a period of happiness and must be distinguished from depression.

Caregivers usually experience the same Kübler-Ross stages, but may take longer to work through the stages. This is often due to being too preoccupied with caring for the ill person to deal with personal emotions. Even when we know ahead of time that someone is going to die, it does not necessarily soften the impact. It still may be difficult to believe that the death has occurred and hard to imagine life without this special person. For caregivers, the actual death can often be the moment when this cycle starts and it is also perfectly normal to go through this cycle more than once, often at the point of diagnosis and then again when death occurs. Most people need comfort and support while they grieve, either from their personal circle of family and friends or from clergy, therapists, or support groups. The bereaved may experience an illusion that the deceased person is physically present. Normal grief generally subsides after one or two years, although some features may continue longer, or may return on holidays or special occasions (the anniversary reaction). The mortality rate is high for close relatives (especially widowed men) in the first year of bereavement.

How Do Children Cope with the Death of a Parent or Sibling?

When a sibling or a parent dies, very young children may not fully understand what has happened and that death is permanent. Children feel many of the same feelings that adults do when someone dies: shock, sadness, or confusion. Children often personalize a death, and they may question if they will also die. The death incident can stir up the child's fears; the child may fear driving if the cause of death is a car accident, or may fear diseases, such as cancer if it is the cause of death. A child may think about the consequences of death and how it will alter his or her life, e.g., remarriage of mother or financial consequences. The presence of support from a family member, friend, or trusted adult usually helps young people to understand their feelings and eventually accept the death.

How Do Adults Cope with the Death of a Child?

The death of a child causes extreme sadness and distress in a family. Whether the death came suddenly or gradually, parents often struggle with guilt that they could not prevent their child's death or even that they outstay their child. Sometimes, after a death, parents might feel the urge to move or change their lives to avoid situations that remind them of their dead child. Elisabeth Kübler-Ross noted that it is usually healthier to face and acknowledge the pain, rather than avoid it.

The Physician's Response to Death

The major responsibility of the medical staff is to give support to the dying patient and the patient's family. Generally, physicians make the patient completely aware of the diagnosis and prognosis. However, a physician should follow the patient's wish as to how much he or she wants to know about the condition. With the patient's permission, the physician may tell the family the diagnosis and other details of the illness. Sometimes, physicians feel a sense of failure at not preventing death. They may deal with this sense by becoming emotionally detached from the patient in order to deal with his or her imminent death. Such detachment can prevent helping the patient and family through this important transition.

Cultural Influences on Bereavement

Although grief is a universal response to major loss, its meaning, duration, and how it is expressed, are all culturally determined. Grief, in turn, is related to cultural beliefs about death. Trying to distinguish "normal" from "abnormal/pathological" grief must be considered in terms of cultural norms.

Clinical Notes

- According to DSM-5, adjustment disorders may be diagnosed following the death of a loved one when the intensity, quality, or persistence of grief reactions exceed what normally might be expected, taking into account cultural, religious, or age-appropriate norms. A new category of bereavement-related symptoms, designated as persistent complex bereavement disorder, was introduced in DSM-5.
- Careful consideration should be given to distinguishing normal sadness and grief from a major depressive episode. In major depression, the depressed mood is more persistent and not tied to specific thoughts or preoccupations, and thoughts show self-critical or pessimistic ruminations. In grief, dysphoria is likely to decrease in intensity over days to weeks and occurs in waves that are likely to be associated with thoughts or reminders of the deceased. The pain of grief may be associated with positive emotions and humor contrary to the pervasive unhappiness and misery characteristic of a major depressive episode (American Psychiatric Association, 2013).

Summary

- There is a widely held assumption that grief proceeds through an orderly series of stages or phases, with distinct features.

- Bowlby viewed grief as a form of separation anxiety response to the disruption of an attachment bond. It involves four phases: numbing; yearning and searching; disorganization and despair; and reorganization phases.
- Elisabeth Kübler-Ross identified five stages of reaction to death and dying: denial, anger, bargaining, depression, and acceptance stages.

Test Your Knowledge

- Outline Bowlby's view of grief.
- Describe Elisabeth Kübler-Ross's identified stages of reaction to death and dying.
- How do children cope with the death of a parent or sibling?
- How do adults cope with the death of a child?

Critical Thinking Question

How could you evaluate the experience of death of a relative from different psychological perspectives?

twenty-one
Psychological Disorders

- This chapter is intended to provide the reader with an overview of the prevalence of psychological disorders, the definition of normality and abnormality, the classification of mental health problems, disorders of childhood and adolescence, psychotic disorders, mood disorders, anxiety disorders, obsessive-compulsive disorder, phobias, and eating disorders.

Introduction

Approximately 1 in 5 of respondents across pooled studies (16.3–18.9 percent) (95% confidence interval) were identified as meeting the criteria for a common mental disorder during the 12 months preceding assessment; 29.2 percent (25.9–32.6 percent) of respondents were identified as having experienced a common mental disorder at some time during their lifetimes. A consistent gender difference in the prevalence of common mental disorder was evident; women having higher rates of mood disorders (7.3 percent: 4.0 percent) and anxiety (8.7 percent: 4.3 percent) disorders than males during the previous 12 months. while men have higher rates of substance use disorders than women (2.0 percent: 7.5 percent), with a similar pattern for lifetime prevalence. There was also consistent evidence of regional variation in the prevalence of common mental disorders. Countries in north-east and south-East Asia in particular displayed consistently lower one-year and lifetime prevalence estimates than other regions. One-year prevalence rates were also low among Sub-Saharan-Africa, whereas English-speaking countries returned the highest lifetime prevalence estimates (Steel et al., 2014).

Among youth in the US, approximately 1 in every 4–5 meets the criteria for a mental disorder with severe impairment across their lifetime in a nationally representative sample of US adolescents. Anxiety disorders were the most common condition (31.9 percent), followed by behavior disorders (19.1 percent), mood disorders (14.3 percent), and substance use disorders (11.4 percent), with approximately 40 percent of those with one class of disorder also meeting the criteria for another class of lifetime disorder. The overall prevalence of disorders with severe impairment and/or distress was 22.2 percent; (11.2 percent with mood disorders; 8.3 percent with anxiety disorders; 9.6 percent behavior disorders). The median age of onset for disorder classes was earliest for anxiety (6 years), followed by 11 years for behavior, 13 years for mood, and 15 years for substance use disorders (Merikangas et al., 2010).

Normality and Abnormality

The concepts of normality and abnormality resemble the two sides of a coin, each is defined only in relation to the other. The boundaries between normality and pathology vary among cultures for specific types of behaviors. The judgment that a given behavior is abnormal and requires clinical attention depends on cultural norms. Awareness of the significance of culture may correct mistaken interpretations of psychopathology, but culture may also contribute to vulnerability and suffering (e.g., by amplifying fears that maintain panic disorder or health anxiety) (American Psychiatric Association, 2013). Thresholds of tolerance for specific symptoms or behaviors differ across cultures, social settings, and families. Hence, the level at which an experience becomes problematic or pathological will differ. Consequently, there are a lot of definitions that propose definitions of normality and abnormality in an attempt to draw a line that distinguishes both concepts.

Normality

According to the World Health Organization (WHO), mental health is defined as a state of well-being in which every individual realizes his or her own potential, can cope with the normal stresses of life, can work productively and fruitfully, and is able to make a contribution to her or his community (World Health Organization, 2004). Despite the importance of moving away from the conceptualization of mental health as a state of absence of mental illness, there are several concerns about potential misunderstandings of identifying positive feelings and positive functioning as key factors for mental health. Murphy (1978) argued that these ideas were laden with cultural values considered important by North Americans. Even for a North American person, it is hard to imagine, for example, that a mentally healthy human threatened by terrorists can experience a sense of happiness and mastery over the environment.

Galderisi et al. (2015) defined mental health as a dynamic state of internal equilibrium which enables individuals to use their abilities in harmony with the universal values of society. Important components of mental health which contribute to the state of internal equilibrium include basic cognitive and social skills; the ability to recognize, express, and modulate one's own emotions, as well as empathize with others; flexibility and ability to cope with adverse life events and function in social roles; and a harmonious relationship between body and mind. All components proposed in Galderisi's definition of mental health may contribute to a varying degree to the state of equilibrium, and each component represents an important but not mandatory aspect of mental health. A fully developed function may balance an impairment in another aspect of mental functioning, e.g., a very empathetic person, highly interested in mutual sharing, may compensate for a moderate degree of cognitive impairment, and still find a satisfactory equilibrium and achieve her or his life goals. Whatever the definition of normal mental health, the following characteristics are usually described as a part of normal person characteristics (Galderisi, Heinz, Kastrup, Beezhold, & Sartorius, 2015):

1. *Appropriate perception of reality*: normal individuals are fairly realistic in appraising their reactions and capabilities and in interpreting what is going on around them.

2. *Flexibility and ability to cope with changes*: these factors are considered important to mental health maintenance. Flexibility refers to the ability to change one's own ideas in the light of new evidence, and adapt to changes and in face of unpredicted difficulties.

3. *Self-esteem and acceptance*: normal people usually appreciate their own worth and feel accepted by those around them. They are comfortable with other people and are able to react spontaneously in social situations. At the same time, they do not feel obliged to completely submit their opinions to those of the group. Feelings of worthlessness, loneliness, and lack of acceptance are prevalent among individuals who are diagnosed as abnormal.

4. *Ability to form affectionate relationships*: normal individuals are able to form close and satisfying relationships with other people. They are sensitive to the feelings of others and do not make excessive demands on others to gratify their own needs. The ability to experience and understand what others feel without confusion between oneself and others enables individuals to communicate and interact in effective ways and to predict the actions, intentions, and feelings of others. The ability to recognize, express, and modulate one's own emotions is also regarded as an important component of mental health.

5. *Basic cognitive and social skills* are important components of mental health in the light of their impact on all aspects of everyday life. Cognitive skills include the ability to pay attention, remember and organize information, solve problems, and make decisions. Social skills involve the ability to use one's own repertoire of verbal/non-verbal abilities to communicate and interact with others. All these abilities are interdependent and allow people to function in their environment.

6. *The basic ability to perform different social roles* and to participate in meaningful social interactions is an important aspect of mental health and particularly contributes to resilience against distress. However, social exclusion and stigmatization often impair social participation.

7. *The ability to exercise voluntary control over behavior*: normal individuals feel fairly confident about their ability to control their behavior. Occasionally they may act impulsively, but they are able to restrain their sexual and aggressive urges when necessary. They may fail to conform to social norms, but in such instances their decisions are voluntary rather than the result of uncontrollable impulses.

Defining Abnormality

A mental disorder can be defined as a clinically significant disturbance in an individual's cognition, emotion regulation, or behavior that reflects a dysfunction in the psychological, biological, or developmental processes underlying mental functioning. Mental disorders are usually associated with significant distress or disability in social, occupational, or other important activities. An expectable or culturally approved response to a common stressor or loss, such as the death of a loved one, is not a mental disorder. Socially deviant behavior (e.g., political, religious, or sexual) and conflicts that are primarily between the individual and society are not mental disorders unless the deviance or conflict results from a dysfunction in the individual, as described above (American Psychiatric Association, 2013). Currently, there is no objective test that determines abnormality. Instead, clinicians usually rely on signs and symptoms, and on subjective criteria for deciding when those symptoms constitute an abnormality that could determine whether an individual has a mental disorder. The following is a summary of the different perspectives used in defining abnormality.

Deviation from Cultural Norms

Every culture has certain standards or norms of acceptable behaviors and ways of thinking. Deviations from cultural norms may be considered abnormal. Culture can influence acceptance or rejection of a diagnosis, the accuracy of diagnosis, treatment decisions and adherence to treatments, and consequently the course of illness and recovery. Cultural habits and traditions can also contribute to either stigma or support in the social and familial response to mental illness. However, opponents of the cultural perspective point to the danger that societies may label individuals as abnormal to justify controlling or silencing them, as Hitler called the Jews abnormal to justify the Holocaust. Additionally, the concept of abnormality changes over time within the same society; many Europeans would have considered men wearing earrings abnormal in the past. Today, such behavior tends to be viewed as differences in lifestyle rather than as signs of abnormality.

Deviation from Statistical Norms

The word abnormal means away from the norm. Therefore, this definition of abnormality is based on deviation from statistical norms: normality is the average, while abnormal behaviors, thoughts, or feelings are statistically infrequent or deviant from the norm. Many characteristics, such as height, weight, and intelligence, cover a range of values when measured over an entire population, e.g., most people fall within the middle range of height, and a few are unusually tall or unusually short. However, according to this definition, a person who is extremely intelligent or extremely happy would be classified as abnormal. Conversely, there are certain types of behavior and experience which are so common as to be normal in the statistical sense, but are regarded as constituting psychological disorders (such as anxiety and depression). Thus, the statistical criterion appears to be neither necessary nor sufficient as a way of defining abnormality.

Maladaptive Behavior and Impaired Functioning

According to this perspective, the most important features that define abnormality are how behavior, thoughts, or feelings affect the adjustment and functioning of the individual among the social group. Accordingly, experiences raise concern if they are maladaptive, that is, if they have adverse effects on the individual or on society. Some kinds of behavior interfere with the adaptation of the individual, e.g., avoidance of riding the bus to work because of fear of crowds, inability to hold a job because of excessive alcohol drinking. Other forms of behavior are harmful to society, e.g., an adolescent who has violent aggressive outbursts, and a paranoid individual who plans to murder a persecutor.

Behavior may be seen as abnormal if it prevents people from achieving their goals, or does not contribute to their personal sense of well-being, or prevents them from functioning as they would wish in their personal, sexual, social, intellectual, and occupational functioning. Impaired functioning means having difficulty in fulfilling appropriate and expected roles in the family, in social and work-related situations, e.g., it is normal to experience sadness at one time or another when experiencing a life stressor, but if sadness becomes so intense or long-lasting, and it interferes with their ability to hold a job or care for their children, it is likely to be considered abnormal. However, it is not appropriate to call someone abnormal just because the person is dysfunctional. The dysfunction might be caused by a physical illness, by an overwhelming but temporary family problem, or by a variety of things other than a psychological disorder. Further, some people who display significant psychological disorders are still able to function reasonably well at school, at work, or at home (Üstün & Kennedy, 2009).

Personal Distress

People usually do not come to clinics because they feel they have met some abstract definition of abnormality, but because of their feelings or behavior that cause their distress. Subjective experience of distress may be the only symptom of the disorder, and the individual's behavior may appear normal to the casual observer, e.g., feelings of anxiety, depression, or agitation, or experiences such as insomnia, loss of appetite, or numerous aches and pains. Experiencing distress is the criterion that people regularly use to define the severity of their psychological problems and their need for treatment. However, personal suffering alone is not an adequate criterion for abnormality, as it may stem from casual everyday life events, and people can display psychological disorders without experiencing distress.

Abnormality as Unexpected Behavior

People usually have generalized expectations about others' typical reactions to particular kinds of situation, this makes a person's behavior predictable to the extent that we know about the situation. However, situations do not have equally powerful influences on behavior, and cannot be used equally to predict a person's behavior. It follows that, it is normal for any individual's behavior to be only partially predictable or consistent and, in turn, it is abnormal for a person to react to a situation or event in ways that could not be reasonably predicted, given what we know about human behavior, e.g., a child who suddenly bursts into tears or crushes his toys with no apparent provocation is behaving unpredictably (Davison, Neale, &, Kring, 2004). Similarly, an anxious person who has fears which are out of proportion to the situation. By this definition, under-reacting is just as abnormal as over-reacting, however, only the latter is usually seen as a problem. Thus, abnormality is defined as deviation from the expected average, whereby what is reasonable or acceptable is simply how most people would be expected to behave. The problem with this criterion is the absence of clear determinants about who decides what is in proportion, and the absence of clear determinants of what is acceptable, expected behavior beyond which it is considered abnormal.

Abnormality as Mental Illness

According to this perspective, abnormal behavior is referred to as psychopathology or psychological disorder, which is classified on the basis of symptoms. The classification is called diagnosis, and the methods used to try to change the behavior are called therapies. If the deviant behavior ceases, the patient is described as cured. This way of talking about psychological abnormality reflects the medical model of thinking, where abnormal behavior is seen as indicative of an underlying illness. However, when we label people as sick or ill, we are removing from them all responsibility for their behavior, just as we do not normally hold someone responsible for having the common cold.

Conclusion: because of difficulties defining a specific set of behaviors that everyone, everywhere, will agree to consider as abnormality, and as no single criterion or perspective is entirely adequate in identifying abnormality, it is appropriate to combine aspects of different perspectives. Thus, the person's behavior, emotional reaction, and the consequences of the behavior of that person are to be considered within the sociocultural context of the person. The effect of age, gender, and culture, as well as the effect of a particular situation and the historical era in which people live should be considered to define what is appropriate when defining the words "appropriate," "expected," and "functional" behavior.

Etiology of Psychiatric Disorders

Attempts to understand the etiology of psychiatric disorders generally fall under one of the three broad perspectives:

1. *Biological perspective (medical or disease model)*: this explains psychological disorders in terms of particular disturbances in the anatomy and chemistry of the brain and in other biological processes, including genetic influences (e.g., Plomin & Asbury, 2005; Plomin & McGuffin, 2003). The medical model gave rise to the idea that abnormality is a mental illness. Neuroscientists and others who adopt a neurobiological model study the causes and treatment of these disorders as they would study any physical illness, assuming that problematic symptoms stem primarily from an underlying illness that can be diagnosed, treated, and cured. Researchers using this approach look for genetic abnormalities that may predispose a person to develop a particular mental health problem by affecting the functioning of the brain. They also look for abnormalities in specific parts of the brain and dysfunction in neurochemical systems in the brain and other parts of the body. Proponents of this perspective generally favor the use of drugs to treat mental health problems.

2. *Psychological perspective*: there are a number of psychological perspectives that look differently at variations in emotions, thinking, or behavior. Common psychological perspectives include:
   a. The psychodynamic perspective emphasizes unconscious conflicts, usually originating in early childhood, and the use of defense mechanisms to handle the anxiety generated by the repressed impulses and emotions. Bringing the unconscious conflicts and emotions into awareness is expected to eliminate the need for the defense mechanisms and alleviate the disorder.

b. The cognitive model suggests that some mental problems stem from maladaptive cognitive processes and can be alleviated by changing these biased cognitions. The way we think about ourselves, the way we appraise stressful situations, and our strategies for coping with them are all interrelated. It is not the negative events that cause psychological problems, but it is our thoughts about those events.

c. The behavioral perspective proposes that maladaptive behaviors are learned. This investigates how fears become conditioned to specific situations and the role of reinforcement in the origin and maintenance of inappropriate behavior.

d. Sociocultural perspectives take the view that mental health problems can be caused by social contexts of the individual, such as gender, age, and marital status; the physical, social, and economic situations in which people live; and the cultural values, traditions, and expectations in which they are immersed (Appignanesi, 2009; Lim, 2006; Sue & Sue, 2008). Sociocultural context influences not only what is and is not labeled "abnormal" but also who displays what kind of disorder and how likely people are to receive treatment for it. Proponents of this perspective look to physical and social environment stressors, such as discrimination and poverty, which can interfere with people's functioning.

The sociocultural factors create differing stressors, social roles, opportunities, experiences, and ways of expression for different groups of people. They shape the disorders and symptoms to which certain categories of people are prone, e.g., symptoms of depression differ, depending on cultural background (Falicov, 2003; Hopper & Wanderling, 2000; Whaley & Hall, 2009). In Western cultures, emotional and physical components of disorders are generally viewed separately, so symptoms of depression tend to revolve around despair and other signs of emotional distress. But in China, Japan, and certain other Asian cultures, emotional and physical experiences tend to be viewed as one, so a depressed person is as likely to report stomach or back pain as to complain of sadness (Nakao & Yano, 2006; Weiss, Tram, Weisz, Rescorla, & Achenbach, 2009). Sociocultural factors can also influence the overall prevalence of disorders, e.g., the higher rates of alcohol abuse among men compared to women in some cultures may be explained by the cultural factor that excessive alcohol consumption is less appropriate for women than for men (Timko, Finney, & Moos, 2005). Also, many kinds of psychological disorders increase in frequency among people living in countries suffering from wars or other stressful conditions (Alhasnawi et al., 2009).

3. *The diathesis-stress model*: the key point of the diathesis-stress model is that the combination and interaction of biological, psychological, and sociocultural factors predispose in varying degrees to a particular disorder, but a certain amount of stress is needed to actually trigger that disorder (Hankin & Abela, 2005; Krueger & Markon, 2006). Whether or not a person actually develops symptoms of a disorder depends on the nature and amount of stress the person encounters (Elwood, Hahn, Olatunji, & Williams, 2009; Turner & Lloyd, 2004), e.g., a person may inherit a biological predisposition to depression or may have learned depressing patterns of thinking, but these predispositions may not be expressed as a depressive disorder unless the person is faced with a financial crisis or suffers the loss of a loved one. In the absence of major stressors, or if the person has adequate skills for coping with them, depressive symptoms may never appear or may be relatively mild (Canli et al., 2006). This model helps to explain why some people develop serious psychological problems when confronted with minimal stress while others remain healthy regardless of how difficult their lives may become.

Classification of Mental Health Problems

An integral part of the medical model is the classification of mental disorder and the related process of diagnosis. Although definitions of abnormality vary, as described before, there is usually a set of culture-general and culture-specific behavior patterns that characterize what most mental health professionals consider to be a disorder. Current systems of classification of mental disorders stem from the work of Kraepelin, who published the first recognized textbook of psychiatry in 1883. Kraepelin claimed that certain groups of symptoms occur together sufficiently often to be called a disease or syndrome. Kraepelin (1896) proposed two major groups of serious mental diseases: dementia praecox (the original term for schizophrenia), and manic–depressive psychosis (Kraepelin, 1902). His classification helped to establish the organic nature of mental disorders, and formed the basis of the *Diagnostic and Statistical Manual of Mental Disorders* (DSM), the official North American diagnostic classification system, and the International Classification of Diseases (ICD) (Chapter 5: Mental and behavioral disorders), published by the World Health Organization. The World Health Organization included the classification of mental disorders in its International Classification of Diseases for the first time in 1949 (ICD-6), while its latest revision, ICD-11 was published in 2018. The *Diagnostic and Statistical Manual of Mental Disorders* (DSM) was first published by the American Psychiatric Association in 1952, and it has been revised regularly to improve the quality of the diagnostic system. Its latest revision, DSM-5, was published in 2013.

The main value of classification of psychological disorders is to determine the nature of people's problems, in order to assign the most appropriate method of treatment. Thus, classifications help in promoting communication about the nature of patients' problems, prognosis, and treatment. It helps in exchanging information about individual cases by offering some agreed terminology, criteria, and labels that can be used to distinguish one patient's disorder from another (Aboraya, Rankin, France, El-Missiry, & John, 2006; Claridge & Davis, 2003; Gelder, Gath, & Mayon, 1989). Classifications are also important in research on the etiology and treatment of mental disorders, and in legal situations. The main categories of the latest edition of the American Psychiatric Association (2013) classification (DSM-5) include:

- Neurodevelopmental Disorders
- Schizophrenia Spectrum and Other Psychotic Disorders
- Bipolar and Related Disorders
- Depressive Disorders
- Anxiety Disorders
- Obsessive-Compulsive and Related Disorders
- Trauma- and Stressor-Related Disorders
- Dissociative Disorders
- Somatic Symptom and Related Disorders
- Feeding and Eating Disorders
- Elimination Disorders
- Sleep–Wake Disorders
- Sexual Dysfunctions
- Gender Dysphoria
- Disruptive, Impulse Control, and Conduct Disorders
- Substance-Related and Addictive Disorders
- Neurocognitive Disorders
- Personality Disorders
- Paraphilic Disorders

Problems with the Classification of Mental Disorders

From the beginning there have been a lot of concerns about the classification of mental disorders. The current criticism seems to echo a long-running debate about the nature of mental health. However, psychiatric professionals continued to elaborate on the original classification system, resulting in newer versions of the DSM and the ICD, despite all the social criticism. These revisions were accompanied by a continuous increase in the number of mental disorders, and improved reliability and validity. However, many critics of the DSM and the ICD see it as an oversimplification of the infinite continuum of human behavior. Reducing complex problems to labels and numbers carries the risk of losing track of the unique human element. Possible risks include misdiagnosis or over-diagnosis, in which people may be labeled as having a disorder simply because their behavior does not always line up with the current ideal. Other concerns about classification include the following:

- *Reliability and validity concerns*: the repeated revisions of the DSM and the ICD have been mainly concerned with diagnostic reliability. However, these classification schemes demonstrate a certain degree of erraticism about how people are diagnosed (Claridge & Davis, 2003). Many diagnoses are so similar that there is a high rate of comorbidity between disorders. Specifying a particular number of symptoms from a long list when diagnosing a particular diagnosis seems very arbitrary, while lowering the threshold for psychiatric diagnoses carries the risk of an undue increase in the number of persons labeled in such a way, with corresponding consequences on them and on the health care system itself (Francis, 2013). On the other hand, subjective interpretation on the part of the psychiatrist may carry the risk of misdiagnosis, e.g., in order to diagnose mania, the elevated mood must be "abnormally and persistently elevated."

- *Diagnoses are based on superficial symptoms*: the DSM is criticized for being a categorical classification that is mainly concerned with collecting the signs and symptoms of mental disorders together based on statistical or clinical patterns, rather than their underlying causes. To overcome this categorical simplification, DSM-5 requires psychiatrists to grade the severity of the patient's symptoms. This ideological shift signals a step away from the simplistic notion that mental disorders are discrete conditions. This incorporation of a dimensional approach is supposed to increase the reliability of diagnosis and make treatments more tailored to patients' needs.

- *Cultural bias*: current diagnostic guidelines have been criticized as having a fundamentally Euro-American outlook.

- *Medicalization and financial conflicts of interest*: the way the categories of the DSM are structured and the substantial expansion of the number of categories refer to an increasing medicalization of human nature. This has been attributed by many to the expanding power and influence of pharmaceutical companies over the past few decades.

- *Stigma*: classifications are often criticized for contributing to the creation of social stigma and discriminating against those with mental illnesses because of the use of diagnostic labels. This can add to the suffering and disability of those who are diagnosed with a mental disorder.

Disorders of Childhood and Adolescence

Like adults, children may experience disturbance in cognition, emotions, behavior, and relationships which impairs their functioning. Community surveys indicate that 7–20 percent of children can be diagnosed as having a psychiatric disorder. Only about 10 percent of affected children receive psychiatric treatment.

Intellectual Disability

Patients with intellectual disability have deficits in intellectual functions, combined with deficits in adaptive functioning. Intellectual disability affects 1–3 percent of the population and has a male:female ratio of 2:1. Severity of intellectual disability ranges from mild to profound, defined on the basis of adaptive functioning, and not IQ scores. Milder forms of intellectual disability occur more frequently in families with low socio-economic status, while severe forms of intellectual disability are independent of socio-economic status. Most patients with intellectual disability have mild or moderate forms.

Etiology

Intellectual disability can be thought of as a final common pathway of a number of prenatal, perinatal, and postnatal disorders that affect brain structure or function. Possible causes include more than 500 genetic abnormalities, inborn errors of metabolism; perinatal or early childhood head injuries; maternal diabetes; mother's substance abuse; toxemia of pregnancy; or rubella. In 30–40 percent of patients with intellectual disability, no clear etiology can be determined. The most common cause of intellectual disability is Down syndrome (trisomy 21) and Fragile X syndrome.

Clinical Manifestations

The onset of manifestations of intellectual disability must be apparent before the age of 18. Parents or pediatricians may suspect that a child has intellectual disability after failure to meet developmental milestones in a number of functional areas (e.g., speech, social skills, or self-care skills). Children with intellectual disability show deficits in intellectual functions, such as reason-

PHOTO 21.1.   A Down's Syndrome Child.

ing, problem-solving, planning, abstract thinking, judgment, academic learning, and learning from experience. Also, the patients show deficits in adaptive functioning that result in failure to meet developmental and sociocultural standards for personal independence and social responsibility. Without ongoing support, the adaptive deficits limit functioning in one or more activities of daily life, such as communication, social participation, and independent living, across multiple environments, such as home, school, work, and community. Assessment of intelligence and adaptive functions by individualized, standardized testing can reveal the diagnosis. Comorbid psychiatric disorders are common in mentally retarded persons, e.g., autism, hyperactivity, aggression, repetitive behavior, enuresis and encopresis, and depression, especially in mild cases.

Investigations can help to assess treatable causes, such as hypothyroidism, phenylketonuria, galactosemia, congenital adrenal hyperplasia; can identify etiological factors such as Fragile X syndrome; and can ascertain a comorbid condition (e.g., epilepsy).

Management

Management of intellectual disability depends on its degree, and the particular abilities of the child. An individualized rehabilitation program is needed to empower skills in deficit areas.

Autism Spectrum Disorder

Autism spectrum disorder (ASD) is a pervasive developmental disorder of childhood onset. It is characterized by persistent deficits in social communication and social interaction across multiple contexts, and restricted, repetitive patterns of behavior, interests, or activities. Autism spectrum disorder occurs in about 1 percent of children. The male : female ratio is 3 : 1 to 4 : 1. There is no single etiologic factor that has been established as a definite cause of ASD, but possible causes include genetic factors, immunological factors, perinatal factors (e.g., obstetric complications), and environmental factors (pollution, lead and mercury poisoning).

Clinical Manifestations

Abnormal clinical findings are evident in early childhood (usually before age of 3). Core symptoms include impairment in social communication and interactions across multiple settings, and restrictive, repetitive, or stereotyped patterns of behavior, interests, or activities.

PHOTO 21.2.   A Child with ASD.

Impairment in social communication and interactions include deficits in social reciprocity, poorly integrated verbal and non-verbal communication; abnormalities in eye contact and body language or deficits in understanding and use of gestures; a total lack of facial expressions and non-verbal communication. These children may show impairment in the ability to initiate and sustain conversations and use repetitive or idiosyncratic language. Language may also be abnormal in pitch, intonation, rate, rhythm, or stress. Those children show deficits in skills necessary to develop, maintain, and understand relationships.

Children suffering from ASD show restricted, repetitive, or stereotyped patterns of behavior, interests, or activities. There may be marked preoccupation with one or more stereotyped and restricted patterns of interest (e.g., a certain toy or T-shirt), an inflexible adherence to specific non-functional routines or rituals (e.g., eating the same meal in the same dish at the same place each day), stereotyped or repetitive motor mannerisms (e.g., whole-body rocking), and a persistent preoccupation with the parts of objects (e.g., wheels of cars).

Approximately 25 percent of children with autistic disorder have comorbid seizures, and approximately 75 percent have intellectual disability. EEGs and intelligence testing are typically part of the initial evaluation. Rarely, some autistic children have specific special skills (e.g., calendar calculation and artistic talent).

Management

ASD is a chronic lifelong disorder with relatively significant morbidity. Behavioral management and educational techniques are used to improve attention, imitation, cognitive skills, communication, and social functioning. Self-help skills, fine and gross motor skills, improve restricted interests, and reduce stereotyped behaviors. Many children with autism require special education or specialized day programs. Early intervention leads to better outcome. Drugs have no role in improving the core symptoms of autism, though they could be useful in the management of comorbid conditions, e.g., epilepsy is treated with anticonvulsants, and low doses of atypical antipsychotics (e.g., risperidone) are used to decrease aggressive or self-harming behaviors.

Attention Deficit Hyperactivity Disorder (ADHD)

ADHD refers to a syndrome found in children, characterized by a persistent pattern of inattention and/or hyperactivity-impulsivity that interferes with functioning or development. The prevalence of ADHD in school-aged children is estimated to be 3–5 percent. The boy:girl ratio ranges from 4:1 in the general population to 9:1 in clinical settings. It is the most common cause of chronic behavioral problems for school-aged children. The etiology of the disorder is unknown, but genetic factors, psychosocial factors, and environmental factors, such as substance exposure, perinatal injury, and lead intoxication have all been implicated. Disturbance in norepinephrine and dopamine neurotransmission is supposed to play a role in the etiology and hence in the treatment of the disorder. Many children with ADHD have abnormalities of sleep architecture, EEG abnormalities, and soft neurologic signs. Brain imaging studies indicate that overall brain volume is smaller in children diagnosed with ADHD when compared with controls. The disorder runs in families and co-occurs with mood disorders, substance use disorders, learning disorders, and antisocial personality disorder.

Clinical Manifestations

The onset of the disorder must be evident before the age of 12 years. Symptoms must be present in two or more settings (e.g., school, home). Symptoms in only one setting suggest an environmental or situational cause. Core symptoms include hyperactivity, impulsivity, and inattention. Preschool-age children are usually brought for evaluation because of marked problem behavior at home. Typically, they stay up late, wake up early, and spend most of their waking hours in various hyperactive and impulsive activities that causes damage and disruption at home. When these children enter school, their difficulties with attention become more obvious. They appear not to follow directions, forget important school supplies, fail to complete homework or in-class assignments, and blurt out answers to teachers' questions before being called on. Because of their inattention and hyperactivity, those children often become known as troublemakers. They fall behind their peers academically and socially because of their symptoms.

Management

The management of ADHD involves a combination of drugs and behavioral interventions. Most children with ADHD respond favorably to psychostimulants (e.g., methylphenidate) and atomoxetine. Behavioral management techniques include positive reinforcement, firm limit setting, and techniques for reducing stimulation (e.g., one playmate at a time; and short focused tasks).

Conduct Disorder

Conduct disorder is defined as a repetitive and persistent pattern of behavior in which the basic rights of others or important age-appropriate societal norms or rules are violated. Disordered behaviors include aggression toward people or animals, destruction of property, deceitfulness, theft, or serious violations of rules (e.g., school truancy, running away from home overnight). Conduct disorder is the childhood equivalent of adult antisocial personality disorder. It is a common disorder in child outpatient psychiatric clinics and is frequently seen comorbid with ADHD or learning disorders. Parental separation or divorce, parental substance abuse, severely poor or inconsistent parenting, and association with a delinquent peer group have been shown to have some relationship to the development of conduct disorder.

Treatment of conduct disorder involves individual and parent management training. Some children may need to be removed from the home and placed in foster care. Medication is used only to treat a comorbid ADHD or mood disorder but not the conduct disorder itself. The long-term outcome depends on the severity of the disorder and the degree and type of comorbidity. Of children with conduct disorder, 25–40 percent go on to have adult antisocial personality disorder.

Psychotic Disorders

Psychotic disorders are a group of disorders in which there is gross impairment in reality testing, which is manifested as delusions, hallucinations, and disorganized behavior. Psychotic Disorders in DSM-5 involves several categories including schizophrenia, schizophreniform disorder, brief psychotic disorder, schizoaffective disorder, and delusional disorder.

Schizophrenia

Schizophrenia is a disorder in which patients have psychotic symptoms and social and/or occupational dysfunction that persist for at least 6 months. Schizophrenia affects 1 percent of the population, including all socio-economic classes. The typical age of onset is the early twenties for men and the late twenties for women. Patients having schizophrenia are at high risk for suicide. Approximately one-third will attempt suicide and 10 percent will complete suicide. Risk factors for suicide include male gender, age <30 years, chronic course, prior depression, and recent hospital discharge.

Etiology

The essential cause of schizophrenia appears to be genetic and constitutional but a large number of biopsychosocial factors may predispose a person to manifest the illness at a particular time in a person's life. Schizophrenia is widely believed to have a neurobiological basis. The most notable theory is the dopamine hypothesis, which postulates that positive symptoms of schizophrenia are due to hyperactivity of the dopamine D2 receptor neurotransmission in the subcortical and limbic brain regions, whereas negative and cognitive symptoms of the disorder can be ascribed to the hypofunctionality of the dopamine D1 receptor neurotransmission in the prefrontal cortex (Toda & Abi-Dargham, 2007). In support of this, studies have shown an increased density of the dopamine D2 receptor in post-mortem brain tissue of schizophrenia sufferers. This theory is also partly supported by the efficacy of antipsychotic drugs (which block dopamine receptors) and the ability of drugs (such as cocaine or amphetamines) that stimulate dopaminergic activity to induce psychosis. Many recent studies have revealed a lot of structural and functional brain abnormalities evidenced through brain imaging of schizophrenic patients. Psychosocial and environmental factors may hinder or help to make the predisposition to schizophrenia, these include various psychosocial stressors and unfavorable early experiences, abnormal parental attitudes, physical illness, head injury, and intoxications. No one finding or theory to date is fully adequate in explaining the etiology and pathogenesis of this complex disease.

Clinical Manifestations

Patients with schizophrenia generally have a history of abnormal premorbid functioning. The prodrome of schizophrenia includes poor social skills, social withdrawal, and unusual (although not frankly delusional) thinking. Inquiring about the premorbid history may help to distinguish schizophrenia from other psychotic disorders. Clinical features of schizophrenia include the following.

- *Disturbances of thought*: The process and the content of thought may be disturbed in schizophrenia. The process of thinking shows loosening of associations in which the individual's ideas shift from one topic to another in ways that appear unrelated. In severe cases, the speech appears incoherent and cannot be understood. Abnormal contents include false beliefs which cannot be corrected by logic and reasoning and which is not keeping with the patient's cultural and educational background, that is, delusions. Delusions are often described according to their content. Any type of delusion could occur in schizophrenia, especially persecutory, religious, reference, influence, thought broadcasting, thought insertion, and thought withdrawal.
- *Disturbances of perception*: The most dramatic disturbance in perception is hallucination: the patient has sensory experiences in the absence of relevant external stimuli. Auditory hallucinations are the most common type of hallucination. This may take the form of voices talking about the patient in the third person, voices making a running commentary on the patient's actions, or voices telling the patient what to do (command auditory hallucination). Visual hallucinations are somewhat less frequent, e.g., seeing strange, dreadful or fantastic creatures. Other types of hallucinations occur infrequently, e.g., smelling a bad odor originating from one's body (olfactory hallucination), tasting a poison in food (gustatory hallucination), or feeling of being pricked by needles (tactile hallucination).
- *Motor and behavioral symptoms*: People with schizophrenia sometimes exhibit bizarre motor activity. They may grimace, adopt strange facial expressions, or gesture repeatedly using peculiar sequences of finger, hand, and arm movements. Some patients may become agitated and show extreme hyperactivity, while others may become totally

unresponsive and immobile, adopting an unusual posture and maintaining it for long periods of time. In cases with catatonic immobility, a person may stand like a statue with one foot extended and one arm raised toward the ceiling.

■ *Disturbances of emotional expression*: People suffering from schizophrenia may be withdrawn and unresponsive in situations that should make them sad or happy. Blunting of emotional expression can conceal inner turmoil, and the person may have angry outbursts. Severe emotional outbursts may appear spontaneously without any apparent provocation. These may take the form of anger, violence, or marked terror which characteristically come out of the blue without warning. Sometimes individuals with schizophrenia express emotions that are inappropriately linked to the situation or to the thought being expressed (emotional incongruity), such as smiling while speaking of disastrous events. Because emotions are influenced by cognitive processes, it is not surprising that disorganized thoughts and perceptions are accompanied by changes in emotional responses.

■ *Negative symptoms*: Negative symptoms of schizophrenia represent a reduction of emotional responsiveness, motivation, socialization, speech, and movement. Negative symptoms may be either primary or secondary. Primary negative symptoms are thought to be etiologically related to the core pathophysiology of schizophrenia, whereas secondary negative symptoms are thought to be derivative of other symptoms of schizophrenia (e.g., delusions or hallucinations), other disease processes (e.g., depression can cause anhedonia, lack of motivation, and social withdrawal), medications (e.g., antipsychotic medications variably produce both akinesia and blunted affect), or the environment (e.g., lack of stimulation in impoverished institutional environments can lead to lack of motivation and initiation of productive activities).

■ *Decreased ability to function*: In addition to the specific symptoms described above, people with schizophrenia have impairment in the ability to carry out their daily life routines. Personal hygiene and grooming may deteriorate, and the individual avoids the company of other people. If the disorder occurs in adolescence, the individual may have diminished ability to cope with school and limited social skills and few friends. Adults suffering from schizophrenia are often unsuccessful in obtaining or holding down a job.

Management

Antipsychotic drugs are the principal treatment of schizophrenia. These medications are used to treat acute psychotic episodes and to maintain patients in remission. The efficacy of antipsychotic drugs is essentially related to their dopamine antagonistic activity and to some extent to serotonin antagonism. Typical antipsychotics act as dopamine antagonists, e.g., chlorpromazine, haloperidol, and trifluoperazine. Their main side effects are extrapyramidal symptoms. Atypical antipsychotics act as dopamine and serotonin antagonists, e.g., risperidone, olanzapine, and clozapine. Their main side effects are metabolic syndrome. Psychosocial treatments, including stable reality-oriented psychotherapy, family support, psychoeducation, social and vocational skills training, and attention to details of living situation (housing, roommates, daily activities), are critical to the long-term management of these patients. Poor prognosis occurs in cases with early onset, history of head trauma, or comorbid substance abuse.

Mood Disorders

Mood disorders are a group of psychological disturbances in which the central symptom is persistent disturbance of mood that is usually accompanied by other characteristic symptoms that cause psychological discomfort, impaired ability to function, or both. Mood disorders in DSM-5 involve one of two large categories: bipolar and related disorders (in which the individual at least has an episode of mania or hypomania that may or may not alternate with episodes of depression, usually with a return to normal mood between the two extremes), or depressive disorders (in which the individual has one or more periods of depression without a history of manic episodes), e.g., major depressive disorder, dysthymia, premenstrual dysphoric disorder, and disruptive mood dysregulation disorder.

Major Depressive Disorder

Most people have periods of feeling sad, lethargic, and being uninterested in any activities, even pleasurable ones, as a normal response to many of life's stresses, especially important losses. Depression becomes a disorder when the symptoms are severe enough to interfere with normal functioning, and continue for at least two weeks, and cannot be explained by situational or other etiologic factors.

Major depression affects about 6–7 percent of Americans, in any given year, and affects about 15 percent of Americans at some point in their life (Kessler et al., 2005d). Women are about twice as likely as men to be diagnosed with major depression (Hammen & Watkins, 2008).

Major depression is a disorder of the whole person, affecting bodily functions, behavior, and thoughts as well as emotions. A person does not need to have all the symptoms of depression to be diagnosed with a disorder, but the diagnosis of depression will be more certain with an increasing number and severity of symptoms. The emotional symptoms of depression differ from everyday blues that one may experience from time to time, by their persistent nature and severity of discomfort and despair. The depressed patient may lose interest and pleasure, and is unable to experience joy even in response to most previously pleasurable activities, a symptom referred to as anhedonia. Depressed people experience reduced appetite, they tend to be very fatigued, and have low energy. Abnormal sleep patterns are another hallmark of major depression. About three-quarters of depressed patients have insomnia symptoms, and hypersomnia is present in about 40 percent of young depressed adults and 10 percent of older patients, with preponderance in females. Sleep onset latency is significantly increased, there is little or no deep sleep, and total sleep time reduced. Rapid eye movement (REM) latency is often shortened, and the duration of the first REM period is increased. Early morning awakening also occurs as the depressed person awakens at 3:00 or 4:00 a.m. and cannot get back to sleep, even if feeling very tired, and exhausted (Nutt, Wilson, & Paterson, 2008).

The cognitive symptoms of depression consist primarily of negative thoughts, with themes of worthlessness, guilt, hopelessness, and even recurrent thoughts of death or suicidal ideation, plans or attempts. The depressed person tends to be passive and has difficulty initiating activities. Episodes of depression can be greatly shortened, and new episodes prevented using either drug therapy and/or psychotherapy. If not treated, the symptoms of major depression can last six months or longer. More than half of people who had an episode of major depression can be expected to have a relapse, usually within two years. With each recurrence, the symptoms tend to increase in severity and the time between major depression episodes decreases (Hammen, 2005).

Bipolar Disorder

Bipolar disorder-I involves having an episode of mania alternating or not with a major depressive episode. In cases of bipolar disorder-II, a hypomanic episode alternates with a major depressive episode. So, the defining feature of bipolar disorder is having manic or hypomanic episodes. The onset of bipolar disorder typically occurs in the person's early twenties. The life-time prevalence is 0.4–1.6 percent. There are no gender differences in the rate at which bipolar disorder occurs.

Manic episodes typically begin suddenly, and symptoms escalate rapidly. During a manic episode, people are exceptionally euphoric, expansive, or excited for one week or more. During manic episodes, patients are energetic, enthusiastic, and full of self-confidence. They talk continually, rush from one activity to another with little need for sleep. Manic patients usually have grandiose plans for obtaining wealth, power, and reputation. Sometimes the grandiose ideas represent delusional beliefs. Manic persons may become agitated or verbally abusive when others question their grandiose claims (Miklowitz & Johnson, 2007), or attempt to interfere with their activities. During manic episodes, patients can become sexually promiscuous, or commit illegal acts. The functioning of manic patients is significantly impaired during a manic episode. Hospitalization is usually required, partly to protect patients from the potential consequences of their inappropriate decisions and behavior.

Etiology

The etiology of mood disorders appears to be multifactorial. A combined biological and psychological model may best explain the mood disorders. However, how these factors precisely interact to cause mood disorders is not clearly understood.

Genetic predisposition vulnerability to mood disorders is suggested by family, twin, and adoption studies. Researchers have consistently found that both major depression and bipolar disorder tend to run in families (Leonardo & Hen, 2006). The first-degree relatives (parents, children, and siblings) studies of people with bipolar disorder have 5–10 times higher rates of both bipolar disorder and depressive disorders than relatives of people without bipolar disorder. Identical twins of individuals with bipolar disorder are 45–75 times more likely to develop the disorder than people in the general population (Farmer, Elkin, & McGuffin, 2007).

Family history studies of first-degree relatives of people with depression find 2–4 times higher rates of depression than others (P. F. Sullivan, Neale, & Kendler, 2000). Interestingly, relatives of depressed people do not have any greater risk of developing bipolar disorder than relatives of people with no mood disorder. This suggests that bipolar disorder has a different genetic basis from that of depression. Twin studies also suggest that depression is heritable but to a lesser degree than bipolar disorder (Sullivan et al., 2000).

Abnormalities at all the stages of neurotransmission of monoamines (norepinephrine, serotonin, and dopamine), particularly in areas of the brain that are involved in the regulation of emotion, such as the hypothalamus (Belmaker & Agam, 2008) are suggested as a cause of depression or bipolar disorder. Since the 1960s, several medications that act on one or more of these neurotransmitters have been developed. Lithium, the drug that effectively alleviates symptoms of bipolar disorder, regulates the availability of glutamate, which acts as an excitatory neurotransmitter in many brain areas (Dixon & Hokin, 1998).

Neuroimaging studies using computerized tomography (CT) scans and magnetic resonance imaging (MRI) have found deterioration in the prefrontal cortex of people with severe unipolar depression or bipolar disorder (Dougherty & Rauch, 2007). This is associated with abnormalities in metabolism in this area of the brain, as revealed by positron emission tomography (PET) studies. Reduced activity in the cingulate gyrus of the prefrontal cortex was found in patients with bipolar disorder, as well as reductions in activity in the thalamus. Similarly, depressed patients show variations in the functioning of the prefrontal cortex, as well as the thalamus, the hypothalamus, the amygdala, and the hippocampus, which are involved in the regulation of responses to stress and in sleep, appetite, sexual drive, motivation, and memory (Southwick, Vythilingam, & Charney, 2005). The precise meaning of these structural and functional brain abnormalities is still unknown.

Traumatic and stressful life events can trigger new episodes of mood disorders (Miklowitz & Johnson, 2006; Southwick et al., 2005). Improving family atmosphere and teaching the patient how to reduce and cope with stressors reduce the risk of relapse of the disorder (Lam & Wong, 2005; Miklowitz & Craighead, 2007). According to cognitive theories, people become depressed because they tend to interpret events in their lives in pessimistic, hopeless ways (Abramson et al., 2002). Aaron Beck grouped the negative thoughts of depressed individuals into three categories, which he called the cognitive triad: (1) negative thoughts about the self; (2) negative thoughts about present experiences; and (3) negative thoughts about the future (Beck, 1976). Negative thoughts about the self include the depressed person's belief that he or she is worthless and inadequate. Depressed people believe that their inadequacies and defects will prevent them from ever improving their situation.

Anxiety Disorders

Most people feel anxious and tense in the face of threatening or stressful situations. Such feelings are normal reactions to stressors. Anxiety is considered abnormal when it occurs in situations that most people can handle with little difficulty. Anxiety is characterized by a feeling of fear accompanied by somatic signs that indicate a hyperactive autonomic nervous system. In the absence of a real threat, these symptoms become maladaptive. Anxiety include a group of disorders in which anxiety either is the main symptom (e.g., generalized anxiety and panic disorders) or is experienced when the individual attempts to control certain maladaptive behaviors (e.g., phobic disorders). Acute and post-traumatic stress disorder involves anxiety following a traumatic event.

There are four types of symptoms of anxiety: (1) physiological or somatic symptoms that resemble fight-or-flight responses, e.g., increased heart rate, perspiration, and muscle tension; (2) cognitive symptoms of anxiety include thoughts about having a heart attack and dying; (3) behavioral symptoms of anxiety include inability to move until help arrives; and (4) emotional symptoms of anxiety involve the sense of dread and terror; many people with anxiety disorders view situations that most people consider benign as threatening, and they worry about those situations even when they are unlikely to occur, e.g., people with social phobias avoid social gatherings.

Generalized Anxiety Disorder

People suffering from generalized anxiety disorder are constantly tense and anxious. They feel anxious about a wide range of life circumstances, when one source of worry is removed, another quickly moves in to take its place, with little or no apparent justification (Craske & Waters, 2005). The anxiety can be attached to virtually any object or to none at all. Because of this, generalized anxiety disorder is sometimes referred to as free-floating anxiety.

Common physical complaints among persons suffering from generalized anxiety disorder include disturbed sleep, fatigue, headaches, dizziness, and rapid heart rate. In addition, the individual continually worries about potential problems and has difficulty concentrating or making decisions. When the individual finally makes a decision, it becomes a source of further worry. Environmental, psychological, and genetic as well as other biological factors are probably involved in the etiology of generalized anxiety disorder.

Panic Disorder

A panic attack is a sudden episode of extreme anxiety that rapidly escalates in intensity. About 28 percent of adults have occasional panic attacks, especially during times of stress (Kessler et al., 2006). These feelings are usually accompanied by feeling dizzy or faint, or having a pounding heart, shortness of breath, a choking sensation, or chest pain. The person may also experience nausea, perspiration, shaking, light-headedness, faintness, chills, or hot flashes. These symptoms are interpreted as indicating a terrible consequence, e.g., I am going to have a heart attack, I am about to die, go crazy, or lose control. This leads to hypervigilance about body sensations, increased arousal of the sympathetic nervous system, more physical sensations, and heightened anxiety, which spirals into a panic attack (Clark, 1986). A panic attack typically peaks within 10 minutes of onset and then gradually subsides. Panic disorder refers to recurrent panic attacks in which the individual is worrying about having further attacks. Panic disorder usually appears between late adolescence and the mid-thirties. The first panic attack may occur after a stressful experience, such as an injury or illness, or during a stressful period of life, such as while changing jobs or during a period of marital conflict (Watanabe, Kazuhisa, & Madoka, 2005). In other cases, the first panic attack cannot be related to life events.

About 20 percent of people with panic disorder also develop agoraphobia. People with agoraphobia fear situations from which escape may be difficult or embarrassing, where they may be trapped in or unable to receive help when having a panic attack, e.g., being alone in wide open spaces, such as an isolated beach, or being in an open crowded place, such as a shopping mall. They may also fear being in tightly enclosed spaces from which it can be difficult to escape, such as a bus, an elevator, or the subway. They may also feel embarrassed that others will see that they are having a panic attack, even though other people are usually not aware when a person is having a panic attack. Lifetime prevalence estimates are 22.7 percent for isolated panic without agoraphobia, 0.8 percent for isolated panic attack with agoraphobia, 3.7 percent for panic disorder without agoraphobia, and 1.1 percent for panic disorder with agoraphobia (Kessler et al., 2006).

Etiology

The definite cause of panic disorder is unknown. Several factors probably contribute to its development including genetic, biochemical and structural and functional brain change, and early family factors. The triple vulnerabilities model states that a biological predisposition toward anxiety, over-sensitivity to physical sensations, and a low sense of control over potentially life-threatening events, combine to make a person vulnerable to panic (Craske & Barlow, 2008).

Twin studies show that an identical twin suffers panic disorder twice as likely fraternal twins (Hettema, Neale, & Kendler, 2001; van den Heuvel, van de Wetering, Veltman, & Pauls, 2000). Gorman et al. (2000) argue that patients inherit a sensitive central nervous system fear mechanism centered in the amygdala, though several other brain areas are also implicated. People with panic disorder also show variations in neurotransmitter systems critical to the fear response, including gamma-aminobutyric acid (GABA) and serotonin. These brain and neurotransmitter abnormalities could cause hyperactivation and poor regulation of fear responses. Some studies show that people with panic disorder have reduced metabolism in the amygdala, the hippocampus, the thalamus, and the brain-stem areas, which are important in regulating responses to fear (Roy-Byrne, Craske, & Stein, 2006).

People who develop panic disorder are often hypersensitive to their body sensations, paying close attention to signs of physical arousal, and may misinterpret body sensations in a negative way, and engage in catastrophic thinking, e.g., increased heart rate after climbing stairs is misinterpreted as the warning signs of a heart attack. Such catastrophic misinterpretations simply add to the physiological arousal, creating a vicious circle in which the frightening symptoms intensify. A full panic attack can be induced in persons having panic disorder by engagement in activities that stimulate the initial physiological changes of the fight-or-flight response, e.g., intentional hyperventilation, breathing into a paper bag, or inhaling a small amount of carbon dioxide (Clark, 1988; Craske & Waters, 2005; Zvolensky & Smits, 2008). In the same way, people with panic disorder remember vividly places where they have had attacks, fear those places, and generalize fear to all similar places. By avoiding those places, they reduce their anxiety, and their avoidance behavior thus highly reinforces their fears. Thus, through classical and operant conditioning, their behaviors lead to agoraphobia.

Phobias

Many people are fearful of certain animals, such as dogs or snakes, or are moderately uncomfortable in particular situations, such as flying in a plane or riding in a glass elevator. This fear seems normal or appropriate, and those people would not be diagnosed with a psychological disorder. A phobia is an intense fear of a stimulus or situation that most people do not consider particularly dangerous. The individual usually realizes that this fear is greater than what most people experience but still feels anxiety (ranging from strong uneasiness to panic) that can be alleviated only by avoiding the feared object or situation. A fear is usually not diagnosed as a phobic disorder unless it is accompanied by significant distress or interferes considerably with the person's daily life, e.g., fear of enclosed places that prevents a person from entering elevators.

The DSM-5 included three categories of phobic disorders among anxiety disorders: (1) specific phobia; (2) social phobia (social anxiety disorder); and (3) agoraphobia. A specific phobia is fear of a specific object, animal, or situation, e.g., intense fears of germs, enclosed places, or darkness. Sometimes, the individual may have a concurrent number of phobias. Specific phobias are quite common, with nearly 8–13 percent of the general population experiencing a specific phobia at some time in their lives (Alonso et al., 2004; Kessler et al., 2005b). Generally, the objects or situations that produce specific phobias tend to fall into four categories:

- *Fear of particular situations,* such as flying, driving, tunnels, bridges, elevators, crowds, or enclosed places.
- *Fear of features of the natural environment,* such as heights, seas, thunder, or lightning.
- *Fear of injury or blood,* including the fear of injections, needles, and medical or dental procedures.
- *Fear of animals and insects,* such as spiders, dogs, cats, slugs, or bats.

PHOTO 21.3. Spider Phobia.

In social phobia, people feel extremely insecure and have an exaggerated fear of being embarrassed in social situations, even if the situation involves performing routine behaviors in front of others, e.g., eating a meal in public, making small talk at a party, or using a public restroom can be distressing for the person with social phobia. The core of social phobia seems to be an irrational fear of being embarrassed, judged, or critically evaluated by others. Although people with social phobia recognize that their fear is excessive and unreasonable, they cannot control their anxiety in social situations (Hofmann & Otto, 2008). Facing a feared social situation, they may begin trembling and perspiring, feel confused and dizzy, have heart palpitations, and may finally have a full panic attack. People with social phobias will make every effort to avoid situations in which others may evaluate them, e.g., taking jobs that are solitary and isolated to avoid other people. In the United States, approximately 6.8 percent of adults suffer from social phobia in a given year. Social phobia typically begins in adolescence and tends to be a chronic problem if it is not treated (Kessler et al., 1998).

Etiology

Freud argued that phobias result when people displace their anxiety about unconscious motives or desires onto objects that symbolize those motives or desires, e.g., fear of horses symbolizes Oedipal fears. Many phobias emerge after a traumatic experience, e.g., a child who suffers a near-drowning experience may develop a phobia of seas (thalassophobia), a child who was bitten by a dog may develop a phobia of dogs, and a student who is laughed at by peers after a hesitant speech in class may develop a phobia of public speaking. Through classical conditioning, the previously neutral stimulus would elicit the anxiety reaction. Many people with such fears avoid the phobic object to reduce their anxiety, and the phobic behavior is maintained through operant conditioning. Phobias related to survival such as snake and spider phobia develop more rapidly and easily due to innate or evolutionary predisposition, this is called *stimulus preparedness*. Such prepared learning or conditioning is highly resistant to extinction (Seligman, 1971). Phobias may also be learned indirectly through observation, e.g., children may share their parents' fears through observation (Muris, Steerneman, Merckelbach, & Meesters, 1996). However, genetic factors may play a role in vulnerability to fear conditioning. The first-degree relatives of phobic people are three to four times more likely than others to have a phobia, and twin studies suggest that this is due, at least in part, to genetics (Hettema et al., 2001).

Acute and Post-traumatic Stress Disorder

Acute and post-traumatic stress disorder (PTSD) is a trauma and stressor-related disorder that develops in response to an extreme physical or psychological trauma. Extreme traumas are events that produce intense feelings of horror and helplessness, such as a serious physical injury or threat of injury to self or to loved ones. Acute stress disorder typically occurs within one month of a traumatic event. It lasts at least three days and can persist for up to one month after exposure to trauma. Acute and post-traumatic stress disorder can develop in survivors of military combat and other sorts of extreme traumas, such as natural disasters, physical or sexual assault, or terrorist attacks (McNally, 2003). Rescue workers, relief workers, and emergency service personnel can also develop PTSD symptoms (Eriksson et al., 2001). Witnessing the injury or death of others can be sufficiently traumatic to develop these disorders.

Three core symptoms that characterize post-traumatic stress disorder include: (1) frequent intrusive recollections of the event, and replaying it in one's mind; (2) avoiding stimuli or situations that may trigger memories of the experience; (3) negative alterations of cognitions and mood associated with the traumatic event; and (4) increased physical arousal associated with anxiety, e.g., easy startling, sleep disturbances, problems with concentrating and remembering, and irritability or outbursts of anger.

Obsessive-Compulsive Disorder

Obsessions are repeated, intrusive, uncontrollable thoughts or mental images that cause significant personal anxiety and distress. Obsessions are not the same as everyday worries which usually have a rational basis. Common obsessional themes include irrational fear of dirt, germs, and other forms of contamination, thoughts about religion and sex, and pathological doubt about having accomplished simple tasks, such as closing the door (Antony, Purdon, & Summerfeldt, 2007). Compulsions are irresistible urges to carry out certain acts or rituals that reduce anxiety. Compulsions may be overt behaviors (such as repeatedly washing hands, or checking doors or windows), or they may be covert mental behaviors (such as counting or self-reciting certain phrases). Regardless of whether the repetitive element is a thought (obsession) or an act (compulsion), the central feature of the disorder is the subjective experience of loss of control. Patients struggle to stop the intrusive thoughts or resist performing the repetitive acts but are unable to do so. Obsessional thoughts are very distressing, and engagement in compulsive behaviors can take a great deal of time and be highly maladaptive. People may experience either obsessions or compulsions. More commonly, obsessions and compulsions occur alongside. Obsessions and compulsions are frequently linked in some way, e.g., a person who has obsessions of contamination washes hands excessively. About 2.3 percent of people develop obsessive compulsive disorder at some time in their lives (Ruscio, Stein, Chiu, & Kessler, 2010). It begins at a young age (Franklin & Foa, 2008).

Etiology

The psychoanalytic explanation of OCD was once the best way to understand this disorder, but its failure to alleviate its manifestations led to its decline. A number of other theories replaced it as a possible explanation, these include behavioral, cognitive, and biological factors.

The behavioral model suggests that compulsions are learned responses that help in reducing or preventing discomfort associated with obsessions. The cognitive model suggests that faulty misinterpretation of intrusive thoughts leads to the creation of obsessions and compulsions. Unwanted cognitive intrusions are experienced by most people, with similar contents to clinical obsessions, but are not believed and consequently cause little or no distress. In people who develop OCD, these intrusive thoughts are appraised as personally important, highly unacceptable or immoral, or posing a threat for which the individual is personally responsible (Salkovskis, 1985). The greater the strength and concerns about these thoughts, the greater the chance that a person will develop OCD. Thus, obsessions begin with a normal, intrusive thought, which interacts with a belief system held by the individual in such a way that causes marked discomfort or anxiety. This anxiety is combined then with an enhanced sense of responsibility and self-blame. People attempt to alleviate distress created by their inappropriate appraisals via some behaviors that temporarily suppress the obsession and the anxiety it arouses. This reduction in anxiety reinforces the behavior, and a compulsion is born, thus perpetuating the cycle of obsessions and compulsions.

While the cognitive-behavioral model has a good explanatory power and has led to the development of effective treatments, it certainly does not completely explain why any one individual has OCD. Biological explanations include genetic, biochemical, structural, and functional brain changes.

In their review, van Grootheest et al. (2005) concluded that OCD symptoms are heritable, with genetic influences in the range of 45–65 percent in children, and 27–47 percent in adults. Most candidate genes that have been studied are involved in the metabolism of neurotransmitters, especially catechol-O-methyl-transferase (COMT), monoamine oxidase-A (MAO-A), dopamine transporter (DAT), dopamine receptors DRD_1, DRD_2, DRD_3, DRD_4, serotonin transporters $5-HT_2A$ and $5HT_1B$. Of these, the most promising for OCD transmission and expression belongs to ones in the serotonin systems (5HTTLPR and $5HT_1B$) and the glutamate systems (Hollander, Braun, & Simeon, 2008).

Caudate nucleus and the orbitofrontal cortex display increased activity in individuals with OCD (Guehl et al., 2008; Saxena, Brody, Schwartz, & Baxter, 1998; Whiteside, Port, & Abramowitz, 2004). The caudate nucleus receives information, along with the putamen, from the cerebral cortex. This information is then processed by the basal ganglia, which then goes through two pathways, the direct pathway and the indirect pathway, through the thalamus and back to the cortex. The direct pathway is excitatory whereas the indirect pathway is inhibitory. OCD may be the result of overactivity of the direct pathway. The orbitofrontal cortex can activate the two pathways resulting in an imbalance of the pathways, resulting in OCD behaviors (Saxena et al., 1998). The orbitofrontal cortex and basal ganglia receive input from serotonergic terminals (Lack, 2015; Lavoie & Parent, 1990; El Mansara & Blier, 1997). Many positron emission tomography (PET) studies of OCD have found an increased metabolism or blood flow in orbitofrontal and anterior cingulate cortex as well as the head of the caudate nucleus (Millet et al., 2013, Parmar & Sarkar, 2016). Functional magnetic resonance imaging (fMRI) studies provide significant correlation between orbitofrontal and anterior cingulated cortices and the mediation of OCD symptoms (Rotge et al., 2008).

Eating Disorders

Eating disorders involve serious and maladaptive disturbances in eating behavior. These disturbances include extreme reduction of food intake, severe bouts of overeating, and obsessive concerns about body shape or weight (American Psychiatric Association, 2013). The two main types of eating disorders are anorexia nervosa and bulimia nervosa, which usually begin during adolescence or early adulthood. Some 90–95 percent of the people who experience an eating disorder are female (Thompson, Roehrig, & Kinder, 2007). Despite the 10-to-1 gender-difference ratio, the central features of eating disorders are similar among males and females (Andersen, 2002).

Anorexia Nervosa

Anorexia nervosa is characterized by refusal to maintain a minimally normal body weight, with a body weight that is 15 percent or more below normal, body mass index can drop to 12 or lower. Persons with anorexia are extremely afraid of gaining weight or becoming fat, in spite of being dangerously underweight, they have a distorted perception of the body size. Although emaciated, patients deny the seriousness of their weight loss, and see themselves in mirror as fat or obese (American Psychiatric Association, 2000).

The severe malnutrition caused by anorexia disrupts the body physiology in ways that are very similar to those caused by starvation. Basal metabolic rate, blood levels of glucose, insulin, and leptin significantly decrease. Other hormonal levels drop, including the level of reproductive hormones. In women, reduced estrogen results in cessation of the menstrual cycle. In males, decreased testosterone disrupts sex drive and sexual function (Crosscope-Happel, Getz, & Hayes, 2000). Anorexia nervosa is associated with skin signs which are the expression of the medical consequences of starvation, and induced vomiting. They include xerosis, lanugo-like body hair, carotenoderma, acne, hyperpigmentation, seborrhoeic dermatitis, acrocyanosis, petechiae, livedo reticularis, interdigital intertrigo, paronychia, acquired striae distensae, and acral coldness (Strumia, 2009).

Bulimia Nervosa

People with bulimia nervosa experience periods of binge eating, consuming large amounts of sweet and high-calorie foods that can be swallowed quickly, such as ice cream, cake, and candy. Binges typically occur in secrecy, and are often triggered by negative feelings or hunger.

People with bulimia nervosa fear gaining weight and are intensely preoccupied and dissatisfied with their bodies. However, people with bulimia stay within a normal weight range or may even be slightly overweight. After bingeing, a patient compensates by purging herself of the excessive food, by self-induced vomiting or by misuse of laxatives or enemas. Once she purges, she often feels psychologically relieved. Some people with bulimia do not purge themselves of the excess food. Rather, they use fasting and excessive exercise to keep their body weight within the normal range (American Psychiatric Association, 2000). Like anorexia nervosa, bulimia nervosa can have a serious physical impact on the body. Repeated purging disrupts the body's electrolyte balance, leading to muscle cramps, irregular heartbeats, and other potentially fatal cardiac problems. Self-induced vomiting erodes tooth enamel by the acidic vomitus, causing tooth decay and gum disease. Frequent vomiting, especially when practiced for long periods of time, can damage the gastrointestinal tract as well as the teeth (Forney, Buchman-Schmitt, Keel, & Frank, 2016).

Etiology

Contemporary Western cultural attitudes toward thinness and dieting probably contribute to the increased incidence of eating disorders today. This seems to be especially true with anorexia, which occurs predominantly in Western or westernized countries (Becker & Fay, 2006). Family interaction patterns may also contribute to eating disorders, e.g., critical comments by parents or siblings about a child's weight, or parental modeling of disordered eating, may increase the risk that an individual develops an eating disorder (Thompson et al., 2007).

Both anorexia and bulimia patients show a decrease in brain activity of the neurotransmitter serotonin (Fumeron et al., 2001). Disrupted brain chemistry probably also contributes to the fact that eating disorders frequently co-occur with other psychiatric disorders, such as depression, substance abuse, personality disorders, and anxiety disorders, including obsessive–compulsive disorder (Thompson et al., 2007). While chemical imbalances may cause eating disorders, they can result from them as well (Smolak, 2009).

Clinical Notes

Psychiatric classification and diagnosis are still problematic. Current psychiatry has not yet achieved a real understanding of mental illnesses, and health professionals still have variable views about what constitutes a mental illness, what makes it different from a physical illness, and how it should be treated. Current symptom-based DSM and ICD diagnostic criteria of mental disorders are usually criticized because there is a lack of real boundaries that separate them from other disorders, lack of consideration of contextual effect, over-reliance on a statistical number of symptoms to make a diagnosis, lack of clear etiological explanation of categories, and insufficient information on treatment or outcome implications of receiving certain diagnosis. However, this does not mean that mental illnesses do not exist or are unscientific, or that psychiatrists and psychologists should abandon making a diagnosis, but it points to the need to consider these limitations when assessing a presumed patient, and to try to find a way to correct it in the future.

Summary

- Pooled studies revealed that nearly 1 in 5 of respondents meet the criteria for a common mental disorder during the 12 months preceding assessment.
- The judgment that a given behavior is abnormal and requires clinical attention depends on cultural norms. Awareness of the significance of culture may correct mistaken interpretations of psychopathology, but culture may also contribute to vulnerability and suffering.
- The World Health Organization defines mental health as a state of well-being in which every individual realizes his or her own potential, can cope with the normal stresses of life, can work productively and fruitfully, and is able to make a contribution to her or his community.
- Galderisi et al. (2015) defined mental health as a dynamic state of internal equilibrium which enables individuals to use their abilities in harmony with the universal values of society.
- A mental disorder can be defined as a clinically significant disturbance in an individual's cognition, emotion regulation, or behavior that reflects a dysfunction in the psychological, biological, or developmental processes underlying mental functioning.
- Different perspectives that are used in defining abnormality include deviation from cultural norms, deviation from statistical norms, maladaptive behavior and impaired functioning, personal distress, abnormality as unexpected behavior, and abnormality as mental illness.
- Attempts to understand the etiology of psychiatric disorders generally fall under one of the three broad perspectives: the biological perspective, the psychological perspective, and the diathesis-stress model.
- The main categories of the latest edition of the American Psychiatric Association classification (DSM-5) (APA, 2013) include: neurodevelopmental disorders, schizophrenia spectrum and other psychotic disorders, bipolar and related disorders, depressive disorders. anxiety disorders, obsessive-compulsive and related disorders, trauma- and stressor-related disorders, dissociative disorders, somatic symptom and related disorders, feeding and eating disorders, elimination disorders, sleep–wake disorders, sexual dysfunctions, gender dysphoria, disruptive, impulse control, and conduct disorders, substance-related and addictive disorders, neurocognitive disorders, personality disorders, and paraphilic disorders.

Test Your Knowledge

- Define the clinical features of each of the following disorders:
    - intellectual disability
    - autism spectrum disorder
    - ADHD
    - conduct disorder
    - schizophrenia
    - major depressive disorder
    - bipolar disorder
    - generalized anxiety disorder
    - panic disorders
    - phobias
    - obsessive-compulsive disorder.
- Outline the difference between acute and post-traumatic stress disorder.
- Outline the difference between anorexia nervosa and bulimia nervosa.

Critical Thinking Questions

- How can you evaluate the current diagnostic classification of mental disorders?
- How can you evaluate the diathesis-stress model of mental disorders?
- What do you think of the idea that psychology should abandon diagnosis?

twenty-two
Treatment of Psychological Disorders

Learning Goals

- This chapter is intended to provide the reader with an overview of the basic categories of treatment in psychiatry:

  1. Psychotherapy: this section will provide a brief overview of behavior therapy, cognitive-behavior therapy, psychoanalysis and psychodynamic psychotherapy, humanistic therapies, group therapy, and family and marital therapy.
  2. Biological therapies: this section will provide a brief overview of the major categories of biological therapies, including antipsychotic drugs, antidepressant drugs, mood stabilizers, antianxiety drugs, stimulant drugs, and electroconvulsive therapy (ECT).
  3. Combining biological and psychological therapies.

Introduction

Management of mental disorders is a complex issue, two distinct categories of interventions are usually used: psychotherapy and biological therapy. A combination of the two categories is common practice.

Psychotherapy

Psychotherapy refers to psychological interventions that share the goal of alleviating human problems and facilitating effective functioning in society. There are many types of psychotherapy, each has its distinctive underlying perspective, and its own approach to improving mental well-being, e.g., psychodynamic psychotherapy assumes that modification of behavior is dependent on the understanding of unconscious motives and conflicts, while behavioral and cognitive-behavior psychotherapy focus on changing habitual patterns of behavior and thinking. Psychotherapy often can be successfully completed in a few months, but in some cases, long-term treatment is needed. It can take place individually, in a group, or with family members.

Despite differences in psychotherapeutic techniques, they mostly share in common a helping relationship between the patient (the client) and the therapist. Regardless of the type of therapy, the client and the therapist should have mutual respect and regard in order to develop a good therapeutic relationship. The client should believe that the therapist understands and is concerned with his or her problems. The patient is encouraged to discuss intimate concerns, emotions, and experiences freely without fear of being judged by the therapist or having confidences betrayed. The therapist, in turn, offers empathy and understanding, provokes trust, and tries to help the patient develop more effective ways of handling problems. In fact, the most successful therapists, regardless of method, are those who form a helpful supportive relationship with their clients. Common techniques of psychotherapy include the following:

Behavior Therapy

Behavior therapy refers to a number of therapeutic methods that are based on the principles of learning, and assume that maladaptive behaviors are learned ways of coping with stress and can be replaced by more appropriate adaptive responses through learning techniques. The achievement of insight is not a goal, and it is not necessary to ensure behavioral change in behavior therapy, e.g., a person with social phobia may overcome fears without having insight about their origin. Behavior therapies attempt to modify behaviors that are maladaptive in specific situations. The behaviors to be changed are specified, first, then the therapist and client prepare a specific treatment program, for the particular problem. Behavior therapy is usually a short duration therapy, lasting about 6–8 weeks. Behavior therapists are easy to train and training is usually cost-effective. Some of the important behavioral techniques will be described briefly.

Systematic Desensitization

Systematic desensitization is a method in which the client undergoes a series of anxiety-provoking stimuli while remaining calm. It is based on the principle of reciprocal inhibition, described by Wolpe. The principle states that if a response incompatible with anxiety is produced at the same time as an anxiety-provoking stimulus, the learned association between anxiety and the feared object weakens until the fear disappears, that is, anxiety is reduced by reciprocal inhibition (Wolpe, 1958, 1964, 1982). The client is first trained to use relaxation techniques to reduce fearful responses, e.g., Jacobson's progressive muscular relaxation in which the client first tenses and then relaxes major muscle groups of the body in a predetermined order, usually beginning at the top of the body and progressing downwards. The person is taught to observe the feeling of the muscles when they are relaxed and to discriminate among various degrees of tension. Sometimes drugs and hypnosis are used to help people who cannot relax. The next step is to create a hierarchy of the anxiety-producing situations, where the patient is asked to list all the conditions which provoke anxiety, then is asked to list them in a descending order of anxiety provocation.

The final step is the systematic desensitization proper, this can be done either in imagery or in reality (in vivo exposure). At first, the lowest item in the hierarchy is confronted (in reality or in imagery). The patient is advised to signal whenever anxiety occurs, and is asked to relax at that time. After a few trials, the patient is able to control anxiety when the maximum anxiety-provoking stimulus can be faced in the absence of anxiety. In vivo exposure is more effective than simply imagining anxiety-producing situations, but it should come later for some clients who have severe intolerable symptoms.

Flooding

The person is directly exposed to the phobic stimulus, while escape is made impossible. Decrease in anxiety and diminution of the phobic behavior result from prolonged contact with the phobic stimulus, under the therapist's guidance and encouragement, and the therapist's modeling behavior. This is used in the treatment of phobias and anxiety disorders, including post-traumatic stress disorder.

Aversion Therapy

Aversion therapy was used for the treatment of conditions which are undesirable but felt pleasant by the patient, e.g., alcohol dependence, and transvestism. The underlying principle is pairing of the pleasant stimulus with an unpleasant response, so that even in the absence of the unpleasant response, the pleasant stimulus becomes unpleasant by association. The unpleasant aversion can be produced by low voltage electric stimulus, or drugs (such as disulfiram in the case of alcohol dependence). Typically, 20–40 sessions are needed, with each session lasting about 1 hour. After completion of treatment, booster sessions may be given. Currently, the use of aversion therapy has declined sharply as it is felt that it may violate the human rights of the patient.

Selective Reinforcement

Selective reinforcement is a technique designed to strengthen or increase specific desired behaviors, e.g., to complete assignments or to participate in class activities. Reinforcement of desirable responses can be accompanied by extinction of undesirable ones. It is used successfully in dealing with a broad range of childhood problems, including bed-wetting, aggression, tantrums, disruptive classroom behavior, poor school performance, and social withdrawal. Similar procedures have been used in treating autism, e.g., reinforcing socially appropriate behaviors such as looking other people in the eyes, or reducing inappropriate behavior, such as temper tantrums. When the reinforcement is withdrawn for some time in the case of undesired response, it is called time-out. Time-out is often used with therapy children with behavioral problems.

Satiation

Satiation refers to repeated presentation of the undesired stimulus for the purpose of reducing the attractiveness and influence of that stimulus. The undesired act is allowed to be performed in excess until the client tires of it. A similar technique is negative practice procedure: the person repeatedly practices the wrongly displayed behavior in order to experience it on purpose, and thus become able to reduce or extinguish it, e.g., a student who was caught spitting on the hallway floor would be made to spit into a cup several times. Both satiation and negative practice carry the risk of establishing a behavior more.

Modeling

Modeling is the process by which people with maladaptive responses learn better strategies by observing and imitating others who display adaptive behavior, e.g., observing a therapist handling a spider can reduce the fears of a person with a spider phobia, making it possible to eventually handle the spider. Observing the behavior of a model, either live or videotaped, is effective in overcoming fears and anxieties because it provides an opportunity to observe someone who goes through the anxiety-provoking situation without getting hurt. Watching videotapes of models enjoying a visit to the dentist or going through various hospital procedures has proved successful in helping both children and adults overcome their fears of such experiences (Thorpe & Olson, 1997).

Cognitive-Behavior Therapy

Cognitive-behavior therapy (CBT) has been proven effective in treating depression, anxiety disorders, eating disorders, drug and alcohol dependence, and sexual dysfunctions. In addition, CBT can help people with psychotic symptoms learn how to manage their symptoms.

The goal of CBT is to replace maladaptive thinking and behavior with more realistic and adaptive ones, by challenging ways of thinking and reacting, thus decreasing self-defeating emotions and behavior and breaking what can otherwise become a negative cycle (Hayes, Villatte, Levin, & Hildebrandt, 2011). This can provide relief from emotional problems and enhance happiness by modifying dysfunctional emotions, behaviors, and thoughts. A typical cognitive therapy schedule consists of about 15 sessions over a three-month period. The cognitive-behavior therapy involves the following steps:

1. *Identification of automatic thoughts* (ATs) which are dysfunctional or negative views of the self, world, or the future based upon already existing beliefs about oneself, the world, or the future. Recording our thoughts in a thought record/diary is a useful tool for this. When we encounter challenging events, it is useful to write down our thoughts so we can start to tune into what we are saying to ourselves in our internal self-talk. Automatic thoughts include self-evaluations, evaluations of others, thoughts about coping strategies and behavioral plans, thoughts of avoidance, and other uncategorized thoughts.
2. *Identification of the cognitive distortions in the automatic thoughts*: create a list of troublesome thoughts and examine them for matches with a list of cognitive distortions. This process will allow us to think about our problem or difficulty in more natural and realistic ways.
3. *Rational argument of cognitive distortions*: once a cognitive distortion has been identified, Socratic questioning or a decatastrophizing technique can be used as a way to uncover and challenge underlying assumptions.

4. *Replace faulty beliefs with realistic alternatives*: replacements for automatic thoughts become evident in the course of refuting the irrational beliefs on which they are based.
5. *Practice*: the above steps 1–4 are useless if not practiced. These include activity scheduling (e.g., recording mood at regular intervals), homework assignments, graded task assignment, behavioral rehearsal, role playing, and diversion and activity scheduling (e.g., recording mood at regular intervals), and raising awareness techniques such as:
   a. The elastic band technique: this is a way to raise awareness through gentle physical sensation like wearing a rubber band around wrist, and snapping it gently whenever you have a negative thought.
   b. Watch your words: verification of the meaning of words, e.g., are you really a useless idiot, or did you just make a mistake?
   c. Look for positives: for every negative thought, there is usually a positive counter-thought, and vice versa.

Psychoanalysis and Psychodynamic Psychotherapy

Psychoanalytic therapy probes into a patient's unconscious through techniques, such as free association and dream analysis. The key assumption of psychodynamic therapies is that people's current problems cannot be resolved successfully without a thorough understanding of their unconscious basis in early relationships with parents and siblings. The goal of the psychoanalyst is to explore the patient's unconscious thoughts to help in dealing with any issues or trauma buried in the unconscious mind to bring conflicts (repressed emotions and motives) into awareness so that they can be dealt with in a more rational and realistic way. The psychodynamic therapies include classic Freudian psychoanalysis and a number of psychodynamic therapies based on modifications of the neo-Freudian theorists (Vakoch & Strupp, 2000).

In Freudian psychoanalysis, patients tell the analyst both what they feel important and what they consider to be unimportant. The method of psychoanalysis involves several significant steps. First, the analyst gathers material with which to work from patients' free associations, the results of transference, dream interpretation and the patients' slips. Second, the analyst begins to form hypotheses about what happened to the patients in the past and what is currently

PHOTO 22.1.   Freud's Couch.

happening to them in their daily life. It is important that the analyst communicates their conclusions only after the patients have reached the same conclusions of their own accord. Resistance occurs when the analyst reveals their conclusions too early to patients due to repression. Overcoming this resistance requires additional time and effort by both the analyst and the patients. Once patients accept the conclusions, they are cured.

In free association, the patient is allowed to communicate unguided, and is encouraged to talk freely about thoughts and feelings and to say whatever comes to mind. The therapist remains passive with a non-directive approach; however, the therapist constantly challenges the existing defenses and points out and interprets resistance and transference (i.e., the client expresses attitudes toward the analyst that are actually felt toward other people who are, or were, important in his or her life). No direct advice is ever given to the patient. The core of the therapy is interpretation. Freud believed that blocking, or resistance results from the individual's unconscious control over sensitive areas and that these are precisely the areas that need to be explored.

In dream analysis, the patient talks about the content of dreams and then free associates to that content. Freud believed that dreams are the royal road to the unconscious, they represent an unconscious wish or fear in disguised form. He distinguished between dreams' manifest content (the obvious, conscious content) and their latent content (the hidden, unconscious content). By talking about the manifest content of a dream and providing free association to that content, the analyst and client attempt to discover the dream's unconscious meaning.

During analysis, transference has either positive and negative effects, when patients view their analysts as parents, role models, or other figures from their past. Transference may cause patients to become concerned with pleasing their analysts and as a result, patients lose their rational aim of getting well.

Freudian psychoanalysis typically needs 50-minute sessions, three to five times per week for at least a year and often for several years. No detailed history taking, mental status examination, or formal psychiatric diagnosis is attempted. During the therapy, the patient typically lies on the couch, with the therapist sitting just out of vision. No other therapy is usually used as adjunct.

Psychoanalytically-oriented and psychodynamic psychotherapy remains centered on the role of people's internal drives and forces, but the duration of therapy is much briefer and less intensive (usually once or twice per week), and advice is given to the patient occasionally. Supporters of this type of therapy state that some of the insights and opportunity for change and growth available from long-term psychoanalysis can be achieved in a shorter time by introducing directive elements and a focus on particular topics. The patient and the therapist may sit opposite each other, face-to-face, or a couch is used. Examples of psychodynamic psychotherapies include interpersonal therapy (IPT), which is a structured, supportive approach that focuses on current rather than past problems. Treatment goals evolve from four main interpersonal problem areas: (1) grief; (2) interpersonal disputes; (3) role transitions; and (4) interpersonal deficits. IPT is usually a time-limited treatment, typically lasting 12–16 weeks, that encourages the patient to regain control of mood and functioning.

Humanistic Therapies

Humanistic therapies are based on the humanistic approach to personality that emphasizes the individual's natural tendency toward growth and self-actualization. Psychological disorders are assumed to arise when circumstances or other people (parents, teachers, and spouses) prevent the people from achieving their potential. When this occurs, people begin to deny their true desires, and their potential for growth is reduced. Humanistic therapies seek to help people to get in touch with their real identities and make deliberate choices regarding their lives and behavior rather than being controlled by external events. The humanistic therapist attempts to increase the client's awareness of underlying emotions and motives. But the emphasis is on what the individual is experiencing in the here and now, rather than in the past. Unlike psycho-analysts, the humanistic therapist does not interpret the client's behavior, or try to modify it as behavior therapists do, because this can impose the therapist's views on the patient. The goal of the humanistic therapist is to facilitate exploration of the individual's own thoughts and feelings and to assist the individual in arriving at his or her own solutions. The most influential human-istic therapies include client-centered therapy, developed in the 1940s by Carl Rogers, and Gestalt therapy, developed by Frederick and Laura Perls.

Client-centered therapy is based on the assumption that each individual is the best expert of himself or herself, and that people are capable of developing solutions to their own prob-lems. Central to this thinking is the idea that the world is judgmental, therefore, many people tend to suppress their beliefs, values, or opinions because these are not supported, are socially unacceptable, or negatively judged. Client-centered therapy provides a supportive environ-ment in which clients can re-establish their true identity. Rogers preferred the term facilitator to therapist, and he called the people he worked with "clients" rather than "patients," because he did not view emotional difficulties as indications of an illness to be cured. To re-establish a client's true identity, the therapist relies on the techniques of unconditional positive regard and empathy. Empathy refers to the ability to understand the feelings that a client is trying to express and the ability to communicate this understanding to the client. These two techniques are central to client-centered therapy because they build trust between the client and therapist by creating a nonjudgmental and supportive environment for the client.

The therapist attempts to see the problems as the client sees them, and adopts the client's view. By warmth, Rogers meant acceptance of individuals' way, including the conviction that they have the capacity to deal constructively with their problems. By listening to and echoing back the clients' own concerns, the therapist helps the client to see themselves as others may see them. This can help them to perceive inconsistencies or biases in their perceptions of the world and other people. Client-centered therapy appears to be successful only with individuals who are fairly verbal and are motivated to discuss their problems. It is not suitable for people who do not voluntarily seek help or are seriously disturbed and unable to discuss their feelings, where more directive methods are usually necessary. Also, it is not used for individuals who feel inse-cure and ineffective in their interpersonal relationships, they usually need more structured help in modifying their behavior.

Gestalt Therapy

Gestalt psychologists emphasize the idea that people actively organize their perceptions of the world. As a result, they believe that people create their own versions of reality and that their natural psychological growth continues only as long as they accurately perceive, remain aware of, and act on their true feelings. Growth stops and symptoms appear, when people are not aware of all aspects of themselves (Perls, 1969; Perls, Hefferline, & Goodman, 1951).

Gestalt therapy focuses on the skills and techniques that permit an individual to be more aware of their feelings. It emphasizes the here and now; it is much more important to under-stand what patients are feeling and how they are feeling rather than to identify what is causing their feelings. Supporters of Gestalt therapy argued that earlier theories spent an unnecessary amount of time making assumptions about what causes behavior. Role playing plays a large role in Gestalt therapy and allows for a true expression of feelings that may not have been shared in other circumstances. Also, non-verbal cues are seen as indicator of how the client may actually be feeling, despite the feelings expressed.

Gestalt therapy seeks to create conditions in which clients can become more self-aware, and self-accepting, and thus ready to grow again. Gestalt therapists usually work in group settings, and use more direct and dramatic methods than client-centered therapy do. Gestalt therapists lead clients to become aware of feelings and impulses that they have denied and to discard feelings, ideas, and values that are not really their own, e.g., the therapist or other group members might point out inconsistencies between what clients say and how they behave. Gestalt therapists pay particular attention to clients' gestures and other kinds of body language that appear to conflict with what the clients are saying (Kepner, 2001). They may also ask clients to engage in imaginary dialogues, or conversations, with parts of their own personalities, with other people, and even with objects (Elliott, Watson, & Goldman, 2004a, 2004b). Like a shy person who can be socially outgoing only while masked at a costume party, clients often find that these dialogues help them get in touch with and express their feelings (Woldt & Toman, 2005). Over the years, client-centered and other forms of humanistic therapy have declined in popularity (Norcross et al., 2002).

Group Therapy

Group therapy or group psychotherapy is a less time-consuming procedure, in which usually 6–12 people can be treated at one time. This was first used by Joseph Pratt (an internist) in 1905, for patients suffering from tuberculosis. Group therapy offers patients and their relatives an opportunity to realize that many others have and share problems which are very similar to their own problems, and that they are not alone in their suffering. Group therapy has been used in a variety of settings: in hospital wards and outpatient psychiatric clinics, with parents of disturbed children, and with teenagers in correctional institutions. Typically, sessions are held once or twice a week, with each session lasting 1–2 hours (often 1½ hours). The patients usually sit in a circle, with equal opportunities for interaction. Psychoanalytic, humanistic, and cognitive-behaviorist therapists have modified their techniques so that they can be used with groups. The therapist usually remains in the background, allowing group members to exchange experiences, comment on one another's behavior, and discuss their own problems as well as those of the other members. However, in some groups, the therapist is quite active, e.g., in a group desensitization session, people who share the same phobias (such as fear of flying or anxiety about tests) may be led through a systematic desensitization hierarchy. In a session for training social skills, a group of shy and unassertive individuals may be coached in a series of role-playing scenes.

Most groups are led by a trained therapist. However, the number and variety of self-help groups that are conducted without a professional therapist are increasing. Self-help groups are voluntary organizations of people who meet regularly to exchange information and support one another's efforts to overcome a common problem, e.g., Alcoholics Anonymous. Other groups help people cope with specific stressful situations, such as bereavement, divorce, and single parenthood.

Group therapy offers several features not found in individual treatment. (1) Group therapy allows the therapist to see clients interacting with one another, which can be helpful in identifying problems in clients' interpersonal styles. (2) Clients discover that they are not alone, as they listen to others and realize that many people have similar difficulties. This realization tends to raise each client's expectations for improvement, a factor important in all forms of treatment. (3) Group members can boost one another's self-confidence and self-acceptance as they come to trust and value one another. (4) Clients learn from one another by sharing ideas for solving problems and giving one another honest feedback about how each member deals with others. (5) Mutual modeling during the group experience makes clients more willing to share their feelings and more sensitive to other people's needs and messages. (6) Group therapy allows clients to try out new skills, such as assertiveness, in a safe and supportive environment.

Family and Marital Therapy

In family therapy and in marital therapy, the focus of intervention is not on the individual but the family as a unit or the marital unit. Whenever there are relational problems within a family or marital unit (either primarily or secondary to a psychiatric disorder), family and/or marital therapy is indicated. There are several varieties of family and marital therapies, such as those based on psychodynamic, humanistic, or cognitive-behavioral approaches, e.g., in a behavioral marital therapy, components of therapy may include problem-solving, communication skills training, writing a behavioral marital contract, and homework assignments.

There are many approaches to marital therapy (also called couples therapy), but most focus is on helping the partners to communicate their feelings, develop greater understanding and sensitivity to each other's needs, and work on more effective ways of handling their conflicts. Some couples enter marriage with very different and often unrealistic expectations about the roles of husband and wife. The therapist can help them clarify their expectations and work out a mutually agreeable compromise. Sometimes the couple negotiates behavioral contracts, agreeing on the behavior changes each person is willing to make in order to create a more satisfying relationship, and specifying rewards and penalties for making, or not making, the desired changes.

In family therapy, the family itself is the client, and treatment involves as many members as possible. It involves treatment of two or more individuals from the same family system, one of whom (often a troubled child or adolescent) is the initially identified client. The term family system highlights the idea that the problems displayed by one family member usually reflect problems in the functioning of the entire family (Cox & Paley, 2003; Nichols, 2007; Williams, 2005). In fact, the goal of family therapy is not just to manage the identified client's problems but also to create greater harmony and balance within the family by helping each member understand the family's interaction patterns (Blow & Timm, 2002). The basic premise of family therapy is that the problem shown by the patient is a sign that the family system is not operating properly. The difficulty may lie in poor communication among family members or in an alliance between some family members that excludes others, e.g., a mother whose relationship with her husband is unsatisfactory may focus all her attention on her son. As a result, the husband and daughter feel neglected, and the son develops problems in school, due to upset by his mother's excessive attention and the resentment directed toward him by his father and sister. Although the boy's school difficulties may be the reason for seeking treatment, it is clear that they are only a symptom of a more basic family problem.

In family therapy, the family meets regularly with one or two therapists (usually a male and a female). The therapist observes the interactions among family members and tries to help each member become aware of the way he or she relates to the others and how his or her actions may be contributing to the family's problems. Sometimes videotape recordings are played back to make the family members aware of how they interact. At other times, the therapist may visit the family at home to observe conflicts and verbal exchanges as they occur in their natural setting. It often becomes apparent that problem behaviors are being reinforced by the responses of family members. For example, a child's temper tantrums or a teenager's eating problems may be inadvertently reinforced by the attention they elicit from the parents. The therapist can teach the parents to monitor their own and their children's behavior, determine how their reactions may be reinforcing the problem behavior, and then alter the reinforcement contingencies.

Effectiveness of Psychotherapy

Though there are difficulties in evaluating the effectiveness of psychotherapy, several reviews of the outcomes of psychotherapy research over the last five decades have concluded that psychotherapy has positive effects and is better than no treatment at all or various placebos (Lambert, Shapiro, & Bergin, 1986; Westen, Novotny, & Thompson-Brenner, 2004). Several controlled studies show that different types of psychotherapy were compared with drug therapy or with controls who received no therapy for a specific disorder. These studies suggest that certain forms of psychotherapy can be highly effective in the treatment of depression, anxiety disorders, eating disorders, substance abuse disorders, and several childhood disorders (Kazdin & Weisz, 2003; Leiblum & Rosen, 2000). Psychotherapy can also help reduce symptoms of autism and schizophrenia and lower the risk of relapse in schizophrenia (Lovaas & Smith, 2003; Spaulding, Johnson, & Coursey, 2001).

Comparing the results of different psychotherapies reveals that there is little difference in effectiveness between different therapies (Lambert & Bergin, 1994; Wampold et al., 1997). Equal efficacy may be explained by the common factors shared by different psychotherapies. It may be these common factors, rather than the specific therapeutic techniques employed, that promote positive change. Another explanation is that certain therapies may be effective for certain problems but relatively ineffective for others. When specific therapies are used to treat a wide range of problems, averaging results over cases may conceal the special strengths of a particular therapy.

Clinical Notes

- Over the last few decades, an extensive body of knowledge has been created on many psychotherapies for all varieties of mental disorders, as well as for physical health problems, across all age groups. This research has shown that psychotherapies are effective in treating many mental disorders, with the consequence that these therapies are included in guidelines as first-line treatments (Weissman & Cuijpers, 2017).
- Currently, there is a variety of available evidence-based psychotherapies. However, some patients may do better on one rather than another form of psychotherapy. It is therefore good to have different choices even if, overall, they may appear the same (Weissman & Cuijpers, 2017).

Summary

- Management of mental disorders is a complex issue, two distinctive categories of interventions are usually used: psychotherapy and biological therapy.
- Psychotherapy refers to psychological interventions that share the goal of alleviating human problems and facilitating effective functioning in society.
- There are many types of psychotherapy; each has its distinctive underlying perspective, and its own approach to improving mental well-being.
- Regardless of the type of therapy, psychotherapeutic techniques have in common a helping relationship between the patient (client) and the therapist; the client and the

therapist should have mutual respect and regard to develop a good therapeutic relationship, while the client should believe that the therapist understands and is concerned with his or her problems.

■ Behavior therapy refers to a number of therapeutic methods that are based on the principles of learning, and assume that maladaptive behaviors are learned ways of coping with stress and can be replaced by more appropriate adaptive responses through learning techniques. These include systematic desensitization, flooding, aversion therapy, selective reinforcement, satiation, and modeling.

■ CBT tries to replace maladaptive strategies with more realistic and adaptive ones, by challenging ways of thinking and reacting, thus decreasing self-defeating emotions and behavior and breaking what can otherwise become a negative cycle.

■ Psychoanalytic therapy try to explore the patient's unconscious thoughts to help in dealing with any issues or trauma buried in the unconscious mind to bring conflicts into awareness, so that they can be dealt with in a more rational and realistic way.

■ Humanistic therapies seek to help people to get in touch with their real identities and make deliberate choices regarding their lives and behavior rather than being controlled by external events. The humanistic therapist attempts to increase the client's awareness of what the individual is experiencing in the here and now, rather than in the past.

■ Group therapy is any type of psychotherapy in which a group of people (usually 6–12) can be treated at one time.

■ In family therapy and in marital therapy, the focus of intervention is not on the individual but the family as a unit or the marital unit.

Test Your Knowledge

■ Describe the different types of behavior therapy.
■ Outline CBT.
■ What is meant by psychoanalytic therapy?
■ What is the goal of humanistic therapies?
■ What is the difference between family therapy and marital therapy?

Critical Thinking Questions

■ How can different types of psychotherapy be used to effectively manage different types of psychopathology?
■ Evaluate the current place of psychoanalytic psychotherapy.
■ Evaluate the current place of humanistic therapies.
■ What are the possible disadvantages of different types of psychotherapy?

Biological Therapies

Biological therapy assumes that mental health problems are similar to physical illnesses, both are caused by biochemical or physiological dysfunctions of the brain. Biological therapies essentially include the use of drugs and electroconvulsive therapy. The discovery in the early 1950s of antipsychotic drugs that relieved some of the symptoms of schizophrenia was a major breakthrough in psychopharmacology. Many individuals, who previously would have required hospitalization became able to function within the community with the help of these drugs. On the other hand, antipsychotic drugs reduced the necessity to physically restrain intensely agitated patients. A few years later, the discovery of antidepressant drugs had a similar beneficial effect on management of severe depression. However, all therapeutic drugs can produce some undesirable side effects, and caution is usually needed when prescribing psychoactive drugs to people with medical problems, as well as pregnant or nursing women.

Antipsychotic Drugs

Chlorpromazine was the first antipsychotic drug, it was administered to psychiatric patients in 1952. Shortly thereafter, two other prototypes of antipsychotics were developed: reserpine (introduced in 1954) and haloperidol (introduced in 1958). Investigations of these three prototype antipsychotics contributed to the formulation of the dopamine hypothesis of schizophrenia and the production of numerous classes of conventional antipsychotics. The various biochemical classes of these drugs were marked by their ability to block D_2 receptors. This group of antipsychotics is now called first-generation, conventional, or typical antipsychotics. Typical antipsychotics were marked by their extrapyramidal side effects, their potential to produce tardive dyskinesia, and increased serum prolactin: all result from D_2 blockage. The conventional antipsychotic medications are classified according to their chemical structure into the phenothiazines, butyrophenones, thioxanthenes, dihydroindolones, dibenzepines, and diphenylbutylpiperidines. They are considered to be equally effective in the treatment of psychotic symptoms of schizophrenia, but vary in their individual properties, side effects, and potency (Miyamoto, Stroup, Duncan, Aoba, & Lieberman, 2003).

Later on, another class of antipsychotics, the prototypical agent of which was clozapine, was developed with less potential for extrapyramidal side effects and tardive dyskinesia. This class is called the second generation antipsychotics or atypical antipsychotics. It produces less D_2 receptors blockage and has serotonin ($5HT_2A$) antagonistic activity. An increased ratio of $5\text{-}HT_2A$ to D_2 receptor antagonism has been proposed as responsible for the efficacy and tolerability of atypical antipsychotics. This group includes risperidone and olanzapine, quetiapine, ziprasidone, amisulpride, zotepine, and sertindole. Atypical antipsychotics are marked by its metabolic side effects (e.g., weight gain, dysglycemia, dyslipidemia). Aripiprazole is an atypical antipsychotic that exceptionally acts as partial DA agonist.

Antipsychotic drugs shorten the length of hospitalization, and are effective in relapse prevention. Studies of people with schizophrenia living in the community find that 78 percent of those who discontinue using the drugs relapse within one year, and 98 percent within two years, compared to about a third of people who continue on their medications (Gitlin et al., 2001; Sampath, Shah, Krska, & Soni, 1992). Unfortunately, about 25 percent of people with schizophrenia do not respond to the antipsychotic drugs (Spaulding et al., 2001).

Antidepressant Drugs

Antidepressants are those drugs which are used for the treatment of depressive disorders or to prevent its recurrence. In 1951, the antituberculous drug isoniazid (INH) was found to have mood-elevating properties in some patients suffering from tuberculosis. A derivative of INH (iaproniazid), which was a MAO inhibitor, was later (1958) introduced for the treatment of depression. The first tricyclic antidepressant (TCA) imipramine was used in 1958 by Thomas Kuhn. Since that time, many antidepressants have gradually been introduced. The exact mechanism of the antidepressants' action is not clearly known. However, it appears from clinical studies that the predominant action of antidepressants is to increase the catecholamine levels in the brain (monoamine hypothesis), either through blocking the reuptake of norepinephrine (NE), serotonin (5HT) and/or dopamine (DA) at the nerve terminals, thus increasing NE, 5HT and/or DA levels at the receptor site, or through down-regulation of the β-adrenergic receptors. Alternatively, the monoamine oxidase inhibitors (MAOIs) act on monoamine oxidase (MAO), which is responsible for the degradation of catecholamines following their reuptake; the final effect is a functional increase in the NE and/or 5HT levels at the receptor site.

The clinical effect of antidepressants may become evident after two or three weeks. Therefore, it is of no benefit to prescribe antidepressants on as-needed basis. They must be administered regularly in appropriate doses to achieve the desired effect. Also, it is essential to continue the antidepressant for a period of a further six months after reaching remission, in the first episode of depressive disorder (and for longer duration in subsequent episodes) to prevent the recurrence of symptoms. Many classes of antidepressants are currently available, these include:

- monoamine oxidase inhibitors (MAOIs)
- tricyclic and tetracyclic antidepressants (TCAs)
- selective serotonin reuptake inhibitors (SSRIs)
- serotonin and norepinephrine reuptake inhibitors (SNRIs)
- dopamine reuptake blocker
- $5\text{-HT}_1\text{A}$ receptor antagonist
- 5-HT_2 receptor antagonists
- 5-HT_3 receptor antagonist
- noradrenergic antagonist

Monoamine Oxidase Inhibitors (MAOIs)

Monoamine oxidase inhibitors (MAOIs) inhibit the activity of the monoamine oxidase enzyme which degrades norepinephrine, serotonin, and dopamine; this inhibition is usually irreversible (e.g., phenelzine) or reversible (e.g., moclobemide). MAOIs is notorious for its tyramine response: when patients taking MAOIs eat tyramine-rich foods such as mature cheese, broad-bean pods, dried, aged, smoked, fermented fish or poultry, unpasteurized beers, and soya products, this can result in a rapid and dangerous rise in blood pressure. MAOIs also interact with opioids, and potentiate the effects of central nervous system depressants, such as the benzodiazepines, barbiturates, and alcohol. Consequently, patients who are prescribed MAOIs need to be warned of these effects and issued with a card listing of the food and drugs to be avoided.

Tricyclic and Tetracyclic Antidepressants (TCAs)

A few years ago, tricyclic antidepressants (TCAs) were the first-line treatment for moderate to severe depression. Now, they are generally reserved for cases in which treatment with more recently introduced drugs have failed.

As a class, the TCAs have a sufficiently long half-life so that a once-daily dose can be given. In practice, for the majority of patients, the dosage of TCAs is titrated against symptoms, balancing improvement against emerging side effects. The commonest problems associated with the TCAs result from antimuscarinic, anticholinergic properties, such as a dry mouth, blurring of vision, constipation or hesitancy in micturition. It is useful to warn the patient in advance about such symptoms. Tolerance to the symptoms usually develops over time. However, it is necessary to avoid TCAs altogether in patients with glaucoma, in whom an acute attack can be precipitated; and in men with prostatic enlargement, who may develop urine retention.

Cardiovascular side effects are potentially dangerous. Postural hypotension is common, particularly in older patients, and can be managed by lowering the dosage. Cardiac arrhythmia and conduction defects can occur, and prolongation of the QTc interval occurs with all the TCAs. They are therefore contraindicated in patients who have had a recent myocardial infarction or a history of heart block. They are also potentially fatal in overdose even in young subjects and those who have no previous history of heart disease. Other side effects include weight gain, increased sweating and sexual difficulties (typically delayed ejaculation in men).

Selective Serotonin Reuptake Inhibitors (SSRIs)

The selective serotonin reuptake inhibitors (SSRIs) increase serotonin levels by blocking its reuptake. These involve fluoxetine, paroxetine, sertraline, fluvoxamine, citalopram, and escitalopram. Common side effects of SSRIs include nausea, trouble sleeping, nervousness, tremors, and sexual problems. Co-prescription of SSRIs with other serotonergic drugs and especially MAOIs can lead to serotonin syndrome. This is characterized by a classic triad of mental status changes, neuromuscular abnormalities, and autonomic hyperactivity. These include anxiety, agitation, confusion, hyperreflexia, clonus, tremors, myoclonus, rigidity, increased heart rate, flushing, hyperthermia, and excessive sweating. Death can occur in severe cases of serotonin syndrome.

Serotonin-Norepinephrine Reuptake Inhibitors

Serotonin-norepinephrine reuptake inhibitors (SNRIs) increase the availability of both serotonin and norepinephrine (such as venlafaxine, desvenlafaxine, and duloxetine). In addition to relieving depression, these drugs have proved helpful in treating anxiety disorders, e.g., panic disorder, and treatment of obsessive compulsive disorder (Humble, 2000; Sansone & Sansone, 2011). They can cause inhibited orgasm, nausea and diarrhea, dizziness, and nervousness.

Dopamine Reuptake Blocker: Bupropion

Bupropion is a mild dopamine and norepinephrine reuptake blocker. It is used for treatment of depression and seasonal affective disorder. It is also used in smoking cessation.

5-HT$_2$ Receptor Antagonists

Two 5-HT$_2$ receptor antagonists, nefazodone and trazodone, are used to treat depression. Trazodone is a serotonin 5-HT$_2$ antagonist and also has some serotonin reuptake inhibiting properties. It has a sedative effect and therefore may be a useful choice in patients with mixed depressive and anxiety symptoms or in those who suffer from insomnia. Conversely, unwanted effects may include over-sedation and dizziness.

Noradrenergic Antagonist

Mirtazapine is an alpha-2 antagonist. By blocking presynaptic alpha-2 adrenergic receptors, it causes an increase in both serotonin and noradrenaline neurotransmission. Mirtazapine also blocks serotonin 5-HT$_2$A, 5-HT$_2$C and 5-HT$_3$ receptors as well as histamine H$_1$ receptors. It has good anxiety-relieving properties and has some sedative properties, so it is a particularly useful drug given as a once-daily dose at night for patients for whom insomnia is a prominent symptom. However, over-sedation can be a problem, and some patients report dizziness. It also stimulates appetite and promotes weight gain, which again is useful in depressed patients for whom loss of appetite is prominent but presents a relative contraindication in patients who are already overweight. Unlike many antidepressants, mirtazapine does not appear to interfere with sexual function. Other unwanted effects can include dry mouth, constipation, and hypotension, and uncommonly mirtazapine can lower the white blood cell count and cause flu-like symptoms.

Selective Noradrenergic Reuptake Inhibitor

Reboxetine is a selective noradrenergic reuptake inhibitor (NARI). Although weight gain and sedation are unusual with reboxetine, insomnia, anxiety, agitation, sexual dysfunction, and side effects similar to tricyclics, such as urinary retention, dry mouth, hypotension, and constipation can occur. Also like the tricyclics, reboxetine is contra-indicated in those with closed-angle glaucoma. Because its mode of action is complementary to SSRIs, it is possible to use reboxetine in combination with one of these drugs in chronic depression or where there is partial response to a serotonergic agent.

Mood Stabilizers

Mood stabilizers are those drugs that are effective in the treatment and prophylaxis of mania and bipolar depression. The most commonly used mood stabilizers include lithium, valproate, carbamazepine, and lamotrigine. Recently, several atypical antipsychotics, such as olanzapine, quetiapine, and aripiprazole have been added to the list of drugs used in maintenance treatment of bipolar disorder.

Lithium

Lithium is the mainstay of bipolar disorder pharmacotherapy for acute mood episodes, switch prevention, prophylactic treatment, and suicide prevention (Machado-Vieira, Manji, & Zarate, 2009). The mechanism of action of lithium is uncertain. It alters the neuronal function through its substitution for or competition with other ions and has an effect on several neurotransmitter systems (e.g., dopamine, acetylcholine, serotonin), enzymes (e.g., glycogen synthase kinase-3, fructose-1,6 bisphosphatase) and second messenger and signal transduction systems. In particular, lithium has been found to decrease both hosphoinositide and cyclic adenosine monophosphate metabolism, possibly through effects on guanine nucleotide-binding proteins. Lithium might also modulate gene expression through its effects on protein kinase-C.

Lithium is primarily excreted unmetabolized through the kidneys. The therapeutic plasma drug concentration range is 0.5–1.2 meq/L. Many of lithium's several adverse effects are dose-related, these include fine tremor, weight gain, polydipsia/polyuria, gastrointestinal upset, impaired coordination, leukocytosis, alopecia, ankle edema, and acne. Other side effects include ECG changes/arrhythmias, disturbances of thyroid function, exacerbations of psoriasis, hypokalemia, hypercalcemia, hypermagnesemia, hyperparathyroidism, and possible renal impairment.

Toxicity often occurs with blood levels above 1.5 meq/L and begins with tremor, nausea, diarrhea, blurred vision, unsteadiness or clumsiness, difficulty in speaking, followed by severe tremor or twitching limbs, increased deep tendon reflexes, confusion, seizures, dysrhythmias, renal failure, coma, and possibly death at higher levels. Chronic lithium toxicity may also occur and may be manifested by light-headedness, drowsiness, apathy, memory difficulties, tinnitus,

Parkinsonian symptoms, myopathy, neuropathy, hypothyroidism, myocarditis, aplastic anemia, tremors, muscle twitching, hyperreflexia, slurred speech, pseudotumor cerebri, chronic interstitial nephritis, renal failure, nephrogenic diabetes insipidus, skin ulcers, localized edema, and dermatitis (Timmer & Sands, 1999).

Reductions in renal clearance (e.g., secondary to hyponatremia, angiotensin converting enzyme inhibitors, some diuretics, fluid volume depletion) may lead to lithium toxicity, whereas osmotic diuretics, aminophylline, and carbonic anhydrase inhibitors may decrease lithium blood levels. Altered electrolyte levels and some medications (e.g., nonsteroidal anti-inflammatory agents) may also increase the risk of chronic toxicity. Recommended baseline, and in some cases follow-up, laboratory tests for patients receiving lithium include a pregnancy test, renal and thyroid function tests, ECG monitoring, and possibly a complete blood count.

Valproate

The effectiveness of valproate in bipolar disorder was first reported in the 1960s. The proposed mechanism of action of valproate includes increasing GABA activity in the brain, neuroplastic effects, as well as blocking sodium channels. Its antikindling and neuroprotective properties may also be relevant to its mood-stabilizing effects. Therapeutic drug concentrations range from 50–125 µg/mL for acute manic/mixed episodes, although lower levels are sometimes employed during maintenance treatment. Valproate metabolism occurs via the cytochrome P-450 system, glucuronidation and beta-oxidation, and valproate has the ability to inhibit the breakdown of other hepatically metabolized medications. Valproate levels may be affected by concomitant use of drugs that induce or inhibit microsomal enzymes.

Dose-related side effects of treatment with valproate include gastrointestinal upset (e.g., nausea, vomiting, and diarrhea), elevation of liver enzymes, tremors, and sedation. Alopecia, increased appetite, polycystic ovarian syndrome, and weight gain may also occur. Rashes, ataxia, pancreatitis, severe and potentially fatal hepatotoxicity (rare and mostly in pediatric patients) and hematologic abnormalities (e.g., thrombocytopenia, leukopenia, coagulation disturbances) may necessitate its discontinuation. Neural tube defects may be seen in infants exposed to valproate early in gestation; lower dosages, supplemental folic acid, and monotherapy may decrease this risk. Valproate should not be given to individuals with clinically significant hepatic disease. Baseline and follow-up investigations for patients receiving valproate include liver function, blood chemistries, and complete blood count.

Carbamazepine

Carbamazepine (CBZ) has been used in the treatment of bipolar disorder, both in acute mania and maintenance therapy, since the early 1970s. CBZ has proved efficacious in the maintenance treatment of bipolar disorder in naturalistic clinical practice, either as monotherapy or in combination with other medications (Chen & Lin, 2012). The precise mechanism of the action of carbamazepine remains unknown, but it decreases the activity of sodium channels and attenuates the activity of the cyclic adenosine monophosphate. Carbamazepine also has effects on several other neurotransmitters (e.g., adenosine, dopamine, serotonin) and the second messenger systems. Therapeutic blood levels for the treatment of acute manic/mixed episodes are targeted for approximately 4–12 µg/ml.

Carbamazepine is metabolized by the cytochrome P-450 system and induces the metabolism of itself and other agents metabolized by that system, thus, an increase in dosage may be necessary after several months of treatment. The metabolism of carbamazepine may also be affected by liver disease. Additionally, blood levels are affected by other agents that have an effect on the cytochrome P-450 system.

CBZ is well tolerated by most patients. Adverse effects include central nervous system effects (e.g., fatigue, diplopia, dizziness, nausea, tremor, ataxia, blurred vision), rashes, hyponatremia, increased liver enzymes, constipation, diarrhea, gastrointestinal distress, vomiting, anorexia, and hematologic abnormalities (e.g., leukopenia). Rare side effects include agranulocytosis, aplastic anemia, systemic hypersensitivity reactions, renal effects, cardiac conduction disturbance, Stevens-Johnson syndrome, thrombocytopenia, and pancreatitis. Recommended baseline, and in some cases follow-up tests for patients being treated with carbamazepine include hematologic, liver function, renal function, and electrolyte tests.

Lamotrigine

Lamotrigine was approved recently as a mood stabilizer for maintenance treatment of bipolar disorder. Lamotrigine is mainly effective against depression as opposed to mania. The mechanism of action of lamotrigine may be related to its inhibition of sodium channels, its antiglutamatergic effect or neuroprotective effects. Metabolism occurs primarily through glucuronidation in the liver, and thus several pharmacokinetic interactions are possible, although effects on cytochrome P-450 enzymes are generally not seen.

The metabolism and blood levels of lamotrigine may also be affected by hepatic and renal impairment. In addition, lamotrigine can induce its own metabolism. Significantly lower dosages should be used in individuals receiving valproate because of pharmacokinetic interactions. Lamotrigine is well tolerated by most patients. The most common complaints include dizziness, stomach upset, headache, unsteadiness, double vision, and cutaneous rash. A serious rash while taking lamotrigine has been reported in about 3 in 1000 adults and 1 in 100 children. Severe rashes have been reported to occur more often when rapid titration schedules are used and in younger individuals, in addition to when lamotrigine is used concomitantly with valproate.

Antianxiety Drugs

Several drugs are used in the management of anxiety disorders. Antidepressants, especially selective serotonin reuptake inhibitors, are currently the first choice in anxiety management. Other drugs include benzodiazepines and non-benzodiazepine drugs, and non-benzodiazepine agonists.

Benzodiazepines

Benzodiazepines derive their name from their molecular structure. They share a common effect on benzodiazepine receptors, which in turn modulate gamma-aminobutyric acid (GABA) activity. Because benzodiazepines have a rapid anxiolytic sedative effect, they are most commonly used for immediate treatment of insomnia, acute anxiety, and agitation or anxiety associated with any psychiatric disorder. In addition, the benzodiazepines are used as anesthetics, anticonvulsants, and muscle relaxants. Because of the risk of dependence, benzodiazepines are not recommended for long-term use. Flumazenil, a benzodiazepine receptor antagonist, is used to reverse benzodiazepine-induced sedation and in emergency care of benzodiazepine overdosage.

Non-Benzodiazepine Drugs

Buspirone is a non-benzodiazepine, azapirone derivative. It is a 5-HT$_1$A partial agonist and a selective dopamine auto receptor antagonist. It also inhibits the spontaneous firing of 5-HT neurons. It does not seem to act on the benzodiazepine receptors. It has no sedative, anticonvulsant or muscle-relaxant properties. It is administered in a dose of 15–30 mg/day, in a thrice daily schedule due to its short half-life. As it has a slower and more gradual onset of action, it usually takes about two weeks before its anti-anxiety effects are evident. Buspirone is preferable in treatment of generalized anxiety disorders, but it is not useful in treatment of panic disorder. The common side effects include dizziness, headache, light-headedness, and diarrhea.

Non-benzodiazepine agonists

Non-benzodiazepine agonists act on the GABA receptors, but at a site distinct from that of benzodiazepines, e.g., zopiclone, zolpidem, zaleplon. They are essentially used as a hypnotic. They have low abuse potential compared with benzodiazepine.

Stimulant Drugs

Methylphenidate (MPH) is the most commonly used stimulant drug. The action of stimulants in ADHD is attributed to the release of DA and their ability to block its reuptake by the dopamine transporter (DAT) at the presynaptic nerve terminal. Radioligand binding studies have demonstrated the direct action of stimulants, particularly MPH, on striatal DAT. The dopamine action of stimulants also explains the appearance of behavioral stereotypes, seen at high doses. Approximately 70 percent of children with ADHD respond to stimulants compared with 13 percent to placebo. Short-term efficacy is more pronounced for behavioral rather than cognitive and learning abnormalities associated with ADHD. Behavioral rebound may appear at the end of the school day, due to loss of the stimulant effect. Children present with afternoon irritability, talkativeness, non-compliance, excitability, motor hyperactivity and insomnia about 5–15 hours after the last dose. If rebound occurs, many physicians add a small afternoon MPH dose or add a small dose of a tricyclic antidepressant. Stimulants have been abused by adults, but the risk of addiction by children with ADHD is low, so stimulants are classified in most countries as potentially drugs of abuse.

Children taking stimulants usually show appetite suppression when starting treatment. For this reason, it is optimally ingested after breakfast and lunch. Even though the daytime appetite is reduced, hunger rebounds in the evening. These effects on appetite often decrease within the first six weeks of treatment. The growth effects of MPH appear to be minimal. Height and weight should be measured at six-monthly intervals during stimulant treatment and recorded on age-adjusted growth forms to determine the presence of a drug-related reduction in height or weight velocity. If such a decrement is discovered during maintenance therapy with stimulants, a reduction in dosage or change to another class of medication can be carried out.

Electroconvulsive Therapy (ECT)

ECT is a procedure during which an electric current is applied to a patient's brain, typically to the temple on the side of the non-dominant cerebral hemisphere, to produce a seizure similar to an epileptic convulsion. The seizure activity is normally attenuated with the short-acting muscular relaxant succinylcholine, and the patient is given short-acting anesthesia. The minimum current required to produce a brain seizure is administered. The muscle relaxant prevents convulsive muscle spasms. The individual usually awakens within a few minutes and remembers nothing about the treatment. The mechanism of action is unknown but the efficacy of ECT is linked to the production of generalized tonic-clonic seizures, not to the electricity itself. One hypothesis about the mechanism of ECT states that it possibly affects the catecholamine pathways between the diencephalon and the limbic system, also involving the hypothalamus. As ECT increases the threshold for further seizures, it may paradoxically act as an anticonvulsant. ECT also causes the down-regulation of β1 receptors in the cortex and the hippocampus. Written and informed consent is required in most countries. ECT is used essentially in the treatment of:

- Major depression with suicidal risk, stupor, poor intake of food and fluids, melancholia, psychotic features, unsatisfactory response to drug therapy, and where drugs are contra-indicated, or have serious side effects.
- Severe psychoses: ECT is not a treatment of first choice in bipolar disorder or schizophrenia, and is employed only when there is risk of suicide, homicide, or danger of physical assault, where drugs are contra-indicated, or if serious side effects or an unsatisfactory response to drug therapy are presumed, and if the patient has very prominent depressive features (e.g., bipolar depression or schizoaffective disorder).

The total duration and number of treatments given depend on the diagnosis, the presence of side effects, and the response to treatment. Usually 6–10 treatments are sufficient, although up to 15 treatments can be given if needed. The treatments should be spaced, so that no more than three ECTs are given per week. Continuous or maintenance ECT is occasionally maintained at less frequent intervals (Tharyan & Adams, 2005). Side effects of ECT are essentially those related to general anesthesia, and the mortality rate is similar to any operative procedure under anesthesia. Both anterograde and retrograde memory disturbances are common. These are usually mild, and recovery occurs within six months after treatment. Unilateral ECT causes much less memory disturbance than bilateral ECT. A postictal period of confusion may occur especially with bilateral ECT, but it is self-limited and requires no treatment. The only absolute contra-indication of ECT is the presence of raised intracranial tension, thus, an examination of the fundus oculi and brain imaging may be needed in certain cases. Relative contra-indications of ECT include: recent myocardial infarction, severe hypertension, a cerebrovascular accident, severe pulmonary disease, retinal detachment, and pheochromocytoma.

Combining Biological and Psychological Therapies

Combined biological and psychological treatments is common practice today, intervening at one level of a person's bio-psycho-social system is assumed to affect all levels of the system, e.g., intervening at the psychological level may cause changes in the patient's biochemistry and social behaviors. It is usually helpful to provide treatment at both the biological and psychosocial levels in the management of depression and the anxiety disorders. Even in disorders like schizophrenia, whose primary cause is biological, supplementing antipsychotic drugs with psychotherapy designed to help the person cope with the consequences of schizophrenia can be very useful in alleviating the impairment in social skills and the ability to function in a job.

Clinical Notes

- Psychopharmacological intervention plays a major role in the management of patients suffering from mental disorders. However, a broad view considers the various psychosocial variables of a patient, to give the best results.
- The main factors that determine the efficacy of pharmacotherapy include establishing a proper diagnosis, and selecting a proven treatment in an adequate dosage for an adequate period.
- The categories of pharmacotherapy may not reflect its actual usage, e.g., antidepressants may be used in many different disorders other than depression, such as generalized anxiety, phobia, obsessive compulsive disorder, management of pain, and premature ejaculation.
- The choice of a drug for a symptom or a disorder depends on its proven efficacy, adverse effects, interactions with other drugs, medical condition, cost, previous experience of the patient, and the agreement of the patient.
- Guidelines for prescribing psychotropic drugs change frequently, so it is important for clinicians to update their knowledge periodically.

Summary

- Biological therapies include essentially the use of drugs and electroconvulsive therapy to treat mental health problems.
- The first-generation antipsychotics are marked by their ability to block D_2 receptors, and hence their extrapyramidal side effects, with the potential to produce tardive dyskinesia, and increased serum prolactin: all the result of D_2 blockage.
- Second-generation antipsychotics produce less blockage of D_2 receptors and have serotonin ($5HT_2A$) antagonistic activity. An increased ratio of $5\text{-}HT_2A$ to D_2 receptor antagonism has been proposed as responsible for the efficacy and tolerability of atypical antipsychotics.
- Antidepressants are those drugs which are used for the treatment of depressive disorders or prevent their recurrence. The predominant action of antidepressants is to increase the catecholamine levels in the brain (monoamine hypothesis), either through blocking the reuptake of norepinephrine (NE), serotonin (5HT) and/or dopamine (DA) at the nerve terminals, thus increasing NE, 5HT and/or DA levels at the receptor site, or through down-regulation of the β-adrenergic receptors. Alternatively, the monoamine oxidase inhibitors (MAOIs) act on monoamine oxidase (MAO), which is responsible for the degradation of catecholamines following their reuptake, with a subsequent increase in the NE and/or 5HT levels at receptor site.
- Mood stabilizers are those drugs that are effective in the treatment and prophylaxis of mania and bipolar depression. The most commonly used mood stabilizers include lithium, valproate, carbamazepine, and lamotrigine. Recently, several atypical antipsychotics, such as olanzapine, quetiapine, and aripiprazole have been added to the list of drugs used in the maintenance treatment of bipolar disorder.
- Several drugs are used in the management of anxiety disorders. Antidepressants, especially selective serotonin reuptake inhibitors, are currently the first choice in anxiety management. Other drugs include benzodiazepines and non-benzodiazepine drugs, and non-benzodiazepine agonists.

■ Benzodiazepines derive their name from their molecular structure. They share a common effect on benzodiazepine receptors, which in turn modulate gamma-aminobutyric acid (GABA) activity. Buspirone is a non-benzodiazepine, azapirone derivative. It is a 5-HT$_1$A partial agonist and a selective dopamine auto receptor antagonist. It also inhibits the spontaneous firing of 5-HT neurons. Non-benzodiazepine agonists act on the GABA receptors, but at a site distinct from that of benzodiazepines.

■ Methylphenidate (MPH) is the most commonly used stimulant drug. The action of stimulants in ADHD is attributed to the release of DA and their ability to block its reuptake by the dopamine transporter (DAT) at the presynaptic nerve terminal.

■ ECT is a procedure during which an electric current is applied to a patient's brain, typically to the temple on the side of the non-dominant cerebral hemisphere, to produce a seizure similar to an epileptic convulsion. ECT is very useful in the treatment of major severe depression with suicidal risk, stupor, poor intake of food and fluids, melancholia, psychotic features, unsatisfactory response to drug therapy, and where drugs are contra-indicated, or have serious side effects. It is also useful in some cases with severe psychoses.

Test Your Knowledge

■ Outline the difference between first-generation and second-generation antipsychotics.
■ Define the different classes of antidepressants.
■ Describe what is meant by a mood stabilizer and its types.
■ What is the difference between benzodiazepines, non-benzodiazepines and non-benzodiazepine agonists?
■ What is mechanism of action of stimulant drugs and what is its indication?
■ Give an account of ECT and its indications.

Critical Thinking Questions

■ How could you evaluate the usage of drugs to treat major mental disorders in the absence of clear-cut evidence about their etiology?
■ In the face of objections that some people and authorities have about the use of ECT, how do you evaluate its current place in the treatment of psychiatric disorders?

twenty-three
Positive Psychology

Learning Goals

- This chapter is intended to provide the reader with an overview of the concept of positive psychology and its different aspects, the factors affecting happiness, and a possible intervention to cultivate positive emotions.

Introduction

Though positive psychology shares some of its ideas with what William James wrote as early as 1902, about the importance of happiness, and with some ideas of the humanistic psychologists who were interested in advancing human fulfillment, positive psychology was founded in 1998 by Martin Seligman and Mihaly Csikszentmihaly. Prior to positive psychology, the focus of psychology was directed toward understanding and alleviating *negative* states, such as emotional problems, the effects of traumatic stress, and problem behaviors, such as violence and drug addiction.

Positive psychology is an umbrella term that includes the scientific understanding of positive subjective experiences (happiness, pleasure, gratification, fulfillment), the study of positive personality traits (strengths of character, talents, interests, values), and the characteristics of positive groups and institutions (families, schools, businesses, communities, societies). These domains form the three pillars of positive psychology (Seligman, 2011; Seligman & Csikszentmihalyi, 2000; Seligman, Steen, Park, & Peterson, 2005):

PHOTO 23.1.   Positive Psychology.

1. *Positive subjective experiences such as happiness and optimism*: this is the first pillar of positive psychology. Positive psychology aims to discover, understand, test, and promote personal factors that allow individuals to flourish. Positive emotions have been found to expand people's mindsets, leading to an increase in personal resources, through discovering new ideas and actions that lead to building up physical, intellectual, social, and psychological resources. Thus, positive emotions are not end states in themselves but are means of cultivating psychological growth and flourishing (Fredrickson, 2001).
2. *Positive personality traits* are the second pillar of positive psychology: the focus is on exploring and enhancing wisdom, creativity, compassion, integrity, self-control, leadership, courage, and spirituality.
3. *Positive organizations and social structures* that might cultivate civility and responsible citizenship are the third pillar of positive psychology: this seeks to foster a positive social environment. These include healthy, responsible, and effective families, neighborhoods, schools, and media.

Learned Helplessness and the Origin of Positive Psychology

While experimenting on classical conditioning on dogs, Martin Seligman discovered a phenomenon which he called "learned helplessness," i.e., dogs tend to fail to act to escape from an electric shock because of a history of repeated failures in previous trials (Seligman, 1975). It was assumed that the dogs had learned that there was nothing they could do to escape the shock, and hence the dogs did nothing when placed in a situation in which escape was possible, because they had learned to be helpless; they did not try because they believed they could not escape. Investigation of the brain mechanisms underlying learned helplessness suggests that the ventromedial prefrontal cortex (vmPFC), is able to help determine what is controllable. In turn, the vmPFC inhibits the brain stem area and calms the amygdala's response, allowing an animal to effectively respond to a stressor and exhibit control (Amat et al., 2005; Maier, Amat, Baratta, Paul, & Watkins, 2006; Maier & Watkins, 2005). Thus, it is possible that the dogs in the early studies did not learn how to relax and take control of the situation rather than learning to be helpless, in other words, it could be the failure to be positive rather than learning to stay negative. Maier and colleagues suggest that both training and input from the vmPFC are necessary for animals to learn how to take control (Maier et al., 2006).

Seligman extended the concept of learned helplessness to explain some psychological problems in humans, including depression. Depressed people frequently have a sense of powerlessness and hopelessness and stay in unpleasant circumstances or bad interpersonal relationships rather than trying to escape or overcome their situation. Seligman proposed that this depressive behavior is a form of learned helplessness. Seligman (1998) eventually developed a program to teach "learned optimism" as a way of overcoming feelings of helplessness, habitual pessimism, and depression.

Happiness and Well-Being

Happiness is an important aspect of positive psychology, however, it forms only one-third of the domain of positive psychology. Positive experiences can be divided into emotion about the past (satisfaction, pride, and the like); the present (happiness); and the future (optimism, hope, and the like). Positive psychology on this view is more than just hedonics (the study of how we feel). The quality of a life is not just the sum total of good moments minus bad moments; the strength, virtue, and meaning of feelings all account for a positive life (Fredrickson, 2001; Schkade & Kahneman, 1998). Thus, happiness is an important but only one aspect of the domain of positive psychology.

Promoting human happiness is the main aim of positive psychology, rather than just repairing negative emotions, such as anxiety and depression. Happiness or well-being can be considered to be comprised of subjective and psychological well-being, both are closely related but are not necessarily interchangeable, a person could feel subjectively happy without leading a virtuous life (Chen, Jing, Hayes, & Lee, 2013; Diener, 1984; Haybron, 2005):

- Subjective well-being (subjective or hedonic experience): happy people usually experience high levels of positive emotions and low levels of negative emotions.
- Psychological well-being (eudaimonic happiness): happy people report high levels of satisfaction of their life as a whole and with important life domains, such as work, health, marriage, and interpersonal relationships.

Predictors of Happiness
Wealth

Although many people may believe that they would be happier if they got a lot of money, research does not support this belief. Wealth was found to make only a minor contribution to the level of happiness and life satisfaction (Boyce, Brown, & Moore, 2010; Sussman & Shafir, 2012). However, being poor can contribute to unhappiness, and earning more money at lower income levels correlates with greater happiness, but additional income beyond the level needed to meet a family's basic needs (about $75,000

PHOTO 23.2   Wealth.

in annual income) has little, if any, effect on personal happiness (Kahneman & Deaton, 2010). The reason that greater wealth does not equate to greater happiness may be due to the tendency of people to judge themselves in relation to others in their social network who are earning much higher amounts, the rise in material desires, and gaining less satisfaction from their family life due to indulgence in work (Frank, 2012; Kasser, Ryan, Couchman, & Sheldon, 2004 Nickerson, Schwarz, Diener, & Kahneman, 2003).

Marriage

Although people complain a lot about their marriages, happier people are more likely to be married or stay married compared with those who are single or divorced (Myers, 1999). However, the causal relations underlying this correlation are not well understood. While happiness may be the cause of marital satisfaction, marital satisfaction may promote happiness. However, investigators find that happiness among recently married couples tends to wear off within two years of marriage, returning back to the pre-wedding baseline (Lyubomirsky, 2012).

PHOTO 23.3.   Marriage.

Friendships

Friendships appear to contribute to happiness. Having close friends is an important ingredient of happiness, and social connections in childhood and adolescence more powerfully predict whether people will be happy in adulthood than does academic achievement (Olsson, McGee, Nada-Raja, & Williams, 2012). Happiness (or unhappiness) spreads through social networks such as friends, family members (Fowler & Christakis, 2008). Thus, being happy may at least partly depend on having happy friends and family members.

PHOTO 23.4.   Friendships.

Religion

Religion is also associated with happiness, and people who regularly participate in religious services are more happy than less frequent attenders (Hout & Greeley, 2012; Kesebir & Diener, 2008). Researchers suggest that the increase of happiness from religious practices arises from the emotional experiences of practicing religious activities, not simply from socializing with others (Hout & Greeley, 2012). Myers (1992) inferred that the effect of religion on happiness stems from giving a sense of purpose and meaning to life and putting ultimate mortality in perspective, its role in accepting life obstacles gracefully, and connecting people to a caring and supportive community.

Health

Cohen et al. (2003) found that individuals who reported high levels of happiness were found to be less vulnerable to the common cold. Danner et al. (2001) demonstrated that positive affective content in handwritten autobiographies of Catholic sisters, collected at the mean age of 22, strongly predicted their longevity six decades later. However, having a serious, disabling health condition is not always a bad experience, as one would assume (Myers, 1992). The relation between health and happiness seems bidirectional, where health can promote happiness to a moderate degree, and happiness can also promote better health. Veenhoven (2008) found a positive correlation between happiness and longevity.

Personality

Dispositional differences in responding to people and events play an important role in happiness levels. Genetic predispositions may account for about 50 percent of variability in happiness (Stubbe, Posthuma, Boomsma, & de Geus, 2005). A lot of evidence suggests that happiness does not depend on external circumstances, but on internal factors, which include one's personality and outlook on life (Lykken & Tellegen, 1996; Lyubomirsky, Sheldon, & Schkade, 2005). Tatarkiewicz (1976) suggested that personality has a dual influence on happiness, as it predisposes an individual to feel joy or sorrow, and it can shape an individual's life in such a way as to cause joy or sorrow. Research has revealed that some personality traits correlate with happiness or unhappiness. Extraversion is more likely to predispose to positive affect and predicts the frequency of positive objective life events, whereas neuroticism predisposes individuals to negative affect and predicts the frequency of negative objective events (Magnus, Diener, Fujita, & Pavot, 1993; Rusting & Larsen, 1997). Other personality traits that were found to be predictors of happiness include self-esteem, optimism, trust, agreeableness, repressive defensiveness, desire for control, and hardiness (DeNeve & Cooper, 1998). Nonetheless, happiness is not genetically determined and can change through the lifetime (Fujita & Diener, 2005; Inglehart, Foa, Peterson, & Welzel, 2008).

Achievement

Happiness is linked to professional achievement. Happiness is not a constant pursuit of pleasure, but it stems from striving for and making progress toward goals derived from one's most-prized values. The feelings of meaning, purpose, and fulfillment typically predict happiness (Kesebir & Diener, 2008). Hence, happy individuals are more likely to graduate from college, have a job, and be less likely to lose it, and are quicker to be reemployed if they are terminated, be evaluated favorably from supervisors, and earn higher incomes (Diener, Nickerson, Lucas, & Sandvik, 2002; Diener & Seligman, 2004).

PHOTO 23.5.   Achievement.

Positive Psychology Interventions

Positive psychology interventions are not programs or treatments that aim at relieving or healing something that is pathological or deficient. These strategies or intentional activities aim to cultivate positive feelings, behaviors, or cognitions (Sin & Lyubomirsky, 2009). There are different types of strategies e.g., three good things, gratitude letter, counting kindness, etc. (Seligman et al., 2005):

- *Three good things exercise*: think of what happened to you each night before you go to sleep, write them down, and think deeply why they went well. This should be repeated daily for one week or more.
- *Gratitude letter*: think of a person who did something that affected your life for the better whom you never properly thanked, and write a letter of gratitude to that person. schedule a visit to the person, and read the letter and discuss with him or her what he or she has meant to you. Seligman believes that expressing gratitude is a key component of personal happiness.
- *Good deed*: try to secretly help someone each day and write about your help in your diary. Doing something good for others can reduce our own stress and makes us feel good, it's called "helpers high."

Clinical Notes

A lot of positive psychology interventions (PPIs) showed beneficial effects on mental health in non-clinical populations. The current literature is inconclusive regarding its effectiveness in clinical settings. However, a recent meta-analysis of the effects of PPIs on well-being and distress in clinical samples with psychiatric and somatic disorders revealed that PPIs have a small but significant effect on well-being compared to control conditions. At follow-up, a significant moderate effect size of PPIs on well-being was observed. The most promising PPIs seem to be those that are therapist-guided (compared to unguided self-help) (Chakhssi, Kraiss, Sommers-Spijkerman, & Bohlmeijer, 2018).

Summary

- Positive psychology is the scientific understanding of positive subjective experiences, the study of positive personality traits and the characteristics of positive groups and institutions.
- Promoting human happiness is a key goal of positive psychology, rather than just repairing negative emotions such as anxiety and depression; however, happiness forms only one-third of the domain of positive psychology.
- Happiness or well-being can be considered to be comprised of subjective and psychological well-being.
- Factors that may affect the level of happiness include wealth, marriage, friendships, religion, health, personality, and achievement.
- Positive psychology interventions are strategies or intentional activities that aim to cultivate positive feelings, behaviors, or cognitions, e.g., three good things, gratitude letter, counting kindness, etc.

Test Your Knowledge

- What is positive psychology?
- How is the focus of positive psychology different from traditional psychology?
- What are the three pillars of positive psychology?
- How is happiness related to positive psychology?
- Give an account of positive psychology interventions.

Critical Thinking Questions

- How does positive psychology relate to happiness?
- How do positive personality traits relate to positive psychology?

References

Aan het Rot, M., Mathew, S. J., & Charney, D. S. (2009). Neurobiological mechanisms in major depressive disorder. *CMAJ : Canadian Medical Association Journal*, 180(3), 305–313.

Aboraya, A., Rankin, E., France, C., El-Missiry, A., & John, C. (2006). The reliability of psychiatric diagnosis revisited: The clinician's guide to improve the reliability of psychiatric diagnosis. *Psychiatry*, 3(1), 41–50.

Abramson, L. Y., Alloy, L. B., Hankin, B. L., Haeffel, G. J., MacCoon, D. G., & Gibb, B. E. (2002). Cognitive vulnerability-stress models of depression in a self-regulatory, psychobiological context. In I. H. Gotlib, & C. L. Hammen (Eds.), *Handbook of depression*. New York: Guilford.

Adair, L. S., & Gordon-Larsen, P. (2001). Maturational timing and overweight prevalence in US adolescent girls. *American Journal of Public Health*, 91, 642–644.

Adorno, T. W., Frenkel-Brunswik, E., Levinson, D. J., & Sanford, R. N. (1950). *The authoritarian personality*. New York: Harper and Brothers.

Ainsworth, M. D. (1964). Patterns of attachment behavior shown by the infant in interaction with his mother. *Merrill-Palmer Quarterly of Behavior and Development*, 10, 51–58.

Ainsworth, M. D. S., Bell, S. M. V., & Stayton, D. J. (1971). Individual differences in strange situation behaviour of one-year-olds. In H. R. Schaffer (Ed.), *The origins of human social relations*. New York: Academic Press.

Ainsworth, M. D. S., Blehar, M. C., Waters, E., & Wall, S. (1978). *Patterns of attachment: A psychological study of the strange situation*. Hillsdale, NJ: Lawrence Erlbaum Associates Inc.

Ajzen, I. (2001). Nature and operation of attitudes. *Annual Review of Psychology*, 52, 27–58.

Albarracin, D., & Vargas, P. (2010). Attitudes and persuasion: From biology to social responses to persuasive intent. In S. T. Fiske, D. T. Gilbert, & G. Lindzey (Eds.), *The handbook of social psychology*. Hoboken, NJ: John Wiley & Sons, Inc.

Albert, D., Chein, J., & Steinberg, L. (2013). The teenage brain: Peer influences on adolescent decision making. *Current Directions in Psychological Science*, 22, 114–120.

Alderfer, C. P. (1969). An empirical test of a new theory of human needs. *Organizational Behavior and Human Performance*, 2(2), 142–175.

Alhasnawi, S., Sadik, S., Rasheed, M., Baban, A., Al-Alak, M. M., Othman A. Y., On Behalf of the Iraq Mental Health Survey Study Group. (2009). The prevalence and correlates of DSM-IV disorders in the Iraq Mental Health Survey (IMHS). *World Psychiatry*, 8(2), 97–109.

Alhola, P., & Polo-Kantola, P. (2007). Sleep deprivation: Impact on cognitive performance. *Neuropsychiatric Disease and Treatment*, 3(5), 553–567.

Alia-Klein, N., Goldstein, R. Z., Tomasi, D., Woicik, P. A., et al. (2009). Neural mechanisms of anger regulation as a function of genetic risk for violence. *Emotion*, 9, 385–396.

Allen, L. B., McHugh, R. K., & Barlow, D. H. (2008). Emotional disorders: A unified protocol. In D. H. Barlow (Ed.), *Clinical handbook of psychological disorders* (4th ed., pp. 216–249). New York: Guilford Press.

Allport, G. W. (1954). *The nature of prejudice*. Garden City, NY: Anchor Books, Doubleday.

Allport, G. W. (1985). The historical background of social psychology. In G. Lindzey, & E. Aronson (Eds.), *The handbook of social psychology*. New York: McGraw-Hill.

Alonso, J., Angermeyer, M. C., Bernert, S., Bruffaerts, R., Brugha, T. S., Bryson, H., et al. (2004). 12-month comorbidity patterns and associated factors in Europe: Results from the European Study of the Epidemiology of Mental Disorders (ESEMeD) project. *Acta Psychiatrica Scandinavica*, 109, 28–37.

Altemeyer, B. (2004). Highly dominating, highly authoritarian personalities. *Journal of Social Psychology*, 144, 421–447.

Altemeyer, B., & Hunsberger, B. (2005). Fundamentalism and authoritarianism. In R. Paloutzian, & C. Park (Eds.), *Handbook of the psychology of religion and spirituality* (pp. 378–393). New York: Guilford Press.

Alter, M. D., Rubin, D. B., Ramsey, K., Halpern, R., Stephan, D. A., Abbott L. F., et al. (2008). Variation in the large-scale organization of gene expression levels in the hippocampus relates to stable epigenetic variability in behavior. *PLoS ONE*, 3, e3344.

Alwin, D. F. (2009). History, cohorts, and patterns of cognitive aging. In H. B. Bosworth, & C. Hertzog (Eds.), *Aging and cognition: Research methodologies and empirical advances* (pp. 9–38). Washington, DC: American Psychological Association.

Amat, J., Baratta, M. V., Paul, E., Bland, S. T., Watkins, L. R., & Maier, S. F. (2005). Medial prefrontal cortex determines how stressor controllability affects behavior and dorsal raphe nucleus. *Nature Neuroscience*, 8(3), 365–371.

Amato, P. R. (2000). The consequences of divorce for adults and children. *Journal of Marriage and Family*, 62, 1269–1287.

Amen, D. G., Stubblefield, M., Carmichael, B., & Thisted, R. (1996). Brain SPECT findings and aggressiveness. *Annals of Clinical Psychiatry*, 8, 129–137.

American Psychiatric Association (2000). Practice guidelines for the treatment of patients with eating disorders (revised). *American Journal of Psychiatry*, 157(Suppl.), 1–39.

American Psychological Association. (2010). *Ethical principles of psychologists and code of conduct*. Available at: www.apa.org/ethics/code (accessed September 8, 2017).

American Psychiatric Association (2013). *Diagnostic and statistical manual of mental disorders* (5th ed.). Arlington, VA: American Psychiatric Publishing.

Amodio, D. M., & Showers, C. J. (2005). "Similarity breeds liking" revisited: The moderating role of commitment. *Journal of Social and Personal Relationships*, 22(6), 817–836.

Amsel, A. (1992). *Frustration theory: An analysis of dispositional learning and memory*. Cambridge: Cambridge University Press.

Andersen, A. E. (2002). Rethinking the DSM-IV diagnosis of eating disorders. *Eating Disorders*, 10, 177–180.

Anderson, C. A., Anderson, K. B., & Deuser, W. E. (1996). Examining an affective aggression framework. *Personality and Social Psychology Bulletin*, 22(4), 366–376.

Anderson, C. A., Berkowitz, L., Donnerstein, E., et al. (2003). Influence of media violence on youth. *Psychological Science in the Public Interest*, 4, 1–30.

Anderson, C. A., & Bushman, B. J. (2002). Human aggression. *Annual Review of Psychology*, 53, 27–51.

Anderson, J. R. (1995). *Learning and memory: An integrated approach*. New York: Wiley.

Andresen, J. (2000). Meditation meets behavioural medicine: The story of experimental research on meditation. *Journal of Consciousness Studies*, 7(11–12), 17–73.

Aneshensel, C. S., Rutter, C. M., & Lachenbruch, P. A. (1991). Social structure, stress, and mental health: Competing conceptual and analytic models. *American Sociological Review*, 56(2), 166–178.

Ansbacher, H. L., & Ansbacher, R. R. (Eds.) (1956). *The individual psychology of Alfred Adler: A systematic presentation in selections from his writings*. Oxford: Basic Books.

Antony, M. M., Purdon, C., & Summerfeldt, L. J. (2007). *Psychological treatment of obsessive–compulsive disorder: Fundamentals and beyond*. Washington, DC: American Psychological Association.

Antrobus, J. (1991). Dreaming: Cognitive processes during cortical activation and high afferent thresholds. *Psychological Review*, 98, 96–121.

Appignanesi, L. (2009). *Mad, bad, and sad: A history of women and mind doctors*. New York: Norton.

Ariely, D. (2008). *Predictably irrational*. New York: HarperCollins.

Arnett, J. J. (2007). Emerging adulthood: What is it, and what is it good for? *Child Development Perspectives*, 1(2), 68–73.

Arnett, J. J. (2011). Emerging adulthood(s): The cultural psychology of a new life stage. In L. Arnett Jensen (Ed.), *Bridging cultural and developmental approaches to psychology: New syntheses in theory, research, and policy*. New York: Oxford University Press.

Arnold, A. P. (2004). Sex chromosomes and brain gender. *Nature Reviews Neuroscience*, 5, 701–708.

Aron, A., Fisher, H. E., Mashek, D. J., Strong, G., Li, H. F. & Brown, L. L. (2005). Reward, motivation and emotion systems associated with early-stage intense romantic love: An fMRI study. *Journal of Neurophysiology*, 94, 327–337.

Aronson, E. (2008). *The social animal* (10th ed.). New York: Worth.

Asch, S. E. (1951). Effects of group pressure upon the modification and distortion of judgment. In H. Guetzkow (Ed.), *Groups, leadership and men*. Pittsburgh, PA: Carnegie Press.

Atkinson, R. C., & Shiffrin, R. M. (1968). Human memory: A proposed system and its control processes. In K. W. Spence, & J. T. Spence (Eds.), *The psychology of learning and motivation* (vol. 2). New York: Academic Press.

Baddeley, A., Eysenck, M., & Anderson, M. (2009). *Memory*. New York: Taylor and Francis, Inc.

Bahrami, B., Lavie, N., & Rees, G. (2007). Attentional load modulates responses of human primary visual cortex to invisible stimuli. *Current Biology*, 17(6), 509–513.

Bailey, J. M., & Pillard, R.C. (1991). A genetic study of male sexual orientation. *Archives of General Psychiatry*, 48(12): 1089–1096.

Balbernie, R. (2001). Circuits and circumstances: The neurobiological consequences of early relationship experiences and how they shape later behaviour. *Journal of Child Psychotherapy*, 27(3), 237–255.

Banaji, M. R., & Heiphetz, L. (2010). Attitudes. In S. T. Fiske, D. T. Gilbert, & G. Lindzey (Eds.), *Handbook of social psychology* (5th ed., vol. 1, pp. 353–393). Hoboken, NJ: Wiley.

Bandura, A. (1965). Influence of models' reinforcement contingencies on the acquisition of imitative responses. *Journal of Personality and Social Psychology*, 1, 589–595.

Bandura, A. (1974). Behavior theory and the models of man. *American Psychologist*, 29, 859–869.

Bandura, A. (1977). Self-efficacy: Toward a unifying theory of behavioral change. *Psychological Review*, 84(2), 191–215.

Bandura, A. (1986). *Social foundations of thought and action: A social cognitive theory*. Englewood Cliffs, NJ: Prentice Hall.

Bard, P. (1934). On emotional expression after decortication with some remarks on certain theoretical views: Part 1. *Psychological Review*, 41(4), 309–329.

Baron, R. A., & Richardson, D. C. (1994). *Human aggression* (2nd ed.). New York: Plenum.

Barrett, L. F., Quigley, K. S., Bliss-Moreau, E., & Aronson, K. R. (2004). Interoceptive sensitivity and self-reports of emotional experience. *Journal of Personality and Social Psychology*, 87(5), 684–697.

Barrett, L. F., & Russell, J. A. (1999). The structure of current affect: Controversies and emerging consensus. *Current Directions in Psychological Science*, 8(1), 10–14.

Bartholow, B. D., Bushman, B. J., & Sestir, M. A. (2006). Chronic violent video game exposure and desensitization to violence: Behavioral and event-related brain potential data. *Journal of Experimental Social Psychology*, 42, 532–539.

Bartholow, B. D., Sestir, M. A., & Davis, E. B. (2005). Correlates and consequences of exposure to video game violence: Hostile personality, empathy, and aggressive behavior. *Personality and Social Psychology Bulletin*, 31(11), 1573–1586.

Batson, C. D. (2011). *Altruism in humans*. New York: Oxford University Press.

Baumeister, R. F., Campbell, J. D., Krueger, J. I. & Vohs, K. D. (2003). Does high self-esteem cause better performance, interpersonal success, happiness, or healthier lifestyles? *Psychological Science in the Public Interest*, 4, 1–44.

Bayliss, D. M., Jarrold, C., Baddeley, A. D., Gunn, D. M., & Leigh, E. (2005). Mapping the developmental constraints on working memory span performance. *Developmental Psychology*, 41, 579–597.

Beck, A. T. (1963). Thinking and depression. I. Idiosyncratic content and cognitive distortions. *Archives of General Psychiatry*, 9, 324–33.

Beck, A. T. (1976). *Cognitive therapy and the emotional disorders*. New York: International Universities Press.

Becker, A. E., & Fay, K. (2006). Socio-cultural issues and eating disorders. In S. Wonderlich, M. de Zwaan, H. Steiger, & J. Mitchell (Eds.), *Annual review of eating disorders: Part 2* (pp. 35–63). Chicago, IL: Academy for Eating Disorders.

Bee, H. L. (1994). *Lifespan development*. New York: HarperCollins College Publishers.

Bell-Pedersen, D., Cassone, V. M., Earnest, D. J., Golden, S. S., Hardin, P. E., et al. (2005). Circadian rhythms from multiple oscillators: Lessons from diverse organisms. *Nature Reviews Genetics*, 6(7), 544–556.

Belmaker, R. H., & Agam, G. (2008). Major depressive disorder. *New England Journal of Medicine*, 358, 55–68.

Belsky, J., Steinberg, L., Houts, R. M., & Halpern-Felsher, B. L. (2010). The development of reproductive strategy in females: Early maternal harshness → earlier menarche → increased sexual risk taking. *Developmental Psychology*, 46(1), 120–128.

Bem, D. J. (1967). Self-perception: An alternative interpretation of cognitive dissonance phenomena. *Psychological Review*, 74, 183–200.

Bem, D. J. (1967). Self-perception: An alternative interpretation of cognitive dissonance phenomena. *Psychological Review*, 74, 183–200.

Berk, L. E. (2001). Private speech and self-regulation in children with impulse control difficulties: Implications for research and practice. *Journal of Cognitive Education and Psychology*, 2, 1–21.

Berkowitz, L. (1994). Is something missing? Some observations prompted by the cognitive neoassociationist view of anger and emotional aggression. In L. R. Huesmann (Ed.), *Human aggression: Current perspectives* (pp. 35–60). New York: Plenum.

Berkowitz, L. (1998). Affective aggression: The role of stress, pain, and negative affect. In R. G. Geen, & E. Donnerstein (Eds.), *Human aggression* (pp. 49–72). San Diego, CA: Academic Press.

Berlyne, D. E. (1960). *Conflict, arousal and curiosity*. New York: McGraw-Hill.

Berman, M., Gladue, B., & Taylor, S. (1993). The effects of hormones, Type A behavior pattern, and provocation on aggression in men. *Motivation and Emotion*, 17, 125–138.

Berman, M. E., McCloskey, M. S, Fanning, J. R, Schumacher, J. A., & Coccaro, E. F. (2009). Serotonin augmentation reduces response to attack in aggressive individuals. *Psychological Science*, 20(6), 714–720.

Berne, E. (1961). *Transactional analysis in psychotherapy: A systematic individual and social psychiatry.* New York: Grove Press.

Berne, E. (1964). *Games people play: The psychology of human relationships*. New York: Grove Press.

Berry, J. W., & Triandis, H. C. (2006). Culture. In K. Pawlik and G. d'Ydewalle (Eds.), *Psychological concepts: An international and historical perspective* (pp. 47–62). Hove: Psychology Press.

Berscheid, E. (2010). Love in the fourth dimension. *Annual Review of Psychology*, 61, 1–25.

Berscheid, E. (2011). Love and compassion: Caregiving in adult close relationships. In S. Brown, M. Brown, & L. Penner (Eds.), *Self-interest and beyond: Toward a new understanding of human caregiving*. New York: Oxford University Press.

Berscheid, E., & Regan, P. (2005). *The psychology of interpersonal relationships*. New York: Prentice-Hall.

Berson, D. M., Dunn, F. A., & Takao, M. (2002). Phototransduction by retinal ganglion cells that set the circadian clock. *Science*, 295, 1070–1073.

Bettencourt, B. A., Talley, A., Benjamin, A. J., & Valentine, J. (2006). Personality and aggressive behavior under provoking and neutral conditions: A meta-analytic review. *Psychological Bulletin*, 132, 751–777.

Biddle, B. J. (1979). *Role theory: Expectations, identities, and behaviors*. New York: Academic Press.

Billings, A. G., & Moos, R. H. (1981). The role of coping responses and social resources in attenuating the stress of life events. *Journal of Behavioral Medicine*, 4, 139–157.

Bird, A. (2007). Perceptions of epigenetics. *Nature*, 447, 396–398.

Bisaz, R., Travaglia, A., & Alberini, C. M. (2014). The neurobiological bases of memory formation: From physiological conditions to psychopathology. *Psychopathology*, 47(6), 347–356.

Bjorklund, B. R. (1995). Language development and cognition. In F. B. David (Ed.), *Children's thinking: Developmental function and individual differences* (2nd ed.). Pacific Grove, CA: Brooks/Cole.

Blagrove, M. (1992). Dreams as a reflection of our waking concerns and abilities: A critique of the problem-solving paradigm in dream research. *Dreaming*, 2, 205–220.

Blagrove, M. (1996). Problems with the cognitive psychological modeling of dreaming. *Journal of Mind and Behavior*, 17, 99–134.

Blair, I. (2002). The malleability of automatic stereotypes and prejudice. *Personality and Social Psychology Review*, 6, 242–261.

Blakemore, C. (1988). *The mind machine*. London: BBC Publications.

Blass, T. (1991). Understanding behavior in the Milgram obedience experiment: The role of personality, situations, and their interactions. *Journal of Personality and Social Psychology*, 60, 398–413.

Blow, A. J., & Timm, T. M. (2002). Promoting community through family therapy: Helping clients develop a network of significant social relationships. *Journal of Systematic Therapies*, 21, 67–89.

Boehm, J. K., & Kubzansky, L. D. (2012). The heart's content: The association between positive psychological well-being and cardiovascular health. *Psychological Bulletin*, 138(4), 655–691.

Bohlen, H. O., & Dermietzel, R. (2006). *Neurotransmitters and neuromodulators: Handbook of receptors and biological effects*. Weinheim: Wiley-VCH.

Bohner, G., Erb, H.-P., & Siebler, F. (2008). Information processing approaches to persuasion: Integrating assumptions from the dual- and single-processing perspectives. In W. B. Crano, & R. Prislin (Eds.), *Attitudes and persuasion* (pp. 161–188). New York: Psychology Press.

Bolger, N., DeLongis, A., Kessler, R. C., & Schilling, E. A. (1989). Effects of daily stress on negative mood. *Journal of Personality and Social Psychology*, 57(5), 808–818.

Booth, A., Shelley, G., Mazur, A., Tharp, G., & Kittok, R. (1989). Testosterone, and winning and losing in human competition. *Hormones and Behavior*, 23(4), 556–571.

Borbély, A. A., & Achermann, P. (1999). Sleep homeostasis and models of sleep regulation. *Journal of Biological Rhythms*, 14(6), 557–568.

Borbély, A. A., & Achermann, P. (2005). Sleep homeostasis and models of sleep regulation. In M. H. Kryger, T. Roth, & W. C. Dement (Eds.), *Principles and practice of sleep medicine*. Philadelphia, PA: Elsevier Saunders.

Bowlby, J. (1951). *Maternal care and mental health*. Geneva: World Health Organization Monograph (Serial No. 2).

Bowlby, J. (1969). *Attachment and loss* (vol. 1): *Attachment*. New York: Basic Books.

Bowlby, J. (1980). *Attachment and loss* (vol. 3): *Loss, sadness and depression*. New York: Basic Books.

Bowlby, J. (1988). *A secure base: Parent-child attachment and healthy human development*. New York: Basic Books.

Bowlby, J., & Robertson, J. (1952). A two-year-old goes to hospital. *Proceedings of the Royal Society of Medicine*, 46, 425–427.

Boyce, C. J., Brown, G. D. A., & Moore, S. C. (2010). Money and happiness: Rank of income, not income, affects life satisfaction. *Psychological Science*, 21, 471–475.

Braisby, N., & Gellatly, A. (2005). *Cognitive psychology*. New York: Oxford University Press.

Braun, S. (2001). Ecstasy on trial: Seeking insight by prescription. *Cerebrum*, 3, 10–21.

Breckler, S. J., Olson, J. M., & Wiggins, E. C. (2006). *Social psychology alive*. Belmont, CA: Wadsworth.

Brehm, J. W. (1966). *A theory of psychological reactance*. New York: Academic Press.

Breiding, M. J., Smith, S. G, Basile, K. C., Walters, M. L., & Chen, J. (2014). Prevalence and characteristics of sexual violence, stalking, and intimate partner violence victimization: National Intimate Partner and Sexual Violence Survey, United States, 2011, *Morbidity and Mortality Weekly Report*, September 5, 63(8).

Brescoll, V. L., & Uhlmann, E. L. (2008). Can an angry woman get ahead? Status conferral, gender, and expression of emotion in the workplace. *Psychological Science*, 19(3), 268–275.

Brewer, W. F. (1974). There is no convincing evidence for operant or classical conditioning in adult humans. In W. B. Weimer, & D. S. Palermo (Eds.), *Cognition and the symbolic processes*. Hillsdale, NJ: Lawrence Erlbaum Associates.

Broadbent, D. (1958). *Perception and communication*. London: Pergamon Press.

Brock, T. C., & Green, M. C. (Eds.). (2005). *Persuasion: Psychological insights and perspectives* (2nd ed.). Thousand Oaks, CA: Sage.

Brooks-Gunn, J., & Reiter, E. O. (1990). The role of pubertal processes. In S. S. Feldman, & G. R. Elliott (Eds.), *At the threshold: The developing adolescent*. Cambridge, MA: Harvard University Press.

Brown, G. L., Ebert. M. H., Goyer, P. F., Jimerson, D. C., Klein, W. J., Bunney, W. E., & Goodwin, F. K. (1982). Aggression, suicide, and serotonin: Relationships to CSF amine metabolites *The American Journal of Psychiatry*, 139, 741–746.

Brown, R. (1974). Further comment on the risky shift. *American Psychologist*, 29(6), 468–470.

Brown, R. (1988). *Group processes: Dynamics within and between groups*. Oxford: Blackwell.

Brown, S. L., & Brown, R. M. (2006). Selective investment theory: Recasting the functional significance of close relationships. *Psychological Inquiry*, 17, 1–29.

Bruner, J. S. (1957). Going beyond the information given. In J. S. Bruner, E. Brunswik, L. Festinger, F. Heider, K. F. Muenzinger, C. E. Osgood, & D. Rapaport (Eds.), *Contemporary approaches to cognition* (pp, 41–69). Cambridge, MA: Harvard University Press.

Bucur, B., Madden, D. J., Spaniol J., Provenzale, J. M. Cabeza, R., White, L. E., & Huettel, S. A. (2008). Age related slowing of memory retrieval: Contributions of perceptual speed and cerebral white matter integrity. *Neurobiology of Aging*, 29(7), 1070–1079.

Budney, A. J., Roffman, R., Stephens, R. S., & Walker, D. (2007). Marijuana dependence and its treatment. *Addiction Science and Clinical Practice*, 4, 4–16.

Bufkin, J. L., & Luttrell, V. R. (2005). Neuroimaging studies of aggressive and violent behavior: Current findings and implications for criminology and criminal justice. *Trauma Violence & Abuse*, 6(2), 176–191.

Bui, K.-V. T., Peplau, L. A., & Hill, C. T. (1996). Testing the Rusbult model of relationship commitment and stability in a 15-year study of heterosexual couples. *Personality and Social Psychology Bulletin*, 22, 1244–1257.

Burgard, S. A., & Ailshire, J. A. (2009). Putting work to bed: Stressful experiences on the job and sleep quality. *Journal of Health and Social Behavior*, 50, 476–492.

Burger, J. M. (1986). Increasing compliance by improving the deal: The that's-not-all technique. *Journal of Personality and Social Psychology*, 51(2), 277–283.

Bushman, B. J., & Anderson, C. A. (2009). Comfortably numb: Desensitizing effects of violent media on helping others. *Psychological Science*, 20(3), 273–277.

Bushman, B. J., & Huesmann, L. R. (2010). Aggression. In S. T. Fiske, D. T. Gilbert, & G. Lindzey (Eds.), *Handbook of social psychology* (5th ed., vol. 2, pp. 833–863). Hoboken, NJ: Wiley.

Busink, R. & Kuiken, D. (1996). Identifying types of impactful dreams: A replication. *Dreaming*, 6(2), 97–119.

Buss, D. M. (2000). *The dangerous passion: Why jealousy is as necessary as love and sex*. New York: The Free Press.

Büssing, A., Michalsen, A., Khalsa, S. B. S., Telles, S., & Sherman, K. J. (2012). Effects of yoga on mental and physical health: A short summary of reviews. *Evidence-Based Complementary and Alternative Medicine*: eCAM, 165410.

Byrne, D. (1969). Attitudes and attraction. In L. Berkowitz (Ed.), *Advances in experimental social psychology*. New York: Academic Press.

Byrne, D., Ervin, C. E., & Lamberth, J. (1970). Continuity between the experimental study of attraction and real-life computer dating. *Journal of Personality and Social Psychology*, 16, 157–165.

Bystron, I., Blakemore, C., & Rakic, P. (2008). Development of the human cerebral cortex: Boulder Committee revisited. *Nature Reviews Neuroscience*, 9(2), 110–122.

Cacioppo, J. T., Gardner, W. L., & Berntson, G. G. (1999). The affect system has parallel and integrative processing components: Form follows function. *Journal of Personality and Social Psychology*, 76, 839–855.

Cacioppo, J. T., & Petty, R. E. (1986). *Communication and persuasion: Central and peripheral routes to attitude change*. New York: Springer.

Cacioppo, J. T., Petty, R. E., Feinstein, J. A, Jarvis, W., & Blair, G. (1996). Dispositional differences in cognitive motivation: The life and times of individuals varying in need for cognition. *Psychological Bulletin*, 119, 197–253.

Cadoret, R. J., Leve, L. D., & Devor, E. (1997). Genetics of aggressive and violent behavior. *Psychiatric Clinics of North America*, 20, 301–322.

Canli, T., Qui, M., Omura, K., Congdon, E., et al. (2006). Neural correlates of epigenesis. *Proceedings of the National Academy of Sciences of the U.S.A.*, 103, 16033–16038.

Carew, T., Castellucci, V. F., & Kandel, E. R. (1979). Sensitization in Aplysia: Restoration of transmission in synapses inactivated by long-term habituation. *Science*, 205, 417–419.

Carlson, D. L. (2010). Well, what did you expect? Family transitions, life course expectations, and mental health. Doctoral dissertation, The Ohio State University, Columbus, OH.

Carlson, M., Marcus-Newhall, A., & Miller, N. (1990). Effects of situational aggression cues: A quantitative review. *Journal of Personality and Social Psychology*, 58, 622–633.

Carr, D., & Umberson, D. (2013). The social psychology of stress, health, and coping. In J. DeLamater, & A. Ward (Eds.), *Handbook of social psychology*. Dordrecht: Springer Netherlands.

Carroll, J. B. (1993). *Human cognitive abilities: A survey of factor-analytic studies*. Cambridge: Cambridge University Press.

Cartwright, D., & Harary, F. (1956). Structural balance: A generalization of Heider's theory. *Psychological Review*, 63(5), 277–93.

Cartwright, R. (2004). Sleepwalking violence: A sleep disorder, a legal dilemma, and a psychological challenge. *The American Journal of Psychiatry*, 161(7), 1149–1158.

Carver, C. S., Johnson, S. L., & Joormann, J. (2008). Serotonergic function, two-mode models of self-regulation, and vulnerability to depression: What depression has in common with impulsive aggression. *Psychological Bulletin*, 134, 912–943.

Carver, C. S., Scheier, M. F., & Weintraub, J. K. (1989). Assessing coping strategies: A theoretically based approach. *Journal of Personality and Social Psychology*, 56(2), 267–283.

Cassidy, J., & Berlin, L. J. (1994). The insecure/ambivalent pattern of attachment: Theory and research. *Child Development*, 65(4), 971–91.

Castelli, L., Zogmaister, C., & Tomelleri, S. (2009). The transmission of racial attitudes within the family. *Developmental Psychology*, 45(2), 586–591.

Castellucci, V. F., Carew, T. J., & Kandel, E. R. (1978). Cellular analysis of long-term habituation of the gill-withdrawal reflex of Aplysia californica. *Science*, 202, 1306–1308.

Castro, J. (2012). Sleep's secret repairs. *Scientific American Mind*, 23(2), 42–45.

Chakhssi, F., Kraiss, J. T., Sommers-Spijkerman, M., & Bohlmeijer, E. T. (2018). The effect of positive psychology interventions on well-being and distress in clinical samples with psychiatric or somatic disorders: A systematic review and metaanalysis. *BMC Psychiatry*, 18, 211.

Chan, D. K-S., Gelfand, M. J., Triandis, H. C., & Tzeng, O. (1996). Tightness-looseness revisited: Some preliminary analyses in Japan and the United States. *International Journal of Psychology*, 31, 1–12.

Chansler, P. A., Swamidass, P. M., & Cammann, C. (2003). Self-managing work teams: An empirical study of group cohesiveness in "natural work groups" at a Harley-Davidson Motor Company plant. *Small Group Research*, 34(1), 101–120.

Charles, S. T., & Carstensen, L. L. (2010). Social and emotional aging. *Annual Review of Psychology*, 61, 383–409.

Charnay, Y., & Léger, L. (2010). Brain serotonergic circuitries. *Dialogues in Clinical Neuroscience*, 12(4), 471–487.

Chen, C. H., & Lin, S. K. (2012). Carbamazepine treatment of bipolar disorder: A retrospective evaluation of naturalistic long-term outcomes. *BMC Psychiatry*, 12, 47.

Chen, F. F, Jing, Y., Hayes, A., & Lee, J. M. (2013). Two concepts or two approaches? A bifactor analysis of psychological and subjective well-being. *Journal of Happiness Studies*, 14, 1033–1068.

Chen, S., & Andersen, S. M. (1999). Relationship from the past in the present: Significant-other representations and transference in interpersonal life. In M. P. Zanna (Ed.), *Advances in experimental social psychology* (vol. 31, pp. 123–190). San Diego, CA: Academic Press.

Choudhary, A. K., Kishanrao, S. S., Dadarao Dhanvijay, A. K., & Alam, T. (2016). Sleep restriction may lead to disruption in physiological attention and reaction time. *Sleep Science*, 9(3), 207–211.

Chyrelle, M. C. (2006). Social anxiety, attributional style, and contemporary dating practices. Doctoral dissertation, Pacific University. Available at: http://commons.pacificu.edu/spp/39

Cialdini, R. B. (2003). Crafting normative messages to protect the environment. *Current Directions in Psychological Science*, 12, 105–109.

Cialdini, R. B. (2009). *Influence: Science and practice* (5th ed.). Boston: Allyn & Bacon.

Cialdini, R. B., Borden, R. J., Thorne, A., Walker, M. R., Freeman, S., & Sloan, L. R. (1976). Basking in reflected glory: Three (football) field studies. *Journal of Personality and Social Psychology*, 39, 406–415.

Cialdini, R. B., & Goldstein, N. J. (2004). Social influence: Compliance and conformity. *Annual Review of Psychology*, 55, 591–621.

Claridge, G., & Davis, C. (2003). *Personality and psychological disorders*. London: Arnold.

Clark, D. (1988). A cognitive model of panic attacks. In S. Rachman, & J. D. Maser (Eds.), *Panic: Psychological perspectives*. Mahwah, NJ: Lawrence Erlbaum Associates, Inc.

Clark, D. M. (1986). A cognitive approach to panic. *Behaviour Research and Therapy*, 24, 461–470.

Clark, M. S., & Lemay, E. P., Jr. (2010). Close relationships. In S. T. Fiske, D. T. Gilbert, & G. Lindzey (Eds.), *Handbook of social psychology* (pp. 898–940). Hoboken, NJ: John Wiley & Sons, Inc.

Coccaro, E. F. (1989). Central serotonin and impulsive aggression. *British Journal of Psychiatry*, 155, 52–62.

Cohen, S., Alper, C. M., Doyle, W. J., Treanor, J. J., & Turner, R. B. (2006). Positive emotional style predicts resistance to illness after experimental exposure to rhinovirus or influenza virus. *Psychosomatic Medicine*, 68(6), 809–815.

Cohen, S., Doyle, W. J., Turner, R. B., Alper, C. M., & Skoner, D. P. (2003). Emotional style and susceptibility to the common cold. *Psychosomatic Medicine*, 65, 652–657.

Cohen, S., Frank, E., Doyle, W. J., Skoner, D. P., Rabin, B. S., & Gwaltney, J. M. Jr. (1998). Types of stressors that increase susceptibility to the common cold in healthy adults. *Health Psychology*, 17, 214–223.

Cohen, S., Tyrrell, D. A., & Smith, A. P. (1991). Psychological stress and susceptibility to the common cold. *New England Journal of Medicine*, 325, 606–612.

Cohen, S., & Wills, T. A. (1985). Stress, social support, and the buffering hypothesis. *Psychological Bulletin*, 98, 310–357.

Cohen-Bendahan, C. C., van de Beek, C., & Berenbaum, S. A. (2005). Prenatal sex hormone effects on child and adult sex-typed behavior: Methods and findings. *Neuroscience & Biobehavioral Reviews*, 29(2), 353–384.

Cohrs, C., & Ibler, S. (2009). Authoritarianism, threat, and prejudice: An analysis of mediation and moderation. *Basic and Applied Social Psychology*, 31(1), 81–94.

Colby, K. M. (1960). *An introduction to psychoanalytic research*. New York: Basic Books.

Collerton, J., Davies, K., Jagger, C., Kingston, A., Bond, J., Eccles, M. P., Robinson, L. A., et al. (2009). Health and disease in 85 year olds: Baseline findings from the Newcastle 85+ cohort study. *BMJ*, 339, b4904.

Collins, N. L., & Miller, L. C. (1994). Self-disclosure and liking: A meta-analytic review. *Psychological Bulletin*, 116, 457–475.

Collins, R. L., Elliott, M. N., Berry, S. H., Kanouse, D. E., Kunkel, D., Hunter, S. B., & Miu, A. (2004). Watching sex on TV predicts adolescent initiation of sexual behavior. *Pediatrics*, 114, e1–e10.

Collins, W. A. (2003). More than myth: The developmental significance of romantic relationships during adolescence. *Journal of Research on Adolescence*, 13, 1–24.

Comte, A. (1903). *A discourse on the positive spirit*. London: Reeves.

Connolly, J. A., & McIsaac, C. (2009). Romantic relationships in adolescence. In R. M. Lerner, & L. Steinberg (Eds.), *Handbook of adolescent psychology* (vol 2): *Contextual influences on adolescent development* (3rd ed., pp. 104–151). Hoboken, NJ: Wiley.

Cook, E. C., Buehler, C., & Henson, R. (2009). Parents and peers as social influences to deter antisocial behavior. *Journal of Youth and Adolescence*, 38(9), 1240–1252.

Cook, T. D., & Campbell, D. T. (1979). *Quasi-experimentation: Design and analysis issues for field settings*. Boston: Houghton Mifflin.

Cook, T. D., Deng, Y., & Morgano, E. (2007). Friendship influences during early adolescence: The special role of friends' grade point average. *Journal of Research on Adolescence*, 17(2), 325–356.

Coon, D. (1983). *Introduction to psychology* (3rd ed.). St Paul, MN: West Publishing Co.

Cooper, J., Mirabile, R., Scher, S. J., Brock, T. C., & Green, M. C. (2005). Actions and attitudes: The theory of cognitive dissonance. In T. C. Brock, & M. C. Green (eds.). *Persuasion: Psychological insights and perspectives*. (2nd ed., pp. 63–79). Thousand Oaks, CA: Sage.

Correll, J., Park, B., Judd, C. M., & Wittenbrink, B. (2002). The police officer's dilemma: Using ethnicity to disambiguate potentially threatening individuals. *Journal of Personality and Social Psychology*, 83(6), 1314–1329.

Correll, J., Park, B., Judd, C. M., Wittenbrink, B., Sadler, M. S., & Keesee, T. (2007). Across the thin blue line: Police officers and racial bias in the decision to shoot. *Journal of Personality and Social Psychology*, 92(6), 1006–1023.

Cottrell, N. B., Wack, D. L., Sekerak, G. J., & Rittle, R. H. (1968). Social facilitation of dominant responses by the presence of an audience and the mere presence of others. *Journal of Personality and Social Psychology*, 9(3), 245.

Cox, M. J., & Paley, B. (2003). Understanding families as systems. *Current Directions in Psychological Science*, 12, 193–196.

Craig, T. Y., & Kelly, J. R. (1999). Group cohesiveness and creative performance. *Group Dynamics*, 3(4), 243–256.

Craik, F. I. M., & Lockhart, R. S. (1972). Levels of processing: A framework for memory research. *Journal of Verbal Learning and Verbal Behavior*, 11, 671–684.

Cramer, P. (2000). Defense mechanisms in psychology today: Further processes for adaptation. *American Psychologist*, 55, 637–646.

Cramer, P. (2006). *Protecting the self: Defense mechanisms in action*. New York: Guilford Press.

Crano, W. D., & Prislin, R. (2006). Attitudes and persuasion. *Annual Review of Psychology*, 57, 345–374.

Craske, M. G., & Barlow, D. H. (2008). Panic disorder and agoraphobia. In D. H. Barlow (Ed.), *Clinical handbook of psychological disorders: A step-by-step treatment manual* (pp. 1–64). New York: Guilford Press.

Craske, M. G., & Waters, A. M. (2005). Panic disorder, phobias, and generalized anxiety disorder. *Annual Review of Clinical Psychology*, 1, 197–225.

Crocker, J., Thompson, L. L., McGraw, K. M., & Ingerman, C. (1987). Downward comparison, prejudice, and evaluations of others: Effects of self-esteem and threat. *Journal of Personality and Social Psychology*, 52, 907–916.

Croft, R. J., Klugman, A., Baldeweg, T., & Gruzelier, J. H. (2001). Electrophysiological evidence of serotonergic impairment in long-term MDMA ("ecstasy") users. *American Journal of Psychiatry*, 158, 1687–1692.

Crosscope-Happel, C., Hutchins, D. E., Getz, H. G., & Hayes, G. L. (2000). Male anorexia nervosa: A new focus. *Journal of Mental Health Counselling*, 22, 365–370.

Croucher, S. (2017). Integrated threat theory. In *Oxford research encyclopedia of communication*. Available at: http://communication.oxfordre.com/view/10.1093/acrefore/9780190228613.001.0001/acrefore-9780190228613-e-490 (accessed September 18, 2017).

Curtis, R. C., & Miller, K. (1986). Believing another likes or dislikes you: Behaviors making the beliefs come true. *Journal of Personality and Social Psychology*, 51(2), 284–290.

Czeisler, C. A., Duffy, J. F., Shanahan, T. L., et al. (1999). Stability, precision, and near-24-hour period of the human circadian pacemaker. *Science*, 284, 2177–2181.

Czeisler, C. A., Zimmerman, J. C., Ronda, J. M., et al. (1980). Timing of REM sleep is coupled to the circadian rhythm of body temperature in man. *Sleep*, 2, 329–346.

Dabbs, J. M., & Morris, R. (1990). Testosterone, social class, and antisocial behavior in a sample of 4462 men. *Psychological Science*, 1, 209–211.

Dabbs, J. M. Jr., Riad, J. K., & Chance, S. E. (2001). Testosterone and ruthless homicide. *Personality and Individual Differences*, 31, 599–603.

Dani, J. A. (2015). Neuronal nicotinic acetylcholine receptor structure and function and response to nicotine. *International Review of Neurobiology*, 124, 3–19.

Dannefer, D. (2003). Cumulative advantage/disadvantage and the life course: Cross-fertilizing age and social science theory. *The Journals of Gerontology: Social Sciences*, 58B(6), S327–S337.

Danner, D. D., Snowdon, D. A., & Friesen, W. V. (2001). Positive emotions in early life and longevity: Findings from the nun study. *Journal of Personality and Social Psychology*, 80(5), 804–813.

Dasgupta, N., & Greenwald, A. G. (2001). On the malleability of automatic attitudes: Combating automatic prejudice with images of admired and disliked individuals. *Journal of Personality and Social Psychology*, 81(5), 800–814.

Davis, J. I., Senghas, A., & Ochsner, K. N. (2009). How does facial feedback modulate emotional experience? *Journal of Research in Personality*, 43(5), 822–829.

Davis, M., & Whalen, P. J. (2001). The amygdala: Vigilance and emotion. *Molecular Psychiatry*, 6(1), 13–34.

Davison, G. C., Neale, J. M., & Kring, A. M. (2004). *Abnormal psychology* (9th ed.). New York: John Wiley & Sons, Inc.

DeNeve, K. M., & Cooper, H. (1998). The happy personality: A metaanalysis of 137 personality traits and subjective well-being. *Psychological Bulletin*, 124, 197–229.

Denrell, J. (2005). Why most people disapprove of me: Experience sampling in impression formation. *Psychological Review*, 112, 951–978.

Derryberry, D., & Tucker, D. M. (1994). Motivating the focus of attention. In P. M. Niedenthal, & S. Kitayama (Eds.), *The heart's eye: Emotional influence in perception and attention* (pp. 167–196). San Diego, CA: Academic Press.

Deutsch, J. A., & Deutsch, D. (1963). Attention: Some theoretical considerations. *Psychological Review*, 70(1), 80–90.

Deutsch, M., & Collins, M. E. (1951). *Interracial housing: A psychological evaluation of a social experiment*. Minneapolis, MN: University of Minnesota Press.

Devine, P. G. (1989). Overattribution effect: The role of confidence and attributional complexity. *Social Psychology Quarterly*, 52(2), 149–158.

Diamond, L. M. (2004). Emerging perspectives on distinctions between romantic love and sexual desire. *Current Directions in Psychological Science*, 13, 116–119.

Diehl, M., & Stroebe, W. (1987). Productivity loss in brainstorming groups: Toward the solution of a riddle. *Journal of Personality and Social Psychology*, 53, 497–509.

Diener, E. (1984). Subjective well-being. *Psychological Bulletin*, 95, 542–575.

Diener, E., Nickerson, C., Lucas, R. E., & Sandvik, E. (2002). Dispositional affect and job outcomes. *Social Indicators Research*, 59, 229–259.

Diener, E., & Seligman, M. E. P. (2004). Beyond money: Toward an economy of well-being. *Psychological Science in the Public Interest*, 5, 1–31.

Dijk D.J., & Lockley S. W. (2002). Integration of human sleep-wake regulation and circadian rhythmicity. *Journal of Applied Physiology*, 92(2), 852–862.

Dishion, T. J., & Tipsord, J. M. (2011). Peer Contagion in child and adolescent social and emotional development. *Annual Review of Psychology*, 62, 189–214.

Dixon, J. F., & Hokin, L. E. (1998). Lithium acutely inhibits and chronically up-regulates and stabilizes glutamate uptake by presynaptic nerve endings in mouse cerebral cortex. *Proceedings of the National Academy of Sciences of the U.S.A.* 95(14), 8363–8368.

Dohrenwend, B. P. (2006). Inventorying stressful life events as risk factors for psychopathology: Toward resolution of the problem of intracategory variability. *Psychological Bulletin*, 132(3), 477–495.

Dollard, J., Doob, L. W., Miller, N. E., Mowrer, O. H., & Sears, R. R. (1939). *Frustration and aggression*. New Haven, CT: Yale University Press.

Domhoff, G. W. (1996). *Finding meaning in dreams: A quantitative approach*. New York: Plenum Publishing Co.

Domhoff, G. W. (2003). *The scientific study of dreams: Neural networks, cognitive development, and content analysis*. Washington, DC: American Psychological Association.

Domhoff, G. W. (2007). Realistic simulation and bizarreness in dream content: Past findings and suggestions for future research. In D. Barrett, & P. McNamara (Eds.), *The new science of dreaming: Content, recall, and personality correlates* (vol. 2, pp. 1–27). Westport, CT: Praeger.

Domjan, M. (2006). *The principles of learning and behavior* (5th ed.). Belmont, CA: Cengage Learning/ Wadsworth.

Dougherty, D. D., & Rauch, S. L. (2007). Brain correlates of antidepressant treatment outcome from neuroimaging studies in depression. *Psychiatric Clinics of North America*, 30, 91–103.

Dovidio, J. F., Brigham, J. C., Johnson, B. T., & Gaertner, S. (1996). Stereotyping, prejudice, and discrimination: Another look. In C. N. Macrae, C. Stangor, & M. Hewstone (Eds.), *Stereotypes and stereotyping* (pp. 276–319). New York: Guilford Press.

Dovidio, J. F., Gaertner, S. L., & Kawakami, K. (2010). Racism. In J. F. Dovidio, M. Hewstone, P. Glick, & V. M. Esses (Eds.), *The SAGE handbook of prejudice, stereotyping and discrimination* (pp. 312–327). London: Sage.

Dovidio, J. F., Kawakami, K., Johnson, C., Johnson, B., & Howard, A. (1997). On the nature of prejudice: Automatic and controlled processes. *Journal of Experimental Social Psychology*, 33, 510–540.

Dovidio, J. F., Piliavin, J. A., Schroeder, D. A., & Penner, L. (2006). *The social psychology of prosocial behavior*. Mahwah, NJ: Lawrence Erlbaum Associates.

Drouyer, E., Rieux, C., Hut, R. A., & Cooper, H. M. (2007). Responses of suprachiasmatic nucleus neurons to light and dark adaptation: Relative contributions of melanopsin and rod–cone inputs. *The Journal of Neuroscience*, 27(36), 9623–9631.

Duclos, S. E., Laird, J. D., Schneider, E., Sexter, M., Stern, L., & Van Lighten, L. (1989). Emotion-specific effects of facial expressions and postures on emotional experience. *Journal of Personality and Social Psychology*, 57, 100–108.

Duncan, G. J., Ziol-Guest, K. M., & Kalil, A. (2010). Early-childhood poverty and adult attainment, behavior, and health. *Child Development*, 81(1), 306–325.

Dunkel Schetter, C. (2011). Psychological science on pregnancy: Stress processes, biopsychosocial models, and emerging research issues. *Annual Review of Psychology*, 62, 531–558.

Dunning, D. (2001). On the motives underlying social cognition. In A. Tesser, & N. Schwarz (Eds.), *Blackwell handbook of social psychology: Intraindividual processes* (pp. 348–374). Oxford: Blackwell.

Dunning, D., Leuenberger, A., & Sherman, D. A. (1995). A new look at motivated inference: Are self-serving theories of success a product of motivational forces? *Journal of Personality and Social Psychology*, 69, 58–68.

Durmer, J. S., & Dinges, D. F. (2005). Neurocognitive consequences of sleep deprivation. *Seminars in Neurology*, 25(1), 117–129.

Eagle, M. N. (2011). *From classical to contemporary psychoanalysis: A critique and integration*. New York: Taylor & Francis.

Eagly, A. H., & Chaiken, S. (1993). *The psychology of attitudes*. Fort Worth, TX: Harcourt, Brace, & Janovich.

Eastman, C. I., Gazda, C. J., Burgess, H. J., Crowley, S. J., & Fogg, L. F. (2005). Advancing circadian rhythms before eastward flight: A strategy to prevent or reduce jet lag, *Sleep*, 28, 33–44.

Easton, C. J., Mandel, D., & Babuscio, T. (2007). Differences in treatment outcome between male alcohol-dependent offenders of domestic violence with and without positive drug screens. *Addictive Behaviors*, 32, 2151–2163.

Eastwick, P. W., Eagly, A. H., Finkel, E. J., & Johnson, S. E. (2011). Implicit and explicit preferences for physical attractiveness in a romantic partner: A double dissociation in predictive validity. *Journal of Personality and Social Psychology*, 101, 993–1011.

Eastwick, P. W., Finkel, E. J., Mochon, D., & Ariely, D. (2007). Selective versus unselective romantic desire: Not all reciprocity is created equal. *Psychological Science*, 18(4), 317–319.

Eidelson, R. J., & Eidelson, J. I. (2003). Dangerous ideas. Five beliefs that propel groups toward conflict. *American Psychologist*, 58(3), 182–192.

Eisenberg, N., Cumberland, A., & Spinrad, T. L. (1998). parental socialization of emotion. *Psychological Inquiry*, 9(4), 241–273.

Eisenberger, N. I., Way, B. M., Taylor, S. E., Welch, W. T., & Lieberman, M. D. (2007). Understanding genetic risk for aggression: Clues from the brain's response to social exclusion. *Biological Psychiatry*, 61, 1100–1108.

Ekman, P. (1992a). Are there basic emotions? *Psychological Review*, 99(3), 550–553.

Ekman, P. (1992b). An argument for basic emotions. *Cognition and Emotion*, 6(3/4), 169–200.

Ekman, P., & Davidson, R. J. (1993). Voluntary smiling changes regional brain activity. *Psychological Science*, 4, 342–345.

Elder, G. H. Jr. (1995). The life course paradigm: Social change and individual development. In P. Moen, G. H. Elder, Jr., & K. Liischer (Eds.), *Examining lives in context: Perspectives on the ecology of human development* (pp. 101–139). Washington, DC: APA Press.

Elliott, R., Watson, J. C., & Goldman, R. N. (2004a). Empty-chair work for unfinished interpersonal issues. In R. Elliott, & J. Watson (Eds.), *Learning emotion-focused therapy: The process-experiential approach to change* (pp. 243–265). Washington, DC: American Psychological Association.

Elliott, R., Watson, J. C., & Goldman, R. N. (2004b). Two-chair work for conflict splits. In R. Elliott, & J. Watson (Eds.), *Learning emotion-focused therapy: The process-experiential approach to change* (pp. 219–241). Washington, DC: American Psychological Association.

Ellis, B. J., Jackson, J. J., & Boyce, W. T. (2006). The stress response system: Universality and adaptive individual differences. *Developmental Review*, 26, 175–212.

El Mansari, M., & Blier, P. (1997). In vivo electrophysiological characterization of 5-HT receptors in the guinea pig head of a caudate nucleus and orbiotofrontal cortex. *Neuropharmacology*, 36, 577–88.

Elwood, L. S., Hahn, K. S., Olatunji, B. O., & Williams, N. L. (2009). Cognitive vulnerabilities to the development of PTSD: A review of four vulnerabilities and the proposal of an integrative vulnerability model. *Clinical Psychology Review*, 29, 87–100.

Emanuele, E., Politi, P., Bianchi, M., Minoretti, P., Bertona, M., & Geroldi, D. (2006). Raised plasma nerve growth factor levels associated with early-stage romantic love. *Psychoneuroendocrinology*, 31, 288–294.

Entringer, S., Epel, E. S., Kumsta, R., Lin, J., Hellhammer, D. H., et al. (2011). Stress exposure in intrauterine life is associated with shorter telomere length in young adulthood. *Proceedings of the National Academy of Sciences of the U.S.A.* 108(33): E513–E518.

Eriksson, C. B., Kemp, H. V., Gorsuch, R. et al. (2001). Trauma exposure and PTSD symptoms in international relief and development personnel. *Journal of Traumatic Stress*, 14, 205–212.

Ernst, F. H. (1971). The OK Corral: The grid for get-on-with. *Transactional Analysis Journal*, 1(4), 231–240.

Ersoy, B., Balkan, C., & Gunnay, T. (2005). The factors affecting the relation between the menarcheal age of mother and daughter. *Child: Care, Health and Development*, 31, 303–308.

Esses, V. M., Jackson, L. M., Dovidio, J. F., & Hodson, G. (2005). Instrumental relations among groups: Group competition, conflict, and prejudice. In J. F. Dovidio, P. Glick, & L. A. Rudman (Eds.), *On the nature of prejudice: Fifty years after Allport*. Oxford: Blackwell Publishing Ltd,

Evans, C. (1983). *Landscapes of the night: How and why we dream*. New York: Viking Press.

Fabiano, G. A., Schatz, N. K., Aloe, A. M., Chacko, A., & Chronis-Tuscano, A. (2015). A systematic review of meta-analyses of psychosocial treatment for attention-deficit/hyperactivity disorder. *Clinical Child and Family Psychology Review*, 18(1), 77–97.

Fahs, B. (2007). Second shifts and political awakenings: Divorce and the political socialization of middle-aged women. *Journal of Divorce & Remarriage*, 47(3–4), 43–66.

Falicov, C. J. (2003). Culture, society, and gender in depression. *Journal of Family Therapy*, 25, 371–387.

Farmer, A., Elkin, A., & McGuffin, P. (2007). The genetics of bipolar affective disorder. *Current Opinion in Psychiatry*, 20(1), 8–12.

Farrell, B. A. (1981). *The standing of psychoanalysis*. Oxford: Oxford University Press.

Fazio, R. H. (1990). Multiple processes by which attitudes guide behavior: The MODE model as an integrative framework. In M. P. Zanna (Ed.), *Advances in experimental social psychology* (vol. 23, pp. 75–109). New York: Academic Press.

Feist, J., & Feist, G. J. (2010). *Theories of personality* (7th ed.). New York: McGraw-Hill.

Feldman, B. L., & Russell, J. A. (1999). The structure of current affect controversies and emerging consensus. *Current Directions in Psychological Science*, 8(1), 10–14.

Feldman, S. (2003), Enforcing social conformity: a theory of authoritarianism. *Political Psychology*, 24, 41–74.

Ferguson, C. J., & Beaver, K. M. (2009). Natural born killers: The genetic origins of extreme violence. *Aggression and Violent Behavior*, 14, 286–294.

Ferguson, M. L., & Katkin, E. S. (1996). Visceral perception, anhedonia, and emotion. *Biological Psychology*, 42(1–2), 131–145.

Festinger, L. A. (1954). A theory of social comparison processes. *Human Relations*, 2, 117–140.

Festinger, L. A. (1957). *A theory of cognitive dissonance*. Evanston, IL: Row, Peterson.

Figueredo, A. J., Sefcek, J. A., & Jones, D. N. (2006). The ideal romantic partner personality. *Personality and Individual Differences*, 41(3), 431–441.

Fischer, A. H. (2000). *Gender and emotion: Social psychological perspectives*. Cambridge: Cambridge University Press.

Fischer, A. H., Rodriguez, P. M., van Vianen, E. A. M., & Manstead, A. S. R. (2004). Gender and culture differences in emotion. *Emotion*, 4, 87–94.

Fisher, S., & Greenberg, R. (1977). *The scientific credibility of Freud's theories and therapy*. New York: Basic Books.

Fisher, S., & Greenberg, R. (1996). *Freud scientifically appraised*. New York: John Wiley & Sons, Inc.

Fiske, A. P., Kitayama, S., Markus, H. R., & Nisbett, R. E. (1998). The cultural matrix of social psychology. In D. Gilbert, S. Fiske, & G. Lindzey (Eds.), *The handbook of social psychology* (4th ed.). Hillsdale, NJ: Erlbaum.

Fiske, S. T. (1993). Social cognition and social perception. *Annual Review of Psychology*, 44, 155–194.

Fiske, S. T. (2004). *Social beings*. Hoboken, NJ: John Wiley & Sons, Inc.

Fiske, S. T. (2010). *Social beings: Core motives in social psychology* (2nd ed.). Hoboken, NJ: John Wiley & Sons, Inc.

Fiske, S. T., Cuddy, A. J., Glick, P., & Xu, J. (2002). A model of (often mixed) stereotype content: Competence and warmth respectively follow from perceived status and competition. *Journal of Personality and Social Psychology*, 82(6), 878–902.

Flack, W. (2006). Peripheral feedback effects of facial expressions, bodily postures, and vocal expressions on emotional feelings. *Cognition & Emotion*, 20, 177–195.

Flack, W., Laird, J. D., & Cavallaro, L. A. (1999). Separate and combined effects of facial expressions and bodily postures on emotional feelings. *European Journal of Social Psychology*, 29, 203–217.

Flanagan, D. P., & Dixon, S. G. (2013). The Cattell-Horn-Carroll Theory of cognitive abilities. In D. P. Flanagan (Ed.), *Encyclopedia of special education* (pp. 368–382). Hoboken, NJ: John Wiley & Sons.

Forgas, J. P. (2008). Affect and cognition. *Perspectives on Psychological Science*, 3, 94–101.

Forgas, J. P., Dunn, E., & Granland, S. (2008). Are you being served …? An unobtrusive experiment of affective influences on helping in a department store. *European Journal of Social Psychology*, 38, 333–342.

Forney, K. J., Buchman-Schmitt, J. M., Keel, P. K., & Frank, G. K. W. (2016). The medical complications associated with purging. *The International Journal of Eating Disorders*, 49(3), 249–259.

Forsyth, D. R. (2010). *Group dynamics* (5th ed.). Belmont, CA: Wadsworth Cengage Learning.

Foulkes, D. (1985). *Dreaming: A cognitive-psychological analysis*. Hillsdale, NJ: Erlbaum.

Foulkes, D. (1999). *Children's dreaming and the development of consciousness*. Cambridge, MA: Harvard University Press.

Fowler, J. H. & Christakis, N. A. (2008). Dynamic spread of happiness in a large social network: Longitudinal analysis over 20 years in the Framingham Heart Study. *British Medical Journal*, 337, 2338.

Fox, J. A. & DeLateur, M. J. (2014). Mass shootings in America: Moving beyond Newtown. *Homicide Studies*, 18(1), 121–145.

Fozard, J. L., Vercruyssen, M., Reynolds, S. L., & Hancock, P. A. (1994). Age differences and changes in reaction time: The Baltimore longitudinal study of aging. *Journals of Gerontology*, 49(4), 179–189.

Frager, R. (1970). Conformity and anti-conformity in Japan. *Journal of Personality and Social Psychology*, 15, 203–210.

Francis, A. (2013). *Saving normal: An insider's revolt against out-of-control psychiatric diagnosis, DSM-5, Big Pharma, and the medicalization of ordinary life*. New York: HarperCollins.

Frank, R. H. (2012). The Easterlin Paradox revisited. *Emotion*, 12, 1188–1191.

Frankenburg, W. K., Dodds, J., Archer, P., Shapiro, H., & Bresnick, B. (1992). The Denver II: A major revision and restandardization of the Denver Developmental Screening Test. *Pediatrics*, 89(1), 91–97.

Franklin, M., & Foa, E. (2008). Obsessive–compulsive disorder. In D. H. Barlow (Ed.), *Clinical handbook of psychological disorders* (pp. 164–215). New York: Guilford Press.

Fredrickson, B. (2001). The role of positive emotions in positive psychology: The broaden-and-build theory of positive emotions. *American Psychologist*, 56. 218–226.

Freeman, E. W. (2010). Associations of depression with the transition to menopause. *Menopause*, 17, 823–827.

Freud, A. (1937). *The ego and the mechanisms of defence*. London: Hogarth Press, and the Institute of Psycho-analysis.

Freud, A. (1946). *The ego and the mechanisms of defense*. New York: International Universities Press.

Freud, S. (1894). The neuro-psychoses of defence. In J. Strachey (Ed.), *The standard edition of the complete psychological works of Sigmund Freud* (vol. 3, pp. 41–61). London: Hogarth Press.

Freud, S. (1896). Further remarks on the neuro-psychoses of defence. In J. Strachey (Ed.), *The standard edition of the complete psychological works of Sigmund Freud* (vol. 3, pp. 157–185). London: Hogarth Press.

Freud, S. (1900). The interpretation of dreams. In J. Strachey (Ed.), *The standard edition of the complete psychological works of Sigmund Freud* (vol. 8). London: Hogarth Press.

Freud, S. (1915). The unconscious. In J. Strachey (Ed.), *The standard edition of the complete psychological works of Sigmund Freud* (vol. 14, pp. 159–204). London: Hogarth Press.

Freud, S. (1920). Beyond the pleasure principle. In J. Strachey (Ed.), *The standard edition of the complete psychological works of Sigmund Freud* (vol. 18, pp. 1–64). London: Hogarth Press.

Freud, S. (1925). Negation. In J. Strachey (Ed.), *The standard edition of the complete psychological works of Sigmund Freud* (vol. 19, pp. 235–239). London: Hogarth Press.

Freud, S. (1949). *An outline of psychoanalysis* (trans. J. Strachey). New York, W. W. Norton.

Friedman, E. M., Williams, D. R., Singer, B. H., & Ryff, C. D. (2009). Chronic discrimination predicts higher circulating levels of E-selectin in a national sample: The MIDUS Study. *Brain, Behavior & Immunity*, 23(5), 684–692.

Friedman, M., & Ulmer, D. (1985). *Treating type A behaviour and your heart*. London: Michael Joseph.

Frijda, N. H. (1986). *The emotions*. New York: Cambridge University Press.

Frydman, M. (1999). Television, aggressiveness and violence. *International Journal of Adolescent Medicine & Health*, 11(3–4), 335–344.

Fujita, F., & Diener, E. (2005). Life satisfaction set point: Stability and change. *Journal of Personality and Social Psychology*, 88, 158–164.

Fumeron, F., Betoulle, D., Aubert, R., Herbeth, B., Siest, G., & Rigaud, D. (2001). Association of a functional 5-HT transporter gene polymorphism with anorexia nervosa and food intake. *Molecular Psychiatry*, 6, 9–10.

Furnham, A., & Wu, J. (2008). Gender differences in estimates of one's own and parental intelligence in China. *Individual Differences Research*, 6(1), 1–12.

Gaertner, S. L., Mann, J., Murrell, A., & Dovidio, J. F. (1989). Reducing intergroup bias: The benefits of recategorization. *Journal of Personality and Social Psychology*, 57(2), 239–249.

Galderisi, S., Heinz, A., Kastrup, M., Beezhold, J., & Sartorius, N. (2015). Toward a new definition of mental health. *World Psychiatry*, 14(2), 231–233.

Gardner, H. (1983). *Frames of mind: The theory of multiple intelligences.* New York: Basic Books.

Gask, L., Evans, M., & Kessler, D. (2013). Personality disorder. *BMJ*, 347, f5276.

Gaskill, M. N., & Díaz, R. M. (1991). The relation between private speech and cognitive performance. *Journal for the Study of Education and Development*, 14(53), 45–58.

Gass, R. H., & Seiter, J. S. (2007). *Persuasion: Social influence and compliance gaining* (3rd ed.). Boston: Allyn & Bacon.

Gawronski, B., Deutsch, R., Mbirkou, S., Seibt, B., & Strack, F. (2008). When "just say no" is not enough: Affirmation versus negation training and the reduction of automatic stereotype activation. *Journal of Experimental Social Psychology*, 44, 370–377.

Ge, X., Kim, I. J., Brody, G. H., Conger, R. D., Simons, R. L., Gibbons, F. X., & Cutrona, C. E. (2003). It's about timing and change: Pubertal transition effects on symptoms of major depression among African American youths. *Developmental Psychology*, 39, 430–439.

Gelder, M., Gath, D., & Mayon, R. (1989). *The Oxford textbook of psychiatry* (2nd ed.). Oxford: Oxford University Press.

Gelder M., Mayou R. & Geddes J. (1999). *Psychiatry* (2nd ed.). Oxford: Oxford University Press.

Gendolla, G. H. E. (2000). On the impact of mood on behavior: An integrative theory and a review. *Review of General Psychology*, 4, 378–408.

Gentile, D. A. (2009). Pathological video game use among youth 8 to 18: A national study. *Psychological Science*, 20, 594–602.

Gentile, D. A., Anderson, C. A., Yukawa, S., Ihori, N., Saleem, M., Ming, L. K., Sakamoto, A. (2009). The effects of prosocial video games on prosocial behaviors: International evidence from correlational, longitudinal, and experimental studies. *Personality and Social Psychology Bulletin*, 35(6), 752–763.

Gentile, D. A., Reimer, R., Nathanson, A. I., & Walsh, D. A. (2014). Protective effects of parental monitoring of children's media use: A prospective study. *JAMA Pediatrics*, 168(5), 479–484.

Gentilucci, M., & Dalla Volta, R. (2007). The motor system and the relationships between speech and gesture. *Gesture*, 7, 159–177.

George, L. K. (1999). Life-course perspectives on mental health. In C. Aneshensel, & J. Phelan (Eds.), *Handbook of the sociology of mental health* (pp. 565–583). New York: Kluwer.

Gershoff, E. T. (2002). Corporal punishment by parents and associated child behaviors and experiences: A meta-analytic and theoretical review. *Psychological Bulletin*, 128, 539–579.

Gershoff, E. T. (2013). Spanking and child development: We know enough now to stop hitting our children. *Child Development Perspectives*, 7(3), 133–137.

Gershoff, E. T., Grogan-Kaylor, A., Lansford, J. E., Chang, L., Zelli, A., et al. (2010). Parent discipline practices in an international sample: Associations with child behaviors and moderation by perceived normativeness. *Child Development*, 81, 487–502.

Ghooi, R. B. (2014). Institutional review boards: Challenges and opportunities. *Perspectives in Clinical Research*, 5(2), 60–65.

Giancola, P. R., Duke, A. A., & Ritz, K. Z. (2011). Alcohol, violence, and the alcohol myopia model: Preliminary findings and implications for prevention. *Addictive Behaviors*, 36(10), 1019–1022.

Giancola, P. R., Josephs, R. A., Parrott, D. J., & Duke, A. A. (2010). Alcohol myopia revisited: Clarifying aggression and other acts of disinhibition through a distorted lens. *Perspectives on Psychological Science*, 5, 265–278.

Gibson, J. J. (1972). A theory of direct visual perception. In J. Royce, & W. Rozenboom (Eds.). *The psychology of knowing*. New York: Gordon & Breach.

Gilestro, G. F., Tononi, G., & Cirelli, C. (2009). Widespread changes in synaptic markers as a function of sleep and wakefulness in drosophila. *Science*, 324, 109–112.

Gilligan, C. (1982). *In a different voice: Psychological theory and women's development.* Cambridge, MA: Harvard University Press.

Gitlin, M., Nuechterlein, K., Subotnik, K., Ventura, J., Mintz, J., Fogelson, D., et al. (2001). Clinical outcome following neuroleptic discontinuation in patients with remitted recent-onset schizophrenia. *The American Journal of Psychiatry*, 158, 1835–1842.

Glaser, R., Kiecolt-Glaser, J. K., Speicher, C. E., & Holliday, J. E. (1985). Stress, loneliness, and changes in herpes virus latency. *Journal of Behavioral Medicine*, 8, 249–260.

Goldinger, S. D., Kleider, H. M., Azuma, T., & Beike, D. (2003). "Blaming the victim" under memory load. *Psychological Science*, 14, 81–85.

Goldstein, N. J., Cialdini, R. B., & Griskevicius, V. (2008). A room with a viewpoint: Using social norms to motivate environmental conservation in hotels. *Journal of Consumer Research*, 35(3), 472–482.

Good, T. L., & Brophy, J. E. (1990). *Educational psychology: A realistic approach* (4th ed.). White Plains, NY: Longman.

Gorman, J. M., Ken, J. M., Sullivan, G. M., & Coplan, J. D. (2000). Neuroanatomic hypothesis of panic disorder, revised. *The American Journal of Psychiatry*, 157, 493–505.

Gotlib, I. H., & Wheaton, B. (Eds.) (1997). *Stress and adversity over the life course.* Cambridge: Cambridge University Press.

Gottman, J. (2007). *Why marriages succeed or fail.* London: Bloomsbury.

Gould, S. J., & Lewontin, R. C. (1979). The spandrels of San Marco and the Panglossian paradigm: A critique of the adaptationist programme. *Proceedings of the Royal Society of London*, Series B, 205, 581–598.

Gove, W. R., & Tudor, J. F. (1973). Adult sex roles and mental illness. *American Journal of Sociology*, 78(4), 813–835.

Grack, C., & Richman, C. L. (1996). Reducing general and specific heterosexism through cooperative contact. *Journal of Psychology & Human Sexuality*, 8(4), 59–68.

Gray-Little, B., & Burks, N. (1983). Power and satisfaction in marriage: A review and critique. *Psychological Bulletin*, 93, 513–538.

Green, S. K., Buchanan, D. R. & Heuer, S. K. (1984). Winners, losers, and choosers: A field investigation of dating initiation. *Personality and Social Psychology Bulletin*, 10, 502–511.

Green, W., & Kowalick, S. (1997). Violence in child and adolescent psychiatry. *Psychiatric Annals*, 27, 745–749.

Greenwald, A. G. (1968). Cognitive learning, cognitive response to persuasion, and attitude change. In A. G. Greenwald, T. C., Brock, & T. M. Ostrom (Eds.), *Psychological foundations of attitudes.* New York: Academic Press.

Gregory, R. (1970). *The intelligent eye.* London: Weidenfeld and Nicolson.

Grigg-Damberger, M. (2007). Normal sleep: Impact of age, circadian rhythms, and sleep debt. *Lifelong Learning in Neurology*, 13(3), 31–84.

Griskevicius, V., Goldstein, N. J., Mortensen, C. R., Sundie, J. M., Cialdini, R. B., & Kenrick, D. T. (2009). Fear and loving in Las Vegas: Evolution, emotion, and persuasion. *Jounal of Market Research*, 46(3), 384–395.

Gross, J. J. (1998a). The emerging field of emotion regulation: An integrative review. *Review of general psychology.* Special issue: *New directions in research on emotion*, 2(3), 271–299.

Gross, J. J. (1998b). Antecedent- and response-focused emotion regulation: Divergent consequences for experience, expression, and physiology. *Journal of Personality and Social Psychology*, 74(1), 224–237.

Grossberg, S. (1995). The attentive brain. *American Scientist,* 83, 438–449.

Guehl, D., Benazzouz, A., Aouizerate, B., Cuny, E., Rotgé, J. Y., et al. (2008). Neuronal correlates of obsessions in the caudate nucleus. *Biological Psychiatry*, 63, 557–562.

Guilford, J. P. (1967). *The nature of human intelligence.* New York: McGraw-Hill.

Guilford, J. P. (1985). A sixty-year perspective on psychological I measurement. *Applied Psychological Measurement*, 9(4), 341–349.

Guilford, J. P. (1988). Some changes in the structure-of-intellect model. *Educational and Psychological Measurement*, 48(1), 1–4.

Gustaffson, J. E., & Undheim, J. O. (1996). Individual differences in cognitive functions. In D. C. Berliner, & R. C. Calfee (Eds.), *Handbook of educational psychology* (pp. 186–242). New York: Macmillan.

Gutheil, T. G., & Gabbard, G. O. (1993). The concept of boundaries in clinical practice: Theoretical risk-management. *The American Journal of Psychiatry*, 150, 188–196.

Hamilton, W. D. (1964). The evolution of social behavior: Parts I and II. *Journal of Theoretical Biology*, 7, 1–52.

Hammen, C. (2005). Stress and depression. *Annual Review of Clinical Psychology*, 1, 293–319.

Hammen, C., & Watkins, E. (2008). *Depression* (2nd ed.). Hove: Psychology Press.

Hammer, L. B., Grigsby, T. D., & Woods, S. (1998). The conflicting demands of work, family, and school among students at an urban university. *The Journal of Psychology*, 132(2), 220–226.

Haney, C., Banks, W. C., & Zimbardo, P. G. (1973). A study of prisoners and guards in a simulated prison. *Naval Research Review*, 30, 4–17.

Hankin, B. L., & Abela, J. R. Z. (Eds.). (2005). *Development of psychopathology: A vulnerability-stress perspective*. Thousand Oaks, CA: Sage.

Harman, S. M. (2005). Testosterone in older men after the Institute of Medicine Report: Where do we go from here? *Climacteric*, 8, 124–135.

Harris, J. A. (1999). Review and methodological considerations in research on testosterone and aggression. *Aggression and Violent Behavior*, 4, 273–291.

Harrison, P. J., & Owen, M. J. (2003). Genes for schizophrenia? Recent findings and their pathophysiological implications. *Lancet*, 361(9355), 417–419.

Hartwig, M., & Bond, C. F. (2011). Why do lie-catchers fail? A lens model meta-analysis of human lie judgments. *Psychological Bulletin*, 137(4), 643–659.

Hawkins, D. L., Pepler, D. J., & Craig, W. M. (2001). Naturalistic observations of peer interventions in bullying. *Social Development*, 10, 512–527.

Hayatbakhsh, M. R., Najman, J. M., McGee, T. R., Bor, W., & O'Callaghan, M. J. (2009). Early pubertal maturation in the prediction of early adult substance use: A prospective study. *Addiction*, 104(1), 59–66.

Haybron, D. (2005). On being happy or unhappy. *Philosophy and Phenomenological Research*, 71, 287–317.

Hayes, S. C., Villatte, M., Levin, M., & Hildebrandt, M. (2011). Open, aware, and active: Contextual approaches as an emerging trend in the behavioral and cognitive therapies. *Annual Review of Clinical Psychology*, 7, 141–168.

Hazan, C., & Shaver, P. R. (1987). Romantic love conceptualized as an attachment process. *Journal of Personality and Social Psychology*, 52(3), 511–524.

Hearold, S. L. (1987). Meta-analysis of the effects of television on social behavior. In G. Comstock (Ed.), *Public communication and behavior* (vol. 1). New York: Academic Press.

Hedge, A., & Yousif, Y. (1992). Effects of urban size, urgency, and cost on helpfulness: A cross-cultural comparison between the United Kingdom and the Sudan. *Journal of Cross-Cultural Psychology*, 23, 107–115.

Heider, F. (1946). Attitudes and cognitive organization. *The Journal of Psychology*, 21, 107–112.

Heider, F. (1958). *The psychology of interpersonal relations*. New York: Wiley.

Henchy, T., & Glass, D. C. (1968). Evaluation apprehension and the social facilitation of dominant and subordinant responses. *Journal of Personality and Social Psychology*, 10, 446–454.

Herek, G. M., & McLemore, K. A. (2013). Sexual prejudice. *Annual Review of Psychology*, 64, 309–333.

Hergenhahn, B. (2009). *Introduction to the history of psychology*. Belmont, CA: Wadsworth Cengage Learning.

Hettema, J. M., Neale, M. C., & Kendler, K. S. (2001). A review and meta-analysis of the genetic epidemiology of anxiety disorders. *The American Journal of Psychiatry*, 158(10), 1568–1578.

Hill, T., Smith, N. D., & Lewicki, P. (1989). The development of self-image bias: A real-world demonstration. *Personality and Social Psychology Bulletin*, 15(2), 205–211.

Hillis, S., Mercy, J., Amobi, A., et al. (2016). Global prevalence of past-year violence against children: A systematic review and minimum estimates. *Pediatrics*, 137(3), e20154079.

Hirshkowitz, M., Whiton, K., Albert, S. M., et al. (2015). National Sleep Foundation's sleep time duration recommendations: Methodology and results summary, *Sleep Health: Journal of the National Sleep Foundation*, 1(1), 40–43.

Hobson, J. A., & McCarley, R. W. (1977). The brain as a dream state generator: An activation–synthesis hypothesis of the dream process. *American Journal of Psychiatry*, 134, 1335–1348.

Hofmann, S. G., & Otto, M. W. (2008). *Cognitive-behavior therapy of social anxiety disorder: Evidence-based and disorder-specific treatment techniques*. New York: Routledge.

Hofstede, G. (1983). Dimensions of national cultures in fifty countries and three regions. In J. B. Deregowski, S. Dziurawiec, & R. C. Annis (Eds.), *Expectations in cross-cultural psychology* (pp. 335–355). Lisse, the Netherlands: Swets and Zeitlinger.

Hohmann, G. W. (1962). The effect of dysfunctions of the autonomic nervous system on experienced feelings and emotions. Paper presented at Emotions and Feelings conference, New School for Social Research, New York.

Hohmann, G. W. (1966). Some effects of spinal cord lesions on experienced emotional feelings. *Psychophysiology*, 3, 143–156.

Hollander, E., Braun, A., & Simeon, D. (2008). Should OCD leave the anxiety disorders in DSM-V? The case for obsessive compulsive-related disorders. *Depression and Anxiety*, 25(4), 317–329.

Holmes, D. S. (1987). The influence of meditation versus rest on physiological arousal: A second examination. In M. A. West (Ed.), *The psychology of meditation* (pp. 81–103). Oxford: Clarendon Press.

Hopper, K., & Wanderling, J. (2000). Revisiting the developed versus developing country distinction in course and outcome in schizophrenia: Results from ISoS, the WHO Collaborative Follow up Project. *Schizophrenia Bulletin*, 26, 835–846.

Horney, K. (1937). *The neurotic personality of our time*. New York: W.W. Norton & Company, Inc.

Horney, K. (1942). *Self-analysis*. New York: W. W. Norton and Company, Inc.

Horney, K. (1950). *Neurosis and human growth: The struggle toward self-realization*. New York: W.W. Norton & Company, Inc..

Horwitz, A. V., White, H. R., & Howell-White, S. (1996). The use of multiple outcomes in stress research: A case study of gender differences in responses to marital dissolution. *Journal of Health and Social Behavior*, 37(3), 278–291.

House, J. S., Kahn, R. L., McLeod, J. D., & Williams, D. (1985). Measures and concepts of social support. In S. Cohen, & S. L. Syme (Eds.), *Social support and health* (pp. 83–108). San Diego, CA: Academic Press.

Hout, M., & Greeley, A. (2012). Religion and happiness. In P. V. Marsden (Ed.), *Social trends in American life: Findings from the General Social Survey since 1972* (pp. 288–314). Princeton, NJ: Princeton University Press.

Howe, C. J. (1980). Learning language from mothers' replies. *First Language*, 1(2), 83–97.

Hull, C. (1943). *Principles of behavior*. New York: Appleton-Century-Crofts.

Humble, M. (2000). Noradrenaline and serotonin reuptake inhibition as clinical principles: A review of antidepressant efficacy. *Acta Psychiatrica Scandinavica Suppl.*, 402, 28–36.

Ilardi, S. S., & Feldman, D. (2001). The cognitive neuroscience paradigm: A unifying metatheoretical framework for the science and practice of clinical psychology. *Journal of Clinical Psychology*, 57, 1067–1088.

Inglehart, R., Foa, F., Peterson, C., & Welzel, C. (2008). Development, freedom, and rising happiness: A global perspective (1981–2007). *Perspectives on Psychological Science*, 3, 264–285.

International Schizophrenia Consortium (2008). Rare chromosomal deletions and duplications increase risk of schizophrenia. *Nature*, 455(7210), 237–41.

Irwin, C. E. Jr. (2005). Editorial: Pubertal timing: Is there any new news? *Journal of Adolescent Health*, 37, 343–344.

Isen, A. M. (1993). Positive affect and decision making. In M. Lewis, & J. Haviland (Eds.), *Handbook of emotion* (pp. 261–277). NewYork: Guilford Press.

Isenberg, D. J. (1986). Group polarization: A critical review and meta-analysis. *Journal of Personality and Social Psychology*, 50(6), 1141–1151.

Izard, C. E. (1990a). Facial expressions and the regulation of emotions. *Journal of Personality and Social Psychology*, 58, 487–498.

Izard, C. E. (1990b). The substrates and functions of emotion feelings: William James and current emotion theories. *Personality and Social Psychology Bulletin*, 16, 626–635.

Jackson, G. R., Felix, T., & Owsley, C. (2006). The scotopic sensitivity tester-1 and the detection of early age-related macular degeneration. *Ophthalmic and Physiological Optics*, 26(4), 431–437.

Jackson, G. R., Owsley, C., & McGwin, G. J. (1999). Aging and dark adaptation. *Vision Research*, 39(23), 3975–3982.

Jakovcevski, I., Filipovic, R., Mo, Z., Rakic, S., & Zecevic, N. (2009). Oligodendrocyte development and the onset of myelination in the human fetal brain. *Frontiers in Neuroanatomy*, 3, 5.

James. W. (1884). What is an emotion? *Mind*, 9, 188–205.

Janis, I. L. (1972). *Victims of groupthink: A psychological study of foreign policy decisions and fiascoes*. Boston: Houghton Mifflin Company.

Janis, I. L. (1982). *Groupthink: Psychological studies of policy decisions and fiascoes* (2nd ed.). Boston: Houghton Mifflin Company.

Jason, L. A., Pokorny, S. B., Sanem, J. R., & Adams, M. L. (2006). Monitoring and decreasing public smoking among youth. *Behavior Modification*, 30, 681–692.

Jemmott, III, J. B., Borysenko, M., Chapman, R., Borysenko, J. Z., McClelland, D. C., Meyer, D., & Benson, H. (1983). Academic stress, power motivation, and decrease in secretion rate of salivary secretory immunoglobulin A. *Lancet*, 321, 1400–1402.

Jenni, O. G., Borbély, A. A., & Achermann, P. (2004). Development of the nocturnal sleep electroencephalogram in human infants. *American Journal of Physiology – Regulatory Integrative Comparative Physiology*, 286, R528–R538.

Jensen, A. R. (1998). Human evolution, behavior, and intelligence. In A. R. Jensen, *The g factor: The science of mental ability*. Westport, CT: Praeger Publishers.

Johnson, E., & Tversky, A. (1983). Affect, generalization, and the perception of risk. *Journal of Personality and Social Psychology*, 45, 20–31.

Jonassen, D. H. (1991). Objectivism versus constructivism: Do we need a new philosophical paradigm? *Journal of Educational Research*, 39(3), 5–14.

Jones, E. E., & Davis, K. E. (1965). From acts to dispositions: The attribution process in social psychology, In L. Berkowitz (Ed.), *Advances in experimental social psychology* (vol. 2). New York: Academic Press.

Jones, E. E., Goethals, G. R., Kennington, G. E., & Severance, L. J. (1972). Primacy and assimilation in the attribution process: The stable entity proposition1. *Journal of Personality*, 40: 250–274.

Jost, J. T., & Hamilton, D. L. (2005). Stereotypes in our culture. In J. F. Dovidio, P. Glick and L. A. Rudman (Eds.), *On The Nature of Prejudice: Fifty years after Allport*. Oxford: Blackwell Publishing Ltd.

Juliano, L. M., & Griffiths, R. R. (2004). A critical review of caffeine withdrawal: Empirical validation of symptoms and signs, incidence, severity, and associated features. *Psychopharmacology*, 176, 1–29.

Julien, R. M. (2008). *A primer of drug action* (11th ed.). New York: Worth.

Kahn, J. R., & Pearlin, L. (2006). Financial strain over the life course and health among older adults. *Journal of Health and Social Behavior*, 47(1), 17–31.

Kahneman, D. (1973). *Attention and effort*. Englewood Cliffs, NJ: Prentice-Hall.

Kahneman, D., & Deaton, A. (2010). High income improves evaluation of life but not emotional well-being. *Proceedings of the National Academy of Sciences*, 107, 16489–16493.

Kalechstein, A. D., De La Garza, R., Mahoney, J. J., Fantegrossi, W. E., & Newton, T. F. (2007). MDMA use and metacognition: A meta-analytic review. *Psychopharmacology*, 189, 531–537.

Kassel, J. D., Stroud, L. R., & Paronis, C. A. (2003). Smoking, stress, and negative affect: Correlation, causation, and context across stages of smoking. *Psychological Bulletin*, 129(2), 270–304.

Kasser, T., Ryan, R. M., Couchman, C. E., & Sheldon, K. M. (2004). Materialistic values: Their causes and consequences. In T. Kasser, & A. D. Kanner (Eds.), *Psychology and consumer culture: The struggle for a good life in a materialistic world*. Washington, DC: American Psychological Association.

Katz, D. (1960). The functional approach to the study of attitudes. *Public Opinion Quarterly*, 24, 163–204.

Katz, P. A. (2003). Racists or tolerant multiculturalists? How do they begin? *American Psychologist*, 58(11), 897–909.

Kaufman, A. S. (1990). *Assessing adolescent and adult intelligence*. Boston: Allyn & Bacon.

Kawakami, K., Dovidio, J. F., Moll, J., Hermsen, S., & Russin, A. (2000). Just say no (to stereotyping): Effects of training in the negation of stereotypic associations on stereotype activation. *Journal of Personality and Social Psychology*, 78(5), 871–888.

Kazdin, A. E., & Weisz, J. R. (2003). *Evidence-based psychotherapies for children and adolescents*. New York: Guilford Press.

Kelley, H. H. (1967). Attribution theory in social psychology. In D. Levine (Ed.), *Nebraska symposium on motivation* (vol. 15, pp. 192–238). Lincoln, NE: University of Nebraska Press.

Kelley, H. H., Berscheid, E., Christensen, A., Harvey, J. H., Huston, T. L., et al. (1983). *Close relationships*. Clinton Corners, NY: Percheron.

Kelman, H. (1958). Compliance, identification, and internalization: Three processes of attitude change. *Journal of Conflict Resolution*, 2(1), 51–60.

Kemeny, M. E. (2003). The psychobiology of stress. *Current Directions in Psychological Science*, 12(4), 124–129.

Kenrick, D. T., Neuberg, S. L., & Cialdini, R. B. (2010). *Social psychology: Unraveling the mystery* (5th ed.). Boston: Allyn & Bacon.

Kepner, J. (2001). Touch in Gestalt body process psychotherapy: Purpose, practice, and ethics. *Gestalt Review*, 5, 97–114.

Kern, W., Dodt, C., Born, J., & Fehm, H. L. (1996). Changes in cortisol and growth hormone secretion during nocturnal sleep in the course of aging. *Journals of Gerontology, Series A, Biological Sciences and Medical Sciences*, 51(1), M3–M9.

Kernberg, O. F. (1978). *Object relations theory and clinical psychoanalysis*. New York: Jason Aronson.

Kernberg, O. F. (2004). *Contemporary controversies in psychoanalytic theory, techniques, and their applications*. New Haven, CT: Yale University Press.

Kesebir, P., & Diener, E. (2008). In pursuit of happiness: Empirical answers to philosophical questions. *Perspectives on Psychological Science*, 3, 117–125.

Kessler, R. C. (2003). The impairments caused by social phobia in the general population: Implications for intervention. *Acta Psychiatrica Scandinavica Suppl.*, 417, 19–27.

Kessler, R. C., Berglund, P., Demler, O., Jin, R., Merikangos, K. R., & Walters, E. E. (2005a). Lifetime prevalence and age of-onset distributions of DSM-IV disorders in the National Comorbidity Survey Replication. *Archives of General Psychiatry*, 62(6), 593–602.

Kessler, R. C., Chiu, W. T., Demler, O., Merikangas, K. R., & Walters, E. E. (2005b). Prevalence, severity, and comorbidity of 12-month DSM-IV disorders in the National Comorbidity Survey Replication. *Archives of General Psychiatry*, 62(6), 617–627.

Kessler, R. C., Chiu, W. T., Jin, R., Ruscio, A. M., Shear, K., & Walters, E. E. (2006). The epidemiology of panic attacks, panic disorder, and agoraphobia in the National Comorbidity Survey Replication. *Archives of General Psychiatry*, 63(4), 415–424.

Kessler, R. C., Demler, O., Frank, R. G., Olfson, M., Pincus, M. A., Walters, E. E., et al. (2005d). Prevalence and treatment of mental disorders, 1990 to 2003. *New England Journal of Medicine*, 352, 2515–2523.

Kessler, R. C., Mickelson, K. D., & Williams, D. R. (1999). The prevalence, distribution, and mental health correlates of perceived discrimination in the United States. *Journal of Health and Social Behavior*, 40(3), 208–230.

Kessler, R. C., Wittchen, H-U., Abelson, J. M., McGonagle, K. A., Schwarz, N., et al. (1998). Methodological studies of the Composite International Diagnostic Interview (CIDI) in the US National Comorbidity Survey. *International Journal of Methods in Psychiatric Research*, 7(1), 33–55.

Khan, S. S., & Liu, J. H. (2008). Intergroup attributions and ethnocentrism in the Indian subcontinent. *Journal of Cross-Cultural Psychology*, 39(1), 16–36.

Kheriaty. A. (2007). The return of the unconscious. *Psychiatric Annals*, 7(4), 285–287.

Kiecolt-Glaser, J. K., Garner, W., Speicher, C., Penn, G. M., Holliday, J., & Glaser, R. (1984). Psychosocial modifiers of immunocompetence in medical students. *Psychosomatic Medicine*, 46(1), 7–14.

Kiecolt-Glaser, J. K., McGuire, L., Robles, T. F., & Glaser, R. (2002). Psychoneuroimmunology and psychosomatic medicine: Back to the future. *Psychosomatic Medicine*, 64, 15–18.

Kiecolt-Glaser, J. K., Preacher, K. J., MacCallum, R. C., Atkinson, C., Malarkey, W. B., & Glaser, R. (2003). Chronic stress and age-related increases in the proinflammatory cytokine IL-6. *Proceedings of the National Academy of Sciences*, 100, 9090–9095.

Kiehl, K. A., Smith, A. M., Hare, R. D., Mendrek, A., Forster, B. B., et al. (2001). Limbic abnormalities in affective processing by criminal psychopaths as revealed by functional magnetic resonance imaging. *Biological Psychiatry*, 50(9), 677–684.

Kihlstrom, J. F., Mulvaney, S., Tobias, B. A., & Tobis, I. P. (2000). The emotional unconscious. In E. Eich, J. F. Kihlstrom, G. H. Bower, J. P. Forgas, & P. M. Niedenthal (Eds.), *Cognition and emotion*. New York: Oxford University Press.

Kirsch, I., Lynn, S. J., Vigorito, M., & Miller, R. R. (2004). The role of cognition in classical and operant conditioning. *Journal of Clinical Psychology*, 60(4), 369–392.

Kitayama, S., Markus, H. R., & Kurokawa, M. (2000). Culture, emotion, and well-being: Good feelings in Japan and the United States. *Cognition & Emotion*, 14, 93–124.

Klein, R. (1991). Age-related eye disease, visual impairment, and driving in the elderly. *Human Factors*, 33(5), 521–525.

Kline, D. W., Kline, T. J., Fozard, J. L., & Kosnik, W. (1992). Vision, aging, and driving: The problems of older drivers. *Journals of Gerontology*, 47(1), P27–P34.

Klinesmith, J., Kasser, T., & McAndrew, F. T. (2006). Guns, testosterone, and aggression: An experimental test of a mediational hypothesis. *Psychological Science*, 17(7), 568–571.

Klonsky, E. D., Oltmanns, T. F., & Turkheimer, E. (2003). Deliberate self-harm in a nonclinical population: Prevalence and psychological correlates. *The American Journal of Psychiatry*, 160, 1501–1508.

Kniffin, K. M, & Wilson, D. S. (2004). The effect of nonphysical traits on the perception of physical attractiveness. *Evolution and Human Behavior*, 25(2), 88–101.

Knudsen, E. I. (2007). Fundamental components of attention. *Annual Review of Neuroscience*, 30, 57–78.

Kohlberg, L. (1969). The cognitive developmental approach to socialization. In A. Goslin (Ed.), *Handbook of socialization theory and research*. Chicago: Rand McNally.

Kohlberg, L. (1976). Moral stages and moralization: The cognitive developmental approach. In T. Lickona (Ed.), *Moral development and behavior: Theory, research and social issues* (pp. 31–53). New York: Holt, Rinehart and Winston.

Kraepelin, E. (1896). *Psychiatrie: Ein Lehrbuch für Studierende und Aerzte* (5th ed.). Leipzig, Germany: Johann Ambrosius Barth.

Kraepelin, E. (1902). *Clinical psychiatry: A textbook for students and physicians*. Abstracted from the 6th German edn of *Lehrbuch der Psychiatrie*. New York: Macmillan.

Kraus, G., & Reynolds, D. J. (2001). The "A-B-C's" of the cluster B's: Identifying, understanding, and treating cluster B personality disorders. *Clinical Psychology Review*, 21(3), 345–373.

Krause, N., & Borawski-Clark, E. (1995). Social class differences in social support among older adults. *Gerontologist*, 35(4), 498–508.

Krieger, J., & Higgins, D. L. (2002). Housing and health: Time again for public health action. *American Journal of Public Health*, 92, 758–768.

Kristenson, M., Eriksen, H. R., Sluiter, J. K., Starke, D., & Ursin, H. (2004). Psychobiological mechanisms of socioeconomic differences in health. *Social Science & Medicine*, 58(8), 1511–1522.

Krosnick, J. A., Judd, C. M., & Wittenbrink, B. (2005). The measurement of attitudes. In D. Albarracín, B. T. Johnson, & M. P. Zanna (Eds.), *The handbook of attitudes* (pp. 21–76). Mahwah, NJ: Lawrence Erlbaum.

Krueger, R. F., & Markon, K. E. (2006). Understanding psychopathology: Melding behavior genetics, personality, and quantitative psychology to develop an empirically based model. *Current Directions in Psychological Science*, 15, 113–117.

Kruger, D. J. (2003). Evolution and altruism: Combining psychological mediators with naturally selected tendencies. *Evolution and Human Behavior*, 24, 118–125.

Kruger, J., & Gilovich, T. (2004). Actions, intentions, and self-assessment: The road to self-enhancement is paved with good intentions. *Personality and Social Psychology Bulletin*, 30(3), 328–339.

Kuhl, P. (2004). Early language acquisition: Cracking the speech code. *Nature Reviews Neuroscience*, 5, 831–843.

Kuhl, P., Williams, K. A., Lacerda, F., Stevens, K. N., & Lindblom, B. (1992). Linguistic experience alters phonetic perception in infants by 6 months of age. *Science*, 255, 606–608.

Kuhn, C. M., & Wilson, W. A. (2001). Our dangerous love affair with Ecstasy. *Cerebrum*, 3(2), 22–33.

Kuiken, D., & Sikora, S. (1993). The impact of dreams on waking thoughts and feelings. In A. Moffitt, M. Kramer, & R. Hoffman, (Eds.), *The functions of dreaming* (pp. 419–476). Albany, NY: State University of New York Press.

Kumkale, G. T., & Albarracín, D. (2004). The sleeper effect in persuasion: A meta-analytic review. *Psychological Bulletin*, 130(1), 143–172.

Kurtines, W., & Greif, E. B. (1974). The development of moral thought: Review and evaluation of Kohlberg's approach. *Psychological Bulletin*, 81(8), 453–470.

Lack, C. W. (2015). The etiology of obsessive-compulsive disorder. In C. W. Lack (Ed.), *Obsessive-compulsive disorder: Etiology, phenomenology, and treatment*. Fareham: Onus Books.

Lagerspetz, K. M. J., & Lagerspetz, K. Y. H. (1983). Genes and aggression. In E. C. Simmel, M. E. Hahn, & J. K. Walters (Eds.), *Aggressive behavior: Genetic and neural approaches* (pp. 89–102). Hillsdale, NJ: Erlbaum.

Lam, D., & Wong, G. (2005). Prodromes, coping strategies and psychological interventions in bipolar disorders. *Clinical Psychology Review*, 25(8), 1028–1042.

Lambert, M. J., & Bergin, A. E. (1994). The effectiveness of psychotherapy. In A. E. Bergin & S. L. Garfield (Eds.), *Handbook of psychotherapy and behavior change*. New York: John Wiley & Sons, Inc.

Lambert, M. J., Shapiro, D. A., & Bergin, A. E. (1986). The effectiveness of psychotherapy. In S. L. Garfield & A. E. Bergin (Eds.), *Handbook of psychotherapy and behavior change* (pp. 157–212). New York: John Wiley & Sons, Inc.

Larzelere, R. E. (2000). Child outcomes of nonabusive and customary physical punishment by parents: An updated literature review. *Clinical Child and Family Psychology Review*, 3, 199–221.

Larzelere, R. E., & Kuhn, B. R. (2005). Comparing child outcomes of physical punishment and alternative disciplinary tactics: A meta-analysis. *Clinical Child and Family Psychology Review*, 8(1), 1–37.

Laumann, E. O. (1969). Friends of urban men: An assessment of accuracy in reporting their socioeconomic attributes, mutual choice, and attitude development. *Sociometry*, 32, 54–69.

Laviolette, S. R., & van der Kooy, D. (2004). The neurobiology of nicotine addiction: Bridging the gap from molecules to behaviour. *Nature Reviews Neuroscience*, 5(1), 55–65.

Lavoie, B, & Parent, A. (1990). Immunohistochemical study of the serotoninergic innervations of the basal ganglia in the squirrel monkey. *Journal of Comparative Neurology*, 299, 1–16.

Lawson, H. M., & Leck, K. (2006). Dynamics of internet dating. *Social Science Computer Review*, 24(2), 189–208.

Lazarus, R. S. (1991). Cognition and motivation in emotion. *American Psychologist*, 46(4), 352–367.

Lazarus, R. S. (1995). Emotions express a social relationship, but it is an individual mind that creates them. *Psychological Inquiry*, 6, 253–265.

Lazarus, R. S., & Folkman, S. (1984). *Stress, appraisal, and coping*. New York: Springer.

LeDoux, J. E. (1995). Setting "stress" into motion. In M. J. Friedman, D. S. Charney, & A. Y. Deutch (Eds.), *Neurobiological and clinical consequences of stress: From normal adaptation to PTSD* (pp. 125–134). New York: Raven Press.

LeDoux, J. E. (1996). *The emotional brain*. New York: Simon & Schuster.

LeDoux, J. E. (2000). Emotion circuits in the brain. *Annual Review of Neuroscience*, 23, 155–184.

Lee, L., Loewenstein, G., Ariely, D., Hong, J., & Young, J. (2008). If I'm not hot, are you hot or not? Physical attractiveness evaluations and dating preferences as a function of one's own attractiveness. *Psychological Science*, 19, 669–677.

Lehman, B. J., & Crano, W. D. (2002). The pervasive effects of vested interest on attitude–criterion consistency in political judgment. *Journal of Experimental Social Psychology*, 38, 101–112.

Leiblum, S. R., & Rosen, R. C. (2000). *Principles and practice of sex therapy* (3rd ed.). New York: Guilford Press.

Leonardo, E. D., & Hen, R. (2006). Genetics of affective and anxiety disorders. *Annual Review of Psychology*, 57, 117–137.

Lerner, J. S., & Keltner, D. (2001). Fear, anger, and risk. *Journal of Personality and Social Psychology*, 81(1), 146–159.

Lerner, M. (1980). *The belief in a just world: A fundamental delusion*. New York: Plenum Press.

Levenson, R. W. (2014). The autonomic nervous system and emotion. *Emotion Review*, 6, 100–112.

Levenson, R. W., Ekman, P., & Friesen, W. V. (1990). Voluntary facial action generates emotion specific autonomic nervous system activity. *Psychophysiology*, 27, 363–384.

Levenson, R. W., Ekman, P., Heider, K., & Friesen, W. V. (1992). Emotion and autonomic nervous system activity in the Minangkabau of West Sumatra. *Journal of Personality and Social Psychology*, 62, 972–988.

Levin, R., & Nielsen, T. A. (2007). Disturbed dreaming, posttraumatic stress disorder, and affect distress: A review and neurocognitive model. *Psychological Bulletin*, 133, 482–528.

Levine, L. E., & Munsch, J. (2018). *Child development: An active learning approach*. Thousand Oaks, CA: SAGE.

Levine, R., Reysen, S., & Ganz, E. (2008). The kindness of strangers revisited: A comparison of 24 U.S. cities. *Social Indicators*, 85, 461–481.

Levine, R., Sato, S., Hashimoto, T., & Verma, J. (1995). Love and marriage in eleven cultures. *Journal of Cross-Cultural Psychology*, 26(5), 554–571.

Lim, R. F. (Ed.). (2006). *Clinical manual of cultural psychiatry*. Alexandria, VA: American Psychiatric Association.

Lips, H. M. (2016). *A new psychology of women: Gender, culture and ethnicity* (4th ed.). Long Grove, IL: Waveland Press.

Locke, E. A., & Latham, G. P. (1990). *A theory of goal setting and task performance*. Upper Saddle River, NJ: Prentice Hall.

Lorenz, K. (1935). Der Kumpan in der Umwelt des Vogels. Der Artgenosse als auslösendes Moment sozialer Verhaltensweisen. *Journal für Ornithologie*, 83, 137–215, 289–413.

Lovaas, O. I., & Smith, T. (2003). Early and intensive behavioral intervention in autism. In A. E. Kazdin, & J. R. Weisz (Eds.), *Evidence-based psychotherapies for children and adolescents* (pp. 325–340). New York: Guilford Press.

Luborsky, L., & Barrett, M. S. (2006). The history and empirical status of key psychoanalytic concepts. *Annual Review of Clinical Psychology*, 2, 1–19.

Luo, S., & Zhang, G. (2009). What leads to romantic attraction: similarity, reciprocity, security, or beauty? Evidence from a speed-dating study. *Journal of Personality*, 77, 933–964.

Lydon, J., Fitzsimons, G., & Naidoo, L. (2003). Devaluation versus enhancement of attractive alternatives: A critical test. *Personality and Social Psychology Bulletin*, 29, 349–359.

Lykken, D. T., & Tellegen, A. (1996). Happiness is a stochastic phenomenon. *Psychological Science*, 7, 186–189.

Lyubomirsky, S. (2012). New love: A short shelf life. *The New York Times*, Sunday Review, December 2, pp. 1, 6.

Lyubomirsky, S., Sheldon, K. M., & Schkade, D. (2005). Pursuing happiness: The architecture of sustainable change. *Review of General Psychology*, 9, 111–131.

Maas, J. B., & Robbins, R. S. (2010). *Sleep for success: Everything you must know about sleep but are too tired to ask*. Bloomington, IN: Author House.

Macdonald, G., & Leary, M. R. (2005). Why does social exclusion hurt? The relationship between social and physical pain. *Psychological Bulletin*, 131(2), 202–223.

Machado-Vieira, R., Manji, H. K., & Zarate, C. A., Jr (2009). The role of lithium in the treatment of bipolar disorder: Convergent evidence for neurotrophic effects as a unifying hypothesis. *Bipolar Disorders*, 11(Suppl. 2), 92–109.

Macrae, C. N., & Quadflieg, S. (2010). Perceiving people. In S. T. Fiske, D. T. Gilbert, & G. Lindzey (Eds.). *Handbook of social psychology* (5th ed., vol. 1, pp. 428–463). Hoboken, NJ: John Wiley & Sons, Inc.

Macrae, C. N., Quinn, K. A., Mason, M. F., & Quadflieg, S. (2005). Understanding others: The face and person construal. *Journal of Personality and Social Psychology*, 89, 686–695.

Madon, S., Guyll, M., Spoth, R. L., & Willard, J. (2004). Self-fulfilling prophecies: The synergistic accumulation of parents' beliefs on children's drinking behavior. *Psychological Science*, 15, 837–845.

Magnus, K., Diener, E., Fujita, F., & Pavot, W. (1993). Extraversion and neuroticism as predictors of objective life events: A longitudinal study. *Journal of Personality and Social Psychology*, 65, 1046–1053.

Mahler, M., Pine, F., & Bergman, A. (1975). *The psychological birth of the human infant*. New York: Basic Books.

Maier, S. F., Amat, J., Baratta, M. V., Paul, E., & Watkins, L. R. (2006). Behavioral control, the medial prefrontal cortex, and resilience. *Dialogues in Clinical Neuroscience*, 8(4), 397–406.

Maier, S. F., & Watkins, L. R. (2005). Stressor controllability and learned helplessness: The roles of the dorsal raphe nucleus, serotonin, and corticotropin releasing factor. *Neuroscience & Biobehavioral Reviews*, 29(4–5), 829–841.

Main, M., & Hesse, E. (1990). Parents' unresolved traumatic experiences are related to infant disorganized attachment status. In M. T. Greenberg, D. Cicchetti, & E. M. Cummings (Eds.), *Attachment in the preschool years* (pp. 161–181). Chicago: University of Chicago Press.

Main, M., & Solomon, J. (1986). Discovery of a new, insecure-disorganized/disoriented attachment pattern. In M. Yogman, & T. B. Brazelton (Eds.), *Affective development in infancy* (pp. 95–124). Norwood, NJ: Ablex.

Maio, G., Haddock, G., Manstead, A., & Spears, R. (2010). Attitudes and intergroup relations In J. F. Dovidio, M. Hewstone, P. Glick, & V. M. Esses (Eds.), *Handbook of prejudice, stereotyping, and discrimination* (pp. 261–275). London: Sage.

Mann, J. J., Waternaux, C., Haas, G. L., et al. (1999). Toward a clinical model of suicidal behavior in psychiatric patients. *The American Journal of Psychiatry*, 156, 181–9.

Marcia, J. E. (1966). Development and validation of ego identity status. *Journal of Personality and Social Psychology*, 3, 551–558.

Margolin, G., & Gordis, E. B. (2000). The effects of family and community violence on children. *Annual Review of Psychology*, 51, 445–479.

Markus, H. (1977). Self-schemata and processing information about the self. *Journal of Personality and Social Psychology*, 35, 63–78.

Markus, H. R., Kitayama, S., & Heiman, R. J. (1996). Culture and "basic" psychological principles. In E. T. Higgins, & A. W. Kruglanski (Eds.), *Social psychology: Handbook of basic principles* (pp. 857–913). New York: Guilford Press.

Marmarosh, C., Holtz, A., & Schottenbauer, M. (2005). Group cohesiveness, group-derived collective self-esteem, group-derived hope, and the well-being of group therapy members. *Group Dynamics: Theory, Research, & Practice*, 9(1), 32–44.

Marshall, M. J. (2002). *Why spanking doesn't work: Stopping this bad habit and getting the upper hand on effective discipline*. Springville, UT: Bonneville Books.

Martin, J. A., & Penn, D. L. (2002). Attributional style in schizophrenia: An investigation in outpatients with and without persecutory delusions. *Schizophrenia Bulletin*, 28(1), 131–141.

Maslow, A. H. (1943). A theory of human motivation. *Psychological Review*, 50(4), 370–396.

Maslow, A. H. (1954). *Motivation and personality*. New York: Harper & Row.

Maslow, A. H. (1968). *Toward a psychology of being*. New York: D. Van Nostrand Company.

Maslow, A. H. (1970). *Motivation and personality* (2nd ed.). New York: Harper & Row.

Matson, J. L., & Lovullo, S. V. (2008). A review of behavioral treatments for self-injurious behaviors of persons with autism spectrum disorders. *Behavior Modification*, 32(1), 61–76.

Matson, J. L., & Smith, K. R. M. (2007). Current status of intensive behavioral interventions for young children with autism and PDD-NOS. *Research in Autism Spectrum Disorders*, 2(1): 60–74.

Matsumoto, D. (2001). Emotion in Asia: Linking theories and data around the world. *Asian Journal of Social Psychology*, 4, 163–164.

Matthes, J., Schemer, C., & Wirth, W. (2007). More than meets the eye: Investigating the hidden impact of brand placements in television magazines. *International Journal of Advertising*, 26(4), 477–503.

Mayford, M, Siegelbaum, S. A., & Kandel, E. R. (2012). Synapses and memory storage. *Cold Spring Harbor Perspectives in Biology*, 4, a005751.

Mazur, A, & Booth, A. (1998).Testosterone and dominance in men. *Behavioral and Brain Sciences*, 21(3), 353–363.

McAndrew, F. T. (2009). The interacting roles of testosterone and challenges to status in human male aggression. *Aggression and Violent Behavior*, 14(5), 330–335.

McConnell, A. R., Rydell, R. J., Strain, L. M., & Mackie, D. M. (2008). Forming implicit and explicit attitudes toward individuals: Social group association cues. *Journal of Personality and Social Psychology*, 94(5), 792–807.

McDermott, R., Tingley, D., Cowden, J., Frazzetto, G., & Johnson, D. D. P. (2009). Monoamine oxidase A gene (MAOA) predicts behavioral aggression following provocation. *Proceedings of the National Academy of Sciences of the U.S.A.*, 106(7), 2118–2123.

McElhaney, K. B., Porter, M. R., Thompson, L. W., & Allen, J. P. (2008). Apples and oranges: Divergent meanings of parents' and adolescents' perceptions of parental influence. *Journal of Early Adolescence*, 28(2), 206–229.

McGrew, K. S. (2009). CHC theory and the human cognitive abilities project: Standing on the shoulders of the giants of psychometric intelligence research. *Intelligence*, 37(1), 1–10.

McNally, R. J. (2003). *Remembering trauma*. Cambridge, MA: Belknap Press of Harvard University Press.

McWilliams, N. (2009). *Psychoanalytic diagnosis* (2nd ed.). New York: Guilford Press.

Meddis, R. (1975). On the function of sleep. *Animal Behaviuor*, 23(3), 676–691.

Mednick, S., Volavka, J., Gabrielli, W. F., et al. (1981). EEG as a predictor of antisocial behavior. *Criminology*, 19, 219–231.

Mehrabian, A., & Blum, J. S. (2003). Physical appearance, attractiveness, and the mediating role of emotions. In N. J. Pallone (Ed.), *Love, romance, sexual interaction: Research perspectives from current psychology*. New Brunswick, NJ: Transaction Publishers.

Meichenbaum, D., Henshaw, D., & Himel, N. (1982). Coping with stress as a problem-solving process. In H. W. Krohne, & L. Laux (Eds.), *Achievement, stress, and anxiety*. Washington, DC: Hemisphere.

Menaghan, E. G. (1983). Individual coping efforts and family studies: Conceptual and methodological issues. *Marriage and Family Review*, 6, 113–135.

Mendoza, J. E., & Foundas, A. (2007). *Clinical neuroanatomy: A neurobehavioral approach*. New York: Springer Science & Business Media.

Merikangas, K. R., He, J., Burstein, M., Swanson, S. A., Avenevoli, S., Cui, L., … Swendsen, J. (2010). Lifetime prevalence of mental disorders in US adolescents: Results from the National Comorbidity Study-Adolescent Supplement (NCS-A). *Journal of the American Academy of Child and Adolescent Psychiatry*, 49(10), 980–989.

Merton, R. K. (1968). *Social theory and social structure*. New York: The Free Press.

Mesoudi, A. (2009). How cultural evolutionary theory can inform social psychology and vice versa. *Psychological Review*, 116(4), 929–952.

Meyer, G. J., Finn, S. E., Eyde, L. D., Kay, G. G., Moreland, K. L., Dies, R. R., & Reed, G. M. (2001). Psychological testing and psychological assessment: A review of evidence and issues. *American Psychologist*, 56(2), 128.

Miklowitz, D. J., & Craighead, W. E. (2007). Psychosocial treatment for bipolar disorder. In P. E. Nathan, & J. M. Gorman (Eds.), *A guide to treatments that work* (3rd ed., pp. 309–322). Oxford: Oxford University Press.

Miklowitz, D. J., & Johnson, S. L. (2006). The psychopathology and treatment of bipolar disorder. *Annual Review of Clinical Psychology*, 2, 199–235.

Miklowitz, D. J., & Johnson, S. L. (2007). Bipolar disorder. In M. Hersen, S. M. Turner, & D. C. Beidel (Eds.), *Adult psychopathology and diagnosis* (5th ed., pp. 317–348). Hoboken, NJ: Wiley.

Mikulincer, M. & Shaver, P. R. (2001). Attachment theory and intergroup bias: Evidence that priming the secure base schema attenuates negative reactions to out-groups. *Journal of Personality and Social Psychology*, 81, 97–115.

Miller, B. L. & Cummings, J. L. (2007). *The human frontal lobes: Functions and disorders* (2nd ed.). New York: Guilford Press.

Miller, G. (1956). The magical number seven, plus or minus two: Some limits on our capacity for processing information. *The Psychological Review*, 63, 81–97.

Miller, G. A., Galanter, E., & Pribram, K. H. (1960). Plans and the structure of behavior. *Systems Research and Behavioral Science*, 5, 341–342.

Miller, N. E., & Bugelski, R. (1970). The influence of frustration imposed by the in-group on attitudes expressed toward out-groups. In R. I. Evans, & R. M. Rozelle (Eds.), *Social psychology in life*. Boston: Allyn & Bacon.

Miller, R. S., Perlman, D., & Brehm, S. S. (2007). *Intimate relationships*. Boston: McGraw-Hill Higher Education.

Millet, B., Dondaine, T., Reymann, J. M., Bourguignon, A., Naudet, F., et al. (2013). Obsessive compulsive disorder networks: Positron emission tomography and neuropsychology provide new insights. *PLoS One*, 8(1), e53241.

Mindell, J. A., & Barrett, K. M. (2002). Nightmares and anxiety in elementary-aged children: Is there a relationship? *Child: Care, Health and Development*, 28, 317–322.

Mirowsky, J., & Ross, C. E. (2003). *Education, social status, and health*. New Brunswick, NJ: Aldine Transaction.

Miyamoto, S., Stroup, T. S., Duncan, G. E., Aoba, A., & Lieberman, J. A. (2003). Acute pharmacologic treatment of schizophrenia. In S. R. Hirsch, & D. R. Weinberger (Eds.), *Schizophrenia* (2nd ed., pp. 442–473). Oxford: Blackwell Science.

Moghaddam, F. M. (2002). *The individual and society: A cultural integration.* New York: Worth Publishers.

Mokdad, A. H., Marks, J. S., Stroup, D. F., & Gerberding, J. L. (2004). Actual causes of death in the United States, 2000. *Journal of the American Medical Association*, 291, 1238–1245.

Monteith, M. J., Ashburn-Nardo, L., Voils, C. I., & Czopp, A. M. (2002). Putting the brakes on prejudice: On the development and operation of cues for control. *Journal of Personality and Social Psychology*, 83, 1029–1050.

Monteith, M. J., Lybarger, J. E., & Woodcock, A. (2009). Schooling the cognitive monster: The role of motivation in the regulation and control of prejudice. *Social and Personality Compass*, 3, 211–226.

Montero, I., & de Dios, M. (2006). Vygotsky was right. An experimental approach to the study of the relationship between private speech and task performance. *Estudios de Psicologia*, 27, 175–189.

Montgomery, C., & Fisk, J. E. (2008). Ecstasy-related deficits in the updating component of executive processes. *Human Psychopharmacology*, 23, 495–511.

Montoya, R. M. (2008). I'm hot, so I'd say you're not: The influence of objective physical. *Personality and Social Psychology Bulletin*, 34(10), 1315–1331.

Moore, R. Y. (2007). Suprachiasmatic nucleus in sleep–wake regulation. *Sleep Medicine*, 8, 27–33.

Morgan, J. P. (Ed.). (2005). *Psychology of aggression.* Hauppauge, NY: Nova Science Publishers.

Morris, J. S., Ohman, A., & Dolan, R. J. (1999). A subcortical pathway to the right amygdala mediating "unseen" fear. *Proceedings of the National Academy of Sciences of the U.S.A.*, 96(4), 1680–1685.

Moscovici, S., & Nemeth, C. (1974). Minority influence. In C. Nemeth (Ed.), *Social psychology: Classic and contemporary integrations*, Chicago: Rand McNally.

Moskowitz, G. B. (2010). On the control over stereotype activation and stereotype inhibition. *Social and Personality Psychology Compass*, 4(2), 140–158.

Moskowitz, G. B., & Ignarri, C. (2009). Implicit volition and stereotype control. *European Review of Social Psychology*, 20, 97–145.

Moskowitz, G. B., Salomon, A. R., & Taylor, C. M. (2000). Implicit control of stereotype activation through the preconscious operation of egalitarian goals. *Social Cognition*, 18, 151–177.

Motivala, S. J., & Irwin, M. R. (2007). Sleep and immunity cytokine pathways linking sleep and health outcomes. *Current Directions in Psychological Science*, 16(1), 21–25.

Mozak, H. H. (1984). Adlerian psychotherapy. In R. Corsini (Ed.) *Current psychotherapies*. Illinois: F. E. Peacock Publishers, Inc.

Müller, M. J., Bosy-Westphal, A., & Heymsfield, S. B. (2010). Is there evidence for a set point that regulates human body weight? *F1000 Medicine Reports*, 2, 59.

Muris, P., Steerneman, P., Merckelbach, H., & Meesters, C. (1996). The role of parental fearfulness and modeling in children's fear. *Behaviour Research and Therapy*, 34(3), 265–268.

Murphy, H. B. M. (1978). The meaning of symptom check-list scores in mental health surveys: A testing of multiple hypotheses. *Social Science and Medicine*, 12, 67–75.

Mustanski, B. S., Viken, R. J., Kaprio, J., Pulkkinen, L., & Rose, R. J. (2004). Genetic and environmental influences on pubertal development: Longitudinal data from Finnish twins at ages 11 and 14. *Developmental Psychology*, 40, 1188–1198.

Myers, D. G. (1992). *The pursuit of happiness: Who is happy and why.* New York: Morrow.

Myers, D. G. (1999). Close relationships and quality of life. In D. Kahneman, E. Diener, & N. Schwarz (Eds.), *Well-being: The foundations of hedonic psychology*. New York: Russell Sage Foundation.

Myers, D. G. (2008). *Exploring psychology* (9th ed.. Special update for DSM-5). New York: Worth Publishers.

Myers, D. G., & Bishop, G. D. (1970). Discussion effects on racial attitudes. *Science*, 169(3947), 778–779.

Myers, D. G., & Lamm, H. (1976). *Psychological Bulletin*, 83, 602–627.

Nakao, M., & Yano, E. (2006). Prediction of major depression in Japanese adults: Somatic manifestations of depression in annual health examinations. *Journal of Affective Disorders*, 90, 29–35.

National Institute on Aging (2007). Exercise and physical activity. Bethesda, MD: U.S. Department of Health and Human Services, National Institutes of Health.

Neisser, U. (1967). *Cognitive psychology.* New York: Appleton–Century–Crofts.

Nelson, T. D. (2006). *The psychology of prejudice* (2nd ed.). New York: Allyn & Bacon.

Nemeth, C. J. (1986). The differential contributions of majority and minority influence. *Psychological Review*, 93, 23–32.

Nettelbeck, T., & Burns, N. R. (2010). Processing speed, working memory and reasoning ability from childhood to old age. *Personality and Individual Differences*, 48(4), 379–384.

Newcomb, T. M. (1953). An approach to the study of communicative acts. *Psychological Review*, 60, 393–404.

Newcomb, T. M. (1968). Interpersonal balance. In R. P. Abelson, E. Aronson, W. J. McGuire, T. M. Newcomb, M. J. Rosenberg, & P. H. Tannenbaum (Eds.), *Theories of cognitive consistency: A source book* (pp. 28–51). Chicago: Rand McNally.

Newheiser, A. K., Hewstone, M., Voci, A., Schmid, K., Zick, A., & Küpper, B. (2013). Social-psychological aspects of religion and prejudice: Evidence from survey and experimental research. In S. Clarke, R. Powell, & J. Savulescu (Eds.), *Religion, intolerance, and conflict: A scientific and conceptual investigation* (pp. 107–125). Oxford: Oxford University Press.

Newton, J. H., & McGrew, K. S. (2010). Introduction to the special issue: Current research in Cattell–Horn–Carroll–based assessment. *Psychology in the Schools*, 47(7), 621–634.

Ng, D. M., & Jeffery, R. W. (2003). Relationships between perceived stress and health behaviors in a sample of working adults. *Health Psychology*, 22(6), 638–642.

Nichols, M. P. (2007). *Family therapy: Concepts and methods* (8th ed.). Boston: Allyn & Bacon.

Nickerson, C., Schwarz, N., Diener, E., & Kahneman, D. (2003). Zeroing in on the dark side of the American dream: A closer look at the negative consequences of the goal for financial success. *Psychological Science*, 14, 531–536.

Nielsen, T. A., & Stenstrom, P. (2005). What are the memory sources of dreaming? *Nature*, 437(7063), 1286–1289.

Nielsen, T. A., Stenstrom, P., & Levin, R. (2006). Nightmare frequency by age, gender and 9/11: Findings from an Internet questionnaire. *Dreaming*, 16, 145–158.

Nielson, D., Goldman, D., Virkkunen, M., et al. (1994). Suicidality and 5-hydroxyindoleacetic acid concentration associated with a tryptophan hydroxylase polymorphism. *Archives of General Psychiatry*, 51, 34–38.

Nocon, A., Wittchen, H-U., Pfister, H., Zimmermann, P., & Lieb, R. (2006). Dependence symptoms in young cannabis users? A prospective epidemiological study. *Journal of Psychiatric Research*, 40, 394–403.

Norcross, J. C., Hedges, M., & Castle, P. H. (2002). Psychologists conducting psychotherapy in 2001: A study of Division 29 membership. *Psychotherapy: Theory, Research, Practice, Training*, 39, 97–102.

Norman, D. A. (1968). Toward a theory of memory and attention. *Psychological Review*, 75(6), 522–536.

North, M. S., & Fiske, S. T. (2013). A prescriptive, intergenerational-tension ageism scale: Succession, identity, and consumption (SIC). *Psychological Assessment*, 25(3), 706–713.

Norton, M. I., Frost, J. H., & Ariely, D. (2007). Less is more: The lure of ambiguity, or why familiarity breeds contempt. *Journal of Personality and Social Psychology*, 92(1), 97–105.

Nutt, D., Wilson, S., & Paterson, L. (2008). Sleep disorders as core symptoms of depression. *Dialogues in Clinical Neuroscience*, 10(3), 329–336.

O'Donovan, A., Tomiyama A. J., Lin, J., Puterman, E., Adler, N. E., Kemeny, M., Epel, E. S. (2012). Stress appraisals and cellular aging: A key role for anticipatory threat in the relationship between psychological stress and telomere length. *Brain, Behavior, and Immunity*, 26(4), 573–579.

Oetzel, R. (1966). Classified summary of research on sex differences. In E. E. Maccoby (Ed.), *The development of sex differences*. Stanford, CA: Stanford University Press.

Ogden, T. H. (1982). *Projective identification and psychotherapeutic technique*. New York: J. Aronson.

Ohayon, M. M., Carskadon, M. A., Guilleminault, C., & Vitiello, M. V. (2004). Meta-analysis of quantitative sleep parameters from childhood to old age in healthy individuals: Developing normative sleep values across the human lifespan. *Sleep*, 27(7), 1255–1273.

Ohman, A., Carlsson, K., Lundqvist, D., & Ingvar, M. (2007). On the unconscious subcortical origin of human fear. *Physiology and Behavior*, 92(1–2), 180–185.

Oliveira, M. A., Hsu, J., Park, J., Clark, J. E., & Shim, J.K. (2008). Age-related changes in multi-finger interactions in adults during maximum voluntary finger force production tasks. *Human Movement Science*, 27, 714–727.

Olson, J. M., & Zanna, M. P. (1993). Attitudes and attitude change. *Annual Review of Psychology*, 44, 117–154.

Olsson, C. A., McGee, R., Nada-Raja, S, & Williams, S. M. (2012). A 32-year longitudinal study of child and adolescent pathways to well-being in adulthood. *Journal of Happiness Studies*, 13, 1–15.

Olweus, D., Mattsson, A., Schalling, D., & Low, H. (1988). Circulating testosterone levels and aggression in adolescent males: A causal analysis. *Psychosomatic Medicine*, 50, 261–272.

Oquendo, M. A., & Mann, J. J. (2000). The biology of impulsivity and suicidality *Psychiatric Clinics of North America*, 23, 11–25.

Osgood, C. E., & Tannenbaum, P. H. (1955). The principle of congruity in the prediction of attitude change. *Psychological Review*, 62, 42–55.

Oskamp, S., & Schultz, P. W. (2005). *Attitudes and opinions* (3rd ed.). Mahwah, NJ: Erlbaum.

Packer, D. J. (2008). Identifying systematic disobedience in Milgram's obedience experiments: A meta-analytic review. *Perspectives on Psychological Science*, 3(4), 301–304.

Papa, M. J., Singhal, A., Law, S., Pant, S., Sood, S., Rogers, E. M., et al. (2000). Entertainment-education and social change: An analysis of parasocial interaction, social learning, collective efficacy and paradoxical communication, *Journal of Communication*, 50, 31–55.

Park, M. J., Mulye, T. P., Adams, S. H., Brindis, C. D., & Irwin, C. E. J. (2006). The health status of young adults in the United States. *Journal of Adolescent Health*, 39(3), 305–317.

Parkinson, B., & Totterdell, P. (1999). Classifying affect-regulation strategies. *Cognition and Emotion*, 13, 277–303.

Parmar, A., & Sarkar, S. (2016). Neuroimaging studies in obsessive compulsive disorder: A narrative review. *Indian Journal of Psychological Medicine*, 38(5), 386–394.

Pascual, A., & Guéguen, N. (2005). Foot-in-the-door and door-in-the-face: A comparative meta-analytic study. *Psychological Reports*, 96(1), 122–128.

Pattyn, N., Neyt, X., Henderickx, D., & Soetens, E. (2008). Psychophysiological investigation of vigilance decrement: Boredom or cognitive fatigue? *Physiology & Behavior*, 93, 369–378.

Paulhus, D. L., Fridhandler, B., & Hayes, S. (1997). Psychological defense: Contemporary theory and research. In R. Hogan, J. Johnson, & S. Briggs (Eds.), *Handbook of personality*. New York: Academic Press.

Pearlin, L. I. (1999). Stress and mental health: A conceptual overview. In A. V. Horwitz, & T. L. Scheid (Eds.), *A handbook for the study of mental health: Social contexts, theories, and systems* (pp. 161–175). New York: Cambridge University Press.

Pearlin, L. I., Menaghan, E. G., Lieberman, M. A., & Mullan, J. T. (1981). The stress process. *Journal of Health and Social Behavior*, 22, 337–356.

Pearlin, L. I., Schieman, S., Fazio, E., & Meersman, S. (2005). Stress, health, and the life course: Some conceptual perspectives. *Journal of Health and Social Behavior*, 46(2), 205–219.

Peleg, G., Katzir, G., Peleg, O., Kamara, M., Brodsky, L., et al. (2006). Hereditary family signature of facial expression. *Proceedings of the National Academy of Sciences*, 103, 15921–15926.

Penner, L. A., Dovidio, J. F., Piliavin, J. A., & Schroeder, D. A. (2005). Prosocial behavior: Multilevel perspectives. *Annual Review of Psychology*, 56, 365–392.

Penner, L. A., Fritzsche, B. A., Craiger, J. P., & Freifeld, T. R. (1995). Measuring the prosocial personality. In J. Butcher, & C. D. Spielberger (Eds.), *Advances in personality assessment* (vol. 10, pp. 147–163). Hillsdale, NJ: Lawrence Erlbaum Associates.

Perez, L. A., Peynircioglu, F., & Blaxton, T. A. (1998). Developmental differences in implicit and explicit memory performance. *Journal of Experimental Children Psychology*, 70, 167–185.

Perls, F. S. (1969). *Ego, hunger and aggression: The beginning of Gestalt therapy*. New York: Random House.

Perls, F. S., Hefferline, R. F., & Goodman, P. (1951). *Gestalt therapy*. New York: Julian Press.

Pesant, N., & Zadra, A. (2004). Working with dreams in therapy: What do we know and what should we do? *Clinical Psychology Review*, 24, 489–512.

Peterson, L. R., & Peterson, M. J. (1959). Short-term retention of individual verbal items. *Journal of Experimental Psychology*, 58, 193–198.

Petitto, L. A., Holowka, S., Sergio, L. E., Levy, B., & Ostry, D. J. (2004). Baby hands that move to the rhythm of language: Hearing babies acquiring sign languages babble silently on the hands. *Cognition*, 93, 43–73.

Petrova, P. K., Cialdini, R. B., & Sills, S. J. (2007). Personal consistency and compliance across cultures. *Journal of Experimental Social Psychology*, 43, 104–111.

Pettigrew, T. F. (1979). The ultimate attribution error: Extending Allport's cognitive analysis of prejudice. *Personality and Social Psychology Bulletin*, 5, 461–476.

Pettigrew, T. F., Tropp, L. R., Wagner, U., & Christ, O. (2011). Recent advances in intergroup contact theory. *International Journal of Intercultural Relations*, 35(3), 271–280.

Phelan, J. C., Link, B. G., & Tehranifar, P. (2010). Social conditions as fundamental causes of health inequalities: Theory, evidence, and policy implications. *Journal of Health and Social Behavior*, 51(1 suppl.), S28–S40.

Phelps, E. A. (2006). Emotion and cognition: Insights from studies of the human amygdala. *Annual Review of Psychology*, 57, 27–53.

Phelps, E. A., & LeDoux, J. E. (2000). Emotional networks in the brain. In M. Lewis, & J. M. Haviland-Jones (Eds.), *Handbook of emotions* (2nd ed.). New York: Guilford Press.

Phelps E. A., O'Connor K. J., Gatenby C., Gore ,J. C., Grillon, C., & Davis M. (2001). Activation of the left amygdala to a cognitive representation of fear. *Nature Neuroscience*, 4, 437–441.

Piaget, J. (1954). *The construction of reality in the child*. New York: Basic Books.

Piaget, J. (1965). *The moral judgment of the child*. New York: Free Press.

Pillemer, K., & Suitor, J. J. (2008). Collective ambivalence: Considering new approaches to the complexity of intergenerational relations. *The Journals of Gerontology, Series B: Psychological Sciences and Social Sciences*, 63, S94–S96.

Pinel, J. P. J. (1993). *Biopsychology* (2nd ed.). Boston: Allyn & Bacon.

Plant, E. A., Kling, K. C., & Smith, G. L. (2004). The influence of gender and social role on the interpretation of facial expressions. *Sex Roles*, 51, 187–196.

Plomin, R., & Asbury, K. (2005). Nature and nurture: Genetic and environmental influences on behavior. *The Annals of the American Academy of Political and Social Science*, 600(1), 86–98.

Plomin, R., & McGuffin, P. (2003). Psychopathology in the postgenomic era. *Annual Review of Psychology*, 54, 205–228.

Plutchik, R., Kellerman, H., & Conte, H. R. (1979). A structural theory of ego defences and emotions. In C. E. Izard (Ed.), *Emotions in personality and psychopathology* (pp. 229–257). New York: Plenum Press.

Pollatos, O., Kirsch, W., & Schandry, R. (2005). On the relationship between interoceptive awareness, emotional experience, and brain processes. *Cognitive Brain Research*, 25(3), 948–962.

Porter, S., & ten Brinke, L. (2008). Reading between the lies: Identifying concealed and falsified emotions in universal facial expressions. *Psychological Science*, 19(5), 508–514.

Poulsen, P., Esteller, M., Vaag, A., & Fraga, M. F. (2007). The epigenetic basis of twin discordance in age-related diseases. *Pediatric Research*, 61(5, Part 2), 38R–42R.

Prinzmetal, W. (1995). Visual feature integration in a world of objects. *Current Directions in Psychological Science*, 4, 90–94.

Quadflieg, S., & Macrae, C. N. (2011). Stereotypes and stereotyping: What's the brain got to do with it? *European Review of Social Psychology*, 22, 215–273.

Rachlin, H., & Jones, B. A. (2008). Altruism among relatives and non-relatives. *Behavioural Processes*, 79, 120–123.

Racsmány, M., Conway, M. A., & Demeter, G. (2010). Consolidation of episodic memories during sleep: Long-term effects of retrieval practice. *Psychological Science*, 21, 80–85.

Radloff, L. S. (1977). The CES-D scale: A self-report depression scale for research in the general population. *Applied Psychological Measurement*, 1, 385–401.

Raine, A. (2005). The interaction of biological and social measures in the explanation of antisocial and violent behavior. In D. M. Stoff, & E. J. Susman (Eds.), *Developmental psychobiology of aggression*. New York: Cambridge University Press.

Raine, A., Buchsbaum, M., & LaCasse, L. (1997). Brain abnormalities in murderers indicated by positron emission tomography *Biological Psychiatry*, 42, 495–508.

Rajmohan, V., & Mohandas, E. (2007). The limbic system. *Indian Journal of Psychiatry*, 49(2), 132–139.

Ranganathan, V. K., Siemionow, V., Sahgal, V., & Yue, G. H. (2001). Effects of aging on hand function. *Journal of the American Geriatrics Society*, 49(11), 1478–1484.

Rapport, M. M., Green, A. A., & Page, I. H. (1948). Serum vasoconstrictor (serotonin): Isolation and characterization. *Journal of Biological Chemistry*, 176, 1243–1251.

Rasch, B., & Born, J. (2008). Reactivation and consolidation of memory during sleep. *Current Directions in Psychological Science*, 17(3), 188–192.

Raynor, L. A., Pankow, J. S., Miller, M. B., Huang, G., Dalton, D., Klein, R., et al. (2009). Familial aggregation of age-related hearing loss in an epidemiological study of older adults. *American Journal of Audiology*, 18(2), 114–118.

Reading, P. (2013). *ABC of sleep medicine*. Hoboken, NJ: John Wiley & Sons.

Rebok, G. W., Smith, C. B., Pascualvaca, D. M., Mirsky, A. F., Anthony, B. J., & Kellam, S. G. (1997). Developmental changes in attentional performance in urban children from eight to thirteen years. *Child Neuropsychology*, 3(1), 28–46.

Reinisch, J. M., Ziemba-Davis, M., & Sanders, S. A. (1991). Hormonal contributions to sexually dimorphic behavioral development in humans. *Psychoneuroendocrinology*, 16(1–3), 213–78.

Reissig, C. J., Strain, E. C., & Griffiths, R. R. (2009). Caffeinated energy drinks: A growing problem. *Drug and Alcohol Dependence*, 99, 1–10.

Reneman, L., Booij, J., de Bruin, K., Reitsma, J. B., de Wolff, F. A., et al. (2001). Effects of dose, sex, and long-term abstention from use on toxic effects of MDMA (ecstasy) on brain serotonin neurons. *Lancet*, 358, 1864–1869.

Reneman, L., Schilt, T., & de Win, M. M. (2006). Memory function and serotonin transporter promoter gene polymorphism in ecstasy (MDMA) users. *Journal of Psychopharmacology*, 20, 389–399.

Repetti, R. L., Robles, T. F., & Reynolds, B. M. (2011). Allostatic processes in the family. *Development and Psychopathology*, 23, 921–938.

Reynolds, C. R., & Suzuki, L. A. (2013). Bias in psychological assessment: An empirical review and recommendations. In J. R. Graham, J. A. Naglieri, & I. B. Weiner (Eds.), *Handbook of psychology* (vol. 10): *Assessment psychology* (2nd ed., pp. 82–113). Hoboken, NJ: Wiley.

Reynolds, P., Hurley, S., Torres, M., Jackson, J., Boyd, P., & Chen, V. W. (2000). Use of coping strategies and breast cancer survival: Results from the Black/White Cancer Survival Study. *Amerian Journal of Epidemiology*, 152(10), 940–949.

Ridings, C. M., & Gefen, D. (2004). Virtual community attraction: Why people hang out online. *Journal of Computer-Mediated Communication*, 10, 1.

Riek, B. M., Mania, E. W., & Gaertner, S. L. (2006). Intergroup threat and outgroup attitudes: A meta-analytic review. *Personality and Social Psychology Review*, 10(4), 336–353.

Riggs, K.J., McTaggart, J., Simpson, A., & Freeman, R. P. (2006). Changes in the capacity of visual working memory in 5- to 10-year-olds. *Journal of Experimental Child Psychology*, 95(1), 18–26.

Robbins, T. W., Ersche, K. D., & Everitt, B. J. (2008). Drug addiction and the memory systems of the brain. *New York Academy of Sciences*, 1141(1), 1–21.

Robins, L. N., Wing, J., Wittchen, H. U., Helzer, J. E., Babor, T. F., et al. (1988). The Composite International Diagnostic Interview: An epidemiologic instrument suitable for use in conjunction with different diagnostic systems and in different cultures. *Archives of General Psychiatry*, 45(12), 1069–1077.

Robinson, G. (2002). Cross-cultural perspectives on menopause. In A. E. Hunter, & C. Forden, *Readings in the psychology of gender: Exploring our differences and commonalities* (pp. 140–149). Needham Heights, MA: Allyn & Bacon.

Robinson, T. N., Wilde, M. L., Navracruz, L. C., Haydel, K. F., & Varady, A. (2001). Effects of reducing children's television and video game use on aggressive behavior: A randomized controlled trial. *Archives of Pediatrics and Adolescent Medicine*, 155(1), 17–23.

Robles, T. F., & Kiecolt-Glaser, J. K. (2003). The physiology of marriage: Pathways to health. *Physiology & Behavior*, 79(3), 409–16.

Rogers, C. R. (1959). A theory of therapy, personality and interpersonal relationships as developed in the client-centered framework. In S. Koch (Ed.), *Psychology: A study of a science*. vol. 3: *Formulations of the person and the social context*. New York: McGraw-Hill.

Rogers, K. (2011). *The brain and the nervous system*. Chicago: Britannica Educational Publishers.

Roid, G. H. (2003). *Stanford-Binet Intelligence Scales: Technical manual* (5th ed.). Itasca, IL: Riverside Publishing.

Rook, K. S. (1998). Investigating the positive and negative sides of personal relationships: Through a glass darkly? In B. H. Spitzberg, & W. R. Cupach (Eds.), *The dark side of close relationships* (pp. 369–393). Mahwah, NJ: Lawrence Erlbaum.

Rose, J. E., Behm, F. M., Westman, E. C., Mathew, R. J., London, E. D., et al. (2003). PET studies of the influences of nicotine on neural systems in cigarette smokers. *American Journal of Psychiatry*, 160(2), 323–333.

Rosenberg, M. J. (1956). Cognitive structure and attitudinal affect. *The Journal of Abnormal and Social Psychology*, 53, 367–372.

Rosenberg, M. J. (1968). Mathematical models of social behavior. In G. Lindzey, & E. Aronson (Eds.), *The handbook of social psychology*, vol. 1. Reading, MA: Addison-Wesley.

Rosenberg, N. L., Grigsby, J., Dreisbach, J., Busenbark, D., & Grigsby, P. (2002). Neuropsychologic impairment and MRI abnormalities associated with chronic solvent abuse. *Journal of Toxicology. Clinical Toxicology*, 40(1), 21–34.

Rosenman, R., Friedman, M., Straus, R. et al. (1970). Coronary heart disease in the Western Collaborative Group Study: A follow-up experience of 4.5 years. *Journal of Chronic Diseases*, 23(3), 173–190.

Ross, L. (1977). The intuitive psychologist and his shortcomings: Distortions in the attribution process. In L. Berkowitz (Ed.), *Advances in experimental social psychology*, vol. 10. New York: Academic Press.

Rotge, J. Y., Guehl, D., Dilharreguy, B., Cuny, E., Tignol, J., et al. (2008). Provocation of obsessive-compulsive symptoms: A quantitative voxel-based meta-analysis of functional neuroimaging studies. *Journal of Psychiatry & Neuroscience*, 33(5), 405–412.

Rotter, J. (1966). Generalized expectancies for internal versus external control of reinforcements, *Psychological Monographs*, 80, Whole No. 609.

Roy-Byrne, P. P., Craske, M. G., & Stein, M. B. (2006). Panic disorder. *Lancet*, 368(9540), 1023–1032.

Ruscio, A. M., Stein, D. J., Chiu, W. T., & Kessler, R. C. (2010). The *Epidemiology of Obsessive-Compulsive Disorder* in the National Comorbidity Survey Replication. *Molecular Psychiatry*, 15(1), 53–63.

Rushton, J. P., & Bons, T. A. (2005). Mate choice and friendship in twins: Evidence for genetic similarity. *Psychological Science*, 16(7), 555–559.

Russell, J. A. (1991). Culture and the categorization of emotion. *Psychological Bulletin*, 110, 426–450.

Russo, J. E., Carlson, K. A., & Meloy, M. G. (2006). Choosing an inferior alternative. *Psychological Science*, 17(10), 899–904.

Rusting, C. L., & Larsen, R. J. (1997). Extraversion, neuroticism, and susceptibility to positive and negative affect: A test of two theoretical models. *Personality and Individual Differences*, 22, 607–612.

Rutland, A., Killen, M., & Abrams, D. A. (2010). New social-cognitive developmental perspective on prejudice: The interplay between morality and group identity. *Perspectives on Psychological Science*, 5(3), 279–291.

Rutter, M. (1972). *Maternal deprivation reassessed*. Harmondsworth: Penguin.

Ryff, C. D. (1989). Happiness is everything, or is it? Explorations on the meaning of psychological well-being. *Journal of Personality and Social Psychology*, 57(6), 1069–1081.

Sadock, B. J., Sadock, V. A., & Ruiz, P. (2015). *Kaplan & Sadock's synopsis of psychiatry: Behavioral sciences/clinical psychiatry* (11th ed.). Philadelphia, PA: Wolters Kluwer.

Sadock, B. J., Sadock, V. A., & Ruiz, P. (2017). *Kaplan and Sadock's comprehensive textbook of psychiatry*. Philadelphia, PA: Wolters Kluwer Health/Lippincott Williams & Wilkins.

Saegert, S., Swap, W., & Zajonc, R. B. (1973). Exposure, context, and interpersonal attraction. *Journal of Personality and Social Psychology*, 25, 234–242.

Salkovskis, P. M. (1985). Obsessional-compulsive problems: A cognitive-behavioural analysis. *Behaviour Research and Therapy*, 23(5), 571–583.

Salovey, P., Mayer, J. D., & Rosenhan, D. L. (1991). Mood and helping: Mood as a motivator of helping and helping as a regulator of mood. In M. S. Clark (Ed.), *Prosocial behavior*, vol. 12:. *Review of personality and social psychology*. Newbury Park, CA: Sage.

Salovey, P., & Sluyter, D. J. (1997). *Emotional development and emotional intelligence*. New York: Basic Books.

Salthouse, T. A. (2009). When does age-related cognitive decline begin? *Neurobiology of Aging*, 30(4), 507–514.

Sampath, G., Shah, A., Krska, J., & Soni, S. D. (1992). Neuroleptic discontinuation in the very stable schizophrenic patient: Relapse rates and serum neuroleptic levels. *Human Psychopharmacology*, 7, 255–264.

SAMHSA (Substance Abuse and Mental Health Services Administration) (2008). *Results from the 2008 National Survey on Drug Use and Health: National findings*. Rockville, MD: Office of Applied Studies, 2009 NSDUH Series H-36, HHS Publication No. SMA 09-4434.

SAMHS (Substance Abuse and Mental Health Services Administration) (2015). *National Survey on Drug Use and Health (NSDUH)*. Available at: www.samhsa.gov/data/sites/default/files/NSDUH-DetTabs-2015/NSDUH-DetTabs-2015/NSDUH-DetTabs-2015.htm#tab2-41b (accessed 18 January 2017).

Sanford, N., & Woodwarda, T. S. (2017). Symptom-related attributional biases in schizophrenia and bipolar disorder. *Cognitive Neuropsychiatry*, 22(4), 263–279.

Sansone, R. A., & Sansone, L. A. (2011). SNRIs: Pharmacological alternatives for the treatment of obsessive compulsive disorder? *Innovations in Clinical Neuroscience*, 8(6), 10–14.

Saper, C. B., Chou, T. C., & Scammell, T. E. (2001). The sleep switch: Hypothalamic control of sleep and wakefulness. *Trends in Neuroscience*, 24, 726–731.

Saper, C. B., Lu, J., Chou, T. C., & Gooley, J. (2005). The hypothalamic integrator for circadian rhythms. *Trends in Neuroscience*, 28, 152–157.

Saxena, S., Brody, A. L., Schwartz, J. M., & Baxter, L. R. (1998). Neuroimaging and frontal-subcortical circuitry in obsessive-compulsive disorder. *British Journal of Psychiatry Supplement*, 35, 26–37.

Scarpa, A., & Raine, A. (1997). Psychophysiology of anger and violent behavior. *Psychiatric Clinics of North America*, 20, 375–393.

Schachter, S. (1964). The interaction of cognitive and physiological determinants of emotional state. In L. Berkowitz (Ed.), *Advances in experimental social psychology*, vol. 1. New York: Academic Press.

Schachter, S., & Singer, J. E. (1962). Cognitive, social, and physiological determinants of emotional state. *Psychological Review*, 69(5), 378–399.

Schaffer, H. R. & Emerson, P. E. (1964). *The development of social attachments in infancy*. Monographs of the Society for Research in Child Development, 29. (Whole No. 3).

Schaie, K. W. (1995). *Intellectual development in adulthood: The Seattle Longitudinal Study*. New York: Oxford University Press.

Schaie, K. W. (2005). *Developmental influences on adult intelligence: The Seattle longitudinal study*. New York: Oxford University Press.

Scherer, K. R., & Ellgring, H. (2007). Multimodal expression of emotion: Affect programs or componential appraisal patterns? *Emotion*, 7, 158–171.

Scherer, K. R., & Wallbott, H. G. (1994). Evidence for universality and cultural variation of differential emotion response patterning. *Journal of Personality and Social Psychology*, 66, 310–328.

Schilt, T., de Win, M. M. L., Koeter, M., Jager, G., Korf, D. J., et al. (2007). Cognition in novice Ecstasy users with minimal exposure to other drugs. *Archives of General Psychiatry*, 64, 728–736.

Schkade, D., & Kahneman, D. (1998). Does living in California make people happy? A focusing illusion in judgments of life satisfaction. *Psychological Science*, 9, 340–346.

Schmader, T., & Johns, M. (2003). Converging evidence that stereotype threat reduces working memory capacity. *Journal of Personality and Social Psychology*, 85(3), 440–452.

Schmader, T., Johns, M., & Forbes, C. (2008). An integrated process model of stereotype threat effects on performance. *Psychological Review*, 115, 336–356.

Schmidt, C., Peigneux, P., & Cajochen, C. (2012). Age-related changes in sleep and circadian rhythms: Impact on cognitive performance and underlying neuroanatomical networks. *Frontiers in Neurology*, 3, 118.

Schnall, S., & Laird, J. D. (2003). Keep smiling: Enduring effects of facial expressions and postures on emotional experience and memory. *Cognition & Emotion*, 17, 787–797.

Schneider, W. J., & McGrew, K. S. (2012). The Cattell-Horn-Carroll model of intelligence. In D. P. Flanagan, & P. L. Harrison (Eds.), *Contemporary intellectual assessment: Theories, tests, and issues* (pp. 99–144). New York: Guilford Press.

Schnittker, J., & McLeod, J. D. (2005). The social psychology of health disparities. *Annual Review of Sociology*, 31(1), 75–103.

Schultz, D. P., & Schultz, S. E. (2007). *A history of modern psychology* (9th ed.). Stanford, CT: Cengage Learning.

Segerstrom, S. C., & Miller, G. E. (2004). Psychological stress and the human immune system: A meta-analytic study of 30 years of inquiry. *Psychological Bulletin*, 130(4), 601–630.

Seligman, M. (1971). Phobias and preparedness. *Behavior Therapy*, 2(3), 307–321.

Seligman, M. E. P. (1975). *Helplessness: Depression, development and death*. New York: W. H. Freeman.

Seligman, M. E. P. (1998). *Learned optimism: How to change your mind and your life* (2nd ed.). New York: Pocket Books.

Seligman, M. E. P. (2011). *Flourish: A visionary new understanding of happiness and wellbeing*. New York: Free Press.

Seligman, M. E. P., & Csikszentmihalyi M. (2000). Positive psychology: An introduction. *American Psychologist*, 55, 5–14.

Seligman, M. E. P., Steen, T. A., Park, N., & Peterson, C. (2005). Positive psychology progress: Empirical validation of interventions. *American Psychologist*, 60, 410–421.

Selye, H. (1936). A syndrome produced by diverse nocuous agents. *Nature*, 138(3479), 32.

Selye, H. (1952). *The story of the adaptation syndrome*. Montreal: ACTA, Inc.

Senécal, C., Julien, E., & Guay, F. (2003). Role conflict and academic procrastination: A self-determination perspective. *European Journal of Social Psychology*, 33, 135–145.

Seymour, R. B., & Smith, D. E. (1998). Psychological and psychiatric consequences of hallucinogens. In R. E. Tarter, R. T. Ammerman, & P. J. Ott (Eds.), *Handbook of substance abuse*. New York: Springer.

Sheldon, W. H., Stevens, S. S., & Tucker, W. B. (1940). *The varieties of human physique*. New York: Harper & Brothers.

Shepard, R. N., & Metzler, J. (1971). Mental rotation of three-dimensional objects. *Science*, 171(3972), 701–703.

Shepherd, J. (2007). Preventing alcohol-related violence: A public health approach. *Criminal Behaviour & Mental Health*, 17, 250–264.

Sherif, M., Harvey, O. J., White, B. J., Hood, W. R., & Sherif, C. W. (1961). *Intergroup conflict and cooperation: The Robbers Cave experiment*, vol. 10. Norman, OK: University Book Exchange.

Shors, T. J., & Matzel, L. D. (1997). Long-term potentiation: What's learning got to do with it? *Behavioral and Brain Sciences*, 20, 597–655.

Siegel, J. M. (2003). Why we sleep. *Scientific American*, 289(5), 72–77.

Siegler, I. C., Poon, L. W., Madden, D. J., Dilworth-Anderson, P., Schaie, K. W., et al. (2009). Psychological aspects of normal aging. In D. G. Blazer, & D. C. Steffens (Eds.), *The American Psychiatric Publishing textbook of geriatric psychiatry* (4th ed., pp. 137–155). Arlington, VA: American Psychiatric Publishing.

Siever, L. J. (2008). Neurobiology of aggression and violence. *American Journal of Psychiatry*, 165, 429–442.

Simon, R. W. (1992). Association of parental role strains, salience of parental identity and gender differences in psychological distress. *Journal of Health and Social Behavior*, 33, 25–35.

Simpson, J. A., Campbell, B., & Berscheid, E. (1986). The association between romantic love and marriage. *Personality and Social Psychology Bulletin*, 12, 363–372.

Sin, N. L., & Lyubomirsky, S. (2009). Enhancing well-being and alleviating depressive symptoms with positive psychology interventions: A practice-friendly meta-analysis. *Journal of Clinical Psychology*, 65, 1–26.

Singer, T., Verhaeghen, P., Ghisletta, P., Lindenberger, U., & Baltes, P. (2003). The fate of cognition in very old age: Six-year longitudinal findings in the Berlin Aging Study (BASE). *Psychology and Aging*, 18, 318–331.

Singhal, A., Cody, M. J., Rogers, E. M., & Sabido, M. (Eds.) (2004). *Entertainment-education and social change: History, research, and practice*. Mahwah, NJ: Erlbaum.

Skinner, B. F. (1956). A case history in scientific method. *American Psychologist*, 11, 221–233.

Skinner, B. F. (1972). *Beyond freedom and dignity*. New York: Vintage Books.

Slavich, G. M., Monroe, S. M., & Gotlib, I. H. (2011). Early parental loss and depression history: Associations with recent life stress in major depressive disorder. *Journal of Psychiatric Research*, 45(9), 1146–1152.

Slopen, N., Lewis, T. T., Gruenewald, T. L., Mujahid, M. S., Ryff, C. D., et al. (2010). Early life adversity and inflammation in African Americans and Ahites in the midlife in the United States survey. *Psychosomatic Medicine*, 42(7), 694–701.

Smith, A. (2009). *The theory of moral sentiments* (250th anniversary ed.). New York: Penguin Books.

Smith, C. A., & Ellsworth, P. C. (1985). Patterns of cognitive appraisal in emotion. *Journal of Personality and Social Psychology*, 48, 813–838.

Smith, C. A., & Ellsworth, P. C. (1987). Patterns of appraisal and emotion related to taking an exam. *Journal of Personality and Social Psychology*, 52, 475–488.

Smith, C. A., & Lazarus, R. S. (1993). Appraisal components, core relational themes, and the emotions, *Cognition and Emotion*, 7(3–4), 233–269.

Smith, E. R., & Queller, S. (2001). Mental representations. In A. Tesser, & N. Schwarz (Eds.), *Blackwell handbook of social psychology: Intraindividual processes*. London: Blackwell Publishers.

Smith, P. K., Dijksterhuis, A., & Chaiken, S. (2008). Subliminal exposure to faces and racial attitudes: Exposure to whites makes whites like blacks less. *Journal of Experimental Social Psychology*, 44, 50–64.

Smith, S. M., McIntosh, W. D., & Bazzini, D. G. (1999). Are the beautiful good in Hollywood? An investigation of the beauty-and-goodness stereotype on film. *Basic and Applied Social Psychology*, 21, 69–80.

Smolak, L. (2009). Risk factors in the development of body image, eating problems and obesity. In L. Smolak, & J. K. Thompson (Eds.), *Body image, eating disorders and obesity in youth: Assessment, prevention and treatment* (pp. 135–156). Washington, DC: American Psychological Association.

Sohlberg, M. M. & Mateer, C. A. (1987). Effectiveness of an attention training program. *Journal of Clinical and Experimental Neuropsychology*, 9, 117–130.

Sohlberg, M. M. & Mateer, C. A. (1989). *Cognitive rehabilitation: Introduction to theory and practice*. New York: Guilford Press.

Sokol, R. J. Jr., Delaney-Black, V., & Nordstrom, B. (2003). Fetal alcohol spectrum disorder. *JAMA: Journal of the American Medical Association*, 290(22), 2996–2999.

Solms, M. (1997). *The neuropsychology of dreams*. Mahwah, NJ: Erlbaum.

Solms, M., & Turnbull, O. (2007). To sleep, perchance to REM? The rediscovered role of emotion and meaning in dreams. In S. Della Sala (Ed.), *Tall tales about the mind and brain: Sseparating fact from fiction*. Oxford: Oxford University Press.

Soloff, P. H., & Chiappetta, L. (2012). Prospective predictors of suicidal behavior in borderline personality disorder at 6-year follow-up. *The American Journal of Psychiatry*, 169, 484–490.

Solomon, C. (2003). Transactional analysis theory: The basics. *Transactional Analysis Journal*, 33(1), 15–22.

Solomon, G. F., Segerstrom, S. C., Grohr, P., Kemeny, M., & Fahey, J. (1997). Shaking up immunity: Psychological and immunologic changes after a natural disaster. *Psychosomatic Medicine*, 59, 114–127.

Somerville, L. H. (2013). The teenage brain: Sensitivity to social evaluation. *Current Directions in Psychological Science*, 22, 121–127.

Sood, S., SenGupta, M., Mishra, P. R., & Jacoby, C. (2004). "Come gather around together": An examination of radio listening groups in Fulbari, Nepal. *Gazette: The International Journal for Communication Studies*, 66, 63–86.

Southwick, S. M., Vythilingam, M., & Charney, D. S. (2005). The psychobiology of depression and resilience to stress: Implications for prevention and treatment. *Annual Review of Clinical Psychology*, 1, 255–291.

Spaulding, W., Johnson, D., & Coursey, R. (2001). Treatment and rehabilitation of schizophrenia. In M. Sammons, & N. Schmidt (Eds.), *Combined treatments for mental disorders: A guide to psychological and pharmacological interventions*. Washington, DC: American Psychological Association.

Spearman, C. E. (1927). *The abilities of man: Their nature and measurement*. London: Macmillan.

Sprecher, S., & Duck, S. (1994). Sweet talk: The importance of perceived communication for romantic and friendship attraction experienced during a get-acquainted date. *Personality and Social Psychology Bulletin*, 20, 391–400.

Stangor, C. (2010). *Introduction to psychology*, vol 1.0.1. Available at: www.saylor.org/site/textbooks/Introduction%20to%20Psychology.pdf (accessed October 8, 2017).

Stanley, S. M., Amato, P. R., Johnson, C. A., & Markman, H. J. (2006). Premarital education, marital quality, and marital stability: Findings from a large, random household survey. *Journal of Family Psychology*, 20, 117–126.

Stasser, G., Taylor, L. A., & Hanna, C. (1989). Information sampling in structured and unstructured discussions of three- and six-person groups. *Journal of Personality and Social Psychology*, 57, 67–78.

Stasser, G., & Titus, W. (1985). Pooling of unshared information in group decision making: Biased information sampling during discussion. *Journal of Personality and Social Psychology*, 48, 1467–1478.

Stasser, G., & Titus, W. (1987). Effects of information load and percentage of shared information on the dissemination of unshared information during group discussion. *Journal of Personality and Social Psychology*, 53, 81–93.

Staub, E. (1978). *Positive social behavior and morality: Social and personal influences.* New York: Academic Press.

Steel, Z., Marnane, C., Iranpour, C., Chey, T., Jackson, J. W., et al. (2014). The global prevalence of common mental disorders: A systematic review and meta-analysis 1980–2013. *International Journal of Epidemiology*, 43(2), 476–493.

Steele, C. M. (1997). A threat in the air: How stereotypes shape the intellectual identities and performance of women and African-Americans. *American Psychologist*, 52, 613–629.

Stefansson, H., Rujescu, D., Cichon, S., Pietiläinen, O. P. H., et al. (2008). Large recurrent microdeletions associated with schizophrenia. *Nature*, 455(7210), 232–236.

Steinberg, L. (1990). Autonomy, conflict, and harmony in the family relationship. In S. S. Feldman, & G.R. Elliott (Eds.), *At the threshold: The developing adolescent.* Cambridge, MA: Harvard University Press.

Steinberg, L. (2001). We know some things: Parent–adolescent relationships in retrospect and prospect. *Journal of Research on Adolescence*, 11, 1–19.

Stephan, W. G., Boniecki, K. A., Ybarra, O., Bettencourt, A., Ervin, K. S., et al. (2002). The role of threats in the racial attitudes of Blacks and Whites. *Personality and Social Psychology Bulletin*, 28, 1242–1254.

Stephan, W. G., Renfro, C. L., Esses, V. M., Stephan, C. W., & Martin, T. (2005). The effects of feeling threatened on attitudes toward immigrants. *International Journal of Intercultural Relations*, 29, 1–19.

Steptoe, A., O'Donnell, K., Badrick, E., Kumari, M., & Marmot, M. (2008). Neuroendocrine and inflammatory factors associated with positive affect in healthy men and women: the Whitehall II study. *American Journal of Epidemiology*, 167(1), 96–102.

Steptoe, A., Wardle, J., Pollard, T. M., Canaan, L., & Davies, G. J. (1996). Stress, social support and health-related behavior: A study of smoking, alcohol consumption and physical exercise. *Journal of Psychosomatic Research*, 41(2), 171–180.

Sternberg, R. J. (1997). Construct validation of a triangular love scale. *European Journal of Social Psychology*, 27(3), 313–335.

Sternberg, R. J., & Grajek, S. (1984). The nature of love. *Journal of Personality and Social Psychology*, 47(2), 312–329.

Stickgold, R., & Ellenbogen, J. M. (2008). Quiet! Sleeping brain at work. *Scientific American Mind*, 19, 23–29.

Strack, F., Martin, L. L., & Stepper, S. (1988). Inhibiting and facilitating conditions of the human smile: A nonobtrusive test of the facial feedback hypothesis. *Journal of Personality and Social Psychology*, 54, 768–777.

Straus, M. A., Sugarman, D. B., & Giles-Sims, J. (1997). Spanking by parents and subsequent antisocial behavior of children. *Archives of Pediatric and Adolescent Medicine*, 151, 761–767.

Strumia, R. (2009). Skin signs in anorexia nervosa. *Dermato-Endocrinology*, 1(5), 268–270.

Stubbe, J. H., Posthuma, D., Boomsma, D. I., & de Geus, E. J. C. (2005). Heritability of life satisfaction in adults: A twin study. *Psychological Medicine*, 35, 1581–1588.

Sue, D. W., & Sue, D. (2008). *Counseling the culturally diverse: Theory and practice* (5th ed.). Hoboken, NJ: Wiley.

Suedfeld, P., & Tetlock, P. E. (2001). Individual differences in information processing. In A. Tesser, & N. Schwartz (Eds.), *Blackwell international handbook of social psychology: Intra-individual processes*, vol. 1. London: Blackwell Publishers.

Sullivan, K. T., Pasch, L. A., Johnson, M. D., & Bradbury, T. N. (2010). Social support, problem solving, and the longitudinal course of newlywed marriage. *Journal of Personality and Social Psychology*, 98, 631–644.

Sullivan, P. F., Neale, M. C., & Kendler, K. S. (2000). Genetic epidemiology of major depression: Review and meta-analysis. *The American Journal of Psychiatry*, 157(10), 1552–1562.

Sumter, S. R., Bokhorst, C. L., Steinberg, L., & Westenberg, P. M. (2009). The developmental pattern of resistance to peer influence in adolescence: Will the teenager ever be able to resist? *Journal of Adolescence*, 32(4), 1009–1021.

Sussman, A. B., & Shafir, E. (2012). On assets and debt in the psychology of perceived wealth. *Psychological Science*, 23, 101–108.

Sweeney, P. D., Anderson, K., & Bailey, S. (1986). Attributional style in depression: A meta-analytic review. *Journal of Personality and Social Psychology*, 50(5), 974–991.

Tajfel, H., & Turner, J. C. (1979). An integrative theory of intergroup conflict. In W. G. Austin, & S. Worchel. *The social psychology of intergroup relations*. Monterey, CA: Brooks/Cole.

Talaska, C. A., Fiske, S. T., & Chaiken, S. (2008). Legitimating racial discrimination: A meta-analysis of the racial attitude–behavior literature shows that emotions, not beliefs, best predict discrimination. *Social Justice Research: Social Power in Action*, 21, 263–296.

Tannenbaum, P. H. (1968). The congruity principle: Retrospective reflections and recent research. In R. P. Abelson, E. Aronson, W. J. McGuire, T. M. Newcomb, M. J. Rosenberg, & P. H. Tannenbaum (Eds.), *Theories of cognitive consistency: A sourcebook* (pp. 52–72). Chicago: Rand McNally.

Tatarkiewicz, W. (1976). *Analysis of happiness*. Warsaw: Polish Scientific Publishers.

Taylor, L. S., Fiore, A. T., Mendelsohn, G. A., & Cheshire, C. (2011). Out of my league: A realworld test of the matching hypothesis, *Personality and Social Psychology Bulletin*, 37, 942–954.

Taylor, S., Peplau, A., & Sears, D. (2006). *Social psychology* (12th ed.). Upper Saddle River, NJ: Prentice Hall.

Taylor, S. P., & Hulsizer, M. R. (1998). Psychoactive drugs and human aggression. In R. G. Geen, & E. Donnerstein (Eds.), *Human aggression* (pp. 139–167). San Diego. CA: Academic Press.

Tesser, A., Millar, M., & Moore, J. (1988). Some affective consequences of social comparison and reflection processes: The pain and pleasure of being close. *Journal of Personality and Social Psychology*, 54, 49–61.

Tharyan, P., & Adams, C.E. (2005). Electroconvulsive therapy for schizophrenia. *Cochrane Database of Systematic Reviews*, (2): CD000076.

Thielen, J. W., Takashima, A., Rutters, F., Tendolkar, I., & Fernández, G. (2015). Transient relay function of midline thalamic nuclei during long-term memory consolidation in humans. *Learning & Memory*, 22(10), 527–531.

Thoits, P. A. (1983). Dimensions of life events that influence psychological distress: An evaluation and synthesis of the literature. In H. B. Kaplan (Ed.), *Psychological stress: Trends in theory and research* (pp. 33–103). New York: Academic Press.

Thoits, P. A. (1995). Stress, coping, and social support process: Where are we? What next? *Journal of Health and Social Behavior*, 35, 53–79.

Thoits, P. A. (2010). Stress and health: Major findings and policy implications. *Journal of Health and Social Behavior*, 51, 41–53.

Thompson, J. K., Roehrig, M., & Kinder, B. N. (2007). Eating disorders. In M. Hersen, S. M. Turner, & D. C. Beidel (Eds.), *Adult psychopathology and diagnosis* (5th ed., pp. 571–600). Hoboken, NJ: Wiley.

Thomsen, L., Green, E. G. T., & Sidanius, J. (2008). We will hunt them down: How social dominance orientation and right-wing authoritarianism fuel ethnic persecution of immigrants in fundamentally different ways. *Journal of Experimental Social Psychology*, 44(6), 1455–1464.

Thorndike, E. L. (1911). *Animal intelligence: Experimental studies*. New York: The Macmillan Company.

Thorpe, G. L., & Olson, S. L. (1997). *Behavior therapy: Concepts, procedures, and applications* (2nd ed.). Needham Heights, MA: Allyn & Bacon.

Timko, C., Finney, J. W., & Moos, R. H. (2005). The 8-year course of alcohol abuse: Gender differences in social context and coping. *Alcoholism: Clinical and Experimental Research*, 29(4): 612–621.

Timmer, R. T., & Sands, J. M. (1999). Lithium intoxication. *Journal of the American Society of Nephrology*, 10(3), 666–674.

Toates, F. (1986). *Motivational systems*. Cambridge: Cambridge University Press.

Toates, F. (2001). *Biological psychology: An integrative approach*. Harlow: Pearson Education Ltd.

Tobler, I. (2005). Phylogeny of sleep regulation. In M. H. Kryger, T. Roth, & W. C. Dement (Eds.). *Principles and practice of sleep medicine*. Philadelphia, PA: W. B. Saunders.

Toda, M., & Abi-Dargham, A. (2007). Dopamine hypothesis of schizophrenia: Making sense of it all. *Current Psychiatry Reports*, 9(4), 329–336.

Todd, A. R., Bodenhausen, G. V., Richeson, J. A., & Galinsky, A. D. (2011). Perspective taking combats automatic expressions of racial bias. *Journal of Personality and Social Psychology*, 100(6), 1027–1042.

Tolman, E. C. (1932). *Purposive behavior in animals and men*. New York: Appleton-Century-Crofts.

Tolman, E. C. (1948). Cognitive maps in rats and men. *Psychological Review*, 55(4), 189.

Tomkins, S. S. (1962). *Affect, imagery, consciousness*, vol. 1: *The positive affects*. New York: Springer.

Tononi, G., & Cirelli, C. (2014). Sleep and the price of plasticity: From synaptic and cellular homeostasis to memory consolidation and integration. *Neuron*, 81(1), 12–34.

Toyohara, J., Sakata, M., & Ishiwata, K. (2010). Human brain imaging of acetylcholine receptors. In P. Seeman, & B. Madras (Eds.), *Imaging of the human brain in health and disease*. New York: Academic Press.

Treisman, A. (1964). Verbal cues, language and meaning in selective attention. *The American Journal of Psychology*, 77(2): 206–219.

Tsai, J. L., Louie, J. Y., Chen, E. E., & Uchida, Y. (2007). Learning what feelings to desire: Socialization of ideal affect through children's storybooks. *Personality and Social Psychology Bulletin*, 33(1), 17–30.

Tsankova, N., Renthal, W., Kumar, A., & Nestler, E. J. (2007). Epigenetic regulation in psychiatric disorders. *Nature Reviews Neuroscience*, 8(5), 355–367.

Tulving, E., & Gold, C. (1963). Stimulus information and contextual information as determinants of tachistoscopic recognition of words. *Journal of Experiemental Psychology*, 66, 319–327.

Turner, R., Wheaton, B., & Lloyd, D. (1995). The epidemiology of social stress. *American Sociological Review*, 60, 104–125.

Turner, R. J., & Lloyd, D. A. (2004). Stress burden and the lifetime incidence of psychiatric disorder in young adults: Racial and ethnic contrasts. *Archives of General Psychiatry*, 61, 481–488.

Tversky, A. (1972). Elimination by aspects: A theory of choice. *Psychological Review*, 79(4), 281–299.

Tversky, A., & Kahneman, D. (1981). The framing of decisions and the psychology of choice. *Science*, 211, 453–458.

Umland, E. M. (2008). Treatment strategies for reducing the burden of menopause-associated vasomotor symptoms. *Journal of Managed Care Pharmacy*, 14(3 Suppl.), 14–19.

UNESCO (2013). *Adult and youth literacy: National, regional and global trends, 1985–2015*. Montreal: UNESCO Institute of Statistics.

Üstün, B., & Kennedy, C. (2009). What is "functional impairment"? Disentangling disability from clinical significance. *World Psychiatry*, 8(2), 82–85.

Vaillant, G. E. (1977). *Adaptation to life*. Boston: Little Brown and Co.

Vakoch, D. A., & Strupp, H. H. (2000). Psychodynamic approaches to psychotherapy: Philosophical and theoretical foundations of effective practice. In C. R. Snyder, & R. Ingram (Eds.), *Handbook of psychological change* (pp. 200–216). New York: Wiley.

Van Bavel, J. J., & Cunningham, W. A. (2009). Self-categorization with a novel mixed-race group moderates automatic social and racial biases. *Personality and Social Psychology Bulletin*, 35, 321–335.

Van Boven, L., Kamada, A., & Gilovich, T. (1999). The perceiver as perceived: Everyday intuitions about the correspondence bias. *Journal of Personality and Social Psychology*, 77, 1188–1199.

Van Cauter, E. (2005). Endocrine physiology. In M. H. Kryger, T. Roth, & W. C. Dement (Eds.), *Principles and practice of sleep medicine* (4th ed.). Philadelphia, PA: Elsevier Saunders.

Van den Heuvel, O. A., Van de Wetering, B. J., Veltman, D. J., & Pauls, D. L. (2000). Genetic studies of panic disorder: A review. *Journal of Clinical Psychiatry*, 61(10), 756–766.

Van Grootheest, D., Cath, D., Beekman, A., & Boomsma, D. (2005). Twin studies on obsessive–compulsive disorder: A review. *Twin Research and Human Genetics*, 8(5), 450–458.

Van Yperen, N. W., & Buunk, B. P. (1990). A longitudinal study of equity and satisfaction in intimate relationships. *European Journal of Social Psychology*, 20, 287–309.

Vartanian, T. P., & Houser, L. (2010). The effects of childhood neighborhood conditions on self-reports of adult health. *Journal of Health and Social Behavior*, 51(3), 291–306.

Veenhoven, R. (2008). Healthy happiness: Effects of happiness on physical health and the consequences for preventive health care. *Journal of Happiness Studies*, 9, 449–469.

Verkuyten, M., & De Wolf, A. (2007). The development of in-group favoritism: Between social reality and group identity. *Developmental Psychology*, 43, 901–911.

Vierikko, E., Pulkkinen, L., Kaprio, J., & Rose, R. J. (2006). Genetic and environmental sources of continuity and change in teacher-rated aggression during early adolescence. *Aggressive Behavior*, 32, 308–320.

Vroom, V. H. (1964). *Work and motivation*. Chichester: John Wiley & Sons, Ltd.

Vyazovskiy, V. V., Cirelli, C., Pfister-Genskow, M., Faraguna, U., & Tononi, G. (2008). Molecular and electrophysiological evidence for net synaptic potentiation in wake and depression in sleep. *Nature Neuroscience*, 11, 200–208.

Vygotsky, L. S. (1962). *Thought and language*. Cambridge MA: MIT Press.

Vygotsky, L. S. (1978). *Mind in society: The development of higher psychological processes*. Cambridge, MA: Harvard University Press.

Vytal, K., & Hamann, S. (2010). Neuroimaging support for discrete neural correlates of basic emotions: A voxel-based meta-analysis. *Journal of Cognitive Neuroscience*, 22(12), 2864–2885.

Wachholtz, A. B., & Pargament, K. I. (2008). Migraines and meditation: Does spirituality matter? *Journal of Behavioral Medicine*, 31(4), 351–366.

Wachtel, P. L. (1997). *Psychoanalysis, behaviour therapy, and the relational world*. Washington, DC: American Psychological Association.

Waisbren, S. E., Brown, M. J., de Sonneville, L. M., & Levy, H. L. (1994). Review of neuropsychological functioning in treated phenylketonuria: An information processing approach. *Acta Paediatrica Supplement*, 407, 98–103.

Walker, I., & Crogan, M. (1998). Academic performance, prejudice, and the jigsaw classroom. *Journal of Community & Applied Social Psychology*, 8(6), 381–393.

Wallas, G. (1926). *The art of thought*. New York: Harcourt, Brace & Company.

Waller, B. M., Cray, J. J. Jr., & Burrows, A. M. (2008). Selection for universal facial emotion. *Emotion*, 8, 435–439.

Walsh, R., & Shapiro, S. L. (2006). The meeting of meditative disciplines and Western psychology: A mutually enriching dialogue. *American Psychologist*, 61, 227–239.

Walters, G. D. (2002). Psychology as the study of mind and behaviour. In S. P. Shohov (Ed.), *Advances in psychological research* (vol. 15, pp. 27–50). New York: Nova Science Publishers Inc.

Wampold, B. E., Mondin, G. W., Moody, M., Stich, E., et al. (1997). A metaanalysis of outcome studies comparing bona fide psychotherapies. *Psychological Bulletin*, 122(3), 203–215.

Wamsley, E. J. & Stickgold, R. (2010). Dreaming and offline memory processing. *Current Biology*, 20(23), R1010–R1013.

Wang, C. S., Kenneth, T., Ku, G., & Galinsky, A. D. (2014). Perspective-taking increases willingness to engage in intergroup contact. *PLoS ONE* 9(1): e85681.

Watanabe, A., Nakao, K., & Tokuyama, M. (2005l). Prediction of first episode of panic attack among white-collar workers. *Psychiatry and Clinical Neurosciences*, 59(2), 119–126.

Watson, J. B. (1919). *Psychology from the standpoint of a behaviorist*. Philadelphia, PA: Lippincott.

Wechsler D. (1939). *The measurement of adult intelligence*. Baltimore, MD: Williams and Wilkins.

Weiss, B., Tram, J. M., Weisz, J. R., Rescorla, L., & Achenbach, T. M. (2009). Differential symptom expression and somatization in Thai versus U.S. children. *Journal of Consulting and Clinical Psychology*, 77, 987–992.

Weissman, M., & Cuijpers, P. (2017). Psychotherapy over the last four decades. *Harvard Review of Psychiatry*, 25(4), 155–158.

Weissman, M. M. (1993). The epidemiology of personality disorders: A 1990 update. *Journal of Personality Disorders*, 7, 44–62.

Weitzman, E. D., Czeisler, C. A., Zimmerman, J. C., et al. (1980). Timing of REM and stages 3 + 4 sleep during temporal isolation in man. *Sleep*, 2, 391–407.

Wells, S., Graham, K., & West, P. (2000). Alcohol-related aggression in the general population. *Journal of Studies on Alcohol*, 61(4), 626–632.

Werker, J., & Desjardins, R. (1995). Listening to speech in the 1st year of life: Experiential influences on phoneme production. *Current Directions in Psychological Science*, 4, 76–81.

West, S. A., & Gardner, A. (2010). Altruism, spite, and greenbeards. *Science*, 327, 1341–1344.

Westen, D., Novotny, C. M., & Thompson-Brenner, H. (2004). The empirical status of empirically supported psychotherapies: Assumptions, findings, and reporting in controlled clinical trials. *Psychological Bulletin*, 130(4), 631–663.

Westen, D., Weinberger, J., & Bradley, R. (2007). Motivation, decision making, and consciousness: From psychodynamics to subliminal priming and emotional constraint satisfaction. In P.D. Zelazo, M. Moscovitch, & E. Thompson (Eds.), *The Cambridge handbook of consciousness*. New York: Cambridge University Press.

Wethington, E., & Kessler, R. C. (1986). Perceived support, received support, and adjustment to stressful life events. *Journal of Health and Social Behavior*, 27, 78–89.

Whaley, A. L., & Hall, B. N. (2009). Cultural themes in the psychotic symptoms of African American psychiatric patients. *Professional Psychology: Research and Practice*, 40, 75–80.

Wheaton, B. (1999). Social stress. In C. S. Aneshensel, & J. Phelan (Eds.), *Handbook on the sociology of mental health* (pp. 277–300). New York: Plenum Press.

Whisman, M. A., & Sbarra, D. A. (2012). Marital adjustment and interleukin-6 (IL-6). *Journal of Family Psychology*, 26(2), 290–295.

White, H. R., Brick, J., & Hansell, S. (1993). A longitudinal investigation of alcohol use and aggression in adolescence. *Journal of Studies on Alcohol, Supplement* 11, 62–77.

Whiteside, S. P., Port, J. D., & Abramowitz, J. S. (2004). A meta-analysis of functional neuroimaging in obsessive-compulsive disorder. *Psychiatry Research*, 15, 69–79.

Whitley, B. E. (1999). Right-wing authoritarianism, social dominance orientation, and prejudice. *Journal of Personality & Social Psychology*, 77(l), 126–134.

Wickens, C. D., & Carswell, C. M. (2006). Information processing. In G. Salvendy (Ed.), *Handbook of human factors and ergonomics* (3rd ed., pp. 111–149). Hoboken, NJ: Wiley Interscience.

Wicklund, R. A., & Brehm, J. W. (1976). *Perspectives on cognitive dissonance*. Hillsdale, N.J: Erlbaum.

Widiger, T. A. (2003). Personality disorder diagnosis. *World Psychiatry*, 2(3), 131–135.

Wierson, M., & Forehand, R. (1994). Parent behavioral training for child noncompliance: Rationale, concepts, and effectiveness. *Current Directions in Psychological Science*, 3, 146–149.

Wilder, D. A., Chen, L., Atwell, J., Pritchard, J., & Weinstein, P. (2006). Brief functional analyses and treatment of tantrums associated with transitions in preschool children. *Journal of Applied Behavior Analysis*, 39, 103–107.

Wilder, D. A., Simon, A. F., & Faith, M. (1996). Enhancing the impact of counterstereotypic information. *Journal of Personality & Social Psychology*, 71(2), 276–287.

Williams, R. A. (2005). A short course in family therapy: Translating research into practice. *Family Journal: Counseling and Therapy for Couples and Families*, 13, 188–194.

Willis, J., & Todorov, A. (2006). First impressions: Making up your mind after a 100-ms exposure to a face. *Psychological Science*, 17, 592–598.

Wittmann, M., & Schmidt, S. (2014). Mindfulness meditation and the experience of time. In S. Schmidt, & H. Walach (Eds.), *Meditation: Neuroscientific approaches and philosophical implications*, vol. 2: *Studies in neuroscience, consciousness and* spirituality. Cham: Springer.

Woldt, A. L., & Toman, S. M. (Eds.). (2005). *Gestalt therapy: History, theory, and practice*. Thousand Oaks, CA: Sage.

Wolpe, J. (1958). *Psychotherapy by reciprocal inhibition*. Stanford, CA: Stanford University Press.

Wolpe, J. (1964). Behavior therapy in complex neurotic states. *The British Journal of Psychiatry*, 110(464), 28–34.

Wolpe, J. (1982). *The practice of behavior therapy*. New York: Pergamon Press.

Wood, W., Lundgren, S., Ouellette, J. A., Busceme, S., & Blackstone, T. (1994). Minority influence: A meta-analytic review of social influence processes. *Psychological Bulletin*, 115(3), 323–345.

Wood, W., & Neal, D. T. (2007). A new look at habits and the habit-goal interface. *Psychological Review*, 114(4), 843–863.

Wood, W., Rhodes, N., & Bick, M. (1995). Working knowledge and attitude strength: An information processing analysis. In R. E. Petty & J. A. Krosnick (Eds.), *Attitude strength: Antecedents and consequences*. Hillsdale, NJ: Erlbaum.

Workman, L., & Reader, W. (2014). *Evolutionary psychology: An introduction* (3rd ed.). New York: Cambridge University Press.

World Health Organization (2004). *Promoting mental health: Concepts, emerging evidence, practice (Summary Report)*. Geneva: World Health Organization.

World Health Organization (WHO). (2014). Global status report on alcohol and health. Available at: www.who.int/substance_abuse/publications/global_alcohol_report/msb_gsr_2014_1.pdf?ua=1 (accessed September 15, 2017).

Yang, Y.-J., & Chiu, C.-Y. (2009). Mapping the structure and dynamics of psychological knowledge: Forty years of APA Journal citations (1970–2009). *Review of General Psychology*, 13(4), 349–356.

Yerkes, R. M., & Dodson, J. D. (1908). The relation of strength of stimulus to rapidity of habit-formation. *Journal of Comparative Neurology and Psychology*, 18, 459–482.

Yoshida, K. A., Pons, F., Maye, J., & Werker, J. F. (2010). Distributional phonetic learning at 10 months of age. *Infancy*, 15(4), 420–433.

Yousif, Y., & Korte, C. (1995). Urbanization, culture, and helpfulness: Cross-cultural studies in England and the Sudan. *Journal of Cross-Cultural Psychology*, 26, 474–489.

Yunesian, M., Aslani, A., Vash, J. H., & Yazdi, A. B. (2008). Effects of transcendental meditation on mental health: A before-after study. *Clinical Practice & Epidemiology in Mental Health*, 4, 25.

Zajonc, R. B. (1965). Social facilitation. *Science*, 149(3681), 269–274.

Zajonc, R. B. (1968). Attitudinal effects of mere exposure. *Journal of Personality & Social Psychology, Monograph Supplement*, 9, Part 2, 1–27.

Zajonc, R. B. (1984). On the primacy of affect. *American Psychologist*, 39, 117–123.

Zajonc, R. B. (2001). Mere exposure: A gateway to the subliminal. *Current Directions in Psychological Science*, 10, 224–228.

Zebrowitz, L., White, B., & Wieneke, K. (2008). Mere exposure and racial prejudice: Exposure to other-race faces increases liking for strangers of that race. *Social Cognition, 26,* 259–275.

Zelinski, E. M., & Kennison, R. F. (2007). Not your parents' test scores: Cohort reduces psychometric aging effects. *Psychology and Aging, 22*(3), 546–557.

Zhu, W. X., Li, L., & Hesketh, T. (2009). China's excess males, sex selective abortion, and one child policy: Analysis of data from 2005 National Intercensus Survey. *British Medical Journal, 338:* b1211.

Zillmann, D. (1988). Cognition-excitation interdependencies in aggressive behavior. *Aggressive Behavior, 14,* 51–64.

Zillmann, D. (2003). Theory of affective dynamics: Emotions and moods. In J. Bryant, & D. Roskos-Ewoldsen (Eds.), *Communication and emotion: Essays in honor of Dolf Zillmann* (pp. 533–567). Mahwah, NJ: Erlbaum.

Zimbardo, P. (2007). *The Lucifer effect: Understanding how good people turn evil.* New York: Random House.

Zimet, G. D., Dahlem, N. W., Zimet, S. G., & Farley, G. K. (1988). The multidimensional scale of perceived social support. *Journal of Personality Assessment, 52,* 30–41.

Zuber, J. A., Crott, H. W., & Werner, J. (1992). Choice shift and group polarization: An analysis of the status of arguments and social decision schemes. *Journal of Personality and Social Psychology, 62*(1), 50–61.

Zuckerman, M. (1979). *Sensation seeking: Beyond the optimal level of arousal.* Hillsdale, NJ: Erlbaum.

Zuckerman, M. (2007). *Sensation seeking and risky behavior.* Washington, DC: American Psychological Association.

Zulley, J. (1980). Distribution of REM sleep in entrained 24 hour and free-running sleep-wake cycles. *Sleep, 2,* 377–389.

Zvolensky, M. J., & Smits, J. A. J. (Eds.). (2008). *Anxiety in health behaviors and physical illness.* New York: Springer.

Index